IRISH SOCIAL POLICY

A CRITICAL INTRODUCTION

IRISH SOCIAL POLICY

A CRITICAL INTRODUCTION

Mairéad Considine and Fiona Dukelow

Gill & Macmillan

Gill & Macmillan Ltd
Hume Avenue
Park West
Dublin 12
with associated companies throughout the world
www.gillmacmillan.ie

© Mairéad Considine and Fiona Dukelow, 2009

978 07171 41562

Index compiled by Grainne Farren
Print origination in Ireland by Carole Lynch
Printed by the MPG Books Group

The paper used in this book is made from the wood pulp of
managed forests. For every tree felled, at least one tree is planted,
thereby renewing natural resources.

A CIP catalogue record for this book is available
from the British Library.

For permission to reproduce copyright material in this book,
the publishers gratefully acknowledge: Derek Speirs,
The National Archives, UK, and enfo (www.enfo.ie).

For

Jim and Rebecca Dukelow

Nora and Tomás Ahern

CONTENTS

LIST OF BOXES, CHARTS, TABLES AND PHOTOS

ABBREVIATIONS

ADC	Aid to Dependent Children
AFDC	Aid to Families with Dependent Children
BMA	British Medical Association
BMW	Border, Midlands and Western region
CAP	Common Agricultural Policy
CECDE	Centre for Early Childhood Development and Education
CEO	Chief Executive Officer
CIF	Construction Industry Federation
CII	Chartered Insurance Institute
CMRS	Conference of Major Religious Superiors
CORI	Conference of Religious in Ireland
COS	Charity Organisation Society
CPA	Combat Poverty Agency
CPAG	Child Poverty Action Group
CSFs	Community Support Frameworks
CSO	Central Statistics Office
CSW	Commission on Social Welfare
DCU	Dublin City University
DEHLG	Department of the Environment, Heritage and Local Government
DJELR	Department of Justice, Equality and Law Reform
DoH	Department of Health
DoHC	Department of Health and Children
DSFA	Department of Social and Family Affairs
DWS	The Developmental Welfare State
ECSC	European Coal and Steel Community
EEA	European Economic Area
EEC	European Economic Community
EES	European Employment Strategy
ERHA	Eastern Regional Health Authority
EOCP	Equal Opportunities Childcare Programme
EPA	Environmental Protection Agency
EPSEN	Education for Persons with Special Educational Needs
ESF	European Social Fund
ESRI	Economic and Social Research Institute
EUETS	EU Emissions Trading Scheme
EU-SILC	EU Survey of Income and Living Conditions

FÁS	Foras Áiseanna Saothair (Irish National Training and Employment Authority)
FDI	Foreign Direct Investment
FERA	Federal Emergency Relief Administration
FOI	Freedom of Information
FUE	Federated Union of Employers
GAIE	Gross Average Industrial Earnings
GDP	Gross Domestic Product
GLEN	Gay and Lesbian Equality Network
GMS	General Medical Scheme
GNP	Gross National Product
GP	General Practitioner
HEA	Higher Education Authority
HIA	Health Insurance Authority
HIQA	Health Information and Quality Authority
HRC	Habitual Residence Condition
HSE	Health Service Executive
ICCL	Irish Council for Civil Liberties
ICOS	Irish Co-operative Organisation Society
ICTU	Irish Congress of Trade Unions
IFA	Irish Farmers' Association
ILO	International Labour Organization
IMA	Irish Medical Association
IMF	International Monetary Fund
INOU	Irish National Organisation for the Unemployed
INTO	Irish National Teachers Organisation
IOM	International Organization for Migration
IPA	Institute of Public Administration
IWLM	Irish Women's Liberation Movement
IWU	Irish Women United
LCAP	Leaving Certificate Applied Programme
LCVP	Leaving Certificate Vocational Programme
LGB	Lesbian, Gay and Bisexual
LGBT	Lesbian, Gay, Bisexual, Trans-gender
LIS	Living in Ireland Survey
MHC	Mental Health Commission
MNCs	Multi-National Companies
n. av.	not available
n.d.	no date
NALA	National Adult Literacy Agency
NAPS	National Anti-Poverty Strategy
NASC	Irish Immigrant Support Centre

NCAOP	National Council on Ageing and Older People
NCCA	National Council for Curriculum and Assessment
NCCRI	National Consultative Committee on Racism and Interculturalism
NCO	National Children's Office
NCPSCP	National Committee on Pilot Schemes to Combat Poverty
NDA	National Disability Authority
NESC	National Economic and Social Council
NESF	National Economic and Social Forum
NHO	National Hospitals Office
NHS	National Health Service
NPAR	National Action Plan against Racism
NSPCC	National Society for the Prevention of Cruelty to Children
NTPF	National Treatment Purchase Fund
NUI	National University of Ireland
OECD	Organisation for Economic Cooperation and Development
*OMC	Office of the Minister for Children *(Chapter 11)
OMC	Open Method of Co-ordination
OMCYA	Office of the Minister for Children and Youth Affairs
OMI	Office of the Minister for Integration
PAYE	Pay As You Earn
PCCC	Primary, Community and Continuing Care
PESP	Programme for Economic and Social Progress
PNR	Programme for National Recovery
PRSI	Pay Related Social Insurance
RIA	Reception and Integration Agency
RSPCA	Royal Society for the Prevention of Cruelty to Animals
RTÉ	Raidió Teilifís Éireann
SERC	Special Education Review Committee
SERPS	State Earnings Related Pension Scheme
SSI	Social Services Inspectorate
TANF	Temporary Assistance to Needy Families
TASC	think tank for action on social change
TD	Teachta Dála (elected representative of Dáil Éireann)
UCC	University College Cork
UCD	University College Dublin
UL	University of Limerick
UN	United Nations
UNFCCC	UN Framework Convention on Climate Change
VEC	Vocational Education Committee
VHI	Voluntary Health Insurance
WHO	World Health Organization
WNHA	Women's National Health Association

WPA   Works Progress Administration
WTO   World Trade Organization

ACKNOWLEDGMENTS

We would like to thank our colleagues and students at the Department of Applied Social Studies, UCC. Particular thanks to Fred Powell for his support, and to Cathal O'Connell and Cynthia Martin for their helpful suggestions and encouragement.

We are grateful to staff at Gill & Macmillan, in particular Marion O'Brien, Emma Farrell and Aoife O'Kelly for their help and support throughout the project, and also to Julie O'Shea for her editorial work.

Finally we would like to thank our families and friends, for their interest and for the many engaging conversations about the book along the way. Special thanks go to John Ahern and David Coughlan for their constant encouragement, and for putting up with the long-running demands of this project.

INTRODUCTION

INTRODUCING SOCIAL POLICY

Social policy is a difficult area to define and it is not easy to provide a neat description that captures the breadth of this area of study. The same may be said for other areas of study at third level but in social policy's case it is probably made more challenging by the fact that the term is not used in everyday discourse and there is no intuitive or common-sense understanding of the area. So, going to college and studying social policy requires a lot more explaining than telling people you are studying science or history, for example. Yet social policy is something which is very closely connected to people's lives. At its core, social policy is the study of how human needs are met and how we respond to risks that human beings face. Whether as individuals, families, communities or societies, people make decisions, or have decisions made for them, about needs such as education and training, healthcare, housing, work, childcare and so on. As well as the many ways in which needs arise through the course of typical life experiences, we also face particular risks, such as being made redundant, becoming ill, dealing with a crisis pregnancy, dealing with a failed or abusive relationship, becoming homeless and so on. Taken together, how we meet needs and deal with risks involves a concern with well-being, welfare or security.

While, at an individual or personal level, we all try to figure out the best thing to do to achieve well-being, given the opportunities and constraints of our particular circumstances, social policy involves the study of this at a collective or societal level; how do societies figure this out? Governments give direction to the level and extent of state intervention and guide the policy priorities in a given country. This in turn involves asking other questions such as: what counts as a need or a risk? What values guide policy and provision? How are limited resources used? What impact does social policy have on different groups in society? How are resources shared or redistributed between different social groups? How is cultural diversity recognised? How are differences dealt with? While words like welfare and well-being have a certain 'feel good' factor, the questions addressed in the study of social policy do not automatically produce positive answers. Different views or perspectives contribute to theoretical and political debates about how best to address these and many other questions that make up social policy. Linked to this, in practice, the design and implementation of actual social policies can often result in insecurity and lack of well-being, in other words, the opposite of welfare. As a result, how needs are met, and how risks are responded to can have very significant implications for the type of society we live in, whether it is broadly equal or unequal, for example, and our position within that society.

THE IMPACT OF SOCIAL POLICY ON PEOPLE'S LIVES

If we look at some of the ways in which social policy relates to people's lives in Irish society, many of these issues and questions become more real. A good starting point is the case of education. If you are reading this book then your participation in the education system will mean that you have had much personal and direct experience of the impact of social policy. Education is a major component of social policy provision and has a major bearing on the early part of our lives and beyond. While day-to-day participation in the education system is quite a personal experience, it is shaped by the policy goals government has for education. For example, only a basic form of education was treated as a need that the state should pay for until the 1960s. Any further education depended on ability to pay or to gain a scholarship, of which there were relatively few. As a result, there were substantial inequalities in Irish society between groups who could afford more than the free education provided until one reached fourteen and those who could not.

At the present time education is tied much more strongly to economic needs than cultural ones, and policy, particularly at third level, is strongly influenced by the need to provide a skilled labour force for our knowledge economy. Another frequently espoused goal is that of equality of opportunity. This broadly means that everyone is given a chance to succeed in the education system and should not face obstacles such as inability to pay for education. While there is still continuity with the past in that the majority of schools are religiously owned, participation in the education system has increased enormously, particularly at third level. In the mid-1980s your likelihood of attending college was one in four; only a quarter of all school leavers went on to third-level education. By the mid-2000s 54 out of every 100 school leavers went on to third-level education. This is set to grow further; the policy goal for 2020 is to have a participation rate of 72 per cent at third level (National Office for Equity of Access to Higher Education, 2008). In other words, the individual decisions we make about going to college and choosing subjects to study are part of this wider policy context guided by economic needs and by the value placed upon equality of opportunity. This is practically expressed through policies such as free fees and/or grants and a widening range of third-level colleges and subjects offered. However, there are ways in which the equal participation of different social groups has not been achieved, despite the fact that overall participation has grown significantly. There are many issues involved here, such as how the education needs of different groups are recognised; how equality of opportunity is interpreted; how much money is spent in the education system; how much money is spent across the different levels of the system; and the extent to which the education system can address inequalities generated outside of the education system. How these issues are debated, researched and addressed in policy make up some of the core elements of education as studied within the discipline of social policy.

Education is taken here as just one illustration of the importance of social policy in shaping the opportunities available to people. Examples could equally be given in the other core areas of social policy. The core areas of social policy study are considered to be social security (usually referred to as social welfare in Ireland), housing, healthcare, education and particular aspects of the social services. The latter refers to the provision of services to particular groups deemed to require more specialist support, traditionally referred to as the personal social services. However, the widening scope of social policy means that while the social services remain central, notable attention to concepts including equality, redistribution, recognition and rights, and to the diverse range of policy areas such as family policy, migration policy, sustainability, and quality of life issues in general, suggest that the domain of social policy has broadened significantly. The key point here is that social policy can and does impact upon the well-being and opportunities available to individuals and their families. Social policy is therefore a subject centrally grounded in the present realities of people's lives, making it relevant and current to all of us who study it.

ABOUT THIS BOOK

This book is about social policy in the Irish context. It offers a way of understanding social policy in Ireland by looking at the past (as in Part I), introducing wider conceptual and theoretical debates and issues (Part II), examining specific social service areas and their development and current position in Ireland (Part III) and, finally, by exploring the position and treatment of social groups and quality of life issues in Ireland (Part IV). In bringing the different elements of social policy together in this way, we hope to provide, but also to go beyond, a descriptive account of issues and events, and encompass a critical examination of them. The analysis of social policy presented here is shaped by attention to core social policy concepts, such as equality, redistribution, rights and social justice, which require openness to question and explore both the achievements and limits of social policy. There is, therefore, a deliberate attempt to draw attention to different interpretations and views about the nature, development, and scope of Irish social policy and its various elements. This approach is taken to heighten awareness of the complexity of social policy processes and debates and to offer an introduction to the discipline which both provokes and challenges discussion about Irish social policy, its limits and its potential.

A BRIEF OUTLINE OF THE BOOK

The book is divided into four parts. In part I, chapters one to three look at the history of Irish social policy, from its emergence in the seventeenth and eighteenth centuries up to the early years of the twenty-first century. This is presented in narrative form in which the dominant themes of various periods are elucidated. Chapter 1 charts the emergence of the earliest social policy measures in Ireland; these are considered with reference to the wider social conditions and prevailing attitudes of the period. The development of social policy in post-independent Ireland, from the 1920s to the 1960s, is examined in chapter 2. Chapter 3 outlines the main influencing factors on the path of Irish social policy from the 1970s to the 2000s. Part one aims to familiarise you with the specific developments that have shaped Irish policy historically before we turn – in part two – to explain core social policy concepts, examine the nature of welfare ideologies and explore some of the contemporary theoretical debates relevant to the study of social policy.

There is a substantial shift of focus in the second part. We move away from the exclusive focus on Ireland in order to introduce a wider conceptual and theoretical backdrop relevant to the study of social policy. Here a broader account of the development of social policy is offered, the influence of a variety of ideological perspectives is considered, and key theoretical debates in social policy are introduced. Specifically, chapter 4 charts the evolution and development of social policy and welfare states outside of Ireland. This provides a broader contextual landscape through which some of the main social policy concepts can be understood. Chapter 5 sketches the major ideologies of welfare by identifying their core values and outlining the basis of their differing views on social policy. Chapter 6 offers an introduction to a variety of theoretical debates that arise, including those related to the analysis of welfare states, the nature and impact of globalisation and the role of the EU in social policy. We return to the Irish experience in the latter part of chapter 6, placing it in a wider context by looking first at historical and political factors of relevance before the major influences and challenges of the Irish welfare state are considered.

The social services are widely considered to be the backbone of social policy; part III concentrates on and critically examines the core social services in Ireland, designed to meet needs in the areas of social security, health, education and housing. These chapters analyse the social service areas with reference to core social policy concepts of relevance. The concept of redistribution, for example, is central to understanding social security, and the notion of equality and its interpretation has significant social implications in areas such as healthcare and education. There are four chapters in this part; the first of these, chapter 7, introduces key concepts associated with social security and outlines its main features, before charting the development of Irish social security policy and examining some key issues related to the provision of social security in Ireland at present. Chapters 8, 9 and 10, dealing with health, education and housing, respectively, address these social services in a similar way; relevant concepts and issues are introduced and examined before turning to the particular development and the contemporary position of the specific social service in the Irish context.

The final part of the book also looks at the impact of the social services but this time from the vantage point of particular social groups. Part IV turns to look at social policy firstly in terms of how it influences the welfare of particular groups in Ireland, while the last chapter moves to consider relatively new questions about how social policy relates to broader debates about welfare in the context of growing concerns about the environment and sustainable development. Specifically, chapter 11 considers the positions of various social groups in terms of social policy, including children, older people, people with disabilities and carers in Irish society. The chapter concentrates in particular on social policy developments relevant to meeting the needs, rights and recognition of these social groups. Chapter 12 examines the position of groups such as Travellers, refugees and asylum seekers, migrant workers and gay, lesbian and bisexual people, for whom issues of diversity and discrimination are relevant in dealing with their rights and recognition in social policy. The final chapter of the book turns the focus of attention to how the boundaries of social policy have shifted due to growing concerns with sustainable development and quality of life. Chapter 13 traces the growing linkage between environmental issues, sustainability and social policy and examines some particular areas that have a bearing on well-being and quality of life that go beyond the traditional ways of looking at social policy and social services. In many ways the issues covered in the final chapter demonstrate how social policy is a discipline that continues to change, yet the core theme of how to figure out how best to secure welfare and well-being is something that remains constant throughout.

HOW TO USE THIS BOOK

This book is intended as an introductory text, which students of Irish social policy can use in several ways. It may of course be read in full but – for those who prefer a more flexible approach to many of the debates and issues covered – it is possible to read relevant parts or chapters of this book on their own. Text boxes are provided which outline a term in the briefest possible way. The term is also highlighted in bold in the text and it is important to consult this as part of your study to gather the full meaning. Our main advice to students using the book as a source of reference that is 'dipped in and out of' is to ensure that supplementary reading is done to build on what is provided here. Recommended further reading is provided at the end of each chapter to aid with this. In addition, because of the nature of the subject matter, it is important to keep abreast of policy developments and to consult key policy documents. More than most subjects, social policy has the additional challenge of being constantly subject to new information and changing circumstances. Aware of this, we point you to some useful websites that should provide updated information on a regular basis. Finally, we have included a number of discussion points which may be of use as part of your study.

PART I

APPROACHING IRISH SOCIAL POLICY: FROM THE PAST TO THE PRESENT

The first part of this book comprises three chapters, which focus on the history and development of social policy in Ireland. It has two main aims, the first is to provide a narrative account of the development of social policy in the Irish context, and the second is to set out the wider historical landscape in which Irish social policy has developed. It helps to create an understanding of what social policy is by approaching it historically, by looking at its emergence, how it has changed over time, and how patterns of both change and continuity can be detected. Looking at the particulars of Irish social policy history serves as a reference point for the broader theoretical and conceptual landscape of social policy, which is dealt with in part II, and the detailed components of Irish social policy, as dealt with in parts III and IV of the book. While some historical elements are developed in detail in this first part, it is not intended to be a comprehensive account of Irish social policy history. Instead, the elements discussed serve as a means of explaining how social policy has evolved, and they draw attention to the most significant factors which have been influential in its development. These themes appear again later in the book in parts which examine the wider theoretical context of social policy and in the more particular analysis of the nature of Irish social policy.

▸ Chapter 1 traces the emergence and growth of social policy in Ireland, from the seventeenth century to the early twentieth century when Ireland gained independence. Some of the most significant influences are outlined and core developments are discussed, including the Poor Law, which was one of the central elements of Irish social policy provision for much of the nineteenth and into the twentieth century.

▸ Chapter 2 is framed by the decades from the 1920s to the 1960s. It looks at some of the key episodes of social policy development in these decades, the main influences on the evolution of social policy in the early phases of independence, and some of the factors which began to change and modernise it over the 1960s and 1970s.

‣ Chapter 3 describes the context in which Irish social policy has developed from the 1970s onwards. It looks at some of the most notable economic and social issues and events that have shaped Irish society since the 1980s, leading to a range of current social policy debates, which are outlined briefly at the end of this chapter.

CHAPTER 1

FROM THE SEVENTEENTH CENTURY TO THE EARLY TWENTIETH CENTURY: THE EMERGENCE OF SOCIAL POLICY IN IRELAND

This chapter sketches the key features of the emergence of social policy in Ireland. This spans early state and charitable activity in the seventeenth and eighteenth centuries, through to the more extensive social policy measures and provisions which emerged during the nineteenth and early twentieth centuries, before Ireland gained independence in 1921. The chapter documents the themes of care and social control which were intertwined in a mix of charitable and state provision during the seventeenth and eighteenth centuries. Provision dealt primarily with the 'problem of the poor'. During this period charitable efforts stand out, but only for categories of the 'deserving poor', principally children and the sick poor. State intervention was minimal, and strongly linked to the control and punishment of the 'undeserving poor'. In the nineteenth century the establishment of the Poor Law continued the concern with poverty and social control, but within the context of a much larger institutional framework. The chapter also identifies the emergence of a more sustained debate about the nature of welfare by the end of the nineteenth century. This encompassed the idea that social policy and state intervention were matters that went beyond the problems of the poor, and resulted in recognition of the needs of some particular groups in the population, including children and older people.

CHAPTER OUTLINE

▸ The first section of the chapter examines the roots of social policy by looking at the elements which existed prior to the nineteenth century.

▸ The second section looks at developments during the nineteenth century, which were dominated by the implementation of the Poor Law in Ireland from 1838.

▸ The final section explores the emergence of a modern strand to social policy development in the early twentieth century.

SECTION 1: EARLY SOCIAL POLICY MEASURES IN IRELAND

> ... there are 34,425 strolling beggars in the kingdom; of which there are not 1 in 10 real objects (of compassion) ... so that we may suppose 30,000 of them able to work. (Arthur Dobbs, Irish Surveyor General, 1729, in Powell, 1989, p. 72)

Early fragments of social policy emerged during the seventeenth and eighteenth centuries, before welfare provision became more easily recognised in the nineteenth century. The historical overview presented here refers directly to social policy developments and initiatives, although this is not how such measures would have been identified at the time. Terms such as relief, correction, and aid, would have been more typically used, reflecting the prevailing ethos of the time. Initially, the maintenance of social order superseded the meeting of needs, despite the existence of large-scale poverty in Ireland. The primary purpose of early provision was to group together people who were considered undesirable to impose some kind of order and control. Undesirability was associated with moving from place to place and being without work if one was physically capable of working or 'able-bodied'. Both of these qualities clashed with the emerging modern values of being settled in one place and at work. Therefore, 'sturdy beggars' who contravened both of these values came in for particular attention. This issue was not exclusive to Ireland; other European countries also perceived beggars as a threat to social stability and implemented measures to deal with them. In the Irish case, the title of one of the earliest pieces of legislation related to social policy includes an extensive list of individuals considered a problem. This was 'An Act for the Erecting of Houses of Correction and for Punishment of all Rogues, Vagabonds, Sturdy Beggars and other Lewd and Idle Persons', which was passed in 1635. The title reflects the concern that idleness and what were construed as illegitimate forms of movement, were to be dealt with using corrective treatment in an environment segregated from the rest of the population. Correction and punishment were implemented by setting people

> **Able-bodied poor** referred to the poor who were assumed to be in a position to physically support themselves.

to labour and by administering 'moderate' whippings. This was intended as deterrent for the rest of the poor as much as a punishment for the idle poor (Powell, 1989). However, the legislation proved inoperable due to lack of financial provisions (Ó Cinnéide, 1969).

The 1635 Act was followed in 1703 by 'An Act for erecting a workhouse in the City of Dublin, for employing and maintaining the poor thereof'. The workhouse, also known as a house of industry, was built near James Street. Nicholls (1856, p. 37), in his history of the Poor Law in Ireland, noted that that this Act was the 'first in which a direct provision is made for the relief of poverty in Ireland'. However, while this Act marks an acknowledgement of poverty, the treatment of the poor was very much linked to the need to maintain order and control. In 1735 an Act was passed to provide a similar workhouse in Cork, which was built on the Watercourse Road (O'Connor, 1995). Again, the title of the Act clearly reveals its purpose: 'An Act for erecting a workhouse in the city of Cork for employing and maintaining the poor, punishing vagabonds, and providing for and educating foundling children'. These workhouses operated jointly as 'foundling hospitals' for abandoned children. Abandonment was not uncommon at the time, caused by family poverty. Funding for the workhouses was to be sourced from special taxes, such as a tax on all imported coal in the case of Cork, and a house tax in the case of Dublin. This legislation represented an early attempt to separate out different categories of need from the general mass of 'idle and lewd' persons. As Evason, Darby and Pearson (1976) note, children were the first to benefit from recognition as a special category requiring more lenient attention. In the case of the Dublin Act, for example, Dublin Corporation was required to care for orphans and to 'apprentice out such children to any honest persons, being Protestants' (cited in ibid., p. 4). In this case early social policy was also used as an instrument of proselytisation, specifically for promulgating Protestantism.

By the 1720s the Dublin workhouse became the Dublin Foundling Hospital, due to the large numbers of children being abandoned by poor families. However, conditions within the Foundling Hospital were incredibly harsh, indicated by the number of children who died in the institution. Between 1790 and 1796, for example, of the 12,768 children admitted, 9,786 died (Raftery and O'Sullivan, 1999). The hospital was later described by the Royal Commission on the Poor Laws of 1909 as 'the most gigantic baby-farming, nursing, boarding-out and apprenticing institutions that these countries have ever seen' (cited in ibid., p. 54). In response to the awful conditions at the foundling hospital, and also the fact that children boarded out from there were brought up as Protestant, many Catholic orphanages were set up by local parishes on a voluntary basis. These orphanages arranged for children to be boarded out to Catholic families, and thus 'rescued' from the proselytising efforts of Protestants.

For adults, 'legitimate' or **'deserving'** beggars were recognised and distinguished from **'undeserving'** or 'sturdy' beggars in an Act passed in 1772. This was 'An Act for badging such poor as shall be found unable to support themselves by labour, and otherwise providing for them, and for restraining such as shall be found able to support themselves by labour or industry from begging'. Beggars were separated into two groups: those whose activity was officially recognised and who were granted a badge to beg; and those who were 'able-bodied' and thus deemed fit to work. The latter were to be punished by being placed in stocks, with a three-hour stint for a first offence, and six hours for every re-offence (Nicholls, 1856). This Act also allowed for the erection of more workhouses, and by 1838 when the Poor Law was implemented, a total of nine workhouses were in operation in Ireland (Farley, 1964).

> **Deserving and undeserving poor** were terms used to distinguish between the poor who deserved support through charity or state provision and those who did not. The deserving poor included orphaned children, the sick and the disabled. In contrast, the undeserving poor, because they were able-bodied, did not deserve support.

Outside of the workhouses, some developments were also taking place in the area of healthcare, although such initiatives came mainly from charities or philanthropists, not the state. According to O'Brien (1999, p. 199):

> ... in the limited imagination of the non-poor, poor people in normal times fitted roughly into two categories: the sturdy beggars and the sick ... The sick poor ... attracted sympathy rather than hostility. This reflected, partly, the popular recognition that sickness was not confined to the lower orders; partly also the realization that, whereas poverty was the result of improvidence and idleness, sickness was an act of God.

Therefore, as O'Brien puts it, 'if you had the misfortune to be poor, you were better off being sick also' (ibid.). This again reflects the distinction between the 'deserving' and 'undeserving' poor. The first voluntary hospital, founded by six surgeons, was opened on Cook Street in Dublin, with a mission to care for the 'maim'd and wound'd poor' (Kelly, 1999, p. 27). This became known as the Charitable Infirmary. Another Charitable Infirmary, known as the North Charitable Infirmary opened in Cork in 1744.[1] Two other voluntary hospitals opened in Dublin, Dr Steeven's Hospital in 1733, initially funded by a legacy left by Dr Richard Steeven, and Mercer's Hospital, opened by Mary Mercer in 1734. Following the establishment of these general hospitals, several more opened, often catering for more specific aspects of healthcare, such as fever hospitals and maternity hospitals, also known as 'lying in' hospitals. The philanthropic efforts of the individuals involved in funding and running these hospitals were in part calculated to enhance their status in the community. And while the poor who availed of the hospitals did not have to pay, they were reminded of their status as objects of charity by being expected to publicly acknowledge their indebtedness (Geary, 2004). All of these hospitals were supported by a 'web of charitable bodies that sprang up alongside them' (Kelly, 1999, p. 27). In Cork, for example, the Charitable and Musical Society raised funds for the North Charitable Infirmary by holding musical performances, and in Dublin, the proceeds of the very first public performance of Handel's Messiah in 1742 went to Mercer's hospital (Geary, 2004). However, charitable funding alone was insufficient, as the level of need among the sick poor was very high, and many of the hospitals went through several phases of expansion as a result. Many of the hospitals eventually received public funding to supplement their charitable income.

These voluntary hospital initiatives did not extend outside of the main cities, and a network of rural hospitals was not established until the 1765 County Infirmaries Act provided for the creation of an infirmary in each county. These were funded by parliamentary grants, grand jury presentments, and donations. However, these hospitals quickly became very run-down, and as Geary (2004, p. 53) notes, the Act 'was imperfect in many respects ... these institutions were too few, too small, and often inconveniently located. They were limited by the method of funding and staffing, and by the absence of proper supervision and control.' Dispensaries also began to emerge in the late eighteenth century, mainly in urban areas. These were designed to provide out-patient care, and included apothecaries, which dispensed medicines to the poor. Apothecaries were essentially the precursors of pharmacies. At that time the practice of an apothecary was described in the language of 'art and mystery' in the 1791 Act aimed at regulating them, reflecting the early status of modern medicine. Again, the dispensaries were a voluntary initiative, meeting the needs of the sick poor on money raised from voluntary subscriptions.

Education was also provided mostly outside of the state framework at this time. Again, voluntary groups were the main actors, and the provision of education was divided along religious lines. Several Protestant societies, such as the Association for Discountenancing Vice and the Baptist Society for Promoting the Gospel in Ireland, ran primary and second-level schools, and their activities were assisted with some public funding, as a means of spreading Protestantism and of increasing the use of the English language (Coolahan, 1981). In contrast, the Penal Laws of the seventeenth century made life very difficult for Catholics, and while Catholic organisations were forbidden to establish schools, an unofficial system of hedge schools operated. Once the Penal Laws were repealed, the growth of Catholic-run schooling became significant, including education provided by the Christian Brothers and the Presentation Sisters. However, unlike the Protestant organisations, these groups did not initially receive state funding.

SECTION 2: IRISH SOCIAL POLICY DEVELOPMENTS AFTER 1800

The nineteenth century began with the Act of Union in 1800, under which Ireland and Britain became one political unit. Ireland lost the political autonomy it had through a devolved parliament, and any further developments depended on decisions taken in London. While state intervention in matters of welfare grew throughout the century, as McPherson and Midgley (1987, p. 9 in Cousins, 2005a, p. 7) note:

> ... the nature of colonial administration gave emerging welfare institutions distinctive features which heavily influenced policy making. Administrations were highly bureaucratic and extremely centralised – designed for control, maintenance of order and downward transmission of policies formulated elsewhere.

The most significant development in terms of welfare in the nineteenth century was the introduction of the Poor Law to Ireland in 1838, which emphasised control and the maintenance of order, and also hardened the distinction between the 'deserving' and 'undeserving poor'. However, before elaborating on this point it should be noted that some other noteworthy developments did take place earlier in the century, marking the emergence of state intervention, particularly in the areas of health and education.

In 1805 legislation was introduced to fund dispensaries in rural areas. If local voluntary subscriptions could be raised then a similar amount would be provided by county grand juries through taxation. However, this initiative was patchy in terms of meeting need. Often, wealthier areas were more likely to raise the initial sums needed through voluntary efforts, yet these areas would be less in need of the services of a dispensary than poor districts. Unequal access to healthcare has therefore a long history: 'then, as now, medical relief was not equally available to all' (Geary, 2004, p. 63). In 1817 the establishment of a network of public lunatic asylums was approved, making Ireland the first country in Europe to experience such a development (O'Brien, 1999). This was an improvement on the previous practice of consigning 'lunatics' to houses of industry, and it mirrored a shift in thinking from punishment to the idea that mental illness could be medically treated. Twenty-two asylums were built between 1810 and 1869, and admission rates increased steadily during the nineteenth century (Malcolm, 1999).

The establishment of a national school system in 1831 was another development which put Ireland ahead of England. Education was increasingly recognised as an asset in developing economic and industrial strength, but in Ireland's case, education was a powerful tool of cultural control in a colonised country. Several commissions were established to examine education in Ireland, and by 1831 the government decided to establish a Board of Commissioners for National Education whose members would be both Catholics and Protestants. This Board was given responsibility for funding and regulating schools. The arrangement was intended to develop multi-denominational schooling, although the system gradually tilted towards denominational education, as none of the religious groupings were happy with a multi-denominational ethos (Coolahan, 1981).

While these initiatives marked some innovative developments, on the whole Ireland was not progressing economically or socially. Unlike Britain, most of Ireland did not experience an industrial revolution; the economy remained largely agricultural, serving both its domestic needs as well as a growing market for food in Britain, owing to its industrial transformation. This also meant that there was a demand for Irish labour in Britain, while Irish cottage industries, particularly textiles, suffered a decline as they couldn't compete with the growth of cheaper factory-produced textiles in Britain (Mokyr and Ó Gráda, 1988). This was compounded by an economic depression in Ireland during the early to mid-1800s, primarily due to events in Britain, where a period of economic austerity reduced demand for Irish produce. Within Ireland, almost all land was owned by landlords who, as Daly puts it, 'represented the peak of the Irish social pyramid' (1981, p. 6). Below them were tenant farmers, many of whom found it difficult to pay rent at this time. Farm labourers, who got work on a temporary basis, also fared badly. There was less demand for their services as farmers couldn't afford to pay them. Landlord–tenant tensions rose as the effects of long leases became apparent: tenant farmers tended to further sub-divide their land, resulting in too many farmers on too small holdings, unable to produce enough for survival or to pay their rents. Some landlords responded by reducing the length of new leases and consolidating farms by evicting small farmers and creating larger farms to rent. The scene was set for escalating levels of poverty and inequality. This was confirmed by the findings of the Poor Law Inquiry Commission, established in 1835 to investigate poverty in Ireland. Although the Commission did not clearly define or set standards for measuring poverty, it concluded that the circumstances of three out of the eight million people in Ireland would allow them to claim relief (Mokyr and Ó Gráda, 1988). This level of poverty was supported by the 1841 census, which recorded one in three families living in one-room cabins (Daly, 1981).

A Poor Law for Ireland

The Poor Law Inquiry Commission was the culmination of several commissions and investigations into the conditions of the poor in Ireland since the Act of Union; however, their various recommendations were rarely acted upon. This inaction changed with the growing feeling that there were too many Irish people availing of the Poor Law in Britain. Movement between the two countries was not uncommon, with a constant stream of migrant workers leaving Ireland for work in Britain, particularly after a regular steamboat service was set up between the two countries in 1815. Some labourers, particularly those who moved their families to Britain, became destitute. Even though they were not entitled to avail of poor relief until after five years of residence, it was, as McLoughlin (1990, p. 118) notes, 'the increasing visibility of these Irish poor on the English scene and their perceived threat to both wages and social order which provided the principal impetus for the 1838 Poor Law Act and the initiation of the workhouse system of relief'. This also indicates that debates about the implications of migration are not exclusive to the contemporary context, dealt with later in this book (see Chapter 12). The Poor Law cast a long shadow over the development of social policy in Ireland, in terms of attitudes, administration, and rules and regulations attached to services, so it is useful to examine its implementation in some detail.

To understand the Poor Law in Ireland, we need to look at its operation in Britain where it was already well established. In 1601 an Act for the Relief of the Poor provided outdoor relief in Britain to 'able-bodied' adults who were poor. Outdoor relief meant that assistance, often in the form of food or clothing, could be given in people's own homes, as opposed to requiring them to enter a workhouse. Two centuries later, however, the dominant ideas about welfare had changed and this approach was thought to be too lenient and too expensive. The 1601 Act was amended in 1834 with a new Act, known as the New Poor Law and entitled 'An Act for the Amendment and Better Administration of the Laws relating to the Poor in England and Wales'. A new principle was introduced called the principle of 'less eligibility'.

Two members of the Royal Commission appointed in 1832 to investigate the Poor Law in Britain, Edwin Chadwick and Nassau Senior, believed that the 1601 Poor Law had actually succeeded in encouraging **pauperism** by giving relief to the 'able-bodied' poor and had therefore made living

> **Pauperism** described a state of complete destitution symbolised by dependence on Poor Law provision.

on relief more attractive than working. The dominant view of poverty at the time was that it was the fault of individuals and their particular character traits, such as idleness, rather than being caused by structural factors outside the control of an individual person, such as lack of work. Thus, it was felt that the existing Poor Law system only encouraged 'the indolence and improvidence of the poor' (Jones, 1910, p. 361). Here again, another issue can be identified which recurs in debate throughout the history of social policy, namely, welfare and its perceived negative effect on character. In order to discourage this effect, Chadwick and Nassau Senior argued that relief to the 'able-bodied' poor should be given in workhouses only, where conditions would be less attractive than the standard of living one could achieve by earning a wage, however low. This was intended to deter those who were not truly destitute, and was otherwise known as the workhouse test.

The Royal Commission therefore advocated the principle 'that the condition of paupers shall in no case be so eligible as the condition of persons of the lowest class subsisting on the fruits of their own industry' (cited in Ó Cinnéide, 1969, p. 286). This principle, known as the 'principle of less eligibility', dictated that relief for the able-bodied should only be available within workhouses. Entering the workhouse meant that one took on the status of a pauper, meaning one was not just poor but completely destitute as, 'destitution not poverty, would be the criterion for eligibility' (Burke, 1987, p. 22). The overall character of the new Poor Law is summed up well by Jones (1910, p. 362):

> Destitution is the result of defective personal character; the firm and regular offer of the workhouse will convert the potential pauper into an independent labourer; in any case, the condition must be made worse than that of the free labourer; thrift, occupational improvement, manly independence, domestic peace, follow in the wake of strict administration. So runs the doctrine …

The Poor Law was transferred to Ireland after the rejection of more progressive proposals made by the Royal Commission of Inquiry into the Condition of the Poorer Classes in Ireland. The Commission, headed by Dr Whately, the Protestant Archbishop of Dublin at the time, took the view that a Poor Law would be inappropriate for Ireland; the conditions were so bad that the principle of 'less eligibility' would prove inoperable. The Commission commented that 'we see that the labouring class are eager for work; that work there is not for them, and that they are therefore, and not from any fault of their own, in permanent want' (cited in O'Connor, 1995, p. 54). The Commission recommended that Ireland's resources needed development to provide employment, and to supplement this, a scheme of assisted emigration was recommended to enable those who could not find work in Ireland to find it abroad.

This view clashed with the dominant ideas underpinning the new Poor Law in Britain and the Commission's recommendations were rejected. George Nicholls, one of the Poor Law Commissioners in England who fully endorsed the ideas behind the new Poor Law, was sent to investigate the feasibility of implementing it in Ireland. He produced a report after a six-week visit to Ireland, in which he emphatically recommended 'that, in Ireland, no relief should be given except in the workhouse. I do not propose to impart a right to relief, even to the destitute poor' (cited in Ó Cinnéide, 1969, p. 288). He felt that the deterrent would be a 'first step, towards effecting an improvement in the character, habits and social conditions of the people' (cited in Burke, 1987, p. 42). In the case of Ireland, this view of poverty as the fault of the individual complemented the racialised view of Irish people in the eyes of their British colonisers. The Irish were perceived as an inferior race and uncivilised in comparison to the English and, following this line of thinking, it was expected that Irish people would naturally exhibit the depraved traits of being poor. So, for example, when Nicholls (cited in Burke, 1987, pp. 41–2) reported his observations about the peasantry in Ireland, he commented that:

> They seem to feel no pride, no emulation; to be heedless of the present, and reckless of the future. They do not … strive to improve their appearance or add to their comforts. Their cabins still continue slovenly, smoky, filthy, almost without furniture or any article of convenience or decency … If you point out these circumstances to the peasantry themselves, and endeavour to reason with and show them how easily they might improve their condition and increase their comforts, you are invariably met by excuses as to their poverty … 'Sure how can we help it, we are so poor' … whilst at the same time (he) is smoking tobacco, and had probably not denied himself the enjoyment of whiskey.

In keeping with the views of Chadwick and Nassau, Nicholls (1856, p. v) felt that the objective of the Poor Law was:

> … to relieve the community from the demoralization as well as from the danger consequent on the prevalence of extensive and unmitigated destitution, and to do this in such a way as shall have the least possible tendency to create the evil which it is sought to guard against …

Nicholls proposed that a Poor Law be introduced to Ireland by dividing the country into 130 Poor Law unions, with a workhouse catering for 800 people in each union, run by a local board of guardians, paid for by a local tax (Poor Law rate), and overseen by a Poor Law Commission located in London. This proposal was quickly accepted and legislated for in the 1838 'Act for the more effectual relief of the destitute poor in Ireland'.

Implementation of the Irish Poor Law

There were two key components to what was considered effective relief in the application of the Poor Law. Firstly, there was no automatic entitlement to relief, and secondly, life within the workhouses was to be highly regulated. The lack of a right to relief meant that entry was at the discretion of the board of guardians, and as it quickly became apparent that the number of workhouses built was completely insufficient, women, children and the aged were prioritised over able-bodied but destitute men. However, if a man was granted relief in a workhouse, his family had to enter the workhouse with him, becoming pauperised as well. Once in the workhouse, regulations and classification systems were a central feature in the way workhouses were managed. The interest in classifying people was part of a wider pattern in the emergence and growth of social scientific knowledge at this time. Early social scientists, such as Bentham, aimed to create a body of knowledge about the social world, in a similar fashion to the way that scientists were producing knowledge and classifying components of the physical world. The more knowledge produced about the social world, the more amenable it would be to reform and improvement. This thinking was applied with zeal in the workhouses; the more groups could be classified, the easier it would be to create order and to reform, and the whole enterprise was thought to operate on precise, scientific grounds as a result (Clark, 2005).

Those entering the workhouse were therefore not treated as a homogeneous group. The classification system in the workhouses, laid down by the *Compendium of the Irish Poor Law; and general manual for Poor Law Guardians and their officers*, published in 1887, was as follows:

1   Males above the age of 15 years
2   Boys above the age of 2 years, and under 15 years
3   Females above the age of 15 years
4   Girls above the age of 2 years, and under 15 years
5   Children under 2 years of age

(cited in O'Mahony, 2005, p. 6).

These groups were to have separate spaces in the workhouse, with different food rations, and they were not supposed to mix. However, this attempt at an ordered state of affairs failed, as the workhouses quickly descended into a dilapidated state. Lack of discipline within workhouses was often attributed to poor implementation of the classification system, and when separate categories were allowed to mix, it was felt that it paved the way for 'moral contagion' (Englander, 1998). Attempts at more stringent implementation of workhouse rules and regulations paled into insignificance as the onset of the famine in 1845 resulted in a crisis for the workhouse system.

The Poor Law during the Great Famine and beyond

The Workhouse is filled beyond what prudence would suggest as safe to the health of the inmate, or that of the city. At most, it can shelter but a few hundreds more – while every lane in the city has its *hundreds* of starving poor – while every parish in the city swarms with THOUSANDS of destitute men, women, and children. (*The Cork Examiner*, 14 May 1847)

During the Great Famine (1845–7) the level of destitution escalated in Ireland due to the failure of the potato crop, which was the main food source for the majority of the population. People who were previously reluctant to enter the workhouse now had to resort to it as the sole source of relief. Overcrowding was the inevitable result. One million people died during the famine, yet state intervention was based on a workhouse system which was designed to cater for approximately 110,000 people. By 1851 there were 217,000 inmates in the workhouses (O'Connor, 1995).

The government's response to this scale of failure was minimal, and significant changes were not implemented until voluntary initiatives paved the way. Voluntary organisations, such as the Society of Friends, otherwise known as the Quakers, raised money to set up a system of soup kitchens. In 1847 there was public outcry in Britain after artists' depictions of the famine were printed in the British media, and this led to a government-funded scheme of soup kitchens to give relief to those who could not gain admittance to the overcrowded workhouses (O'Connor, 1995). Subsequently, in June 1847, a significant piece of legislation was introduced, in the form of the Irish Poor Relief Extension Act, 1847. The Act introduced a right to relief and allowed boards of guardians to provide outdoor relief. Outdoor literally meant outside of the workhouse, and relief was given in the form of food only, by 'relieving officers'. A system of deterrence also accompanied outdoor relief. Only certain groups of people were entitled; these included the sick, the aged, and the widowed, provided they had two or more dependent, legitimate children. Relief for the able-bodied was still limited to the workhouse for fear that giving outdoor relief would encourage idleness among those capable of working. The Poor Law Commissioners' decision to begin displaying the names of those receiving indoor and outdoor relief acted as another deterrent. While the list was to inform the ratepayers who were funding the service, it also acted as a measure of fraud detection by encouraging 'all trustworthy persons in the union' to give information 'on circumstances of persons receiving relief' (First Report of the Irish Poor Law Commissioners, 1848, cited in Burke, 1987, p. 135). This practice continued until the 1920s. The provision of relief became a little more generous by 1880 with the introduction of the Relief of Distress Act, which extended outdoor relief to all categories of need. One component of the contemporary social welfare system, the Supplementary Welfare Allowance, can be traced back to the introduction of outdoor relief.

An assisted emigration scheme also emerged out of the crisis of the workhouse system during the famine. Boards of guardians became empowered to assist workhouse paupers to emigrate to other British colonies experiencing a labour shortage, especially Canada and Australia, where there was a shortage of women. Boards of guardians were particularly keen to arrange for the emigration of their female inmates because after the worst of the famine was over, the population within the workhouses tended towards a greater proportion of women, as more work became available for men. There was a fear that women and children would become a long-term burden and they were described as 'permanent deadweight' (Moran, 2004a, p. 123). At the same time, however, females deemed suitable for emigration had 'to be imbued with religion and morally pure' (*Limerick and Clare Examiner*, 31 May 1848, in ibid., p. 130). As for those remaining in Ireland, it was felt that if the surplus poor emigrated, improvement would follow for the rest of the population. As Duffy (2004, p. 80) points out, 'the idea of overpopulation as an "encumbrance on society", restricting improvements in moral and social order and civilisation, was fashionable in colonial discourse'. Emigration under the Poor Law system began in 1849 and continued until 1906, during which time approximately 45,000 people were assisted to emigrate (Moran, 2004b). This figure is part of a much larger number of people who emigrated from Ireland in the decades after the famine. Many were assisted by voluntary organisations and by landlords. Voluntary organisations financed schemes to help the poor to emigrate in search of better lives. Some landlords found emigration schemes attractive, calculating that it would cost them less to assist people to emigrate than to continue funding them via the workhouse, given the rising Poor Law rates they had to pay during the famine.

The rise in levels of sickness and disease was an inevitable consequence of the famine, and legislation was introduced in 1846 to require Poor Law unions to build fever hospitals on workhouse grounds. This expanded the role of the Poor Law system in providing healthcare, as previously workhouses only had a sick ward. Pauper graveyards also became part of the system after

1847, as Poor Law unions were empowered to buy extra land to open graveyards to cope with the large numbers dying in the workhouses and fever hospitals. The role of the Poor Law system in administering health services expanded greatly in 1851, as the boards of guardians took over the running of dispensaries, thus extending the 'outdoor' nature of relief available under the Poor Law. This was legislated for under the Medical Charities (Ireland) Act, 1851. Under this legislation, the existing dispensaries were reorganised across the Poor Law unions. Each Poor Law union was divided into a number of dispensary districts, and services were to be funded by the poor rate. Under this arrangement boards of guardians had to look after dispensary buildings, supply medicines and pay the dispensary doctor attached to each district. Dispensary doctors were charged with the care of people who couldn't afford to pay for their own healthcare and who had obtained a ticket from the management committee appointed by the board of guardians to run the service. The tickets issued were known as black and red tickets, black indicating that the bearer was entitled to receive care and medicine at the dispensary, and red indicating that the nature of the recipient's condition required home visits by the doctor (Cassell, 1997). The decision as to who was entitled to a ticket was left to the discretion of the management committee, who judged each individual case. The legislation used the words 'poor persons' as opposed to paupers when referring to who could access free healthcare from a dispensary; however, no guidelines to aid decision-making were included in the legislation. As a result, while the right to healthcare was not introduced, the legislation expanded the numbers of people who could potentially be granted free medical relief. Following this, the role of the Poor Law in providing hospital care was also expanded through the Poor Law (Ireland) Amendment Act, 1861. This provided for the conversion of workhouse infirmaries into general hospitals, where poor persons with non-contagious diseases could be admitted. This reflected the fact that after the famine, as well as the growing proportion of women in the workhouses, other groups whose admission was growing included the aged and the sick.

Within the workhouse hospitals nuns became an important part of the nursing staff and by 1903 nuns were responsible for the nursing duties in 84 unions (Luddy, 1999). Nuns performing nursing work were attractive to boards of guardians because they generally offered to work for low pay and they 'would bring with them into the workhouse all those virtues with which "good" women were credited. They would also, more importantly, create a docile and passive inmate and a more moral female patient' (ibid., p. 107). The influence of the nuns was welcomed at this time because, by the 1850s, as Luddy documents, female poverty and the rising number of women presenting at the workhouses was conflated with sexual immorality. The presence of nuns was therefore perceived to help prevent the risk of moral contamination these women posed. Visiting ladies committees, often made up of the wives of landowners, also sought to have some effect on the character and welfare of female inmates, particularly children (O'Connell, 1880).

The growth of the Catholic Church as a provider of social services from the mid-nineteenth century

The inclusion of nuns on the staff of workhouse hospitals was part of a growing trend of Catholic involvement in welfare provision. As already discussed, charitable activity was already long-established; however, the mid-nineteenth century marked the development of a stronger and more organised Catholic Church in Ireland. It was particularly keen to take over existing activities, such as small local orphanages, and to develop bigger institutions in the fields of health, education and childcare, with women and children foremost in their work. Their activity also focused on countering the conversion efforts of Protestant charities. However, both groups had similar attitudes to the poor they set out to help. As Preston (1998, p. 106) notes, 'many charities noted in their statement of intent that they helped only those who "deserved" aid'. Thus, the distinction between the 'deserving' and 'undeserving' poor was not exclusive to state-provided welfare. This was clearly evident in the titles of some of the charities, for example, the Dublin-based 'House of Protection for Distressed Young Women of Unblemished Character' and the 'House of Refuge for Industrious and Distressed Females of Good Character'. Both of these were Catholic charities that aimed to train destitute women in skills such as laundry to enable them to gain employment (ibid.). For women who had 'fallen', whose character was considered redeemable, there was the female penitentiary or 'Magdalen' system, which aimed to house and reform women. Magdalen homes initially targeted prostitutes and subsequently unmarried mothers. The first Magdalen home was established in Dublin in 1767, but as congregations of religious women grew, a network of larger Magdalen asylums formed, including, most notably, homes run by the Good Shepherd Sisters, such as homes opened in Waterford in 1858, and in Sundays Well in Cork, in 1869 (Finnegan, 2001). A strict disciplinary regime was followed in the Magdalen homes, based on penitence and obedience, with laundry work, carried out in silence, being the women's daily activity. Far from being unknown to the wider community, these homes advertised for laundry as a way of funding their operations:

> The Magdalen Asylum Laundry. [Waterford]
> The Community of the Good Shepherd beg to inform the public that in the new Magdalen Asylum Laundry, under their care, washing is done most carefully and satisfactorily as can be testified by the gentry of both County and City. The Community earnestly solicit the

County and City Clubs, and also private families to send their washing, as the work in the Laundry at present is not sufficient to keep the penitents employed, and is besides, inadequate for the maintenance of the daily increasing numbers who make application for admission. The Magdalen Asylum Laundry van will call to any place in and around the City for washing, and will deliver it in due time when done. (*Waterford Chronicle*, 14 December 1895, cited in Finnegan, 2001, p. 47)

Besides the Magdalen homes, disciplinary control also featured heavily in the industrial and reformatory schools which began to open from the late 1850s. These were funded by the state but managed by religious groups. The first schools opened in Dublin; the first reformatory school in Drumcondra in 1858, and the first industrial school in Sandymount in 1869. The industrial schools operated on the principle of taking children 'in their early childhood, training them to industry and good conduct' (cited in Raftery and O'Sullivan, 1999, p. 63). The children placed in industrial schools included those whose parents were poor and considered to be unfit or unable to look after their children, as well as orphans, and children of unmarried mothers. Many of these children would have previously ended up in the workhouses, now they were brought up in the industrial schools, in an environment considered more appropriate for them. But there were other considerations as well. Echoing some of the logic behind the Poor Law, the industrial school system was considered:

> ... by far the cheapest and best in every point of view, since it saves the expense of prosecuting and imprisoning the children; and what is more important, by preventing them from becoming criminals, protects the community from the losses and evils they would inflict upon it. (ibid.)

Reformatories catered for children who had been sentenced by the courts after committing an offence – usually something minor. Running these schools was an attractive proposition for the Catholic Church, because it gave them an opportunity to 'save the souls' of these children, and the institutional model of care represented 'an efficient means of maintaining the maximum control over the recipients of this care' (ibid., p. 57). Thus both types of school expanded rapidly, despite the fact that the early inspectors of the schools were critical both of the expansion of the system and the substandard levels of care they found in many of the schools.

SECTION 3: ADVANCES IN IRISH SOCIAL POLICY IN THE LATE NINETEENTH AND EARLY TWENTIETH CENTURY

> That one-half of the world knows not how the other half lives is a truth, not always acknowledged by us, but one that is strikingly emphasised when one descends into the lives and homes of those who are destined to live perpetually on the border line of subsistence, and work out a hand-to-mouth existence from day to day. (MacSweeney, *A Study of Poverty in Cork City*, 1915, p. 93)

Some important developments came late in the nineteenth century which marked the roots of modern social policy. These were underpinned by a change, or at least a partial shift, in attitudes about poverty and poor people, and in thinking about welfare, which occurred in general and not just in Ireland. The view of poverty as a personal failing was challenged by links established between poverty and problems beyond individual control, such as unemployment. The idea that welfare was something for the poor only, which rich people paid for but didn't avail of, and the impulse to control recipients of relief faded somewhat. Welfare began to be perceived as a matter of rights, where an individual's needs were met as a member of society or as a citizen, not a matter of charity calibrated by notions of what was deserved. As a result, 'the deserving poor were transformed into "needy fellow citizens"' (Dross, 2002, p. 86). However, this was not a rapid transformation; changes were often the outcome of conflict between those who maintained the view that the Poor Law was the most effective solution for social problems, and those who felt that people should be compensated for the problems encountered in an industrial society, such as unemployment and old age.

In Britain, emerging research about the extent of poverty, the growing strength of the labour movement, and the establishment of the Fabian Society, all contributed to the push towards newer social policy developments that would eventually supersede the Poor Law. (These themes are dealt with in more detail in Chapter 4). These social policy developments, which were implemented in Ireland as well, were not so radical as to completely overthrow the Poor Law system; instead, developments occurred whereby particular categories of people were regarded, not as paupers, but as entitled to welfare as a right. The first legislation contributing to a structure of provision outside the Poor Law was the Workmen's Compensation Act, 1897. This Act was significant because it was based on the recognition that a person's inability to work could be due to accidents at work, for example, which merited compensation, rather than leading to destitution and the workhouse. The passing of this Act marked the beginnings of a period in which there was 'a very decided advance in the cause of social legislation' (Shannon Millin, 1917, p. 306).

The introduction of non-contributory old age pensions, which had long been campaigned for as a matter of right completely detached from any notion of pauperism, was a particularly notable advance. The Old Age Pension Act, 1908, meant that people over 70 could qualify for a pension, and the rate at which they received the payment depended on their means. However, there were some conditions attached to entitlement. One of the reasons the pension was introduced was because of the high numbers of aged poor residing in workhouses, and it was felt that a pension would help this group leave behind the workhouse and the 'disreputable inmates' with whom they were forced to live. Consequently, to ensure that the pension went to the 'deserving aged' only, several disqualifications applied. These included being in receipt of outdoor relief, being convicted under the 1898 Inebriates Act, and being detained in a lunatic asylum. Those who '"habitually failed to work" according to their ability, opportunity and need for their maintenance' (Farley, 1964, p. 18) were also disqualified. At the same time, the introduction of a state pension was quite a radical departure from previous welfare provision, and older people in Ireland fared particularly well, as the rates set were referenced against wages and living standards in Britain which were higher than in Ireland. For many men it meant that they returned to live with their extended families, with the pension contributing something to the household income, while it enhanced the status and independence of many older women (Guinnane, 1993). There was, however, the feeling that the initial number of claimants in Ireland did not accurately reflect the actual number of people who were over 70. This was complicated by the fact that a system of birth registrations was not fully functioning until 1864. As a result, some people got their pension early, with divine intervention getting the better of the pension administrators, as evidenced below:

> Grateful thanks to the Sacred Heart of Jesus for obtaining my Old Age Pension five years before it was due. (Thanksgiving notice published in a provincial newspaper cited in Ó Gráda, 2002, p. 134)

A Children's Act, commonly known as the Children's Charter, was also introduced in 1908. It was the first comprehensive piece of legislation to deal with children and was considered progressive in its time. The Act sought, in the words of its instigator Herbert Samuel, to rescue children from the 'bad home' (cited in Dawson, 1910, p. 388). It provided for tighter regulation and inspection of the guardians of children and protected children against assault, ill treatment and danger to life or health by any person caring for them. This Act and its later amendments, as Raftery and O'Sullivan (1999, p. 21) point out, 'was to form the legislative basis for child welfare services in Ireland for much of the twentieth century'.

Alongside legislation in these areas, progress was notable in relation to housing and rural development, demonstrated by several pieces of legislation which dealt with circumstances specific to Ireland. These circumstances had to do with increasing unrest, particularly in relation to land matters under colonial rule. One strand of this was the establishment of the Congested Districts Board in 1891, which was charged with the task of developing the poorer western regions of the country and dealing with congestion, or overcrowding. It attempted to consolidate unviable small holdings by buying up and then redistributing land, and it also aimed to create sustainable livelihoods by developing agricultural and fishery resources. This was, as Fahey and McLaughlin (1999, p. 120) note, 'a unique experiment in state-led development at the time'. It went strongly against the grain of minimal intervention and minimal redistribution which had been the prevailing state ethos. The Board was also active in building new houses and improving the existing housing stock and in this respect it was part of a larger housing initiative which again was unique to Ireland. A series of Labourers' Acts in the late nineteenth and early twentieth century were designed to build houses for rent by landless agricultural labourers, and a total of 41,000 houses were built by 1921. This initiative was, according to Aalen (1992, p. 140, in ibid.), 'the first public housing programme in the British Isles and probably in Europe'. The rural example led to pressure for similar funding of urban housing and in 1908 a Housing Act was passed to provide for urban housing development. Consequently, the provision of urban housing was well ahead of British provision in the early decades of the twentieth century (Fahey, 2002).

One final significant development prior to Ireland gaining independence in 1921 was the introduction of the National Insurance Act, 1911. This again gave workers something to rely on as a right, outside of the Poor Law, and established the beginnings of insurance-based social security. The Act was based on contributory insurance, with contributions coming from three sources, the employee, the employer and the state. The proposed Act was composed of two parts. The first part provided health insurance giving entitlements to medical benefits, including a free general practitioner service and free medicines (on prescription) that would be set apart from the dispensary service. The second part provided national insurance giving benefits in the event of sickness or unemployment. Thus, the structural causes of unemployment were gaining some recognition and the language of the 'able-bodied poor' began to fade. Despite the security offered to workers by the Act, it was opposed by many groups in Ireland, including the Catholic Church, the medical profession and the Irish Party on grounds such as cost and whether a predominantly agricultural country needed such a measure (Powell, 1992). On foot of this opposition, a compromise was reached which meant that while the National Insurance Act was applied to Ireland, medical benefit was excluded. This meant that an opportunity to develop an insurance-based health system was lost. Another long-lasting implication of this Act was the **male breadwinner model** of social security which underpinned the legislation. The Act operated on the assumption that the man, as head of the household, was the most important or sole wage earner. Women, whether married or single, were considered less important earners in this scheme of things and were treated differently in terms of contributions and benefits (Yeates, 1997). These differences, though modified over time, have had long-lasting effects in terms of inequalities between men and women in the social security system.

> The **male breadwinner model** describes the extent to which welfare states and social security systems, in particular, have been 'gendered' with certain assumptions about the roles of women and men in society.

Despite this discrimination against women, many women's groups were active in Ireland at this time, and women became more involved in public life beyond charity work. As Luddy (2002, p. 72) notes, 'by the beginning of the twentieth century women had created a diverse group of formal organizations that allowed them political expression. In addition to reform societies, which had originally been connected with women's philanthropic work, unionist, nationalist, suffrage, cultural and labour organizations had also been created.' The first suffrage society in Ireland had been established by Isabella Tod in 1871; in 1908 the Irish Women's Franchise League was formed and 'the vote' was finally granted to women over 30 in 1918. Local government reform in the late nineteenth century also widened women's participation, by affording them elected positions as Poor Law guardians and members of urban and district councils. Jenny Wyse-Power, for example, a prominent nationalist activist, who continued to argue for equality for women after Ireland gained independence, was one of the first women to be elected on to a board of Poor Law guardians in Cork, where she served between 1903 and 1911.

In overall terms, the range of activity and organisations of women fighting for equality and the improvement of social conditions in Ireland at this time (including the Irish Women's Workers Union and United Irishwomen) combined with the contribution of women (such as Cumann na mBan – the 'League of Women') to the nationalist agenda, seemed promising in terms of the possibility of social reform once Ireland gained independence. Within the nationalist movement the promise of equality in the 1916 Proclamation, and the principles included in the Democratic Programme adopted by Sinn Féin at the first session of the Revolutionary National Assembly or Dáil Éireann in January 1919, provided some grounds for optimism. For example, the democratic programme promised the abolition of the Poor Law and placed a strong emphasis on redistribution and equality. (See Chapter 6 for more on the Democratic Programme).

Finally, and specifically with regard to gender equality, the activism of women's groups in Ireland during the early twentieth century provided further grounds for optimism about the capacity for change. The hard-fought success of the suffrage movement in securing the right to vote for women in the form of the Representation of People Act, 1918, served as a concrete example of what was possible. Despite the age restriction contained in the Act (only women over 30 were entitled to vote initially), a small group of Irish feminists continued to highlight wider impediments to equality:

> We want equal pay for equal work, equal marriage laws, the abolition of legal disabilities, the right of women to enter the hitherto banned learned professions, women jurors and justices, in short, the complete abolition of various taboos and barriers – social, economic and political – that still impede women's progress and consequently that of the race. (Editorial from the *Irish Citizen*, 1919 cited in Cullen Owens, 1984, p. 132)

However, these aspirations were all but ignored in Ireland in the years that followed. The equality demands of women in early twentieth-century Ireland were given some short-lived credence but ultimately did not result in change. This change was to take the better part of the century to achieve and forms part of a more complex story about the development of social policy which is continued in the next two chapters.

CHAPTER SUMMARY

▸ This chapter provided an account of the emergence and development of welfare measures in Ireland since the seventeenth to the early twentieth century. The earliest measures were balanced between aid and punishment, and aimed exclusively at the poor. However, the poor were categorised into 'deserving' and 'undeserving' groups, with aid for the former and punishment for the latter.

▸ State provision grew during the nineteenth century with the introduction of the Poor Law to Ireland. The network of workhouses established under the Poor Law represented a large-scale effort to deal with poverty in Ireland; however, the thinking behind the system remained essentially the same as heretofore.

▶ By the late nineteenth and early twentieth century, other factors became significant in the development of welfare. One was the growth of the Catholic Church as a charitable provider of welfare, but the impulse to categorise and control was something it shared with existing state provision. Another strand, which we would recognise today as the roots of modern social policy, is the shift away from workhouse provision towards cash payments in the form of pensions and national insurance.

▶ However, the development of social policy is not a simple story of linear progress, where each new phase succeeds in eradicating the influences of a less developed past. The history of social policy, from the past to the present, can be marked as much by repetition and regression as by progression, as different strands and influences have varying weight over time, depending on the wider political, economic and cultural context.

Discussion points

▶ Think about your local area in terms of early social interventions. Trace the origins of county hospitals, schools, voluntary associations, etc., and locate their development in the wider history of social policy.

▶ Examine the differences between the Whately Commission and Nicholl's proposal for a Poor Law for Ireland in terms of solutions to the problem of poverty.

▶ Assess the importance of the social policy measures of the early twentieth century, a) at the time, and, b) in terms of their long-term impact on the Irish welfare state.

Further reading

Burke, H. (1987) *The People and the Poor Law in Nineteenth Century Ireland*, The Women's Education Bureau: West Sussex.

Luddy, M. (1995) *Women in Ireland 1800–1918: A documentary history*, Cork: Cork University Press.

Powell, F. W. (1992) *The Politics of Irish Social Policy 1600–1990*, New York: Edwin Mellen Press.

Raftery, M. and O'Sullivan, E. (1999) *Suffer the Little Children: the inside story of Ireland's industrial schools*, Dublin: New Island.

Notes

1   The Charitable Infirmary in Dublin later became Jervis Street Hospital. The hospital was closed in 1987 and the site was subsequently developed as the Jervis Street shopping centre. The North Charitable Infirmary in Cork remained open until 1988 and has since become a hotel.

CHAPTER 2

FROM THE 1920s TO THE 1960s: THE DEVELOPMENT OF SOCIAL POLICY IN IRELAND

This chapter examines the context in which social policy developed in Ireland from 1921, when the country gained independence, to the 1960s, when it entered a period of modernisation and change. The chapter profiles two broad phases, from 1921 to the late 1950s, and from the late 1950s to late 1960s. From the perspective of social policy, the first period was marked by very little progress. The early decades of independence had the hallmarks of a state finding its feet, trying to carve out an identity and attempting to impose order, with few resources available, on social policy. At the same time there was little inclination to progress social policy; not only were the economic conditions limiting, so too was the social and cultural environment in which the new state operated, which was dominated by the Catholic Church and a rural vision for Irish society. The second period marks a gradual change away from the economic and social conditions that inhibited social policy developments in the earlier decades of independence. Gradual reform led to the expansion of the main social services together with some recognition of the needs of people and groups who had been neglected by the main actors and interests that had shaped social policy until the 1950s.

CHAPTER OUTLINE

▸ Section one examines social policy developments and the context in which they emerged during the period from the early 1920s to the end of the 1940s.

▸ The second section examines the 1950s as a decade of crisis, characterised by economic failure, large-scale unemployment and emigration, which ultimately provoked change in economic terms at least.

▸ The third section examines developments from the late 1950s which led to growth in the economy, and the gradual development and expansion of the main social services, as well as some, albeit limited, recognition of groups hitherto neglected in terms of social policy provision.

SECTION 1: THE 1920s TO THE LATE 1940s – THE EARLY DECADES OF INDEPENDENCE AND THE DEVELOPMENT OF SOCIAL POLICY

1920s: economic conservatism and the influence of the Catholic Church

Contrary to the promising signs for the development of social policy as discussed at the end of the previous chapter, economic and religious influences gained the upper hand over concerns with equality and social rights once Ireland achieved independence. Thus, the early decades of independence were marked by a conservative and cautious approach to welfare expenditure. In addition, there was a strong Catholic influence on policymaking; a value system based on rural, patriarchal family living was adhered to; and there was little appetite for redistributive policies, leaving class distinctions and unequal relations between women and men undisturbed and obscured by a vision of a harmonious agrarian society.

In the first decade of independence (1921–32) a party called Cumann na nGhaedheal (a new party composed of those within Sinn Féin who accepted the 1921 Treaty with Britain that granted Ireland independence as a free state, renamed Fine Gael in 1930) held power and governed the country through what O'Connor Lysaght (1991, p. 49) describes as 'refurbished' versions of institutions that existed under colonial rule. A key element of this refurbishment was a highly centralised approach to policymaking, which has remained more or less intact since then. At the centre of this was the Department of Finance, which kept a very strong check on government expenditure. Another theme inherited from the previous century was a suspicion of welfare and its effect on character, with government ministers fearful that any expansion of state welfare would make people overly dependent. For example, in 1924 the Minister for Local Government, P. J. Burke argued that:

> One of the most serious defects of the Irish character is this tendency to dependence of one kind or another ... The number of people who lead a parasitic existence ... [was] increasing relative to the number of people who are striving to make an honest living. (cited in Ó Gráda, 1997, p. 91)

Cumann na nGaedheal's attitude towards welfare therefore displayed a strong similarity to the thinking behind the introduction of the new poor law in both Britain and Ireland in the 1830s. The Old Age Pension was one of the first social policy measures to bear the brunt of these attitudes, and very early on there was, as Ó Gráda (2002, p. 148) puts it, 'signs of nerves' about how much pensions were costing. Thus, in 1924 pension payments were reduced, and income taxes were also reduced from 25 per cent to 15 per cent between 1924 and 1926.

These changes were also influenced by the state of the economy and the power of the key economic actors. The Irish economy was in a poor state after independence, hampered by the effects of colonisation and a subsequent civil war which meant that there was little industrial infrastructure and few resources with which to develop it. Furthermore, agricultural interests and actors lay at the heart of class politics and represented a more influential force in comparison to the labour movement and the working classes. As Garvin (2005, pp. 34–5) notes:

> There was a new, and large, middle class of over 200,000 farmers with between fifteen and 100 acres, which dominated society and politics because of its massive collective presence in the form of demographic weight, cultural centrality and electoral political clout.

Securing the prosperity of the farming classes was therefore an important goal for the government and the economic strategy of Cumann na nGaedheal was to use agriculture as the motor for growth of the economy. Its aim was to reduce the costs of production by lowering taxation and limiting government expenditure.

Other areas of social policy also suffered under this regime. The substance of the poor law remained, with some changes made to its administration. Under the Local Government (Temporary Provisions) Act of 1923 many workhouses were closed and the remainder became county homes, and outdoor relief was renamed 'home assistance'. Home assistance was the only payment available other than pensions and national insurance payments, so any person in need and not entitled to these had to apply to their County Council for this payment. A poor person was defined under the scheme as a 'person who is unable to provide by his own industry or other lawful means the necessaries of life' (cited in Ó Cinnéide, 1970, p. 3). This had its roots in poor law legislation and remained unchanged until the 1970s. Each application was assessed by an assistance officer. The relieving officers of famine times were renamed assistance officers; however, assistance officers continued to be commonly known as relieving officers. No national standards were developed to guide assessment or payment levels, so these differed from county to county. The means-testing involved a household or family means test, which meant that the income of other people in a household was taken into account in making a decision. For the most part, poverty was recognised only in a very narrow way, and a family would have to display destitution in order for the applicant to receive assistance. Assistance payments lasted on average for one month only, after which time a new application would have to be made. The system continued to be highly stigmatising, and it was women who bore the brunt of this. More women than men applied for home assistance for themselves and their children. These women included widows, deserted wives and unmarried mothers. In the case of unmarried mothers, assistance officers had the additional task of:

> ... assisting unmarried mothers with the many problems arising from their condition; making contact with their parents or with doctors; arranging adoptions and maternity hospital accommodation or facilities in homes for unmarried mothers; helping to arrange for the rehabilitation of these girls. (cited in ibid., p. 9)

This was one of the routes by which unmarried mothers found themselves in county homes and Magdalen homes, which continued to operate for much of the twentieth century.

The Catholic Church, women and social policy

> The Church speaks to the State as fully an equal, not as a subordinate part, or in any way dependent on, or drawing its powers from, the State. (Coyne, 1951, p. 132)

This brings us to another powerful force shaping social policy in Ireland for most of the twentieth century, namely the Catholic Church. Once the country gained independence the Church sought to consolidate its position in Irish society, particularly in terms of culture and morality. The Church saw itself as equal to the state and having a higher authority than any other group in society when it came to commenting on or criticising state activity. As asserted by Coyne (1951, p. 132) 'Catholic principles recognize a still deeper right of criticism than that which is conferred on citizens or organizations by constitutions or the natural law'. And while the Church was in the business of securing people's eternal salvation, in practice this meant that the Church felt it had as much authority on social questions as moral questions, because it did not see the two as mutually exclusive spheres. This was made clear in *Quadragesimo Anno*, a papal encyclical written by Pope Pius XI in 1931:

> We must lay down the principle, long since clearly established by Leo XIII, that it is Our right and Our duty to deal authoritatively with social and economic problems ... the deposit of truth entrusted to Us by God, and Our weighty office of declaring, interpreting and

urging, in season and out of season, the entire moral law, demand that both the social order and economic life be brought within our supreme jurisdiction. (cited in ibid., p. 136)

Much of its focus on authority and morality was expressed through attempts to control women and families, seen as the foundation of social order in the newly independent state. For women, the Church prescribed the role of motherhood, which included strict regulation of sexuality. This thinking resulted in policies that discriminated against women, as their rights were curtailed in many areas, and instead of pursuing the vision of equality contained in the 1916 Proclamation, discrimination and inequality was legitimised by the state. As Clancy (1999, p. 209) notes, 'often, the parliamentarians articulated perspectives and ideas that appeared to be untouched by principles of equality that had been articulated some thirty years earlier'. For the state as for the Church, the regulation of sexuality and sexual desire by tying them to marriage, in which women were subordinate partners, was central to social order and social control. This need to maintain order was heightened in the early decades of independence as the new state tried to define its national identity in the aftermath of colonisation. This suited the economic interests of the land-owning class as well, as the emphasis on land ownership dominated all other spheres of life, including decisions about marriage. Children born outside of wedlock upset this order of things and, as Inglis (2005, p. 17) observes, 'the economic strategy of a farmer intent on improving his standard of living could be ruined by the transgressive actions of his daughters'.

As for economic and civil rights, the 1925 Civil Service Regulation (Amendment) Bill sought to exclude women from senior positions in the civil service by confining the qualifying examinations to men only. However, several women's groups, including the Irish Women's Citizens' and Local Government Association, mounted a campaign against this Bill and the legislation was not enacted (Beaumont, 1997). This attempt at discrimination was followed in 1927 by the Juries Act which exempted women from jury service. However, women's groups did manage to modify the legislation by forcing an amendment whereby women were included in a list of people (which also included vegetarians!) who were exempted, but who could apply to serve on juries (McCarthy, 2006). Referring to Article 3 of the Free State Constitution which spoke of equality between men and women, Kevin O'Higgins, the Minister for Justice who introduced the Juries Bill, said, 'a few words in a Constitution do not wipe out the difference between the sexes, either physical or mental or temperamental or emotional' (cited in Clancy, 1999, pp. 210–11). This illustrates legislators' view of women at the time: fundamentally different to men in a way that did not warrant equality with men.

Regarding the regulation of sexuality, three influential reports were written between 1927 and 1931. In 1927, the *Report of the Committee on Evil Literature*, and the *Report of the Commission on the Relief of the Sick and Destitute Poor including the Insane Poor* were both published. These were followed in 1931 by the *Report of the Committee on the Criminal Law Amendment Acts (1880–85) and Juvenile Prostitution*, which was referred to as the Carrigan report. However, this report remained unpublished due to what was regarded as the sensitive nature of its content. The recommendations of the *Report of the Committee on Evil Literature* and the Carrigan report became the basis for both the 1929 Censorship of Publications Act, which prohibited literature advertising contraceptives, and the 1935 Criminal Law Amendment Act, which went further by prohibiting the importation and sale of contraceptives. For both committees, as McAvoy (1999, p. 254) notes, 'birth control and "vice" appear to have been intrinsically linked'. The 1935 legislation was also aided by a 1930 papal encyclical entitled *Casti Connubii* which condemned the use of contraception, abortion and sterilisation, regardless of the circumstances.

In the Irish context the legislation was seen as a means of controlling what was perceived to be widespread sexual laxity and immorality, as concern grew over the numbers of unmarried mothers (Luddy, 2001). This concern also occupied the members of the Commission on the Relief of the Sick and Destitute Poor including the Insane Poor. There was a feeling that the number of unmarried mothers residing in county homes was a strain on resources, and there was also uneasiness about unmarried mothers residing in the same institutions as the 'deserving' poor and sick (McAvoy, 1999). The Commission suggested that unmarried mothers be divided into two categories, those capable of being reformed and 'less hopeful cases'. It recommended that the first group could be reformed by character and training, while the second group should be subjected to a period of detention in a county home or special institution, such as a Magdalen home. This obsession with sexuality and morality meant the state ignored the deeper social problems that women were experiencing, such as poverty, inadequate education and a lack of opportunities (ibid.).

Children also bore the brunt of this avoidant attitude towards real social problems and the impulse to impose order and institutional solutions. This was demonstrated by the continued use of industrial schools. As Ferriter (2004, p. 325) notes, 'by 1924 there were more children in industrial schools in the Irish Free State than there were in all of the industrial schools in England, Scotland, Wales and Northern Ireland combined. Abolished in England in 1933, the system was tenaciously clung to in Ireland.' Conditions within the Catholic-managed schools were incredibly tough, and the Church also resisted fostering or adoption. In the eyes of the Church these options posed a risk to the religious welfare of the children involved. However, the institutional care that the Catholic Church provided left children open to starvation, abuse and neglect, as highlighted by inspections of the schools; yet nothing was done by either church or state to improve or abolish the system.

1930s: the influence of early Fianna Fáil governments

> If there are to be hair shirts at all, it will be hair shirts all round. Ultimately I hope the day will come when the hair shirt will give way to the silk shirt all round. (de Valera, 1932, in Moynihan, 1980, p. 205)

By the early 1930s Fianna Fáil was in government, having taken power from Fine Gael in 1932. Fianna Fáil was a new party founded by de Valera in 1926, comprising people within Sinn Féin who opposed the 1921 treaty. Fianna Fáil took a more active stance on social problems, based on its electoral strategy of a cross-class alliance, designed to overpower Fine Gael and its more well-off supporters. It succeeded in holding office, with Fine Gael in opposition, for a very long time, thus 'closing off the openings available to other left-wing and radical groupings in Ireland', which had long-term consequences for the development of social policy (Hutton, 1991, p. 56). (See Chapter 6 for more on this point). However, during the 1930s Fianna Fáil did succeed in implementing some positive social policy measures, particularly in the area of housing, and to a lesser extent in the area of social welfare. The Church still remained dominant, with its armour strengthened by the publication of the aforementioned papal encyclical *Quadragesimo Anno* in 1931. The encyclical stated that 'it is an injustice ... a grave evil and a disturbance of right order, for a larger and higher association to arrogate to itself functions which can be performed efficiently by smaller and lower societies' (cited in Powell, 1992, p. 232). This is known as the principle of **subsidiarity** and the implication for the state is that it should not take on the responsibility for providing social services where needs could be met by smaller entities, such as individuals themselves, their families or voluntary organisations. In the Irish context this became a mechanism which shaped the relationship between the state and families; the state only intervened in ways which were consistent with the Church's perspective on men, women and families.

> **Subsidiarity** is a principle which originates in, but is not exclusive to Catholic social teaching, which considers that matters of policy and provision should be handled by the smallest, most local or least centralised unit possible.

The state of the economy and the economic policy Fianna Fáil chose to pursue was another factor shaping social policy. A worldwide economic depression during the 1930s impacted on Ireland through a dramatic rise in unemployment, with the numbers on the Live Register of unemployed rising from a figure of 29,331 in December 1931 to 102,619 in December 1932 (Powell 1992). Fianna Fáil's approach to the economy was to pursue a policy of protectionism, which was instrumental in shaping Irish society according to Fianna Fáil's vision of a country that was self-sufficient, non-materialistic and able to shake off any external influences, whether cultural or economic. Economic protectionism was implemented by imposing high import taxes on foreign goods and by discouraging foreign investment in the Irish economy. Instead, Irish industries were to be encouraged to produce Irish goods for Irish consumption, and consumption itself was to be restrained by the value of frugality. While this policy was never very successful in its own right, it was exacerbated by the onset of an economic war with Britain. This stemmed from de Valera's refusal to transmit land annuities that Britain were owed as a result of the previous century's Land Acts, which facilitated the return of land from landlords to tenants in the dismantling of colonial structures. The British government retaliated with the imposition of duties on the importation of Irish agricultural produce and restrictions on the importation of Irish cattle. This had an adverse effect on Irish trading, which suffered a decline of 25 per cent in the 1930s, and living standards, which were already below par with Britain, dropped further (Cousins, 1995).

While the state of the economy meant that little wealth was generated, Fianna Fáil partly carved out its identity by distinguishing itself from the harsher approach Cumann na nGaedheal took to social policy. It used the pensions issue in particular to mark itself out as different, and once in government it eased the means test applied to pensions. And while Cumann na nGaedheal's greatest activity in social policy was in housing, as it built approximately 14,000 homes for small holders in congested districts and for urban artisans, Fianna Fáil became even more active in housing. On the one hand, this allowed Fianna Fáil to gain extra electoral support, especially from people who might otherwise vote for the Labour Party; on the other hand, its housing policy efforts, especially in relation to rural housing, reflected an important symbolic vision on de Valera's part. As Walsh (1999, p. 50) explains:

> For de Valera, the labourer epitomised the cultural and economic values of a rural idyll. But the idyll was tarnished by poverty, poor health and housing conditions. The resulting high levels of emigration caused uneasiness in government circles. It was felt that a cottage and small plot at a low rent would provide the labourer with a mainstay at all times and root him in Ireland. It was not envisioned that this would lead to a luxurious life-style.

Thus, de Valera equated rural cottage living with the goodness of frugality, and in a speech in July 1928 he recommended that the Irishman:

> ... give up the idea of having around him the cushions and all the rest that a servant in the mansion might have ... If he goes into the cottage, he has to make up his mind to put up with the frugal fare of that cottage. (de Valera, 1928, in Moynihan, 1980, pp. 154–5)

Thus, a Housing Act introduced in 1932 allowed for compulsory acquisition of land, and increased the finance available to local authorities for cottage building. As a result, between 1931 and 1942, 82,000 dwellings were constructed and a further 11,000 condemned houses were demolished (Curry, 2003). In 1936 a Labourer's Act provided for the sale of cottages to labourers; however, the Act defined a labourer very widely, to encourage home ownership among rural dwellers. This marked the beginnings of the strong preoccupation with home ownership in Irish housing policy. This continued throughout the twentieth century as more and more groups of people were considered eligible to buy the homes they were renting from a local authority. Owning a house was posed as a shield against insecurity and was supported by all political parties. For example, in a Dáil debate in 1944, Davin, a Labour Party TD, declared that:

> Everybody realises that in the long run the home is the sheet-anchor on which economic defence in adversity rests. If you can ensure tenants of labourers' cottages an interest in their homesteads, you root them in the land; not only do you root them in the land but you give them a source of permanence there. You give them a defence against the temporary economic blizzards which unfortunately blow across their abodes from time to time. (Davin, 1944, cited in Walsh, 1999, p. 59)

The unemployment problem also required a response, which took the form of the 1933 Unemployment Assistance Act. This was designed to provide for the many unemployed people without entitlement to unemployment benefit or whose entitlement had expired. Until this time the only other payment they would have been able to avail of was home assistance. However, when unemployment assistance was introduced, the severity of means-testing meant that far less people actually received payment than those who initially applied. Only 60,000 people had qualified out of 200,000 applicants by May 1934 (Powell, 1992). Strong protest from the unemployed poor resulted in some changes to the means-testing. However, it could not be said that social assistance contributed in any significant way to the alleviation of poverty. Also telling of attitudes of the time was the resistance to the introduction of the Act because of the impact it was felt it would have on families. For example, Seán MacEntee, Minister for Local Government and Public Health, protested that parental authority in rural areas had 'been gravely weakened' and he suggested that the payment should be made to the father 'where his general character from the point of view of industry and sobriety warrants such payment', otherwise it should be paid to the mother (cited in Daly, 1999a, p. 9).

Another means of dealing with the unemployment problem was to further restrict women's right to work. In 1932, Fianna Fáil introduced a marriage bar that required women to retire from teaching and from the civil service upon marriage. Women's right to work was further curtailed in the Conditions of Employment Bill, 1935, which gave power to the Minister for Industry to restrict the number of women in industry. This was debated in terms of fitness for work, and women were not considered fit for many forms of employment. This view was bolstered by the assumption that the man in a family would be the breadwinner and that the growth of female employment would threaten male employment. These issues went unopposed by the trade union movement, with the exception of the Irish Women Workers' Union and some female senators, such as Kathleen Clarke, who continued to argue for equal pay and equal rights for women. However, as Hutton (1991, p. 59) notes:

> general thinking on the social position of women, and the pressures of an economy with a high rate of unemployment and only limited room for expansion, meant that such views carried little weight either within the Labour and trade union movement, or outside it.

As a result, as Conroy-Jackson (1993, p. 77) put it, 'unemployment was merely a theoretical concept as far as women were concerned'.

Social policy and the 1937 Constitution: inscribing different models of citizenship for men and women

> Everyone knows there is little chance of having a home in the real sense if there is no woman in it, the woman is really the home-maker. (de Valera, 1937, cited in Beaumont, 1997, p. 174)

This thinking on the position of women was cemented in the new Irish Constitution, introduced by de Valera in 1937. Ireland already had a Free State constitution, however, this was felt to be too heavily laden with 'the "repugnant symbols" of imperialism' (Keogh, 1987, p. 6). In de Valera's constitution, colonial influences were replaced by religious influences, as well as nationalist and republican strands of thinking. Catholic social principles were strongly evident, especially in sections relating to the family (Article 41), education (Article 42), religion (Article 44) and social policy (Article 45). Much of this was informed by correspondence between de Valera and John Charles McQuaid. At the time McQuaid was president of Blackrock College, run by the Holy Ghost Order, where both de Valera and his children were educated. McQuaid later became the Archbishop of Dublin; a role he used to ensure there was a sustained Catholic influence on social policy developments. During the time de Valera prepared the constitution, McQuaid supplied him with copious notes on Catholic social principles, much of which were derived from relevant papal encyclicals (ibid.). The eventual constitution granted the Catholic Church a special position in Article 44.2, which read:

> The State recognises the special position of the Holy Catholic Apostolic and Roman Church as the guardian of the Faith professed by the great majority of the citizens. (Constitution of Ireland, 1937)

However, the article went on to recognise other minority religions in the state, much to the disappointment of the Catholic Church who wanted something more exclusive in the constitution. The Catholic Church's special position remained in place until the 1960s when a constitutional review led to a referendum which removed Article 44.2.

A draft of the constitution was published in May 1937. Many women's organisations, such as the Joint Committee of Women's Societies and Social Workers, and the Irish Women's Workers Union, were opposed to several of the articles for undermining women's rights and for posing differentiated citizenship for men and women. In particular, they were opposed to Article 41.2 on the family, which is based on very different roles, rights and responsibilities for men and women. It reads:

> 41.2.1   In particular, the State recognises that by her life within the home, woman gives to the State a support without which the common good cannot be achieved.
>
> 41.2.2   The State shall, therefore, endeavour to ensure that all mothers shall not be obliged by economic necessity to engage in labour to the neglect of their duties in the home.
> (Constitution of Ireland, 1937)

This article reflects a sexual division of labour and different models of citizenship for men and women. As described by Connelly (1999, p. 24), the constitution posits a model in which:

> the ideal woman will marry, will have children within marriage, and will devote herself to the care of her husband and her children,

putting her "duties in the home" above any consideration of employment outside the home. The ideal man will also marry, will also have children within marriage, and will provide for the material needs of his wife and children through participation in public life.

The Irish Women Worker's Union opposed the wording of Article 41.2.1, arguing that 'work' instead of 'life' would be a more accurate description of women's activities in the home. More fundamentally, the union didn't see the need for special recognition of women as mothers within the home when no reference was made to work that women might do outside of the home. The Joint Committee of Women's Societies and Social Workers was critical of Article 41.2.2 because it feared that it could be used to confine women to the sphere of the home; it was aware that provisions in the 1935 Conditions of Employment Bill were already making this fear a reality (Beaumont, 1997).

In responding to criticism of Article 41, both the Catholic Church and de Valera articulated the view that this did not deny women the choice to remain single and work, rather it simply provided a protected position for women who did make the choice to marry. However, both also held the view that the natural place for women was in the home. For example, McQuaid wrote to de Valera that 'nothing will change the law and fact of nature that woman's natural sphere is the home. She is perfectly free not to marry or to marry, to choose this or that career' (McQuaid, cited in Coughlan, 1987, p. 153). Despite the opposition of various women's groups, this article remained unchanged in the final version of the constitution.

The idea of an all-encompassing sexual difference between men and women appeared again in Article 45, where a reference was made to the state's intention to protect women and children from unsuitable 'avocations' because of their 'inadequate strength'. The women's groups opposition succeeded in having the phrase 'inadequate strength' dropped (O'Callaghan, 2002). However, the final version of Article 45.4.2 still assumes a sexual division of labour:

> The state shall endeavour to ensure that the strength and health of workers, men and women, and the tender age of children shall not be abused and that citizens shall not be forced by economic necessity to enter avocations unsuited to their sex, age or strength. (Constitution of Ireland, 1937)

All of this was endorsed with satisfaction by the Catholic Church. For example, Rev. Shannon, writing in *Christus Rex*, observed that 'state policy towards females is regulated by a constitution which invokes the paramountcy of the supernatural and embodies the wisdom of Catholic sociology on the primacy of family life' (1955, p. 158). This wisdom is further revealed in his statement that 'satisfaction and completion are … impossible for women unless her racial purpose, her urge to union and motherhood be provided with adequate fulfilment' (ibid.). Rev. Shannon sealed this view by criticising modern feminism for encouraging 'hordes of thwarted females vainly seeking justification as independent free persons by pursuit of male interests, male work and male ambitions' (ibid.). It seemed that independence and freedom were for men only.

1940s: developments in relation to children and to health

In the 1940s, one of the most significant developments in social policy was the introduction of a Children's Allowance in 1944. The Irish Women's Citizen's and Local Government Association had been promoting the idea of a children's allowance since the 1920s, suggesting that it would contribute to child welfare, and at the same time give wives 'a sense of contributing to her share of the family exchequer' (United Irishwomen, 1926, in Beaumont, 1997, p. 176). However, the eventual implementation of the Act did not quite meet their aspirations, as the payment was to be made to the father as the head of the household. Yet, as a social policy measure, Ó Gráda (2002) suggests that it was the most radical development since the introduction of the Old Age Pension Act in 1908. Part of its significance lay in the fact that it was introduced as a universal payment as opposed to a means-tested payment. That is, it was made available to all families with children, regardless of their income. Additionally, the expenditure involved represented a big commitment for the government, as it initially added 25 per cent to the government's existing income maintenance expenditure, all the more significant for occurring during World War II (Cousins, 1999). The financial implications of the Act did not go unopposed, as again the Department of Finance voiced its conservative opinion. It argued that 'the principle has not been generally accepted that the State has responsibility for the relief of poverty in all its degrees' (cited in ibid., p. 42). The department only recognised 'the relief of destitution: i.e. extreme cases where employment and the minimum necessities of existence are lacking' (ibid.).

This reflected attitudes towards poverty that had prevailed since the nineteenth century; however, as Cousins suggests, the 1930s and 1940s became a time when 'the domains of life for which the state was perceived as having some responsibility were expanding' (ibid., p. 50). The 'domain of life' that was relevant here was family poverty, and Lemass, the Minister for Industry and Commerce who introduced the Children's Allowance, couched it in terms of alleviating the poverty experienced by large families. Thus, the payment was initially only made to families with three or more children. As already mentioned, the payment was to be made to the father, as the head of the family. The Irish Women's Citizen's and Local Government Association arguments to the contrary were cast aside by Lemass who argued that 'we should regard the father as the head of the family and responsible for the proper utilisation of family income' (cited in ibid., p. 47).

The introduction of the Children's Allowance was also approved by the Catholic Church, which was of the opinion that it did not contravene the principle of subsidiarity. In its view the payment would supplement the family wage, not supplant it. However, three years later, another universal scheme, this time in the area of healthcare, did not meet with the same approval by the Church, which gave rise to a key episode in social policy development in the twentieth century: the mother and child scheme controversy.

This controversy revealed the extent not only of Church control and influence on social policy, but also the power of the medical profession in shaping health policy. Health services had not progressed very far since independence. The health status of the population did not compare favourably with other European countries, and hospitals 'were old, rundown, ill-equipped to the extent that they were more of a danger or hazard to health than they were capable of restoring patients to health' according to Noël Browne (1986, p. 141), the Minister for Health during the inter-party government of 1948–51. The basis of the mother and child scheme already existed in Fianna Fáil's plans for health reform during the late 1940s. These plans were prompted by growing concern about the health status of the population. For example, medical inspections required for those emigrating resulted in findings that were a 'great shock to all engaged in health administration' (Hurson, 1944, in McKee, 1986, p. 159). Ill health particularly affected the poorest sections of the population whose living conditions were very meagre and lacked adequate sanitary facilities. These conditions affected children in particular, and the mortality rate for infants was very high. In 1945 the Department of Local Government and Public Health prepared proposals for the development of the health services, which over time were intended to cover the whole of the population.

The mother and child element of the scheme was designed to provide a comprehensive package of healthcare free to mothers and children up to 16 years, exclusive of both compulsion and means-testing. The scheme was to be delivered through the dispensary system, which would be improved, with extra staffing and upgraded or new accommodation. Services provided in the dispensary would be augmented by home visits during the child's early years and school visits once a child reached school age (McCarthy, 2004). It was felt that this would be an effective way of tackling the health problems that came to the fore in the 1940s. It would also represent a very definite move forward in terms of developing Ireland's welfare state and expanding social rights. However, the idea of a welfare state was not welcomed by everyone. The Department of Finance again rowed in with its conservative views, with McElligott, the Secretary of the Department of Finance, feeling that comprehensively provided state healthcare would have a detrimental effect on character:

> There was at one time in the country the belief – perhaps it still persists – that to take a 'red ticket' involved a certain loss of caste and that the doctor should be paid if the money could be found at all. That very proper pride will surely be steadily diminished if the farmers' sons and daughters can get this medical benefit without any transfer of cash. That spirit of independence was very valuable, and I am not actuated by financial considerations when I say that it is a pity that it should be helped to disappear. (McElligott, 1944, in McKee, 1986, p. 166)

Nevertheless, a Health Act, reflecting the Department of Local Government and Public Health's proposals, was passed in 1947. However, Fianna Fáil lost power in a general election in 1948 that saw the formation of a coalition government, consisting of Fine Gael, the Labour Party and Clann na Poblachta, of which Browne was a member. Browne became the new Minister for Health and had the task of implementing part 3 of the 1947 Act, which comprised the mother and child scheme. For the Church, however, this signalled the advent of overly interventionist state provision and it opposed the notion of universal entitlement to healthcare for mothers and children. The banner of subsidiarity was brought to bear in their opposition:

> The right to provide for the health of children belongs to parents not the State. The State has a right to intervene only in a subsidiary capacity … It may help indigent or neglectful parents; it may not deprive 90% of parents of their rights because of 10% necessitous or negligent parents. (Staunton, 1950, in Powell, 1992, p. 257)

The Church also opposed the scheme on the grounds that there was no guarantee that the healthcare delivered would be in accordance with Catholic social principles, fearing that the care provided would include things such as advice on birth control, and that Catholic women might be cared for by Protestant doctors. Therefore the scheme was held by the Archbishop of Dublin Dr McQuaid to be 'entirely and directly contrary to Catholic teaching on the rights of the family, the rights of the Church in education, the rights of the medical profession and of voluntary institutions' (cited in

Whyte, 1971, p. 143) It seemed that the Catholic Church was defending everybody's rights but those who needed the service.

The medical profession was also strongly opposed to the scheme. Its preference, as outlined in a plan previously submitted to the Department of Local Government and Public Health, was for 'free medical relief for the poor, a contributory service for wage earners, and the preservation of the upper income field as a battleground for the more enterprising practitioners' (cited in McKee, 1986, p. 163). Essentially, the medical profession felt that the scheme threatened its right to practice and profit from private medicine; therefore it opposed the idea of a mother and child scheme without means-testing.

Browne did not agree with the reasoning of either the Church or the medical profession. In a series of exchanges Browne had with the Church and with other members of the inter-party government, he was adamant that means-testing was not the way to proceed and the differences became irreconcilable. The outcome was that Browne was forced to resign and the new Fianna Fáil government, elected in 1951, introduced a new Health Act

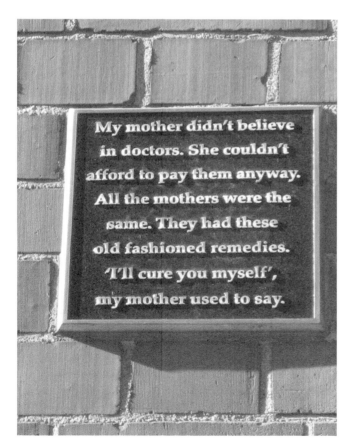

Plaque at Bride Street, Dublin, from an oral history project with residents of Iveagh Trust Housing. Source: author's photograph.

My mother didn't believe in doctors. She couldn't afford to pay them anyway. All the mothers were the same. They had these old fashioned remedies. 'I'll cure you myself', my mother used to say.

in 1953, which contained a scheme similar to that of the mother and child scheme. There were, however, some vital differences. In keeping with the wishes of the Church and the medical profession, a means test was imposed and services were to be made available only until a child reached six weeks as opposed to sixteen years. Once Browne resigned he published correspondence between himself and the Church in the *Irish Times* newspaper. This made public for the first time the strength of church-state relations. However, it also shielded the power of the medical profession to obstruct change. The 1953 Act was still unpalatable to the medical profession and a compromise was reached by the promise of the development of a voluntary insurance scheme, which would assist people in paying for private care. As McKee (1986, p. 192) comments:

> Not only did the medical profession secure the restrictions it wanted to the mother-and-child scheme, but it was able to determine the nature of the whole Irish health service on the lines of the proposals put forward by the Medical Association of Éire in the mid-1940s. In place of the Department of Health's ideal in 1945 of a free medical service for all, the government offered in 1956 what the I.M.A. had long considered to be a far more suitable alternative – the voluntary health insurance scheme …

An opportunity to develop a comprehensive health service, free at the point of use, was lost, the legacy of which has endured to the present time.

SECTION 2: THE 1950s – ECONOMIC FAILURE, UNEMPLOYMENT AND EMIGRATION

During the 1950s the economy became the main focus of attention and by the end of the decade the policy of economic protectionism finally came to an end. The failure of protectionism as the cornerstone of economic policy became more apparent in the aftermath of World War II when other European countries experienced post-war economic growth and improved standards of living. While Ireland did experience some of the benefits of post-war economic growth, by the 1950s this had faded away. Balance of payments crises in the 1950s highlighted the unsustainability of protectionism as goods imported far exceeded goods exported. Demand for imports was dampened by higher taxes and public spending cutbacks. The result was a stagnant economy. Between 1949 and 1956, for example, whereas British national income grew by 21 per cent and income grew by 40 per cent in continental Europe, Ireland could only manage an 8 per cent growth (Jacobsen, 1994). Things worsened in the late 1950s; between 1955 and 1959 Irish gross national product grew by less than 0.5 per cent per year (O'Hanlon, 2004). Behind the economic data, life was characterised by lack of jobs and emigration. By 1957, unemployment peaked at 78,000 people. Agricultural employment was in particular decline, and the numbers employed in occupations such as 'relatives assisting', agricultural labourers and domestic servants were diminishing. Government cutbacks also affected particular trades, especially building. However, an equally worrying trend was the rising emigration levels, which were a direct consequence of unemployment and without which, unemployment numbers would have been much higher. Emigration levels also peaked in 1957, with 78,000 people leaving the country that year. This was part of a larger net loss of 408,800 people between 1951 and 1961 (O'Hanlon, 2004).

The levels of unemployment and the hardship experienced by people trying to survive on what were very meagre unemployment payments provoked protest, particularly in the form of unemployed movements. The Dublin Unemployed Association was set up in 1953 and remained active for about a year. It used public demonstrations to highlight the problems unemployed people and their families were facing and to campaign for the provision of work. In 1957 another group, the Unemployed Protest Committee, emerged, and committees were set up in Cork and Waterford as well as Dublin. It succeeded in having the first unemployed candidate, Jack Murphy, elected as a TD for Dublin South Central in the 1957 general election that saw Fianna Fáil back in government after a brief spell of coalition government between 1954 and 1957. On the whole, however, the unemployed movements had little of their demands met beyond small-scale relief schemes provided by the government (Kilmurray, 1988).

Emigrating rather than struggling with unemployment seemed to be the more common choice. Living standards were undeniably higher in Britain, where most people emigrated. In addition, life as an emigrant was also preferable to many, particularly women, who had more options and rights abroad (Yeates, 2004; Clear, 2004). Many women who emigrated worked in domestic service, and the Irish Housewives Association pointed out that 'the domestic worker in Great Britain gets recognition as a human being while she does not get it here' (cited in Delaney, 2000, p. 185). Also, there were many more opportunities for married women. In Britain 47 per cent of Irish-born married women participated in the labour force, compared to only 7 per cent in Ireland (O'Hanlon, 2004). Many of these women worked in professions such as nursing, reflecting the fact that emigration gave these women the opportunity to develop their careers; an option that the marriage bar denied them in Ireland. The growth of the welfare state in Britain also highlighted the underdeveloped and stigmatising versions of welfare offered in Ireland. Donál MacAmhlaigh, in an account of his life as an Irish emigrant labourer in

England in the 1950s, wrote of the way that the British welfare state highlighted the class inequality and degradation that existed in parts of Ireland:

> It has many qualities that are closer to Christian values than much at home in Ireland … at home, such as I saw of it, if you can get a ticket to go to the doctor, you have to wait in an old ruin of a house. Look around you and all you see is poverty, despair and dirt, both on people themselves and on their clothes. The people go in to the doctor as they used to go into the aristocrats or the landlords long ago – shaking with humility. In England he'll give you to understand that you are a person and not a beggar. (cited in Ferriter, 2004, p. 478).

However, the government response to emigration was generally one of ambivalence. While there was some acknowledgement of the problem of low standards of living in Ireland, a more common response was to suggest that Irish emigrants were unpatriotic. For example, in 1950, the Irish journalist and novelist Aodh de Blacam (1950, pp. 279–88 in ibid., pp. 471–2) argued that:

> No normal man or woman, able to make a living at home, prefers a living abroad for the sake of an increase in salary. What is a hundred pounds' increment when balanced against separation from one's kindred, one's own class fellows, one's home town and nation, the rearing of one's children in the right spiritual environment? The flight from Ireland, now that we have control of its resources and our personal future, is abnormal, morbid and one might add absurd.

Official recognition of emigration came with the decision to set up a Commission on Emigration and Other Population Problems during the coalition government of 1948–51. It reported in 1954, during the period of the second coalition government, between 1954–7 (this time a coalition of Fine Gael, the Labour party and Clann na Talmhan). The Commission was, as Connolly (2004, p. 87) notes, the first 'conscious effort made by an Irish administration to study population trends with particular emphasis on emigration'. The Commission received submissions from groups throughout the country who put forward various reasons for emigration, as well as ways to halt it. A submission from Connemara, Co. Galway, suggested that the media had a role to play in emigration:

> Films make the young emigrant more at home when he goes abroad than he used to be. He already knows Bing Crosby and Mickey Mouse. Dublin is less known than Boston. Dáil Éireann is only something in the papers. (cited in ibid., p. 92)

Another submission suggested that girls who wished to emigrate should be prohibited from doing so for one year, and that a system of marriage dowries be introduced. A further submission suggested that a tax on bachelors would help prevent female emigration, assuming that much of it was due to the wish to improve their chances of marriage: 'Girls want husbands. Therefore if men emigrate, girls must also' (ibid., p. 93). Going beyond Mickey Mouse and bachelor taxes, the Irish Country Women's Association, in its submission, pointed to the lack of status and lack of opportunities for women in Ireland, and the fact that living in rural Ireland was simply drudgery for women working in the home, as many had to make do without running water, and services such as electricity were limited. Even if houses did have electricity, often the sole socket fitted would be used to power a radio rather than any labour-saving devices, reflecting male power within the household (Daly, 1997).

Most of the Commission's recommendations centred on economic development; however, it seemed pessimistic about the likelihood of achieving it: 'development – agricultural and industrial – and the rising standard of living which the population seeks, call for a programme of large-scale and long-term investment which far exceeds the present volume of domestic savings' (Commission on Employment and Other Population Problems, 1954, p. 168, in Connolly, 2004, p. 99). The Commission also acknowledged the need to improve welfare through diet, clothing and housing. It focused particularly on the need for rural development, through measures such as rural electrification, and the improvement of postal, telephone, transport and health services. Its recommendations highlighted the fact that agriculture and rural living were still very much at the forefront of Irish identity. The Commission was very conscious of movement from rural to urban areas, as well as abroad, and it called on educators to avoid fostering an 'urban mentality'. The report also suggested that there was an insufficiently developed sense of responsibility towards the family, with a new generation more concerned with individualistic material interests than national well-being (Ferriter, 2004).

SECTION 3: THE LATE 1950s TO THE LATE 1960s – ECONOMIC GROWTH AND THE GRADUAL EXPANSION OF SOCIAL POLICY PROVISION

In itself, the publication of the Commission's report did little to halt emigration. However, by the late 1950s increasing attention was given to the state of the economy and the need to find new solutions for the lack of economic progress. In November 1958, the government published a *Programme for Economic Expansion* which was the impetus for a new path of industrial development. This was preceded by an influential paper written by T. K. Whitaker in May 1958, entitled *Economic Development*. At this point Fianna Fáil was again back in power and its outlook began to change as Seán Lemass took over leadership of the party from Eamon de Valera in 1959. Prior to that he had been the Minister for Industry and Commerce and had been campaigning for a change of direction in economic policy. By 1958, in the *Programme for Economic Expansion* the government admitted the need to 'redefine the objectives of economic policy' (Government of Ireland, 1958, p. 7) in order to tackle emigration and unemployment, and to prevent Irish standards of living falling further behind the rest of Europe, which was now forging ahead with the creation of the European Economic Community (EEC) in 1958. The programme aimed to enhance agricultural production but it also envisaged more radical changes in industrial policy, re-orienting industrial production away from native producers and meeting the needs of Irish consumers. As the programme put it, 'we must be prepared to welcome foreign participation, financial and technical, in new industrial activities aimed at exports' (ibid., p. 36). A strong role for the state was envisaged through the financing of various schemes designed to encourage industrial development, the promotion of exports through the agency Coras Tráchtála Teo., and the attraction of foreign investment through the Industrial Development Authority. Alongside these measures aimed at stimulating private enterprise, the state also provided for the expansion and development of its own activities in steel, shipping, public transport, electricity, turf, civic aviation, telephones, mining and tourism. These policies were developed and implemented over a series of economic programmes, the first one covering the period 1959–63, the second intending to cover 1964–70, and a third one covering 1969–72.

This change of direction in economic policy began to yield some results in the 1960s, but what did it mean for social policy and the overall character of society? A well-known comment about this time is Murphy's (1979, p. 3) observation that 'the 1950s and 1960s are two sharply contrasting periods … Truly, it was the worst of decades followed by the best of decades'. While this might accurately reflect the economic changes that were beginning to take place, the same could not be said for developments in social policy. Within the economic programmes an emphasis was placed on productive spending, which meant that social policy had to take a back seat. In Whitaker's view, trying to achieve economic growth whilst also attempting to improve social services would amount to burning the candle at both ends:

> The way towards stabilisation and eventual reduction of taxation clearly lies (*inter alia*) in deferring further improvements in the social

services until a steady growth in real national income is well established. If resources are being used to the maximum to provide productive employment and raise all round living standards, it is impossible to devote them at the same time to improvements in social welfare – the national candle can not be burned at both ends. (Whitaker, 1958, in Kaim-Caudle, 1967, p. 104)

Despite these sentiments, some benefits did accrue to social policy. One of the first areas of social policy to benefit from the change in economic policy was education. The 1960s saw a shift away from an elite model of education to a mass model, with a growing role for the state. Until this time, the state had minimal input into the education system, preferring to leave provision to the various churches. However, special attention was given to education in the *Second Programme for Economic Expansion*. Here, education was justified as productive spending, reflecting the popularity of the idea of education as human capital in the 1960s; in other words, investment in people by educating and training them was regarded as an important source of economic growth. A report entitled *Investment in Education* followed in 1965, which was jointly published by the Irish government and the OECD. Not surprisingly, it found that significant class and regional inequalities existed in education participation rates and, given the rate of economic growth, the education system would not be fulfilling the needs of the economy by the 1970s. The report observed that workforce problems 'are to a large extent bound up with the question of participation, since increased numbers of certificants must largely come from those who otherwise would not be participating in the educational system at that level' (OECD, 1965, p. 326). Expanding the education system and increasing participation would, therefore, be both economically prudent and contribute to equality of opportunity.

A major step forward was the introduction of free post-primary level education in 1967–8, so that people would no longer have to come from a wealthy background or gain a scholarship to remain in school until their Leaving Certificate. As for third level, which was even more elitist at the time, a Local Authority (Higher Education Grant) Act was passed in 1968 to enable students from less well-off backgrounds to participate in third-level education. This was followed by a major expansion of the third-level sector, with the establishment of Regional Technical Colleges in particular. Increasing opportunities in education gave people greater chances of social mobility, and ownership of property or land became less influential in determining one's life chances.

Social mobility coincided with another kind of movement as more people moved from rural to urban areas. Ireland became more and more urbanised in the 1960s and 1970s. The 1971 census was the first to show that a greater number of people were living in urban than rural areas and any earlier attempts at keeping a check on the growth of an 'urban mentality' came undone. This rural-to-urban migration was facilitated by the growing output of houses, both in the private and the public sector. A model of mass housing development, involving the construction of maximum units for minimum cost, was adopted by the local authority housing sector, epitomised by the construction of large housing estates such as Ballymun in Dublin. The construction of large exclusively owner-occupied estates took off particularly in the 1970s. The demand for housing grew as the population increased and many of the emigrants who left in the 1950s returned as job prospects improved. There was a big increase in the proportion of people who owned their own homes.

In terms of healthcare, a White Paper entitled *The Health Services and their Further Development*, published in 1966, focused on streamlining the health system. The White Paper proposed that specialised healthcare could be most effectively organised from national and regional centres. The Health Act which followed in 1970 provided for the creation of eight regional health boards. Another milestone was the replacement of the dispensary system of healthcare with the General Medical Service in 1972. This finally ended the red ticket system. These were replaced by medical cards which allowed a choice of doctor and chemist to those who were eligible.

The social welfare system also expanded in the 1960s and 1970s, as new needs and new groups of people were recognised. This was true of the 1970s in particular, reflecting the fact that increases in expenditure in the 'non-productive' area of social welfare came later than 'productive' spending in areas such as education and housing. Much of the expansion in the system concerned the needs of women who had hitherto been largely excluded from the social welfare system on the grounds that most women were sustained by their breadwinner husbands. However, many of the payments introduced were for women as wives and mothers without husbands. The introduction of an unmarried mothers payment in 1973, for example, marked the first significant recognition of single mothers in Ireland, and Kennedy (2001, p. 219) remarks that its introduction was like 'stepping on to a new planet'. (See Chapters 7 to 10 for more detailed exploration of social service developments.)

Outside of the main social services, various reports and commissions signalled the emergence of some attention towards minority groups and to the area of services traditionally known as the personal social services, catering for specific needs beyond the remit of mainstream income, housing, health and education services. These included a report on Travellers in 1963, entitled *Report of the Commission on Itinerancy*. This report at least recognised the Travelling population in Ireland, which at that time were referred to as itinerants, but, paradoxically, the main thrust of the report was the absorption of the Travelling population into the settled community, thus negating their specific identity. People with intellectual disabilities, then referred to as the mentally handicapped, were the subject of the *Report of the Commission of Inquiry on Mental Handicap*, 1965, while older people were the concern of the 1968 report *The Care of the Aged*. A long overdue report on children in industrial and reformatory schools was published in 1970. This was the *Report on the Industrial and Reformatory Schools System*, which is known as the Kennedy report, named after the chairperson of the reporting body, District Justice Eileen Kennedy. This report finally marked the end of the era of industrial and reform schools, which were to be replaced with smaller residential centres and special schools.

A common theme of all three reports was the recognition of a need to move away from institutional forms of care and services towards more community-based care. The voluntary nature of much of the provision for these groups was also recognised, as in many cases voluntary organisations delivered the only services available in the absence of state provision. Despite expanding state provision during the 1960s, these reports encouraged the further development of voluntary provision, but with more formalised state funding and support. Thus, a trend developed of more state-sponsored but not state-delivered services (Donoghue, 1998a). Funding for voluntary initiatives had been strengthened by a provision in the 1953 Health Act, and the establishment of health boards in the 1970s moved this forward, particularly through community care programmes under which voluntary initiatives were seen as key to the delivery of community care. This trend was reinforced by the establishment of the National Social Services Council in 1971 whose remit was to encourage and stimulate new voluntary action (ibid.).

The expansion of social service provision and the recognition of the needs of groups that were previously hidden or treated in discriminatory or unjust ways had, therefore, mixed effects. New social services were characterised by a heavy reliance on means-tested as opposed to universal services, most notably in social security and health. In addition, the recognition of particular groups, such as women in the social security system, did not necessarily mean an end to discriminatory treatment. In the case of Travellers in some ways the 1963 report read more as a legitimisation of continued discrimination and lack of recognition than any fundamental change in attitude towards this group. Furthermore, the limits of state investment were particularly apparent in the case of groups such as people with disabilities and older people; voluntary groups were still expected to be at the forefront of provision in these areas.

CHAPTER SUMMARY

▶ This chapter profiled the main developments in the Irish economy and society from the 1920s to the 1960s and broadly considered their impact on social policy developments.

▶ For the most part it can be said that developments in social policy left a lot to be desired. Powerful interests and conservative attitudes combined with lack of economic development conspired to inhibit the emergence of new welfare programmes and ultimately the welfare state in Ireland.

▶ This lack of development impacted on the most vulnerable and minority groups, including the poor, children and women in particular.

▶ Signs of growth and innovation were evident by the 1960s and the needs of some previously excluded and/or hidden groups gained a degree of recognition. However, significant inequalities and social injustices persisted, which is a theme we turn to in the next chapter.

Discussion points

▶ Choose one or more of the various actors in Irish society during the period of the 1920s to the 1960s – such as the Catholic Church, prominent politicians, farmers and business interests, and women's groups – and assess their influence on social policy developments.

▶ If a policy of economic protectionism had not been pursued from the 1930s to the 1950s do you think Irish social policy would have developed differently?

▶ Research the experiences and the extent of social policy provision for particular groups during the early decades of independence, such as unmarried mothers, children in industrial schools, Travellers, older people.

Further reading

Browne, N. (1986) *Against the Tide*, Dublin: Gill and Macmillan.
Ferriter, D. (2004) *The Transformation of Ireland 1900–2000*, London: Profile Books.
Litton, F., (ed.) (1982) *Unequal Achievement: The Irish Experience 1957–1982*, Dublin: IPA.

Ó Gráda, C. (1997) *A Rocky Road: The Irish Economy since the 1920s*, Manchester: Manchester University Press.

Tweedy, H. (1992) *A Link in the Chain: the Story of the Irish Housewives' Association 1942–1992*, Dublin: Attic Press.

CHAPTER 3

FROM THE 1970s TO THE PRESENT: SOCIAL POLICY IN CONTEXT

The decades from the 1970s to the present have been marked by a series of intense social and economic changes which have been substantial in their effect on Irish society in general and on the evolution of social policy in particular. This chapter sets the context for understanding the development of social policy in Ireland since the 1970s by examining wider economic, political and social realities of relevance. Seen in this way, this chapter does not serve as a direct continuation of the previous two; rather it charts the broader political, economic and social backdrop to the development of social policy in recent decades. Part three of this book provides a detailed analysis of the core areas of Irish social policy over this period. This chapter sketches the major themes that are pertinent to that analysis and offers some insight into the broadened yet contested domain of Irish social policy in recent years.

Despite the expansion of social policy in the 1960s, by the early 1970s a growing critique emerged about the continuing failure of government in a number of areas, but primarily in relation to poverty and inequality. However, the more radical edge to political and social questioning present in the 1970s was overtaken by an altogether more austere and conservative climate during the 1980s. The economic crisis of the 1980s was shaken off in the most dramatic fashion over the course of the 1990s, with rapid and unprecedented economic growth. After decades of underinvestment, and in response to a chronic need for modernisation, investment in the social services increased substantially. The 1990s and 2000s have seen massive social change, and some major advances in social policy, but significant challenges remain.

CHAPTER OUTLINE

▸ The first section outlines the wider context of, and key advocates for, social change, which emerged during the 1970s, and it briefly considers the economic landscape, which by the end of the decade looked ominous.

> ▸ The second section reviews the particularly fraught decade of the 1980s, characterised by economic recession, emigration, unemployment and conflict over matters such as divorce and abortion, and considers the consequences of these issues for social policy.
>
> ▸ The third section sketches the intense economic and social change that has occurred since the 1990s and examines the broader impact by bringing key aspects of Irish social policy into sharper focus.

SECTION 1: SOCIAL CHANGE DURING THE 1970s

The turnaround in the Irish economy generated extra resources for some basic reforms and improvements in the main social services by the late 1960s, as profiled in Chapter 2. Yet, the 1960s and 1970s were also witness to a period of acute social and cultural change which in many ways highlighted continuing problems rather than progress in the way social policy was developing. Differing responses emerged to issues such as poverty and gender inequality over the course of the 1970s. It was a decade of radicalism and protest for some organised groups, including community and women's groups and the trade union movement. These groups made their voices heard in different ways and ultimately left their mark by pushing for change in core social policy areas, including gender equality, access to public services, responses to poverty, and in highlighting the potential of local communities and groups. Awareness was generated and this challenged the status quo and questioned, in particular, the more conservative values which had influenced social policy throughout its development in Ireland. New issues and debates emerged which facilitated some reluctant but long overdue reform. Ultimately, though, the decade might well be characterised in social policy terms as something of a false dawn, given the hostile ideological and economic climate which came to prevail in the 1980s.

The issues which came to the fore in the 1970s arose as a result of the late modernisation of Irish society and the shift away from an assumed view of Ireland as traditional, insular and self-sustaining. The economic policies pursued since the late 1950s had challenged this view in economic terms, but the implications of modern perspectives on issues such as the position of women, work and the family raised substantial social questions. Broader fora for the discussion of social change had also emerged. These had been developing over the previous decades, particularly in relation to the media, for example. In the 1940s, the average size of a newspaper was four pages and the first radio news bulletin of the day was at noon (Gageby, 1979). By the 1960s, these media had grown substantially, as had social reporting, represented, for example, by newspaper articles written by Michael Viney in the 1960s on previously relatively hidden subjects such as unmarried mothers, alcoholism and childhood deprivation.

The introduction of television (Teilifís Éireann) in 1961 also had a significant impact. By 1970 there were 438,000 TV licences, and television became a 'major conduit of imported mass cultural influences' (Lee, 1979, p. 173) which 'coincided with the spread of a questioning mentality and a receptivity to change' (ibid., p. 172). The Catholic Church was one of the established actors in social policy that was now subjected to this questioning mentality as, 'before the mid-1960s, it was unheard of for an Irish bishop to submit himself to interview' (Whyte, 1979, p. 79). The Catholic Church itself also developed a more critical view of the state's activity in social policy and 'government departments were increasingly likely to be criticised for not doing enough, rather than for doing too much' (ibid., p. 76). This partly reflected the influence of the second Vatican Council, held in Rome between 1962 and 1965, which reviewed the position of the Church in a modernising world, and oriented its message more towards the need for social justice. Another more practical element also came into play, namely a falling-off in vocations, which led to a gradual decline in the number of religious working in key areas of the social services such as hospitals and schools.

The renewal of the Irish women's movement acted as a significant force for change, and highlighted how social policy developments still left a lot to be desired in terms of women's welfare. One consequence of this was the establishment of the Commission on the Status of Women in 1970. This was the result of campaigning by a long-established women's group, the Irish Housewives Association, which joined with other groups to form an ad hoc committee of women's organisations for the purpose of lobbying the government to set up the commission. The commission's terms of reference included the task of making 'recommendations on the steps necessary to ensure the participation of women on equal terms and conditions with men in the political, social, cultural and economic life of the country' (Commission on the Status of Women, 1972, p. 7). The bulk of the commission's work focused on equal pay and equal work conditions for women, as well as equality in areas such as social welfare and taxation. It found, for example, that single women made up 81.4 per cent of all working women, and in the manufacturing sector, women's pay varied from 51.1 per cent to 66 per cent of men's pay. The commission's recommendations on equality between men and women, along with Ireland's entry to the EEC, finally forced the government to begin to dismantle the discriminatory architecture of policies towards women.

Another strand of the women's movement was represented by the emergence of more radical groups, which focused on the broader aim of equality for all women, rather than solely on the matter of equal treatment. These groups included the Irish Women's Liberation Movement (IWLM), formed in 1970, and Irish Women United (IWU), formed in 1975. They challenged the confining roles mapped out for women in Irish society and criticised the raft of discrimination against women in areas such as social welfare, employment, law, education, and also raised, albeit to a lesser extent, issues of sexuality. The aims of the IWLM, listed below, demonstrate some of the core issues for which the women's movement mobilised for change. It also signalled supporters' unhappiness with many of the reforms already occurring, which did not go far enough in dealing with such problems as poor housing conditions and inequalities in education and social welfare:

1 One Family, One House
2 Equal Rights in Law
3 Equal Pay Now, Removal of the Marriage Bar
4 Justice for Widows, Deserted Wives, Unmarried Mothers
5 Equal Educational Opportunities
6 Contraception – a Human Right (in Smyth, 1988, p. 335).

Another significant outcome of the women's movement at this time was the emergence of a number of new voluntary agencies (Connolly, 1996). These included the Well Woman Centre, Women's Aid, Adapt, the Rape Crisis Centre and Cherish. These organisations represented the development of a self-help philosophy, and at the same time pointed to major gaps and a lack of recognition of women's needs and issues on the part of the state, particularly in areas such as domestic violence, rape, and single motherhood.

The emergence of many of these women's groups along with other community-based organisations marked a shift in emphasis from 'charity' towards an ethos of participation and empowerment (Donoghue, 1998a). Participation and empowerment were important values in the growth of community activism in the 1970s. In addition to women's groups, these values were also manifested in tenants' groups and housing action groups in particular, who were critical of the economic development as it was unfolding, especially in terms of its effects on poorer communities in both urban and rural areas. Curtin and Varley (1995, p. 380) identify this as oppositional community action, characterised by criticism of state action founded on structural analysis which showed that far from alleviating inequality 'the state played an important role in underpinning patterns of disadvantage'. This analysis was also reflected in the establishment of an EEC anti-poverty programme in Ireland which, as Donoghue (1998b, p. 20) notes, 'provided another building block in community activism as this emphasized the structural causes of poverty and promoted a process of community empowerment'.

Emerging frameworks for economic and social policy

Another significant force for economic and social policy change in Ireland was entry into the EEC. The national debate about joining the EEC was largely cast in terms of the economic benefits that would follow, as Ireland was still far behind the rest of the EEC in economic terms. While the social and cultural implications of membership were not a key concern, joining at least signified that Ireland was opening up to outside influences. Following a long preparatory period during the 1960s in which an earlier application for membership fell through in 1963 (FitzGerald, 1998) and a constitutional amendment which required a referendum (in which 83 per cent voted in favour); Ireland became a member of the Community in 1973. Membership of the EEC was to allow greater access to external markets both for indigenous industry and for multi-national companies located in Ireland. Membership offered new economic prospects, with less reliance on the UK market for exports. Farmers benefited through the higher prices they received for their produce under the Common Agricultural Policy (CAP). Income levels were 55–60 per cent of the Community average at the time of accession, which meant that Ireland would also benefit from the wider distributive policies of the EEC (ibid.), and significant grants were subsequently received through the European Social Fund and the Regional Development Fund (Kennedy et al., 1988; Mac Sharry and White, 2000).

Apart from the economic interests served by membership of the EEC, its role in securing greater rights for women during the 1970s, which complemented the role of the women's movement, is also important. Membership meant that Ireland had to pay much more attention to equality policies, specifically in relation to equality of opportunity for women in the workforce, even though its first impulse was to try to resist this implication of EEC membership. A process of gradual reform followed with the introduction of the Anti-Discrimination Pay Act in 1974 and the Employment Equality Act in 1977, along with the establishment of the Employment Equality Agency in 1977 to oversee the operation of this legislation (Bacik, 2004). (See Chapter 6 for greater detail on the overall influence of EU membership on Irish social policy.)

At the level of national policymaking the establishment of the National Economic and Social Council (NESC) in 1973 also played a role in the development of social policy in Ireland. The emergence of a new national body whose members (now referred to as the **social partners**) had a range of interests and where the specific terms of reference involved reviewing social and economic issues for consideration by government was noteworthy, both as an emerging structure of national social partnership and in terms of enhancing 'the flow of information and intelligence available to such decision makers as [choose] to take cognisance of them' (Lee, 1989, p. 365). Work was

> **Social partners** are representatives of particular groups (including trade unions, employers/business, farmers and the community/voluntary sector) that may be consulted and/or engage in a process with government to secure agreement on specific aspects of policy.

produced by the NESC in its early years examining previously neglected debates in Irish social policy, including universal and selective provision of services, issues of distribution and the objectives of social policy at that time. Insightful comments offered by the NESC (1975, p. 13) illustrate the nature of the debate, which continue to resonate:

> Agreement about what would constitute an ideal distribution of income and wealth may be difficult to achieve. Again, however, differences must not be overstated. There is agreement that income should be redistributed to the disadvantaged to assure them not only of the necessities but also of the basic amenities of life. However, there are differences of view on the extent to which this should be carried. There is also agreement that every member of our society should have every incentive to contribute to the full extent of his capacities to the welfare of the community – but there are differences of view, for example, about the size of the income differentials that may be necessary to ensure that this happens.

Significant too, particularly for the time, was the NESC (ibid., p. 16) position that:

> … the Council has been concerned with the concept of social policy that should guide its thinking and its future work. Narrow definitions of social policy that limit it to social services must be rejected. In its work, the Council will be concerned with the social (i.e. the distributional) effects and implications of all major policies.

Subsequent work produced by the NESC during the 1970s did reflect this overall philosophy, although maintaining such a focus over the longer term, particularly with less favourable economic circumstances, proved difficult. It is important to note that while the NESC makes policy recommendations to government, these do not have to be accepted or implemented. Nevertheless, the emergence of an advisory body with such a focus represented a major boost for the development of social policy debate in Ireland at that time.

Responding to poverty

After the 'feel good years' of the 1960s, the 1970s provided more realism about the expectation that the rising tide could lift all boats. Specifically, the 'rediscovery of poverty', as it became known, saw the emergence of evidence, first in the US and UK and later in Ireland, that 'poverty hadn't gone away'. In their landmark study of poverty in the UK, Abel-Smith and Townsend (1965) were instrumental in re-conceptualising poverty and its measurement. Their approach was based on a relative understanding of poverty, which considered the circumstances of individuals relative to the rest of the society in which they lived.

In Ireland, the first research incorporating this perspective was presented at the Kilkenny Conference on Poverty in 1971. Research undertaken by Ó Cinnéide (1972) found that at least 24 per cent of the population fell below the poverty line, based on social welfare rates in the North and South. His later work revised this figure to 27 per cent (Powell, 1992). This research confirmed the existence of significant social problems which others had also highlighted. It displayed the inadequacies of Irish welfare provision and its limited capacity to deal with poverty. This pioneering work marked the beginning of more sustained attention to, and research into, the causes and incidence of poverty in Ireland. The initial political response of the Fine Gael/Labour coalition government of 1973–7 came through the establishment of an advisory Committee, the National Committee on Pilot Schemes to Combat Poverty (NCPSCP), whose role it was to coordinate pilot schemes funded by the EEC poverty programme. However that funding came to an end in 1980 as did the NCPSCP, although its final report called for the establishment of a national agency (Curry, 2003). The Combat Poverty Agency (CPA) was subsequently established in 1986.

Notwithstanding the positive impact of the pilot schemes in some local areas and the fact that they raised the issue of poverty in Ireland more generally, Brown notes that (1981, p. 149), 'the problem of poverty remains marginal to economic and social planning at both national and Community level and there is little apparent conviction that this is an issue of the first priority.' The reliance on the EEC to both fund and shape the policy responses to poverty also indicates its secondary status as an issue in Ireland at that time.

Economic frailties of the 1970s

In the midst of this re-conceptualisation of poverty, economic growth continued although it was not failsafe. The expansionary economic model of the 1960s and the shift to a more open economy remained central. The policy of promoting Foreign Direct Investment (FDI) continued, and by

1973 one-third of all manufacturing jobs were in Multi-National Companies (MNCs) (Ó Gráda, 1997). Employment growth was strong, with non-agricultural employment rising by an average of 2.2 per cent per annum from 1973–80 (Kennedy, 1993). In fact, Ireland enjoyed its first period of net inward migration, with immigration of 109,000 recorded for 1971–9 (Blackwell, 1982). The arrival of MNCs, while broadly welcomed for the economic opportunities they would provide, was only one element in the overall employment landscape. Home-grown or indigenous industry struggled to keep pace with the growth in FDI and competition from imports made it difficult for existing industries. There were other distortions in the employment expansion of the 1970s too; the state was the major employer of the decade, with five of every ten jobs created outside of agriculture being located in the public sector (Sexton, 1986).

These frailties in the employment situation were compounded by other troubling economic indicators. Internationally, the so-called 'oil crises' had led to a massive increase in the cost of oil, resulting in a worldwide recession. Inflation (and greater wage demands) became a significant difficulty in Ireland over the course of the 1970s. In addition, government borrowing emerged as an issue after the long-standing policy of balancing current expenditure with current revenue was abandoned in 1972 (Kennedy et al., 1988). Notwithstanding the severe economic outlook, domestic demand and economic growth continued. By the end of the decade, however, cracks were beginning to appear in the Irish economy; PAYE workers protested over their dissatisfaction with the equity of the tax system; demands for wage increases were considered increasingly unsustainable; and the national debt was mounting. The 1980s ultimately became the payback decade for the economic laxity of previous years.

SECTION 2: ECONOMIC CRISIS AND THE SOCIAL CHALLENGES OF THE 1980S

> Will the last TD to leave the Dáil please switch off the light at the end of the tunnel? (Browne, in *Magill*, January 1982, p. 21)

The 1980s is not a decade that is fondly remembered – massive emigration, high unemployment, high interest rates, high inflation, cutbacks in social services and inadequate social welfare payments made life a tough grind for many families trying to make ends meet. The country was in the midst of a heavy and unrelenting economic recession for much of the 1980s, the origins of which are frequently attributed to political decisions taken in the previous decade. The general election of 1977 is noteworthy for more than the fact that the largest overall majority was secured by one political party in Ireland. Fianna Fáil returned 84 seats out of 148, with 50.6 per cent of the total vote (Lee, 1989), and their manifesto is frequently referred to as an ambitious and expensive programme for government, which it transpired the country could ill afford. Borrowing was used as a bolster to government spending during the 1970s at a time when it could have done without. On this, T. K. Whitaker (1986, p. 15) observed, 'By then we had already been so misusing our borrowing potential that we had little leeway for stimulating the economy when genuine need arose.' And as the 1980s wore on, that need was unrelenting. Government borrowing had reached crisis point, with the external debt estimated to be of the order of £10,000 per person at work in 1986 (ibid.). The national debt rose from 68 per cent of GNP in 1970 to 129 per cent of GNP by 1986. As the debt level rose so too did the cost of servicing it, with four out of every five pounds collected in income tax needed to cover the interest on the national debt alone (Mac Sharry, 2000a). In addition, the steady decline in the numbers at work in agriculture, along with serious job losses in the manufacturing sector throughout the 1970s and 1980s outstripped the gains made in creating new employment. Larger scale factory closures, which had a very serious impact on local economies and many families, included Ferenka in Limerick in 1978 and the Ford car and Dunlop tyre manufacturing plants in Cork in 1980.

The connection between unemployment and poverty was clearly exposed, and the shortcomings in social service and welfare provisions became more apparent in the Ireland of the 1980s. The inadequacy of the social infrastructure in place meant that by now it was clear that many social groups continued to live on the margins, due to poverty and a lack of opportunities and the fact that the services on which many were reliant belonged to an earlier era. Poverty studies indicated the extent to which the social services and welfare system fell short (Kennedy, 1981). In particular, unemployed people and their children, women, single-parent families, older people, people in institutional care and the Travelling community were identified as being at particular risk of poverty (Fitzgerald, 1981). Furthermore, poverty was not only the preserve of 'at-risk' groups; there was evidence of a 'working poor' phenomenon, with at least one person working in almost half of the poorest 30 per cent of households (Trench and Brennan, 1980).

The economic difficulties were compounded by a lack of political stability in government, particularly during the early 1980s. There were three governments between mid-1981 and the end of 1982 when a Fine Gael/Labour coalition secured office until 1987. The mounting problems in the public finances were a persistent difficulty which led to spending cuts in key areas of the public services such as the closure of some hospitals and strict controls on public service recruitment and pay (Maguire, 1998). It was the nature of the proposed spending cuts which ultimately led the Labour Party to withdraw from that coalition government early in 1987.

Demographic pressures and unemployment: the consequences

> Never have so many been dependent on so few for so much. (Tansey, in *Magill*, July 1989, p. 45)

The demographic profile of the country in the early 1980s presented a considerable challenge in terms of the massive need for employment and the availability of social services. The fact that fertility rates in Ireland remained high until 1980, long after the post-war baby boom had subsided elsewhere, meant that there was a large cohort of young people and families for whom social services were needed. In economic terms this is understood as a high-dependency ratio, that is, the number of 'dependants' in proportion to those 'economically active'. Fahey and Fitz Gerald (1997, p. 98) explain the impact of the high-dependency ratio at that time: 'The mid-1980s witnessed peak levels of *economic* dependency ... a small workforce was supporting a very large child population, a very large number of unemployed and a reasonably large elderly population. The number of women in home duties was also very large.' This demographic profile imposed a heavy financial burden on the state, an impact felt more acutely in the context of persistently high unemployment and corresponding demands on the health, education and social welfare systems. Unemployment increased from just below 10 per cent of the workforce in 1981 to almost 17 per cent by 1987. The costs of the severe economic recession were not only felt by the state, however. Individuals and families bore the burden of a lack of work and income, and ran the risk of potential negative impacts on physical and mental health and familial and marital relations (see Breen, 1987, for a review of relevant literature of the time). The phenomenon of long-term unemployment became a particularly difficult feature of the unemployment crisis at this time. One study of the experiences and views of some long-term unemployed people in Tallaght (Ronayne and Creedon, 1991) illustrates the depth of feeling, with participants expressing the following views:

> The longer I am unemployed, the more unemployable I become. (ibid., p. 40)

> Being unemployed takes your dignity away. You are demeaned while you are asking for your legitimate entitlements. (ibid., p. 47)

I applied for a job in the Square and they said I was too old. I'm 32. (ibid., p. 53)

Research produced by the Economic and Social Research Institute (ESRI) in 1987 indicated that three out of five households where the head was unemployed fell below the poverty line (Callan et al., 1989). A study of the scale and impact of the poverty experienced by women in Ireland, also based on the 1987 ESRI research, found that 274,000 adult women (slightly over 30 per cent) lived in poverty (Daly, 1989). In addition, female participation in the labour force remained low throughout the decade, with a 30 per cent female participation rate in 1985 (CSO, 2006). Over half of all women worked full-time in the home in 1987 (Daly, 1989). Women who did work outside the home continued to earn less than men. In 1987, the average gross weekly wage of women in industry was 40 per cent below that of men. In short, despite some important legislative changes during the 1970s, the continued absence of opportunities or infrastructure (e.g. childcare) along with the persistence of traditional attitudes about the role of women in society, denied many women the chance of labour force participation on the same basis as men. The significant achievements of the women's movement during the 1970s certainly helped to expose the structural inequalities which persisted for women, but the reluctance of government to engage in more substantial policy reform was also clear. The lack of work undoubtedly compounded the situation, however.

Given the historical and long-standing problem with the lack of adequate employment, it is interesting to note that – the unemployment movements of the 1950s notwithstanding – the first national organisation to represent unemployed people was not established until 1987 (Allen, 1998). This organisation, the Irish National Organisation for the Unemployed (INOU) came to play a key role in advocating the rights of unemployed people, particularly at a time when the recognition of those rights was under considerable threat elsewhere (see Chapter 4). This is not to say that they had it all their own way but the INOU played a part in representing the needs of this group and by the 1990s it sought to influence employment policies and continued to argue for full employment when few believed it to be possible (Larragy, 2006). The emergence of representative bodies such as the INOU was to become more significant in terms of the broader issue of policymaking in Ireland during the 1990s, as we will see below.

Emigration

The lack of work resulted in renewed emigration on a scale comparable with 1950s Ireland. The net outflow of emigrants totalled 130,000 for the years 1983–8. More men than women emigrated. In the 1981–6 intercensal period, for every 1,000 men who emigrated, 736 women emigrated. Young people in particular left: 70.6 per cent of those who emigrated between 1981 and 1986 were aged 15–24. Another significant trend, perhaps mirroring the expansion of education since the 1960s, was that in contrast to the tradition of those from lower socio-economic groups emigrating, by the 1980s, there was a relatively even distribution of people across the classes emigrating (NESC, 1991). The proportion of university graduates that emigrated during this period highlighted the scale of the problem; in 1988, for instance, 26.1 per cent of graduates left the country (Ó Gráda, 1997). Commonly referred to as the 'brain drain', the loss of so many of the best-educated was a significant cause for concern. O'Toole (1988) wrote that the scale of graduate emigration meant that the main beneficiaries of graduate-level education were foreign governments and companies.

The government response appears to have been yet again one of ambivalence, exemplified by Minister Brian Lenihan's famous remark that 'after all, we can't all live on a small island' in an interview published in *Newsweek* in October, 1987:

> I don't look on the type of emigration we have today as being in the same category as the terrible emigration of the last century. What we have now is a very literate emigrant who thinks nothing of coming to the United States and going back to Ireland and maybe on to Germany and back to Ireland again. The younger people in Ireland today are very much in that mode ... It [emigration] is not a defeat because the more Irish emigrants hone their skills and talents in another environment, the more they develop a work ethic in a country like Germany or the US, the better it can be applied in Ireland when they return. After all we can't all live on a small island. (Lenihan in Whelan, 1987)

Social policy development during the 1980s: emerging recognition but few resources and little reform

In the midst of the problems of rising unemployment and high levels of welfare dependency the government commissioned the first ever review of the Irish social welfare system in 1983. The *Report of the Commission on Social Welfare* was published in 1986 and made many recommendations for reform of the system, not least of which related to improving the adequacy of social welfare payments and the establishment of a minimum adequate income. The report, however, came at the height of the economic crisis, thereby making it difficult to act swiftly on its recommendations. The government statement (cited in Curry, 2003, p. 35) on its publication makes this clear:

... in present circumstances and for the immediate future it would be beyond the capacity of the country to fully implement the Commission's proposals. This is an unpalatable reality but it must be borne in mind in the context of considering all the Commission's proposals.

Nevertheless, the report was widely publicised and its relevance was indisputable in the context of the significant demands on the social welfare system at that time. The recommendations of the Commission did influence subsequent policy decisions in the area over the next number of years (see Chapter 7).

Despite the scarce resources of the 1980s, policy documents were drawn up in a number of previously neglected areas of social policy. In an examination of the mental health services *The Psychiatric Services: Planning for the Future* (1984) provided the policy framework for de-institutionalisation and the development of community-based services where possible, although issues did arise with its implementation. With regard to the needs of older people, a working party completed a report in 1988 entitled *The Years Ahead, A Policy Document for the Elderly,* which reviewed relevant health and welfare services; however, many of its recommendations remained unimplemented until recent years. *A Green Paper on Services for Disabled People* (1984), published by the Department of Health, marked the beginning of greater recognition of the needs of people with disabilities in Ireland, although it was into the 1990s and 2000s before much of the necessary legislation was enacted. The position of the Travelling Community was considered in the *Report of the Travelling People Review Body* (1983) and it made a significant advance (from the earlier *Commission on Itinerancy,* produced in 1963) in recognising the distinct identity of Travellers in Ireland, although this was not developed upon (Crowley, 1999). Neither were any particular resources made available to affirm this recognition (ibid.). The *O'Sullivan Report* (1980) and the *Costello Report* (1984) reviewed the position of youth work in Ireland and made recommendations about the future development of the area but these were not implemented (Jenkinson, 1996). In response to the problem of emigration, NESC published a report in 1991 entitled the *Economic and Social Implications of Emigration.* It made recommendations both to try and halt the flow of emigration and to assist those who emigrated to Britain in particular and who were struggling. Ultimately, however, the issue of emigration was resolved by an upturn in the economy rather than any specific government efforts in the area.

In short, the 1980s saw the emergence of greater attention to the needs of many different and previously neglected sectors of Irish society but this was not necessarily translated into policy implementation. It seemed that such groups would need to demand political attention and policy change and many subsequently did (see below).

The stalled 'liberal agenda' and Irish solutions to Irish problems

In addition to economic troubles and the challenges these posed for social policy during the 1980s, the decade was marked by a resurgence of Catholic social teaching and conflict in areas such sexuality, contraception, divorce, the family, and the role of the state in the lives of individuals generally. As Inglis (2002, p. 7) puts it, 'While there is no evidence of a causal connection, the economic recession coincided with the emergence of a new strident Catholic morality.' The advances made by the women's movement and the increased attention given to issues of equality in the 1970s did not result in a seamless process of change in social values and attitudes in Irish society during the 1980s. This decade was to be a bleak one for many Irish women in particular; in Smyth's assessment (1993, p. 265) '... women were subjected to unprecedented social, psychic, and moral battering.'

Contraception

The public debate generated by the women's movement about the availability of contraceptives during the 1970s and the decision of the Supreme Court in the McGee case (ruling that there was a right to marital privacy under the constitution) did not result in legislative change until 1979. The Fine Gael/Labour coalition had produced a Bill to allow for the importation, manufacture and sale of contraceptives but it was defeated (Kennedy, 2001). A political solution was finally delivered in the legislation passed in 1979 by then Minister for Health, Charles Haughey, which allowed for contraceptives to be available but under prescription and to bona fide married couples only. This was the legislative compromise put forward, in response to opposition to the availability of contraceptives by many. This period saw a sustained campaign against the legalisation of contraceptives by such groups as The Council for Social Concern and The League of Decency. It was in this context that the contraception legislation enacted in 1979 was assessed as, 'a genuine attempt to accommodate to the old values *and* the new, an impossible task, breeding a piece of legislation ignored in practice and condemned on all sides' (Kerrigan, 1983, p. 8). As then Secretary General of the Department of Health, Margaret Hayes (1995, cited in Kennedy, 2001, p. 233) recalled:

> The key phrase in the bill was that contraception was to be available on prescription for *bona fide* family planning purposes. We felt that it was as far as we could go in terms of public acceptability but it did pave the way for subsequent amendments.

Subsequent amendments were eventually passed; first with the Family Planning Act, 1985, which legalised contraceptives, and then in 1993, partly as a consequence of the fear surrounding the spread of the HIV virus, the sale of condoms was more widely permitted.

Private morality

The extent of state regulation of matters of private morality was exemplified in the case of a female teacher who lost her job when, in February 1984, the Employment Appeals Tribunal upheld the right of her employer (a religious order) to sack her on the basis that she had become pregnant by the married man with whom she lived. This dismissal was later upheld in the High Court in July 1984 (Inglis, 2002). In January of the same year, a fifteen-year-old school girl gave birth at the foot of a grotto in County Longford, where both she and the baby died. Also in the same year, the case of the Kerry Babies came to prominence when the Garda investigation into the death of two new-born babies collapsed and was followed by a Public Tribunal of Inquiry into the case. The Tribunal lasted 84 days, during which time there was much public vilification of the woman at the centre of the case, despite the fact that the case being made was rejected by one of the expert witnesses for the prosecution (ibid.).

The married nuclear family remained the preferred model to be followed in Irish law, although the absence of rights for children born outside of marriage was identified as an issue for consideration by the Law Reform Commission in 1983. It argued that in the constitutional protection of marriage the law should not deny the rights of children born outside of marriage. It recommended 'that the legislation remove the concept of illegitimacy from the law and equalise the rights of children born outside marriage with those of children born within marriage' (cited in Kennedy, 2001, p. 234). A Supreme Court ruling in 1984 held that the Succession Act, 1965, gave no succession rights to illegitimate children and that the Act was in accordance with Article 41 of the constitution (ibid.). The traditional married Irish family was that which was protected in legal terms although the Status of Children Act, which was passed in 1987, provided greater recognition to the guardianship, maintenance and inheritance rights of the children of unmarried parents. With regard to marriage breakdown, the right to divorce was rejected by 63.5 per cent of those who voted in June 1986, notwithstanding the fact that polls conducted as early as 1977 had indicated that public opinion would favour the legalisation of divorce in Ireland (Magill, 1977). The influence of the Catholic Church, which may have been perceived to be waning, was considerable, in both the abortion and divorce referenda held during the 1980s, and highlighted the sustained influence of Catholic social teaching on social policy in Ireland.

Abortion

The 'moral' tensions which began in the 1970s spilled over to divisive effect with the emergence of a lobby for an abortion referendum in 1980. Already illegal under the 1861 Offences Against the Persons Act, abortion became an issue in the context of proposed legislative change in the UK and, probably more importantly, as a result of the issue of abortion referral, which was not a crime in Ireland. The movement gained ground with the establishment of the Irish Society for the Protection of the Unborn Child in 1980. Other groups subsequently entered the fray (including The Irish Catholic Doctors' Guild and The Responsible Society), culminating in the emergence of the Pro-Life Amendment Campaign in April 1981 (Brennan, 1982; Kerrigan, 1983). Following nearly two years of divisive debate, an abortion referendum was carried by a two-to-one majority which, by virtue of the wording, made abortion unconstitutional in Ireland in 1983.

The Eighth Amendment to the Constitution, Article 40.3.3., reads as follows:

> The State acknowledges the right to life of the unborn and, with due regard to the equal right to life of the mother, guarantees in its laws to respect, and, as far as practicable, by its laws to defend and vindicate that right.

The impact of the amendment quickly became apparent when Irish courts ruled that information on the procurement of an abortion abroad could not be made available in Ireland. Ultimately, in 1992, this was challenged in the European Court of Human Rights, which found that a ban on information on abortion was contrary to Article 10 of the European Convention on Human Rights. In February of that year, the law was applied to prevent a 14-year-old girl who became pregnant as a result of rape from travelling abroad for an abortion. Ultimately, the Supreme Court ruled that an abortion was permissible if the girl was suicidal and there was therefore 'a real and substantial risk to the life, as distinct from the health, of the mother'. The X case, as it became known, caused public outcry and the government was forced to respond. In November 1992 the government proposed three further amendments to Article 40.3.3. These covered the 'substantive issue' of abortion, the right to information and the freedom to travel. The amendment to the 'substantive issue' was not carried (and many on both sides of the debate claimed victory), but the right to information and travel were passed (Bacik, 2004).

After almost ten years, there was, at least, clarity about freedom to travel and the right to information. However, the emergence of the C Case in November 1997 came as a stark reminder of what had evolved since 1983, when a girl in the care of the state, who was also pregnant as a result of rape, sought to have a termination. The Eastern Health Board applied and was permitted by the Courts to enable the girl to travel to Britain for an abortion (Galligan, 1999). However, the position with regard to abortion in Ireland continues to remain unclear and as Mr Justice Niall McCarthy (in Kennedy, 2002, pp. 115–16) pointed out in 1992, '… the failure by the legislature to enact the appropriate legislation is no longer just unfortunate; it is inexcusable.' It was not until the late 1990s that the issue was again taken up by government (see below). In the meantime, at least 37,000 Irish women travelled to the UK for a termination during the 1980s alone. Over 48,000 women are estimated to have travelled over the course of the 1990s (Irish Family Planning Association, n.d.).

Responding to the economic crisis: cutbacks and consensus

> If countries really can go broke, then by late 1986, early 1987, Ireland, cast in the role of Celtic pauper, was emerging as a prime candidate for bankruptcy. (Mac Sharry and White, 2000, p. 356)

Fianna Fáil was returned to office in 1987 and although they ran an election campaign slogan 'Health Cuts Hurt the Old, the Sick and the Handicapped: There is a Better Way', their budgetary actions quickly placed them in retrenchment mode. Cutbacks in public services, which included the closure of hospital beds, the lack of maintenance of basic social infrastructure, such as school buildings, the selling off of local authority houses, an early retirement scheme, a freeze on recruitment and the postponement of special pay awards in the public service, indicated their intent. Reflecting on *The Challenge of 1987*, the then Minister for Finance Ray Mac Sharry (2000a, p. 63) recalled that:

> On the election of the government, the Taoiseach and I quickly agreed a common approach. We recognised we had to seize the initiative from the spending departments, and do so from the outset … We also knew, and fully accepted, that major financial surgery would have to be performed. Except this time, the operation would have to be carried out on the patient without the benefit of an anaesthetic.

The first edition of *Poverty Today*, published by the CPA in December 1987, indicates the nature of the cutbacks planned. The National Social Service Board (the organisation with responsibility for the development and support of community information centres throughout the country, later renamed Comhairle) was initially to be abolished, although, following protests from the voluntary sector (Acheson et al., 2004), its functions were actually limited instead. The CPA also had to revise its objectives in view of a 50 per cent cut in staff and resources applied to the organisation in 1988 (CPA, 1987). The reduction in the Department of Education budget had a serious effect on the services and supports offered by the Vocational Education Committee (VEC); and the National Adult Literacy Agency (NALA) also had its budget cut by one-third (Trench et al., 1987). In addition, young people on AnCO (now FÁS) training schemes had their allowances reduced by one-third (CPA, 1987). Reviewing the impact of the AnCO cuts on Traveller training schemes, Trench et al. (1987, p. 6), writing in *Magill* at the time, considered that 'The £10 cut in trainee allowances to £20 may persuade some of the teenagers to go elsewhere; they could expect to earn more from begging.'

1987 General Election poster. Source: *Magill*, May 1987, p. 61. Derek Speirs.

The implementation of the cutbacks was most acutely felt by some of the most vulnerable members of Irish society. Trench et al. (1987), for example, outline how cutbacks were affecting the lives of individuals, through a series of measures implemented by different Health Boards around the country. The Midland Health Board, for instance, introduced charges for appeals to medical card refusals and for claims for refunds on money spent on medicines. In the Eastern Health Board the number of incontinence pads provided for a four-year-old child with spina bifida was reduced. Hospital closures were common and a total of 1,470 general hospital beds were closed by February 1988 (Dáil Éireann, 9 February 1988, written answers – hospital closures) and this figure does not include beds closed in other hospitals. In the area of housing, both the Home Improvements Grants Scheme (introduced in 1985) and the Builders' Grants for New Dwellings (introduced in 1986) were abolished in 1987 (Curry, 1998). In addition, local authority house-completion rates reached an all-time low by 1989 (Silke, 1999). (Chapters 7 to 10 provide a more detailed assessment of the impact of the cutbacks of this decade.)

Consensus: social partnership and 'the national interest'

The mood was grim, but several factors appear to have coalesced to create a greater sense of shared purpose around the need for economic and fiscal reform. In September 1987, Alan Dukes, leader of the opposition, gave a speech to the Tallaght Chamber of Commerce at which he committed the support of the Fine Gael party to government efforts to deal with the economic difficulties of the time (Mac Sharry, 2000b). The 'Tallaght Strategy', as it became known, offered a significant vote of confidence to the government to persevere with its economic reform, despite the hardships it would bring in the short-term. The second noteworthy development of the time was that negotiations were underway between the social partners and the government to deliver a new national agreement. The opening statement of the agreement, the Programme for National Recovery (PNR), indicates the prevailing mood. 'The Government, the ICTU, the FUE, the CII, the CIF, the IFA, Macra na Feirme and the ICOS, conscious of the grave state of our economic and social life, have agreed on this Programme to seek to regenerate our economy and improve the social equity of our society through their combined efforts' (Government of Ireland, 1987, p. 5). A number of factors were highlighted in the programme, which indicate the scale of the economic difficulties confronting policymakers at the time:

(a) a Gross Domestic Product per capita which is only 64 per cent of the European Community average,

(b) a National Debt of over £25 billion which is equivalent to more than one and one-half times of our Gross National Product and the servicing of which consumes annually one-third of Exchequer tax revenue,

(c) an Exchequer borrowing requirement of 10.7 per cent of Gross National Product in 1987 to finance both current and capital expenditure. This is among the highest budgetary deficits in the European Community,

(d) high nominal and real interest rates which are a barrier to investment,

(e) an unemployment rate of 18.5 per cent of the work-force amounting to 242,000 persons, of whom 73,000 are under 25

years of age. This is one of the highest rates of unemployment in
the European Community,

(f) employment in agriculture which continues to decline steadily
at a rate almost twice the European Community average,

(g) net emigration estimated currently at close to 30,000 and which
is equivalent to the natural increase in the population, and

(h) no overall growth in the volume of investment in equipment over
the past 5 years compared with an increase of 20 per cent in the
European Community. (ibid.)

Both in Ireland and abroad the economic situation showed signs of
improvement from 1988 onwards. Economic growth averaged 4.7 per cent
per annum in the period 1987–91 and this was notably higher than the EU
average of three per cent (Bacon, 1997). In addition, employment in the
non-agricultural economy rose by 14,000 per annum between 1987 and
1991 and in the private sector by 18,000 per annum over the same period
(ibid.). The debt to GNP ratio started to fall as did interest rates. The
economic recovery in the UK meant the appreciation of Sterling which
helped to make Irish wage levels more competitive. A tax amnesty returned
a larger than expected revenue windfall to the government and a doubling
of EU structural funding provided an opportunity to invest in some capital
projects (Honohan, 1999). It took somewhat longer for the improved
economic circumstances to filter down to the population at large.
Emigration and persistent unemployment continued for the remainder of
the 1980s and into the early 1990s. Unemployment dropped back to 13 per
cent by 1990 thanks to a total increase in employment but also sustained
emigration. As Kennedy (1993, p. 7) points out, 'The reduction in
unemployment, however, owed far more to resumption of high emigration
than to employment growth. While employment rose by 47,000 from 1985
to 1990, emigration in that period amounted to 164,000.' It was clear,
therefore, that in employment terms Ireland was still unable to provide
adequate opportunities for those in need of them, but over the course of
the 1990s there was much more change to come.

SECTION 3: THE 1990s AND 2000s – NEW TIMES AND A NEW IRELAND?

Given the bleakness of the 1980s, the election of feminist lawyer Mary
Robinson as President of Ireland in 1990 offered a powerful representation
of the potential for social change in Ireland. For the first time, a woman

occupying the highest office in the state presented for many the opportunity to imagine a different vision for Irish society. Her inaugural speech was testament to this, her address to the women and men of Ireland, and her acknowledgement of the Irish diaspora offered recognition and hope of a new kind. The style of presidency adopted was open and inviting, particularly for women and community groups. Her connectedness with civil society was explicit (Brown, 2004). Commenting on this and also the timing of this presidency, Brown (ibid., p. 362) notes that '... the kind of self-confidence Robinson had engendered enabled many ordinary citizens to feel that their own participation in society was a real resource, in a decade when the foundations of the Irish social structure seemed to fracture' (Brown, 2004, p. 364). The 1990s was indeed the period in which cracks began to appear in many of the core institutions, including church and state.

Confronting the past and dealing with the present

The Catholic and largely conservative Ireland of the 1980s described above might feel like something far removed from the Ireland of today. However, when perspectives on, and attitudes to, core areas of debate such as the family, access to abortion, and the rights of minority groups are examined, a complex and more opaque picture of Irish society and its values emerge. Ireland learned a lot about other elements of its hidden and often very painful past over the course of the 1990s. The appalling abuses suffered in Industrial Schools were exposed and victims spoke, many for the first time, about their experiences. In 1996, RTÉ broadcast 'Dear Daughter' which dealt with the abuses in the Goldenbridge Orphanage (Kennedy, 2001). Three years later, a three-part documentary series 'States of Fear' gave a harrowing account of the abuses suffered in Industrial Schools (see Raftery and O'Sullivan, 1999).

Earlier in the 1990s the Kilkenny Incest Case and The West of Ireland Farmer Case, as they were known, highlighted in a very stark way, the extreme abuse that could happen within the confines of the family; these cases exposed the inadequacies in the Irish child protection system but, undoubtedly, they also raised public consciousness about the existence of child abuse and contributed to the full implementation of the Child Care Act, 1991 (the legislation which details the responsibilities of the state with regard to the protection of children), by 1996. There was a significant increase in notified cases of child abuse throughout the 1990s (Ferguson and O'Reilly, 2001), probably reflecting the growing awareness of the issue. Accounts of clerical sex abuse also came to light, the pain of which, for many victims, was compounded by the non-management/mismanagement of the issue by senior religious figures in many dioceses. The failure of the Catholic Church to respond effectively to allegations of child sexual abuse among some of its practicing priests (see, for example, Report of the Ferns Inquiry,

2005) has damaged its reputation in the public mind, both in Ireland and elsewhere.

The second divorce referendum took place in the context of government support, which pointed to a growing number of marital separations and the government estimated that approximately 80,000 people were affected by the mid-1990s (Kennedy, 2001). The referendum, held in November 1995, was carried by the narrowest of margins: 50.28 per cent voted in favour and 49.72 per cent against. This was hardly an overwhelming endorsement of the right to divorce in Ireland and a result particularly noteworthy in the context of the cross-party political support which existed for the referendum. The result gives some insight into the cross-section of opinion held on such matters in 1990s Ireland. The 1990s was also the decade in which 'corruption' entered popular discourse through the exposure of a number of high-profile incidents; including business interests and a number of national politicians, the abuse of children in state care and negligence in the health services (for a detailed account see Collins and O'Shea, 2001; Keogh, 2005).

In 1999 the government produced a *Green Paper on Abortion*, a cabinet committee was established, and the All-Party Committee on the Constitution considered the matter. The Protection of Human Life in Pregnancy Bill was subsequently published in October 2001 (Kennedy, 2002). In terms of the substantive issue, the debate on the referendum centred around the implications of the passing of an amendment which, on the one hand, would have the effect of criminalising abortion (with a possible penalty of up to 12 years' imprisonment, or a fine, or both) and, on the other, would clarify issues that arose post the X case. In the event, the turnout was low (42.89 per cent) and the referendum was rejected by another remarkably narrow margin – 50.42 per cent to 49.58 per cent (ibid.). More recently, the 2007 Ms D. case highlighted once again the need for legislation in this area. In this case a 17-year-old girl, in the care of the HSE and carrying a foetus that would not live for more than three days outside the womb, was forced to go to the courts to establish her 'freedom to travel'. The HSE had taken the view that a court order was necessary to allow the girl to travel. It seems likely that further cases of this kind will appear before the courts in the continuing absence of appropriate legislation.

Economic prosperity during the 1990s

> Ireland's transformation is so dazzling ... one of the most remarkable economic transformations of recent times: from basket case to 'emerald tiger' in ten years. (*The Economist*, 17 May 1997, in Sweeney, 1999, p. 8)

An international economic downturn between 1991 and 1993 saw unemployment rise again, with over 300,000 or 21 per cent of the labour force registered unemployed in January 1993. Youth unemployment was an even more serious problem, with 27 per cent of young people (under 25) unemployed in the middle of 1992 (Kennedy, 1993). However, since that time there has been very rapid growth in the Irish economy, with annual growth rates of over eight per cent between 1993–8, and total employment growing by a quarter over the same period (O'Connell, 1999). Unemployment dropped from 12.3 per cent in 1995 to 4.3 per cent in 2000. In fact, employment in Ireland grew by an average of 4.2 per cent per annum over the ten year period to 2001, which compared very favourably with the lower growth rates recorded in other countries at that time (O'Hagan and McIndoe, 2005). The common practice of 'going where the work is', which had continued to haunt Irish families and communities, finally saw a welcome break. Over the course of the 1990s emigration was not only halted, large scale immigration became a new reality for Ireland. Ruhs (2004, p. 3) points out that:

> ... between 1995 and 1999, Ireland's average annual net migration rate was the second highest in the EU-15, surpassed only by that of Luxembourg. And ... by 2002, the estimated share of non-nationals in Ireland's population had surpassed those of the UK and France, countries with much longer immigration histories.

This represented an unprecedented turnaround in Ireland's experience of migration, which would have been unimaginable during the 1980s.

The 'Celtic Tiger' label was applied to the Irish economy after Kevin Gardiner of the Investment Bank Morgan Stanley on 31 August 1994 compared the Irish economy to the East Asian tiger economies (O'Hearn, 1997). Much has been written about the unprecedented growth in the Irish economy over the course of the 1990s, however, the core economic changes, as summed up by Barry (1999, p. 1) in a comparative context are as follows:

> Ireland's economic performance over the last decade has been spectacular, not only in terms of its own historical experience but in an international comparative context also ... Irish GNP expanded by almost 70 per cent in the 10 years from 1987, during which time the US expanded by only 27 per cent, the 15-country EU by 24 per cent, and the UK by 20 per cent. Ireland has had a long-standing problem with low levels of job creation. By 1997 there were 23 per cent more jobs in the economy than in 1987. The US created 17 per cent net new jobs over this period, the UK 5 per cent and the EU15 only 3 per cent.

This was a remarkable about-turn in economic fortunes, and all in a relatively short period of time. Assessments of the factors that contributed to the success of the Irish economy during the 1990s vary in emphasis. Firstly, there was an improvement in external economic conditions generally and an intensification of global economic activity which provided a suitable climate to continue the policy of supporting FDI and attracting MNCs to locate in Ireland. The internal dynamics of the Irish economy were also more favourable. Social partnership was considered to have brought about greater stability in industrial relations and the conditions for economic competitiveness and growth had been enhanced through various grants, incentives and tax reform. There was an easing of the demographic pressures which had imposed heavily on the need for social services, and the availability of a young, well-educated, English-speaking workforce was an important 'selling point' to potential foreign investors. The impact of EU membership (the single market, European monetary union and the benefit derived from structural and cohesion funds) is also among the factors widely regarded as important in creating the conditions for unparalleled economic growth (see Fitz Gerald, 2000; O'Connell, 1999; Sweeney, 1999). In short, Ireland developed over the course of the 1990s to become a much more flexible, open and globalised economy. (The debate about the implications of this economic trajectory for Irish social policy is considered in Chapter 6.)

A new climate for the development of social policy?

While the transformation of the Irish economy was indeed astounding, it had implications for social policy. For the first time in her history, Ireland generated employment sufficient to meet demand, and it had resources available on an unprecedented scale to develop and invest in the social services and in key areas of infrastructure. In terms of the social services, health and education have seen much greater levels of investment and many important policy developments over the course of the 1990s. In many ways this was the decade to 'play catch-up', as the cutbacks of the 1980s had taken their toll on social services that had endured decades of underinvestment and were in serious need of modernisation. The social welfare system, for example, underwent considerable reform during the 1990s in terms of meeting the targets set by the 1986 Commission on Social Welfare and in modernising its operations through the provision of more accessible information on citizens' rights and entitlements.

Specifically with regard to poverty and **social exclusion**, the development of the National Anti-Poverty Strategy (NAPS) in 1997 provides a

> **Social exclusion** is a concept increasingly used to refer to the consequences of poverty and inequality, where people are 'left out' and unable to participate fully in society.

useful illustration of social policy innovation during the 1990s. The NAPS provides the official definition of poverty adopted in Ireland and set specific policy targets for poverty reduction; Ireland was the first of the EU member states to adopt these targets (which continue to be subject to review). The structural developments attached to its implementation (e.g. a designated Cabinet Sub-Committee, the establishment of a NAPS unit in the Department of Social and Family Affairs, and latterly the setting up of the Office for Social Inclusion) and the targets developed in this regard are noteworthy policy initiatives which have served to focus attention on poverty and inequality, which, as we have seen, were a long time in the making. The NAPS (1997) achieved its target of reducing consistent poverty well in advance of the date set, but it is important to note that the definitions of poverty in use in Ireland continue to be the subject of debate, particularly if framed within the wider conceptual framework of redistribution, as discussed in Chapter 7.

The widening agenda, actors and scope of social policy

A number of factors combined to focus attention on core social policy issues over the course of the 1990s, not least of which included the growth in resources available to deal more effectively with issues such as poverty and social exclusion. The more explicit campaigning and lobbying activities of many organisations during the 1990s also helped to put the rights of particular groups on the political agenda. The 'politicisation of disadvantage' (Donoghue, 1998a) brought greater attention to the unmet needs of marginalised groups, and the work of the community and voluntary sector has been central in this regard. Disability rights campaigners, for example, although not a singular group, became a more visible and influential force during the 1990s and 2000s. In terms of social partnership, the formal engagement of the community and voluntary sector with the process also evolved over the course of the 1990s. First invited to participate in the national social partnership talks in 1997, when Partnership 2000 was negotiated, the insider-outsider dilemma has emerged as one that faces many of the participating organisations. Many within the sector remain critical and sometimes cynical about their involvement and the extent to which they really have a say in the final agreements (see Chapter 6).

If social policy developments in the area of poverty and inequality are considered central to the notion of redistribution then the emergence of more sustained attention to issues of discrimination and exclusion highlight the relevance of the concept of recognition for social policy discourse. The recognition of various marginalised groups in Irish society was an issue that gained prominence over the course of the 1990s and from which stemmed a number of key developments. The National Consultative Committee on

Racism and Interculturalism (NCCRI) was an independent body set up in 1998 to develop an inclusive approach to combat racism and to promote an intercultural society by providing advice and training to government and non-government organisations, monitoring racist incidents, providing information and raising public awareness. As the first national organisation with such a remit, it has played an important role in challenging racism and been a vital advocate for many of the newer members of Irish society.

The establishment of the Equality Authority in 1999 represents another step in improving the recognition and protection of individuals and social groups in Ireland. The passing of significant equality legislation including the Equality Acts 1998 and 2004 and the Equal Status Acts 2000 and 2004 marked a milestone in the development of the '**equality agenda**' in Ireland. This legislation now prohibits discrimination (in

> The **equality agenda** refers to the pursuit of recognition and equality for all individuals and groups in society.

the provision of goods and services, employment, training, advertising, collective agreements and other opportunities to which the public generally has access) on nine grounds: gender, marital status, sexual orientation, family status, disability, age, race, religion and membership of the Travelling Community. These laws, while vital to facilitating recourse against discrimination, are arguably weak in terms of some aspects of their application and in the exceptions allowed. The research commissioned by the Equality Authority has highlighted some notable barriers to the realisation of equality for all (see Chapters 11 and 12). In overall terms, the work and impact of the Equality Authority (and the associated legislation) stands to become one of the most positive social policy initiatives of recent times, if the necessary legislation and resources continue to be provided to pursue its work over the longer term.

In short, developments since the late 1990s appear to reflect a growing level of political acceptance of the necessity to listen to and address the needs of particular social groups and their representatives in the Irish context. The key question emerging now though is the extent to which this has resulted in particular groups 'being heard', tangible policy change and a more inclusive, supportive or equal society. The final part of the book considers these issues in greater depth.

A 'deepening dualism' in Irish social policy?

Taken in absolute terms, there was unprecedented investment in social and public services during the economic boom years. Social expenditure, for example, rose from €6.8 billion in 2000 to €12.1 billion in 2005 (Kirby, 2008). This, however, should not be interpreted as an unequivocal expansion of the Irish welfare state or the extension of social rights in Ireland. This is argued on three grounds. Firstly, this has occurred from a low and late starting point given the 'delayed development' of the Irish welfare state, which was playing 'catch-up' for much of the 1990s. Secondly, and contrary to a lot of popular opinion, social spending remains low in Ireland, particularly if considered in comparative terms. Social expenditure is generally calculated as a share of GDP/GNP; based on GDP and data from 2001, Ireland had the lowest level of social expenditure of the EU-15 (Timonen, 2005). A different calculation method moves Ireland from this bottom spot to third last (after Portugal and Spain; see ibid. for details). Timonen's (2003, 2005) research confirms Ireland's overall status as a 'low spender' in comparative terms. Finally, and more broadly, it seems that social rights remain a **contested concept** in Ireland; while there undoubtedly have been improvements in the services to which individuals are entitled there have also been limits to the quality of, or access to, certain entitlements (relative to what might be available in the private or commercial sector). This contradiction is illustrated in parallel developments since the mid-1990s which demonstrate the emergence of a more distinctive benefit to be drawn from the private as opposed to the public sphere (see 'deepening dualism', NESC, 2005, below). Access to healthcare and housing, the rise of the private school phenomenon in education and the growth of private sector care services for older people provide some notable examples. These trends point to the fact that market choices in key areas were consolidated during this era, but only for those who could afford to pay. Social policy developments since the 1990s, therefore, might be characterised as reformist and expansionary but the outcomes were not always inclusive or redistributive.

> A **contested concept** is one that is subject to differing interpretations around which there is no universal agreement of meaning.

In 2005 the NESC published an important report on the future direction of the Irish welfare state, entitled *The Developmental Welfare State* (DWS). Pointing to the radical social and economic changes that have occurred, the NESC states that 'it is both opportune and necessary to re-visit the basic architecture and core objectives of Ireland's social policies and welfare state, and in several key respects to reform them' (NESC, 2005, p. 2). The report identifies the 'hybrid nature' of social protection and it draws particular attention to the high level of reliance on means-testing in the Irish welfare state. Risks associated with 'deepening dualism' (ibid., p. 163) are identified. This involves 'a growing majority who are able to supplement very basic levels of public service provision with additional protection they purchase for themselves', while 'a significant minority', 'rely nearly entirely on public provision, and in doing so are further removed from the mainstream of Irish society and less likely to experience mobility into it' (ibid.). It lays out a vision for the Irish welfare state incorporating three core areas: services, income supports and activist measures. The development of, and access to, services (education, health, childcare, eldercare, housing, transport and employment services) are highlighted in terms of their potential benefit to the economy, in promoting social cohesion and in addressing social exclusion (generating what the report terms a 'services dividend'). Income supports (progressive child income supports, working age transfers for participation, minimum pension guarantee and capped tax expenditures) are framed in terms of acknowledging need at different stages of the lifecycle.

The current social partnership agreement *Towards 2016: Ten-Year Framework Social Partnership Agreement 2006–2015* adopts the 'lifecycle approach' advocated by the NESC (2005). The key lifecycle stages identified relate to children, people of working age, older people and people with disabilities. While broadly welcomed by the social partners, the challenge now is to work on the commitments made in the agreement, and there has been some criticism of the lack of progress in certain areas to date. Returning to the NESC (2005) report, it is worth noting that the DWS has received a mixed but remarkably low-key response. It has been the source of some criticism (see Kirby, 2008; Murphy and Millar, 2007) but the fact that the fundamental issues raised about the future direction of the Irish welfare state have not enjoyed anything like the public and political reaction that might be expected from such a document, is significant. The lack of debate may be symptomatic of a wider ambivalence or reluctance to be explicit about 'the direction' of the Irish welfare state. However, the fact that certain dualist aspects of the social services, such as two-tier access to hospital care, are a source of public and political discussion raises a contradiction in the focus of Irish welfare debate. This is to say that problems of dualism are examined, but frequently without reference to the wider distributional policies and problems that contribute to the existence of dualism in the first place.

The late 2000s: austerity returns

> I want to make it absolutely clear that we are battling the most severe global economic and financial conditions for a century. The decisions we are making now will determine whether we throw away the economic progress we have achieved or whether we give ourselves and our children a prosperous future. That is how stark this situation is and that is why we have been taking the difficult decisions that we have. (An Taoiseach, Brian Cowen, October 2008)

Apart from a dip in economic growth during 2001–2, Ireland's economic growth continued apace (with average growth rates for the five years from 2002–7 in excess of five per cent), but 2008 witnessed a sharp reversal of these trends. Ireland is once again in an economic recession, the depth and scale of which will only be clear in time. The budget surpluses dried up and have been replaced by deficits and a concentration of effort about how best to revive the economy. Rising levels of unemployment, emigration and increased government borrowing (given the significant shortfall in exchequer returns) are some of the challenges that now arise. Economic factors (external and internal) coalesced to produce what some commentators have referred to as 'the perfect storm'. Global economic conditions began to deteriorate from the mid-2000s and the financial and associated credit crisis of 2008 is said to be unparalleled in living memory. Internally, the over-reliance of the Irish economy on the construction industry over the last decade and the sharp decline in property prices resulted in a radical reversal of the economic fortunes of Ireland in a short space of time.

Against this economic backdrop, it is likely that the development of social policy will again be relegated in terms of priority. Indications from Budget 2009 have not been positive. Some of the most important agencies established during the 1980s and 1990s to combat poverty, racism and discrimination have been abolished or have had their budgets severely cut. The CPA, which was established in 1986 and has provided over 20 years' of social policy research, expertise and advice to government, wider organisations and community groups alike, is to be subsumed into the Department of Social and Family Affairs. The impact of the loss of such an independent voice, whose mandate was to work for the elimination of poverty, may be significant. The NCCRI has had all of its funding removed. Both the Equality Authority and the Irish Human Rights Commission have had their budgets cut by 43 per cent and 24 per cent, respectively (O'Gorman, 2008). The cumulative effect of these decisions cannot be fully known or evaluated at this time, but these developments do not bode well for the realisation and recognition of rights in Irish society in the immediate future.

Finally, the imperative of economic development, which has so dominated and shaped the Irish political landscape, may continue to be instrumental in the approach to social policy if the appropriate financing and provision of social services are presented as anathema to economic growth. Alternatively, economic and social policy may be seen in a less oppositional and more interdependent way. To fully get to grips with this debate as it might apply to Ireland, the level of the welfare effort as delivered through the social services and its effect on different social groups requires closer examination. These are considered in parts three and four of the book, respectively. Part two first sets out a broader historical, conceptual and theoretical framework necessary for the study of social policy out of which more complex questions about the precise nature of Irish social policy can be addressed.

CHAPTER SUMMARY

▸ This chapter outlined the social, political and economic backdrop to the development of social policy in Ireland since the 1970s.

▸ In overall terms, the 1970s did not live up to the expectations of that decade although some important breakthroughs were made, particularly with regard to rights of women.

▸ The 1980s were marked by a series of tribulations – economic, political, social and moral – providing a hostile climate for the development of social policy. Emigration and unemployment were endemic, and, with limited resources and spending cuts, the social services were under significant strain.

▸ The 1990s bore witness to a period of significant economic growth and rapid social change in Irish society. Despite the fact that there were noteworthy advances in the late 1990s and the early 2000s, Irish social policy is marked by certain continuities and contradictions. These include the persistence of poverty, relatively high levels of inequality, improved welfare provision in certain areas but with limited commitment to 'rights-based' social services and a growth in private sector reliance for those in a position to pay.

▸ In short, the notable social policy achievements of the early 2000s are circumscribed by clear limits. These tensions are likely to be brought into much sharper focus in the context of managing government spending in the current economic recession.

Discussion points

▸ As the Minister responsible for a particular area of social policy (e.g. health, social welfare, housing, etc.), prepare four short speeches which outline the main policy problems and priorities in 1979, 1989, 1999 and 2009.

▸ Select any decade (from the 1970s to the 2000s) and analyse the major influences on social policy during that time.

▸ Do rising tides lift all boats? Consider with reference to the Irish welfare state.

▸ Analyse the implications of 'deepening dualism' in the Irish welfare state.

Further reading

Kennedy, F. (2001) *Cottage to Crèche: Family Change in Ireland*, Dublin: IPA.

Keogh, D. (2005) *Twentieth Century Ireland: revolution and state building* (second edition), Dublin: Gill & Macmillan.

Kirby, P. (2002) *The Celtic Tiger in Distress: Growth with inequality in Ireland*, Basingstoke: Palgrave.

National Economic and Social Council (2005) *The Developmental Welfare State*, Dublin: NESC.

Nolan, B., O'Connell, P. J. and Whelan, C. T. (eds) (2000) *Bust to Boom?: The Irish Experience of Growth and Inequality*, Dublin: IPA.

PART II

EXPLAINING SOCIAL POLICY: CONCEPTS, POLITICS AND IDEOLOGY

This part of the book moves away from the exclusive focus on Irish social policy in order to examine broader themes of relevance. This approach is taken to provide some insight into the theoretical context in which social policy is located. While the direction of Irish social policy often defies neat categorisation, this does not negate the need to think critically about wider themes and issues that arise. Consideration of how social policy evolved elsewhere and what influenced such developments is important. Perspectives on welfare and the role of social policy are also explored and while it might be argued that these have been less explicit in the Irish context, their overall influence on social policy remains central. Another dimension of the study of social policy requiring attention is the theoretical debates about the nature of, and influences on, contemporary welfare states and approaches to welfare.

The overall aim is to outline the main developments and perspectives which have influenced the broad direction of social policy and to explore some of the key contemporary theories and debates, which are relevant to the analysis offered in parts III and IV of the book. Some of the main social policy concepts and ideas that inform much contemporary discussion are outlined in this context. Specifically, this is done firstly by explaining the factors that have influenced the nature and development of social policy in general terms in Chapter 4, before attention is focused on the different ways of approaching and thinking about social policy, particularly in political and ideological terms, as considered in Chapter 5. More weight is now being given to the changing contexts within which welfare states operate, and focus is increasingly placed on economic, political and social pressures as they impinge on social policy. Chapter 6 explores some of these themes and debates in order to set the Irish experience in this broader context.

▸ Chapter 4 sketches the wider course of social policy from the mid-nineteenth century through to present issues and debates about the nature and sustainability of welfare states. Attention is given to key events and debates in order to illustrate, in narrative form, the different paths taken in terms of social policy and welfare provision.

▸ Chapter 5 introduces the different views and values brought to bear on social policy; it examines different perspectives or ideologies of welfare and considers their implications for welfare and social policy issues.

▸ Chapter 6 charts some of the key areas of debate in contemporary social policy, including attention to globalisation and its consequences and the development of EU social policy. The latter part of the chapter considers the position of Irish social policy in this wider context.

CHAPTER 4

SOCIAL POLICY AND THE WELFARE STATE: ORIGINS, DEVELOPMENTS AND REFORM

The aim of this chapter is to offer a wider exploration of the origins and development of welfare and social services from the latter part of the nineteenth century onwards. Part one of the book outlined the nature and impact of Poor Law provision and subsequent welfare developments specifically in the Irish context. The present chapter maps the broader context for welfare provision and the development of welfare states, offering a point of contrast between the experience in Ireland and elsewhere. There is a particular focus on Britain, where the historical development of social policy was 'shared' in terms of early inherited legislation and because of its subsequently differing welfare trajectory. Such an examination provides another dimension to the study of social policy because, in contrast to the relatively delayed development of the discipline in Ireland, in other countries, social policy, or social administration as it was previously called, became the subject of academic scrutiny, and matters of social policy were the subject of much debate from the latter part of the nineteenth century onwards.

This chapter identifies a range of influences on the development of welfare provision, including the emergence of new ideas, political movements and changing social attitudes, along with economic expansion which shaped the context for social change and reform over the course of the twentieth century. There are, however, limitations to offering such a 'potted history' of welfare provision and what we provide is a sketch of wider social policy developments and debates which should be followed up with supplementary reading. The chapter does outline some of the core concepts that inform different perspectives on the role of social policy and considers, in broad terms, some of the major influences on the development of the welfare state and its reform in recent decades.

CHAPTER OUTLINE

▶ The first section of the chapter offers a historical narrative which traces the growing attention given to the 'social question' since the latter part of the nineteenth century. The emergence of competing ideas about the organisation of society, the development of economies, and questions about meeting basic needs and acknowledging risks are considered.

▶ The key welfare and social policy developments of the early to mid-twentieth century are examined in the second section. The foundations of the welfare state, which were laid in the early part of the century and subsequently developed, are explored, along with the wider political, economic and social influences, including the emergence of a more collectivist perspective by the mid-twentieth century.

▶ The final section of the chapter considers the shifting welfare debates of the latter part of the twentieth century, particularly in terms of the increasing contestation of some of the core assumptions on which the welfare state was built. It also briefly deals with the politics of welfare state reform since the 1980s and outlines the wider perspectives which have come to bear on welfare discourse in the twenty-first century.

SECTION 1: KEY DEVELOPMENTS OF THE NINETEENTH AND EARLY TWENTIETH CENTURIES – THE EMERGENCE OF WELFARE AND 'THE SOCIAL QUESTION'

Individualism and the ethos of the Poor Law

The earlier examination of the Irish Poor Law highlighted its severity and its categorisation of poverty and poor people as 'deserving', 'undeserving', 'able-bodied' and 'impotent poor'. The implementation of the Poor Law, particularly as seen in its emphasis on personal responsibility, individual failure and associated negligence, held an underlying philosophy of individual and familial responsibility in which collective responses to poverty were kept to an absolute minimum. In other words, the overriding concern was to protect the

> **Individualism** is a belief that confers a central role on individuals in maintaining their own well-being.

ethos of **individualism** and to promote individual responsibility, including, where necessary, to contain and control those in abject poverty, rather than to make any acknowledgement of the structural causes which contributed to the situation. Furthermore, while the assessment of the Poor Law in our opening chapter focused primarily on the experience in Ireland, the philosophy of the time was similar elsewhere. For example, in Germany a system of poor relief was also in operation where legislation basically placed responsibility for the poor with local rather than national government. In Rosenhaft's (1994, p. 26) account of this period in Germany, she asserts that:

> State law fixed the obligations of the municipalities, but it implied neither an obligation on its own part nor a right to support on the part of the poor; indeed, those who were dependent on poor relief were deprived of most civil rights, including the franchise. Nineteenth-century poor law represented the minimum intervention necessary to protect public order against the threat posed by unrelieved hardship.

Katz's (1986, in Conley, 2003, p. 225) assessment of public welfare as provided through poor houses in the United States during the nineteenth century is harsher:

> Poorhouses, which shut the old and sick away from their friends and relatives, were supposed to deter the working class from asking for poor relief. They were, in fact, the ultimate [defense] against the erosion of the work ethic in early industrial America. Miserable, poorly managed, underfunded institutions, trapped by their own contradictions, poorhouses failed to meet any of the goals so confidently predicted by their sponsors.

Notwithstanding the obvious hardships endured, the legacy of poor relief remains important because it was the first system of state intervention to deal with poverty and deliver a most basic form of provision, albeit one of last resort. Ultimately, the Poor Law system marked the opening phase in what was to become a more complex and less grudging acceptance about the role of the state in the provision of welfare and social services.

The emphasis on individual responsibility had been a hallmark value of the early nineteenth century; people were responsible for their own welfare; and failure to provide adequately for one's self and one's family was commonly seen as the result of personal failings. This individualism, based on a *laissez-faire* philosophy, stressed the importance of self-responsibility at the core of Victorian values, in which class boundaries were also rigid. The class system was part of 'the natural order of things' and as such people were not expected to move beyond the class into which they were born. The wider implications of this way of thinking were evident in relation to children for instance, who 'should be seen but not heard' and also in relation to the dependent roles ascribed to women in society. In addition, institutions remained the preferred option in catering for people with disabilities and those with mental illness. Ultimately though, the family was and continued to be the primary source of welfare for individuals. Outside providers, where available, were really only called upon if absolutely necessary. The aim of Victorian governments, after all, was 'to provide a framework of rules and guidelines designed to enable society very largely to run itself' (Harris, 1990, p. 67 in Lewis, 1999, p. 14).

A number of forces did coalesce, however, to bring about some shift in the level of state intervention in support of people and their needs. Taken together, these influences marked the emergence of a changed climate in terms of attitudes to human need, risk, different life stages and vulnerabilities. This is not to say that a shift in opinion about the provision of welfare was universal, linear or the result of unanimous support. However, the arrival of competing theories and ideas about how best to provide and support individuals and their families, and the identification of needs specific to certain groups (such as workers, children and older people) paved the way for the provision of welfare and social services on significantly changed terms over the course of the twentieth century.

Social change, activism and philanthropy

The mid-nineteenth century was a period of immense social and economic change. Industrialisation and urbanisation in countries like Britain, Germany and America prompted massive social change, from rural to urban living, growing specialisation of skills required in work, and the emergence of the factory as a major site of production and employment. The 'social consequences of industrialisation' according to Fraser (1984, p. 5), 'provided the fieldwork with which social policy had to deal, and they were broadly of three sorts, affecting the individual, his work and his environment'. In terms of the individual, people found themselves having to relate to each other, and to authority, in a more sophisticated but sometimes less secure way. Fraser (ibid.) explains this change:

> In place of the security of a cohesive *vertical* social structure in which every individual had a formal or informal connection with those above and below, there was the uncertainty of a mass society in which a *horizontal* class structure gradually emerged.

In terms of work, the nature and types of activity changed enormously and the demand for particular skills grew, while others were made obsolete. The monitoring and regulation of these new places of employment were to become critical to the protection of workers and as such emerged as a formative feature of state intervention affecting the lives of individuals.

Known as *Arbeiterschutz* in Germany, the regulation of working conditions was important in 'the developing system of industrial wage labour' (Rosenhaft, 1994, p. 26). Tampke (1981), for example, describes early social legislation that existed in Prussia to cover employees in the coal mining industry. From 1776 (and enforced until 1865), work in the mines was restricted to eight hours, with a guaranteed minimum income and medical treatment for accident or illness and payments during such periods. No women and children were permitted to work in the mines at this time. Further legislation introduced in 1839 placed some wider restrictions on the employment of children and an office for inspection of factories was set up to supervise these regulations. In the case of the UK, the Children's Employment Commission in Mines and Factories 1842 highlighted the inadequate regulation and sometimes shocking working conditions which prevailed during the industrial revolution. Legislation began to regulate conditions of employment through a series of Factory Acts over the course of the century, which culminated in the abolition of child labour from factories and workshops in 1901.

Industrialisation also bore witness to the earliest work-related benefits (now known as occupational benefits); these are benefits accruing to the employee from the employer as part of the conditions of employment. Some large-scale and wealthy employers provided accommodation through the development of 'model villages' attached to their factories. Examples of such housing developments include those undertaken by W. H. Lever, Wedgewood, Rowntree and Cadbury in the UK. Some of the first pensions were delivered as work-based occupational benefits in the 1870s by railroad companies such as Grand Trunk Railway and American Express in the USA and Canada. Critically though, these welfare initiatives were at the discretion of employers and therefore only available to some employees.

At its most basic, the impact of industrialisation and urbanisation as it emerged in the nineteenth century (although not in Ireland) was that it highlighted in even more stark terms, the welfare risks presented by poverty and poor housing conditions, overcrowding and inadequate sanitation. Taken together, these problems emerged as **'social risks'** that had the potential to damage the existing social structure of

> **Social risks** refer to possibilities that are beyond the control of an individual; they are shared in the sense that there are certain risks to which all of us are exposed in various ways.

society and, over time, these were acknowledged as issues that were not going to go away without significant investment and intervention by a larger body. Public health measures were among the first which gave recognition to large-scale needs. Inadequate systems of sewerage and drainage, access to water, street cleaning and overcrowding were the main areas for which local authorities or municipalities were given responsibility. The first Public Health Act, introduced in the UK in 1848, was potentially ground-breaking but it appears to have been poorly implemented. The subsequent Sanitation Act, 1866, and the Public Health Act, 1875, outlined to greater effect the functions and duties of the local authorities in these matters (Fraser, 1984). Similarly, municipal boards of health were also introduced in the major cities of America, although their effectiveness in the early years was also limited (Trattner, 1999).

Some of the most notable developments of this period occurred outside of the domain of the state, in civil society. The emergence and growth of what we now call the voluntary or third sector, goes back to this time when a lead role was played by voluntary groups in highlighting and responding to welfare needs and issues. One element of this was the practice of forming support systems within social groups and communities, known as **mutual aid**, which grew during the nineteenth century. Examples of these mutual aid organisations include cooperatives, housing associations, credit unions and Friendly Societies. Friendly Societies worked on the basis of people of particular trades or guilds each contributing a certain amount per week, in return for which an amount could be received in the event of a death in the family, illness and so on. As a preventative or proactive welfare strategy taken up by individuals who could afford it, this was a system of basic self-insurance, which became very popular. The Manchester Unity of Oddfellows was the largest society in Britain, with over half a million members in 1876 (Green, 1999), and Britain had an estimated six million Friendly Society members by 1904 (Thane, 1996). However, Friendly Societies too had their drawbacks as a source of welfare; they were mainly closed associations, available only to those who had work and income sufficient to contribute. Eventually, their costs began to mount and some ended in bankruptcy. Yet mutual aid in some ways reflected the principle of shared (or socialised) risk which subsequently formed the basis of many of the social security systems around the world.

> **Mutual aid** refers to non-state reciprocal help or support; it can be financial or social in orientation.

In terms of the voluntary sector more generally, charitable groups grew and were at the forefront of seeking to address issues of poverty and human need. Specifically the significance of **philanthropy** grew over the

> **Philanthropy** refers to charitable and altruistic activity (conventionally carried out by middle-class individuals) for the benefit of individuals and society as a whole.

course of the nineteenth century. Upper middle-class women in particular engaged in charitable work, especially in larger urban areas. The growth of the sector and the widening variety and scope of organisations are particularly evident from about 1870 onwards when a number of high profile organisations, representing different interests and causes, were established. Prominent examples of such organisations that were subsequently established in several countries include the Dr Barnardos Home, the Society of Saint Vincent de Paul, the Salvation Army, the Peabody Foundation and the Charity Organisation Society.

Motivations for engagement in such charitable work may have varied, but for some the threat of the spread of disease or crime prompted intervention by the middle class. Outside of this the poor housing conditions which prevailed in many of the new urban areas prompted some philanthropic activity and investment during the latter part of the nineteenth century. Regardless of the motivation, the growth in charitable activity during this period was remarkable, particularly among women, with an estimated 500,000 female volunteers in the UK in 1893 (Thane, 1996). The charitable sector was also very significant in terms of its resources. By the end of the nineteenth century £8 million per annum was transferred to charities in London, more than the total national Poor Law expenditure at that time (ibid.). The pioneering and lobbying roles of volunteers in dealing with aspects of social provision are also noteworthy. Individual women and women's groups advocated the introduction of a wide range of social measures such as the provision of school meals, medical inspections, improvement in the quality of food and better maternity services. In terms of the volunteerism of women overall, as Thane (1996, p. 18) points out, 'Though unpaid, many of them were highly committed professionals. They created new approaches to social policy, some of which (e.g. district nurses, health visitors) were later adopted by the statutory sector.'

One such example was the Charity Organisation Society (COS), originally called the Society for Organising Charitable Relief and Repressing Mendicity, founded in the UK in 1869. A significant voluntary organisation in the history of welfare and social policy, the COS sought to cooperate with the Poor Law provisions and to better organise and coordinate the activities of charitable agencies; branches were established in Germany, France and in America (Trattner, 1999; Ziliak, 2004). The stated aims of the COS included, 'to promote, as far as possible, the general welfare of the poor by means of social and sanitary reforms, and by the inculcation of habits of providence and self-dependence' (COS in Mooney, 1998, p. 69). This was done through the development of the casework approach involving direct work with individuals and their families, an approach which subsequently became influential in social work.

However, the wider ethos of personal responsibility and self-help which underpinned the work of the COS distinguished between 'deserving' and 'undeserving' cases. This philosophy of promoting self-help and individual responsibility was not without its critics, mainly because, as Jones (2000, p. 36) asserts:

> Their approach, both with their clients and with more compassionate relief organizations, was so abrasive that it earned much of the opprobrium which has since been directed against philanthropy in general. Their diagnosis of the problems of large-scale Victorian philanthropy was sound enough; but their proposed cure gave the whole movement a bad name.

Overall, the growth of voluntary welfare provision in the latter part of the nineteenth century is significant for a number of reasons. It offered practical assistance, agitated for reform, was often motivated by an underlying religious philosophy and was frequently shaped by varying belief systems. Some of these beliefs tended to promote and re-enforce the ethos of personal responsibility which was discretionary in its allocation of welfare. In addition and notwithstanding its very pioneering role in many countries, private philanthropy was, by its nature 'unevenly spread and frequently could only offer palliatives rather than fundamental solutions to the problems it encountered' (Stevenson, 1984, p. 24). Ultimately though, 'in 1870, and still in 1900, support from agencies of either central or local government was the least sought and usually the last resort. The family was almost certainly the first resort' (Thane, 1996, p. 19). This illustrates the relatively low priority accorded to social issues at the time and reflects the culture of individualism which prevailed. Furthermore, the emerging social policy of the time was arrived at by means of a complicated, reluctant and reactionary response to events and issues, and not based on any long-term strategy about meeting human needs. As Fraser (1984, p. 117) argues:

> … any explanation which does not emphasise the practical, pragmatic, unplanned, *ad hoc* response of the state is in a major respect deficient. It cannot be over emphasised that social policies and their administration were geared to meet real and pressing problems … It was the pressure of facts, and unpalatable ones at that, which produced unexpected and (by most) undesired administrative growth.

Knowledge, democracy and ideology

Increased political activism and the emergence of political rights over the latter part of the nineteenth century and particularly 'one person, one vote' meant that individuals could finally express, through the ballot box at least, a preference for a certain point of view. As Flora (1981, p. 353) puts it, 'the development towards mass democracy inevitably brought new tasks for governments, but it equally strengthened the legitimacy of their demands for resources.' Enfranchisement was a crucial development of the time, and the emergence of the trade union movement and the right of individuals to associate in groups marked a new phase in highlighting social divisions. Trade union legislation passed during the 1870s (Trade Union Act, 1871, and the Conspiracy and Protection of Property Act, 1875) in Britain gave recognition to unions before the law and made peaceful protest legal. The concurrent emergence of Marxist philosophy during the latter part of the nineteenth century offered a radical way of thinking about the unequal relationship between the working class and the owners of the means of production, highlighting the insecurity of workers' lives and the nature of class divisions endemic to the capitalist system (see Chapter 5). The growth of the labour movement also brought the working conditions and the everyday experiences of ordinary working people into sharper focus. Events such as the international trade union conference held in 1890 sought a reduction in the number of working hours per day, restrictions on dangerous occupations, a ban on women working in mines and on night work and the provision of four weeks' maternity leave (ILO, 1921, in Rowbotham, 1994). These resolutions were not binding, but they did help to highlight the need for regulation of the workplace for both men and women. These types of initiatives contributed to a more sustained debate about the nature of society and the role of the state in taking some responsibility in regulating and protecting workers' rights. The debate was shaped by considerations outside of the factories too, with living conditions also emerging as an issue worthy of investigation.

Early surveys provided the first scientific appreciation of the scale and depth of poverty which persisted in Poor Law times. In Britain, the first attempt to quantify the scale of the problem of poverty was in the form of research conducted in the late 1880s by Charles Booth in London and by Seebohm Rowntree in York. These landmark studies marked the emergence of social inquiry into the nature and prevalence of poverty. Despite taking different approaches to the measurement of poverty, when the findings were compared Rowntree concluded that 'we are faced with the startling probability that from 25 per cent to 30 per cent of the town population of the United Kingdom are living in poverty' (cited in Thane, 1996, p. 8). Both recorded the statistical incidence of poverty using particular indicators and wider impressions of poverty. What Booth did for the first time was to lay claim to the identification of poor people and poverty in Britain. In that sense, according to Jones (2000, p. 50):

... his contribution to the development of social policy and methods of social investigation was greater than he knew. He was the first person to ask 'Who are the poor?' and to replace stereotypes and prejudice with factual answers.

Rowntree subsequently developed his approach to analysing poverty, by conducting over 11,000 working-class household surveys to establish family budgets and expenditure. Most notably, his distinction between primary poverty (where earnings were insufficient for physical survival) and secondary poverty (where resources were sufficient for physical survival but not much else), represented a turning point in understanding poverty because he challenged the conventional wisdom that the absence of poverty equated with mere physical efficiency. In other words, Rowntree saw poverty in relative terms, viewing secondary poverty as 'no less a cause of concern for its involuntary character and demeaning effects as primary poverty' (Thane, 1996, p. 8). In addition, he highlighted the possibility of a cycle of poverty in the life of a labourer at distinct times, including childhood, the early years of one's family and child rearing and old age (Fraser, 1984). In short, Rowntree presented the first indication of the need for a more sophisticated discussion about more appropriate responses to poverty, a debate which continues to the present day.

The emergence of the Fabian Society in the 1880s was also an important development for social policy, as it too sought to highlight the problem of poverty through the use of social scientific research. It centred on a group of upper middle-class intellectuals, based in London and including such people as H. G. Wells, G. B. Shaw and Sidney and Beatrice Webb. **Fabianism** became significant for the new ideological agenda it put forward for a more collectivist philosophy, which sought to promote a gradual move towards socialism.

> **Fabianism** describes the perspective of the Fabian Society which challenged conventional wisdom by arguing for a more extensive/interventionist role for the state in matters of welfare.

The Fabians were essentially socialist in their thinking but they differed substantially from Marx in their belief that society could be reformed incrementally. Their arguments were based on the idea of social reform and the promotion of the values of collectivism. The Fabians advocated state intervention in the organisation of society, seeing it as a largely positive and benevolent force. They were to become pivotal to the development of the discipline of social policy, with their emphasis on awareness-raising through empirical research into social issues, in order to make, in Shaw's words, 'the public conscious of the evil condition of society under the present system' (cited in Lee and Raban, 1988, p. 15). The Fabian Society was also influential in the establishment of the Labour Party in Britain in 1900.

By the end of the nineteenth century some important social policy developments were apparent: there was direct state intervention in areas of education and public health, and evidence of a growing momentum in relation to the protection of employees. In short, democratisation, political activism and social change became key drivers of an agenda that demanded a different approach to meeting human needs. The debates that surrounded the securing of political rights, the establishment of rights for workers and the management of social change paved the way for more sustained attention to questions about the organisation of society and the role of the state. The foundations for state welfare were being laid, and it is to some of its defining features that we now turn.

SECTION 2: THE EARLY TO MID-TWENTIETH CENTURY – EMERGING WELFARE EFFORT AND SOCIAL POLICY

The emergence of more concrete state intervention gained pace in the first decade of the twentieth century and thus began a century in which matters of welfare provision and welfare state development came to occupy a much more prominent position in political and social policy debate. A distinct body of literature has more recently emerged which offers a number of theories that aid in our overall understanding of the development of state welfare. The earliest of these theories (e.g. Wilensky, 1975) emphasises the significance of structural features including the stage of capitalism, economic development, and industrialisation. Others (e.g. Korpi, 1983) stress the importance of 'power resources', the mobilisation of workers and the reflective sway of political traditions and parties in influencing the direction of welfare states. More recently, Esping Andersen's (1990) analysis of welfare state development highlights the significance of historical legacy and the influence of political structures along with the potential for working-class mobilisation. The debate on exact cause and effect is complex precisely because countries' political cultures and policy processes differ, although the stage of economic development (or the 'logic of industrialisation') remains important to our overall understanding (Cousins, 2005b). (See Chapter 6 for a wider discussion of the different 'worlds of welfare'.) This section briefly outlines some of the formative developments which shaped the nature of state welfare as it evolved during the twentieth century.

The establishment of the first system of compulsory social insurance in Germany in the 1880s marked a watershed in the development of social security benefits. German workers now had a right to protection (by means of a minimal benefit) in the event of illness, accident, disability or old age. Although widely considered groundbreaking, Bismarck's introduction of this system of social insurance was motivated primarily by concerns about the growing strength of the Social Democratic Party and socialist trade unions in Germany rather than a wider progressive vision about the capacity of social security. In the event, Bismarck's original plan was to have low, non-earning related contributions and benefits, but what emerged was contribution-led (both employers and employees contributed to the plan), with separate schemes for 'blue collar' and 'white collar' workers and civil servants (Clasen, 1994). The development of these policy initiatives in Germany did have a wider impact, particularly in Scandinavia, where some committees were established to review Bismarck's initiatives in the area of social insurance. State contribution to accident, sickness and old age insurance was introduced in Sweden between 1891 and 1913 (Berend, 2005).

Landmark welfare measures were subsequently introduced in many countries, although the basis of their introduction was quite different in certain cases. A non-contributory old age pension was set up in Denmark in 1891 and in New Zealand in 1898. Similarly in the UK and Ireland, the Old Age Pension Act, 1908, provided state pensions on a non-contributory basis. Payments were low but their provision on a basis separate from the Poor Law and not reliant on previous work-based contributions was significant. (Chapter 7 offers further explanation of the distinction between social insurance and assistance-based provision; what is of note here is the differing origins of the welfare systems in place.)

The emergence of welfare provisions in these core areas represented the beginning of an acknowledgement of distinct phases of the life course with which particular needs, risks and vulnerabilities are associated. The social security initially offered was largely designed to protect individuals as workers, but the introduction of protective legislation for children and the provision of old age pensions indicated a growing awareness of the needs of people as individuals and an acknowledgement of 'lifecycle risk'. The harsh living conditions of the time and the sometimes awful treatment of children, for instance, became a matter of public consciousness by the latter part of the nineteenth century. The establishment of Societies for the Prevention of Cruelty to Children in the USA, the UK and in Ireland contributed to raising awareness about the welfare of children in general. In the UK the 1889 Children's Charter (the Prevention of Cruelty and Protection of Children Act) provided the first legal basis for state intervention in child–parent relations. This meant that anyone found to be ill-treating a child could be prosecuted. Legislation pertaining to the protection of children was further developed in the UK with the introduction of the National Society for the Prevention of Cruelty to Children (NSPCC) inspectors in the 1904

Prevention of Cruelty Act. These inspectors had the right to remove children from their homes on the grounds of abuse or neglect, on the approval of a Justice of the Peace (NSPCC n.d.). In short, the early twentieth century saw the first challenge to conventional views about the position and status of children in society at that time. This marked the beginning of a very long road in the struggle for the recognition of children as individuals in their own right, also subject to certain risks, and also entitled to protection.

Other important social policy developments of the early twentieth century indicated the dawn of a more extensive role for the state in key areas of social policy. In the UK, for example, the introduction of labour exchanges and the National Insurance Act, 1911, paved the way for benefits to be provided during periods of sickness and unemployment. The rise in the level of state provision was matched with a wider span of taxation measures. The 1909 'People's Budget', introduced by Lloyd George in Britain, contained new land taxes, including a levy on land sales and a tax on the capital value of undeveloped land. The 'Liberal Reforms' of this period were not thought to have had much impact on the distribution of income although the recognition of an 'underserved social surplus' as Lund (2002, p. 84) puts it, 'offered the potential for more radical social and economic change in the direction of social justice'.

From welfare efforts to welfare systems: developments and debates

Sweden continues to be popularly recognised as the 'model' welfare state, although that characterisation has been open to some debate in recent times. In historical terms Sweden was indeed at the forefront of welfare state development, and while influenced by the Bismarckian initiatives of the 1880s, the Swedish application is assessed as more inclusive than was actually the case in Germany. Collective ideals had been actively promoted in political terms since the late 1920s. Known as the People's Home Speech, Prime Minister elect Hansson of Sweden made a famous parliamentary speech in 1928 (in Olsen, 1992, p. 98, cited in Salonen, 2001, p. 146):

> The basis of the home is community and the feeling of togetherness. The good home knows no privileged or disadvantaged individuals, no favourites and step-children. There, one does not look down upon another; there, nobody tries to gain an advantage at the cost of another, the strong one does not hold down and plunder the weak. In the good home equality, consideration, helpfulness prevail. Applied to the great people's and citizens' home, this would mean the breaking down of all social and economic barriers, which now divide citizens into privileged and disadvantaged, into rulers and dependants, into rich and poor, propertied and miserable, plunderers and plundered.

The subsequent and sustained success of the Social Democratic Party, which held power from 1932 to 1976, was undoubtedly a significant factor in the welfare state that subsequently developed in Sweden.

The USA followed a different trajectory in terms of state welfare developments, and local and voluntary sources remained the primary sources of assistance outside of the family. This was the case until the economic depression and unemployment crisis of the 1930s, even though many groups had long argued the merits of state or federal provision in certain instances. Piven and Cloward's (1993) seminal study of public welfare in the United States illustrates the scale of the problems facing local councils, with some not paying their employees, public services being curtailed and many on the verge of bankruptcy. Literally millions of people were affected by this crisis.

The election of Franklin D. Roosevelt in 1933 offered a new political leader, apparently more open to ameliorating the difficulties associated with such large-scale unemployment. The Federal Emergency Relief Administration (FERA) was established and for the first time provided federal assistance in the delivery of support to unemployed persons in the USA. However, while it brought welcome support to the many unemployed, the scheme itself was short-lived and the emphasis quickly shifted to work-based schemes for the 'able-bodied' unemployed. The Works Progress Administration (WPA) was set up, providing an average of two million jobs per annum in its first five years, although this was still far short of what was required. The abolition of FERA in 1936 indicated the ongoing reluctance of the federal state to provide assistance for people affected by unemployment (ibid.). These people had no option but to rely on local agencies which, once again, were under pressure to provide relief.

This is the wider backdrop to the Social Security Act, 1935, which introduced a national social insurance pension, a federal system of unemployment insurance (administered by individual states) and a system of Aid to Dependent Children (ADC). These were significant developments in securing welfare provisions but it is important to note that, for example, in the case of unemployment insurance payments, these were set at local level, coverage was for a limited period, and many workers were actually not covered by the scheme (Trattner, 1999). The ADC was also administered locally on the basis of stringent means-testing and strict eligibility criteria, indicating the conditional nature of the new schemes and the limits of state welfare expansionism in America at this time. Characterisations of a 'work and relief state' (Amenta, 1998, in Clarke, 2001, p. 115) and a 'semi-welfare state' (Katz, 1986, in ibid., p. 118) illustrate the defining features of this important period in American social policy history and stand in contrast to the more comprehensive approach to welfare provision which subsequently emerged in many European countries.

This more comprehensive approach to welfare was largely influenced by a new approach to economic management which emerged and became highly influential in economic and social policy for much of the twentieth century. The work of the economist J. M. Keynes was central to the argument for a role for the state in economic matters and in the development of employment policy from the late 1930s onwards. The fact that he offered the first academic and theoretical rationale for state intervention in the economy was to prove vital in subsequent economic and social planning.

In basic terms, Keynes provided economic justification for state intervention in the workings of the market economy. Specifically, he suggested that the state could intervene to regulate the worst aspects of economic cycles in order to engage in 'demand management' (and thus economic growth) and to maintain employment, where

> **Keynesian economics**, so named after economist J. M. Keynes, advocated state intervention in the economy (as appropriate to the economic conditions which prevailed), challenging the long-standing classical economic laissez-faire position.

appropriate. **Keynesian economics**, as it became known, was instrumental to the development of the welfare state, particularly with its attention to the role of government and the importance of employment policy to the wider welfare agenda. Critically, the impact of Keynesianism may be seen in terms of a break with the predominance of the classical economics of the past. As Mullard and Spicker (1998, p. 29) point out, 'Keynesians sought to offer a revolution in thinking about government and economy and therefore aimed to break with the classical paradigm that a *laissez-faire* economy was the only solution for the well-being of a society.' In offering an economic rationale for greater state intervention, Keynesian economics became the mechanism by which more extensive state provisions and supports were both possible and justifiable and its impact was immense.

> The great day has arrived. You wanted the State to assume greater responsibility for individual citizens. You wanted social security. From today you have it. (*Daily Mirror*, 5 July 1948, in Fraser, 1984, p. xxi)

Published at the height of the Second World War in 1942, *Social Insurance and Allied Services*, the *Beveridge Report* as it became known, is probably the most well-known social policy report of the twentieth century. A best-seller, it contained a blueprint for the provision of social services in Britain and went much further than the initial terms of reference laid out for the report. The author, William Beveridge, was set the task of sorting the muddled system of social insurance which had evolved over the years. What he produced was a report which offered a plan for the future of social policy in Britain. In the guiding principles put forward in his report, Beveridge (1942, pp. 41–2) managed to capture the wider political situation of the time:

> Now, when the war is abolishing landmarks of every kind, is the opportunity for using experience in a clear field. A revolutionary moment in the world's history is a time for revolutions, not for patching.

In the second principle, he offered a vision of welfare which is much more all-encompassing than social insurance alone:

> … organisation of social insurance should be treated as one part only of a comprehensive policy of social progress. Social insurance fully developed may provide income security; it is an attack upon Want. But Want is one only of five giants on the road of reconstruction and in some ways the easiest to attack. The others are Disease, Ignorance, Squalor and Idleness.

Healthcare, education, housing and work were the antidotes to these social problems and the reconstruction which followed World War II allowed for the development of core social services. Acknowledgement of the range of issues which arise in meeting human needs marked a watershed in defining the role of the social services in providing welfare. In so doing, the idea of a baseline or 'national minimum' under which no one should fall, became a new but feasible policy objective, which appeared to promote and appeal to people's sense of social solidarity, particularly in the aftermath of the war. In addition, the centrality of employment, as a policy objective and as the economic linchpin on which welfare provision was possible, was clear. Availability of work was accepted as a central element of social and economic policy for the future. Critically though, while a responsive and expanded role for the state was being carved out in the formative years of the British welfare state, this was not to happen at the expense of economic progress. While advocating a greater role for the state in the abolition of want and in meeting basic needs, Beveridge saw that an appropriate balance had to be struck:

> The third principle is that social security must be achieved by cooperation between the State and the individual. The State should offer security for service and contribution. The State in organising security should not stifle incentive, opportunity, responsibility; in establishing a national minimum, it should leave room and encouragement for voluntary action by each individual to provide more than that minimum for himself and his family.

The collectivist philosophy at the core of a national minimum was clearly circumscribed by a keenness to see individual responsibility maintained in any new welfare balance. 'Reluctant collectivists' (George and Wilding, 1985) was the term subsequently used to describe advocates of this approach to welfare provision.

Turning this plan into a policy reality in Britain became the job of the Labour Party, elected after a landmark election victory in 1945, in which they secured the first majority in their history. In general terms, the Labour Party was considered to be a solid supporter of the Beveridge Report and efforts were made to implement the proposals in the years that followed. While these were not realised in full (Glennerster, 1995), some core areas of policy saw milestone developments during the lifetime of the Labour government. They had inherited the 1944 Education Act which had abolished fees for secondary education along with the legislation enacted for the provision of Family Allowances. The **universal provision** of a payment for the second and subsequent children of all families (as provided for in the Family Allowances Act, 1945) on a non-means-tested and non-contributory basis represented the introduction of the first quintessential universal benefit in Britain (which as documented in Chapter 2 had been introduced in Ireland a year previously on a similar basis). Wider elements of public policy incorporated state control of key components of the economy, and many major industries were nationalised or held in public ownership in the UK at this time. Civil aviation, coal, transport, electricity and gas were all nationalised by the Labour government in the UK during the late 1940s.

> **Universal provision** refers to the delivery of a social service or social security as a matter of right, satisfying a certain core criterion without the use of a means test or other measure of differentiation.

UK Ministry of National Insurance poster advertising the Family Allowance Act, 1945.
Source: The National Archives, UK.

Between the years 1945 and 1951 much was done to consolidate the organisation of the health and social security systems in Britain. While the mother and child scheme controversy exposed the various opponents of a collectivist vision with regard to healthcare in Ireland, in the UK Aneurin Bevan succeeded in passing the National Health Service Act, 1946, despite the objections of many within the medical profession. Private consultant practice was allowed to continue but the Act provided a national health service, largely paid for through general taxation, with a small contribution from the national insurance fund. Services to be provided by the NHS included free treatment by the citizen's doctor of choice, free prescriptions and no charge for hospital visits or stays (ibid.).

The extent to which the suffering experienced during the Second World War and the reconstruction required for national recovery in Britain precipitated support for the welfare state project is debated, but these factors were undoubtedly a crucial part of the context within which the Beveridge Report was received. There is evidence that the report also made the headlines in Ireland and that its popularity prompted a debate about the nature of Irish social policy (Ó Cinnéide, 2000). (This is considered in more detail in Chapter 7.) The report was also subject to considerable academic and political scrutiny in Germany, even if the ideas around social insurance were 'by no means a novelty in German eyes' (Hockerts, 1981, p. 324). A *Report on Social Security in Canada* was produced in 1943, (the author of which had worked with Beveridge) which, while it 'was not as comprehensive as its British counterpart, it nevertheless firmly placed Canada in the Keynes-Beveridge tradition' (Lightman and Riches, 2001, p. 51). Some of the major developments of the Canadian welfare state, including universal family allowances and old age pensions, were introduced in 1945 and 1952, respectively.

Overall, this period was marked by a significant shift in thinking around welfare. The focus moved from 'individuals with problems' and 'troubles' which needed to be 'fixed' to an acknowledgement of the possibilities and positives associated with a more **collectivist approach**, with universal provision of some basic level of welfare and social services. This shift in direction was identified by the International Labour Organisation in 1950 and they refer to a 'new conception' in the development of social security during this period (Oakley, 1994).

> A **collectivist approach** sees groups, communities and societies as the basic unit of social structure. Need and risk are to be met on a 'shared' rather than individualised basis, thereby apportioning greater responsibility to society (often through the medium of the state) in meeting same.

Understanding the events as the expansion of citizenship, T. H. Marshall's seminal essay 'Citizenship and Social Class' (1949) offered an historical evolutionary analysis of the development of **citizenship** rights in Britain. He saw citizenship as evolving from the emergence of civil rights (the right to freedom of expression, freedom of religion and justice before the law) during the

> **Marshallian citizenship** refers to T. H. Marshall's three-prong identification of citizenship rights as having civil, political and social elements. His particular conception of social citizenship was constructed around the role of the state in abating class inequalities in the context of the nation state.

eighteenth century, the establishment of political rights (the right to vote and the right to stand for public office) over the course of the nineteenth century, and the development of social rights (the right to a modicum of economic welfare and security) in the twentieth century. He defined citizenship as a 'status bestowed on those who are full members of a community' (Marshall, 1964, p. 84) and the social element of this as the 'whole range from a right to share a modicum of economic welfare and security to the right to share to the full in the social heritage and to live the life of a civilised being according to the standards prevailing in the society' (ibid.). He suggested that the institutions most closely connected with this idea of social citizenship were the educational system and social services. Reflecting the shift away from thinking about individuals with problems that needed fixing, he emphasised the common experiences that social rights would produce, regardless of one's class position, and suggested that social citizenship would modify the pattern of social inequality. One of the most important aspects of this which Marshall highlighted was a new common experience where 'all learn what it means to have an insurance card that must be regularly stamped (by somebody) or to collect children's allowances or pensions from the post office' (ibid.).

In short, civil and political rights were viewed as necessary components of the development of capitalism, and the emergence of social rights offered a solution to some of the inequalities inherent in capitalist society. The expansionary phase of welfare provision which existed in Britain at that time was clearly relevant to such an analysis, although subsequent assessments of Marshall's theory of citizenship have challenged its core assumptions and questioned its broader application. This is an issue we will return to at the end of this chapter and in the final part of the book.

SECTION 3: WELFARE STATES IN THE MID- TO LATE TWENTIETH CENTURY – CONSOLIDATION, REFORM AND ADAPTATION TO NEW REALITIES

The period after the Second World War was a formative time in the development of social policy, establishing the basis of comprehensive social service provision and social welfare arrangements. The so-called 'golden era' of the welfare state lasted from the late 1940s until the mid-1970s. During this time a range of services were set up, and access improved and widened, particularly in the areas of health, education and social security. Looking at welfare states across Europe, Cousins (2005b) outlines how benefits expanded in the period 1950–70, pointing to a significantly wider reach of such welfare provisions during this period. Social policy moved from concentrating on how best to deal with the poor and the poorest to looking at how access to social services might be the preserve or entitlement of all citizens. However, the more expansive idea of access based on citizenship was a problematic one. In the case of women, it quickly emerged that they were treated as 'second-class' citizens with regard to welfare provision, while some groups, notably immigrants, were denied access to services on the basis of not being citizens.

Returning to the British example and Beveridge's welfare state, it was evident, even at the time of the publication of his report, that Beveridge had worked on the basis of re-enforcing particular 'social norms', particularly with regard to the role of women in society. As his report indicates, 'housewives as mothers have vital work to do in ensuring the adequate continuance of the British race and British ideals in the world' (Beveridge, 1942, p. 52, in Williams, 1989, p. 125). In 1943, Abbott and Bompass highlighted the unequal treatment of married women where Beveridge had proposed that women's social insurance rights should be removed on marriage, that contributions would be voluntary rather than compulsory and that benefits would be payable at a lower rate to that of men (Pratt, 2006). The predominance of these assumptions paved the way for a model of welfare provision which was based on what is now known as the male breadwinner model, with married women assigned a dependent status within the family and not recognised as individuals in their own right. A strong male breadwinner model persisted in the UK and Germany, while the positions in countries such as Sweden and Denmark made greater advances (Lewis, 1992, 1997). Feminists have continued to challenge these assumptions (see Chapter 5), but these views about the role of women were widely held and are said to have been in keeping with the 'social norms' of the time. In Pratt's (2006, p. 128) words:

Beveridge's belief in the two-parent, male breadwinner family unit as the basis of social solidarity was a widely held, mainstream political opinion and it is important that the social changes that he failed to foresee and which led to the undermining of his model should not obscure that fact.

Nevertheless, it is important to point out too that the legacy of this traditional male breadwinner model of welfare provision was long-lived. The dependent status imposed on women and constructed around particular familial and domestic ideals severely restricted the lives of women, and much of the invisible work done by women in the home continued to be ignored. Williams (1989) argues that the model of solidarity espoused by Beveridge allowed for institutional inequalities not only in the treatment of women but that the rights of other groups were also not vindicated by such an approach to welfare provision. The residency requirements attached to many welfare provisions excluded many 'non-citizens' living in Britain from accessing the social services, even though it was within these services that many migrant people worked. As Williams (1989, p. 162) puts it:

> When Beveridge announced his attack on the five giants – Want, Squalor, Idleness, Ignorance and Disease – he hid the giants Racism and Sexism, and the fights against them, behind statues to the Nation and the White Family.

In short, Williams argues that the welfare state as it developed was designed to meet the needs of white British families that conformed to the married, two-parent 'norm'.

Similar issues also came to the fore in the USA, and, ultimately, the Civil Rights movement of the 1960s became central to the demands for welfare reform. Apart from the obvious unrest caused by racial discrimination and conflict, the limitations of the existing welfare provisions also came in for greater scrutiny. The federal–local mix of welfare provision and in particular the conditions attached to the ADC highlighted the 'moral' conditions that were attached to benefit receipt. According to Gordon (1994, p. 298, in Clarke, 2001, p. 118):

> ADC was unique among all welfare programs in its subjection of applicants to a morals test. The most frequent measurement of a 'suitable home' was sexual behaviours. The presence of a man in the house, or the birth of an illegitimate child, made the home unsuitable. These provisions also permitted racist policies. For example, black–white relationships were particularly likely to make a child's home declared unsuitable. The search for these 'moral' infractions produced intense supervision and invasions of privacy.

Apart from these shortcomings of the welfare state, other political, economic and social issues also presented the impetus for welfare debate and reform. A number of problems emerged in the late 1960s and 1970s to provide a much less supportive climate for the 'welfare state' project, which many believed had failed or at least fallen short of its stated objectives. In the 1960s, the 'rediscovery' of poverty, as it became known, highlighted some real problems with the capacity of the welfare state to address issues of poverty and inequality. A study conducted by Abel-Smith and Townsend (1965) entitled *The Poor and the Poorest* demonstrated the extent of the problem, particularly among large low-income families in Britain. A number of direct action groups campaigned on this issue, including the Child Poverty Action Group (CPAG) and the Low Pay Unit (Jones, 2000). A more stringent critique, based on a revival of Marxist thinking, or neo-Marxism, also emerged (O'Connor, 1973; Ginsburg, 1979; Gough, 1979; Offe, 1982, 1984) which provided a challenging assessment of the role of the welfare state in promoting and protecting capitalism. In general terms, this literature highlighted the 'contradictions of the welfare state' in providing the necessary conditions for the maintenance of capitalism.

The 1970s also saw the emergence of community development projects which facilitated important work with people, mainly in disadvantaged areas. Jones (2000), for example, identifies the emergent Welfare Rights and Law Centres movements in the UK as important in providing welfare information and advice. At a more general level, the growth in community development was a clearer indication of the critical shortcomings of the welfare state in meeting the needs of local communities and groups. It is clear that the ethos and culture of the traditional welfare state was under increasing pressure to be more responsive and less rigid than the original and very traditional structures would allow.

Feminist agitation for legislative and other policy reforms to address the discriminatory structure of the welfare state gained ground and a number of issues were tackled such as inequalities in pay and in the formal labour market. Consequently, the Equal Pay Act, 1970, and the Sex Discrimination Act, 1975, were passed in the UK (Dale, 1997) and similar legislation was passed in Ireland (as outlined in Chapter 3). While such reforms were welcome and long overdue, they primarily addressed the inherent discrimination which existed and could no longer be ignored.

In Sweden, in contrast, 'a different conception of equality' (Lewis and Aström, 1997, p. 37) was adopted from the late 1960s onwards which went beyond regulation of the formal labour market and included the introduction of separate taxation and expansion in public daycare facilities for children. A system of parental insurance was introduced in 1974 and developed in subsequent years (ibid.). These initiatives were way ahead of what was happening in this area in most other countries and women's labour market participation rates were considerably higher in Sweden as a result. Sweden was undoubtedly a policy leader in women's rights and family policy, not least when compared with Ireland, where the marriage bar had just been lifted at the time these initiatives were being developed in Sweden. The initiatives mentioned here highlight the difference in approach to these issues but they also illustrate the extent to which the welfare state project continued to be developed in Sweden throughout the 1970s, notwithstanding the political resistance which was building up elsewhere.

In economic terms, the oil crises of the early 1970s, rapid inflation and increasing unemployment meant that Keynesian economics was no longer considered the panacea in addressing the worst excesses of the economic cycle. Workers were unhappy too, with high inflation eroding the real value of their wages and in some cases threatening their jobs. With the economic justification for state intervention and welfare provision under attack, the political and ideological grounds for state intervention became increasingly difficult to defend. As the then UK Labour Minister, Anthony Crosland put it in 1975, the 'party is over' (in Hill, 2003, p. 36). Similarly, academics confirmed the onset of the 'crisis of the welfare state', although this, in retrospect, turned out to be largely intellectual (Alber, 1988) and ideological rather than a 'practical crisis' of its ability to perform day-to-day functions.

In short, criticisms of the welfare state project were grounded in differing perspectives and shaped by conflicting ideological values, but the cumulative effect remained significant: there was an appetite for significant change, most palpably demonstrated in the collapse of support for the Labour Party in Britain in the late 1970s and by the 18 years of Conservative government which followed from 1979 to 1997. The wider resurgence in right-wing thinking was evident in national politics elsewhere too, with the election of Ronald Reagan in the USA in 1980 and the success of the Conservative Party in Canada which won a considerable majority in 1984 (Mishra, 1990). While the political and economic climate undoubtedly changed and became more hostile to the welfare state, it is important to note that welfare states in Europe continued to grow, and spending also rose between 1970 and 1980 (Cousins, 2005b). The question that arises now is whether the economic and political challenges mounted against the 'welfare state project' were effective in their application in the years that followed and it is therefore to the 1980s that we now turn.

Rolling back the welfare state

Reducing the role of the state in all aspects of economic and social life was the major objective of the **New Right**. The New Right was the generic term used to describe

> **The New Right** is an all-encompassing title for the right-wing values that gained prominence during the 1980s. Various strands of thinking have been influential, including neo-liberalism and neo-conservatism.

the objectives of a powerful mix of neo-liberal and neo-conservative thinkers and politicians whose ideas became prominent by the late 1970s. This largely anti-collectivist thinking was exemplified by the Thatcher government elected to office in the UK in 1979. Following the theoretical guidance of Fredrick Von Hayek, in social terms Margaret Thatcher valued, 'a society in which the vast majority of men and women are encouraged and helped to accept responsibility for themselves and their families, and to live their lives with a maximum of independence and self-reliance' (Thatcher, 1977, cited in George and Wilding, 1985, p. 22).

The New Right philosophy sought to reduce the role of the state in the lives of individuals and aimed to radically reform the welfare state, which, it was argued, had created over-reliance and was inefficient, wasteful and in need of an overhaul. For example, in Britain over 200 advisory bodies or 'quangos' were abolished shortly after the 1979 election and these included commissions such as those examining the distribution of wealth and a council working on the development of the personal social services. Official statistical services were also curtailed and their purpose defined primarily in terms of the needs of government (Jones, 2000). The overall approach sought to re-enforce classical liberal values of individualism and the merits of the free market, the principles of which were also to be adopted by the public service.

The application of market principles to key areas of the public service took many forms, including the sale of local authority houses to tenants and the **privatisation** or selling of shares in key previously nationalised utilities such as British Gas and British Telecom. The emergence of **New Public Management** during the 1980s sought to apply private sector practices in the management, budgets and finance of the public service. In turn, outcomes were

> **Privatisation** refers to the process through which previously state-owned companies (often utilities, such as electricity, transport) are sold by the state to private enterprise.

> **New Public Management** refers to the development of a business and commercial ethos and management style in the public service.

measured much more closely in terms of performance and efficiency. Application of new public management principles included the creation of internal markets within the social services in Britain, most notably in health, local government and education, and certain core functions (e.g. cleaning, catering, etc.) were put out to tender. In terms of the core social services, this also involved the introduction of 'quasi-markets' or some level of market competition within the social services. In practice this meant that while the state continued to fund (or purchase) elements of a service, it might not be the actual provider. **Contracting out** is the term used to describe this process and it is a notable policy development of this period in the UK in particular, although it is now increasingly common elsewhere, including in Ireland. This has led to both voluntary and private providers entering formal service agreements with the state around the delivery of particular social services. For the voluntary sector, challenges include how best to maintain their identity, lobbying functions and autonomy in such situations. Lewis (1999, p. 17) explains the dilemma:

> **Contracting out** refers to the process by which certain services within the public sphere are put out to tender to private enterprise or voluntary sector organisations.

> While government has held out a larger role for them in social service provision, government is also in a position to say what it will contract with them to do. Voluntary organisations may be in the process of becoming alternative, rather than supplementary or complementary, providers of welfare, but in a situation in which the state determines the conditions of provision without taking responsibility. This form of welfare pluralism does not position voluntary agencies as mediating institutions, but tends rather to see them as instruments of the state, which raises difficult questions for agencies about both identity and function.

Since the 1980s in particular, new markets have emerged for the private sector in the social services in areas outside of their more typical areas of housing and pensions. This changing welfare mix became one of the more enduring features of welfare reform in subsequent decades.

For the New Right, extolling the virtues of the free market meant tackling the vested interests outside the state as well. Taking on the trade unions, which the Conservative Party in Britain had viewed as too powerful, was also central to restoring the values of capitalism. A combination of legislation and infamous standoffs (most notably with the miners) led to confrontation between state and workers on a scale not seen for many years. The lack of work weakened the union position, as unemployment was a very real prospect. Films such as *Brassed Off* (1996) and *Billy Elliot* (2000) offer a vivid insight into the very real social tensions and divisions which emerged in Britain at the time. Unemployment rose in the UK from 1.2 million in 1979 to over 3 million in 1984 (Jones, 2000), but according to the New Right it was the market and not the state which would solve the unemployment problem.

In economic terms, things were worse after the return of the Conservatives before there were any signs of recovery. Unemployment also rose in the USA during the same period. It wasn't just the scale of the unemployment that was problematic; cutbacks and tighter eligibility criteria applied to unemployment compensation in the USA meant that only 25 per cent of those unemployed received benefits by 1984, compared with 75 per cent in 1975 (Mishra, 1990). Similarly in the UK, social security was made increasingly conditional. Examples include the application of penalties to unemployed people who refused training or left jobs; the abolition of two of the pre-existing universal welfare benefits (the maternity grant and the death grant) which were replaced with means-tested schemes and the reform of the national pension system, the State Earnings Related Pension Scheme (SERPS), to encourage people away from it and into private schemes (Hill, 2003).

The hostile ideological climate in Britain, which was also in evidence in the USA, undermined the solidarity basis of welfare provision and portrayed many welfare recipients as 'deviants'. There was ridicule of those whose lives did not conform to traditional conservative family values (e.g. Lilley, 1992, in Becker, 1997) and wire grilles were installed in some social security offices, indicating the poor relations that existed between clients and some officers at the time (Jones, 2000). A wider academic discourse re-enforced the confrontational approach to welfare debate, with Murray (1984) and others referring to an 'underclass' of society. However ill-defined (see Lister, 1996, for a detailed account of the debate), the term was frequently taken to refer to individual or familial behaviour which can contribute to poverty and welfare dependency. The 'underclass' debate was trenchantly argued, along with other 'dependency politics' (Mead, 1992) theories, which put forward the view that the welfare state sapped people's initiative and enterprise and encouraged dependency on the state. This too was cogently rebutted (Dean and Taylor-Gooby, 1992), most forcibly by reference to the absence of work in the first instance and the severity of the social exclusion experienced by many of the most disadvantaged social groups. In particular, the 'welfare-to-work' basis for the provision of social protection became the new 'tough love' approach to social policy.

This welfare-to-work theme or **'workfare'** continued through the 1990s and is well illustrated in social policy developments in the US. In 1994 the AFDC was replaced with a programme called Temporary Assistance to Needy Families (TANF) which imposed work requirements and time limits on lone mothers receiving assistance from the scheme. The Personal Responsibility and Work Opportunity Reconciliation Act, 1996, similarly sought that families be independent through work. In practice, this meant a maximum of two years' benefit before the state could begin withdrawing support. Furthermore, the

> **Workfare** refers to welfare arrangements in which a requirement to work (or train) is a condition of eligibility. The 'growing conditionality' of welfare entitlements has been a particular feature of welfare policy in liberal welfare states.

Act aimed to promote marriage and two-parent families; in fact, states could refuse additional benefit for any child born whose mother was already in receipt of welfare (Clarke and Piven, 2001). The Act, and in particular the abolition of the AFDC resulted in a measure which, as Trattner (1999, p. 397) explains, 'eliminated any national entitlement to welfare, reflected a resurgence of a number of fundamental themes of colonial poor law, its more unworkable, or at least unfair and punitive provisions, namely local responsibility, restrictions on providing aid to "strangers", and the "work or starve" mentality for the able-bodied'.

Similar to the welfare ethos of the nineteenth century, the 1980s New Right philosophy promoted resurgence in individualist values, demonstrated through a rhetoric that extolled the virtues of free market economics and a limited state. In addition, the capacity and virtue of charity was espoused as a viable alternative to state provision of social services. However, notwithstanding the evident impact of New Right thinking on the nature of welfare benefits and the increased conditions attached to them, it is important to note that the welfare state did, broadly speaking, 'survive' the plans to dismantle it. This is true even in countries like the UK, where the impact of New Right politics was greatest. At the same time, these welfare states did not emerge unscathed as we have discussed here. Analysing the social policy legacy of the New Right can only be fully explored in the context of what followed and to which we now briefly turn.

Welfare states under pressure I: adapting to new political and economic realities?

The 1990s and 2000s have been marked by greater attention to the need to reign in costs associated with social expenditure, and appeals for welfare 'cost containment' are commonplace. This is evidenced in the welfare reform debates and the increasingly mainstream acceptance of globalisation as a force to be reckoned with in terms of managing national economic and social policies in recent times (see Chapter 6).

In political terms, the 1990s saw a marked shift in political thinking on the left, specifically the redefining of social democratic values (e.g. the emergence of New Labour), the causes and consequences of which continue to be debated (discussed in Chapter 5). The emergence of a Third Way offered a perspective that was not bound by old paradigms and approaches to political debate, and, crucially, it is argued, this approach acknowledges the changed nature of society (especially in terms of globalisation) and the need to change with it. Applying this to economic and social policy meant taking more nuanced positions on social rights, or as some would argue, withdrawing from the 'old' unconditional approach offered by Marshall's notion of social rights in favour of 'no rights without responsibilities'.

This shift in thinking provided the basis for some continuity with the welfare reforms instigated in the 1980s, while at the same time developing key priorities for promoting equality of opportunity (although not equality of outcome) through investment in children and in education. In terms of economic policy, it became increasingly clear that in the case of the UK, for example, New Labour was more pro-market than their 'old Labour' predecessors and it sought to stress the benefits of the market and in that sense make a clear break with its more socialist leanings of the past. In terms of the welfare state, this translated into greater continuity rather than a reversal of the social service reforms introduced by the Conservatives during the 1980s. For example, the imposition of tighter 'jobseeking' requirements were initially introduced in The Jobseekers Allowance Act, 1996, which attached stricter conditions to the receipt of unemployment benefits (Clasen et al., 2006). The change in government in 1997 maintained the emphasis on labour market participation, and subsequent measures introduced sanctions up to and including the withdrawal of benefits for failure to take up one of four offers of work/training (Dwyer, 2004a). The significance of these incremental changes has been characterised in terms of the 'creeping conditionality' (ibid.) of social security in Britain in recent years. The point here is that the 'reversal' that might have been expected post the New Right era of the 1990s did not quite materialise.

Since the emergence of the welfare 'containment' argument of the 1970s, welfare discourse has been marked by attempts to characterise the overall direction of welfare reforms. Welfare retrenchment, austerity, adaptation, re-structuring and re-calibration are among the concepts and characterisations that have gained prominence in the analyses of welfare states in recent decades. New social risks (Taylor-Gooby, 2004a; Bonoli, 2007) have also been identified which distinguish between the risks dealt with by traditional welfare states and those which now require attention. In general terms, welfare states offer greatest protection to those with a full-time, long-standing employment record, and the 'de-standardisation of employment' (Bonoli, 2007, p. 500) away from the full-time, job-for-life model exposes the risks exemplified by the position of part-time workers, often women. The increased participation of women in the labour market since the 1970s, as Bonoli (ibid., p. 499) points out, 'is obviously not a source of social risk per se ... Rather, a new risk stems from the inability to combine motherhood and child rearing with paid employment.' Other caring responsibilities are also recognised in this framework of analysis (as has been highlighted by feminists for many years – see Chapter 5) which acknowledges that 'traditional patterns of care impose stresses on women seeking paid work and generate a demand for provision from alternative sources – men, the private sector, and the state.' (Taylor-Gooby, 2004b, p. 3). Changes in family forms are also highlighted in terms of 'new social risks', again, not because they are problematic but because welfare states are ill-equipped to deal with their needs. Expansion of private sector provision of welfare services is included in Taylor-Gooby's account of 'new risks' because of the risks apparent where provision is inadequate and/or unregulated.

Post-industrialisation has given way to substantial changes in employment; jobs in manufacturing have declined and the service industry has grown, and long-term unemployment has emerged as a significant risk for those whose skills are not transferable (Bonoli, 2007). The traditional welfare state model offered protection to such (usually male) workers, but low-skill workers today are exposed to the risk of unemployment and/or the possibility of being paid a 'poverty wage' (ibid., p. 499). The concept of the 'working poor' is not a new one, but the expansion in the service sector and the nature of much of the employment therein does not provide the same job security or prospects for worker mobilisation as previously. The impact of globalisation, changing demographics and associated demands on welfare states have shaped and continue to impact on contemporary discourses of welfare. Generally speaking, the result has been a tightening up of eligibility and contribution criteria in an attempt to manage the costs of social provisions to which welfare states are exposed.

However characterised, it is not possible to put together a 'one size fits all' assessment of the health or otherwise of welfare states. Nevertheless, it is possible to identify two broad trends in social policy over the last decade: the emphasis on welfare-to-work (availing of, and access to, paid employment) as illustrated above; and more sustained efforts to contain social expenditure (largely imposed through stricter conditions attached to service and benefit eligibility). Containment of major social protection commitments (most notably pensions) has been a widespread feature of all welfare states over the course of the 1990s. At the same time, there is some evidence of welfare states developing new initiatives in the historically neglected area of care (particularly for children and older people), although the welfare mix of these arrangements is likely to be much more influenced by long-term cost considerations than was previously the case. In short, welfare states grapple with a variety of demands and as Kautto and Kvist (2002, p. 195) put it, 'during the 1990s reference to "external pressures" from the European and global context began to supplement older concerns and established criticism against welfare state arrangements based on internal pressures.'

Whatever the precise manifestations of these pressures in individual countries, it is important to note that social expenditure has not collapsed, or anything close. Drawing on OECD data for pensions and family spending for 20 countries, Cousins (2005b) points out that spending has continued to rise in all but two countries (Ireland and the Netherlands). The increasing numbers in receipt of state pensions, particularly in many of the mainland European countries, accounts for the increased expenditure on pensions. The increased spending on family policy points not to welfare states in abeyance but an effort in many cases to address the difficulties related to family and labour market policies mentioned earlier in the chapter. There is now a good deal of acceptance that while there has been extensive welfare state reform in recent times this does not necessarily amount to retrenchment, although that is probably now much more possible in the climate that has developed in the last decade or so (Taylor-Gooby, 2001). This is a theme to which we return in the context of contemporary economic and political pressures, particularly those related to globalisation and its impact, in Chapter 6.

Welfare states under pressure II: adapting to new cultural realities?

While we have concentrated on the political and economic trends in the welfare state's fortunes since the 1980s, culture and cultural change have also played a part in the new realities of the welfare state. Some authors (Smith, 1998; Clarke, 2004) have talked about the 'cultural turn' in the social sciences. This entails both new perspectives on analysing social change and acknowledging that issues of identity, recognition and representation go beyond the economic realm, social class identity and inequalities. However, this is a complex and contested area, which provokes much debate. While feminist thinking has been a long-standing alternative to class-based analysis and has long been critical of the ways in which social policy develops to exclude or discriminate against women, in more recent times, specifically in the 1970s, new theories were emerging that posed a much more all-encompassing challenge to ways of thinking and acting in the modern world. These theories included postmodernism and poststructuralism. Vastly oversimplifying, these theories questioned the basis upon which we 'know' reality and produce knowledge, and our faith in values such as progress, universalism and the attainability of social justice.[1] Immediately it would appear that such a way of looking at the world doesn't have much to do with social policy or that, more dramatically, it attacks its foundations.

Postmodern theory, developed by the likes of Lyotard, Jameson and Baudrillard, encompassed trends in areas such as architecture and consumer capitalism; however, its meaning has provoked quite sceptical and critical responses (Coughlan, 2005), and the term is used by some in quite a derisive way. As for post-structuralism – represented in particular by the work of Foucault on power and discourse and his detailed studies of areas such as criminality, sexuality and madness – this has had more long-lasting political effect. Foucault was interested in the notion of discourse which he defined as a system of representation which regulates the meanings and practices which can and cannot be produced. In other words, instead of understanding welfare simply as policies which act upon the social world and aim to improve it, Foucault understood welfare as a discourse and a practice that played a key role creating and regulating what we know as the social world and people within in at a particular point in time. This approach also entailed a deconstruction of any appeals to universal truths and representations. If we take this on board, then questions about how reality is represented become political; as Bertens (1995, p. 7) puts it:

> The end of representation thus leads us back to the question of authorship, to such political questions as 'Whose history gets told? In whose name? For what purpose?' (Marshall, 1992: 4). In the absence of transcendent truth it matters, more than ever, who is speaking (or writing), and why, and to whom.

This has direct relevance and practical application for what has been called the rise of identity politics since the 1980s, which is aptly summarised by Isin and Wood (1999, p. 1):

> For at least two decades political struggles in the West had no longer been waged solely in the name of socialism, with redistribution and equality as its twin principles. Instead, a cultural politics emerged where various groups demanded rights ranging from political representation to affirmation of group difference ... Various social movements, such as those of women, gays, 'racial' and ethnic 'minorities', have charged that behind the veil of 'universal citizenship' and 'equality before the law' there lay systemic forms of domination and oppression that misrecognized and marginalized them.

Within social policy analysis Williams's (1989, 1992, 1994) work in particular has exemplified something of this approach, drawing attention to identities that were hidden behind the veil of 'universal citizenship'. Earlier in the chapter some of the problems associated with the 'social norms' assumed in Beveridge's welfare state and Marshall's conception of social citizenship were examined. Looking at this in a theoretical sense from the point of view of cultural difference and identity politics, Williams (1992) employed the term 'false universalism' to look at how social policies and social rights purport to treat everyone equally but have the effect of privileging a 'false universal' that is usually the white, middle-class, able-bodied heterosexual male over other identities. While not going so far as to say that universalism is an impossibility, Williams suggested that the tension or challenge in social policy is 'between universal principles and policies, on the one hand, and the recognition of diversity, on the other' (ibid., p. 209). This is an on-going challenge and is particularly salient at the present time with reference to diversity stemming from immigration and debates about multi-culturalism, inter-culturalism and integration (see, for example, Chapter 12).

Not all social policy analysts were as open to the challenges and implications of this kind of theory and politics. In the mid-1990s a debate took place between Taylor-Gooby and others about the merits or otherwise of adopting a postmodern approach to social policy. Taylor-Gooby's contribution cut to the heart of the negative implications of postmodernism for social policy at a time when there was a resurgence of neo-liberalism and issues of class inequality, privatisation and welfare retrenchment were more significant than ever. He therefore argued that 'postmodernism functions as an ideological smokescreen, preventing us from recognising some of the most important trends in modern social policy' (Taylor-Gooby, 1994, p. 385). In contrast, Mann (1998), drawing on the example of Williams's work, suggested that there were certain affinities between critical social policy and a postmodern approach. Taking a more positive position, Penna and O'Brien (1996) argued that there were merits to particular strands of postmodernism and poststructuralism in their own right for social policy. They highlighted Foucault's work in particular and argued its relevance for the disability movement and the feminist movement, for example. In some ways these 'headline' debates have now passed, and issues of identity, culture and discourse have become part of mainstream social policy analysis; however, it is important to be aware of the wider theoretical context in which these issues emerged and the various positions adopted in social policy analysis towards them.

CHAPTER SUMMARY

▸ This chapter traced the emergence of the welfare state in the context of the main factors that have influenced its development over the late nineteenth and twentieth centuries.

▸ There were a number of formative influences on the development of welfare debate in the latter part of the nineteenth century, including political activism, philanthropy and the establishment of democratic rights. The Poor Law was the first element of welfare provision in many countries until developments in the latter part of the nineteenth century saw the emergence of state intervention in public health and education. The first social security measures were introduced from the 1880s onwards and developed in the first decade of the twentieth century.

▸ The next phase of welfare state development occurred after the Second World War when a more collectivist approach to welfare provision saw the establishment of social services along with a more comprehensive approach to social security. This expansionary phase lasted through to the 1970s, although the 'welfare state project' came under increasing scrutiny for its assumptions about citizenship, work and the role of women. In addition, its failure to provide the antidote to poverty and the rising costs associated with the welfare state led to mounting criticism of its objectives and results.

▸ The period of the 1980s saw the New Right promote welfare retrenchment in many countries, and a wider discourse of welfare state reform followed over the course of the 1990s. This subsequent debate has drawn attention to a range of economic, political, social and cultural questions about the nature of social policy.

Discussion points

▸ Take an area of welfare state provision in a particular country (e.g. pensions, unemployment, etc.) and research the extent of provision available and entitlement conditions in 1870, 1920, 1990 and 2009. Draw on your findings to create an 'information leaflet' for each of the dates in question.

▸ Choose a concept (e.g. citizenship, collectivism, individualism, etc.) and analyse its significance in the evolution of welfare and social policy debate.

▸ Discuss the proposition that the Beveridge approach to welfare was formative but flawed.

▸ Critically appraise the main perspectives on the contemporary dilemmas of the welfare state.

Further reading

Cousins, M. (2005) *European Welfare States: Comparative Perspectives*, London: Sage.

Jones, K. (2000) *The Making of Social Policy in Britain: From the Poor Law to New Labour* (third edn), London: The Athlone Press.

O'Brien, M. and Penna, S. (1998) *Theorising Welfare: Enlightenment and Modern Society*, London: Sage.

Williams, F. (1989) *Social Policy: a critical introduction: issues of race, gender and class*, Cambridge: Polity.

Notes

1   See, for example, Sarup (1993) and Carter (1998).

CHAPTER 5

POLITICAL IDEOLOGIES, WELFARE AND SOCIAL POLICY

The study of social policy is complex for many reasons, not least because of the range and breadth of disciplines, ideas and values that impact on its development. As the previous chapters have shown, the development of social policy has historically been influenced by a range of factors, with different and competing political ideas and perspectives central among these. Ideologies of welfare are an important area of study because they influence the nature of social policy debate and shape political positions on the core role and objectives of social policy, which in turn impacts on individuals' well-being and quality of life. Ideologies of welfare may be understood as a set of ideas and associated principles or values which, when taken together, offer a rationale for a particular approach to welfare and social policy issues. Ideologies of welfare have evolved, prior to, and in tandem with, welfare state development and as such are of themselves subject to some modification, particularly over time and in light of changing circumstances. However, that is not to imply that ideologies of welfare are 'highly moveable', because at their core there should be some 'first principles' that continue to influence their thinking, even in the context of social change.

This chapter provides an outline of some of the major ideological perspectives on welfare, which are influential in political debate on many matters of importance to social policy. The key principles underpinning the different perspectives on welfare are outlined and the implications of each political ideology is explored with reference to issues such as welfare and social service delivery, the role of the state (and other welfare providers), the significance and interpretation of equality, and the overall function and scope of social policy.

CHAPTER OUTLINE
▸ The first section of this chapter examines the relevance of welfare ideologies to the study of social policy. Attention is then given to the parameters of left and right that so often accompany discussion of ideological positions, and to other important concepts, notably liberty

and equality, that are critical to our overall understanding of the approaches taken to welfare and social policy.

▸ The core features of a number of key perspectives on welfare, including liberalism, conservatism, social democracy, socialism, the 'Third Way', feminism and greenism are outlined in section two. While this is not an exhaustive examination of relevant 'isms', a number of the key perspectives that aid in our understanding of the interplay between politics, ideology and social policy are outlined.

SECTION 1: UNDERSTANDING PERSPECTIVES ON WELFARE

Political ideas and perspectives on welfare

Take a topic such as education and its provision. Should it be free or should it be paid for? Should third-level education be freely provided or should people pay for it? Should people at risk of leaving school early be paid to attend? Should pupils be free to wear clothing and jewellery that has religious significance? Should free school meals be provided to all pupils? Should school meals include a choice of all foods, or only those which are healthy and 'good for you'? There are no wrong or right answers to these questions, rather they are a matter of debate, involving different values and perspectives about the role of the state, the position of religion, the importance of individual freedom and choice, the extent to which equality should be pursued, and views about individual behaviour and how it can or should be influenced and changed. In debating these issues most of us will have some sort of opinion and reasons for our viewpoint, and it is likely that our responses will be influenced by our life experiences, including educational experiences and opportunities, social class, religious beliefs and familial values. While we might not recognise our views in terms of a fully fledged ideology or coherent set of values and ideas, at the same time, as Heywood (2003, p. 3) suggests, 'whether consciously or unconsciously, everyone subscribes to a set of political beliefs and values that guide their behaviour and influence their conduct.'

Social policy is strongly influenced by political beliefs and values that belong to different ideological traditions. An important aspect of the influence of ideology on social policy is the extent to which the various ideologies differ. Social policy is therefore an inherently political subject. As Lavalette and Pratt (2006a, p. 4) assert, '"social policy" is in fact an intensely political – and contested – activity. It encapsulates an important arena of modern social life in which competing ideologies clash.' Social policies are not devised and implemented in a political vacuum, but are subject to conflicting and contested aims and values. Another important aspect of ideology in relation to social policy is the relationship between principles and practice. An ideology, in outlining its 'first principles' or ideals is normative in its prescriptions about how certain issues *should* be dealt with. Its normative component is important to acknowledge, because it highlights the 'vision' or 'ideal' being put forward. The reality of course is often different. Real life, politics and current issues frequently call for a more pragmatic approach, and the realpolitik often results in a dilution of core values in the transition from theory to practice. This does not make ideologies redundant; it simply acknowledges the political (and other) realities within which they are applied.

Left and right

At a basic level, competing ideologies are often identified in terms of left and right of the political spectrum. This left/right analogy of political ideologies provides a popular shorthand characterisation of the political domain. However, its application needs to be considered carefully, mindful of the context in which it is used and in light of perspectives such as feminism and greenism that don't fit neatly within its confines and are often marginalised from discussion as a result. In addition, according to Heywood (2003, pp. 17–18):

> The weakness of the linear spectrum is that it tries to reduce politics to a single dimension, and suggests that political views can be classified according to merely one criterion, be it one's attitude to change, view of equality or economic philosophy. Political ideologies are in fact highly complex collections of beliefs, values and doctrines, which any kind of spectrum is forced to oversimplify.

Nevertheless, the left/right characterisation of political ideas (and political parties) remains in widespread use, and it does offer a useful opening prism within which to identify some of the defining concepts associated with welfare perspectives and the differing positions taken. The left/right labels originate from the seating arrangements taken in the French Parliament after the 1798 revolution. In general terms, the 'left wing' approach to social policy is associated with state intervention, collective provision, universalism and a concern with addressing inequalities and delivering social rights. The right is typically regarded in social policy terms for its emphasis on the free market, individualism and limited welfare provisions.

Table 5.1 Right- and left-wing approaches to social policy

Right	Left
Individualism	Collectivism
'Negative' freedom	'Positive' freedom
Pro-market	Pro-state
Advocates private and/or charitable provision of welfare/social services	Advocates statutory provision of welfare/social services
Selectivism	Universalism
Rights defined primarily in the context of civil and political domain (e.g. equal treatment before the law)	Rights considered in a more extensive way; attention to the civil, political, economic and social domains
Equality – understood in a formal sense – fair and same treatment for all	Equality – understood in structural or relational terms – emphasises the need to address inequalities through state intervention, redistribution, positive discrimination, etc.
Equality of opportunity – minimalist approach	Equality of opportunity – maximalist approach and for some a commitment to equality of condition
Meritocratic	Egalitarian

Simply put, it can be argued that what distinguishes left and right is the starting point adopted. For the right, the individual is the primary focus; for the left, society, and the way it is organised and structured, needs to be examined in order to fully understand, include and respond to all individuals. In addition, differences in ideology can usefully be identified by way of reference to two core issues: liberty (or freedom) and equality (George and Wilding, 1985) and the position taken in respect of them.

Freedom and equality

Writing in 1958, Isaiah Berlin (1909–1997) distinguished between positive and negative freedom. Positive freedom refers to the notion of being 'free to do' something and negative freedom refers to 'freedom from' interference or constraint. Applying this analogy to the ideological context, the right stresses the need for individual liberty or freedom, in the 'negative' sense, to be free from interference, including from the state. The right, broadly speaking, also argues that social issues such as poverty are best addressed through 'natural' free market forces and accepts that a certain level of inequality is inevitable. In contrast, the left sees equality as an objective to be pursued by society; it acknowledges a range of forces which present as obstacles to equality and seeks to address these barriers. Individual liberty is also valued by those on the left, but their approach to freedom, characterised as 'positive', suggests that in order for individuals to really be 'free', they must have opportunity, or in other words, they must be facilitated to exercise their freedom. Individuals who do not have the means or the opportunity do not have their right to freedom vindicated. Fitzpatrick (2001, p. 54) explains the dilemma as follows:

> In a formal sense it is true that the beggar is free to dine at the Ritz, just as the banker is free to sleep under a bridge, but this conception of liberty deprives the principle of any meaningful content. For the Left, being prevented from doing something implies more than physical constraints, it also implies financial constraints (so the beggar *is* less free than the banker).

At its most basic, equality refers to 'the removal of disadvantage' (Spicker, 1988, p. 125), but the extent to which this is to be pursued is the subject of considerable debate. In other words, the concept of **equality** is complicated by the fact that its interpretation is wide and varied and the precise (and intended) meaning of 'equality' is often not clear.[1] In brief, distinctions between equality of opportunity and equality of outcome are frequently drawn to offer greater clarity.

Equality refers to the principle of addressing unequal circumstances which prevail in society. The extent to which equality is perceived and pursued differs widely, with divergent interpretations of the concept (e.g. equality of opportunity versus equality of condition).

Equality of opportunity refers to addressing existing obstacles or disadvantage to the extent that a 'level playing field' or 'equal starting point' is achieved. In other words, equality of opportunity believes in improving the life chances or opportunities of individuals, particularly those thought to be disadvantaged.

A policy which illustrates this principle is investment in early start education programmes in disadvantaged areas to support young children to 'start off on an equal footing'. In this approach to equality, the principle of meritocracy remains protected, whilst improving 'prospects' at an early stage. Equality of outcome (or social equality), on the other hand, takes account of a much wider set of structural factors (including the overall distribution of resources), which present as barriers to equality. Baker et al. (2004, p. 33) employ the term 'equality of condition' to identify the more complex nature of barriers to equality acknowledging that 'inequality is rooted in changing and changeable social structures, and particularly in structures of domination and oppression.' So, for example, in the area of education, equality would be promoted, not just at 'the first point' of entry to the education system, but would provide equality of access in a lifelong framework of opportunity. More importantly, policy would acknowledge and address the fact that equal educational opportunity is contingent on a much wider range of structural factors being addressed, such as income, employment, caring responsibilities and so on (see Chapter 9 for more on equality of educational opportunity). In practical political terms, the fundamental issues raised and the nature of the reform required by this perspective means that it is most commonly associated with those we might consider more firmly on the left.

Contemporary context of ideological debate

In terms of the wider political context, the 1990s bore witness to considerable challenge to the old dichotomies of left and right political ideologies. The collapse of communism across Eastern Europe resulted in a new era in international politics, which was no longer defined in terms of communism versus capitalism. Fukuyama (1992) wrote of 'the end of history' in which he argued that liberal democratic capitalism would inevitably prevail. Sociologist Anthony Giddens (1994, p. 12) argued that the time had come for 'a reconstituted radical politics, one which draws on philosophic conservatism but preserves some of the core values hitherto associated with socialist thought'. This represented a call for movement beyond the old boundaries of right and left. These arguments were to become highly influential in the political domain over the course of the 1990s, with the emergence of the Third Way (discussed below).

Notwithstanding the political changes of the last 20 years, conceptions of freedom and equality remain contested, and these particular debates are of critical importance to defining the aims and scope of social policy, and in analysing any perspective under review. In this context, it is important to note too that the distinction between 'old' and long-established political ideologies such as liberalism and the 'newer' perspectives offered by feminism, for instance, is not applied here. All of the perspectives, new and old, add to our understanding of the significance of competing ideas about the nature of welfare provision and ultimately aid in the overall appreciation and analysis of our own and others' positions.

SECTION 2: POLITICAL IDEOLOGIES AND PERSPECTIVES ON WELFARE

This section provides an outline of the main features of a number of the most influential ideologies of welfare. The discussion of each ideology is relatively brief, the aim being to provide a useful starting point from which to examine ideologies of welfare and their impact on social policy.

Liberalism

To understand the liberal perspective, it is important to note at the outset that modern liberalism has a distinct meaning in political and ideological terms that is different to the meanings drawn from both the classical and neo-liberal positions. This distinction rests primarily on the less hostile approach adopted by modern liberals to the role and functions of the state. The everyday use of the term 'liberal' for instance is considered to be 'progressive', 'tolerant' or 'broadminded' in terms of social issues in particular. This may present as a point of confusion in ideological terms, with classical and neo-liberalism more clearly associated with the right of the political spectrum. Focus here is centred on the core values of the classical liberal position which in social policy terms is noted for its emphasis on individualism, the free market and a limited role for the state.

Classical liberalism draws on the work of the widely regarded 'founding father' of economics Adam Smith (1723–1790), who is best known for arguing the benefits of free market capitalism in generating wealth. This, he believed, would be best achieved by leaving market forces to produce the best outcome in terms of competition, prices and wealth generation, without interference by the state. The application of a *laissez-faire* (leave alone to do) philosophy to the workings of the economy is believed to provide greater benefit to all; for Smith, an 'invisible hand' guides and promotes general prosperity, even when this is not the primary objective. In other words, left to its natural devices, the economic rules of supply and demand will ensure competitors in markets, which will be good for consumers, promote economic growth and result in overall prosperity.

Individualism is seen as a core value to be protected. George and Wilding (1985, p. 21) explain individualism in terms of two elements: 'a theory of society' which posits the view that 'social phenomena can only be understood through an understanding of the actions of individuals' (ibid., p. 22). In addition, it involves 'a set of political maxims about how society should be organised ... The primary maxim is that much which is currently undertaken by the state would be better undertaken by individuals' (ibid.).

In other words, it is the role of individuals, rather than any other entity which should be emphasised in organising society and in analysing social issues. The individual is, therefore, the basic source of action, freedom and responsibility. The personal freedom or liberty associated with this individualism is celebrated although it is defined in the negative sense of being 'free from' interference and state coercion. Individualism promotes self-responsibility, and liberals argue that individuals know what is best for them, and how this should be achieved. In pure terms, the only condition attached to this objective is that individuals do not harm others in the pursuit of their own interests. In order to protect against that possibility, classical liberals accept the need for a legal/justice system to ensure the right to due process before the law in the event that another individual's right to freedom is breached.

In terms of equality then, it is acceptable in so far as it provides 'equality of general rules, that is that laws apply to all citizens equally – equality of civil and political rights – and equality of opportunity' (ibid., p. 24). Specifically in terms of equality of opportunity, anti-collectivists do not find that objectionable because, in their view, 'it does not presuppose any particular social arrangements as desirable' (ibid.). Ultimately, because liberalism sees individuals as autonomous and independent beings, it subscribes that such individuals will fare best in a free market context and are opposed to the notion of social rights and state intervention as far as practicable (see below).

Libertarianism

Libertarianism is the term used to describe a perspective which values individual liberty over all other principles. It defines freedom in negative terms and refutes the need for state intervention (outside of the requirement for a legal and justice system). Pure libertarians also reject state intervention in the economy, in society and in the private affairs of individuals. In short, libertarians are 'on the right' in terms of the economy, but in following through on their principles may be considered to be 'on the left' in matters of personal liberty, and the non-regulation of individual behaviour, in so far as it doesn't harm another. For instance, a pure libertarian is likely to argue that drug taking is a matter of personal choice and individuals are free to make such choices, even if such activities are detrimental to an individual, if not to others.

The pursuit of equality is also dismissed, given that redistribution would require people who are in a position to do so to pay tax; this is considered an imposition on individuals' freedom. For example, one of the best known libertarian thinkers Robert Nozick (1938–2002) argues that 'taxation of earnings from labor is on a par with forced labor' (Nozick, 1974, p. 169). In economic terms, libertarians therefore reject the concept of redistribution and the associated welfare state, seeing such interventions as anathema to individual liberty and compromising of the benefits of free market forces, in which individuals as consumers can maximise choices in relation to their own personal welfare. Taken overall, libertarians relegate the role of the state as far as practicable, in defence of individual freedom. Libertarianism adopts a radically anti-state position with regard to matters of welfare, and its ideas enjoy greatest support in think tanks, such as in the USA.

Libertarianism is examined here because the application of its principles to the sphere of the economy resonates with the classical liberal position, but an important distinction needs to be made: many of the most eminent thinkers of the classical liberal perspective acknowledged a role for the state in certain matters of social policy. One of the foremost thinkers within the classical liberal tradition Friedrich von Hayek (1899–1992), for example, considered that people may have to be compelled to protect against need arising, particularly with regard to unemployment, illness and old age, 'those common hazards of life' (Hayek, 1960, in George and Wilding, 1985, p. 36). This departure from the principles outlined earlier, is circumscribed by serious concern that goalposts will quickly shift, away from meeting these basic minimum needs to something much more demanding in terms of taking individuals' resources and damaging the values of freedom and individualism and undermining free market capitalism in the process. In addition, the pursuit of social justice is rejected as inherently flawed and unachievable. Hayek (1976, cited in Lund, 2006, p. 114) argued that social justice is 'entirely empty and meaningless'. Moreover, in Hayek's view, the notion of social justice presents a threat 'to most other values of a free civilisation' (ibid.). George and Wilding (1985, p. 36) provide a succinct assessment of the dangers envisaged by this perspective:

> Welfare state policies, if not tightly limited in a way which the anti-collectivists recognise as politically almost impossible, represent a dangerous shuffle down the road to egalitarianism and socialism.

The critique of the welfare state, which gained ground in the latter part of the twentieth century, has been largely influenced by these starting principles of individual freedom, individualism and the merits of the free market. For instance, the 'conception of the welfare state', according to Hayek (1960/2006, p. 224) 'has no precise meaning', and has not been adequately defined. In addition, the term welfare state 'does not designate a definite system' (ibid. p. 226) and he argues, 'what goes under that name is a conglomerate of so many diverse and even contradictory elements that, while some of them may make a free society more attractive, others are incompatible with it or may at least constitute potential threats to its existence' (ibid.). More importantly perhaps, from this point of view, are the consequences that stem from the welfare state. Aside from compromising individual freedom, the welfare state is thought to be paternalistic by deciding what is best for individuals. In addition, the state provision of a range of services is thought to produce distortions in welfare markets, through monopolistic provision, leading to inefficiency, bureaucracy, over-regulation (of individuals, business and the economy in general), and poor value for taxpayers' money (see Chapter 4 for some illustration of the application of these arguments during the 1980s).

Public choice theory

The emergence of public choice theory, most notably in the USA since the 1960s, has provided an additional strand to the critique of the welfare state. Taking a 'politics without romance' (Buchanan, 2003, p. 13) approach, in which economic analysis is applied to politics, it is argued that the absence of limits to the role of government is flawed and that 'bureaucratic over-supply' cannot be curbed. Public choice theory offers the view that both politicians and public servants are motivated primarily by the need to maintain their position and get elected, and the promises offered at election time are not necessarily in the best interests of the country but can in some cases amount to a collage of different policies designed to secure re-election. In this view, politicians are considered to act in their own best interest, unrestrained by economic considerations of cost or the long-term consequences of their promises and actions. This particular assessment of politics and those elected to public office uses economic theory to account for political and policy decisions and does not incorporate wider societal phenomena into its analysis. The solutions offered by public choice theory are similarly derived and include privatisation and the imposition of strict spending limits on governments.

Neo-liberalism

In present day terms, neo-liberalism reasserts the merits of the (global) free market, in what Heywood (2003, p. 55) describes as 'a form of market fundamentalism'. According to this view, the welfare state is said to have failed in reaching its objectives, not least in terms of tackling relative poverty and pursuing social justice which neo-liberals view as inherently flawed and infinitely contestable. Instead, 'they see a clear and fundamental distinction between the legal and political rights at the core of classical liberalism and the putative claims of a right to welfare' (Pratt, 2006a, p. 21). This allows a clear distinction to be drawn between civil and political rights on the one hand and social and economic rights on the other. Realigning the discourse of rights in this way is significant and it facilitates a return to the values associated with classical liberalism. Adopting a firmly anti-welfare position, neo-liberals seek the dismantling of the welfare state and the dissolution of welfare rights, in favour of individual responsibility and market provision of social services. Neo-liberalism has been an influential perspective since the 1980s and its manifestations are particularly evident in the political rhetoric of the right, especially, but not exclusive to, political systems where the liberal perspective has always held sway (e.g. the USA). Espousal of neo-liberal ideas are also to be found in think tanks that are supported by interests seeking to promote their particular perspective (Pratt, 2006a); examples include the CATO Institute in the USA and the Institute of Economic Affairs in Britain. Economic globalisation has often been used as a rationale to justify and promote the neo-liberal agenda. Its impact on alternative perspectives on welfare may yet be its greatest legacy, acting as a 'pull factor', drawing competing perspectives in their direction. This argument is considered later in the chapter, particularly in the context of the redefining of the values of some of those on the left (see below). First, table 5.2 indicates the key features of the liberal perspective on welfare.

Table 5.2 Main features of the liberal perspective on welfare

Advocates individualism and personal responsibility

Favours the free market and minimal state intervention

Sees a clear distinction between civil and political rights on the one hand and social and economic rights on the other

Rejects the welfare state, the attempt to overcome relative poverty and the pursuit of equality and social justice

Favours individual, private or charitable providers of welfare

Minimal, selectivist and conditional approach to benefit and social services where they are provided

Conservatism

Conservatism is a position commonly associated with an affinity for tradition and order and a resistance to change; 'a philosophy of limits and restraint' (Fitzpatrick, 2001, p. 125). Conservative ideas first emerged in the context of significant economic and social change in the late eighteenth and early nineteenth century and challenged the growth of liberalism, socialism and nationalism at this time. The core principles of conservatism include tradition, pragmatism, human imperfection, organic society, hierarchy, authority and property ownership (Heywood, 2002). Edmund Burke (1729–1797) is commonly associated with the emergence of conservative thinking and his 'change in order to conserve' philosophy has been an important element in refining the thinking itself (ibid.). In terms of tradition, conservatives regard established institutions, customs and practice as important in recognising established wisdom, appreciating it and providing a sense of identity. They believe in pragmatism in order to deal with reality and 'to do what works', so to speak. Humans are regarded as fallible (and sometimes flawed) and in need of security and protection. This belief, along with their acceptance of hierarchy and authority and in particular their emphasis on individual obligations and duties, provides the justification for a tough approach to crime and justice and a commitment to 'strong' government in dealing with such matters. In practical terms, the conservative perspective seeks to contain and manage forces of social change, particularly those that may be thought to present a threat to social order. The family, for instance, is viewed as an essential element of society and, although averse to state intervention in other instances, conservatives argue that the state can have a central role in maintaining core social structures, rather than risk the upheaval and uncertainty that could accompany more dramatic social change.

Conservative thinking evolved to 'progressive conservatism' during the 1940s in the UK context at least. The impact of Harold Macmillan's *The Middle Way*, published in 1938, influenced the shift towards more 'planned capitalism' and a greater acceptance of social reform by the Conservative Party by the latter part of the 1940s. This became apparent in their subsequent governments of the 1950s, which steered a moderate 'middle way' between the economic and the social, although this was not embraced by all and wasn't sustained in the long term (Ritschel, 1995). More recently, the conservative perspective is often recognised in terms of the New Right and the Thatcher era of Conservative government in Britain. While this provides a useful example of conservative politics in ascendancy, it would not in fact be considered a 'strictly' conservative era, in the sense that the economic policies adopted drew heavily on the classical liberal position (Pinker, 2008). This neo-liberal turn of the 1980s was not 'typically' conservative; in fact the social policies later adopted by the Conservative Party, such as measures designed to promote the 'work ethic' and end 'welfare dependency' along with the 'back to basics' approach of the 1990s, could be argued to be more reflective of traditional conservative thought (see Chapter 4 for specific policy examples).

Neo-conservatism

Neo-conservatism draws on the economic liberal perspective in terms of the role and functions of the free market and, in general terms, shares with it a negative view of the capacity and role of the state in matters of human welfare. However, it seeks to restore traditional values, particularly those associated with 'the family, religion and the nation' (Heywood, 2002, p. 50), and takes the view that the state, as an authority, has a very important role, in maintaining social order. In short, it maintains a relatively liberal position on the economy but accepts and sometimes advocates robust state intervention to uphold and maintain its traditional values, particularly in the context of the nation state.

Finally, in the context of the USA there is common reference to the neo-conservative strand of political thinking, exemplified by the Bush administration (2001–2009), in which conservatism has been pushed to new boundaries. Arguing the merits of unilateral decisions in the common good, this has emerged as a controversial approach, particularly in terms of its impact on international relations in recent years. More specifically in terms of social policy, neo-conservatism in the USA has been associated with promoting privatisation of social security and seeking to encourage the role of religious and other voluntary agencies to provide welfare. In addition, the promotion of the 'ownership society' as espoused by Republican policies highlights the liberal influence which promotes individualism. Former US Vice-President, Dick Cheney (in Rosenbaum, 2005), speaking in 2005, provided an illustration of this vision:

> One of the great goals of our administration is to help more Americans find the opportunity to own a home, a small business, a health care plan or a retirement plan. In all of these areas, ownership is a path to greater opportunity, more freedom and more control over your own life, and this is a goal worthy of a great nation. Everyone deserves a chance to live the American dream, to build up savings and wealth and to have a nest egg for retirement that no one can ever take away.

The turmoil evident in the financial and property markets in the USA during 2008 has, however, led to increased questioning of the legitimacy of such goals.

Table 5.3 Main features of the conservative perspective on welfare

Advocates traditional social values and personal (and familial) responsibility

Favours the free market over state intervention in general terms but does see situations where 'strong' state intervention is appropriate, e.g. law and order and matters of 'national interest'

Obligations and duties also seen as an element of citizenship (which is often framed in national terms)

Sceptical of the welfare state on the grounds of its potential to damage 'traditional' institutions and the organising principles of society, e.g. the family, work ethic

Favours individual (and familial), private or charitable providers of welfare

Minimal and conditional approach to benefit and social service provision

Conservatism and Christian democracy

Conservatism shares some characteristics with the Christian democratic tradition which has been influential in countries like Italy, France and Germany since the Second World War. However, it should be noted that the Christian democratic tradition, while sharing the conservative approach to social order and stability, is more accepting of a role for the state, albeit defined by religious principles, particularly Catholic ones, and drawing on concepts such as subsidiarity. This refers to the ideal of support being availed of at the lowest level possible, i.e. the family as first resort followed by local rather than national sources. The concept of the 'social market economy' is also employed and demonstrates the balance that is sought by Christian democracy in social and economic terms. According to Heywood (2003, pp. 89–90):

> A social market is an economy that is structured by market principles and largely free from government control, operating in the context of a society in which cohesion is maintained through a comprehensive welfare system and effective public services. The market is thus not so much an end in itself as a means of generating wealth in order to achieve broader social goals.

In addition, Christian democrats tend to emphasise the role of significant organisations (and institutions) in society, such as the Church, trade unions and business representatives and in so doing accord them a particular 'status' in a corporatist approach to policymaking. The party of the Christian Democratic Union of Germany (CDU, 2008) provides an illustration of the contemporary Christian democratic perspective, stating, 'The Christian Democratic Union of Germany is the people's party of the centre. We seek to serve people from all levels and groups in our country.' The basis of this perspective is further explained:

> The foundation upon which our politics rest is the Christian understanding between people and their accountability before God. Our basic values of freedom, solidarity, and justice are formed therefrom. The CDU is open to anyone who supports the dignity and freedom of all people and their basic convictions.
>
> A humane pathway, guided by Christian principles: that is the compass and standard for our politics. Upon this foundation, we proceed to help further develop our community in an ever-changing world. We will continue down this path with courage and strength in order to give our children and grandchildren a brighter future in the 21st Century. (ibid.)

Returning briefly to the Conservatist perspective, the 'intellectual renewal' of the Conservative Party in the UK, launched in 2005, points to an interesting review of their core values. Pinker (2008, p. 75) suggests that 'there are already some indications that the party is beginning to reaffirm and reinterpret the values of traditional conservatism in its process of "intellectual renewal".' In the first of a series of Green Papers entitled *Opportunity Agenda* (2007, p. 3), the Conservatives outline their position:

> Conservatives have always believed that if you trust people, they will tend to do the right thing. That if you give people more responsibility, they will behave more responsibly. That if you give people more power and control over their lives, they will make better decisions than those the state would make on their behalf.
>
> This does not mean *no* role for the state. While we must be aware of the limitations of government, we should never be limited in our aspirations for government: to protect our security; to guarantee the provision of high quality, efficient public services, and to work tirelessly for social justice and a responsible society.
>
> But politicians should stop pretending they can fix every problem, and start trusting people, families, businesses, communities and all the myriad institutions of civil society more. We believe in social responsibility, not state control. That there is such a thing as society, it's just not the same thing as the state. This is the right approach for the post-bureaucratic age, and the right way to help people meet their aspirations in the new world of freedom.

The Conservative Party's attempt to re-vitalise itself, which in some respects is not dissimilar to New Labour during the 1990s, may make for less clear ground between them, as illustrated in the discussion of the Third Way below.

Socialism

There is a range of thinking to be considered under the umbrella term of socialism. Marxism, socialism, communism and Fabianism are the major perspectives representing different 'shades' of the left. Social democracy was similarly borne out of the emergence of socialism, although, in overall terms, its post-World War II trajectory has put clearer distance between it and contemporary socialism and it is therefore dealt with separately below. In the broadest sense, socialism developed initially in response to challenges associated with the emergence of capitalism, over the course of the nineteenth century, although some eminent socialist thinkers (such as Comte de Saint-Simon (1760–1825) and Robert Owen (1771–1858)) pre-date this period. The impact of industrialisation and urbanisation (as outlined in the previous chapter) raised new and fundamental questions about the beneficiaries of the social change that had occurred. The growth of the trade union movement and emerging recognition of need, poverty and social class brought about a new political era, where class divisions and associated inequalities were no longer to be ignored, in political and ideological terms at least. Since that time socialist thinking has offered a critique of the development of capitalism and its shortcomings.

The starting point of socialist thinking is collectivist and humanitarian in orientation. In other words, it is argued that people do not live in isolation from one another and therefore society needs to be viewed in terms of the structural forces and dynamics that make up its being, and how these impact on individuals in society. Human well-being is of central importance. In taking this approach, socialism is clear that the way society is organised, and the manner in which control and ownership of resources are distributed, is critical. The various strands of socialist thought are linked by a shared identification of class as 'the key parameter of social inequality' (Ginsburg, 2003, p. 94) and a concern with the pursuit of social equality, although the means of its achievement differ substantially. Equality of outcome (rather than equality of opportunity) is a core objective of socialism, with emphasis placed on the right of all human beings to share in the available resources of a society.

Socialism is also concerned with individual freedom, although the socialist conception of freedom is fundamentally different to that held by liberals (as outlined earlier). Writing in 1949, Richard H. Tawney (1880–1962) (cited in George and Wilding, 1985, p. 74) provides a good illustration of their position on freedom:

> The increase in the freedom of ordinary men and women during the last two generations has taken place, not in spite of the action of governments, but because of it … The mother of liberty has, in fact, been law.

Government 'facilitation' of freedom is not necessarily a position on freedom that all socialists would accept; Marxists, in particular, are likely to reject the possibility of enhanced individual liberty in the context of capitalism at all. The varieties of socialism that have emerged present a challenge in the overall conceptualisation of this perspective of welfare. For instance, it is often thought that socialism and Marxism are 'more or less' the same thing; this is not the case. As Baradat (2000, p. 185) puts it, 'All Marxists are socialists, but not all socialists are Marxists.' Crucially, a distinction is to be made between socialists who seek an evolutionary approach to socialism and those who advocate revolutionary means to secure socialism. The gradualist (or reformist) approach of the Fabian socialists contrasts with the revolutionary (or transformative) approach of Marxism.

Fabian socialism

Fabian socialists are collectivist in orientation; their ideas are based upon the values of freedom, equality and fellowship, along with democratic participation and humanitarianism (George and Wilding, 1985). Influenced by the key thinkers within the Fabian Society[2] (see previous chapter), they seek improvements in society through democratic means to address the inequalities precipitating from capitalism. In his book *The Future of Socialism* (1956) Anthony Crosland (1918–1977) offered the following reflection on the results of inequality:

> If social mobility is low, as it must be in a stratified society, and people cannot easily move up from the lower or middle reaches to the top, then the ruling elite becomes hereditary and self-perpetuating; and whatever one may concede to inherited or family advantages, this must involve a waste of talent. (Crosland, 1956, p. 215 in George and Wilding, 1985, p. 71)

Inequality is seen as an outcome of capitalism which threatens social cohesion, is wasteful in economic terms and 'diminishes people's basic humanity' (George and Wilding, 1985, p. 72). In contrast to Marxists, Fabian socialists seek a gradual or 'evolutionist' strategy in changing the organisation of society in order that a collectivist and redistributive socialist agenda can be pursued, through parliamentary politics and democratic means. They believe strongly in the need for, and capacity of, government and reject the anti-collectivist position on state intervention adopted by classical liberals, as indicated by Tawney (1953, p. 87, in Deakin and Wright, 1995, p. 140):

> It is constantly assumed by privileged classes that, when the state refrains from intervening in any department of economic or social affairs, what remains as a result of its inaction is liberty. In reality, as far as the mass of mankind are concerned, what commonly remains is, not liberty, but tyranny.

In their writings they also consider issues of class conflict and its impact, although not to the same extent as is done within the Marxist tradition (see below).

One of the most influential social policy thinkers of the twentieth century, Richard Titmuss (1907–1973), advocated universalist and comprehensive social services, regarding this as central to promoting social solidarity, in which access could be assured to all. This would provide the bedrock of a better society by promoting social cohesion in a manner not possible where distinctions are made between individuals (as happens when services are means-tested, targeted, etc.). In addition, Titmuss offered an analysis of welfare divisions which challenged the conventional wisdoms around the provision of welfare. Specifically, he argued that it was more accurate to analyse the various systems of welfare that existed, i.e. not just social welfare but also occupational welfare and fiscal welfare. In this respect, he encouraged a fuller analysis of welfare, not just the welfare provided through social services. Titmuss provided an important conceptual tool of welfare analysis that takes a more systematic approach to the tools of redistribution and their respective impact. This is an issue considered in the context of social security in Chapter 7.

Fabian socialism was highly influential in the architecture of the 'original' welfare state in Britain. It sought to provide a comprehensive and accessible range of services for its citizens (discussed in Chapter 4). This position was based on the capacity of the state to deliver social citizenship rights, but this became a matter of some debate as the 'traditional top-down approach … where the state decided what was good for people and then delivered it, resulted in a failure to meet the real needs and preferences of individuals and families' (Pratt, 2006b, p. 43). This was an issue taken up by actors on both the left and the right in the 1970s in Britain.

Table 5.4 Main features of the socialist perspective on welfare

Advocates social equality and is humanitarian in orientation – seeks to meet basic human needs and to protect and promote social rights

Favours collectivism and national ownership, highlighting the inequalities associated with the free market

Sees social rights as critical to the protection and promotion of human welfare

Sees the potential of the welfare state in moving in the direction of a more socialist type of society through a substantial commitment to redistribution

Favours state intervention in the provision of a comprehensive range of welfare and social services

Universal and comprehensive provision of basic social services and supports

Marxist socialism

Marxism shares a commitment to social equality and individual freedom with evolutionary socialism; 'from each according to his abilities, to each according to his needs' was to be the distributive principle of communism, and its core values are derived primarily from its fundamental critique of capitalism. Based on the writings of Karl Marx (1818–1883), in which he provided 'a relentless critique of the inhumanity of the capitalist system as it existed during his lifetime' (George and Wilding, 1985, p. 96), Marxism highlights the injustices of the class system inherent to capitalism and the unequal and exploitative relations at the core of its existence. The nature of the relationship between the owners of the means of production (the capitalists or bourgeoisie) and workers (the proletariat) highlights the divisions and inequalities that exist within capitalism, the alienation that results and the class conflict that is inevitable. This critique is founded on a 'materialist conception of history' where, according to Marx (cited in ibid., p. 99):

> The mode of production in material life determines the general character of the social, political and spiritual processes of life. It is not the consciousness of men that determines their existence but, on the contrary, their social existence determines their consciousness.

The inevitable class conflict would give rise to revolution, making way for a classless society organised on the basis of common ownership, where the state would 'wither away' (Dean, 2008, p. 88). However, this did not happen in any of the countries (such as the former USSR, Cuba, North Korea) where communism took hold. This fact has given rise to much scepticism about the application of Marxist theory in practice. Nevertheless, it is clear that Marxist theory offers a cogent critique of capitalism and its shortcomings; how it assesses the welfare state and the structures that have emerged to deal with the worst excesses of capitalism is the issue to which we now turn.

Neo-Marxism

Neo-Marxism refers to the revival in Marxist theory since the 1970s, which offers a critique of contemporary capitalism and examines the position of the welfare state in that context. The term welfare state is generally rejected in favour of reference to 'welfare capitalism' as a more accurate reflection of reality. The development of welfare provisions is largely seen as the outcome of class conflict but not necessarily as a decisive victory for the working class. From a neo-Marxist perspective these measures support and uphold capitalism, providing and maintaining the conditions in which capitalism continues to prosper. According to this view the welfare state 'is a device to stabilise rather than a step in the transformation of capitalist society' (Offe, 1982, p. 12). Offe argues this on three main grounds: (1) the welfare state is ineffective and inefficient, (2) it is repressive and (3) it offers a false perspective on the organisation of society where:

> ... the structural arrangements of the welfare state tend to make people ignore or forget that the needs and contingencies which the

welfare state responds to are themselves constituted, directly or indirectly, in the sphere of work and production. (ibid., p. 13)

Taking these in turn, first the welfare state is considered ineffective because it has largely failed to address the disparities in income distribution between labour and capital and because it compensates for capitalism rather than dealing with the causes of need and insecurity (i.e. capitalism) in the first place. The social control or 'repressiveness of the welfare state' is illustrated by Offe (ibid.) in terms of the requirements imposed for the receipt of benefits, many of which seek to re-enforce particular views such as the 'deserving' client. Lavelette (2006a, p. 55) has more recently pointed to the social control exercised 'within the daily functioning of welfare services and institutions' where, for example, aspects of education, juvenile justice and family support services involve regulation of families, children and young people. Finally, the 'politico-ideological control function' (Offe, 1982, p. 13) of the welfare state refers to the impact of the welfare state in diffusing rather than challenging the causes and effects of capitalism on individuals. In other words, the welfare state produces a false sense of social harmony which glosses over the fundamental inequalities that persist within the capitalist system.

Table 5.5 Main features of the Marxist perspective on welfare

Advocates transformation to achieve social equality, where human needs take precedence over market forces and the interests of the few

Favours collectivism and shared ownership, highlighting the persistent inequalities associated with capitalism

Seeks to protect and promote social rights, but does not see the capacity for these to be realised in a capitalist context

Sees the welfare state (welfare capitalism or welfarism) primarily as a vehicle for protecting capitalism, rather than the means of realising socialism.

Acknowledges that some welfare provisions owe their existence to working-class mobilisation, which have improved the lives of workers, but that many forms of welfare are also to the benefit of capitalism (e.g. health and education for a fit and educated workforce)

Highlights the 'social control' function of the welfare state

Social democracy

The social democratic perspective is one that has evolved and, some would argue, changed significantly over the course of the twentieth century. Its origins date back to the emergence of workers' movements during the latter part of the nineteenth century and the subsequent establishment of social democratic, labour or workers' political parties across Europe. This coincided with a period during which democracy was still in its infancy and full voting rights had not been secured for all citizens. Its belief in the importance of democracy is one of its earliest defining features, as illustrated by Berger (2002, p. 17) who quotes the 1869 Eisenach programme of the German Social Democratic Workers' Party:

> ... political freedom is the most indispensable precondition for the economic emancipation of the working classes. Hence the social question is indivisible from the political question. The solution to the former is conditional on the solution of the latter, and possible only in the democratic state.

The social democratic perspective was initially influenced by both Marxist thinking and the Fabian socialist position but, ultimately, the orientation of social democracy was largely guided by the evolutionary approach advocated by the latter. Social democracy was also historically noted for its enthusiasm for the welfare state project, including nationalisation and public ownership. The 1945 British Labour Party manifesto, entitled *Let us Face the Future*, gives an indication of this position, seeking 'the establishment of the socialist commonwealth of Great Britain – free, democratic, efficient, progressive, public-spirited, its material resources organised in the service of the British people' (Lee and Raban, 1988, p. 40). In short, the core features of 'old' social democracy included a socialist vision, a positive interpretation of freedom in the context of democracy, and a concern about inequality and the need to tackle it, mainly through state interventions to promote redistribution. The objective was to humanise capitalism, to address the inequalities that arise while at the same time acknowledge that resources have to be generated before they can be redistributed. In other words, while socialist in aspiration, the social democratic perspective married this with an acceptance of economic imperatives as the necessary mechanism for generating wealth and through which redistribution could address class divisions and associated inequality.

The high point of social democracy is commonly acknowledged to coincide with 'the golden era of the welfare state', from the end of World War II until the mid-1970s. Sweden emerged as the archetype for post-war social democracy, and the Keynesian rationale for economic and social planning offered a policy mechanism through which the welfare state project could be pursued. However, Keynesian economic principles were increasingly challenged during the 1970s, leading to significant difficulties in delivering their objectives. The previous chapter provides greater detail about these events; what is noteworthy in terms of the social democratic perspective is the 're-think' that was undertaken, marking the beginning of a phase of social democracy in transition. The social democrats/socialists that were in government at stages during the 1980s in countries like France, Spain, Greece, Australia and New Zealand (Callaghan, 2003) focused, of necessity, on economic stability and, 'by 1990, after a decade in which many socialist projects had either collapsed or been jettisoned, the left-wing exuberance of the 1970s had almost completed disappeared' (ibid., p. 129). Thus began a period of reflection by many social democrats on their principles and core values which ultimately resulted in the emergence of the 'Third Way' during the 1990s. The table below sets out the defining features of social democracy.

Table 5.6 Main features of the social democratic perspective on welfare

Advocates collectivism, cooperation, equality and social justice

Socialist in orientation but circumscribed by a belief in gradualism and ultimately accepting of the need to generate wealth in order to redistribute it

Recognises the centrality of social rights in promoting equality

Seeks a comprehensive welfare state to deliver the social rights associated with citizenship

Favours state intervention to address the inequalities generated by capitalism; supports the welfare state and redistribution in this endeavour

Universal and comprehensive provision of basic social services and supports

The Third Way

The 'Third Way' position emerged during the 1990s as a response to the problems that were perceived to exist within 'old style' social democracy. This was said to be 'modernised social democracy' (Blair, 1998, p. 1) or 'social democracy renewed' (Blair, 2001, p. 10, in Page, 2005, p. 287). Others disagree, arguing that Third Way ideals are ambiguous and closer to neo-liberalism than is articulated. There is no consensus about whether Third Way values should or do represent 'new' social democracy, although its impact is widely accepted as significant in political terms, even if it is interpreted and applied differently.

The Third Way is most commonly associated with the emergence of 'New Labour' in Britain in 1997, but it was also prominent during in the Clinton era (1993–2001) in the USA and in the Schröder period in Germany, as exemplified by the 1999 joint publication with Tony Blair, entitled *Europe: The Third Way – die Neue Mitte* or (the 'new centre'). The welfare state reforms undertaken in Sweden over the course of the 1990s might also be characterised as 'Third Way', with greater evidence of consideration of the economic implications of social policies. Coalition governments in Belgium and the Netherlands during the late 1990s also adopted Third Way policies, although, interestingly, the term itself was embraced more explicitly by the liberal partners in both governments (Hoop, 2004). The main principles associated with the Third Way cannot therefore be characterised in a singular fashion; it is impossible to present a 'one size fits all' explanation of its main features, and closer attention to its interpretation and application in various countries is essential.[3]

Giddens (1998, 2000) has undoubtedly become the most prominent intellectual force behind the Third Way project over the last decade. His work provides a detailed account of the reasons to modernise social democratic thinking, challenging what might be considered the outmoded views of the left, noting the impact of globalisation and advocating a new 'Third Way' approach for new times. Much attention has since been given to the examination of 'Third Way' meaning and its associated policy trajectory, although Giddens (2007) argues, 'Nothing much should be read into the term itself. The "Third Way" is a label for the need to update left-of-centre thinking in the light of the big changes sweeping through the world, especially the influence of globalisation.' Former British Prime Minister (from 1997–2007) Tony Blair is the politician most noted for the espousal of the Third Way philosophy, which he outlined as follows: 'Our mission is to promote and reconcile the four values which are essential to a just society which maximises the freedom and potential of all our people – equal worth, opportunity for all, responsibility and community' (Blair, 1998, p. 3). The main values of the Third Way have been variously characterised in the years that followed; by Le Grand as community, opportunity, responsibility and accountability (CORA); by Lister as responsibility, inclusion and opportunity (RIO); and by White as opportunity, responsibility and community (Barrientos and Powell, 2004). The Third Way is particularly noted for a language of compromise and 'a rhetoric of reconciliation' (Powell, 2008, p. 93); examples include 'economic dynamism as well as social justice', 'enterprise as well as fairness' (ibid.). In this respect, the Third Way clearly draws on the values of the right and the left, making its core ideological make-up difficult to discern. Returning to the concepts of liberty and equality may help in teasing out these issues.

Firstly, with respect to liberty, the argument might well be made that this is implicit in the principles highlighted by Third Way protagonists, although as Dahrendorf (1999) observes, 'I have read most of the publications around the idea of a Third Way and I have been increasingly struck that … one word hardly ever appears and never in a central place. That word is "liberty".'

Beech (2006, p. 144) addresses the issue of liberty in the context of New Labour and similarly observes that 'the importance of freedom is not often mentioned.' Having said this, Beech's overall assessment considers the Third Way's concentration on 'opportunity for all' and its many applications, arguing that this can be taken as demonstrated commitment to a positive notion of liberty, even if reciprocity for entitlements represents a marked break with the 'old' labour position of the past.

In terms of equality, the Third Way philosophy appears to accept equality as critical to social inclusion. Specifically, equality of opportunity is put forward as the objective to be realised. This marks a distinction from 'old left' values that saw equality more in terms of social equality or equality of outcome. Equality of outcome is rejected, according to Brown (1999, p. 42 in Page, 2005, p. 286), because 'predetermined results imposed, as they would have to be, by a central authority and decided irrespective of work, effort or contribution to the community, is not a socialist dream but other people's nightmare of socialism.' Giddens (2000, p. 85) similarly argues that 'There is no future for the "egalitarianism at all costs" that absorbed leftists for so long.' Instead, in Giddens's (ibid., p. 86) view:

> The contemporary left needs to develop a dynamic, life-chances approach to equality, placing the prime stress upon equality of opportunity. Modernizing social democrats also have to find an approach that reconciles equality with pluralism and lifestyle diversity, recognizing that the clashes between freedom and equality to which classical liberals have always pointed are real.

The Third Way espouses equality of opportunity and equality of respect for all, 'whatever their background, capability, creed or race' (Blair, 1998, p. 3). Families and communities are to be supported to realise the potential of all. The welfare state is central to providing such supports, but it is not the welfare state of old, and the re-conceptualisation of the welfare state is at the core of Third Way thinking.

Some of the traditional features of the welfare state are highlighted by the Third Way as inefficient and the old objectives at odds with the social and economic realities that now prevail. In short, the welfare state should be active and responsive, promote self-responsibility and self-realisation, be prudent yet caring and target resources to those most in need of them. Communities should be supported to be strong, and anti-social behaviour is not to be tolerated. There are a few well-worn phrases that capture the essence of the Third Way position, particularly as applied by New Labour in Britain including, 'work is the best form of welfare', the welfare state should provide a 'hand up not a hand out', and it is time to be 'tough on crime,

> **Communitarianism** situates individuals in the context of the wider community. Variously interpreted, this concept implies a rejection of pure individualism while also promoting the duties of individuals within communities.

tough on the causes of crime'. In this respect it can be argued that the Third Way is also influenced by **communitarianism**, which highlights the rights *and* the duties of individuals to themselves and to the wider community.[4] Finally, in addition to the 'rights with responsibilities' approach to welfare comes an enthusiastic endorsement of the market and market-based principles, from which the public sector could and should learn. As Giddens (2000, p. 58) puts it, 'Third way politics looks to transform government and the state – to make them as effective and quick on their feet as many sectors of business have now become.'

The implications of the Third Way perspective for social policy appear to depend on the context in which they are applied. The most enduring example to date is probably Britain where assessments vary.[5] In short, this Third Way success has seen access to work and social rights coupled with conditions, i.e. no rights without responsibilities, and partnership and cooperation with the various welfare providers replacing the monopolistic and inefficient welfare state. Public ownership is no longer the necessary bedrock of economic planning. Equality of opportunity means greater investment in disadvantaged areas, and access to education is the key to promoting mobility for all. Is this twenty-first century social democracy? It seems too soon to know for sure. What we can conclude with are the defining features of the Third Way, as evidenced in recent years.

Table 5.7 Main features of the 'Third Way' perspective on welfare

Advocates a 'new' approach which combines emphasis on equal worth and opportunity with responsibility for all

Accepts capitalism as providing the means of promoting human welfare

Recognises social rights with which come responsibilities

Supports a 'dynamic' and sustainable welfare state

Favours judicious and targeted state intervention to tackle disadvantage, with emphasis placed on equality of opportunity; moving away from the universalist and more substantive position on equality held by many of its political predecessors

Conditional approach to some aspects of welfare provision; core emphasis on work (formal paid employment)

Feminism

Feminism is often thought of as a social movement of the twentieth century particularly associated with the women's liberation movement of the 1960s and 1970s; it has in fact a much longer history, with women highlighting aspects of women's inequality throughout the nineteenth century. The suffrage movement, the involvement of women in trade unions, and voluntary, community and advocacy work (although not so called at the time) marked the arrival of 'first wave' feminism, and the beginnings of a very long and continuing debate about the nature of women's rights. The so-called second wave refers to the period of the late 1960s and 1970s, during which time women again mobilised to challenge continuing discrimination and raise fundamental questions about existing assumptions regarding the role and position of women. In contemporary terms, there is no singular definition of feminism. In fact, it is more accurate to acknowledge the variety of feminisms that have developed over time. In this context, the different types of feminist ideology are briefly outlined here, some of which connect their overall perspective to the ideologies discussed above. bell hooks (2000, p. 1) provides a concise definition to begin with: 'Simply put, feminism is a movement to end sexism, sexist exploitation, and oppression.' Her (ibid.) explanation of the appeal of this definition is worth noting too:

> I liked this definition because it did not imply that men were the enemy. By naming sexism as the problem it went directly to the heart of the matter. Practically, it is a definition which implies that all sexist thinking and action is the problem, whether those who perpetuate it are female or male, child or adult. It is also broad enough to include an understanding of systemic institutionalized sexism.

The possibilities for and of feminism are drawn together by hooks in a way that dispels many of the myths that frequently surround feminism.

Feminism may be seen as a political ideology in its own right, or as one that aligns itself with other perspectives to promote a particular type of feminism. Drawing on the liberal values outlined earlier, liberal feminism, for example, seeks equal rights and equal treatment for women and men. In their pursuit of 'formal' equality, emphasis is placed on the rights of women to be protected and promoted, primarily with reference to the public sphere (Williams, 1989), and liberal feminists are reformist in orientation. Little attention is given to the private domain, although this is an issue to which greater prominence has been given by other feminists (see below).

Socialist feminism, in contrast, offers an assessment of the position of women in society that highlights the nature of the inequalities that persist in the unequal relations in capitalist society. Whilst critical of the relative neglect of the oppression of women in classical Marxist thinking, socialist feminism often draws on the Marxist perspective to highlight structural dimensions of inequality that are relevant. The effects of capitalism are therefore considered in terms of its impact on women's lives in the formal sphere of the paid labour market and within the household context. In Young's (1981, p. 58, in McLaughlin, 2003, p. 51) assessment, for example, 'the marginalization of women and thereby our functioning as a secondary labour force is an essential and fundamental characteristic of capitalism'. The concept of **patriarchy** is also applied in this context and has been variously defined by feminists. Interpretations of patriarchy (introduced to feminist thought in Kate Millet's *Sexual Politics*, 1970) have evolved over time but at its core it refers to both the structures and relations of male power involved in the subordination of women in society. For socialist feminists, then, what is of concern is the interplay between capitalism and patriarchy and its impact on the lives of women. This marks an important distinction from liberal feminism because it is an effort, as Williams (1989, p. 64) explains, 'on the one hand to acknowledge the significance of institutionalized power relationships between men and women which produce gender inequalities, and, on the other, an acknowledgement that capitalism gives rise to *differential* experiences of oppression by women of different classes.' This emphasis on the structured relations between men and women in society and on the needs and position of all women, and how they may differ are issues not acknowledged in the liberal feminist position.

> **Patriarchy** refers to both the structures and relations of male power involved in the subordination of women in the private and the public domain.

Radical feminism emerged during the second wave of the women's movement in the late 1960s, when the wider political climate was also shaped by several demands for social change. In political terms, the message of radical feminism was built around two main concepts; that of patriarchy and the notion that 'the personal is political'. In drawing attention to what was traditionally understood as the 'private' sphere, radical feminists highlighted what they saw as other (and previously hidden) areas of oppression, particularly with regard to sexuality and the family. In this way, as Bryson (1992, p. 181) explains, 'radical feminist analysis insists that male power is not confined to the public worlds of politics and paid employment, but that it extends into private life; this means that traditional concepts of power and politics are challenged and extended to such personal areas of life as the family and sexuality, both of which are seen as instruments of patriarchal domination.' In practical terms, many radical feminist activists played a vital role in establishing and developing important services such as well-woman and health clinics and refuges for women experiencing domestic violence and in advocating the individual rights of women to define their own sexuality (Williams, 1989). In opening these wider questions of power relations and how they relate to welfare rights and equality for women, the contribution of the feminist perspective is put in context by Williams (1989, p. 55): 'The idea that the relations of power between men and women deserve political and theoretical assessment, sets feminism apart from the major traditions of Western political thinking – liberalism and Marxism.'

However, one of the criticisms most frequently levelled at feminism in general is that its agenda is predominantly shaped by white middle-class heterosexual women, to the neglect of others. Black feminists were among the first to highlight some of the shortcomings associated with feminism, particularly its failure to acknowledge the diversity of women who are part of the wider feminist struggle. In particular, many Black feminists have taken issue with the application of the concept of patriarchy that implies that a certain 'universal solidarity exists between women as women' (ibid., p. 71) and that 'stressing *men* as oppressors implies a collective sense of power used by *all* men' (ibid.). In other words, the differences between women (and between men) are ignored through the articulation of a universal patriarchy that fails to take account of other social divisions, such as race. bell hooks (1986, p. 126 in ibid., pp. 72–3), for example, argued that what is needed is a 'liberatory radical theory of socialism that would more adequately address interlocking systems of domination like sexism, racism, class oppression, imperialism and so on'. The recognition of difference(s) has subsequently become an important theme in feminist literature in which recognition and respect for difference is emphasised, but through more fluid understandings of women and men, their many experiences and values. While beneficial in terms of highlighting diversity of experience and in giving voice and recognition to 'others', its 'fluidity' may seem to give little definite policy direction, but this would be to ignore its influence in the articulation of values around equality of respect (see below).

Another major development within feminist thinking since the 1980s is the significant attention that has been given to the entire conceptualisation and position of care in society (e.g. Ungerson, 1987; Williams, 2001; Lynch, 2007). The emergence of the notion of a **feminist 'ethic of care'** brings to the fore a range of critical issues about the way that society is structured and the assumptions that have been made about the positions of

> The feminist 'ethic of care' highlights the need to conceptualise and take account of care issues, both with regard to the cared for person and the carer, in order to promote and realise a more inclusive type of citizenship.

caring, care givers and receivers of care. In short, the ethics of care literature draw attention to the centrality of the care of all human beings, explores the various ethical components of care and highlights the ways in which this issue is one requiring much more substantial political and policy attention. Sevenhuijsen (2003), for example, highlights interdependence and relationality as key elements of the ethic of care, in which care is also seen as 'a continuous social process' (ibid., p. 184). For this to be recognised in real terms, Sevenhuijsen (ibid., p. 193) argues for the development of 'a "caring citizenship", an ideal in which caring is part of collective agency in the public sphere'. In Lister's view (2003, p. 200) what is required in policy terms is:

> … a policy framework that is able to incorporate care as an expression of difference into the citizenship standard itself but in a way that does not undermine progress towards gender equality, thereby balancing practical and strategic gender interests. Rather than replace citizen-the earner with citizen-the carer, policy needs to create the conditions for a *'gender-inclusive'* citizenship through which citizen-the earner/carer and carer/earner can flourish.

Feminism, arguably more than any other perspective on welfare, has challenged the 'traditionalism' of the original welfare state project and has sought a fuller engagement with the pursuit of equality and respect for difference in social policy. Feminist perspectives offer a forceful critique of the exclusionary nature of citizenship (e.g. Young, 1989; Lister, 2003; Siim, 2000) and continue to highlight the limitations attached to the gendered assumptions underpinning the welfare state (see Chapter 4), particularly with regard to the family, work and care. The male breadwinner model, for example, has highlighted the dependent status often imposed on women (Lewis, 1992, 1997), and feminism exposes the difficulties with the public/private divide that has long existed in the field of welfare and its implications for the full realisation of social citizenship for women. The consequence of this divide is that 'women have been faced with a choice between a universalistic claim based on the principle of their equality with men or a particularistic claim based on their difference from men.' (Lister, 2003, p. 197). The concept of 'differentiated universalism' is proposed which could overcome the 'either/or' dilemmas that have long presented difficulty for feminism. Lister (ibid., p. 199) has called for a feminist theory of citizenship to be part of 'feminist praxis' which will need to 'be rooted in a *politics of solidarity in difference*', in common cause of inclusiveness.

In practical policy terms, the feminist agenda has made most ground in the pursuit of formal equality in the 'public' sphere, although this too remains a 'work in progress' given that many feminists argue that this cannot be seen in isolation from the 'private' domain of the family, household division of labour, care and so on. Radical feminism, in contrast, has undoubtedly challenged inequality in a more substantial way and has helped to 'lift the lid' on some of the most challenging aspects of women's oppression, particularly in the 'private' sphere, notably in terms of violence experienced by women, sexual exploitation, bodily integrity and self-defined sexual identity. Black feminism offers a cogent rationale for the need to consider together, rather than in parallel, the various social divisions that exist. Recognition of difference has brought about a more diverse account of the lives of women, and their different needs and values. The development of the feminist ethic of care and the related re-conceptualisation of citizenship offer significant potential in advancing the feminist agenda in social policy terms overall. However, the contemporary struggle relates to the practical and political challenges associated with realising this endeavour in a context in which the concept of citizenship remains contested and in many ways continues to be gender-blind and exclusionary in its application (see also Chapter 11 on this point).

Table 5.8 Main features of the reformist and radical feminist perspectives on welfare

Reformist feminism	Radical feminisms
Liberal feminism	Socialist feminism (SF) Radical feminism (RF)
Seeks 'formal' equality for women –equal treatment for men and women	Emphasises the oppressive nature of capitalism and the patriarchal structures contained therein (SF)
Largely confined to the public sphere	Highlights the oppression of women through the persistence of patriarchy in the public and private spheres (RF)
More recent feminist literature has attempted to address both equality and difference in order to realise a more inclusive approach to welfare, social policy and citizenship.	

Greenism

The 1970s saw a flourishing of movements and debates about the environment. These encompassed questions about the relationship between society and the environment, the nature and extent of environmental problems, such as pollution, the loss of biodiversity and species habitat, and the risks of nuclear power, and what needed to be done about them. Dryzek (2005, p. 225) suggests that 'in the last three decades or so green radicalism has come from nowhere to develop a comprehensive critique of the environmental, social, political and economic shortcomings of industrial society. As such, it represents perhaps the most significant ideological development of the late twentieth century.' In addition, green thinking has influenced mainstream politics, as evidenced by the growth of environmental policy as an area of government, and the appropriation of green ideas by existing political ideologies. To make sense of the diversity of green thinking, different strands are typically divided into two overarching approaches. These are variously described as 'dark' versus 'light' green, deep versus shallow green, radical versus reformist, or technocentric versus eco-centric approaches.

Here we will use the radical versus reformist divide to explore in more detail the key differences between core green thinking and the adoption of green thinking by existing political ideologies. The adoption of green ideas by existing left- and right-wing ideologies, including social democracy and liberalism, is generally reflective of a reformist approach. This approach does recognise environmental problems; however, it believes that either capitalist markets will always produce solutions to overcome problems such as dwindling resources, and continued growth will be ensured; or that by careful economic and environmental management, problems can be overcome to the extent that it is possible to have both economic growth and environmental protection. The former approach has also been described as a cornucopian view and it typically represents a more right-wing version of greenism, while the latter tends to be a more left-wing response to environmental problems. In either case faith is placed in the usefulness of conventional scientific, technological and economic knowledge and expertise, hence the designation of technocentrism by O'Riordan (1981). It follows that this view stresses management over participation, and individuals and local communities do not have a significant role to play in dealing with environmental problems. Debates about values are also of minimal importance. This view is therefore **anthropocentric**. Generally, the reformist approach does not envisage radical alteration of society and its institutions; however, those on the left advocate gradual change (Pepper,

> **Anthropocentrism** refers to valuing the non-human world, such as plants and animals, for instrumental reasons, that is, for how it can benefit humans.

1996). Much contemporary environmental and sustainable development policy can be located within this approach and will be explored in greater detail in Chapter 13 on sustainable development and quality of life.

Radical greenism, in contrast, sees itself as a distinct ideology, exemplified by a slogan of the German green party, 'neither right nor left but in front'. Broadly speaking, green political parties espouse radical green ideas. While green parties have not been very successful in elections, generally not gaining the support of more than 10 per cent of the population, as Dryzek (2005, p. 219) notes, 'the real impact of green parties may be in the degree to which they have forced more established "grey" parties, and the political system as a whole, to craft responses to the green electoral threat.' Beyond party politics, while various strands of the wider green movement may not be successful in terms of creating large-scale change, many radical green ideas which were once seen as far out, have become common practice or gained greater acceptance and created more awareness over time. From green political parties to direct action groups to alternative communities, there is within deep green thinking a considerable diversity of positions including eco-socialism, eco-feminism, deep ecology, social ecology and environmental justice movements. Some of these positions have opposing ideas, some are quite theoretical while others are more practical and it would not be possible to discuss the range of ideas in detail here.[6] We will look briefly at some of the main ideas illustrative of the overall approach.

The idea of limits is central to radical green thinking; the human world is understood as part of a global ecosystem and is therefore subject to ecological laws. These laws ultimately constrain human action, particularly in terms of economic and population growth (Pepper, 1996). In other words, the natural world simply cannot sustain unlimited economic and population growth. Radical green thinking (with the exception of eco-socialism), therefore, rejects both capitalism and socialism because both are underpinned by industrialism premised on the notion of continued economic growth (George and Wilding, 1994). Acceptance of the limits to growth implies that there must be a reduction in economic growth and consumption, and population. Some radical greens therefore advocate the notion of a steady state economy as proposed by Herman Daly. Daly critiqued the 'growthmania' of conventional economics which views economic growth as the solution to every problem, be it social, economic or environmental. A steady state economy in contrast is 'an economy with constant stocks of artefacts and people' where the throughput of people and goods is 'limited in scale so as to be within the regenerative and assimilative capacities of the ecosystem' (Daly, 1995, p. 331). This would involve, among other things, a policy of birth control. Daly, for example, advocated a birth quota system, while other less fundamental greens propose policies such as education and making contraception widely available, which have a greater possibility of acceptance.

Even if unlimited growth were possible, radical greens question the desirability of limitless consumption, arguing that it makes for individualistic, competitive, acquisitive and ultimately unequal societies. They argue that ending the perpetual search for economic growth and material prosperity is an intrinsic good because it leads to richer and more fulfilling lives. In addition, radical greens argue that the pursuit of economic growth aimed at continuously rising living standards distracts from the need for radical redistributive policies within and between countries which is needed in the context of limits to growth.

Radical greens also advocate decentralisation and small-scale participatory democracy. This would have environmental benefits because the creation of small-scale self-sufficient communities would cease the environmental destruction caused by large-scale globalised industrial production. It is also argued that this would have social benefits because 'a decentralized, participatory and egalitarian society is one that recognizes each person's value as an important and respected member of the community' (Garner, 1996, p. 38). This would encourage conservation, reduce waste and pollution, and be more participatory. The main trade and exchange would be within eco-regions, and this would entail less movement of people and goods. There are many problems with the practical application of bio-regionalism, and in the more immediate term radical greens emphasise community values such as participation, empowerment and self-reliance, sharing of resources, and local solutions to local problems and local needs. Promotion of the third sector and the social economy are seen as ways of realising these values and principles in practice. This is part of the wider aim to transform society along the lines of communalism where 'economic relations are intimately connected with social relations and feelings of belonging, sharing, caring and surviving' (O'Riordan, 1989, pp. 89–90 in Pepper, 1993, p. 36). Influenced by the work of André Gorz in particular, the reduction of working time and the introduction of basic income policies are seen as means of achieving this transformation. Again these policies are difficult to implement; Les Verts in France, for example, had short-lived success with reducing the length of the working week.

In contrast to the reformist trust in science and technology, radical greens are critical of or at least ambivalent about resorting to complex large-scale technology used in areas such as industry, agriculture and medicine (George and Wilding, 1994). This, they believe, encourages over-consumption of resources and potentially creates further problems. The production of bio-fuel as a solution to climate change, for example, leads to the problem of rising food costs which particularly affect those on low incomes. Informed by writers such as Ivan Illich, radical greens advocate alternative technologies 'partly because they are considered environmentally benign, but also because they are potentially 'democratic'. That is, unlike high technology, they can be owned, understood, maintained and used by individuals and groups with little economic or political power' (Pepper 1996, p. 38). Finally, this approach is **eco-centric** as opposed to anthropocentric in the sense that there is deep respect for nature in its own right, not just in terms of how it can benefit humans. In this view, nature contains its own purpose which should be respected as a matter of ethical principle, termed bio-ethics (O'Riordan, 1981). Respect is central here because, as most radical green thinkers

> **Eco-centrism** takes seriously the fact that humankind is part of the global eco-system; human action is therefore subject to ecological laws and limits, and the non-human parts of the eco-system are given equal respect as humans and are intrinsically valued.

acknowledge, the implementation of ideas such as species equality would be untenable. In practice, typical policies include banning or phasing out blood sports, animal experiments and intensive livestock farming (George and Wilding, 1994). This approach to the non-human world also informs the radical green view of relationships between people, which should similarly be informed by principles of respect, equality and social justice.

As for an overall assessment of the effect of green thinking on policymaking and the welfare state, green parties have had some influence, usually as a coalition partner in governments which are primarily social democratic, with Germany being a notable example. However, in this type of situation green parties generally have to become more pragmatic and be prepared to compromise on their ideas if they are to gain power, but this is not unlike the experience of many other ideologies in practice. However, it can be said that environmental issues have become part of mainstream government, and having extensive environmental policies and legislation is becoming as important as having economic and social policies. In this respect, for example, Meadowcroft (2005) has proposed that we are witnessing a gradual shift from the welfare state to the ecological state. This does not mean that environmental policies supplant economic and social policies but that they move from something marginal to something more central.

Table 5.9 Main features of the environmental perspectives on welfare

Reformist environmentalism	Radical environmentalism
Anthropocentric	Eco-centric
Existing institutions such as capitalist economy and liberal democracy capable of solving environmental problems	Need for participatory democracy, decentralisation and emphasis on local economic solutions and sharing/redistribution of resources
Economic growth and environmental protection possible	Limits to growth, need for new economic policies, such as steady state economy or social economy

CHAPTER SUMMARY

▸ This chapter discussed the importance of political ideologies in social policy debate. It provided a brief conceptual map of political perspectives in terms of their key thinkers and core values. These values shape positions on welfare and matters of social policy and illustrate the political nature of social policy decisions and outcomes.

▸ The political spectrum of left and right is frequently used to distinguish different perspectives on the role of the state and the objectives of social policy. The concepts of liberty and equality are particularly important in the analysis of ideologies of welfare.

▸ The liberal perspective emphasises individual freedom as a core value to be protected. Classical liberalism applies this principle to the workings of the economy through its laissez-faire philosophy. It rejects the welfare state, highlighting what it sees as an inefficient and monopolistic creation which damages individual freedom.

▸ The socialist perspective sees class divisions and inequality as the inevitable outcome of capitalism and it advocates a collective approach to society and its organisation. Different socialist perspectives exist, some Marxist and others of a less radical and more gradualist character.

▸ The feminist perspective challenges certain assumptions about the role and rights of women in society. Feminism has sought to address not only overt discrimination but also to highlight the gender-blind and hence exclusionary construction of key aspects of social policy, including citizenship, social rights and the welfare state.

▸ The green perspective stresses the limits to growth and the need to consider the finite nature of resources. Policies need to acknowledge and address issues of environmental sustainability. In this context, there are different 'shades of green', some reformist and others radical.

Discussion points

▸ Select and design a social policy statement for an ideological perspective of your choice. Include in this some pointers on the implementation of the policy objectives outlined.

▸ Select and critically examine the main features of an ideological perspective with reference to its impact on social policy.

▸ Analyse the work of a key political thinker/activist and assess his/her contribution to social policy discourse.

▸ Select a specific social policy topic (e.g. poverty, inequality, citizenship) and describe the approaches that two alternative ideological perspectives would advance in respect of it. Critically analyse the implications in terms of social policy.

Further reading

Fitzpatrick, T. (2001) *Welfare Theory: an introduction*, Basingstoke: Palgrave.

George, V. and Wilding, P. (1994) *Welfare and Ideology*, Hemel Hempstead: Harvester Wheatsheaf.

Heywood, A. (2003) *Political Ideologies: an introduction* (third edn), Basingstoke: Palgrave Macmillan.

Lavalette, M. and Pratt, A. (eds) (2006) *Social Policy: Theories, Concepts and Issues* (third edn), London: Sage.

Useful websites

The Political Compass website: http://www.politicalcompass.org/
Consult political party and think tank websites and policy documents.

Notes

1 See Baker et al. (2004) and Fitzpatrick (2001) for further exploration of these issues.

2 The Fabian Society emerged as the first 'think tank' in the UK (Katwala, 2004) and it continues to review and research matters of social policy today.

3 Bonoli and Powell (2004), for example, provide a useful cross-country text on the Third Way.

4 See Deacon, A. (2002) for a useful analysis of the various strands of communitarian thought.

5 Driver and Martell (1998); Hale, Leggett and Martell (2004); Levitas (2005) and Powell (2002) are useful sources in this regard.

6 See Dryzek and Schlosberg (2005) and Carter (2007) for more on the range of green ideas and debates.

CONTEMPORARY THEORIES AND DEBATES IN SOCIAL POLICY: IRELAND IN A WIDER CONTEXT

The previous chapter approached welfare analysis by considering the range of political ideologies that influence social policy. This chapter looks at welfare analysis from the vantage point of recent theoretical paradigms in the study of social policy, particularly those which consider the external factors and the internal influences on national social policy. These include, firstly, welfare regime theories which develop typologies of welfare. These give an insight to the commonalities and differences across diverse groupings of welfare regimes and the historical trajectories they have followed. Secondly, in common with other areas of the social sciences, the impact of globalisation has become increasingly dominant in discussions of welfare states and their futures. This is considered in the context of social policy in this chapter, with particular attention to 'economic globalisation', given its predominance in influencing the scope and limits of welfare states. Thirdly, the chapter briefly lays out the development of EU social policy and considers some of the issues that arise.

After laying out some of the broader parameters of contemporary social policy debate in section one, section two attempts to locate Ireland in a wider theoretical domain in order to connect to, and link the external and internal factors of relevance. To do this, we return to themes of the previous chapter (in which we considered political ideologies and perspectives on welfare and social policy) to understand more fully the ideological influences on politics and social policy in the Irish context. We then examine the Irish welfare state with reference to the wider themes examined in this chapter. This sets a backdrop for understanding the contemporary position of Ireland, placing it in this broader theoretical domain.

CHAPTER OUTLINE

▶ Section one provides an introduction to the welfare typologies and 'worlds of welfare' debate; it introduces the concept of globalisation and theories of its impact on social policy and welfare reform and outlines the development of EU social policy.

▶ Section two examines the position of Ireland in this broader theoretical social policy context. Attention is given to political ideologies and the perspectives on welfare that have influenced the development of Irish social policy before the contemporary position is considered with reference to the influence of the EU and the impact of globalisation on the Irish welfare state.

SECTION 1: WELFARE REGIMES, GLOBALISATION AND THE INFLUENCE OF THE EUROPEAN UNION ON SOCIAL POLICY

Welfare regimes and 'worlds of welfare'

This section briefly maps out the typologies of welfare that have emerged in social policy discourse and some of the debates associated with them. At its most basic, welfare regime theory attempts to classify or group welfare states in terms of common characteristics, taking a number of variables (such as political values and their influence, working class mobilisation, social spending and degrees of universality of certain social services) on the basis of which, welfare states may be understood to occupy a particular 'family', 'cluster' or 'world of welfare'. This area of study has contributed significantly to understanding the development of welfare states and accounted for different historical trajectories of welfare provision across countries. However, the development of any welfare state is influenced by a large range of factors, including and not least 'country-specific dynamics' and it is therefore extremely difficult to incorporate all of these into any 'ideal typology' of welfare states. The Irish welfare state provides a case in point and this is an issue to which we return below. First the major typologies of welfare are outlined.

While the work of Richard Titmuss (1974, p. 30) represented one of the first attempts at 'model-building', Esping Andersen's (1990) contribution remains the benchmark study in this area, marking the starting point for much comparative theorising in social policy. Taking three core elements of social security; pensions, sickness and unemployment arrangements, a de-commodification index was generated to empirically analyse the extent to which entitlements were granted which did not depend on participation in the labour market. De-commodification was developed as a key conceptual tool of analysis in his study, ranking in order of generosity 'the degree to which individuals, or families, can uphold a socially acceptable standard of living independently of market participation' (ibid., p. 37). The other major element of this analysis is the consideration of 'the welfare state as a system of stratification' by which is meant that the welfare state itself 'is not just a mechanism that intervenes in, and possibly corrects, the structure of inequality; it is, in its own right, a system of stratification. It is an active force in the ordering of social relations' (ibid., p. 23). On this point, the typologies drew attention to the fact that welfare states may produce systems of social stratification and social divisions. Levels of stratification relate to the extent to which access to welfare is structured by social class. Three political factors were of particular significance: the degree of power of the Left (working-class mobilisation), electoral support for Catholic conservatism and the historical level of authoritarian rule. Correlations were established between the nature of the benefit system and the regime type, confirming that politics does matter. The overall significance of Esping Andersen's study lies in the fact that it combines attention to theorising the influences on, and an empirical examination of, a large number of welfare states. On the basis of the analysis of OECD and other international data of 18 countries, three welfare regime types are identified: liberal, corporatist and social democratic.

According to Esping Andersen's study, liberal welfare states, such as the USA, Canada and Australia, demonstrate a low level of de-commodification. In these countries there is a strong emphasis on the protection of the 'work-ethic', a predominance of means-tested assistance and modest social insurance benefits, with strict entitlement criteria which encourage private or market-based provision of welfare. The conservative/corporatist cluster is exemplified by countries such as Germany, Austria, Italy and France. This cluster displays the influence of the Christian democratic tradition, with subsidiarity a core influencing principle. Social insurance is the defining feature of this cluster and is based on the standard employment relationship and status-based occupational arrangements. As a result, this system emphasises stratification and the male breadwinner ideology, thereby re-enforcing the traditional position of the family and limiting the redistributive capacity of the welfare state overall. The social democratic regime is the third identified and includes Sweden, Norway and Denmark. This regime provides the highest level of social protection and displays the greatest de-commodifying capacity of the three identified. It is characterised by a high degree of universalism and a commitment to equality. Social insurance is solidaristic and universal, 'yet benefits are graduated according to accustomed earnings' (ibid., p. 28). Greater consideration is given to the needs and support of the family and the social rights of women than in the others regimes identified.

In overall terms, the identification of these welfare regimes provides a framework for understanding and analysing welfare states, although, as Esping Andersen (ibid., pp. 28–9) himself points out:

> ... welfare states cluster, but we must recognize that there is no single pure case. The Scandinavian countries may be predominantly social democratic, but they are not free of crucial liberal elements. Neither are the liberal regimes pure types. The American social-security system is redistributive, compulsory and far from actuarial. At least in its early formulation, the New Deal was as social democratic as was contemporary Scandinavian social democracy. And European conservative regimes have incorporated both liberal and social democratic impulses. Over the decades, they have become less corporativist and less authoritarian.

Esping Andersen's study and its conclusions have since been widely discussed. It has been argued that more than three 'worlds of welfare' exist and that the 'three worlds of welfare' approach tends to sideline the more difficult cases of countries that don't fit into the three welfare regime types. The inadequate attention given to the position of women has also been highlighted. These issues are examined below.

Aspects of the 'worlds of welfare' debate

A number of authors have since argued the need to consider the existence of other regimes. Using 'a "families of nations" perspective', Castles and Mitchell (1993, p. 93) add a fourth 'radical' welfare state regime that includes Australia, New Zealand and the UK. They present historical evidence for this group as 'social policy innovators' (ibid.) at different points, with a 'legacy of radical egalitarianism' (ibid., p. 123) not adequately reflected in the liberal regime. Leibfried (1992) identifies four 'worlds of welfare': the Scandinavian countries, the 'Bismarck' countries (Germany and Austria), Anglo-Saxon countries (US, UK, Australia and New Zealand) and the 'Latin-Rim' countries of Spain, Portugal, Greece, Southern Italy (and to a much lesser degree France). The fourth type is distinguished by its residualism and the lack of an explicit right to welfare; it is influenced by traditional values of welfare reliant on family-oriented provision and characterised as a 'rudimentary welfare state'. Ferrera (1996) similarly identifies a distinct 'Southern model', where in terms of social protection, for instance, relatively generous provisions exist in some areas (e.g. pensions) while basic provisions for those without contributory-based entitlements are not necessarily assured. Moving beyond Europe to East Asian welfare states, specifically Japan and Korea, Kwon (1997) has argued that although some similarities exist, these countries do not fit into the conservative welfare regime type and the case is made for a distinct East Asian welfare regime type. The challenges associated with welfare state 'typologising' (Cousins, 2005b, p. 107) are also evident when the cases of some individual countries are examined. Ireland, for example, proved difficult to classify in the Esping Andersen study, appearing as it did across clusters, as a 'highly moveable feast' (Cousins, 1997, p. 226). Arts and Gelissen (2002, p. 151) also consider this issue with reference to the 'hybrid cases' of the Netherlands and Switzerland. The Netherlands, they explain, has been assigned to different regimes by different authors, a point accepted by Esping Andersen, as illustrated by his reference to the 'Dutch enigma' (Esping Andersen, 1999, p. 88 in ibid.). It may be the case that 'the three worlds approach is over-inclusive' (Cousin, 2005b, p. 120) in this respect, and that there may well be 'more worlds than we have dreamt of' (Cousins, 1997, p. 232).

The feminist perspective has also been critical to the development of approaches to welfare state theorising since the 1990s, particularly in highlighting the extent to which the position of women has been overlooked in traditional analyses of welfare provision. Many feminists, including Lewis (1992, 1997) for example, asserted that the neglect of gender in Esping Andersen's analysis of welfare arrangements was a significant shortcoming. The lack of attention to the value of unpaid work frequently carried out by women means that 'concepts such as "decommodification" or "dependency" have a gendered meaning that is rarely acknowledged' (Lewis, 1997, p. 161) until relatively recently. Lewis explains this in plain terms: 'While Esping Andersen (1990) writes of de-commodification as a necessary prerequisite for workers' political mobilization, the worker he has in mind is male and his mobilization may depend as much on unpaid female household labour as state policies' (ibid.). In this context, Lewis draws attention to the male breadwinner model as it has been subscribed to in welfare states over the course of their development, serving to demonstrate the differing extents (using strong, modified and weak male breadwinner models) to which women have had particular roles (and relationships with the labour market) assigned to them.

In more general terms, the case for creating a more inclusive framework of analysis has increasingly been made. Daly and Lewis (2000), for instance, have highlighted the need to extend the analysis to include the previously neglected concept of care, in a way that considers cash benefits and services and incorporates the different domains of care work – public, private, voluntary and informal. In addition, they argue that the concept of social care 'can also enhance the quality and depth of welfare state analysis in general. In this regard it can lead to a more encompassing analysis, helping to overcome both the fragmentation in existing scholarship between the cash and service dimensions of welfare states and the relative neglect of the latter' (ibid., p. 296). (See also feminist section in Chapter 5.)

Taking into account the limitations of de-commodification in this regard, the argument has also been made to think more in terms of de-familialisation (McLaughlin and Glendinning, 1994, in Lewis, 1997). Jensen (2008) has recently argued the need to develop a distinction between welfare arrangements that relate to de-commodification and those that relate to de-familisation because 'even though both concepts actually refer to transfers as well as services … it might be helpful to view decommodification as predominantly linked to transfers, and defamilization as predominantly linked to welfare services' (ibid., p. 152). The nature, impact and future of all care work, how it is understood and its position in policy terms, is a critical issue for social policy overall. Its inclusion in 'mainstream' social policy is an issue to which we return in the final part of this book.

In short, the body of scholarship that has emerged in this area demonstrates both the significant complexity but also the potential associated with developing frameworks for the comparative analysis of welfare. Sainsbury (2006), for example, has utilised welfare regime theory together with immigration policy regimes as a method through which to explore immigrants' social rights in a comparative perspective (largely absent from analyses of welfare regimes in the past). Finally, the growing attention being drawn to the need to include feminists and ethnic minorities concerns into comparative analysis holds out considerable possibilities for furthering our critical understanding of gendered and racialised dimensions of welfare state development.

Globalisation and social policy

Another defining feature of social policy discourse since the 1990s has been the considerable attention given to the impact of globalisation on welfare states and its affect on social policy in general. Everyday and often-cited symbols of globalisation abound and include such examples as the proliferation of the internet, the global recognition and infiltration of many product brands, the prevalence of MNCs and the existence of global financial markets. However, while processes of globalisation are largely accepted as illustrative of the concept overall its definition 'defies universal agreement' (George and Page, 2004, p. 1). This is hardly surprising given the range of perspectives and meanings attached to the concept, reflecting the complexity of the concept and the processes related to it. That said, George and Wilding's (2002, p. 19) definition of globalisation, from a political economy perspective, is a useful one: 'Globalization is the increasing inter-connectedness of the world through the compression of time and space brought about by advances in knowledge and technology as well as by political events and decisions.' Notwithstanding the challenges of definition and interpretation, it is clear that if we accept globalisation as a 'force' that has taken on greater significance in recent years, it is important to consider its relevance more specifically in the context of the politics of welfare and social policy. In ideological terms, interpretations of its significance vary but in overall terms, as Mullard and Spicker (1998, p. 122) note:

> For the right, globalisation confirms the need to create competitive labour markets, deregulation, more privatisation, reducing the role of government and reducing taxation. By contrast, globalisation confirms to the left the weakness of government and the limitations of reformist and revisionist policy.

Most significant in this context, has been the extent to which economic globalisation has become embedded in the rhetoric of neo-liberalism, providing an 'irreversible' type rationale for global capitalism. On the other hand, an anti-capitalist movement has also emerged over the last decade, providing an opposing perspective, which Lavalette (2006b, p. 289) describes as 'a truly global movement'. He suggests that events such as the World, European and Asian Social Forums 'are massive celebrations of diversity and opposition to the consequences of neo-liberal economics. It is perhaps here, in a "people's globalisation", that the seed-bed of an "other world" which prioritises the welfare needs of all will start to take shape' (ibid.). While this is far from certain, voices for a global social policy are increasingly being heard.

The last decade has seen an emerging body of scholarship (Deacon with Hulse and Stubbs 1997; Deacon, 2007; Yeates, 2001, 2008) which develops the idea that social policy issues are increasingly global 'in scope, cause and impact' (Yeates, 2008a, p. 11). This approach particularly seeks to attend to the roles and contribution of transnational actors in their many forms, not just the high profile international actors but also forces and actors 'from below' (Yeates, 2001, p. 164), such as non-governmental organisations and social movements, with the aim of examining the related processes and impacts on global social policy formation and change. The significance of organisations and actors such as the World Bank, the IMF, the ILO, the OECD, and the UN in global social policy discourse has also been highlighted. Previously, the role and impact of such organisations was mainly analysed in terms of developing and former communist countries, but greater attention to the processes related to global social policy highlights the influence of supra-national actors on the domain of national social policy and the emergence of supra-national policies, particularly in areas of redistribution, regulation and rights (Deacon, 2007). Coming from such a perspective, the development of a global social policy agenda has the capacity to offer a significant alternative to the global economic agenda which has dominated in recent times (See Deacon, 2007; George and Wilding, 2002; Yeates 2001, 2008).

Economic globalisation, post-industrialism and welfare states

Apart from the impact of the concept of globalisation on politics and modes of governance, it is the economic consequences of globalisation that have attracted most focus in discussions of welfare and social policy to date. Specifically, post-industrialisation and economic globalisation have both been significant factors shaping economies in the wake of the economic crisis of the 1970s and 1980s. The shift towards post-industrialisation describes the move from manufacturing to service- and knowledge-based economic activity. Economies across Europe have gradually become post-industrialised as they experience a decline in manufacturing-based employment and a growth in service- and information technology-based occupations. Changes in the world of work are reflected in the shift away from the standard employment relationship towards more atypical forms of employment.

The idea of jobs for life and the security attached to them has been replaced by calls for flexibility and the need for constant innovation. **Economic globalisation** has intensified this shift towards post-industrialism. Economic globalisation refers to the process whereby production and commerce have become increasingly more mobile and internationalised, and as a result countries experience greater competition in terms of attracting foreign investment in particular. Both of these economic trends have been unfolding in an environment in which right-wing or neo-liberal held orthodoxy still holds considerable influence.

> **Economic globalisation** describes the process whereby economies operate on a more open basis and are influenced by increasingly 'global' financial imperatives around trade, investment and competitiveness.

The key elements of economic globalisation relate to areas of global financial markets, trade, foreign direct investment, multi-national corporations and labour markets and mobility (Fitzpatrick, 2001; George and Wilding, 2002). As Fitzpatrick (2001) points out, the global nature of financial markets undoubtedly offers the most solid justification for those holding the view that globalisation is a reality. The changed nature of capitalism has meant that stock market investment has become the standard feature of global economic activity; this is 'a capitalism concerned with dealing in stocks and shares and currencies not with trade or industrial development' (George and Wilding, 2002, p. 28). The fact that financial markets have become the major source of investment means that there has been a shift in the onus of responsibility (away from long-term investment) in favour of shareholders and the maximisation of their share price. Potential consequences include the risk of less 'productive investment' (ibid., p. 29), thereby affecting employment levels, patterns and security and increasing pressure on countries 'to be seen as safe places for international capital' (ibid.). The 2007 sub-prime lending 'crisis' and the subsequent collapse of some major banks in 2008 offered an illustration of the shortcomings of largely unregulated global financial markets, generating much commentary about the extent to which different economies were 'exposed' to the resulting risks.

The pressure on national governments to 'maintain their competitiveness' occurs both in the context of a more open trade environment and in the context of maximising the attractiveness of their countries for potential investors in their economies. Foreign Direct Investment (FDI) is a term that has become particularly familiar in the Irish context (see Chapters 2 and 3), given the economic policy of the Irish state since the 1960s. According to Fitzpatrick (2001, p. 167): 'FDI occurs when an investor owns and/or invests in an enterprise located in a country other than that of the investor.' FDI, while massively significant in the economic policy of some countries, is not a truly global phenomenon in the sense that most investment goes from developed countries (most notably the USA, Europe and Japan) to developed countries. Only 30 per cent of all FDI went to industrially developing countries in 1997, the remainder was invested in advanced industrialised countries (George and Wilding, 2002).

The existence of MNCs is one of the most frequently cited examples of globalisation, but of course, like the other factors outlined here it is not that they are 'new' as such (Ford, for instance, located in Ireland in 1917). However, as potential employers and wealth generators in the areas in which they choose to locate, MNCs continue to hold significant leverage with national governments. Apart from their FDI influence, MNCs represent a substantial interest in the world economy, accounting for 70 per cent of world trade (George and Wilding, 2002). It is not surprising, therefore, that much debate surrounds the profit-making activities of MNCs, particularly in terms of the power and influence of their brands and their attention to issues of labour standards in their countries of location (Klein, 2000). Although some argue that the impact of MNCs is overstated (and that many MNCs maintain their 'home-based' employment etc.), the potential effect on employment prospects and employment standards is global in context, which means that their role must be considered in the context of welfare rights and social policy. As Fitzpatrick (2001, p. 167) notes, while there is no evidence of the existence of a 'global labour market', the view has been put forward that there is 'an international division of labour with industrial capital relocating to low-wage countries in the developing world and so contributing to the hollowing out of domestic labour markets' (ibid.).

Globalisation and social policy trajectories

In briefly laying out the various 'components' of economic globalisation, we need to be clear that these economic challenges are not universally accepted; many stress the long history of world trade and the less than global qualities of FDI as it has developed. More significant perhaps, is the point that the pervasiveness of the arguments does not render states 'powerless' or offer a thesis of 'global economic inevitability'; individual governments undoubtedly 'feel the heat' of these pressures and react and plan as they see fit. In this regard, there are a number of different 'strands' or 'perspectives' on globalisation as it relates to welfare states and social policy. Sykes (2008) usefully characterises these in terms of four main perspectives on globalisation and social policy development:

1 globalization causes welfare retrenchment through capitalism's dominance
2 globalization has little effect upon welfare states
3 globalization's effects on welfare states are mediated by national politics
4 welfare states generated globalization and limit its future development (Sykes, 2008, p. 432)

Drawing on Sykes' analysis, in the first perspective emphasis is placed on the potential force of globalisation to generate economic pressures that ultimately result in greater inequality in employment and put a strain on systems of social security and on social solidarity overall. According to this view, welfare state retrenchment is inevitable, particularly where neo-liberalism is strong. The overall tendency within this perspective is to consider the strength of capitalism as enhanced by economic globalisation to the extent that a 'race to the bottom' is inevitable and that the welfare state is a necessary casualty of the neo-liberal agenda. This perspective has been the subject of some criticism although its value in pointing out a potentially radical and controversial welfare trajectory should not be ignored.

The second perspective, in contrast, argues that pressures on welfare states exist aside from globalisation that are actually largely domestic in origin, although globalisation may often be offered as the reason why welfare restructuring needs to take place. Sykes (2008) indicates the contribution of Pierson (2001) in this regard. Specifically, Pierson (2001, p. 82) argues:

> ... while welfare states indeed face unprecedented budgetary stress, it seems likely that this stress is primarily related to a series of 'post-industrial' changes occurring within advanced industrial democracies themselves, as the employment profiles of affluent societies have become increasingly service-based, as their welfare states have matured, as populations have aged, and as radical changes in household structures have taken place.

This perspective highlights how globalisation can be over-emphasised to the neglect of existing internal pressures on welfare states and social policy.

The third perspective acknowledges pressures brought to bear by globalisation on welfare states but considers that these pressures can and often are mediated by national governments and their actions. Sykes points to Esping Andersen (1996) as an example of this position, where they acknowledge the need for economic competitiveness and openness among nation states in order to respond effectively to globalisation, but they do not see this as marking anything like the end of the welfare state. In fact, they suggest that welfare states will be forced to change, but not necessarily to decline. Taylor-Gooby's (2001) review of the welfare state reform of the 1990s also notes the resilience of welfare states in the context of these (and other) pressures but anticipates that more radical reform is possible in the wake of that phase of welfare state adaptation.

Sykes' fourth perspective on globalisation and social policy development, as exemplified by Rieger and Leibfried (2003) takes a different starting point, arguing that welfare states, although not purposefully, provided the necessary conditions for allowing economic globalisation to take shape. Sykes (2008 p. 433) outlines how, according to this view:

> ... the development of welfare provisions allowed for the subsequent development of a free-market economy on an international scale. International trade and the 'globalizing' of the economy internationally had occurred before, but the difference in the post-Second World War period was that the welfare state was now able to lessen the social effects of free trade by countering the effects in terms of unemployment and lowering of incomes of certain groups.

In this context the historical and continuing role of national governments in matters related to globalisation is important and although certain pressures exist, these are influenced by national social policies. Yeates (2001, p. 26) explains this perspective as one which 'emphasizes the contribution of social policies to the globalization process'. The strengths of this approach are thus illustrated in terms of its acknowledgement of the central role of the state and its social policies in positioning and responding to globalisation. This perspective, as Yeates (ibid., p. 28) asserts, 'draws attention to the importance of values, beliefs, perceptions and political action in determining the extent to which states (and other actors) are able to adopt, formulate and successfully implement, globalizing strategies.'

In short, approaches and interpretations of globalisation and its effects on social policy continue to differ widely; this in itself illustrates that questions about its impact on welfare trajectories now and into the future remain open. That said, mention has already been made of different approaches to welfare and the nature and interpretations of 'pressures' brought to bear on welfare states in macro-terms, since the 1990s in particular. This pressure has been particularly evident in the 'mature' European welfare states and has also been an issue of increasing concern to the EU.

Social policy and the European Union

Origins and evolution of EU social policy

Founded in the 1950s with six member states, the EEC sought to expand the trade links and build on the objectives of the European Coal and Steel Community (ECSC). The Treaty of Rome, signed in 1957, provided the legal framework for the EEC and the establishment of its various institutions. Articles 117–28 of the Treaty mentioned social policy matters, including employment, training, working conditions, social security, collective bargaining, and the principle of equal pay (Hantrais, 2008). However, apart from the equal pay principle, these were not legally binding. In fact, according to the European Parliament (2000):

> Social policy was considered as an adjunct to economic policy and remained broadly speaking an accompanying policy. The only practical achievements recorded between 1958 and 1974 were the implementation of freedom of movement for migrant workers and the associated social security arrangements ... and the establishment of the European Social Fund.

This may be accounted for by the fact that **subsidiarity** (formally set out in the Maastricht Treaty, 1992) has been a guiding principle in the operation of the EU. Referring to the 1992 Communication, Kleinman (2002, p. 90) explains that the EU can only act 'when its aims can be better achieved at European rather than at national level, and the burden of proof is on the European institutions to show that action is necessary at that level, and also to show that binding instruments are necessary rather than support measures and framework directives.' Adherence to this principle has largely maintained the status of national social policy. In addition, as the membership of the EU has grown, the diversity of welfare systems and the challenges associated with attempts at 'harmonisation' have become more apparent (Hantrais, 2008). Notwithstanding these issues, the contribution of the EU to national social policymaking and social policy discourse in general needs to be considered. This section briefly sketches the background and some of the main features of contemporary EU social policy debate, beginning with developments during the 1970s.

By the 1970s there was a growing awareness that the common market alone could not deliver social cohesion and a new initiative, the Social Action Programme, was established in 1974. This was 'designed to achieve the three goals of full and better employment; an improvement in living and working conditions; and greater involvement of management and labour' (Kleinman, 2002, p. 85). A number of pilot poverty programmes were established from 1975, which, while limited in terms of their overall impact, raised the profile of issues of poverty and social exclusion at EU level. At national level, the evolution of these programmes was important in developing different approaches to tackling poverty and social exclusion (e.g. support for community development activities and area-based initiatives) (Frazer, 2007).

Separately, a series of directives (which are legally binding on all member states and enforceable in law) on equal treatment (arising out of Article 119 of the Treaty of Rome) delivered during the 1970s and 1980s were crucial to the development of policies of formal gender equality in many member states. In short, defining features of emergent EU social policy can be identified in terms of a concern with social cohesion in tandem with economic development; equal access to protection, rights and equity within the workplace; and investment and support for local and regional disadvantaged areas.

During the late 1980s, the Commission President Jacque Delors was keen to develop EU social policy, particularly in the context of strengthening the single European market as achieved through the Single European Act, 1986. The Community Charter of Basic Social Rights for Workers (1989) emerged as another social policy development noted for its recognition of the rights of workers and the rights of men and women on an equal basis. It also marked the first recognition of the rights of older people and people with disabilities at this level (Harvey, 2003). However, references to citizens, as opposed to workers, evident in earlier drafts, did not appear in the final version (Hantrais, 2000). The Charter was not acceptable to the Conservative government in the UK and they chose to 'opt out' (although the New Labour government subsequently signed up in 1997). In terms of the impact of the Charter, opinions differ between those who were critical of its non-binding legal nature and those who assess it as setting the scene for more extensive social policy measures in the longer term (Daly, 2008). A Social Chapter was not included in the Maastricht Treaty (owing to the veto by the UK government) although a Protocol on Social Policy was agreed by the other member states, and this was followed by a Green Paper (1993) and subsequently a White Paper on European Social Policy in 1994 (see Kleinman, 2002 for discussion).

The Amsterdam Treaty 1997 provided some strengthening of the social objectives, as indicated by the inclusion of specific reference to established areas such as employment, vocational training, education, young people and equal pay, along with developing objectives in the area of equality, particularly in terms of gender 'mainstreaming', equal opportunities and equal treatment and combating discrimination. Specifically, the Treaty states:

> Without prejudice to the other provisions of this Treaty and within the limits of the powers confirmed by it upon the Community, the Council, acting unanimously on a proposal from the Commission and after consulting the European Parliament, may take appropriate action to combat discrimination based on sex, racial or ethnic origin, religion or belief, disability, age or sexual orientation.

The treaty also provided official recognition of the European objective to combat social exclusion and the possibility of initiating programmes in this regard. The Racial Equality Directive 2000/43/EC and the Employment Equality Directive 2000/78/EC were subsequently adopted and illustrate the role taken up by the EU in challenging discrimination and promoting equality in the workplace.

At the same time, on the economic front, low economic growth rates, 'ageing populations' and rising unemployment meant that the impact of post-industrialisation (and the spectre of economic globalisation) became particularly evident in a number of European member states. Consequently, employment trends and prospects became a central focus of the EU over the course of the 1990s. The European Employment Strategy (EES) was launched following the inclusion of employment as a 'common concern' in the Amsterdam Treaty and the Luxembourg Jobs Summit held in 1997. The objectives of the EES include a commitment to a high level of employment in the EU and the establishment of a number of structures including an Employment Committee and a 'country surveillance procedure' to monitor and offer guidance and recommendations for member states on the basis of the National Action Plans on Employment (now National Reform Programmes) submitted by the member states. Statistical indicators (drawn up by the Employment Committee) have been developed (and revised) under this strategy.[1]

The EES objectives were initially formulated with attention to four pillars: entrepreneurship, employability, adaptability and equal opportunities.[2] The first pillar focused on supporting the efforts of new and small businesses to maximise their potential for growth and development. The second of these pillars concentrated on the issue of unemployment, particularly long-term and youth unemployment. It also sought to improve the situation of early school leavers. The other component of the second pillar reflected the growing focus on activation policies, seeking a move away from passive type supports (see Chapter 7 for explanations). The third pillar of adaptability referred to the need to 'modernise work organization' in order to develop and upgrade the skills of workers and to promote efficiency. The equal opportunities pillar sought to promote equal opportunities for men and women in the labour market through the availability of childcare, career breaks, part-time work and parental leave. Member states were also encouraged to address 'gender gaps' and 'facilitate return to work'. The European Social Fund (ESF) was the major funding source for initiatives in these areas. This four-pillar framework was subsequently revised in 2003 and replaced with a three-pillar model (outlined below). The methodology developed in the implementation of the EES has since become an important component of the approach to other aspects of social policy in recent years (see Social OMC below).

EU social policy for the twenty-first century?

The Lisbon Strategy marks another stage in the 'uneven' history of social policy in the EU. The major objective arising from the Lisbon European Council (March 2000) was the aim of making the EU 'the most competitive and dynamic knowledge-based economy in the world capable of sustainable economic growth with more and better jobs and greater social cohesion' by 2010 (ibid.). Economic, employment and social policy were formally brought together in what became known as the 'Lisbon triangle' (and to which the environmental pillar was added in 2001). Targets were then set to increase the employment rate within the EU to 70 per cent, a 60 per cent target for women and a 50 per cent target for older workers (55–64 years), which was added at the Stockholm European Council in 2001 (ibid.). The target of increasing investment in research and development to 3 per cent of Europe's GDP was agreed in Barcelona in 2002.

Specifically in terms of poverty and social inclusion, the Lisbon Strategy agreed 'on the need to take steps to make a decisive impact on the eradication of poverty' (Council of the European Union, 2002 p. 4). Four Common Objectives were put forward: i) to facilitate participation in employment and access by all to resources, rights, goods and services, ii) to prevent the risks of exclusion, iii) to help the most vulnerable and iv), to mobilise all relevant bodies (see ibid. for details of objectives).

First officially unveiled at the Lisbon Council meeting in 2000, the **Open Method of Co-ordination** (OMC) refers to the process of policy deliberation and development provided for in a framework of: 'political coordination without legal constraints. Member States agree to identify and promote their most effective policies in the fields of Social

> The **Open Method of Co-ordination** refers to the process whereby member states agree, develop and monitor policy developments, targets and outcomes through cooperation and in 'non-directive' terms.

Protection and Social Inclusion with the aim of learning from each others' experiences' (European Commission, 2008a). This involves agreeing common objectives and indicators and member states preparing national strategic reports (formerly national action plans) as per the guidelines issued by the EU.[3] These reports are evaluated by the Commission and the Council and a Joint Report is issued which provides a synthesis of the position across the member states on a range of issues, prioritises key areas and highlights examples of good practice (see Joint Reports for details). In this context, peer review and 'mutual policy learning' are seen by some as a particularly innovative element of the OMC. Others are critical of this 'soft' approach to policymaking, which is not legally binding and does not have any sanctions attached, unlike areas of economic policy.[4]

Notwithstanding this debate about the effectiveness of the OMC, the development of a range of common indicators[5] has been a notable outcome in terms of both strengthening the comparability of EU data and in establishing a framework through which progress in key aspects of social policy can be assessed (see Atkinson et al., 2002; O'Connor, 2005; Nolan, 2006a). These social indicators have been used in the preparation of National Action Plans since 2003, 'marking a fundamental sea-change in the way policy with respect to social inclusion is framed. It provides policy-makers for the first time with a basis on which the starting positions and progress over time in the different Member States in terms of key areas of social concern can be reliably compared' (Nolan, 2003, p. 12).

Returning briefly to the wider aims of the Strategy, poor economic growth and a critical review of its implementation (Kok Report) generated some concern. In 2005, the Commission report for the Spring Council stated:

> While many of the fundamental conditions are in place for a European renaissance, there has simply not been enough delivery at European and national level. This is not just a question of difficult economic conditions since Lisbon was launched, it also results from a policy agenda which has become overloaded, failing co-ordination and

sometimes conflicting priorities. (European Commission, 2005, in Dieckhoff and Gallie, 2007, p. 480)

Consequently, the Lisbon Strategy was re-launched, with a revised focus. The EES was re-visited and its guidelines are now delivered along with macroeconomic and microeconomic policy and are set for a three-year period. Member states continue to submit National Implementation Reports annually. Three priorities are identified:

1   Attract and retain more people in employment and increase labour supply and modernise social protection systems;
2   Improve adaptability of workers and enterprises;
3   Increase investment in human capital through better education and skills. (European Commission, 2007a)

In short, greater emphasis was placed on the need to strengthen the bases for economic growth, and the new guidelines on economic and employment policy failed to include attention to social exclusion. This was to be dealt with separately and the 'streamline reforms' introduced in 2006 saw the introduction of National Reports on Strategies for Social Protection and Social Inclusion. These replaced the previous National Action Plans on Social Inclusion with a wider set of policy objectives to include social inclusion, pensions, health and long-term care. Social exclusion is no longer dealt with as a self-standing issue but has rather been subsumed into a much larger policy agenda. The primary goals of this streamlined approach are outlined as follows:

The overarching objectives of the OMC for social protection and social inclusion are to promote:
(a)   social cohesion, equality between men and women and equal opportunities for all through adequate, accessible, financially sustainable, adaptable and efficient social protection systems and social inclusion policies;
(b)   effective and mutual interaction between the Lisbon objectives of greater economic growth, more and better jobs and greater social cohesion, and with the EU's Sustainable Development Strategy;
(c)   good governance, transparency and the involvement of stakeholders in the design, implementation and monitoring of policy. (European Commission, 2008b)

Further detail is provided under the headings of i) a decisive impact on the eradication of poverty and on social exclusion, ii) adequate and sustainable pensions and iii) accessible, high-quality and sustainable healthcare and long-term care (ibid.).

It seems that the new direction adopted in the revised Lisbon Strategy may represent something of a 'step backwards' in terms of social policy. According to Daly (2008, p. 7), the concept of social exclusion adopted has been modified significantly:

> First, rather than addressed by universalistic type measures, there is now a strengthened reference to social exclusion as a process affecting the most marginalised. Secondly, activation has become more prominent; the term 'active social inclusion' is now used, defined to mean participation in the labour market. This in turn has meant that the references to social exclusion have fallen away as the programme has developed; notions of social inclusion have come to replace those of social exclusion. Thirdly, the efficiency of policies and their interaction has become a dominant concern (with 'modernisation' as the subtext). There is a shift of focus to 'operationalisation' and what was formerly a political goal (mobilisation) is now to serve the ends of better policy design and delivery. Fourthly, the attention to prevention as such is gone.

Similarly, Dieckhoff and Gallie (2007, p. 499) note that apart from the possibility of better employment rates, 'the reformed Lisbon processes led to few policy initiatives that could be expected to make a significant reduction in the vulnerability of the socially disadvantaged.' Notwithstanding these criticisms it is also finally worth noting Daly's (2008, p. 16) observation that 'Despite its watering down, social Lisbon still constitutes an ambitious programme, especially in the context of the limited EU engagement with social policy to date.' In short, Lisbon is now charting new ground in terms of developing the path of EU social policy, although its real impact will only be known in time.

Finally, one of the most recent EU initiatives of note is the development of common principles of 'flexicurity'. The Commission (2007, p. 10) defines **flexicurity** as 'an integrated strategy to enhance, at the same time, flexibility and security in the labour market'. The salience of this concept has grown because of the need

> **Flexicurity** is an emerging concept which seeks to address contemporary labour market challenges, in pursuit of both flexibility and security.

to meet the revised Lisbon objectives on employment, to address the 'segmentation of the labour market' (ibid., p. 9) in which some workers are less protected and to help 'employees and employers alike to fully reap the opportunities presented by globalisation' (ibid., p. 10). The emergence of this concept would seem to build on the activation policies and the productive factor developed in employment policies over the course of the 1990s. During this time there was, as Hemerijck (2003, p. 19) notes, 'a manifest convergence of employment and social policy objectives'. The balance between these objectives is clearly still being settled and the application of the concept of flexicurity is likely to generate much debate within and between member states.

The social policy agenda of the EU remains a 'work in progress'. On the one hand, it is unconstrained by a 'fixed position' or rigid association with older traditions of welfare provision and there is some evidence to suggest that it is in fact reasonably well placed to promote a social policy agenda that incorporates 'new social risks'. As Larsen and Taylor-Gooby (2004, pp. 183–4) observe, 'new risks figure more prominently in the European Union than in national social policy activity.' Allied with this is the EU's attention to issues of equality and workers' rights, and its promotion of activation policies demonstrates its potential to bring about change (see the case of Ireland below). On the other hand, it has limitations, owing to its institutional character and origins. The capacity of the EU to influence and/or shape national social policy is circumscribed by a number of factors. These include the economic rationale that brought it into being and whose economic fortunes it now seeks to revive, current 're-calibration' efforts to bring about sustainable welfare states (which remains largely a national responsibility), the political support of its enlarged group of members (new and old) and the precise relationship to its member states (i.e. subsidiarity) and indeed other global actors (as mentioned earlier in the chapter). Its capacity for policy innovation, the space it offers for social policy 'dialogue' and 'learning' may, in time, provide the framework for a more sustained and sustainable EU approach to social policy, but this is not yet certain.

SECTION 2: ANALYSING IRISH SOCIAL POLICY – INFLUENCES AND CHALLENGES

In order to make sense of these contemporary theoretical debates in the context of Irish social policy, it is first necessary to consider in greater detail some of the specific dynamics that have played a part in shaping social policy debate in Ireland. The historical development of Irish political and ideological debate on welfare is first considered here to put the contemporary theoretical analysis of Irish social policy in its wider context. The first part of this book mapped the complex story that is the development of Irish social policy; the analysis offered now seeks to explore some of the factors that have shaped the ideological discourses on welfare in Ireland, as they have evolved. The previous chapter mapped out what might be considered the 'grand narratives' related to ideologies of welfare which are of historical and contemporary significance to social policy. Some of these perspectives have been and are influential in Ireland, although Irish welfare debate tends not to be characterised in terms of the 'isms' profiled earlier. There are (and historically have been)[6] those who take a broadly 'left' or 'right' wing approach to politics, welfare and social policy, but it is mainly the smaller political parties that are mostly clearly identified in these terms. The reasons for this are complex but the political culture that developed in post-colonial Ireland has certainly been a factor, to which we first turn.

The early political and ideological landscape

The origins of the two largest political parties (Fianna Fáil and Fine Gael) in Ireland arose from the differing positions adopted on the Anglo-Irish Treaty of 1921 and the civil war that followed. A policy of abstention from the Dáil had been followed by anti-treaty Sinn Féin but by 1926 declining party support led Eamon de Valera to propose that if the oath of allegiance was dropped, then abstention could be reviewed. This was not accepted and Fianna Fáil (The Soldiers of Destiny) was established by Eamon de Valera following the split with Sinn Féin in 1926. Fine Gael was founded in 1933 when Cumann na nGaedheal, the National Centre Party and the National Guard (Blueshirts) merged (Coakley, 1993). The Labour Party emerged out of the Irish Trade Union Congress in 1912 and was officially established as a political party in 1922 (ibid.). In terms of the nationalist question, the Labour party failed to offer a clear position, relegating them as Coakley (ibid., p. 18) puts it, to 'that of third party in a three-party system'. There were a number of other factors that contributed to the relatively weak position held by the Labour party in Ireland, particularly when considered in comparative European terms, to which we will return below. In short, however, the political developments of the first decade of the Irish Free State were largely defined by the politics of nationalism in the fledgling state. These historical events were formative in shaping the political landscape in Ireland in terms of 'the national question', over and above traditional left/right distinctions or wider concern for 'the social question' around which there was also much to consider, as Chapter 2 illustrated.

Apart from the divisions relating to the adequacy of the Treaty as a long-term settlement for Anglo-Irish relations in the context of Irish independence, the legitimacy of the Irish Free State was the central concern. In addition, the continued dominance of agriculture as the major economic activity meant that the land reforms of the early twentieth century were a significant feature in shaping the make-up of the newly formed state. However, as Breen et al. (1990, p. 3) point out, 'although the size and commercial value of farm holdings varied greatly, these inequalities were simply not on the agenda for debate in the State's early years. The attainment of security of tenure and, later, ownership had, by the 1920s, made rural Ireland deeply conservative.'

The wider emergence of a more conservative ethos during the 1920s, as exemplified by the Cumann na nGaedheal government, stood in marked contrast to the previous decade of protest and upheaval, and while poverty and harsh social conditions hadn't gone away, Irish politics was not primarily motivated by these issues. In Breen et al.'s (ibid.) view, 'class divisions were strong and manifest but did not translate into the most significant cleavages in defining party politics.' The reality of the early years of Irish political independence was that it was preoccupied by issues of legitimacy and stability of the new state and many of the notably socialist aspirations laid out in the Democratic Programme outlined at the first Dáil meeting in January 1919 were quickly forgotten:

> We declare in the words of the Irish Republican Proclamation the right of the people of Ireland to the ownership of Ireland, and to the unfettered control of Irish destinies to be indefeasible, and in the language of our first President, Pádraig Mac Phiarais, we declare that the Nation's sovereignty extends not only to all men and women of the Nation, but to all its material possessions, the Nation's soil and all its resources, all the wealth and all the wealth-producing processes within the Nation, and with him we reaffirm that all right to private property must be subordinated to the public right and welfare.
>
> We declare that we desire our country to be ruled in accordance with the principles of Liberty, Equality, and Justice for all, which alone can secure permanence of Government in the willing adhesion of the people.
>
> … It shall be the first duty of the Government of the Republic to make provision for the physical, mental and spiritual well-being of the children, to secure that no child shall suffer hunger or cold from lack of food, clothing, or shelter, but that all shall be provided with the means and facilities requisite for their proper education and training as Citizens of a Free and Gaelic Ireland.
>
> The Irish Republic fully realises the necessity of abolishing the present odious, degrading and foreign Poor Law System, substituting therefore a sympathetic native scheme for the care of the Nation's aged and infirm, who shall not be regarded as a burden, but rather entitled to the Nation's gratitude and consideration. Likewise it shall

be the duty of the Republic to take such measures as will safeguard the health of the people and ensure the physical as well as the moral well-being of the Nation. (Dáil Éireann, Volume 1, 21 January 1919, Democratic Programme)

The Irish political landscape began to take on a more enduring shape during the 1920s with the establishment of the Fianna Fáil party, which emerged as a successful political force almost immediately after its formation. It won 44 seats in its first election in 1927, initially forming a government with the support of the Labour Party in 1932, but subsequently holding power in its own right until 1948 (Collins and Cradden, 1997). During that period, Fianna Fáil demonstrated a more interventionist inclination than that previously displayed by Cumann na nGaedheal, and it managed to appeal to a broader spectrum of voters with important social policy interventions, including housing and social welfare measures (see Chapter 2), thus improving its position among urban and rural voters. Fianna Fáil had quickly become 'a classic "catch-all" party, drawing its support from almost all sections of Irish society' (ibid., p. 28). This was a huge challenge to the advancement of the Irish Labour Party, as Fianna Fáil had managed to attract votes from working-class people that might otherwise have been expected to support Labour. In addition, while there were clear class divisions in Ireland, both urban and rural, and an active (but fractious) trade union movement, the absence of large-scale industrialisation and associated employment meant that Ireland 'possessed a relatively small industrial proletariat – the natural constituency for a party of labour' (ibid., p. 29). This resulted in a relatively weak social democratic tradition, marking it apart from much of the rest of Europe.

The success of Fianna Fáil in the 1930s and 1940s meant that the wider political culture that developed was not defined by sharp ideological divisions of right and left, but continued to be steeped in matters of state legitimacy and national identity and, in these, the Catholic Church also played a crucial role. On this point McLaughlin (2001, p. 227) offers the following assessment:

The ideologies of Catholicism and nationalism fused to shape both the nature of the state and the relationship between the state and society. In no other European state, with the exception of Poland, was such a close relationship established between the Catholic Church and national identity and it played the pivotal role of bestowing legitimacy and authority on the new nation state (Schmitt, 1973). Organizationally, the Church provided the institutional links between the new political, economic and social élites and the masses.

The significant influence of the Catholic Church on the development of Irish social policy has already been highlighted (see part one of the book). Its wider impact on the development of ideological discourses of welfare was also important, complementing as it did, the long-standing liberal ethos (see Fanning, 2003, 2004). Looking at the wider 'role of historiography in interpreting the ideological history of social policy', Fanning (2004, p. 6) points to 'past inter-relationships between liberalism and Catholicism in Ireland' (ibid.), which provides a telling account of the subsequent trajectory of the Irish welfare state. The mutually re-enforcing nature of these perspectives meant that while the merits of a welfare state were being considered in Britain during the 1940s, in Ireland the Catholic Church remained central to the delivery of welfare.

The Church was the main provider of a range of basic social services (in education, health and in the care of people with disabilities) on which people were reliant and which otherwise would have had to have been provided by the state. In taking on such an immense field of provision, the Church came to hold significant influence, both in its relationship with the state and with individual citizens. As organisers of, and front line workers in, the social services the religious within the Church were well-placed to promote the values of Catholicism, as was their focus, and, according to Fahey (1998, p. 415): 'The primary purpose of social service provision for the Catholic church was to disseminate and safeguard the faith, not to combat social inequality or reform society.' In short, the conditions were set for the blurred boundaries that existed between church and state at that time. One illustration of this is found in Archbishop McQuaid's position on the mother and child scheme when making the case for its rejection:

> We shall have saved the country from advancing a long way towards socialistic welfare. In particular, we shall have checked the efforts of Leftist and Labour elements, which are approaching the point of publicly ordering the Church to stay out of social life and confine herself to what they think is the Church's proper sphere. (cited in Horgan, 2000, p. 144)

Catholic social teaching was undoubtedly a formative influence on the development of welfare ideologies in Ireland. Its prominent position in Irish society during the first half of the twentieth century in particular helped to maintain a Catholic conservative perspective which was shared by both Fianna Fáil and Fine Gael up until the late 1950s at least. In addition, subsidiarity and its application to the field of welfare provision, and views on the sanctity of the family, the centrality of marriage, and the position of women re-enforced a traditional world view, which was largely mirrored in the mainstream political domain (with the exception of a small number of dissidents; see Chapter 2). The influence of Catholicism on mainstream political thinking in Ireland appears to have some parallels with the Christian Democratic perspective that was influential in other European countries in terms of the impact of the principle of subsidiarity on wider political discourse and the development of a corporatist framework, although this should not be taken too far. As Mair and Weeks (2005, p. 137) point out, 'uniquely among the Catholic countries of western Europe, Christian Democracy has never emerged as a distinct political movement in Ireland. It was never needed by the church.'

The 1960s was a decade of rapid social change, which saw greater attention to both economic and social conditions. The emergence of the discussion group Tuairim, which sought to solve 'the social, economic, political and cultural problems of modern Ireland' (cited in Puirséil, 2005, p. 20), and the founding of the Irish public/social policy journal *Administration* during the 1950s provided emerging fora for debate. Although the journal was initially distributed to public servants it gained a wider audience through its subsequent association with the Institute of Public Administration (IPA) (Fanning, 2008).

In political terms, Fianna Fáil led with a new outward-looking approach to the economy. In this context and conscious of what one commentator referred to as Fine Gael's 'unfavourable party image', specifically 'the party which big farmers, professional men and merchants tend to join' (cited in Bew et al., 1989, p. 113), Fine Gael sought to re-position itself as illustrated in its 1965 electoral document *The Just Society*. This move is further explained by Bew et al. (ibid., p. 114):

> The champions of a new course in Fine Gael ... argued that a real opening for advance was available by attacking the limitations of Fianna Fáil economic 'programming' and putting forward a more directed strategy of economic planning, social welfare and even the talk, unprecedented for a party with such reactionary traditions, of redistribution of income and social justice.

The leader of Fianna Fáil, Seán Lemass, similarly claimed a move to the left in 1963, and Labour, instead of claiming its ground, 'found itself hopelessly outmanoeuvred' (Puirséil, 2005, p. 26). In overall terms, though, the possibility of a political discourse that had a social policy dimension had finally emerged in Ireland. Other factors aided in this too; the setting up of the Economic and Social Research Institute (initially the Economic Research Institute) in the 1960s marked an important milestone for the development of social scientific research in Ireland. In addition, there was considerable effort made by a diverse range of groups and communities to raise issues of social policy from the late 1960s onwards, and expectations were high that the 1970s would deliver significant social improvements (see Chapter 3). This activism was vital in the development of social policy discourse in a country that historically lacked an explicit political left/right divide on social issues and that did not have a tradition of independent economic and social policy 'think tanks' as existed elsewhere.

However, deteriorating economic conditions and the wider political climate in which the right was in ascendance meant that 'Fine Gael's "social democracy" would be attenuated rather than deepened in the late 1970s' (Bew et al., 1989, p. 118). Fianna Fáil took a different approach; they argued for economic development, social solidarity and social cohesion. Mair and Weeks (2005, p. 147) explain the Fianna Fáil position of the time:

> It argued that any patterns of inequality and poverty could best be eradicated by increasing the size of the national cake. It stressed the need for social solidarity, framed in a more general corporatist ideology, which, by emphasising the importance of 'the national interest', deliberately set its face against any attempts to translate social conflict into politics.

Here we are provided with a useful synopsis of the Fianna Fáil perspective; its emphasis on 'the national interest' and social solidarity to appeal to a support base that would not focus on social and class divisions, but rather 'come together' to avoid such challenges, with 'give and take' all round. Addressing the fiftieth Fianna Fáil Árd-Fheis in April 1981, the then Taoiseach, Charles J. Haughey (in Mansergh, 1986, p. 480), outlined his view on the appeal of Fianna Fáil:

> ... the reason we adhere to Fianna Fáil, the reason that time and time again the broad mass of the Irish people have given their endorsement to this Party rather than to any other, turned to it in times of crisis, continued to give it their support in time of difficulty, is because it represents, not this pressure group or that sectional interest, this class or that creed, but because, in the broad sweep of its membership and their faith and devotion to their own country, there resides what one can well call 'the Spirit of the Nation'.

This position has served Fianna Fáil well; it has been in government from 1932–48, 1951–4, 1957–73, 1977–81, February to November 1982, 1987–94 and 1997 to the present. The success, or the hegemonic[7] role of the party, has been at the core of many debates about the nature of politics in Ireland. This discussion remains important in the contemporary context, to which we now turn.

Politics and social policy in Ireland

Corporatism, consensus and coalition

The contemporary genesis of social partnership goes back to the efforts made by Fianna Fáil in 1987 to establish the basis of a national agreement with the social partners which marked the beginning of a new phase of politics and policymaking in Ireland. Fianna Fáil has always been and continues to be the political party most closely aligned to, and with most extensive experience of, social partnership. Fine Gael has always been more lukewarm in its assessment of it, but ultimately did agree the fourth national social partnership agreement (Partnership 2000) while in government during the 1990s. The Labour Party was historically more sceptical of social partnership, with the then leader, Dick Spring, describing the first agreement as 'the con-trick of the century' where increases in public sector pay were to be delivered at the expense of 20,000 jobs (in Allen, 2000, p. 114). However, by the time they were in government during the 1990s, Labour had come to a more positive assessment of its benefits.

Such a positive view of social partnership is also more broadly held and it is often credited as a significant factor in the economic growth of the 1990s and early 2000s. However, Allen (ibid.) argues that right-wing policies have been initiated through the guise of social partnership. Ongoing tensions have also been identified. Boucher and Collins (2003), in their analysis of Irish social partnership, highlight what they see as two different and conflicting paths being taken at the same time, one corporatist and the other neo-liberal. Ó Cinnéide (1999) highlights how the Irish approach to social partnership has shifted key policymaking away from elected representatives to senior civil servants and representatives of the social partners. Specifically with regard to the community and voluntary sector, Meade (2005, p. 351) argues that their 'objective of securing participation within state policy making structures has been counter-productive. The sector has been afforded a tokenistic form of recognition: a presence shorn of influence, participation without power.' Despite, or maybe because of, these contradictions, the culture and type of corporatism or social partnership that has 'grown-up' in Ireland has acted to promote a consensus type of politics, seeking compromise over confrontation. This, it could also be argued, has had a 'diluting effect' on ideological and political difference on matters of economic and social policy.

Coalition governments have been another defining feature of Irish politics in recent decades (the last overall majority secured by Fianna Fáil was in 1977). Every government since then has been formed by a coalition of parties which has not always been made up of the most likely of 'bed-fellows'. Fine Gael and Labour have formed the basis of six governments since the 1940s. The so-called Rainbow government of 1994–7 is the most recent (with Democratic Left who subsequently merged with the Labour Party), although many would argue that Labour is 'naturally' closer to Fianna Fáil than Fine Gael in ideological terms at least. On the other hand, Fianna Fáil has formed four governments with the Progressive Democrats (a small right-wing liberal party) since the 1980s, which appears to have resulted in a firmer centre-right position for Fianna Fáil than that associated with them in the past.

Contemporary political positions

The cross-class support enjoyed by Fianna Fáil has sustained its electoral success for much of the twentieth century. Its appeal to 'the Spirit of the Nation' remains a notable element of party rhetoric. The broad cross-class support base developed by Fianna Fáil has continued through a distinctly pragmatic approach to ideology; the needs of the nation and 'the national interest' can then be served in a variety of ways, as the now Fianna Fáil TD, Martin Mansergh (2001, cited in Rafter, 2002, p. 75) explains:

> Fianna Fáil has been deemed as a catch-all party, as one that tries to be all things to all people. Opponents wish that Fianna Fáil would plump for a particular constituency, instead of trying to maintain a broad appeal. While committed to equality of opportunity, rights and treatment, and to outcomes that lift the whole population above the persistent poverty level, we have the advantage of being pragmatic as to the means. Certainly, since the 1950s, we can put together a mix of policies, some of which in terms of inspiration come from the Left, and others from the Right. Our critics, needless to say, rarely want to look at the whole picture.

This pragmatism facilitates an ability to appeal to different constituencies as appropriate and it is also useful in the formation and delivery of coalition governance. It also makes characterisations of the overall position of the party notoriously difficult. However, the overall economic and social policy orientation of Fianna Fáil does appear to have moved to the right in the last 20 years or so (e.g. a private and public mix in the provision of housing and healthcare). It could alternatively be argued the Fianna Fáil offers its own distinctive 'Third Way' (see O'Dea, 2000). For example, in a reference to Budget 2006, the former Taoiseach, Bertie Ahern (2006) said:

> At the core of this week's Budget was a practical republicanism which reflects the interests of all sections of society. It showed a balance

between protecting a successful economy and using the fruits of success to help those in need. We reject the tired ideologies of those of the right and left who believe there is a conflict between a strong economy and a strong society.

Since Fianna Fáil has been in government for all but two and a half years since 1987, it can be argued that the contemporary position of welfare and the social services in Ireland has been significantly shaped by its perspective and approach to social policy. However, and notwithstanding the particular success of Fianna Fáil in promoting its mantra as 'the party of government' in recent times, there have been a number of important political developments, over the last 25 years, which have given greater breadth to political and ideological debate in Ireland, and these are now considered.

Traditionally regarded for its conservative and mainly middle-class support, Fine Gael was led, somewhat reluctantly, down a more liberal tolerant path during the 1980s by their then leader Dr Garrett FitzGerald. He was clear that certain social issues, such as contraception, divorce and the position of women had to be considered and policies reformed (FitzGerald in Browne, 1981). These issues were subsequently pursued by the Fine Gael–Labour coalition of 1982–7 and the debates that followed brought church and state into conflict on matters of private morality. There was also a demonstrated commitment to other social policy issues, although the severity of the economic crisis meant that the economy took precedence over many of the aspirations outlined (see Chapter 3 for details). This period of Fine Gael's history, while a nightmare in terms of the economic conditions that prevailed, marked an important effort, by an unlikely political party, to continue the challenge started by others during the 1970s.

Fine Gael has only formed one other government since 1987 when it was the lead party in the Rainbow coalition of the mid-1990s. The party currently defines itself as 'a party of the progressive centre' and explains: 'That means we act in a way that is right for Ireland, regardless of dogma or ideology. Fine Gael bases its policies and its ideas for the future of Ireland on its core beliefs' (Fine Gael, 2008). These are outlined as equality of opportunity, enterprise and reward, security, integrity and hope (ibid.). Taking these core values, Fine Gael, in common with most centrist parties, presents a position that favours an equality of opportunity approach to social provisions, although it notes education and health as 'rights, not privileges' (ibid.). It seeks to promote and support business and enterprise and frequently advocates on matters of consumer interest.

The emergence of the Progressive Democrats (PDs) in the mid-1980s (established as a result of a split from Fianna Fáil in 1985) presented an alternative, with a more definitively liberal and right-wing agenda compared to the existing parties. It advocated radical reform of the economy, including tax reform and privatisation. Its electoral performance varied; the party won 14 seats in its first election in 1987, while 2 TDs were returned in 2007. The party of the Progressive Democrats was wound up in 2008 following its poor general electoral result in 2007.

In their 23-year history, the PDs spent more time in government (always with Fianna Fáil) than in opposition, and the ideology of the PDs has been most evident in government policies in areas of personal taxation, in health policy, and immigration policy. The former party leader, Mary Harney, speaking to the American Bar association in 2000, offered an analysis of the position of Ireland in terms of 'Boston versus Berlin' that is often cited when analysing Irish economic and social policies. In her assessment:

> Political and economic commentators sometimes pose a choice between what they see as the American way and the European way.
>
> They view the American way as being built on the rugged individualism of the original frontiersmen, an economic model that is heavily based on enterprise and incentive, on individual effort and with limited government intervention.
>
> They view the European way as being built on a strong concern for social harmony and social inclusion, with governments being prepared to intervene strongly through the tax and regulatory systems to achieve their desired outcomes.
>
> Both models are, of course, overly simplistic but there is an element of truth in them too. We in Ireland have tended to steer a course between the two but I think it is fair to say that we have sailed closer to the American shore than the European one. (Harney, 2000)

This approach, she argued, has worked for Ireland; considerable economic growth was achieved through reducing taxation, without dismantling the welfare state or abandoning the notion of social inclusion (ibid.). The argument itself was the source of much comment, not least by those who asked if ever or for how long this approach would work.

On the left, and specifically in terms of the Labour Party, the early 1990s looked promising. Their presidential candidate, Mary Robinson, a feminist and key political figure in challenging the conservative approach to matters of social policy, was elected President of Ireland in 1990. Two years later Labour enjoyed the most successful election in its history, returning 33 TDs to the Dáil. While this result was significant and paved the way for a coalition government with Fianna Fáil in 1992, this electoral success was short-lived and ultimately 'Labour enjoyed what with the benefit of hindsight was a false dawn' (O'Halloran, 2005, p. 65). The Labour Party has never been as successful electorally since that period. The breakthrough of other small parties (such as Sinn Féin and the Green Party) with an orientation to the left of the political spectrum has undoubtedly been one reason for this, even though the Labour Party merger with Democratic Left in 1999 (a smaller left-wing party) might have been expected to yield greater electoral dividends. This stands in marked contrast to the considerable resurgence enjoyed by Labour in the UK in recent times, although not too much should be read into this observation, given the markedly different political landscape there. It does, however, raise the issue of the 're-branding' of social democratic parties that has been so popular since the 1990s, which has been an exercise not really engaged in by the Irish Labour Party. In this context, it is noteworthy that the Labour Party is the most explicit of the Irish political parties in outlining its core values and ideology, which are presently laid out as follows: 'The four principles on which Socialism is based are **Freedom, Equality, Community** and **Democracy**' (Labour Party, 2008). In terms of equality, its stated principles identify not only economic rights but also political and social ones. For example, on the issue of third-level education fees, it remains committed to a no-fees policy (as introduced by Labour Minister Niamh Bhreathnach in 1996).

Further to the left, there have been a number of small but radical socialist parties in Ireland over the years (e.g. the Worker's party, Democratic Socialist Party, the Communist Party of Ireland), but none has enjoyed significant electoral success. The Socialist Party currently offers the most radical position on the left in Ireland, arguing for 'public ownership and democratic socialist planning of the key areas of economic activity' (Socialist Party, 2008) and providing stringent critique of capitalist interests. It is a very small party that had its first significant electoral success in 1997 with the election of its only TD, Joe Higgins in Dublin West, although he lost his seat in 2007. He remains an ardent socialist campaigner in Ireland and the party also has a small number of high-profile local councillors.

Sinn Féin dropped its policy of abstention from the Dáil in 1986 (Bew et al., 1989) and its major electoral breakthrough in the Republic came in 2002 with the return of five TDs to the Dáil. However, the optimism held for election 2007 was misplaced as the party lost one seat. Sinn Féin claims a long heritage to the republican and nationalist cause, North and South (the politics of which is beyond the scope of discussion here). The party now presents in a less openly 'socialist vein' than previously and appears to have attuned its position to the political realities that pertain.[8] In terms of social policy, the Sinn Féin General Election Manifesto of 2007 (Sinn Féin, 2007) offered a critique of the policy decisions of previous governments, with a clear left-wing orientation demonstrated by a strong emphasis on the need to improve social services to vindicate social rights, although the economic basis underpinning its manifesto was the subject of some criticism.

The growth in support for the Green Party in recent years marks an important milestone in the evolution of political perspectives in Ireland. The origins of the Irish Green Party date back to the Ecology Party of Ireland, founded in 1981, which changed its name to the Green Alliance in 1983 and then to the Green Party in 1987. Its first national electoral success came in 1989 with the election of the first Green Party TD, Roger Garland in Dublin South (Green Party, 2008). Its most significant electoral breakthrough came in 2002 when six TDs were returned to the Dáil; this number held in the 2007 election. Its policies, which were often met with derision from the mainstream parties in the not so distant past, have enjoyed growing consideration in recent years, probably helped by the prevailing global environmental debates.

The Green Party entered government (with Fianna Fáil and the Progressive Democrats and supported by a number of independent TDs) for the first time in 2007[9] and was given two ministries in environment-related portfolios. In keeping with the Green approach (outlined in Chapter 5), the party demonstrates its central concern with environmental issues in a global context in its stated principles (Green Party, 2008). While it may be difficult to discern its specific position on matters of national social policy, the Green Party has developed a comprehensive range of policy position statements in recent years, which in social policy terms demonstrate attention to the delivery of social services and quality of life issues. Its attention to issues such as taxation and social justice (Green Party, 2007), for example, provides evidence of a left-orientation to its position in Ireland.

Looking briefly beyond the political system, the role of voluntary and community organisations (representing many different groups and issues) in contributing to contemporary Irish political and social policy debate should not be ignored. Given the mixed economy of welfare provision in Ireland, it is not surprising that many such organisations have developed considerable knowledge and expertise in areas of social policy and have been a critical voice in highlighting social problems and the shortcomings of government and social policy. The contribution of the sector in this regard has probably received more attention due to its participation in social partnership since the 1990s, but its role in advocating for particular groups and highlighting important issues long pre-dates its entrance to partnership. The Conference of Religious in Ireland (CORI) is a particularly high-profile example of such an organisation that has, since its establishment in 1981, made an important contribution to social policy discourse in Ireland.

The 2000s have seen the emergence of some new fora for economic and social debate in Ireland. These include TASC (think tank for action on social change), set up in 2001, which demonstrates a strong social justice orientation; and recent publications (in a diverse range of areas, including feminism, public–private partnership, pensions, housing, transport and local government) have made an important contribution to contemporary critical social policy discourse in Ireland. The establishment of the neo-liberal Open Republic Institute provides a right-wing, free market assessment of Irish economic and social policy. Launched in 2007, the Iona Institute is a relatively new organisation influenced by Catholic social teaching and dedicated to the promotion of marriage and religious practice in Ireland. It is too early to assess the impact of such groups, but the emergence of more distinctly oriented groups in recent years is in itself significant. In short, the politics of twenty-first century Ireland may see the expression of a more diverse range of ideological perspectives than previously; the extent to which this will challenge the positions or the dominance of the larger political parties remains to be seen.

Irish social policy and the EU

The overall effect of EU membership on Ireland has been variously analysed over the years.[10] There is no doubting the economic impact of EU membership on Ireland, initially loosening economic dependence on Britain and providing access to European markets, and in terms of the effects of the Common Agricultural Policy and European Monetary Union. In addition, the huge inflow of structural funds has also been significant. Over 17 billion euros has been received by Ireland in structural and cohesion funds since 1973 and a wide range of programmes have been delivered in that time. In this context, EU membership is widely regarded as a key factor in Ireland's most recent phase of economic growth. The focus here, however, is confined to a very brief outline of the impact of EU membership on Irish social policy, where we point to evidence of both direct and diffuse EU influence on its development. However, it should be noted that the guiding EU principle of subsidiarity continues to define the limits of its intervention, particularly in terms of social policy and welfare states. Nevertheless, there are some areas in which EU influence is noteworthy, including gender equality, workers' rights, and financial support for economic and social priorities, including anti-poverty, local partnership and other initiatives.

Direct EU influence on Irish social policy is most plainly identified in terms of directives which, since the early days of membership in the 1970s, had the effect of changing the status quo in specific areas. For example, the unequal position and discriminatory treatment of women in the Irish labour market, which the women's movement in Ireland played a key role in campaigning against at the time (see Chapter 3), began to be tackled. Five EU Directives issued between 1975 and 1986 were of particular significance in challenging gender discrimination in the workplace, specifically on the basis of equal pay for work of equal value; equal treatment for women and men in relation to employment, social security payments and occupational social security schemes; and equal treatment for self-employed men and women (Doyle, 1999). On the principle of equal pay for men and women (arising from Article 119 of the Treaty of Rome), Kennedy (1997, p. 139) has remarked that it 'probably has had more impact on social welfare policy in Ireland than any purely domestic initiative'. Other relevant social policy advances include the introduction of parental leave (as per the EU directive issued in 1996) and the working time directive (first issued in 1993 and subsequently amended). More recent EU developments in the area of equality have also been noted. For example, the Secretary General of the ICTU David Begg (2004, p. 46) cites the improvements gained for job-sharers/part-time workers through the EU, resulting in 'progress that would not otherwise have been made.'

FitzGerald (2004, p. 74) explains the importance of the structural funds to Ireland, facilitating 'a much larger scale of investment than the Irish state could ever have afforded on its own ... Whilst these funds did not directly promote economic growth, they removed many bottlenecks that would otherwise have inhibited growth generated by private and public enterprise.' The structure of the funds has evolved over time but their impact in economic and social policy terms can be seen in the major spending areas. As outlined by Kirby (2008), these include infrastructure (e.g. transport, roads), human resources (e.g. education, training), support for the private sector (e.g. grants to new industries) and income supports (most notably to farmers).

The early EU poverty programmes[11] have been noted for their impact on poverty in raising the profile of the problem, highlighting the structural dimensions of poverty, developing greater understanding of the causes of poverty and introducing the concept of social exclusion. The programmes have also provided funding (through the structural funds) for specific area-based projects (such as the PAUL Partnership in Limerick city). Development of the principles of participation and multi-dimensionality (i.e. to include a range of actions and actors using an area-based plan) in the implementation of such initiatives has also been significant (Frazer, 2007; Langford, 1999). The development of local partnerships[12] since the mid-1980s also demonstrates the capacity of policy innovation to develop new ways of approaching and responding to unemployment and social exclusion. The importance not only of the direct funding but also the effect of the accountability sought by the EU regarding the nature of problems and the specifics of the programmes put in place has been noted. Policy 'learning' and 'experimentation' have been a more diffuse outcome of EU membership, but in social policy terms this has been important, both in terms of 'modernising' and developing new approaches to social issues and social problems, and the learning and expertise garnered by policymakers and actors/interest groups alike.[13] The development of EU common indicators for social inclusion is a noteworthy example in this regard (see Nolan, 2006a).

The introduction of the emerging discourse of social inclusion/exclusion during the 1980s to Ireland was undoubtedly hastened by the EU approach to social policy. Langford's (1999, p. 101) assessment of the anti-poverty programmes and those delivered through the community support frameworks (CSFs) notes that their impact has been seen 'at levels other than funding programmes. The language, concepts and analysis of EU social policy have permeated, vertically and horizontally, through Irish social institutions.' This is illustrated through social policy developments of the 1990s such as the establishment of the National Economic and Social Forum (NESF), the emergence of the National Anti-Poverty Strategy (NAPS) and the broadening of participation in the national social partnership process to include the community and voluntary pillar (ibid.).

The extent to which the developing and broadening 'parameters' of Irish social partnership are the result of diffuse EU influence is, of course, debatable, but it is worth noting the usefulness of social partnership in contributing to the 'social dialogue' ethos of the EU and in meeting the requirements of the more recent OMC. Hardiman (2005, p. 32) cites a senior civil servant on the OMC reporting requirements: 'If social partnership did not exist, it would have to be invented.' However, it is clear from what we know of the politics of Irish social partnership that this point should not be overstated because 'without the core deal on incomes and industrial relations, there would, in effect, be no social partnership' (ibid.). Regardless of one's overall assessment of social partnership, it does appear, as Hardiman (2006, p. 368) observes, that: 'Social partnership has become intricately involved with obligations incurred at EU level.' Where this leaves Irish 'social partnership' in the event of no national pay agreement is as yet unclear.

In overall terms, therefore, there is evidence of EU influence on Irish social policy, directly in the form of legally binding directives and in the significant funding of projects with economic and social gain. The socially funded projects allowed for investment, policy experimentation, policy learning and dialogue, yielding some new approaches to social policy development. Finally, its overall impact on social policy discourse in Ireland, while difficult to quantify, would seem to be substantial (e.g. social inclusion, activation), both in terms of developing the concepts and in the quantification of needs and risks (e.g. social indicators, national action plans, etc.). How these influences play out in terms of overall welfare effort and quality of life in Ireland remains 'one to watch', as EU social policy continues to evolve (in a way that seems to be partially an adjunct to employment objectives) and has, in any event, limited capacity to intervene as outlined earlier. In this context it is worth noting that the traditional (and many would argue the most important) domain of social policy, i.e. redistribution of resources and policy interventions to address inequalities in society, remains the responsibility of the Irish state.

Globalisation and the Irish welfare state

In this final part of the chapter we transfer our focus from the impact of the EU on Irish social policy to the broader field of globalisation and its impact on the Irish welfare state. There is no doubt that, economically speaking, Ireland has changed enormously since the 1990s. While Ireland has had an open or 'globalised' economy since the 1960s, this has intensified since the 1990s, particularly in terms of trade, exports, inward FDI, and by the mid-2000s, also in terms of outflow of FDI (Sweeney, 2003).

Mainstream economic interpretations of the impact of economic globalisation on Ireland have been very positive about its effect on the Irish economy in terms of growth and its overall effect on Irish society. More critical readings display greater concern about the dependent position of Ireland, particularly with regard to FDI. This places constraints on social policy expenditure (O'Hearn, 2003) or means that such expenditure has to be 'competition proofed' before it is justified. O'Hearn (2001, p. 200) describes Ireland's position as an 'intermediating periphery' within the Atlantic economy, 'the point through which US products flowed into European markets and in which profits were accumulated and removed back to North America' (ibid., p. 202). As an intermediating peripheral nation, O'Hearn argues that Ireland has had little ability to control how economic globalisation affects it, other than by adhering to neo-liberal prescriptions for growth. O'Hearn (2003, p. 47) suggests that a key outcome of rising growth is rising inequality; therefore, we are now seeing 'a level of class inequality that was previously unknown in modern Ireland'. Although he argues that the state is operating in the context of 'severe constraints' imposed by dependence on foreign investment, he suggests that these did not quite necessitate the level of public spending restraint and tax reform that occurred during the 1990s. The outcome is that 'Ireland remained, along with the United Kingdom and the United States, one of the most shabby, low-welfare states of the OECD' (ibid., p. 52). When applied to social policy this understanding of the process of globalisation ties in with Sykes's first perspective on the effect of globalisation on social policy (globalisation causes welfare retrenchment through capitalism's dominance) which essentially views the welfare state as something that gets in the way of a country's successful exposure to economic globalisation.

An alternative account of Ireland's global integration that makes greater room for the state is evident in the work of Kirby (2002, 2006) who argues that the state is best understood as a competition state, following Cerny (1997). Kirby pays more attention to the relationship between economic development and social development in Ireland, and his overall argument is that the picture is a complex one of 'economic success and social failure' (Kirby, 2002, p. 5). This is argued despite the fact that 'the Irish state has not been lacking in extensive social action' (ibid., p. 139). Agencies such as the Combat Poverty Agency, the Equality Authority and the Irish Human Rights Commission are, as Kirby (2006, p. 112) points out, 'all devoted to addressing these major problems in Irish society'. This then would seem to heighten the contradictions where, on the one hand, the state appears to act to address social problems but, on the other, there is evidence that points to failures in the social services and the extent of relative poverty in Ireland (ibid.). The reasons for this can be traced back to the role of the state as a competition state. As Kirby (2002, p. 141) remarks:

> The correlation of economic success with social failure, which characterises the Irish case, is no accident. It derives from the central feature of Ireland's industrialisation, namely its high level of dependence on inward investment. This industrial policy has required low levels of taxation on wealth and corporate profits in order to attract foreign investment, resulting in relatively low levels of social spending.

Unlike O'Hearn's conclusion that the state simply weakens under this pressure, the concept of the competition state allows us to see that the state has not declined but instead expands its intervention and regulation in the name of competitiveness and marketisation. As Cerny (1997, p. 263) puts it, 'the challenge of the competition state is said to be one of getting the state to do both more and less at the same time.' The shift from a welfare state to a competition state 'marks a decisive shift in the nature of state regulation: from a regulation that sought to harness market forces for the welfare of society to one that seeks to impose competitive disciplines on society for the good of the market' (Kirby, 2006, p. 118). The implication is that government puts the welfare of the market players ahead of that of its citizens (ibid.). This critical interpretation of the role of the Irish state, suggests that if 'Ireland copes with globalisation by concentrating first and foremost on competing' (Dukelow, 2005, p. 127), then the mediating effects of state intervention should not be assumed to be positive in terms of the overall welfare of its citizens.

Contemporary welfare capitalism in Ireland

The opening section of this chapter noted the significance of the evolving scholarship related to welfare typologies and 'worlds of welfare'. What has been explored here highlights the complexity and challenges associated with such endeavour when 'country specifics' are considered.[14] Much has changed in Ireland and elsewhere since Esping Andersen's original study of welfare regimes, where Ireland failed to rank in a way that was consistent with the 'worlds of welfare' identified. Displaying both liberal and corporatist features, Cochrane (1993, p. 15) has described the Irish welfare state as 'an uneasy mix of corporatism and liberalism'. Ginsburg (2001) notes how Ireland has displayed some of the characteristics of the 'Southern European model' in terms of its economic development, the Catholic influence and the role of the voluntary sector in social service provision, while also demonstrating a liberal orientation, like that of Britain, as demonstrated in the low coverage of social insurance, the use of means-testing and poverty levels. The issues of economic globalisation and the role of the state are also considered by Ginsburg (ibid., p. 183):

> While neither the British nor the Irish welfare regimes are anything like clear examples of the liberal model, they certainly have many liberal features that have been enhanced by their state-sponsored exposure to economic globalization in the 1980s. The style and substance of that state sponsorship has, in many respects, differed substantially, with the Irish government adopting a neo-corporatist managerialist approach and the British government taking a more hard-nosed anti-corporatist, neo-liberal approach.

The role of 'partnership' has become an increasingly important component in the overall assessment of the position of Ireland in recent years; McLaughlin (2001, p. 224), for instance, notes its influence as 'the recurring theme linking the various stages of Irish social welfare development'. Daly and Yeates's (2003, p. 94) comparative assessment of British and Irish social security similarly point to 'the new corporatism' in Ireland out of which 'was born a positive view of the role of social policy, in itself and as part of a strategy in managing economic restructuring'. They suggest that there is evidence of divergence from shared liberal origins and argue that, in contrast with Britain, 'The development trajectory in Irish social protection is one of gradual expansion and inclusion' (ibid., p. 95).

In contrast, O'Connor's (2003, p. 398) analysis of Irish welfare state development posits the view that the Irish welfare state, 'is clearly liberal in orientation', as demonstrated by the nature of the income inequalities even with the targeted nature of much of the social protection expenditure and the reliance on market provision to complement the provisions in place (ibid.). Some similar points of weakness in the Irish welfare state have also been identified by the NESC (2005) (see Chapter 3 for details).

O'Connor's assessment brings together some of the other factors at work in the Irish case. As she explains:

> The lesson from Ireland as a late developing open economy and liberal welfare state within the EU is that convergence may be actively pursued in its economic dimensions while historical patterns are maintained in key aspects of the welfare state narrowly conceived. (O'Connor, p. 400)

For O'Connor, emphasis is placed on the need to examine the different actions and interventions of the state, to give recognition to the possibility that 'its actions may have quite different consequences in the areas of economic and social development', in which 'an innovative and flexible developmental state is compatible with a liberal welfare state' (ibid.). It may also be argued that the fact that economic and social policy objectives have never been on a par, and not always taken in tandem, resulted in an economically driven approach to social policy (see part one of the book).

Examining the version of corporatism that emerged in Ireland since the 1980s, Boucher and Collins (2003) also raise another of the tensions inherent in the Irish model which, they argue, 'involved creating a consensus among Ireland's elite to take the country in two apparently contradictory directions at once: towards European neo-corporatism and toward American neo-liberalism' (ibid., p. 302). On the basis of their analysis,[15] they assert that given the significance of American companies in Ireland, the social partners 'had to domesticate a wave of American led globalization and new levels of European integration. In so doing, they refashioned the liberal corporatist welfare state into a form of Irish neo-liberal corporatism that is symbolically situated somewhere between Boston, Berlin and London' (ibid., p. 313).

No longer in a position to highlight the benefits of exceptional economic growth rates, the Irish government may find it increasingly difficult to justify or mediate the tensions at the core of Ireland's position. Alternatively, there may simply be a re-assertion of the Irish social policy trajectory of 'solidarity without equality' (Ó Riain and O'Connell, 2000, p. 339) and the weak redistributive effort that has long defined its being. The next part of the book considers this possibility in an analysis of Irish social services.

CHAPTER SUMMARY

▸ The study of social policy requires close attention to theories, issues and developments beyond the nation state. Conceptualisations of shared and distinct characteristics of welfare states and their associated outcomes have received considerable attention since the 1990s in particular. The development of welfare theorising has served to highlight commonality and difference at macro-level. It has also raised fundamental questions about 'what' and 'who' counts in terms of 'measuring' welfare efforts and outcomes.

▸ The social policy of the European Union has evolved over time. It has become an important agenda setter for member states, not so much in terms of 'hard law' (although this has been important in terms of employment equality), but through the pursuit and funding of new approaches to social policy issues and problems. The actual effect of EU social policy on the overall welfare effort of member states remains more limited, as the principle of subsidiarity largely maintains member state responsibility in the overall sense. On the other hand, the promotion of policy dialogue and policy learning has generated a particular influence on national social policy discourse and instruments, as evidenced in the case of Ireland.

▸ Globalisation has become a central theme of social policy analysis over the last decade. Its interpretation remains a matter of much debate, particularly in terms of its impact on welfare states and their futures. This debate also applies in Ireland; assessments vary widely between those who see Ireland's position in unambiguously positive economic and social terms and others who highlight the social consequences of embracing (and some would argue prioritising) economic globalisation.

▸ The contemporary position of Irish social policy has been shaped by a diverse range of factors from the historical, political and socio-cultural context of the twentieth century, membership of the EU, delayed and then rapid economic development, the strategy underpinning economic growth and economic globalisation, the nature of Irish politics and ideology and the main tenets and politics of Irish social partnership.

▸ The Irish version of welfare capitalism, while generally now seen to be in neo-corporatist mode (as a result of social partnership), actually simultaneously courts and posits messages of liberalism and neo-corporatism. In a country accustomed to an archetypal mixed welfare economy, which has a long history of balancing needs with self-responsibility, the contradictions identified and heightened by more recent rapid social change are not new. Irish social policy remains subordinate to economic priorities, as evidenced in the tension that exists between economic objectives and social policies.

Discussion points

▸ Take Sykes's four main perspectives on globalisation and social policy development and identify some examples that could be used to illustrate each perspective.

▸ Evaluate the impact of the European Union on the development of recent Irish social policy. If Ireland was not a member of the EU, how do you think policies in areas such as equality and social inclusion would have fared?

▸ Research the core values and policy positions of the main political parties in Ireland. Chart and justify their positions from left to right on the political spectrum.

▸ Analyse the development of Irish social policy with reference to i) history, politics and ideology, ii) economic development, iii) EU membership and iv) globalisation.

Further reading

Coakley, J. and Gallagher, M. (eds) (2005) *Politics in the Republic of Ireland* (fourth edn), London: Routledge in association with PSAI Press.

Cousins, M. (2005) *Explaining the Irish Welfare State: An Historical, Comparative and Political Analysis*, New York: The Edwin Mellen Press.

Hantrais, L. (2007) *Social Policy in the European Union* (third edn), Basingstoke: Palgrave Macmillan.

O'Donnell, R. (ed.) (2000) *Europe: The Irish Experience*, Dublin: Institute of European Affairs.

Vij, R. (ed.) (2007) *Globalization and Welfare: A Critical Reader*, Basingstoke: Palgrave.

Yeates, N. (ed.) (2008) *Understanding Global Social Policy*, Bristol: Policy Press.

Useful websites

European Anti-Poverty Network website: www.eapn.org

European Union website: www.europa.eu.int

Irish Government website: www.irlgov.ie – provides links to the Houses of the Oireachtas, Dáil Debates and Government Departments

Consult Irish political party websites for relevant policy documents, campaigns and election manifestos.

Notes

1 http://ec.europa.eu/employment_social/employment_strategy /develop_en.htm

2 See http://ec.europa.eu/employment_social/elm/summit/en/ backgr/pilars.htm for details.

3 See Guidance Note for Preparing National Strategy Reports on Social Protection and Social Inclusion 2008–2010. Available from: http://ec.europa.eu/employment_social/spsi/docs/social_inclusion /2008/080207_guidance_note_nsrs_cln_en.pdf (and individual member state reports for details).

4 See Begg (2004), Daly (2006), Hemerijck (2003), Jacobsson (2004), O'Connor (2005), Radaelli (2003), Taylor-Gooby (2004) for an exploration of this debate.

5 See http://ec.europa.eu/employment_social/spsi/common_ indicators_en.htm for updates.

6 Note the contribution of thinkers and activists to political and social debate in pre-independent Ireland. See, for example, Lane and Ó Drisceoil (2005).

7 See Allen (1997), Bew et al. (1989).

8 See O'Malley (2006) for a wider analysis of Sinn Féin ideology.

9 See the Agreed Programme for Government 2007–2012 (Government of Ireland, 2007a) for policy detail.

10 See, for example, Cromien (2000), FitzGerald (2000, 2004), Gray (1997), Laffan (2000, 2004), Mangan (1993), McAleese (2000), Ó Cinnéide (1992, 1993), O'Donnell (1992, 2000).

11 See Langford (1999) for details of the programmes in Ireland.

12 See Walsh, Craig and McCafferty (1998) for a detailed account of the emergence and main features of local partnership in Ireland.

13 See Laffan (2000), Larragy (2006), O'Donnell (2000a), O'Hara and Commins (2003), Ryan (2000) for a discussion of related points.

14 See Cousins (1997) and O'Donnell (1999) for a discussion of these issues, particularly as they relate to Ireland.

15 Analysis of the evolution of social partnership and the influence of US firms, their work practices and management approaches.

PART III

ANALYSING SOCIAL POLICY I: SOCIAL SERVICES

This part of the book returns to the Irish context, presenting a critical examination of the most important elements of social policy provision as delivered through the social services. The level and quality of social service arrangements and their outcomes remain the central benchmark of social policy in any given country. It is vital, therefore, to be familiar with the key ideas and structures that shape the social services and the policy objectives that underpin the different elements of the social services. In order to fully appreciate the contemporary debates at issue in welfare terms, each of the areas is examined in its own right and the analysis is anchored in an exploration of relevant social policy concepts. There are four chapters in this part, dealing with social security, health, education and housing policy. Each chapter begins with an overview of the various approaches to provision and draws attention to core concepts of influence in the respective social service areas. From this starting point, the historical development of each of the areas in the Irish context is discussed, before the final sections of the chapters move to consider contemporary debates and challenges that arise.

▸ Chapter 7 provides an account of social security policy; what it is, who benefits and the different ways needs can be met through different types of social security provision. The concepts of social justice and redistribution are used to promote a more analytic understanding of the aims and objectives in this area. The chapter then looks at Irish social security policy; its development, the current system and the policies underpinning its core objectives. The final section addresses key contemporary debates, such as the shift towards activation.

▸ Chapter 8 analyses health policy with regard to the concepts of equity and efficiency and their influence in shaping the provision of healthcare. A historical overview is provided and the main features of the current system are explained. The final section addresses major debates that exist around health inequalities, the relationship between public and private care, and current reform of the health system, including the links between reform, equity and efficiency.

▶ Chapter 9 examines education policy with particular attention given to the concept of equality of opportunity. The historical development of the Irish education system is outlined and the key features of the current system are discussed. The final section considers contemporary debates, including inequalities in access to, and participation in, education.

▶ Chapter 10 reviews housing policy with attention to issues such as access, affordability and residualisation. An historical overview provides a backdrop to understanding the particular shape of the Irish system and its aims and objectives. The current system is explained in terms of the balance between the different tenure types, and the main elements of current housing policy and provision. The final section addresses issues such as housing need and homelessness, segregation, affordability, and the future sustainability of contemporary housing patterns.

CHAPTER 7

SOCIAL SECURITY POLICY

Social security is one of the most central aspects of social policy provision. Virtually everyone is connected in some way to the social security system, whether as a recipient of a particular payment, as a contributor via taxation, or both. It is a central expression of how we live in society and how far duties and rights extend. While social security may be represented as quite a technical system of finance and payments, it is underpinned by competing ideological traditions and values, which have different views of the system and its purpose. These range from the idea that social security is about reducing inequality in society, to the idea that it is about providing a meagre safety net to those who have no other source of income. Social security, therefore, represents both an expression of particular values and a substantial commitment in terms of resources. The values informing the system and the costs associated with it have been at the centre of the debate emerging in the 1970s about welfare states in crisis; a debate which continues in the form of discussions about welfare reform. Questions about the precise role of social security, its affordability and its adaptability to changing economic and social circumstances are among those being raised in this period of change and reform.

CHAPTER OUTLINE

▸ The chapter begins with an examination of social security policy in general, by defining it and looking at the factors that underpin its emergence and development, with particular reference to the concepts of social justice and redistribution. This section also looks at the main types of social security payments and the models or systems of social security associated with different types of payments. Some of the main elements of social security reform evident since the 1980s and 1990s are also discussed.

▸ The second section turns to the specifics of the social security system in Ireland, covering its development and its core characteristics from the nineteenth century up to the 1980s. This section examines the main influences that shaped the system over time which allows us to locate it within the models discussed in the first section.

> ▶ The third section examines the contemporary Irish social security system, focusing on reform since the 1990s and the main issues and challenges it currently faces. This is located within the wider context of debate and reform of social security systems.

SECTION 1: SOCIAL SECURITY – DEFINITIONS, VALUES AND SYSTEMS

Defining social security

Social security is a term that is used interchangeably with terms such as social protection, social welfare and income maintenance. In Ireland, the term most commonly used is social welfare; however, internationally the term social security is more commonly used. Despite the variations in the term, the key word 'social' indicates that the system implicates all of society or that it is a shared system that broadly involves everyone, whether as a contributor or recipient or both (Millar, 2003). The second element of the term, whether called security, protection or welfare, points to a similar meaning: that the system is about ensuring security, protection or well-being in a financial sense in the face of particular needs or contingencies. These arise out of circumstances which impinge on an individual's and family's abilities to generate their own income, such as unemployment, ill health, disability, separation, caring duties, or insufficient income due to low-paid work, etc. Social security is therefore about ensuring income in the event of these circumstances. Income provided through social security means that individuals are not left to rely on the market, families or charity if particular circumstances arise.

Needs and the particular economic and social conditions which give rise to them are not stable over time. For example, levels of unemployment rise and fall, and the consequent demands on the social security system change over time. Patterns of family formation also change, as manifested in trends such as the decline in the model of male breadwinner families and the increasing prevalence of one-parent families, especially lone-mother families (Kilkey and Bradshaw, 1999). Change is also apparent in the fact that the needs and risks recognised by social security systems have grown over time, and as a result, the scope of social security systems has widened greatly since their inception in the late nineteenth century. Correspondingly, government expenditure and contributions in the form of tax have grown substantially. For example, in 1960 the EEC average for social security transfers as a percentage of GDP was 9.7 per cent (OECD, 1992), while by the year 2000 the average for the EU-15 was 16.1 per cent (OECD, 2002). The rise in expenditure has meant that levels of taxation, which fund social security, have also risen. As Sjöberg, (1999, p. 277) shows, 'in 1930, an industrial worker paid on cross-national average 1.6 per cent of his or her gross income in direct income taxes and 2.3 per cent in social insurance contributions. In 1990, these figures had risen to 20.7 per cent and 9.9 per cent respectively.'

Social security, redistribution and social justice

Social security systems are also an expression of particular values or normative concerns. As Millar (2003, p. 7) points out, 'social security provisions involve various forms of redistribution that are an expression of our values as a society and our commitment to social and economic justice.' Money collected through taxation and social insurance contributions gets distributed in the form of unemployment payments, pensions, maternity benefits, etc. Therefore, as Rowlingson and McKay (2005, p. 39) suggest, 'the social security and tax systems can, to some extent, be seen as two sides of the same coin. One collects money in for government, the other distributes it to people.'

While factors such as the political context and levels of national wealth determine the amounts of money involved and who gets what, the foundation of these decisions rests on notions of justice, specifically distributive or social justice. Distributive or social justice are terms that can be used interchangeably, but they basically refer to 'how a society or group should allocate its scarce resources or product among individuals with competing needs or claims' (Roemer, 1996, p. 1 in Lund, 2006, p. 107). Justice in this sense involves rights and duties; it means 'giving people what is due to them, and not giving them what is not due to them' (Swift, 2001, p. 11). In this sense it goes beyond charity to mean 'what it is morally required that we, perhaps collectively through our political and social institutions, do to and for one another. Not just to what it would be morally *good* to do, but what we have a duty to do' (ibid.). The notion of social justice began 'creeping into use from about 1850 on' (ibid. p. 9) and by the early twentieth century, 'theorizing about social justice became a major concern' (Miller, 1999, p. 4 in Lund, 2006, p. 108). This coincided with changes in thinking about people's position in society, so that it was no longer seen as something rigidly fixed, either by nature or by God, but something which could be affected by government intervention. With this change in thinking, ideas such as social justice became meaningful.

Debates about justice drew on many perspectives and groups, including the Fabians and the New Liberals, all of which had particular views on what was just or fair in terms of government intervention in the areas of taxation and the development of social security. However, it was not the idea of social justice alone that gave rise to social security systems. Debates about social justice coincided with the growth of industrialisation and national wealth, and the growth of democracy and rights as discussed in Chapter 4.

Justice, wealth and work came together in the notion of giving pensioners their due in return for duties fulfilled during their working years, as illustrated in points made by Lloyd George in debates about the introduction of old age pensions in 1908 in the UK and Ireland:

> A workman who has contributed health and strength, vigour and skill, to the creation of the wealth by which taxation is borne has made his contribution already to the fund which is to give him a pension when he is no longer fit to create that wealth. (Lloyd George, 1908/2000, col. 565)

Lloyd George also anticipated the expansion of social security and the duties of the state over the twentieth century during the same debate when he argued that:

> These problems of the sick, of the infirm, of the men who cannot find means of earning a livelihood, though they seek it as if they were seeking for alms, who are out of work through no fault of their own, and who cannot even guess the reason why, are problems with which it is the business of the State to deal; they are problems which the State has neglected too long (ibid., col. 585).

Forty years later, in 1948, access to social security was considered a fundamental human right, as proclaimed in the 1948 Universal Declaration of Human Rights (Articles 22 and 25) (Dixon, 1999).

Three types of social security

As Sjöberg (1999, p. 275) notes, 'social policy programmes will differ in their redistributive outcomes depending on how the link between risks, contributions and benefits is designed.' Broadly speaking, there are three different ways in which social security programmes are designed. These are insurance-based programmes, assistance-based programmes and universal programmes. Most welfare states have a mix of programmes; however, one type usually tends to be more dominant, depending on factors such as levels of economic development, the relative power of different actors, such as trade unions and employers, and attitudes towards social security. The type of social security system a country has is therefore a good indicator or expression of its overall welfare state regime. Each design or type of programme is examined here in turn and brief reference is made to the welfare regime it is most closely associated with.

Social insurance

Insurance-based programmes are also known as contributory programmes. These involve specific contributions, usually made by workers, employers and the state. These contributions form an insurance fund which is used to cover risks such as unemployment, sickness and retirement. Payments made into the fund are usually income-related. That is, the higher one's salary, the greater the contribution made, and payments made from the fund may be either pay-related, so that those earning more receive more; or they may be made at a flat rate, whereby every recipient receives the same regardless of their prior income. Unemployment and sickness payments made from the fund are usually limited by time. This kind of social security involves a limited sense of redistribution, where only those workers deemed eligible to contribute can benefit from the scheme. The type of redistribution which occurs is known as **horizontal redistribution**, which means a redistribution of income from those earning a regular income to those who are not. This can occur during periods of

> **Horizontal redistribution** occurs across similar income groups, such as during different lifecycle stages, when resources are distributed from working people to retired workers through pensions.

unemployment, or across the life cycle, from people of working age to those who are retired. Social insurance is also built upon the values of collective responsibility and solidarity. Responsibility is collective in the sense that contributions are drawn from three strands: workers, employers and the state. Solidarity is also based on these three strands, alongside the notion of a shared response to social risks.

Since the inception of insurance-based programmes there has been a gradual widening of participation over time. Initially, only a handful of occupations were included, whereas now virtually all occupations, as well as part-time workers and the self-employed are included. The widening process has also meant increasing inclusion for women. Married women, for example, were typically excluded in earlier programmes, while the inclusion of part-time workers has had the greatest impact on women, as they make up the majority of part-time workers. However, social insurance continues to offer little security to those who have interrupted histories of employment, and often it is women who fall into this category. In addition, insurance does not offer protection for those who may never enter the labour market, as the opportunity to make contributions does not arise in this case. Insurance-based payments are, therefore, often referred to as earned rights, based on attachment to the labour market.

The idea of insurance and the notion that the state could calculate risks and thus devise insurance systems to cover those risks were concepts that gained ground during the nineteenth century. As Dixon (1999, p. 53) notes:

The word 'insurance' conjured up images of security, respectability and virtuous providence. In the language of social security, insurance concepts replaced Poor Law concepts: 'needs' became 'contingencies', 'deserving beneficiaries' became 'the insured' and 'poor taxes' became 'contributions'.

As noted in Chapter 4, over the course of the 1880s, Germany became the first country to introduce social security under Bismarck. Following Germany's example, other European countries also introduced social insurance programmes. These programmes came about in a relatively short time span across Europe, from the 1890s to the first decade of the twentieth century. Social insurance combined a sense of justice with increased technical ability. For example, during debates on the introduction of national insurance covering sickness and unemployment in the UK and Ireland in 1911, Churchill referred to the idea of compulsory national insurance as a 'scientific expression to a powerful impulse of just and humane endeavour' (Churchill, 1911/2000, col. 503). He went on to say that:

> There is exhilaration in the study of insurance questions because there is a sense of elaborating new and increased powers which have been devoted to the service of mankind. It is not only a question of collective strength of the nation to render effective the thrift and the exertions of the individual, but we bring in the magic of averages to the aid of the millions (ibid., col. 509).

'The magic of averages to the aid of the millions' became a somewhat faded concept during times when demands on social insurance grew, and, as we will see later in the chapter, there has been much debate in recent years on the future of social insurance systems. Countries where insurance-based programmes are dominant belong to the conservative/corporatist welfare regime, of which Germany is still one of the main members. Other countries in which this model is influential include France, Austria and the Netherlands.

Social assistance

The second design template for social security involves assistance-based payments. These are also known as non-contributory payments. Here eligibility is decided on the basis of need, which is usually organised through categories. For example, some of the early categories of need recognised for the purposes of social assistance included old age, blindness, widowhood and being orphaned. Under social assistance systems need is measured through means-testing. Thus, having means, including income and assets below a certain threshold, qualifies one for payment. This method is intended to ensure that resources go to those most in need and this is referred to as a selective or targeted approach to social security. Payments are funded through general taxation, and here the principle of **vertical redistribution** applies: income

> **Vertical redistribution** refers to redistribution up and down the income scale, usually, but not always, from higher income groups to lower income groups.

gets redistributed between different income groups, generally from higher income groups to lower income groups.

As with insurance-based programmes, the needs recognised under assistance-based programmes have also grown over time, from needs associated with old age and widowhood, to needs associated with caring, disability, etc. Assistance payments tend not to be as generous as insurance-based payments and they have more of a direct lineage with the Poor Law, which is marked by their **selective** focus on need and means-testing. As

> **Selectivism** is an approach which targets payments to particular groups, usually based on need and measured by means-testing.

Marshall (1965, in Dixon, 1999, p. 43) notes, '"need" per se does not generate a "right" to social security; it merely justifies "public charity".' However, these types of payments have a stronger redistributive effect than insurance-based payments, exhibiting what Korpi (1992, p. 19) refers to as a 'steep redistributive gradient'. Yet this targeted approach may also have a stigmatising effect, unlike payments based on the principle of rights.

Countries that rely predominantly on assistance-based payments in their social security systems belong to the liberal welfare regime. Here assistance-payments are based on the minimum necessary to alleviate poverty, and social insurance-based programmes tend not to be pay-related. In Europe, the UK has become the closest proponent of this model of welfare in more recent times.

Universal payments

In the case of universal benefit payments or comprehensive payments, as Ploug and Kvist (1996) note, the distinction between assistance and insurance is blurred. Payments are funded both from general taxation and insurance and they are made available to everyone. A basic minimum is guaranteed for everyone, with supplementary payments to workers to help preserve living standards. As a result everybody is 'guaranteed a certain income irrespective of their attachment to the labour market, just as people with attachment to the labour market are guaranteed an above minimum income in the event of certain social contingencies' (ibid., p. 55).

This system places a heavier emphasis on equality and redistribution than the two previous models, and both horizontal and vertical redistribution take place. In contrast to the liberal model, payments aim to prevent poverty rather than alleviate it. In addition, 'social security is seen primarily as an individual social right, with entitlement exclusively dependent on citizenship' (ibid., p. 56). This means, as Titmuss (1965/1987) noted, that the principle of **universalism** overcomes the discriminatory or stigmatising effects associated with assistance-based services in particular. At the same time a high value is placed on participation in the labour market to help generate the resources to fund such a system. Thus, there is a long tradition of activation measures in countries with universal or comprehensive systems to assist with maintaining a high level of labour market participation, which we will discuss further below. Countries that have traditionally based their social security systems on comprehensive or universal payments include the Nordic welfare states, most notably Sweden, Denmark and Finland.

> **Universalism** is an approach which provides social policy programmes and payments to all, regardless of means.

Table 7.1 **Summary of the key characteristics of the main social security systems**

Social security type	Qualifying criteria	Source of funding
Insurance-based	Available to those who have made the necessary insurance contributions	Social insurance fund
Assistance-based	Available to those in need, based on means-testing	General taxation
Universal	Available to all those in need of the payment	General taxation and social insurance

Fiscal welfare and occupational welfare

Besides these forms of social security, there are two other aspects of social security to be considered; namely, fiscal welfare and occupational welfare. These were first explored by Richard Titmuss, who developed the idea of the social division of welfare, to include social welfare – encompassing the three types of social security discussed above – fiscal welfare and occupational welfare (Titmuss, 1956/1987).

Fiscal welfare refers to exemptions, deductions and credits under income tax, where 'the tax saving that accrues to the individual is, in effect, a transfer payment' (ibid., p. 48). Examples include tax relief on private pension contributions and private health insurance. Fiscal welfare is becoming increasingly popular, with governments tending to use the tax system rather than cash benefits to transfer income . Income transferred in this way has the potential to be regressive, as access to tax benefits may, in certain cases, disproportionately benefit those who earn higher incomes, particularly where they are provided at the marginal rate of income tax.

Occupational welfare or the 'social policy of the firm' as Martin Rein (1982) calls it, refers to benefits, in cash or in kind, provided by employers. This may include income maintenance provisions such as pensions, redundancy payments and sickness benefits, and may also extend to items such as health insurance and education and training grants. Some of these are payments that companies are obliged to pay, referred to as statutory payments, and the state plays a role in regulating the schemes. In other cases payments and benefits are voluntarily made, to attract and reward the workforce. As noted by Titmuss, they duplicate and overlap with social and fiscal welfare and may 'function as concealed multipliers of occupational success' (Titmuss, 1956/1987, p. 51). In this sense they may serve to redistribute resources regressively, as greater benefits accrue to those who are better off. Occupational welfare can also be very unevenly spread across companies, and not only do higher earners tend to benefit more, there is also a difference between male and female workers, with men tending to benefit more from occupational schemes (Farnsworth, 2004). However, occupational welfare is increasingly encouraged by governments because as Farnsworth notes, 'contemporary political and economic pressures have reduced the room for governments to borrow and raise additional revenue from higher personal and corporate taxes' (ibid., p. 437).

Where does the Irish system fit?

The Irish social security system has its roots in the liberal model of welfare. The main reason for this was the colonial link with Britain. The main elements of the emerging liberal social security system in Britain spanning the late nineteenth and early twentieth century were also introduced in Ireland. This inheritance had a strong influence on subsequent developments in the Irish social security system which tended towards assistance-based means-tested payments over comprehensive social insurance. Developments within welfare regime theory, as discussed in Chapter 6, have pointed to other influences besides liberalism on the Irish welfare state, such as Catholic social teaching and agrarianism, which mean that Irish welfare development also shared similarities with southern European states. These influences are discussed in more detail in section two, where it can be seen that their effect coalesced with the underlying liberal ethos of the system. More recently, debate has centred on the question of whether the system has diverged from its liberal roots since the 1990s, given the influence of economic growth and social partnership and the expansion of insurance-based and universal elements of the system. This issue is considered in more detail in section three where it is suggested that the significance of a liberal ethos still cannot be discounted.

Recent reform of social security systems

As discussed in Chapter 4, the 1950s to the 1970s was known as the golden age of welfare, when welfare states grew significantly and social security systems in particular expanded. Their scope was widened and **replacement ratios** rose so that the amount of income from earnings replaced by social security grew (Glyn, 2006). However, the 1980s was a decade of crisis that provoked much debate about social security. A combination of economic recession and rising unemployment meant that social security systems found that their main sources of revenue, that is, tax and insurance contributions, were declining at the same time as the demands on them were increasing. This contributed to the notion of a fiscal crisis confronting welfare states. At the same time, welfare states and social security systems, in particular, were being attacked in more ideological terms. Right-wing ideology was on the ascendant and it had very different views of justice and responsibility, prioritising the individual over the social. This had implications for taxation, which from a right-wing perspective on social justice was often seen as unjust, and from a right-wing perspective on the economy was seen to stifle economic activity. Social rights were also criticised for placing too much emphasis on rights and not enough on responsibility. Commentators such as Charles Murray and Laurence Mead focused attention on what were considered the perverse effects of social security, especially on character (Deacon, 2002). Instead of providing security, payments were considered to make people **dependent** and reluctant to work. Right-wing policy solutions focused on a means-tested approach to social security combined with workfare.

> **Replacement ratio** is the ratio of income received through welfare payments compared to the income received in work. Social security systems often aim to set welfare payments at a particular replacement ratio.

> **Welfare dependency** is a (contested) term which emerged from the New Right critique of social security. It suggests that welfare recipients are not only financially dependent on welfare but psychologically dependent, losing their sense of self-reliance and motivation to work.

Moving to the 1990s and into the twenty-first century, international trends in social security did not quite fulfil the predictions made in the previous decade about the demise of welfare states and social security. Social security systems were not obliterated by the right-wing attack. As Gilbert and Van Voorhis (2003, p. 1) note:

Today we know that rumours about the impending divestiture of the welfare state circulating in the mid 1980s were greatly exaggerated. Although there was much concern about the fiscal capacity of the welfare state and its moral legitimacy, the frequently cited 'crisis' never erupted into a full-blown emergency.

However, a sense of crisis has been replaced by debates about restructuring. The extent of change and its causes are still subject to varying interpretations; some see expansion, some survival, some retrenchment (Adelantado and Caderón, 2006). Regardless of the varying interpretations, key elements of the debate include post-industrialisation and economic globalisation as discussed in Chapter 6. These have both been significant factors shaping economies in the wake of the crisis of the 1970s and 1980s. However, both of these economic trends have been unfolding in an environment in which right-wing or neo-liberal thinking still holds considerable influence. This, as noted by Euzéby (2002, p. 40), can have serious consequences for social security and how it operates:

> The mad race for market share and the competition to attract and retain foreign investment have meant that public authorities in many countries are tempted to resort to measures involving reducing the level or duration of payment of certain social security benefits so as to reduce the fiscal and social burden of enterprises on their territory.

This is not just a matter of cutting the financial costs of social security; neo-liberal globalisation has also undermined the value of commitment to social justice and redistribution. As Deacon (2002a, p. 26) notes, 'the case for equity and for universalism in social provision has been seriously eroded within the global discourse about social policy in the past ten years.' Thus, ideas about social justice and collective responsibility, which underpinned the introduction of social security schemes in the late nineteenth and early twentieth century, have been replaced by themes such as individual responsibility, employability and opportunity. These echo what Zimmerman (2006, p. 35) refers to as the 'semantic field' of post-industrialism, 'determined by the concepts of flexibility, self-sufficiency, adaptability, competencies, individual responsibility, project-based working, and re-skilling'.

Socio-demographic trends are also having an impact on social security and its future. One of these is the ageing of populations, particularly in OECD countries, where 'the proportion of the population aged 65 and over is expected to increase throughout the next three decades, from the current 15 to 17 per cent to around 25 per cent in most countries' (Sarfarti and Bonoli, 2002, p. 3). If the share of older people rises in contrast to the share of those of working age, then the affordability of pensions becomes an issue. Another socio-demographic trend impacting on social security systems is changing household structures, as families move from a model of a male breadwinner to a dual earner model, with increasing female labour force participation rates. Greater participation in the labour force means that women move from having derived rights to claiming social insurance payments in their own right. However, this has also raised issues such as the need for greater recognition of caring within social security systems and an examination of ways in which the work/life balance can be enhanced.

These trends have led to the re-structuring of social security systems in a number of ways, two of which are particularly significant, namely cost containment and connecting welfare to work. With regard to cost containment, payments related to old age, unemployment, sickness, disability and lone parenthood have been subjected to measures such as tightening of eligibility criteria or conditions attached to payments, amounting to a process Kersbergen (2000) calls 'creeping disentitlement', which has the effect of dampening demand and therefore keeping costs under control. Some of the conditions attached to payments such as undertaking training while receiving an unemployment payment are part of the broader efforts to connect welfare with work. The focus of social security therefore shifts from literally being about income maintenance to employment promotion and this has become a major feature of the direction in which social security systems are moving. This is variously referred to as activation, insertion or workfare and such policies are increasingly targeted at people of **'working age'**. This means that the policy focus has extended to people for whom it was previously legitimate not to participate in the labour market. Therefore, as Bonoli and Sarfarti (2002, pp. 466–7) note, policy measures 'are being expanded to encompass social groups for whom in the past it was more acceptable not to work, such as mothers, older people, single mothers and persons

> **Working age** is a term increasingly used in connection with social security systems, to encompass all people, not just the unemployed, in relation to measures that seek to progress people from welfare to work.

with disabilities'. In this way social security systems attempt to meet the challenges of changing socio-demographic patterns by channelling them through the same route in which the needs of the more traditionally unemployed are being met. At the same time, words such as the unemployed and unemployment are disappearing from the lexicon of social security systems, to be replaced by 'employability', 'job-seeking' and the needs of 'people of working age'.

Aside from the fact that concepts such 'working age' are contested (Levitas, 2001), the speed and the extent to which these policy changes are taking place varies (Gilbert and Van Voorhis, 2003). One of the most influential factors in the process of reform is the type of social security system in existence in a particular country. Continental social security systems, for example, have found it difficult to adapt quickly, since 'being founded on waged work, they are even more vulnerable to the economic and demographic changes of recent decades because they are badly affected by the ageing of the population, growing unemployment, the end of the prospect of full employment and the introduction of a new norm: flexibility' (Zimmermann, 2006, p. 34–5). Liberal welfare states, which already place a strong emphasis on targeting and means-tested provision may find adaptation and re-structuring easier to cope with; however, the price to pay is higher levels of poverty.

SECTION 2: THE DEVELOPMENT OF SOCIAL SECURITY IN IRELAND

Pre-independence

As indicated in Chapter 1, Ireland's early welfare infrastructure was dominated by the Poor Law, with subsequent developments involving provision for unemployment and old age originating in Britain. Thus, prior to gaining independence Ireland had a basic structure of Workmen's Compensation (1897), Old Age Pensions (1908) and National Insurance covering sickness and unemployment (1911) in place. This reflected a mix of assistance-based programmes (represented by Old Age Pensions) and insurance-based programmes (represented by Workmen's Compensation and National Insurance). Various amendments and extensions to these programmes occurred up to 1921, including the introduction of a Blind Pension for people over 50, and the inclusion of dependants' allowances for wives and children in national insurance payments. Despite these changes, the overall thrust of the social security system remained one of poverty alleviation through minimal payment levels. In the Irish context this minimalism was reinforced by the resistance of various Irish actors, including the Catholic Church and the Irish Party, to the introduction of national insurance in Ireland. An amended version of national insurance was implemented in Ireland which included sickness benefit, but not medical benefit. This had important consequences for the future development of the Irish social security system which set it apart from the way in which social security developed in other European countries. As noted by McCashin (2004, pp. 23–4), 'it separated the systems of social insurance and health care at an early point in their development. In the future, many countries would build on medical benefit arrangements to develop equal access to health care through social insurance for all of the population.' This was not to be in the Irish case, the consequences of which are explored further in Chapter 8.

Another important point to note in terms of the development of the system is that with the exception of the Old Age Pension, which treated men and women equally, there was greater coverage of men than women in the fledgling social security system. This was evident, for example, through the inclusion of the more male-dominated occupations in the initial national insurance design, such as building, engineering, iron founding and saw milling, and the exclusion of private domestic service, which was typically female employment. The introduction of dependants' allowances for wives and children, but not for husbands, also set the system on the path of a male breadwinner model.

1920s–1940s

After independence, some of the key factors contributing to the development of social security, such as industrialisation, wealth and a commitment to social justice, were in scarce supply. The Irish social security system shared similar developments with the rest of Europe, such as dismantling Poor Law structures, dealing with rising unemployment, developing children's allowances and more comprehensive insurance systems. Yet the Irish system continued to be less comprehensive and at the low end of the scale in terms of expenditure.

In addition to the colonial legacy, indigenous factors reinforced the largely liberal nature of developments post-independence. These factors included a lack of resources, as poor economic development inhibited the development of extensive or generous social security programmes. Lack of industrial development also meant that agriculture remained the backbone of economic activity for much of the twentieth century. For this reason, Fahey (2002) and Carey (2005) argue that agrarianism, that is, the influence of agricultural interests, is a significant factor in the path of development taken by the Irish welfare state and the social security system in particular. The predominance of small family farms, which provided relatively secure subsistence-based lifestyles, bolstered arguments that Ireland did not need extensive social insurance-based programmes which were designed to meet the needs of industrial workers. In addition, it was argued that social insurance contributions were unaffordable for many farmers and other agricultural workers. Social assistance programmes funded from general taxation were felt to be more appropriate in the Irish context. This preference for a liberal-oriented welfare state also sat comfortably with the Catholic Church.

The Church promoted charity over state payments in response to need, and as noted in the previous section, social assistance is closer in character to charity than social insurance. Overall, however, as Fahey and McLaughlin (1999, p. 125) note, the Church held 'a suspicion of state schemes of income distribution and other social services' and this stance mirrored liberalism's preference for a minimal state. Yet, in the domain of social welfare, Cousins (2003, p. 196) likens the Church to 'the dog which does not bark'. It did not directly provide or intervene in the area of social welfare, and Catholic charities such as the Society of Saint Vincent de Paul traditionally saw their role as primarily one of 'the "moral uplifting" of the poor' (ibid., p. 197) rather than the provision of relief.

One final factor militating against expansive developments in social welfare was the prevailing attitude among a number of key government ministers and civil servants over the early decades of the post-independence era. This was particularly the case with J. J. McElligott, the Secretary of the Department of Finance between 1927 and 1953, described by Ó Gráda (1997, p. 227) as the 'Dr No' of Irish economic policy. Influenced by fiscal liberalism, he made every effort to keep state expenditure to a minimum and to foster a character of self-reliance. Thus, poverty alleviation at minimal levels was a recurring theme. This dovetailed with a reluctance to redistribute resources through taxation. Taxation was considered a necessary social evil, with governments preferring, in the words of T. K. Whitaker, to allow 'money to fructify in the pockets of farmers, businessmen and individuals' (Whitaker, 1983, p. 81 in Coleman and Considine, 2006, p. 4). Thus, taxation rates were kept low and during the 1920s approximately 60,000 people paid tax (ibid.).

Turning to actual developments during the first decades of independence, reform began with the partial dismantling of the Poor Law in the 1920s. Counties replaced Poor Law unions as the administrative units for poor relief, and the system came under the remit of the Department of Local Government and Public Health. Workhouses were either closed or converted to county homes. These became 'safety net' institutions for destitute groups for whom there was no social security provision or who needed care beyond what was available in families or through charities. As listed by Garvin (1944, p. 168), such groups included the homeless who were 'infirm or of advanced age ... certain mentally deficient classes of the more harmless types ... and unmarried mothers'.

In terms of cash payments, developments as discussed in Chapter 2 included the replacement of Outdoor Relief with Home Assistance in 1923, the introduction of Unemployment Assistance in 1933, the introduction of Widows and Orphans Pensions in 1935, and the introduction of Children's Allowances in 1944. The introduction of Children's Allowances is particularly significant because it was the first universal payment introduced in Ireland, made available to everyone who had three or more children, funded from general taxation and not tied to insurance or assistance-based principles, as was the case with children's allowances in many other European countries (Kaim-Caudle, 1967).

Late 1940s and the 1950s

The late 1940s and early 1950s were an important time in the development of social security. Many European countries were entering into a period of expansion and improvement of their social security schemes, in the aftermath of World War II. Ireland also participated in this general trend. The initial stimulant for reform in Ireland was the publication of the Beveridge report in Britain in 1942 (as discussed in Chapter 4). The report, as Ó Cinnéide suggests, 'created a stir in Ireland' (2000, p. 21) and questions were raised as to whether Ireland could also develop its social security system along the lines proposed by Beveridge for Britain. This was not countenanced by the government at the time, which criticised Beveridge-style proposals for being too costly and unsuitable to Irish conditions. Yet, as Cousins (2003, p. 131) points out, Lemass did concede that 'the report had created a high conception of social security standards and had made Irish provisions appear inadequate, almost parsimonious.'

Outside of government circles, Dr John Dignan, the Bishop of Clonfert produced a pamphlet, published in 1945, known as the *Dignan Plan*, which proposed a system of comprehensive insurance, influenced not only by the Beveridge plan but also by developments in other continental European welfare states. If implemented this would have represented a major departure from the existing system, and it also represented thinking which deviated from the Catholic Church's position on social security. While Dignan proposed a more comprehensive form of social insurance, including health insurance, similar to the Beveridge plan, he also proposed that it include both pay-related contributions and benefits, as were developing in continental Europe. Again, this was rejected by the government which was not happy with the lack of costing in the proposals, and, in a rare case of role reversal, the government also criticised the cleric's proposals for not leaving enough room for charity (Kaim-Caudle, 1967).

The starting point for actual reform was administrative reorganisation, with the creation of a separate Department of Social Welfare in 1947. This department took over social welfare programmes previously scattered between the Departments of Local Government and Public Health, Finance, and Industry and Commerce. One of the first actions of the department was to produce a White Paper outlining proposals to combine the existing insurance-based payments and to develop them into a more comprehensive social insurance system. The White Paper was published in 1949 under William Norton, the Minister for Social Welfare and leader of the Labour party in the inter-party government of the time. While not embracing Dignan's proposals for pay-related payments, Norton's proposals were still considered quite radical. They were opposed by the more traditional attitude to social services held by the Fine Gael Minister for Finance in the same government, who thought that 'social services were not something to be proud of – they should be used like medicine, and kept in a locker until they were required to treat disease or illness' (McCullagh, 1998, p. 184 in Ó Cinnéide, 2000, p. 25). Norton's proposals included the creation of one social insurance scheme incorporating the existing insurance schemes, which would be open to all employees except self-employed persons, and contributions and benefits would be at a flat rate for the majority. New insurance payments, namely, contributory retirement pensions at 65 for men and 60 for women, and a death benefit payable on the death of a contributor or a member of his family, were also proposed. The proposal contained many aspects of the Beveridge report, such as a flat rate system and the assumption of a male breadwinner. The flat rate system was preferred because it would leave room for the habits of saving and thrift, would be less costly to administer and would reduce the moral dangers associated with malingering (Kaim-Caudle, 1967). Despite some negative reaction to Norton's White Paper on the grounds of cost and suspicion about the expansion of state responsibility, legislation was drafted. However, this was not enacted due to the fall of the inter-party government in 1951.

The new Fianna Fáil government implemented a restricted version of the proposals in the Social Welfare Act of 1952, an approach described by Bew and Patterson (1982, p. 63 in Cousins, 2003, p. 173) as 'mild social reform with financial orthodoxy'. The legislation retained the flat rate system, but made it less comprehensive by imposing an income ceiling and excluding particular categories of workers altogether. Benefits were also less comprehensive as the legislation did not provide for a contributory pension and a death grant. However, it did include a maternity allowance, payable for twelve weeks and improvements to sickness and disability benefit.

This Act, as Carey (2005, p. 305) notes, had 'long-term consequences for the redistributive character of the Irish welfare state'. The redistributive potential of the Act was curbed by the exclusion of higher earners, by the exclusion of the self-employed, including farmers, and by the creation of a modified system for public servants. Overall, therefore, despite the advances made in relation to social insurance, the system was still heavily based on social assistance. The system also continued to discriminate on the basis of gender, particularly in the case of married women. Unless married women were employed, and most were not, they did not qualify for benefits.

However, married women who were employed and subsequently claimed a benefit were paid at a lower rate than unemployed married men. The difference lay in assumptions about dependency in marriage. Unemployed married women received less because they were assumed to be dependent on their husbands. In the case of married unemployed men this assumption meant that they automatically received a dependant allowance for their wives, regardless of whether their wives were employed or independently receiving benefit (Cousins, 2005a).

Subsequent to these reforms, the introduction of the Disabled Persons Maintenance Allowance in 1954, administered by the Department of Health, was another notable development in the 1950s. This represented a widening of the system by recognising the financial needs associated with having a disability. This was a means-tested payment and it took disabled persons who did not qualify for Unemployment Benefit or Assistance out of the Home Assistance net.

1960s and 1970s

Following the economic and social changes of the 1960s and 1970s, the social welfare system also changed and grew, but largely in an incremental rather than a systematic way. Several new schemes, as well as modifications to existing ones, were introduced. Some were insurance-based, others were assistance-based. Some involved the implementation of earlier proposals, others were in response to newly recognised needs and gaps in the system which gained greater visibility as a result of the changing social and cultural environment, as profiled in Chapters 2 and 3.

The 1960s saw the implementation of some of the measures proposed in the previous decade related to social insurance. These included the introduction of a contributory Old Age Pension in 1961. This became available to people on the basis of fulfilling certain social insurance contribution requirements, as an alternative to the means-tested non-contributory pension. In addition, a contributory Retirement Pension was introduced in 1970, with retirement set at 65. Between 1973 and 1977 the pension age for the old age pension was reduced from 70 to 66. The age discrepancy remains between the different pensions so that 'Ireland now has a pension with a retirement condition at age 65 and a pension without a retirement condition at age 66' (Cousins, 2005a, p. 219). Workmen's Compensation was replaced by an Occupational Injuries scheme in 1967; this provided a social insurance-based payment to workers for work-related injuries and illnesses. On the social assistance front, Smallholders Assistance was introduced in 1966 which was a means-tested payment made to small farmers, who had been excluded from the Social Welfare Act in 1952.

The 1960s are also significant for the first recognition of informal caring in the social security system. This came about with the introduction in 1968 of a Prescribed Relative Allowance. This was paid as an increase in pension payments to pensioners who required full-time care in their homes, to be provided by a 'prescribed female relative', such as a daughter, who lived with the pensioner. However, the scheme remained very restrictive in terms of the female relatives who qualified and the payment was made to the old age pensioner not the carer. In addition, the carer was not allowed to participate in paid employment. The payment also reflected the assumption that caring was a female role.

The 1970s brought much more activity, as the benefits under social insurance expanded, and a range of new assistance-based payments were also introduced. Social insurance benefits were extended in the early 1970s by the introduction of Invalidity Pensions (which were made payable to individuals who had long-term illness and who had been claiming disability benefit), Death Grants and payments to deserted wives. Pay-related benefits were introduced for unemployment and disability payments in 1974. New assistance-based payments were introduced which were targeted at women in particular. These included Deserted Wives Allowance (1970), Unmarried Mothers Allowance (1973), Prisoners' Wives Allowance (1974) and Single Women Aged 58 to 68 Allowance (1974). These payments represented a response to the lack of provision for women in the absence of a male breadwinner. Heretofore, the only payment available to these categories of women was Home Assistance. This was also replaced by Supplementary Welfare Allowance in 1977, which made a minimum payment a legal right.

While the changes during the 1960s and 1970s increased the scope of the social security system, they were still problematic. Cook (1986, p. 78) argues that 'the highly categorical system of social insurance became even more highly categorised' and that the system:

> … became extremely complex. The identification of the appropriate benefit and separate claims procedures often made the establishment of welfare rights difficult, particularly when certain schemes were stigmatising to claimants, and the visibility and cause of claimant status were reinforced by the categorical nature of the system.

This problem applied to women in particular, who were predominantly left to rely on the highly categorical social assistance-based payments. Their inclusion in the system therefore was on the basis of being 'a separate but unequal category within the system both as women and as mothers' (Conroy-Jackson, 1993, p. 91). The Single Women Aged 58 to 68 Allowance illustrated the fragmented categorical nature of the system and the unequal position of women. It was created to meet the needs of women who worked informally as family carers and whose relative may have availed of the Prescribed Relative Allowance. However, if this person died the carer had no means of support other than Home Assistance until they reached the age of the non-contributory Old Age Pension, hence the very particular category of Single Women Aged 58 to 68 Allowance.

However, by the end the 1970s, the social insurance element of the system was also gradually widening and becoming more comprehensive. In 1974 social insurance was extended to all full-time employees as the income ceiling was abolished and by 1979 the system became fully pay-related. At this stage, as Cousins (2000, p. 33) notes, 'in many ways, the Irish system was moving away from the classic Beveridgean flat rate approach towards a more continental pay-related model.'

1980s: social security in the context of economic crisis

The shift towards a continental system did not continue into the 1980s. For much of this decade Ireland was transfixed by an incredibly severe economic crisis as discussed in Chapter 3. Consequently, the social security system had to cope with mass unemployment and rising numbers of people claiming Unemployment Assistance, as people's entitlement to Unemployment Benefit ran out. In 1966 20 per cent of the population were beneficiaries of social security payments. By 1985 37.4 per cent of the population were beneficiaries, and unemployment-related payments accounted for 55 per cent of this growth (Curry, 1986). Social security expenditure as a percentage of GDP rose substantially between 1980 and 1985, from 16.8 per cent to 21.8 per cent (OECD, 2008a). Unlike the UK where Thatcherism dominated the 1980s and both the social security system and its beneficiaries came under attack, right-wing thinking and critique remained muted in the Irish context. It has been suggested that the sheer scale of need and reliance on the social security system and in particular the enormous rise in unemployment in the 1980s took precedence (Ó Riain and O'Connell, 2000). That is not to say that no attempts were made to curb rising costs and rising levels of dependency on the social security system. For example, pay-related benefits were reduced in 1984, only five years after they were introduced. A 'genuinely seeking work' requirement was applied to claimants of unemployment benefit, which added an element of conditionality to Unemployment Benefit as a right. Previously, this requirement only applied to claimants of Unemployment Assistance (Cousins, 2005a). Attempts were also made to maintain people with families in low-paying employment, with the introduction of Family Income Supplement in 1984. Various schemes were introduced to provide work (such as a Social Employment Scheme in 1985), encourage job seeking (through Jobsearch 1987) and promote further education (through an Educational Opportunities Scheme in 1986). Such measures mark the origins of more extensive activation in the 1990s and 2000s as discussed in section three below.

One positive aspect of social security in the 1980s related to improvements for women, which went against the tide of cutbacks and crisis. An EU directive on equal treatment in social security in 1979 meant that many of the inequalities married women experienced in the social security system surrounding rates, duration of benefit and assumptions about dependency were removed, but at a slow pace (Cook and McCashin, 1997). Also, maternity leave was introduced in 1981 which provided 14 weeks' leave from work. This was implemented alongside a new Maternity Allowance intended to replace women's income from work while on maternity leave.

Commission on Social Welfare

The 1980s are also significant for the fact that this decade marked the first comprehensive review of the social security system. This was conducted by a Commission on Social Welfare (CSW), appointed in 1983 to review the overall system and make recommendations 'having regard to the needs of modern Irish society' (CSW, 1986, p. 1). The commission was also asked to assess the redistributive effects of government policies and to recommend any changes needed 'to ensure that the net effects of such transfers taken together secure the objectives of social equity and do not operate to facilitate misuse of the system or create a disincentive to employment or investment' (ibid.). Overall, the terms of reference were more a reflection of the haphazard way that the system developed than a need for a right-wing inspired overhaul. The commission reported in 1986 and made recommendations consistent with a gradual development of the existing system.

It recommended the broadening of the insurance base together with the enhancement of means-tested schemes, to respond to those in greatest poverty and to address the gap or hierarchy between those treated most generously in the social security system (old age pensioners and widows) and those treated the most parsimoniously (the unemployed and those claiming supplementary welfare allowance). However, it envisaged that if the social insurance element of the system were to expand, then, eventually, the role of social assistance would diminish. It also outlined some guiding principles for the future development of the system. This was the first time any principles were articulated in connection with social security policy and these were adequacy, redistribution, comprehensiveness, consistency, and simplicity. One of key recommendations related to adequacy and it recommended that a minimally adequate social welfare payment should amount to approximately half the net average industrial earnings.

The report received a mixed reaction. At government level, as Curry (1986), the chairman of the commission noted, the reaction focused on cost implications. This led to the decision to postpone the implementation of any recommendations, as economic circumstances did not permit the expenditure entailed. Some economists, notably Dowling (1986), were highly critical of the report. Dowling argued that the report was unscientific and ideologically biased and he favoured the development of a more targeted social assistance-based system over an insurance-based system (echoing a neo-liberal perspective). Yet his criticisms were countered by McCashin (1986), who argued that Dowling's approach was equally ideologically biased.

What looked like the beginnings of a more ideologically divided debate on social security and its functions was contained by the subsequent development of a partnership approach to policymaking. The first social partnership programme in 1987 included an agreement not to cut social welfare payments and, gradually, over the course of agreements in the 1990s some of the main CSW recommendations were implemented. These included the broadening of the social insurance base to include part-time and self-employed workers, increasing benefits, reducing the gap between the highest and lowest payments, and simplifying some of the complexity around the range of different means tests used and the range of different categorical payments for similar needs. Some of these changes are discussed further in section three.

Table 7.2 Summary of social security measures introduced 1908–89

Year	Insurance-based payments	Assistance-based payments	Universal payments
1908		Old age pension	
1911	Unemployment benefit		
1920	Sickness benefit	Blind pension	
1923		Home assistance	
1935	Widows' and orphans' pensions	Widows' and orphans' pensions	
1944			Children's allowance
1961	Old age pension		
1966		Smallholders' assistance	
1967	Occupational injuries		
1968		Prescribed relative allowance	
1970	Retirement pension	Deserted wives' allowance	
	Invalidity pension		

Year	Insurance-based payments	Assistance-based payments	Universal payments
1973	Deserted wives' benefit		
1974	Pay-related benefit	Unmarried mothers' allowance	
1977		Single woman's allowance; Prisoner's wives' allowance	
1984		Supplementary welfare allowance	
1989		Family income supplement Lone parents allowance	

Source: adapted from Curry (2003)

SECTION 3: FROM THE 1990S TO THE PRESENT – REFORM AND CONTEMPORARY ISSUES IN IRISH SOCIAL SECURITY POLICY

In the Irish context the effects of economic globalisation and post-industrialisation proved very successful in economic terms, transforming the severe economic crisis into a period of unprecedented growth in the space of a decade from the mid-1980s to the mid-1990s. This led to some debate about whether the greater availability of economic resources together with the process of social partnership altered the overall identity of the social security system.

Daly and Yeates (2003), for example, argued that the Irish social security system is gradually diverging from the liberal UK system to become more inclusive and expansive, contrary to attempts at cost containment that have prevailed elsewhere. Therefore, in a reversal of the historical relationship with the UK, payments have become more generous, a greater range of needs are being recognised, particularly in relation to caring and children, and a greater number of payments are being developed on an insurance or universal basis. In addition, NESC (2005, p. 35) draws attention to the hybrid character of the social security system – a 'mix of means-tested, insurance based and universalist income support and service arrangements' – and suggests that this works to its advantage because it may be 'more robust in adapting to globalisation and shifts in values than purebred "pedigree specimens" of welfare states'.

Against both of these assessments, however, Murphy and Millar (2007), for example, point to some enduring liberal characteristics of the system, most significantly the heavy reliance on means-tested payments, to which Ireland's comparatively high levels of poverty and income inequality are related (O'Connor, 2003). It can also be noted that the liberal features of the system come into sharper focus during times of economic recession, such as is happening during the late 2000s when the long phase of economic success originating in the 1990s has come to an end.

Within this overall debate, this section looks at two key areas in which the Irish social security system has undergone reform in the last two decades. These are the introduction of activation measures and greater attention to poverty and anti-poverty initiatives. These issues form a major part of the changing and expanding nature of the social security system. However, examination of trends in relation to activation and poverty policy also points to the limits of reform in these areas. These limitations are linked to the continuing influence of the system's liberal inheritance and the fact that redistribution within the system is generally quite circumscribed, focusing on those at the lowest end of the income distribution scale and leaving wealth and privilege undisturbed (Kirby, 2001; O'Flynn and Murphy, 2001).

For the most part, changes to the system from the 1990s onwards have been strongly aligned with the needs of the economy, with little attention given to issues of inequality or redistribution, or debate about the nature and direction of the Irish social security system. Once basic needs are catered for in the social security system, it is assumed that economic growth will take care of the rest, which resonates with the 'trickle-down' theory the state promulgated during the opening of the economy in the 1960s. In addition, during periods of economic trouble, such as, for example, in the dip in economic growth in the early 2000s and the sharper downturn in the late 2000s, the tendency is to incrementally reduce benefit entitlements and impose greater conditions on eligibility. Therefore, in addition to Kersbergen's (2000) notion of 'creeping disentitlement' as discussed earlier in the chapter, in the Irish context a notion of 'creeping conditionality' (a concept already highlighted in the context of welfare reform in Chapter 4) also comes into play.

First we set the scene for examining activation and anti-poverty measures in the contemporary social system by briefly reviewing the expenditure pattern in social security and the main social security developments since the 1990s.

Table 7.3 Expenditure on social protection as a percentage of GDP in the European Union, 1990–2005

	1990	1996	2000	2005
Belgium	26.8	30.0	26.5	29.7
Bulgaria	n. av.	n. av.	n. av.	16.1
Czech Republic	n. av.	n. av.	19.5	19.1

	1990	1996	2000	2005
Denmark	30.3	33.6	28.9	30.1
Germany	25.4	30.5	29.3	29.4
Estonia	n. av.	n. av.	14.0	12.5
Ireland	19.1	18.9	14.1	18.2
Greece	22.7	23.3	23.5	24.2
Spain	20.4	22.4	20.3	20.8
France	27.7	30.8	29.5	31.5
Italy	24.1	24.8	24.7	26.4
Cyprus	n. av.	n. av.	14.8	18.2
Lithuania	n. av.	n. av.	15.3	12.4
Latvia	n. av.	n. av.	15.8	13.2
Luxembourg	23.5	26.2	19.6	21.9
Hungary	n. av.	n. av.	19.3	21.9
Malta	n. av.	n. av.	16.5	18.3
Netherlands	32.5	30.9	26.4	28.2
Austria	26.7	29.5	28.1	28.8
Poland	n. av.	n. av.	19.7	19.6
Portugal	15.5	21.6	21.7	n. av.
Romania	n. av.	n. av.	13.2	14.2
Slovenia	n. av.	n. av.	24.6	23.4
Slovakia	n. av.	n. av.	19.3	16.9
Finland	25.5	32.1	25.1	26.7
Sweden	32.9	34.8	30.7	32.0
United Kingdom	23.1	27.7	26.9	26.8
EU–15	25.4	28.7	27.0	27.8
EU–25	n. av.	n. av.	26.6	27.4
EU–27	n. av.	n. av.	n. av.	27.2

Source: Amerini (1999) and Petrášová (2008)
n. av. not available

Table 7.3 shows that the overall trend in social expenditure across the EU has remained relatively stable since the early 1990s despite various efforts at reform and cost containment across welfare states. Looking specifically at the Irish pattern, expenditure has remained well below the EU average. Ireland clusters with some Southern European and Eastern European countries in this regard. Variations in the Irish pattern are a product of growth both in GDP and in social security expenditure; however, as GDP growth has outpaced growth in social security expenditure, overall effort has not changed significantly from 1990 to 2005. Nevertheless, Ireland has had one of the highest annual growth rates in social expenditure per capita in real terms; between 2000 and 2005 the average annual rate of growth was 9.3 per cent (Petrášová, 2008).

Some of this growth in expenditure is related to developments with regard to payments. The main innovation since the early 1990s has been greater recognition of carers, with the introduction of Carer's Allowance in 1990 and Carer's Benefit in 2000. A new universal payment for children, the Early Childcare Supplement was introduced in 2006. However, the universal nature of payments has been curtailed by the habitual residence condition introduced in 2004 on foot of EU enlargement. This imposes a two-year residency condition on a number of assistance-based and universal payments (see Chapter 12 for more on this). With regard to older people, a Pre-Retirement Allowance was introduced in 1990 for those over 55 and in receipt of Unemployment Assistance. Reflecting the high levels of unemployment at the time, this allowance did not require its recipients to sign on the Live Register. With respect to pensions, there has been a growing emphasis placed on private/personal provision of supplementary pensions beyond what is provided by the social security system. In this context, the introduction of Personal Retirement Savings Accounts in 2002 was designed to be a flexible 'product', accessible to all to facilitate an improvement in supplementary pension cover in Ireland. However, this initiative has not been a success and the future of pension policy is currently under review (McCashin, 2007). Finally, various efforts have been made to streamline and re-name existing payments, signified by the introduction of Disability Allowance (1996), One Parent Family Payment (1997) and Farm Assist (1999). These replaced and consolidated existing payments in these areas and in some cases adjusted regulations to afford recipients greater incentive to combine work and welfare. In 2006 a more wide-ranging, name-changing exercise was implemented in an attempt to re-orient several elements of the social security system from a 'passive' to an 'active' focus. This change is dealt with in more detail in the section on activation below. The main reports and policy documents, which will be referred to in the remainder of the chapter, are listed in box 7.1.

Box 7.1 Key social security policy developments since the 1990s

1996   Report of the Expert Working Group on the Integration of Tax and Social Welfare Systems

1996   Social Insurance in Ireland

1997   Sharing in Progress: National Anti-Poverty Strategy

2001   Report of the Social Welfare Benchmarking and Indexation Group

2002   Building an Inclusive Society: Review of the National Anti-Poverty Strategy under the Programme for Fairness and Prosperity

2005   The Developmental Welfare State

2006   Government Discussion Paper, Proposals for Supporting Lone Parents

2007   National Action Plan for Social Inclusion 2007–2016

Activation, welfare and work

Since its roots in early 1980s reforms, activation is becoming a larger part of the Irish social security system. This is in line with the increasing emphasis on activation across all European welfare states and with developments in EU policy through the EES and the Lisbon Strategy (as discussed in Chapter 6). Activation involves a 'shift in the inclusion discourse from "inclusion through decent income provisions" towards "inclusion, through participation in work" (van Berkel and Hornemann Møller, 2002, p. 1). In the Irish context this is similarly espoused by the Department of Enterprise, Trade and Employment (2003, p. 41), which states that 'the best way to tackle social exclusion is through a job'. However, there has been no major policy development or strategy developed in relation to activation and the direction it should take.

In common with many other aspects of the Irish social security system this seems to have evolved in an ad hoc way over time, often as a response to EU developments. Yet, in comparative terms, Ireland appears to have embraced activation measures more fully than many other European welfare states, in expenditure terms at least. For example, Vis (2007) identified Ireland as the country which has undergone the greatest change in terms of expenditure on activation in a comparative study of 16 countries over the 1980s to the 2000s.

Activation gathered pace by the mid-1990s when economic growth had little effect on unemployment, particularly long-term unemployment, and concern was also rising about poverty and unemployment traps in the way the social security and taxation systems were working. A key element of activation policy is the Back to Work Allowance introduced in 1993 which allows recipients to retain a portion of their social welfare payments for a period after taking up employment. This is complemented by similar schemes for education (Back to Education Allowance introduced in 1990) and for self-employment (Back to Enterprise Allowance introduced in 1999).

The Expert Working Group on the Integration of Tax and Social Welfare Systems (1996) examined the impact of **unemployment traps** and **poverty traps**, which were obstacles to becoming and remaining employed. Over the latter part of the 1990s and into the 2000s a number of measures have been implemented to curtail the effects of unemployment traps and poverty traps. These include tax reform, including a reduction in the rates of income tax and the introduction of a minimum wage; and a more tapered withdrawal of benefits associated with Back to Work and related schemes; a more generous application of Family Income Supplement; and an increase in earnings disregards associated with the amount one is allowed to earn while retaining certain benefits, such as One Parent Family Allowance. Altogether, these measures aim to positively incentivise people to move from welfare to work and remain in work, or in other words, to make work pay.

> **Unemployment traps** occur when the interaction between the social security system and the taxation system creates a situation where there is no financial incentive for a person to move from welfare to work.

> **Poverty traps** occur in work, at a particular income threshold, when the effects of income tax combined with the withdrawal of in-work benefits leaves the worker less well off compared to when they were earning a lower gross wage.

Other incentives designed to encourage people to work, acting more as 'sticks' than 'carrots' include the curtailment of entitlements associated with social insurance. While the social insurance base broadened to include the self-employed and part-time workers over the course of the late 1980s and early 1990s in line with CSW recommendations, some of the benefits associated with social insurance were cut back. For example, while social insurance contributions continue to be pay-related (up to certain limits), social insurance benefits returned in full to a flat-rated system by 1994. Qualification requirements for benefits were lengthened, meaning that a greater number of contributions have to be made before one is entitled to payments such as Unemployment Benefit, Disability Benefit and contributory pensions. The length of time one can claim Unemployment Benefit has also been shortened for certain claimants. Benefits were also made taxable, such as Disability Benefit in 1993. These changes as Murphy (2006, p. 92) notes, 'reflect policy restructuring designed to increase work incentives rather than being caused by fiscal pressures'.

In addition, a certain element of compulsion is involved in the growing individual engagement with recipients of social security payments in efforts to 'activate' them. Since 1998 when Ireland produced its first National Employment Action Plan as part of the EES, a process referred to as a 'prevention process' has been instigated. This involves targeting and reviewing people claiming social welfare, and referring them to the employment, training or active labour market programmes provided by FÁS, including Community Employment, Job Initiative and Social Economy programmes. Following the re-launch of the Lisbon Strategy in 2005, Ireland's National Employment Action plans have been replaced by a National Reform Programme, the first of which covers 2005 to 2008. Within this programme, prevention and activation measures have intensified. A review of the prevention process in 2005 found that it increased individual job searching, promoted exit from the Live Register and increased Departmental savings (Department of Enterprise, Trade and Employment, 2006). It recommended that the threshold for engagement with FÁS should start sooner, at three instead of six months, and that it be widened to include 55–64-year-olds, lone parents, 16–24-year-olds and people with disabilities. The first two of these recommendations were implemented in 2006. For the older unemployed, activation is occurring in conjunction with the phasing out of the Pre-Retirement Allowance from 2007. Its removal is seen as a measure preventing older people using it as a means of avoiding the take-up of work, as well as fulfilling the Lisbon goal of a 50 per cent labour force participation rate for older workers.

Of the groups mentioned above, lone parents and people with disabilities in particular signify the shift to regarding all people aged 18–64 as people of 'working age' and potentially part of the labour force. Within the National Reform Programme this shift is associated with the challenge of meeting the Lisbon objectives of a 70 per cent labour force participation rate overall and maintaining Ireland's economic growth. Another driver is the changing composition of social security recipients. In the 1980s the main challenge facing the social security system was the problem of unemployment and the escalation of numbers claiming Unemployment Benefit and especially Unemployment Assistance. By the mid-1990s unemployment subsided; however, payments associated with lone parenthood and disability grew in place of the reduction in the numbers of unemployed recipients (NESC, 2005). For example, the total number of One Parent Family Payment recipients grew by 44.3 per cent between 1997 and 2007, while the total number of Disability Allowance recipients grew by 106.2 per cent over the same period. Attention has therefore turned towards the activation of these groups.

The re-positioning of lone parents as people of working age to be included in activation processes is underway. A government discussion paper, *Proposals for Supporting Lone Parents* (Department of Social and Family

Affairs, 2006a), was issued for consultation in 2006. This paper proposed the introduction of a new Parental Allowance for low-income families with young children to replace both the One Parent Family Payment and Qualified Adult Allowances in social assistance payments. The proposals shift the focus away from lone parenthood as a category towards low-income families. It also proposed the introduction of compulsory engagement with employment services once the youngest child reaches a certain age, for example age 5 or 7, and the withdrawal of the payment at another (older) age threshold. Currently, the One Parent Family Payment is paid without any employment or activation conditions until the youngest child reaches 18. In 2007 a pilot initiative of the non-income elements of the new scheme, including childcare, education and training, was introduced in Coolock in Dublin and in Kilkenny; however, the full scheme is yet to be implemented (Department of Social and Family Affairs, 2008a). Plans are also in train to develop more targeted employment supports for people with disabilities (ibid.). To date, however, greater attention has been given to the activation of One Parent Family Payment recipients.

In terms of the system more broadly, a number of key social security payments underwent a name change in the Social Welfare Law Reform and Pensions Act in 2006, to signify a more substantial shift from passive to active forms of social security. Mirroring the broader trends discussed in section one, a semantic shift has occurred away from the traditional categories associated with old age, unemployment and, to a lesser extent, disability. Old age has disappeared from the social security lexicon, unemployment has been transformed into job seeking and Disability Benefit has been changed to Illness Benefit to signify something more temporary than the permanence associated with disability. The Social Welfare Law Reform and Pensions Act 2006 provided for the following name changes:

▸ Old Age (contributory) Pension -> State Pension (contributory)
▸ Old Age (non-contributory) Pension -> State Pension (non-contributory)
▸ Retirement Pension -> State Pension (transition)
▸ Disability Benefit -> Illness Benefit
▸ Unemployment Assistance-> Jobseeker's Allowance
▸ Unemployment Benefit -> Jobseeker's Benefit

Announcing these changes, the then Minister for Social and Family Affairs referred to lone parents and people in receipt of illness and disability payments in terms of their employment potential, and mentioned that 'the challenge is to make sure that in an economy as successful as ours that we do not overlook or neglect the employment contribution that any individual can make' (Brennan, cited in Department of Social and Family Affairs, 2006b). Murphy and Millar (2007, p. 82) note that, a 'productivist re-ordering' of social policy is occurring, which aligns social needs with economic needs. This also has consequences for how poverty is addressed within the social security system.

Social security, adequacy, poverty and anti-poverty policy

The social security system has a bearing on the extent of poverty, in particular overall poverty levels and who is at risk of poverty, because poverty and reliance on social security are strongly related. As Walsh (2007, p. 13) puts it, 'poverty and welfare policies can be seen as two sides of the one coin. Poverty trends are heavily influenced by government welfare and tax policies which influence the income levels of the population.' Historically, as outlined in section two, Irish social security development has been marked by a tradition of low levels of assistance-based payments to preserve the incentive to work whilst covering basic needs. Attesting to the inadequacy of this approach, the 'rediscovery of poverty' in Ireland, as discussed in Chapter 3, revealed that between 24 to 27 per cent of the population were in relative poverty in the early 1970s. Since the 1980s there has been a growing focus on poverty research and policy developments around the adequacy of social security payments and anti-poverty measures.

The first national poverty survey was carried out by the ESRI in 1987. This was followed by a series of studies from 1994 to 2001, called the Living in Ireland Survey (LIS), also carried out by the ESRI. In 2003 the LIS was replaced by a new survey called the EU Survey of Income and Living Conditions (EU-SILC), which the EU requires each member state to carry out annually as part of its social inclusion policy under the OMC. The Central Statistics Office (CSO) carries out this survey. Compared to the 1980s and early 1990s a systematic body of data is now available on poverty which serves as a useful tool in the adoption of policy targets and in monitoring their progress. In addition, as McCashin (2004) notes, the findings of these surveys serve as an important resource for agencies such as the CPA and other voluntary organisations to lobby for social security reform and improve the position of groups particularly vulnerable to poverty. Yet it must also be noted that the profusion of poverty research has 'subtly changed the focus of social policy from equality in income and wealth distribution to poverty reduction' (Kirby, 2001, p. 22). This is a point we will return to at the end of this section.

The first official consideration of the issue of welfare adequacy was contained in the CSW's discussion of adequacy and its recommendations in 1986. Although its recommendations were not officially adopted as policy targets, the lower targets set out by the CSW were achieved for all social security payments by 1999. More recently, adequacy has been considered by a group formed under the *Programme for Prosperity and Fairness* to examine a new benchmark for welfare adequacy. This group, known as the Social Welfare Benchmarking and Indexation Group, recommended that a minimally adequate welfare payment should be based on 27 per cent of Gross Average Industrial Earnings (GAIE), with a longer-term target of 30 per cent. This recommendation influenced the adoption of targets for welfare payments under the revised National Anti-Poverty Strategy in 2002.

This brings us to the subject of anti-poverty policy which gained considerable momentum in the late 1990s with the adoption of a *National Anti-Poverty Strategy* (NAPS) in 1997. Taking poverty data from the 1994 LIS, the NAPS set out a ten-year plan to reduce levels of poverty and tackle it in a multi-dimensional way, looking not just at social security, but also addressing areas such as educational disadvantage and long-term unemployment. This was the first time targets were set out to reduce poverty. Furthermore, the strategy preceded EU action in this area, which involves national action planning on poverty and social inclusion from 2000 onwards as part of its open method of coordination on social inclusion (see Chapter 6). However, EU social inclusion policy and the adoption of social indicators have subsequently become an important part of policy in the Irish context. Because of the unprecedented level of economic growth in the years following the NAPS, a revised strategy was published in 2002 with more ambitious targets in relation to poverty reduction by 2007. With the expiry of the original 10-year framework, a new policy, *NAPinclusion* or the *National Action Plan for Social Inclusion 2007–2016*, was launched in 2007 to guide policy until 2016, so that it runs concurrently with the current social partnership agreement *Towards 2016*.

Having outlined the overall framework of policy developments in relation to poverty research, adequacy and anti-poverty measures, we will now consider the relationship between the three of them in more detail and look at the impact this has had on poverty and social security. A critical aspect of policy on poverty has to do with how it is officially defined and measured, as this becomes the basis for government action in the area. In the Irish context there is a certain disconnection between the overall definition of poverty and the kind of poverty that is measured and used in policy targets.

In the NAPS 1997 a relative definition of poverty was outlined as the government's understanding of poverty. This definition, therefore, focused on exclusion from a generally acceptable standard of living and the norms and practices associated with this. This has been the definition the government has adhered to since:

People are living in poverty if their income and resources (material, cultural and social) are so inadequate as to preclude them from having a standard of living which is regarded as acceptable by Irish society generally. As a result of inadequate income and resources people may be excluded and marginalised from participation in activities which are considered the norm for other people in society. (Government of Ireland, 2007b, p. 20)

However, the kind of poverty recognised for measurement refers to exclusion from a basic as opposed to a generally acceptable standard of living. This is termed consistent poverty and it is based on a relative income measure and basic deprivation:

This measure identifies the proportion of people, from those with an income below a certain threshold (less than 60 per cent of the median income), who are deprived of one or more goods or services considered essential for a basic standard of living. (ibid., p. 24)

Basic deprivation is measured with reference to a list of eight items considered essential for a basic standard of living. These were devised by the ESRI in its poverty research in 1987. As Walsh (2007, p. 18) notes, 'the consistent poverty measure has also attracted some criticism'. However, this criticism has mostly been on methodological grounds, and the fact that the indicators used were set in 1987 when standards of living were much lower. In 2006 the ESRI revisited the list of basic deprivation indicators and 'reconfigured' them to produce an up-to-date, robust and reliable indication of consistent poverty (Maître et al., 2006). The result of their work is set out in table 7.4, which shows the deprivation index used in research until 2006 and the new list to be used from the 2007 EU-SILC onwards.

Table 7.4 Basic deprivation indicators used to measure consistent poverty

Basic deprivation index: 1987–2006	Revised basic deprivation index: 2007 onwards
Persons are in consistent poverty if they experience enforced deprivation of **one or more** items from the list:	Persons are in consistent poverty if they experience enforced deprivation of **two or more** items from the list:–
– Two pairs of strong shoes	– Two pairs of strong shoes
– A warm waterproof overcoat	– A warm waterproof overcoat
– Buy new rather than second-hand clothes	– Buy new rather than second-hand clothes

Basic deprivation index: 1987–2006	Revised basic deprivation index: 2007 onwards
– Eat meals with meat, chicken, fish (or vegetarian equivalent) every second day	– Eat meals with meat, chicken, fish (or vegetarian equivalent) every second day
– Have a roast joint (or its equivalent) once a week	– Have a roast joint (or its equivalent) once a week
– Go without heating during the last 12 months through lack of money	– Go without heating during the last 12 months through lack of money
– Go without substantial meal due to lack of money	– Keep the home adequately warm
– Going into debt to meet ordinary living expenses	– Buy presents for family or friends at least once a year
	– Replace any worn out furniture
	– Have family or friends for a drink or a meal once a month
	– Have a morning or afternoon or evening out in the last fortnight, for entertainment

Source: adapted from Maître et al. (2006)

Regarding trends in poverty over time, table 7.5 outlines the findings in relation to relative and consistent poverty from 1994 to 2006. Research is based on a representative sample of the population and income thresholds are set at between 70 per cent and 50 per cent of the median income of the sample. The 60 per cent median income line is the one most frequently used in policymaking with regard to poverty indicators and targets. The median income refers to the income at the halfway point between the highest and the lowest income encountered among the survey participants. The continuity of the data must be treated with caution because of the slightly different methodology used in the LIS compared to the EU-SILC. This applies in particular to findings related to consistent poverty which displayed a major increase in the changeover from the LIS to the EU-SILC in 2003. The overall trend, however, has been for the level of consistent poverty to fall. In contrast, trends in relation to relative poverty give more of an insight into overall levels of inequality over the period of economic change since the mid-1990s. The proportion of the population in relative poverty grew over the period 1994 to 2001 and has begun to decline since 2003, yet relative poverty levels are still above the level they were at in 1994.

Table 7.5 Percentage of persons at risk of poverty (60 per cent median income line) and percentage of persons in consistent poverty (60 per cent median income line) 1994–2007

	1994	1997	1998	2000	2001	2003*	2004	2005	2006	2007
Relative poverty	15.6	18.2	19.8	20.9	21.9	19.7	19.4	18.5	17.0	16.5
Consistent poverty	8.3	7.8	6.0	4.3	4.1	8.8	6.8	7.0	6.9	5.1

Source: Whelan et al. (2003) and CSO EU-SILC various years
Note: *LIS differs from EU-SILC beginning in 2003 so the data is not directly comparable.

How does this relate to poverty reduction and income adequacy targets? The original poverty reduction target in NAPS (1997) was to reduce the level of consistent poverty from 9 to 15 per cent (depending on the median income threshold used) to 5 to 10 per cent by 2007. As can be seen from the table above, consistent poverty rates fell quite quickly from 1997 to 2001 and this target was achieved well before 2007. Consequently, a revised NAPS strategy was agreed in 2002, entitled *Building An Inclusive Society: review of the National Anti-Poverty Strategy Under the Programme for Prosperity and Fairness*. This strategy aimed to reduce consistent poverty to below 2 per cent and potentially eliminate it altogether. In addition, influenced by the recommendations of the Social Welfare Benchmarking and Indexation Working Group (2001) the strategy also adopted a target in relation to the value of welfare payments. It set out to reach a rate of €150 per week in 2002 terms for the lowest rates of social welfare by 2007. This target was equivalent to 30 per cent of GAIE at the time. Evaluating the progress on consistent poverty is complicated by the fact that the survey series changed from the LIS to the EU-SILC. If we look at the EU-SILC on its own, however, consistent poverty has been falling since the survey began in 2003. Yet the overall decline has been quite slight. As for welfare payment levels, the target of 30 per cent of GAIE was achieved by the 2007 Budget due to a series of payment increases, particularly in the budgets between 2005 and 2007.

It would appear, therefore, that the government has performed quite well in reducing poverty and improving social security payments. However, this evaluation hinges very much on accepting consistent poverty as the measurement against which to benchmark policy. While this is Irish practice, European policy on social inclusion and social indicators uses a relative poverty benchmark, which is referred to as the 'at risk of poverty' rate. This measure records the percentage of the population under the 60 per cent median income level, and is 'state-bounded'. In other words, it refers to the median income in each country, not an EU-wide median income (Fahey,

2007). This percentage is referred to as those 'at risk of poverty' to capture the likelihood of being in relative poverty. According to this indicator Ireland performs poorly in comparison to other EU countries:

Table 7.6 At risk of poverty rate across the EU 2006

EU-25	16	Lithuania	20
EU-15	16	Luxembourg	14
Belgium	15	Hungary	16
Bulgaria	14	Malta	14
Czech Republic	10	Netherlands	10
Denmark	12	Austria	13
Germany	13	Poland	19
Estonia	18	Portugal	18
Ireland	18	Romania	19
Greece	21	Slovenia	12
Spain	20	Slovakia	12
France	13	Finland	13
Italy	20	Sweden	12
Cyprus	16	UK	19
Latvia	23		

Source: Eurostat, n.d.

This poor performance in comparative terms demonstrates the fact that action on reducing and eliminating poverty is still bound by a broadly liberal conception of social security and redistribution in Ireland. This means that social security payments are still preserved at a relatively low level, and relative poverty does not merit as much action as consistent poverty. The Irish government is therefore particularly critical of the EU measure of poverty and its relevance in the Irish context. It argues that:

> The 'at risk of poverty' indicator has particular limitations as a measure of poverty in the case of Ireland in recent years. It takes no account of overall living standards and fails to reflect the fact that the 60% median income threshold increased by 88% from €102.44 in 1997 to €192.74

in 2005 ... All groups in society have benefited from economic growth, therefore, the main value of the indicator is in identifying particular groups which may have difficulty keeping pace with living standards generally. (Government of Ireland, 2007b, p. 25)

In essence, the government argues that relative poverty is not particularly meaningful at a time when everyone's living standards have increased during a period of economic growth, and if one were to take a European-wide measure of living standards in relation to relative poverty then Ireland's position would be much more favourable. High levels of relative poverty are therefore portrayed as an effect of rising living standards during the economic boom, and it is expected that relative poverty will decrease in the longer term. Therefore, the *NAPinclusion* notes that recent reduction in the Irish 'at risk of poverty' rate (which stood at 19.7 per cent in 2003, for example) 'may indicate that the distorting effect of significant structural changes may no longer be a major factor' (ibid.). This echoes the 'rising tide will lift all boats' philosophy commonly referred to during the 1960s and 1970s, which assumed that wealth generated by economic growth would eventually 'trickle down' through the different income groups in society.

Looking at the wider picture of income inequality and redistribution, Nolan and Maître (2007) examine what can be termed the state's redistributive effort, by comparing income levels before and after state intervention in relation to taxation and social security transfers. In this regard Ireland has a similar redistributive record to the UK and both countries compare unfavourably with other North European and Scandinavian welfare states. This can be attributed to fact that the latter countries achieve greater redistribution through their taxation and social security regime. In relation to social security transfers in particular, these, as Nolan and Maître (2007, p. 36) note, 'play a smaller role in reducing the numbers falling below relative income poverty thresholds in Ireland than in many other Member States. This is mostly because the scale of social transfers is more limited than elsewhere.' This pattern of limited redistribution reflects Ireland's long-standing status as a liberal welfare regime, which, along with the UK, sets it apart from other European welfare states. This is illustrated in terms of measures such as the 'at risk of poverty' rate and income inequality (referred to as the Gini coefficient) in the EU social indicators. Therefore, contrary to arguments about the distorting effects of Ireland's recent growth, as Nolan and Maître (ibid., p. 37) argue, 'to understand Ireland's level of income inequality in comparative perspective it is the effects of deep-seated institutional differences of this type – rather than the impact of the recent economic boom – that need to be understood.'

NAPinclusion 2007–2016: combining anti-poverty policy with activation

NAPinclusion or the *National Action Plan for Social Inclusion 2007–2016* is the successor to NAPS and it details the government's approach to poverty and targets until 2016. The plan commits the government to reducing consistent poverty to between 2 and 4 per cent by 2012 and eliminating it by 2016. However, the method by which it aims to do this has changed since NAPS. There the focus centred on reaching adequate levels of social welfare payment, whereas in the current plan activation policy takes precedence over further improvements to the adequacy of social security payments. As it remarks, the plan 'has been prepared in a different context to the original 1997 National Anti-Poverty Strategy. Income support targets (social welfare rates and pensions) have now been achieved and, ... there is greater emphasis on services and activation as a means of tackling social exclusion' (Government of Ireland, 2007b, p. 55). Accordingly, the goal for income support measures for children and those of working age is to maintain their existing value. Mention is made of enhancing income support for people with disabilities and pensioners, but only if resources allow. In terms of services and activation, the plan outlines a proposal for a new *Social and Economic Participation Programme* within the Department of Social and Family Affairs. The aim of this programme is, '... to move from the current largely passive approach to one where the Department will engage with all people of working age in receipt of social welfare at the initial claim stage in order to deliver more intensive engagement on an individual basis' (ibid., p. 44).

This proposal partly reflects the recommendations made by NESC (2005) for greater engagement with social security clients, including greater tailoring of services to meet individual needs, conditional 'on the obligation and need for welfare recipients and public authorities alike to periodically review the extent to which the recipient's best interests are being facilitated by the arrangements governing their access to an income', as NESC (ibid., p. 221) rather ambiguously puts it. However, issues of conditionality or the details of what 'intensive engagement' will entail are not elaborated upon in *NAPinclusion* and it remains to be seen how this programme will be implemented.

In overall terms, however, *NAPinclusion* reflects a strengthening of the view that employment is the answer to social inclusion and to poverty. As Minister Brennan, the Minister for Social and Family Affairs (2004–7) put it, 'movement into employment is the best way out of poverty' (Brennan, cited in Department of Social and Family Affairs, 2006c). While that may be the case for the majority of people, it downplays the role of the social security system in relation to poverty prevention and social inclusion. This is particularly critical for social security recipients who are not of 'working age', such as children and older people, and of those of 'working age' who for whatever reason cannot work, such as those with high levels of caring responsibilities, or those whose disability prevents them from working. Some of these groups, such as children, one-parent households and people with disabilities, along with the unemployed, are at a particularly high risk of both consistent and relative poverty. Social security policies which focus primarily on a 'welfare-to-work' philosophy and target consistent poverty with minimal commitment to redistribution may end up, as Murphy (2006, p. 96) argues, creating a 'pauperisation of segments of society' which is 'directly attributable to a conscious policy decision to keep social welfare payments low'.

Furthermore, the focus on activation and employment as the solution to social exclusion and poverty is facing new challenges during a period of economic recession. Since early 2008 unemployment began to rise steadily, from an annual average rate of 4.4–4.5 per cent from 2004–7 to a rate of 6.7 per cent by late 2008. Consequently, the numbers claiming Job Seeker's Benefit and Job Seeker's Allowance are also beginning to rise significantly. In addition, government revenue began to decline quite rapidly, which has an impact on the level of resources available for social services. In a continuation of past responses to economic difficulties, signified by 'creeping disentitlement' and 'creeping conditionality', Budget 2009 contains proposals to curtail the benefits (by reducing the length of period for which the payment lasts) and increase the conditions (by raising the number of contributions needed to qualify) attached to Jobseeker's Benefit. The first response to rising unemployment, therefore, is an attempt to curb the cost implications it has for the social security system; the greater challenge is the relevance of the re-orientation of the social security system towards a 'welfare-to-work' philosophy when the opportunities to work are in decline.

CHAPTER SUMMARY

▸ The first section of the chapter examined the relationship between social justice, redistribution and social security and reviewed the range of approaches to the formation and development of social security systems, including social insurance, social assistance and universal type systems with reference to these concepts. The section also looked at the challenges faced by all social security systems in recent times, with economic and socio-demographic trends impacting on the values and cost base of all systems in various ways. Within this context, the trend of re-orienting systems towards the needs and activation of people of 'working age' was noted in particular.

▸ The second section reviewed the development of the Irish system and explained the reasons why its development has strongly relied on social assistance-based payments with limited potential for redistribution. The gradual growth of the system to include recognition of a wider range of needs, but within a highly categorical framework since the 1960s, was also discussed. This section ended with a review of the 1980s; a decade which posed serious challenges for the social security system and under which it managed to stay intact without major erosion.

▸ Section three considered reforms within the system since the 1990s. Economic growth provided greater resources which enhanced anti-poverty measures and trends towards activation within the system. However, issues such as the focus on consistent poverty have meant that the system has not changed from one of limited redistributive potential. In the current period of economic recession the risk is that the limited improvements made since the early 1990s will be undermined by the underlying lack of commitment to equality and redistribution.

Discussion points

▸ Explain the differences between social insurance and social assistance-based social security payments.

▸ Examine the differences between relative and consistent poverty.

▸ Discuss the influence of the concept of 'working age' on the treatment of various groups of people within the Irish social security system, e.g. one-parent families, people with disabilities, older people.

▸ Is 'the best way to tackle social exclusion … through a job' (Department of Enterprise, Trade and Employment, 2003, p. 41)?

Further reading

Cantillon, S., Corrigan, C., Kirby, P. and O'Flynn, J. (eds) (2001) *Rich and Poor: perspectives on tackling poverty in Ireland*, Dublin: Oak Tree Press with the CPA.

Cousins, M. (ed.) (2007) *Welfare Policy and Poverty*, Dublin: IPA and CPA.

Cousins, M. (2003) *The Birth of Social Welfare in Ireland*, 1922–52, Dublin: Four Courts Press.

McCashin, A. (2004) *Social Security in Ireland*, Dublin: Gill & Macmillan.

Useful websites

Department of Social Welfare: www.welfare.ie

Office for Social Inclusion: www.socialinclusion.ie – responsible for coordinating government policy on social inclusion.

CHAPTER 8

HEALTH POLICY

The notion of struggle or indeed crisis is a familiar one in the context of Irish health policy. Health is the most contested and debated area of social policy in contemporary Irish society and gains an enormous amount of media attention. Stories about waiting lists, public versus private patients, chaotic accident and emergency services, misdiagnoses, unhygienic hospitals, elder abuse in nursing homes and the 'black hole' of health expenditure abound. These issues raise wider questions about the extent to which equity or equal access for all is pursued, the way the Irish health system is organised and managed, and the extent to which scarce resources are put to the most efficient use. These questions are not exclusive to the Irish healthcare system but are shared across all healthcare systems at a time when health policy is undergoing what appears to be constant reform. This chapter aims to look, therefore, at the broad context of healthcare and current healthcare issues before examining the particular way in which the Irish system developed and the current key issues and challenges it faces.

CHAPTER OUTLINE

▸ Section one introduces the area of health policy. It examines some of the core concepts and issues associated with healthcare, including the diversity of systems in which states create and deliver healthcare policy, and it also briefly reviews some contemporary reform issues.

▸ Section two discusses the development of health policy in Ireland, and looks at how some of the overall concepts and issues have evolved in the Irish context.

▸ Section three examines the contemporary Irish healthcare system, focusing on policy reform since the 1980s and the issue of equity of access to healthcare in particular.

SECTION 1: HEALTHCARE CONCEPTS, HEALTHCARE SYSTEMS AND RECENT TRENDS

Healthcare concepts

Health is a fundamental resource for human life and human flourishing. Ill health can have a ripple effect, leading to problems in other areas of our lives, such as the ability to obtain and remain in employment and to participate in society. Conversely, good health can be an important resource in overcoming social disadvantage (Braveman and Gruskin, 2003). However, health is not evenly distributed; good or ill health varies among individuals. We commonly consider these differences as a matter of luck or of biological inevitability and therefore as something outside our control. For example, we talk about being 'blessed' with good health or 'struck' down with an illness and we accept certain differences in the health of younger compared to older people, and men compared to women. These differences do not invoke a sense of unfairness.

Health inequality

Moving on to the interpretation of health differences in social policy, the term health inequality is used to refer broadly to differences in health status. However, it has a range of meanings. Graham (2007) identifies three interpretations of health inequalities. These are differences in health status between (1) individuals, (2) population groups and (3) groups occupying unequal positions in society, such as people in poverty or ethnic minorities. The first meaning focuses on individualised patterns of health and simply sees them as differences among 'ungrouped' people. The second approach acknowledges a social pattern to health, in other words, different groups in the population, such as older people, women, or social classes, vary according to health status. The third meaning explicitly links health differences with people's unequal position in society. These differences in interpretation matter in terms of policy formation and practical consequences. They can influence commitments to measuring health inequalities and the allocation of resources to address these inequalities (Braveman, 2006). For example, in the UK during the 1980s and 1990s when the Conservative party was in power, health policy was framed in terms of health variations rather than inequalities, whereas succeeding Labour governments reverted to the term health inequalities combined with a commitment to reduce the gaps in key health differences.

Health inequity and health equity

The use of the term health inequality, associated with Graham's third interpretation, suggests an acknowledgement of injustice. In contrast, terms such as variations or disparities, reflecting the first and second of Graham's interpretations, describe a situation without necessarily implying there is anything to be done about such inequalities. When health differences are considered unjust these are referred to as **health inequities**. If health inequalities are acknowledged as unfair then health policy becomes concerned with the challenge of trying to ensure equity. This involves a movement beyond the commitment to equity as an ethical principle, to trying to achieve equity in a practical and measurable way.

> **Health inequity** exists where differences in health are present across different income and social groups, and are considered to be avoidable and unfair.

The WHO suggests that 'health equity has two important strands: improving average health of countries and abolishing avoidable inequalities in health within countries. In both cases ... the aim should be to bring the health of those worse off up to the level of the best' (WHO, 2008, p. 29). The policy implications of this generally extend beyond the remit of health policy to include areas that affect the social determinants of health such as income distribution, housing and education. However, in the realm of health policy at a broad level, equity involves consideration of 'need rather than underlying social advantage ... in decisions about resource allocation that affect health' (WHO, 1998, p. 10). In other words, need for healthcare should be the chief determinant of the allocation of healthcare resources.

This focus on need can be present in policy in a number of different ways. Culyer and Wagstaff (1993) identify four definitions: equal utilisation, distribution according to need, equal access and equal health outcomes. Mooney (1983) divides approaches into horizontal equity and vertical equity. Horizontal equity implies equal treatment for equal need and vertical equity implies different treatment for different need, specifically, more resources for greater need. These definitions range from relatively narrow interpretations, such as equal access, to interpretations that have more far-reaching implications, such as equal health outcomes. However, all definitions involve concepts that are difficult to measure, such as health need and health outcomes.

Public health systems in general articulate some notion of fairness around how healthcare is provided; however, in practice, this may be quite vague or ambiguous. Generally speaking, European health systems have evolved over time towards a system of universal access: the public health system is made available to every one on an equal basis. This means offering universal coverage to the core elements of the system, without payment at the point of use. This, for the most part, was achieved by almost all European states by the 1980s (Freeman, 2000). This embodies the principle of equal access to available care for equal need, or the principle of horizontal equity.

Efficiency

Health systems are not informed by ethical principles alone; they also have to work under economic principles, most importantly, the principle of efficiency. Healthcare has the potential to absorb what seems like limitless amounts of money. As health services have to be paid for and resources are not unlimited, it is important that the most efficient use of resources available is made. The allocation of resources, therefore, involves a trade-off between fairness and efficiency.

Simply defined, economic efficiency is about 'making the best use of limited resources given people's tastes' (Barr, 2004, p. 66). LeGrand et al., (1992, p. 41) define an efficient level of healthcare 'as one that maximizes the difference between benefits and costs'. In economic theory this is about finding the point where the distance between the benefits and costs of producing a particular good is the greatest. For example, an efficient number of hospitals within a city would be the number of hospitals where the gap between the costs of building and running the hospitals and benefits produced by the hospitals is the greatest. Opening another hospital would cost more than the benefits to be gained from having another hospital in the region. However, like equity, efficiency is a contested concept. One of the main reasons is because efficiency can be difficult to measure, particularly when it comes to measuring benefits. As Duff (1997, p. 62) points out, 'it is extremely difficult to define what maximum benefit or output means in healthcare. For example, it could be the number of days it takes to heal after taking a prescription, or how well one feels, or some other indicator.' As well as difficulties with measuring efficiency, there is also ongoing debate about whether markets or governments are best placed to deliver efficient healthcare.

Efficiency and market allocation of healthcare

Market mechanisms frequently tend to be associated with economic efficiency. Libertarians, for example, argue that health should be treated like any other commodity and that people should buy whatever healthcare their income and preferences permit. From a libertarian perspective this is an efficient allocation of healthcare. However, there are many reasons why markets fail or do not produce an efficient outcome in the case of healthcare. Many of the reasons also produce inequitable outcomes but here we focus on the problems associated with efficiency.

Barr (2004) outlines a number of reasons why pure market healthcare is inefficient. Firstly, consumers of healthcare do not possess adequate information to make fully informed healthcare choices. Medical information can be technically complex, mistaken choices can be expensive and in some cases irreversible, and there may not be time to compare different health 'products', particularly if the health condition needing treatment is acute. Secondly, there are problems with a purely private health insurance market. For example, many health conditions are considered uninsurable. These include chronic illnesses that are present before health insurance is taken out, and, as genetic testing becomes more advanced, individuals may not be covered for conditions for which they display a genetic predisposition. Third and fourth, insurance of any kind is subject to problems of adverse selection and moral hazard, and health insurance is particularly susceptible to these problems. Adverse selection refers to cases where individuals who have greater health problems are more likely to opt for health insurance in light of this information. The person insured has more information than the insurer and this imbalance may turn into a bad risk for the insurer in the event of many claims being made. Moral hazard occurs where insured people may take less health precautions or consume more health services, knowing they are protected by insurance. It can also occur when a healthcare provider's decisions (e.g. a doctor's decisions) about an insured person's healthcare are not constrained by that person's ability to pay for treatment. Finally, private healthcare does not generate positive externalities associated with public health expenditure. This occurs particularly in the case of communicable diseases. For example, if only those who are willing and able to pay for vaccination are protected then the full gains of vaccination are not realised and the outcome would be socially inefficient (LeGrand, 1982). All of these problems contribute to inefficient consumption of healthcare, leading in some cases to under-consumption of healthcare and in others to over-consumption.

Aspects of government intervention

Governments intervene in healthcare not just to achieve some kind of equitable outcome but also to try to achieve efficiency. This intervention can take many forms, such as regulation (e.g. regulation of doctors, hospitals, and of private health insurance providers), public funding (e.g. through social insurance or taxation), public production and allocation (e.g. through national health systems). Government intervention is discussed in more detail in the following section on healthcare systems.

The notion of efficiency and market-based healthcare has become prominent in the last few decades as healthcare budgets went through a phase of expansion in the 1950s and 1960s that could not be continued when economies hit a slowdown during the 1970s. The adoption of market concepts is evident in a number of trends, such as the use of quasi- or internal markets, setting incentives for budgetary efficiencies, and privatisation of services. The first two attempt to make public systems conscious of costs and competition, while the latter represents a shift from public to private provision. The adoption of market concepts is discussed in greater detail later in relation to recent trends across the different healthcare systems.

From healthcare concepts to healthcare systems

Three main types of healthcare system have been identified: national health-based systems, social insurance-based systems and private insurance-based systems. One of the first typologies was produced by the OECD in 1987, which constructed a continuum, from the principle of social equity to patient sovereignty, and located each model along this continuum as follows:

Table 8.1 A continuum of healthcare systems

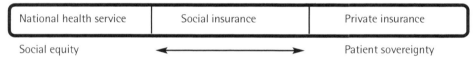

National health service	Social insurance	Private insurance

Social equity ⟵―――――――――⟶ Patient sovereignty

Source: OECD, 1987

The OECD classification focused on funding as the main element influencing the organisation of healthcare systems, which in turn impacts on the balance between equity and individual choice. This classification system was developed in the context of concerns about the cost of health and how to pay for it, and how to make the most efficient use of money spent on healthcare, which increasingly preoccupied debate.

Since the OECD study others have identified further significant factors that shape individual country's health systems and, in particular, institutional factors external to the health system. This broadened the focus of health system typologies beyond health economics. One such typology is offered by Moran (1999, 2000). He adds to our understanding of what healthcare is about and how policy is shaped because, as he observes, 'health care facilities in modern industrial societies are great concentrations of economic resources – and because of this they are also the subject of political struggle' (Moran, 1999, p. 1). In other words, health policy is more than providing a social service which is healthcare, but involves the production, consumption and governance of healthcare. Moran's work draws attention to the politics of healthcare, in particular the distributive struggles about who gets what kind healthcare and who pays for it, and the role of healthcare within an economy.

Moran introduces the concept of the healthcare state to denote the set of institutions related to governance of the production, provision and consumption of healthcare. He defines the healthcare state as 'that part of any state concerned with regulating access to, financing, and organising the delivery of, healthcare to the population' (Moran, 1992, p. 79). Moran suggests that the healthcare state has three 'faces'. The first concerns welfare and setting out access to health services. The second relates to the economic activity of regulating the industrial aspects of health, primarily the production of pharmaceuticals and medical equipment. The third involves the regulation of health interests, which include not just industrial interests, but very significant professional interests, especially doctors', whose actions, particularly relating to their power in deciding the consumption of healthcare, are a key component in understanding healthcare provision and policymaking.

Taking these elements of healthcare into account brings additional dimensions into focus and helps to broaden our understanding of both historical and contemporary healthcare policy. Moran puts forward a typology involving four basic types: secure and insecure command and control type systems, corporatist systems and supply systems. The first two roughly correspond with the national health model, the third with social insurance and the fourth with private insurance.

National health systems

In this system, healthcare is publicly provided on a universal basis and funded through general taxation. All citizens are therefore entitled to basic healthcare, including hospital and GP services and medicines, which they do not pay for at the point of use. Healthcare infrastructure such as hospitals and primary care services are either publicly owned and/or controlled. This type of healthcare system was first established in New Zealand in 1938; however, it is most directly identified with the British system, founded in the 1940s as part of the Beveridge reforms. As it is strongly motivated by equity, need rather than the ability to pay is the main factor influencing healthcare in this system. This is espoused in the 1944 White Paper on the National Health Service in the UK as follows:

> The Government want to ensure that in future every man, woman and child can rely on getting all the advice and treatment and care which they may need in matters of personal health; that what they get shall be the best medical and other facilities available; that their getting these shall not depend on whether they can pay for them, or any other factor irrelevant to the real need. (cited in LeGrand, 1982, p. 23)

This model was also adopted in Scandinavian countries, including Denmark and Sweden. Moran refers to this as a command and control system because the state is heavily implicated in the control and allocation of resources, through administrative mechanisms. This allows for the pursuit of an equitable distribution of healthcare between people of different social classes and between different regions, and for the pursuit of efficiency through administrative means such as rationing.

Moran's account differentiates between secure and insecure command and control systems. The latter include national health type systems developed later, specifically in Italy (1978), Portugal (1979), Greece (1983) and Spain (1986). These systems have been described as 'formally ambitious but under resourced' (Freeman, 2000, p. 6), meaning that they have not been able to reach the level of equal resource distribution that the earlier systems achieved. Moreover, as Moran (2000) notes, these later systems have had to survive in a harsher economic climate, compared to the 'golden age' in which the earlier national systems grew. However, the older established systems are also struggling with less resources and rising costs. Therefore, both the secure and insecure systems share similar problems, and administrative and payment-related reforms mean that the universal character of these systems is being eroded, especially since the 1990s.

Social insurance-based systems

These are also referred to as Bismarckian or corporatist type health systems. The reference to Bismarck reflects the fact that Germany was the first country to develop this type of health system in the 1880s. Since then, other western European countries such as the Netherlands, France and Austria have developed similar systems as has Japan, and Singapore also shares elements of an insurance-based system (Burau and Blank, 2006). Under this system, healthcare is paid for by insurance, based on employer and employee contributions. Insurance funds are non-profit based, and different insurance funds may be organised along occupational or regional lines. These funds usually contract services from both public and private hospitals and from independent doctors (Freeman, 2000).

The social character of the insurance system means that it has similarities with the tax-based national health model and differences that set it apart from private insurance. It is usually compulsory and it is essentially a collectivist system, where risk is pooled without taking account of differences in health status between contributors. Also, as Freeman (2000) points out regarding funding, there is little ultimately to distinguish national health and social insurance-based systems, as both are essentially funded through taxes.

This type of system was initially geared towards the more well-off proportion of the working class, and workers were segmented into different groups, with payments and benefits varying from group to group according to the status of different workers. However, over time insurance-based systems have become more comprehensive. Yet, as Moran (2000, p. 157) notes, 'their governing structures, especially the way sectional interests are empowered, poorly equip them to adapt to the challenge of social and economic change'. The issue of rising costs is therefore difficult to resolve under this system.

Private health insurance systems

In contrast to the systems outlined above, private health insurance companies enter the health insurance market in order to make a profit and they operate predominantly in countries with weak public healthcare provision. This model is also referred to as the supply healthcare state (Burau and Blank, 2006; Moran 2000). Insurance payments are funded by individual and/or employer contributions. They also differ from social insurance on the basis that private insurance is voluntary in nature and the cost of insurance is usually risk-related. This means that differences in the health status of individuals are reflected in different premiums. For example, people with a history of particular illnesses, such as back pain or heart problems, may have to pay higher premiums, and payments may also be loaded if an individual engages in what is considered risky behaviour such as smoking. Private health insurance, therefore, does not have the solidaristic quality of social insurance systems. In reality, much private health insurance is not paid directly by individuals but by their employer. In the USA, for example, where this model is most widespread, approximately 76 per cent of workers were covered by employment-based health insurance in 1996 and only 3 per cent of individuals paid for insurance themselves (Cooper and Schone, 1997, in Moran, 2000).

The logic of private markets has clear implications for the system: costs continue to rise as health is first and foremost a commodity from which profit is to be made, and there is also a significant market for medical innovation (Moran, 2000). The system is also the least equal in terms of access to healthcare; individuals who cannot afford private insurance or who are not in employment which offers health insurance are left to a public system which is strictly means-tested. This affects approximately 45 million Americans under 65 years of age who do not have health insurance (Ham, 2005). The two main forms of public healthcare in the US are Medicare (for older people) and Medicaid (for people on low incomes), both of which were introduced in the 1960s. However, as Navarro (1989) notes, the benefits and standards are comparatively meagre so as to encourage the take-up of private insurance and to limit the use of public health programmes, thus keeping public costs to a minimum. This goes against the trend of the universalisation of health coverage, which is common to both the social insurance and national health systems which predominate in Europe. In this context the US is painted as a welfare laggard, particularly in terms of healthcare. However, advocates of such a system argue that it promotes individual choice or patient sovereignty, because individuals choose what insurance to take out, what doctors to see and what hospitals to go to. Consequently, it is argued that this choice promotes competition between health providers which helps to ensure efficiency, and the supply-led nature of the system drives innovation in medical technology (Moran, 1999).

Where does the Irish healthcare system fit?

While no country fits exactly within any of the models and every country can to some extent be considered a mixed system, this is particularly true in the Irish case. The Irish healthcare system contains elements of the national health type system and elements of the private system. In terms of publicly provided services, basic hospital care is available to everyone and funded primarily from general taxation, while GP care is only available free to approximately 30 per cent of the population, predominantly on the basis of means-testing. Private care is a significant feature of the Irish healthcare system, with approximately 50 per cent of the population paying for private healthcare insurance, the main benefit being access to private hospitals and timelier care. However, a distinctive feature of the Irish system is the fact that much of this private care is delivered within the public system. This has produced many inequities and inefficiencies, which will be discussed in sections two and three of the chapter.

Common trends and issues across healthcare systems after World War II

At least two significant trends are discernable across healthcare systems over the last 50 to 60 years. The first is the growth of public healthcare provision to the point where a basic package of healthcare became universally accessible. The only exception to this trend has been the United States, where, as evident in table 8.2, the coverage of publicly funded healthcare has actually declined.

Table 8.2 Coverage by publicly funded healthcare schemes in selected OECD countries

	1960	1975	1997	2005
USA	20.0	40.0	45.0	27.3
UK	100.0	100.0	100.0	100.0
Germany	85.0*	90.3*	92.2	89.6
Canada	71.0	100.0	100.0	100.0
Japan	88.0	100.0	100.0	100.0

	1960	1975	1997	2005
France	76.3	96.0	99.5	99.9
Italy	87.0	95.0	100.0	100.0
Ireland	85.0	85.0	100.0	100.0

Source: Moran (1999) and OECD (2007)

Note: * 1960 and 1975 figures are for the former West Germany, 1997 and 2005 figures are for the unified Federal Republic.

The second and related trend has been the growth in healthcare expenditure over the same period. Table 8.3 shows that the total expenditure (both public and private) on health as a percentage of gross domestic product has risen significantly since the 1960s. The rate of growth has been relatively consistent over time. Again, the USA stands out as exceptional, having a particularly high level of health expenditure, over half of which is private and is explained by its particular healthcare system as already discussed.

Table 8.3 Total national expenditure on health as a percentage of GDP in selected OECD countries

	1960	1975	1990	2006
USA	5.1	7.0	11.9	15.3
UK	3.9	4.5	6.0	8.4
Germany*	n. av.	8.4	8.3	10.6
Canada	5.4	7.0	8.9	10.0
Japan	3.0	5.7	6.0	8.2**
France	3.8	6.4	8.4	11.1
Italy	n. av.	n. av.	7.7	9.0
Ireland	3.7	7.3	6.1	7.5

Source: OECD (2008b)

Notes:
* 1975 figure is for the former West Germany, 1990 and 2006 figures are for the unified Federal Republic.
** 2005 figure
n. av. not available

Data about the growth in expenditure must be juxtaposed with current debates in health policy. As Lenaghan (1997a) notes, healthcare is in a state of constant reform. Much of this reform is related to the rising costs of healthcare and the desire for cost containment. As a result, many states are attempting to row back on their commitments to funding healthcare entitlements.

There are a number of reasons why the cost of healthcare is increasing. These include demographic changes, changes in the nature of illness and disease, rising expectations, and medical progress. The demographic profile of Western nations has changed considerably, with a decline in birth rates coupled with an increase in life expectancy, meaning that populations are ageing and, of course, older people tend to need greater healthcare. While the origins of many systems were tied to concerns about workers' health, in contemporary healthcare systems the health problems of those outside the labour market require as much if not more attention. This includes not just older people but also the chronically (long-term) sick, as the incidence of chronic illness has risen in recent decades. This is partly a reflection of medical progress which has allowed people with chronic illnesses to live longer, yet this also means that greater demands are made of health services in treating the chronically ill.

The point about chronic illness is related to two other phenomena: medical progress and rising patient expectations. People have become more informed about the illnesses they are experiencing and the quality of care they can expect from health providers (Lenaghan, 1997b). This is linked, on the one hand, to the impact of the sociological critiques of medicine and medical authority stemming from the 1970s and the rise of health activism, and, on the other, to the impact of the increasing accessibility of medical information. The rise of health activism, particularly through patient interest groups, means that some groups of patients at least may no longer accurately be depicted as a 'repressed interest' within the system (Alford, 1975). Advances in medicine and medical technology also put increasing pressure on healthcare systems. Advances tend to be related to high-cost technologies and procedures involving highly skilled labour. Initially these may be accessed by patients with private insurance, which in turn puts pressure on public systems to make the procedures and medicines available on the grounds of equity.

If these are the issues influencing rising costs, on the flip side, healthcare states have been trying to contain costs even though the data on healthcare expenditure does not reflect a very successful programme of cost containment. Trends in relation to cost containment are manifested in diverse ways across the different healthcare systems because of their different funding mechanisms. In the national healthcare type systems rationing services has become more significant. Rationing has always been part of the way these systems operated; however, it has become more problematic compared to the 1950s, when many of these systems were established and rationing was more easily accepted. The use of waiting lists is one of the most well-known methods of rationing. These may be used in conjunction with target setting and performance management, with the aim of reducing waiting times and waiting lists, for example. Restricting the use of certain drugs and services in public healthcare systems is another form of rationing. The use of restrictive lists has become more common in both national health and social insurance-based systems. Limiting the availability of certain services and medicines has prompted a rise in the take-up of private health insurance in countries with national health type systems, which erodes the equitable base of the public health system. For example, in the UK in 2000 11.5 per cent of the population had private medical insurance compared to 4 per cent in 1975 (Mossialos and Thomson, 2002, in Barr, 2004).

Social insurance-based systems have also responded to the problem of rising costs by introducing some market principles to the operation of insurance funds. For example, in 1996 the German healthcare system introduced free choice of insurance funds for workers. This led to competition among different funds, with funds which practiced some limited forms of risk selection emerging as more successful in terms of managing costs. This has put pressure on all funds to curtail their solidaristic nature, so that members with higher health risks have to pay higher premiums. In this way the boundaries between social and private health insurance systems become blurred (Moran, 2000).

However, a shift towards private health insurance is not the answer to cost containment, if the experience of the US is anything to go by. As already noted, this type of system is the least successful at controlling rising health costs. In turn, the cost of private health insurance is continually rising, putting it out of reach of many individual subscribers. Co-payments are another form of cost curtailment, which is particularly evident in the newer national health systems in Southern Europe. This means that people availing of 'universal' health services are required to part-finance their use of a service. This is particularly the case with the Italian healthcare system. In Portugal and Greece, meanwhile, there is still heavy reliance on private health insurance (Moran, 2000). Similar trends can be observed in the Irish system.

In many ways, all examples of cost curtailment are evidence of attempts to shift the costs of healthcare from states to the individual. This is a regressive or inequitable step as it most affects those with the least ability to pay or to take out private insurance. Many of these issues and challenges will be returned to in the specific context of the contemporary Irish healthcare system in section three. First, in section two we look at the historical development of the Irish system, tracing its roots and subsequent development over the twentieth century and locating it within the broader context for understanding healthcare outlined in this section.

SECTION 2: THE DEVELOPMENT OF THE IRISH HEALTHCARE SYSTEM

Pre-independence

Early state involvement in healthcare across Europe was tied to the urgency of the 'hard facts' of sickness and the threat the spread of disease posed to the population at large. Healthy populations were necessary for state-building or state-stabilising projects in the context of industrialisation and war (Steffen et al., 2005). Early hospitals, like workhouses, served as institutions to contain the sick and prevent contagion. Public health measures originating from the mid-1800s onwards were similarly concerned with controlling outbreaks of disease and epidemics. However, that said, developments sprung as much from voluntary charitable efforts as they did from the state. These charitable efforts were often religiously motivated and there is a long history of religious bodies caring for the sick across Europe prior to state intervention as noted in Chapter 1.

The capacities of medicine, attitudes towards health and the demand for healthcare were very different to what prevails today, and these factors also played a significant part in the development of early health policy or medical relief. In Ireland and elsewhere hospitals were not associated with cure but were places of last resort. Admission to hospital was a sign of inability to pay for care in the home which was seen as preferable. Thus, there was a divide between the rich and the poor, with the rich accessing the services of private physicians and surgeons in their own homes. This allowed them to minimise the risk of contagion. In the case of mental illness, those with enough money tended to send their insane to private institutions in England or the Continent (Finnane, 1981), while the insane poor had to enter existing houses of industry. The rich/poor divide also applied to maternity care. Women who had the means to do so delivered their children at home, while poorer women went to the maternity or lying-in hospitals to deliver their babies (Barrington, 1987).

The earliest Irish hospitals and dispensaries, built in the early to mid-1700s, were the product of private charitable efforts. The hospitals were classed as 'charitable infirmaries' and later known as voluntary hospitals. Early state provision was essentially a matter of filling the gaps left by voluntary efforts in the form of county infirmaries and rural dispensaries. By the mid-1800s more vigorous and sustained state effort in the area of healthcare for the sick poor came about under the Poor Law, which provided an administrative framework for an expanding range of healthcare services. The Poor Law institutions took over the running of dispensaries in 1851 and services were provided to all those deemed unable to afford medical help, not just the destitute. The country was divided into 723 dispensary districts, each having a salaried dispensary doctor, who was also allowed to work privately. Workhouse infirmaries gradually accommodated more sick people, especially those not treatable in the existing network of infirmaries, and their role gradually transformed into one of a general hospital (Earner-Byrne, 2007). The dispensary doctor's role also gradually expanded over time to include public health functions.

The public health movement of the mid-nineteenth century was primarily concerned with attempting to control the spread of infectious diseases such as typhus and cholera, which were a major problem of the time, especially in urban areas. Other public health measures included the Births and Deaths Registration (Ireland) Act, 1864, the Public Health Act, 1878, and the Compulsory Vaccination (Ireland) Act, 1885. These acts represented the growth of state intervention in health in the name of prevention, regulation and control. However, the implementation of these acts was not without problems. There was an air of apathy and helplessness among the public health authorities who were hampered by reluctance to impose the higher taxes necessary to fund services, and the scale of poverty and squalor (Barrington, 1987).

As was the case previously with the development of infirmaries, voluntary efforts often took the lead in public health measures. For example, women, through the Women's National Health Association (WNHA), were particularly active in providing sanitorium beds for the sufferers of tuberculosis and educating people about its prevention and lobbying for better services. A similar trend applied in the case of maternity and child welfare, which became more of a public health concern in the late 1800s due to high levels of mortality and morbidity among mothers and babies across the UK. The WHNA was also actively involved in urban maternity committees provided for under the Notification of Births Act, 1915. These were populated by women active in the WHNA and the Infant Aid society who set about establishing baby clubs to assist new mothers (Earner-Byrne, 2007).

Backtracking a little to the late nineteenth century, the 1880s is commonly identified as the period when there was a marked increase in state involvement in healthcare (Freeman, 2000). This was signalled by the development of insurance programmes covering the cost of workers' health needs. The focus of state involvement in health, therefore, widened beyond the needs of the sick poor, and insurance provided benefits such as sickness, maternity and funeral benefits, as well as access to medical treatment. A number of other significant developments may also be observed around this time. Major scientific discoveries relevant to health occurred in the nineteenth century, including growing knowledge about bacteria, radiology and anaesthesia. This allowed health intervention to shift from control and containment to more radical individual interventions that would restore people to health. These discoveries augmented the power and status of medical doctors at the expense of other health practitioners. Doctors became important actors influencing the way states developed their health policies and services. They were significant, in particular, for their ability to organise themselves as professionals and form pressure groups. For example, Moran (1999) notes that the British Medical Association (BMA) was a historical prototype, providing a model which many other groups emulated.

The introduction of health insurance was one of the first episodes which drew doctors and the state into a tighter relationship. In the case of health insurance in Germany, for example, the growing strength of doctors meant that their acceptance of a health insurance system came with costly demands, such as a 'fee-for-service payment, and higher rates of remuneration; for free patient choice of doctor, and for limits to social insurance coverage (to protect private practice)' (Freeman, 2000, p. 23). Similar claims were made by doctors in other countries, including Ireland. The growth of the medical industry is another significant development, having its roots in this period (Moran, 1999). By the early to mid-twentieth century this fed into the gradual changing status of hospitals, which were transformed from places to be avoided to places in demand from the middle classes seeking out the benefits of medical advances and curative possibilities.

In the Irish case, increased state involvement in healthcare was dependent on developments in Britain. A collective insurance-based response to the health needs of workers was not introduced in the UK until 1911 when health insurance was introduced as part of the National Insurance Act as discussed in Chapter 1. This entitled workers under a certain income limit to medical benefit which took them out of the dispensary service and gave them free use of GP services and medicines. While the Act was not passed without controversy in Britain, with the BMA in particular having difficulties with it, in Ireland the health insurance part of the Act was not passed at all.

There was a mixed reaction to the initial 1911 Bill in Ireland; however, the strength of those who opposed the Bill outweighed those in favour of it. The Irish Party, for example, was concerned about the costs of the scheme and it was considered an unfair form of taxation. The medical profession was divided over the Bill, as private practitioners stood to lose fee-paying patients to the insurance system while dispensary doctors would gain as they were designated as the doctors to treat insured patients. The ICTU was in favour of medical benefit (Murray, 2006). However, the strongest opposition came from the Catholic Church which, paying scant regard to the needs of the working class, saw nothing in it for agricultural and business interests (Barrington, 1987; Powell, 1992). These issues and the interaction of the various interest groups led to an eventual settlement that excluded medical benefit in the implementation of the National Insurance Act in Ireland. Social insurance as a funding mechanism for GP services did not therefore take root. The dispensary service remained, with eligibility targeted through income and need. For everyone else, GP services would continue to be accessed privately. Some health-related measures were included in the second part of the Act, including sickness, maternity and disability benefits as cash payments, and sanatorium benefit in the form of treatment in a sanatorium or hospital for tuberculosis.

This episode represented a significant juncture in the history of Irish health policy. The introduction of health insurance in various forms across Europe from the 1880s onwards set countries on a path of gradually extending access to medical services. The non-implementation of this part of the Act in Ireland meant that the country lacked this foundation stone on which to build health services and improve access over the course of the twentieth century.

1920s and 1930s

In common with the other social services, few changes occurred in the area of healthcare once Ireland gained independence. Administrative changes came on foot of the Ministers and Secretaries Act, 1924, which led to the creation of a Department of Local Government and Public Health. This created a centralised authority for the administration and development of services under the remit of a minister. Administrative reform did not lead to new services; old ones were recycled. Thus, workhouses were converted into public hospitals, either in the form of county homes (to cater mainly for older people), county hospitals (one per county to act as the main hospital) or district and local hospitals. Most counties had county homes and hospitals, and district hospitals were spread among 18 counties. The 1929 Commission on the Relief of the Sick and Destitute Poor was severely critical of the services provided under this framework, finding the network of public hospitals under-funded and inadequate (Robins, 1960). Two of the biggest health problems of the early twentieth century, infant mortality and tuberculosis, were neglected. Mother and infant services were left mainly to voluntary initiatives. Tuberculosis services shared a similar fate, with a shortage of accommodation a particular problem. Consequently, while other countries experienced an improvement in the death rates due to the disease, the rate of decline in Ireland was minimal.

By the 1930s the focus turned to attempting to rationalise the network of hospitals. This was prompted by the financial crisis experienced by the voluntary hospital sector, giving rise to the hospital sweepstakes. In particular, voluntary hospitals in Dublin were finding it difficult to fund the rising costs of hospital care. This led to increasing acceptance of fee-paying patients which invoked the criticism that these hospitals were no longer true to their charitable origins (Barrington, 1987). The introduction of the hospital sweepstakes became a major source of funding and 'a remarkable means of evading the constraints imposed by relative underdevelopment on the funding of health services' (Murray, 2006, p. 49). The Public Charitable Hospitals Act, 1930, legalised sweepstakes on horse races for the purposes of raising funds for hospitals.[1] The sweepstakes were very successful during their first decade, and they marked 'the first step towards much greater involvement by public authorities in the affairs of hospitals ... as unprecedented amounts of money became available for hospital development, the state, in its role of guardian to the common good, was challenged to develop a hospital policy for the whole country and for both voluntary and public hospitals' (Barrington, 1987, pp. 111–12). The increasing cost of, and demand for, hospital care and specialist treatment also posed a challenge as these had the potential to widen the gulf between the rich and poor in terms of accessing healthcare. The problem for government, therefore, 'was how to ensure that the poor benefited from medical progress to the same extent as those who could afford to pay' (ibid., p. 119). The issue of private versus public healthcare and equity of access, therefore, has a long history in Ireland.

Fianna Fáil established a Hospitals Commission in 1933 to survey existing services and set about planning a coherent approach to future hospital provision in both local authority hospitals and voluntary hospitals. The commission recommended 12 main hospital centres and the amalgamation of some of the voluntary hospitals so as to improve their facilities and coordinate their services. Part of the rationale for these developments was an attempt to have some equality of treatment between fee-paying patients and non-fee paying patients, make efficient use of services, and avoid a situation where private patients would be treated in voluntary hospitals and the poor in public hospitals. Public hospitals on the whole were less popular and some still held the stigma of their workhouse origins (Robbins and Lapsley, 2008). The commission recommended that voluntary hospitals be required to maintain a certain proportion of non-fee paying patients and it is around this time that the practice of a public/private mix in hospitals emerged. Consultants in the voluntary hospitals and to a lesser extent in the local authority hospitals were allowed to use private beds and hospital services for private patients, treating non-fee paying patients in return (NESF, 2002a).

The commission also recommended that voluntary hospitals be publicly supervised and inspected, as a condition of receiving funding through the sweepstakes. The sweepstakes themselves were now to be administered through a Hospital Trust Fund. This was not welcomed by the voluntary hospitals who offered minimal cooperation with the commission and the trust fund (Daly, 1999b). The fund also became the source of finance for the construction of new public hospitals, whose numbers far exceeded that recommended by the commission (Barrington, 1987). The easy availability of this funding obscured questions of rationalisation and efficiency, storing up problems for later decades. In addition, despite this intense period of capital investment, the overall health status of the population left a lot to be desired. Life expectancy lagged behind the UK, infant mortality was still high and tuberculosis remained a significant problem. This state of affairs was in part a reflection of the fact that services required to address these issues continued to be under-resourced.

1940s and 1950s

The 1940s marked the emergence of a new phase in state involvement in healthcare across Europe, with growing universalisation of access to healthcare (Freeman, 2000). This did not occur without opposition from existing interests within each country's health system, and the more radical reforms tended to arise in countries which had particularly strong left-wing parties twinned with less than coherent opposition from existing interests such as the medical profession and insurance funds (ibid.).

In Ireland, developments in healthcare were influenced to a degree by the creation of the welfare state in Britain (see Chapter 4) and developments leading to the establishment of the NHS in 1948. While Aneurin Bevan, the Minister for Health in Britain, succeeded in overcoming opposition to the NHS, attempts to widen access to health services in Ireland entailed much more of a struggle with structural interests in the system. These included the medical profession, the Catholic Church and the Catholic-owned voluntary hospitals. All feared further state encroachment into existing practices, which would mean a loss of autonomy, damage to the prevailing Catholic ethos, and, in the case of medical practitioners, potential loss of income from private practice. These oppositional forces came to a head in the mother and child controversy during the late 1940s and early 1950s. This has already been described in detail in Chapter 2; here the focus is on the implications the episode had for the overall development of the healthcare system, and, in particular, how events in Ireland can be understood in the wider context of universalisation of access over this period.

Widening access to health services in Ireland was initiated by proposals put forward by the Department of Local Government and Public Health in

1945 in the *Report of the Departmental Committee on Health Services* and were envisaged to lead to 'a national health service embracing all classes within its scope, recognising no limitation of effectiveness on mere economic grounds, and treating the people from the health point of view as a unit' (Department of Local Government and Public Health, 1945, para. 189, in McKee, 1986, p. 165). The report recommended a wide-reaching reorganisation of the health services; counties would become responsible for comprehensive family medical services, available free to the whole population on a phased basis. This would see the end of the dispensary system. It entailed greater numbers of medical staff, especially GPs, and the service was to be paid for primarily through general taxation. Hospital and specialist services were to be organised on a regional basis, with the country divided into three regions, Dublin, Cork and Galway (Robins, 1960). The mother and child scheme proposed was one of the stepping stones towards this eventual outcome as it would extend services free of charge, to all mothers and children up to the age of 16. This was to be implemented as part 3 of the 1947 Health Act, within the new Department of Health created in 1947.

However, the power of the Church and the medical profession against Noël Browne, the Minister for Health, succeeded in blocking its implementation. The Church opposed universal access to the service, arguing instead that a means-tested service would be more appropriate. Means-testing would allay their fears of an overly interventionist state and would ensure that the influence the Catholic Church had on delivery of health services would remain strong. The medical profession was also opposed to the scheme, and wanted the state to continue to provide free services to the poor only, leaving ample room for private medicine.

The eventual outcome was a new Health Act in 1953 that offered a much more limited mother and child service, as part of wider reforms prepared by the new Minister for Health James Ryan after Fianna Fáil's return to power in 1951. These reforms included the extension of free hospital services, which again met with opposition from the Church and the medical profession, but was overcome this time round (ibid.). This Act put forward three categories of eligibility for health services based on income categories. While it has since been modified, this arrangement set in the 1950s remains the cornerstone of access and entitlement in the Irish healthcare system.

> ## Box 8.1 Categories of eligibility for public health services in the Health Act, 1953
>
> – **Category one**: those with the lowest incomes, eligible for all publicly provided health services free of charge, including GP, medicines and public hospitals. Initially 35 per cent of the population qualified as category one users. Essentially the situation of category one people did not change as they already had access to these services under public medical assistance.
> – **Category two**: the middle-income earners, initially comprising 50 per cent of the population. Their access to health services increased because now they were eligible for public hospital services for free or at a nominal charge, and for the new mother and child services. However, this access did not extend as far as GP services.
> – **Category three**: the highest income earners, who were not eligible for free public health services, except those related to tuberculosis; 15 per cent of the population made up category three health users. This group had to pay for their own hospital services and were not eligible for free mother and child services.

The whole episode significantly curtailed efforts to develop a universal health service free at the point of use, which would have seen the majority of the medical profession working for the public service and paid a salary. Under the 1953 legislation the public/private mix in public hospitals became more entrenched because the legislation provided for payments to consultants treating public patients in voluntary hospitals and 'this became the norm in subsequent years' (NESF, 2002a, p. 44). In addition, Voluntary Health Insurance (VHI) was introduced in 1956 in response to the continuing opposition by the Irish Medical Association (IMA) to the 1953 reforms because of the loss of private patients. A state-sponsored VHI Board was set up offering insurance cover on a non-profit basis for the hospital costs incurred by category three health users and the hospital costs incurred by category two users who opted for private care. Its introduction opened up the avenue for further private medicine paid for by private insurance. Although it was initially intended to cater for the small number of people not entitled to public care, this turned out not to be the case. Another legacy of this time, as Murray (2006, p. 51) notes, is the fact that 'restricted availability of family planning services, sterilisation procedures and infertility treatments remains a feature of today's Irish health care system'. This reflects the continuing influence of a Catholic ethos in parts of the health system.

However, the period also brought some positive developments. For example, while Noël Browne was Minister for Health he availed of the Hospital Trust Fund to embark on a major programme of upgrading and building hospitals, making a greater range of diagnostic tools and surgical procedures available in county hospitals. This expansionary programme was continued by successive governments in the 1950s in order to meet the demands for healthcare as a result of increased entitlements to public healthcare following the 1953 Act. For tuberculosis sufferers, extra beds in existing hospitals as well as new sanatoria improved services. Building on the efforts of earlier doctors, such as Dr Dorothy Price working with children who acquired the disease, Noël Browne also recognised the significance of vaccination against the disease, and the implementation of a nationwide vaccination programme in the early 1950s meant that by the end of the decade, the disease ceased to be a major problem (Ó hÓgartaigh, 1999).

1960s and 1970s

During the 1960s and 1970s the focus of the health system turned towards administrative reform and continuing attempts to rationalise services, which were expanding greatly. There were more hospitals and services to run, and they were in demand by the larger proportion of the population who were entitled to free services, as category one and two health users together amounted to approximately 85 per cent of the population. New health issues were also emerging. While health improved in terms of tuberculosis, life expectancy and infant mortality, new health problems were replacing them, especially heart disease, cancer, diseases related to ageing, drug and alcohol dependency and deaths due to accidents. Costs rose significantly; as a proportion of GDP, health expenditure increased from 3.7 per cent in 1960 to 5.1 per cent in 1970 (OECD, 2008b). Despite this growth, debates about expanding access and entitlement continued. During the 1959 election, for example, the Labour Party put forward proposals for a universal health service funded mainly out of taxation, while Fine Gael proposed something similar funded mainly by health insurance. Both parties made similar proposals in the following election in 1965. That election saw Fianna Fáil back in power, with a new Minister for Health Donogh O'Malley, who published a White Paper entitled *The Health Services and their Further Development* in 1966. This paper is significant for being the road map for many of the developments in the health services which have occurred since. However, at the outset the paper declared that the state did not have 'a duty to provide unconditionally for all medical services free of cost for everyone' (Barrington, 1987, p. 261), which basically meant a confirmation of the existing arrangements about eligibility.

The White Paper recommended that category one individuals be granted a choice of doctor and a choice of pharmacist instead of receiving drugs directly from the dispensary doctor, and doctors would be obliged to treat category one patients in the same facilities as private patients. These changes signalled the end of the dispensary system, to be replaced by a General

Medical Scheme (GMS). The overall aim was that there would be no difference in access to GP services between public and private patients. However, the creation of the GMS was problematic. The main issue at stake was how doctors would be paid. The Department of Health favoured a capitation scheme where doctors got paid a lump sum, whereas doctors lobbied for a fee per service arrangement. The fee per service system would be potentially more costly; however, doctors argued that it would help to remove the distinction between private and public patients, and ensure a better quality service. The issue was not resolved until 1972 when a fee per service system was introduced. While the end of the dispensary system and the introduction of choice were most welcome, the fee per service arrangement had many flaws in practice. As Barrington (ibid. p. 277) points out, it 'reinforced many of the defects of Irish general practice: the reluctance to form group practices, poor practice premises, minimal record keeping, excessive competition for patients, and a preoccupation with treatment rather than prevention', the legacy of which is still evident.

The White Paper also assessed trends and problems in hospital services. It ascertained that county hospitals were no longer suitable as the main hospitals for a region and that these needed to be based in larger regions and tied to regional rather than county-based administration. The White Paper also envisaged that local authorities at county level would no longer be the main administrative unit and that local rates would play less of a role in funding hospital services. The White Paper therefore paved the way for the introduction of health boards in the 1970 Health Act as discussed below. While this administrative reform represented a loss of control for local authorities, they were compensated by the reduced burden on local rates. By 1973 it was decided to phase out local health funding completely and this was achieved by 1977 (Hensey, 1988).

The task of formulating a plan to regionalise the hospitals was given to a Consultative Council on the General Hospital Services in 1967, chaired by Professor Patrick Fitzgerald, a voluntary hospital consultant. The Fitzgerald report, as it became known, proposed a systematic but controversially received plan for the future development of the hospitals. The report recommended fewer and larger hospitals, namely 12 general hospitals and 4 regional hospitals. The 12 general hospitals would each have 300 beds to cover a population of 120,000 people, and would offer all the main services, with two consultants per speciality. Twelve existing county hospitals would be designated general hospitals and the rest would become community health centres. Four regional hospitals (two in Dublin, one each in Cork and Galway) would have 600 beds and operate as general hospitals for the area as well as providing more specialised services for the larger region. It recommended a separate administrative system for hospitals, which would oversee the development of both public and voluntary hospitals. The report was not well received at local level, with each area defending its own general hospital against what was perceived as downgrading to a community health centre, and regional hospitals were considered too far away from many rural areas (Barrington, 1987).

The 1970 Health Act introduced many of the changes outlined in the 1966 White Paper. It provided for the establishment of eight regional health boards which came into being in October 1970. Taking over from county-based administration, they became the main operational centres for administering and delivering services. To appease local interests in the face of hospital rationalisation, local authority representatives comprised the majority of board members. In addition, a public inquiry was to be held before any hospital would be closed. Other health board members included representatives from the medical professions, including doctors, dentists, pharmacists and nurses, and people appointed by the Minister for Health. The work, which was carried out by a management team under the Board, was divided into three areas: community care services (preventative, GP, dental and public health, social work and community welfare), general hospital services, and 'special' hospital services (psychiatric; disability – intellectual, physical, sensory; addiction services). A central coordinating body, Comhairle na n-Ospidéal, was created to regulate the appointment of specialists and consultants to health boards and voluntary hospitals. Hospital consultants comprised the majority of the members of this body.

Eligibility for hospital services was extended in 1979 when Charles Haughey, the then Minister for Health, implemented a plan for free hospital care for all user categories of the health service. However, category three users were still liable to pay for consultant charges. On the whole, the 1970s delivered another phase of expansion which entailed significant increases in expenditure. While all health funding was now under the control of central government this did not actually put a brake on expenditure. Health expenditure increased from 5.1 per cent of GDP in 1970 to 8.3 per cent in 1980. In 1970, Irish health expenditure just exceeded the OCED average of 5.0 per cent, while by 1980, Irish expenditure was well above the OECD average of 6.6 per cent of GDP (OECD, 2008b). This increase can partly be explained by the rise in population during the 1970s. In addition, as local areas were no longer being taxed for health services, this unleashed more vigorous demands for the development of services in local areas, while simultaneously strengthening local resistance to any plans to demote particular hospitals.

Freeman (2000) identifies the period from the 1940s to the 1970s in general as one of universalisation of access, but how did the Irish system fare? The only thing that came near to universalisation of access was hospital care, which was now available free to 85 per cent of the population. This represented a certain acceptance of the expansion of the public health system, and Barrington (1987) points out that the reforms of this period de-politicised health conflicts, and the state's relationship with consultants, GPs and voluntary hospitals became less conflictual. Yet the other side of this alliance was the 'perpetuation of private practice and the maintenance of high incomes, the independence of voluntary hospitals and professional involvement at all levels in the administration of the health services' (ibid., p. 280). Also, 15 per cent of the population still had to pay hospital consultant fees and 70 per cent of the population had to pay GP fees.

Equally significant is the way in which private practice evolved since this time, especially in the hospital sector, which makes the Irish system quite distinctive. As Nolan (2006b, p. 633) puts it, 'the public health system has a symbiotic relationship with private health insurance not seen in other European countries.' Essentially, the private and public system are not two separate systems, but are closely intertwined, with the public system absorbing much of the costs of the private system, because a significant amount of private healthcare is delivered in public hospitals. Thus, hospital consultants retained the right to treat their private patients in public hospitals using public system facilities and staff, while public hospitals only charged for the cost of providing accommodation. This produced a build-up of inequities and inefficiencies in the system, which became more acute in the following decades as the public system suffered under economic recession and more people opted to access hospital care privately through health insurance.

SECTION 3: THE CONTEMPORARY IRISH SYSTEM – REFORM SINCE THE 1980s AND CONTINUING ISSUES AND CHALLENGES

The 1980s marked a turning point, not only for the Irish healthcare system but internationally. Governments have struggled with cost containment but, as we have seen in section one, this does not mean expenditure has fallen; in most countries, health expenditure has continued to rise but there is a greater desire for efficiency. In the Irish case, as Wiley (2005, p. 5171) puts it, expenditure since the 1980s has been a story of 'two halves', with quite severe contraction in the 1980s followed by expansion in the 1990s and beyond. However, increased expenditure has been accompanied by actions to keep spending under control. In some respects this has entailed a shift in activity from publicly provided healthcare to private healthcare. However, the manner in which this is being carried out has raised questions about efficiency as well as equity, while the enduring public/private mix in the public healthcare system also raises efficiency and equity concerns, particularly in the context of the cutbacks in the 1980s which have had a long-lasting effect on the health system. Within this overall context, equity of access has emerged as one of the key issues and challenges in the contemporary Irish healthcare. This is expressed in the idea that Ireland has a two-tier health system. This issue is the main focus of the final section of the chapter. This section first sets the scene by looking at the overall pattern of expenditure and the broad evolution of health policy and organisational reform since 1980. The key policy documents and developments concerning the issue of equity of access and main developments within the health system which have a bearing on this, including changes to the eligibility structure, waiting list initiatives, modifications to the public/private mix, issues in relation to private health insurance, the growth of private hospitals and co-location, and developments in primary care, are also examined. Finally, this section also briefly reviews the relationship between health inequalities, the health system and the wider social determinants of health.

Expenditure on health exceeded the OECD average in the early 1980s and the cutbacks beginning in 1987 mark a turning point when Irish expenditure on health fell below the OECD average and remained quite low until an upward trend began again in 2001. However, while total expenditure greatly increased since the early 2000s this is still not enough to bring it to the OECD average which has been steadily rising throughout the period (see table 8.4 below). Overall, the pattern suggests that current expenditure is still making up for deficits from the late 1980s and over the 1990s. This provides an alternative perspective to the idea that increased health expenditure is simply falling into a 'black hole' for which no benefits have been gained, an argument which gained ground during the early 2000s and which continues to be influential.

Table 8.4 Irish Health expenditure as a percentage of GDP compared to the OECD average, 1980–2006

Year	Ireland	OECD average**
1980	8.3	6.6
1985	7.5	6.7
1990	6.1*	7.0
1995	6.7	7.7
2000	6.3	7.8
2005	8.2	8.9
2006	7.5	8.7

Source: OECD (2008b)

Notes:
* break in the series in 1990. In 2003 the OECD re-classified what counts as health expenditure in Ireland and excluded what could be defined as social spending; this had the effect of somewhat lowering overall expenditure as a percentage of GDP, and health expenditure back as far as 1990 was re-classified in this manner. Therefore, expenditure levels before and after 1990 are not strictly comparable.
** calculated from range of countries where data is available

Turning to the overall pattern of health policy development and reform, the observation that health systems are undergoing constant reform as noted in section one is certainly true in the Irish case. Since the 1980s there has been a profusion of policy documents covering strategy and planning, and reviews and reports into particular issues and problems. In chart 8.1 below the main policy developments are outlined and broadly categorised into four areas. These include overall strategic plans for the health service; reports dealing with issues of funding, staffing and organisational change; reports dealing with the reorientation of the health services towards health promotion and/or addressing specific contemporary health problems; and, finally, the more recent phenomenon of reports and investigations into specific areas where the health services have failed particular individuals and groups of people. In focusing on equity of access in particular this section will refer mainly to policies in the first two categories.

Chart 8.1 Health policy developments, 1980s–2000s

Principal strategy documents	System overview/ funding, staffing and organisational reform	Health promotion and specific health issues	System problems and failures
1984 Planning for the Future 1986 Health – the Wider Dimensions 1994 Shaping a Healthier Future 2001 Quality and Fairness – A Health System for You	1989 Commission on Health Funding 1990 Dublin Hospital Initiative Group (Kennedy Reports)	1987 Promoting Health through Public Policy 1996 Cancer Services in Ireland – A National Strategy 1996 National Alcohol Policy	1997 Report of the Tribunal of Inquiry into the Blood Transfusion Service Board 2002 Protecting our Future – Report of the Working Group on Elder Abuse

Principal strategy documents	System overview/ funding, staffing and organisational reform	Health promotion and specific health issues	System problems and failures
2001 Primary care – A New Direction	1999 Interim Report on the Task Force on the Eastern Regional Health Authority 1997 1999 White paper on private health insurance 2001 Audit of the Irish Health system for value for money 2002 Report of the National Task Force on Medical Staffing (Hanly Report) 2003 Report of the Commission on Financial Management and Control Systems in the Health Service (Brennan Commission)	2001 National Drugs Strategy 2001–2008 2002 Traveller Health – National Strategy 2002–2005 2002, 2004 National Strategic Taskforce on Alcohol Interim Reports 2005 Obesity – the policy challenges 2005 Reach Out: National Strategy for Action on Suicide Prevention 2006 Strategy for Cancer Control in Ireland 2008 Tackling Chronic Disease – A Policy Framework for the Management of Chronic Diseases	2002 Report into the death of baby Bronagh Livingstone 2002 Report of the Tribunal of Inquiry into the infection with HIV and Hepatitis C of persons with Haemophilia and related matters 2005 Report of the Panel established to conduct an independent review of the events surrounding the death of Róisín Ruddle 2006 Lourdes Hospital Inquiry: An Inquiry into peripartum hysterectomy at our Lady of Lourdes Hospital, Drogheda

Principal strategy documents	System overview/ funding, staffing and organisational reform	Health promotion and specific health issues	System problems and failures
	2003 Audit of the Structure and Functions of the Irish Health Care System (Prospectus Report)		**2006** Report of Dr Deirdre Madden on post-mortem practice and procedures
	2004 Health Service Reform Programme (Composite Report)		**2008** Management, Governance and Communications – Issues arising from the review of breast radiology services at Midlands Regional Hospital Portlaoise (Fitzgerald Report)
	2005 Review of Governance and Accountability Mechanisms in the GMS schemes		**2008** Report on Independent Review of Symptomatic Breast Care Services at Barrington's Hospital, Limerick, September 2003–August 2007

Organisational reform

Before we look specifically at the issue of equity of access, another significant contextual issue in the organisation of health services needs to be noted. In 2005 the health boards were abolished and replaced with the Health Service Executive (HSE). The need for organisational reform had been recognised as far back as the 1989 Commission on Health Funding. Its major conclusion and recommendation was that the solutions to healthcare lay in administration and management: 'the kernel of the Commission's conclusions is that the solution to the problem facing the Irish health services does not lie primarily in the system of funding but rather in the way that services are planned, organised and delivered' (Commission on Health Funding, 1989, p. 15). It recommended, among other things, the creation of a health executive authority that would have overall responsibility for managing the health services, separate from the Department of Health. This proposal was, however, too radical a step for the government to take at the time. In the meantime some minor reform in the form of the establishment of the Eastern Regional Health Authority (EHRA), replacing three area health boards in the Dublin region, took place in 1999 (Curry, 2003).

Reflecting the influence of new public management thinking (see Chapter 4), issues of managerial reform, accountability and quality reappeared again in *Shaping a Healthier Future* (1994) and in *Quality and Fairness – A Health System for You* (2001). Both of these documents raised the need for more effective and **evidence-based** decision-making procedures, and the need to improve financial, professional and organisational accountability. The eventual establishment of the HSE was also triggered by a number of reports commissioned in the early 2000s by the Department of Health and Children (as the Department was renamed in 1997). These were the Brennan Commission, the Prospectus Report and the Hanly Report. By 2001 an upward trend in health expenditure was emerging and the Brennan Commission was given the remit to assess health expenditure. The Hanly Report was commissioned in response to an EU working time directive and it recommended some far-reaching changes to staffing, so that the health service would be transformed from a consultant-led to a consultant-provided service. The Prospectus Group had the task of assessing the organisation of the health services with a view to how they could be streamlined.

The *Health Service Reform Programme* (Department of Health and

> **Evidence-based** decision-making is an idea originating in medicine and now applied across the social sciences, but which is open to debate. It rests on the notion that decision-making, policy and practice should be based on the best available research knowledge in order to improve quality and effectiveness.

Children, 2003) outlined the government's decisions on how to reform the health system on foot of the three reports. The biggest decision was to abolish the health boards, the EHRA and a number of other agencies and replace them with the HSE. In the new system there are four regional HSE areas: West, South, Dublin Mid-Leinster and Dublin North-East. The HSE began its work in January 2005. Its service functions are divided into three core areas: National Hospitals Office (NHO) (which replaces Comhairle na nOspidéal); Primary, Community and Continuing Care (PCCC); and Population Health. The focus of the Department of Health and Children has shifted from day-to-day matters to policy development and oversight, to complement the work of the HSE. In 2007, another major body, the Health Information and Quality Authority (HIQA), was established and its role is to contribute to the effectiveness of decision-making and the quality of care provided.

This reform process remains unsettled. Since it was established, the HSE has been subjected to a barrage of criticism, relating to, for example, the adequacy of the health budget and the appropriateness of budgetary decisions, and for being overly centralised without clear lines of accountability, leading to administrative and other failures, highlighted by a number of high-profile cases involving mis-diagnoses and inappropriate care. In summer 2008 it was announced that the HSE would undergo some restructuring to improve accountability and the integration of services. The NHO and the PCCC are to be integrated under one director, reflecting the need to have greater integration between hospital and primary care services. Furthermore, it is proposed that the Population Health directorate be replaced by a new directorate of planning. At regional level, new managers are proposed, who would have overall responsibility for the healthcare budget for their area. This would mark something of a return to the regional health board system. As ever with health services, it is likely that proposed and implemented reforms will be the subject of on-going debate.

In addition, from the perspective of equity of access, as Wren (2004, p. 4) has commented:

> It is hard to argue with greater accountability, more streamlined decision making or better regional hospital care delivered by more senior doctors. But no one in Government appears to be starting from the point of view that this state should offer accessible, affordable healthcare to all its people delivered according to need not income. The Government's limited definition of the problem leads it to limited solutions.

It is to this problem, namely equity of access, and the evolution of solutions since the 1980s that we now turn.

Emergence of concern about the two-tier health system

The issue of inequity of access, commonly referred to as the two-tier system of healthcare, unfolded during the mid- to late 1980s in the context of two significant trends: public health cutbacks and private health expansion. Looking firstly at cutbacks and cost containment, as evident in table 8.4 above, public health expenditure began to decline by the late 1980s. One of the most visible ways in which health services were cut back was through hospital closures, and the 1980s represented the first serious rationalisation of hospital services in contrast to earlier decades when such plans were not followed through. Part of the rationale for cutting hospital services was to promote alternatives such as community care, as envisaged in *Planning for the Future* (1984), and prevention and primary care as opposed to 'repair', as envisaged in *Health the Wider Dimensions* (1986). However, in the climate of fiscal restraint at the time these ideals were not adequately realised. Many district and long-running voluntary hospitals closed (see box 8.2), but not without strong resistance from the communities affected. For example, the closure of Barrington's hospital in Limerick was particularly contentious, prompting large protest marches in the city. (It subsequently re-opened as a private hospital in 1994.) Overall, approximately 6,000 hospital beds were eliminated during the late 1980s and early 1990s (Curry, 2003). In terms of hospital beds per 1,000 of population, the number fell from 9.1 in 1987 to 6.7 in 1997 (OECD, 2008b). Other examples of cost containment included the controversial introduction of co-payments for health service charges in 1987, whereby hospital users who did not possess a medical card became liable for a charge for overnight hospital stays and out-patient visits. The General Medical Scheme (GMS) was also reformed. The rising cost of the system had been an issue as early as 1975; however, again, it wasn't until a climate of severe fiscal restraint prevailed that GP resistance to reforming the system was overcome. In 1988 the method of payment to GPs changed from a per use system to a per capita system, on the basis that this cost less money to provide. Doctors were also given individual prescription targets in a bid to reduce the cost of prescriptions under the GMS.

Box 8.2 Hospital closures during the mid-1980s

- Auxiliary District Hospital, Kilkenny
- Bagnelstown District Hospital, County Carlow
- Barrington's Hospital, Limerick
- Brownswood District Hospital, Enniscorthy
- Cork Eye, Ear and Throat Hospital
- County and City Infirmary, Waterford
- Dr Steeven's Hospital, Dublin

- Jervis Street Hospital, Dublin
- Kilrush District Hospital
- Lismore District Hospital, County Waterford
- Monkstown Hospital
- North Infirmary, Cork
- Royal Victoria Eye and Ear Hospital, Dublin
- St Laurence's Hospital
- St John of God's Hospital's Maternity Unit, Cahercalla
- St Mary's Geriatric Hospital, Drogheda
- St Vincent's District Hospital, Tipperary
- Thurles District Hospital

Source: Dáil Éireann (1988)

Growth of private healthcare

Over the 1980s the provision of private health services grew and the public/private mix in the system became more entrenched. These trends stemmed in part from the implementation of a common consultants contract in 1981. This contract put consultants in health boards and voluntary hospitals on the same footing. It provided for a salaried consultant service in all public hospitals and allowed consultants to practice privately, either in the public hospital in which they carried out their salaried work or in a private hospital. Health board hospital consultants were now contractually treated in the same way as consultants in voluntary hospitals. Crucially, however, this contract did not provide for a monitoring of consultant time devoted to public patients, and the extent to which consultants could engage in private practice was unspecified and potentially unlimited. Wren (2003, p. 57) argues that this paved the way for the expansion of private medicine and 'turned heavily state subsidised, private medicine into a growth industry'. Regarding private hospitals, the Mater Private and the Blackrock Clinic both opened in Dublin in 1986. The Mater Private was established by the Sisters of Mercy to replace an existing private hospital run by the order. It was subsequently sold to a management group in 2000 as falling numbers of religious staff meant that the Sisters of Mercy could no longer run it. The Blackrock Clinic was established by Jimmy Sheehan, an orthopaedic consultant, who promoted the notion of health as a commodity:

> The state cannot provide for everyone. That is what they tried to do in the Communist states and they failed miserably. I think health is a bit like housing. People are entitled to different levels of housing. If they want to put their effort into providing for better housing, they

have to work very hard for it and people have forgotten about that in relation to their own health. (Sheehan, 2002, in Wren, 2003, p. 69)

The growth in private medicine paralleled the growth in private health insurance. Private health coverage grew from 26.1 per cent of the population in 1979 to 34.4 per cent by 1990, although people who opted for treatment in the new private hospitals were obliged to subscribe to more expensive insurance programmes at the insistence of the Minister of Health at the time. As for the public/private mix, the volume of private activity in public hospitals grew. In the context of health cutbacks the extra revenue hospitals could raise by providing private bed accommodation acted as an incentive to transform public wards into private wards and the proportion of private beds in public hospitals grew from approximately 10 per cent in 1972 to 20 per cent by 1987 (Wren, 2003). The combination of public hospital cutbacks with the growth in private health services in both private and public hospitals prompted concern that Ireland had an unfair two-tier service. As section two documented, the public/private mix has evolved over many decades; however, the sense that this was a problem did not become widespread until the 1980s (NESF, 2002a) when the implications of the two-tier system became more visible due to the cutbacks.

What is the two-tier system?

Essentially the two-tier system refers to two tiers in both access and care in the public hospital system. Two-tier access became particularly apparent in the face of hospital bed closures as public patients experienced growing waiting times for care, while private patients avoided these waiting times and received private care in the same hospitals much faster. The phenomenon of two-tiered care also became apparent, as private patients benefit from a consultant-provided service, whereas care for public patients is consultant-led. This arrangement reflects the fact that consultants are paid a fee per patient in the private system, while their remuneration for the treatment of public patients is salary-based. When this is combined with the fact that 'frontline services are mainly provided by non-consultant hospital doctors many of whom are in the early stages of their training or not in formal training posts' (Medical Manpower Forum, 2001, p. 19), quality of care has the potential to be especially poor for public patients. 'Long waiting times, additional tests, referrals to other junior doctors and a reluctance to seek senior opinion at times have serious implications for both diagnosis and treatment of the patient' (ibid.).

This situation is exacerbated by the way in which the public/private mix works in the Irish system. Essentially, the private component of the public health system does not pay its own way but is publicly subsidised. Although modified slightly in recent years as discussed below, public subsidisation occurs

Protest against
health cuts, 2008.
Source: author's
photograph.

in three principal ways. Firstly, public hospitals do not charge the full costs of
providing private care. In research commissioned by the government and
carried out by the ESRI, Nolan and Wiley (2001) found that public hospitals
charge insurance companies approximately half the cost of providing private
care. This in turn means that insurance subscription rates do not reflect the full
cost of private care, and, finally, these costs are lowered further by the
provision of tax relief on insurance premiums. In essence, public money
subsidises private healthcare, a situation which can be considered an inefficient
use of scarce public resources and an inequitable one, given the faster access
and superior care afforded to private users of hospital care. Returning to
definitions of health equity discussed in section one, while equity of access is
broadly defined in terms of equal access for equal need, in this situation,
income rather than medical need determines access to hospital care.

Policy responses to inequity of access

Commission on Health Funding, 1989

The notion of a two-tier health service became a matter of increasing public
concern in the late 1980s. The main governmental response was to establish

a Commission on Health Funding (referred to hereafter as 'the Commission') in 1987, with the remit to show how an equitable, comprehensive and cost-effective service could be funded. The Commission took the idea of equity of access to mean 'equal access for equal need' and it went on to outline a horizontal view of equity in practice:

> ... for those services which are considered necessary on the criterion of comprehensiveness, access of patients should be determined on the basis of their individual need for the service, rather than on, for example, their geographical location or their ability to pay. The concept requires not alone that those meeting the criteria of need should have formal entitlement to the services; it also requires that the necessary services are available to satisfy their entitlement, that these services are of high quality and are available within a reasonable period. (Commission on Health Funding, 1989, p. 64)

To achieve equity of access the Commission recommended that there should be greater demarcation between private and public hospital beds, and that a common waiting list be established between public and private patients so that beds would be allocated on the basis of medical priority not ability to pay. It also recommended the abolition of tax relief for private insurance and the abolition of category three eligibility to health services so that all hospital services would be publicly available to all users.

At the same time the Commission did not see a problem with private insurance as an individual choice. It stated that it did 'not consider it inequitable that private insurance should enable individuals to obtain speedier or otherwise unavailable treatment, *provided* that comprehensive and cost-effective publicly-funded health services are available within a reasonable period of time to all those assessed as in need of them' (ibid., p. 13). It therefore envisaged private health insurance as having a supplementary role to public health care.

Shaping a Healthier Future, 1994

Concern with equity of access continued as a key theme in the two main strategic policy documents subsequently published by the Department of Health. In 1994 *Shaping a Healthier Future* was the first major strategic overview of the health service since the 1966 White Paper. The conceptualisation of equity remained similar to the Commission's formulation and again there was little concern about the effect of the private system on equity of access. However, the document did address equity in relation to differences in health status and the health status of particular disadvantaged groups, including Travellers. It therefore defined equity as follows:

Access to healthcare should be determined by actual need for services rather than ability to pay or geographic location. Formal entitlement to services is not enough; those needing services must have them available within a reasonable period. Furthermore, the pursuit of equity must extend beyond the question of access to treatment and care, and must examine variations in the health status of different groups in society and how these might be addressed. (Department of Health, 1994, p. 10)

In relation to equity, the strategy did not see a problem with the public and private mix, and the two-tier system of eligibility to health services. It stated, for example, that the government was 'committed to maintaining the position of private practice, within the well established public/private mix' (ibid., p. 36). It put forward a four-year action plan, with over 200 targets, including measures to reduce premature mortality in relation to cardiovascular diseases, cancer and accidents. In terms of equity, it recommended uniform rules for determining eligibility across the different health boards, reducing waiting times for public patients and focusing on the health needs of particular disadvantaged groups.

Quality and Fairness – A Health System for You, 2001

In 2001, a more far-reaching strategic policy document, based on a consultative process, was published. This 7–10 year programme offered a comprehensive strategy for all aspects of the health services. It made a much stronger statement about the problem of inequity of access and clearly acknowledged that the public/private mix was part of the problem, in particular in terms of physical capacities of hospitals and how consultants allocated time between public and private patients. Adopting a similar approach to equity of access as the 1994 document it went on to specifically refer to the contrasting experiences of private and public patients in public hospitals:

One of the key concerns of the Health Strategy is to promote fair access to services, based on objectively assessed need, rather than on any other factor such as whether the patient is attending on a public or private basis. This is a particular concern in the area of acute hospital services. The current mix of public and private beds in the public system is intended to ensure that public and private sectors can share resources, clinical knowledge, skills and technology. This mix raises serious challenges, which must be addressed in the context of equity of access for public patients. (Department of Health and Children, 2001a, p. 43)

In addition, it made specific reference to the two-tier nature of the health service: 'the strategy must address the "two-tier" element of hospital treatment where public patients frequently do not have fair access to elective treatment' (ibid., p. 48).

The strategy proposed four guiding principles for the health service; these included three already proposed by *Shaping a Healthier Future*, namely quality, accountability and equity, plus the goal of people-centredness. It translated the four principles into four national goals: better health for everyone (including health promotion, quality of life issues, and targeting and reducing health inequalities), fair access, responsive and appropriate care delivery and high performance. These were then translated into 121 actions to be met over the period up to 2010. Instead of transforming the public/private mix or the funding basis of the system, the strategy promised substantial investment in the public health system as a way of overcoming inequity of access. It therefore proposed to increase the capacity of the public hospital system by introducing 3,000 new hospital beds and it promised to end waiting times of longer than three months for hospital treatment by the end of 2004.

Changes in eligibility to health services

Following the Commission's report, changes to the eligibility framework were implemented in 1991 as part of the commitments contained in the second social partnership agreement, the *Programme for Economic and Social Progress* (PESP). These changes meant that universal coverage of hospital care was finally achieved. Unlike earlier times when the eligibility framework was introduced in 1953 and extended in 1979, this time there was no opposition to the change being introduced. Consultants no longer perceived the extension of public hospital care as a threat to their private income, as the number of people opting for private health insurance was rising substantially. In any case the government remained committed to the public/private mix. In the PESP the role of private practice in public hospitals and the role of voluntary health insurance were strongly endorsed and this has been upheld by subsequent governments:

> The Government are committed to maintaining the position of private practice both within and outside the public hospital system. The Government also recognise the crucial role played by voluntary health insurance. In gradually implementing the new system the Government will be sensitive to the need to ensure that the public hospital system caters adequately for the requirements of private patients and that the important role and contribution of voluntary health insurance is not diminished in any way. (Government of Ireland, 1990, p. 28)

An unanticipated change to the medical card eligibility system occurred when all people aged over 70 became eligible for a medical card in 2001. This represented recognition of the greater health needs of older people, yet its universal application meant that the change could be said to be inefficient as it took no account of income. Older people with high incomes who could afford GP costs now found themselves receiving this care free of charge. Major controversy was caused by the 2009 Budget when it was proposed to impose means-testing on medical cards for the over 70s. In response to swift and effective protest by older people the proposal was altered to exclude only those with relatively high incomes (€36,500 for a single person and €73,000 for a couple) from the scheme on a self-assessment basis.

Returning to the 2001 health strategy, it promised to significantly increase the numbers of people eligible for a medical card by raising income thresholds, reviewing them annually and prioritising families with young children and children with disabilities. However, the economic downturn in 2002 meant that this proposal was not implemented. An alternative, more targeted form of expansion occurred in 2005 with the introduction of a means-tested GP Visit card for families on relatively low incomes but not low enough to be eligible for a full medical card. This card covers the cost of visiting a GP but does not cover medical prescriptions. Other forms of assistance are also available to category two users, as outlined in box 8.3 below.

Box 8.3 Categories of entitlement to public health services from 1991 onwards

– **Category one:** those with the lowest incomes, plus the majority of the over 70s. These groups are entitled to all publicly provided health services free of charge, including GP care, medicines, public hospital services, and maternity and infant care services. Altogether, coverage extends to approximately 30 per cent of the population.

– **Category two:** the remainder of the population. Category two users have access to public hospital care subject to relatively small charges and are eligible for maternity and infant care services. GP services are not included, with the exception of those who qualify for a GP Visit card on a means-tested basis (coverage in 2006, 1.22 per cent). Category two users are eligible for subsidies under the drugs payment scheme, if the cost of purchasing medicine exceeds a certain threshold in a month (coverage 36.03 per cent in 2006), and are also entitled to certain drugs free of charge under a long-term illness scheme (coverage 2.51 per cent in 2005). Tax relief is also available on medical costs encountered. (HSE, 2007a)

Medical card eligibility continues to be a contentious issue. The system represents a form of vertical equity where resources are concentrated on those with lowest incomes and who would therefore have difficulty in meeting their medical needs from their own resources. Yet it is argued that this targeted approach does not fully reach those with greatest needs and not all people at risk of poverty have a medical card (CPA, 2007). A key problem is that thresholds for medical cards and GP visiting cards are not increased annually and are not linked to wage rises; therefore, levels of eligibility have declined since the 1980s and 1990s (see table 8.5 below). In addition, if medical cards for the over 70s are excluded, the proportion of the population covered has fallen to approximately 26 per cent in recent years (Burke, 2007). O'Carroll and O'Reilly (2008) also point to the more frequent reviewing of medical card holders since 2001. While this promotes efficiency by cancelling payments to GPs in overlooked cases where, for example, medical card holders have died or emigrated, in the majority of cases, people have their cards withdrawn because they did not return their form in the time allowed. In particular, there is a discrepancy between eligibility and possession of medical cards for the most vulnerable groups, including homeless people, Travellers and asylum seekers.

Table 8.5 Number of medical card holders and medical card holders as a proportion of the total population, various years

Year	No. of persons	Percentage of total population
1972	864,106	29.0
1976	1,193,909	37.0
1980	1,199,599	35.6
1986	1,326,048	37.4
1990	1,221,284	34.9
1996	1,252,385	34.6
2001	1,199,454	31.2
2005	1,155,727	29.5
2006	1,221,695	28.8

Source: The General Medical Service (Payments) Board/ Primary Care Reimbursement Service, Annual Reports, various years

Private insurance

The 1989 Commission's recommendations on the subsidisation of insurance premiums were partially implemented as the amount of tax relief available to private health insurance subscribers was reduced between 1994 and 1996. Tax relief at the highest income tax rate was abolished; however, subsidisation continues at the standard rate of tax. This change did not deter people and the numbers subscribing to health insurance have been rising steadily, reaching 51.2 per cent of the population by 2007 (Health Insurance Authority, 2008).

Following changes to the eligibility framework in 1991, the need to have insurance to cover hospital costs (with the exception of co-payments) was eliminated. In this sense, private insurance for hospital costs moved from having a substitution function to a duplication function (OECD, 2004a). Private insurance therefore supplements or duplicates public care and, as seen in section one, in other European countries where private insurance performs this function the level of take-up is relatively low. However, the high levels of private health subscription in Ireland would suggest that health insurance is not perceived as duplication but as a way of overcoming the deficits of the public health system. This has been confirmed in research into motivations for subscribing to private health insurance (Watson and Williams, 2001; HIA, 2008). In the HIA survey, for example, 90 per cent of subscribers to private health insurance disagreed that public services were adequate, and 74 per cent of subscribers together with 48 per cent of non-subscribers felt that having private health insurance meant getting a better service. In addition, the HIA survey found that 14 per cent of medical card holders had private health insurance. While some of this percentage may be accounted for by the over 70s, Watson and Williams's (2001) study found that 10 per cent of medical card holders had private health insurance in 1994, several years prior to the introduction of medical cards for the over 70s.

Significant changes have taken place in the health insurance market since the mid-1990s. The VHI monopoly on private health insurance ended in 1994 when the Health Insurance Act of 1994 permitted other companies to compete in the Irish market on foot of an EU Directive on Non-Life Insurance. BUPA was the first company to enter the Irish market in 1997. The directive also provided for regulation of the insurance market and, in the Irish system, this meant that new insurance providers had to conform to the rules the VHI operated under, namely, open enrolment, community rating and lifetime cover. These rules mean that anyone can subscribe to health insurance; that everyone, regardless of age or health status, pays the same premium; and that coverage is not subject to a particular age limit. A risk-equalisation scheme was also established in 1996, to level the playing field between the VHI and the newer providers. It was feared that the VHI would be at a disadvantage, having older and potentially sicker subscribers, while newer competitors could 'cherry pick' lower risk groups, namely younger, healthier people. If this were to happen it would pose a threat to community rating. The implementation of the scheme was halted as BUPA argued that it was weighted in favour of the VHI.

In 1999 the government published a White Paper, *Private Health Insurance*. In broad terms, it endorsed the high levels of private insurance in Ireland and its connection with the public/private mix in public hospitals. In this context it was seen as a source of revenue for public hospitals; however, it sought to reduce the extent to which private health insurance was subsidised by aiming to phase in full charges for private beds in public hospitals over a 5–7 year period. Premiums were increased in the early 2000s in response to this; however, the charges levied still amount to approximately 60 per cent of the cost of care (CPA, 2007).

In relation to competition and risk equalisation, the White Paper aimed to modify the arrangement somewhat by introducing lifetime community rating. This would mean that insurance companies could apply a higher charge to people who took out health insurance at an older age. However, it remained committed to the risk-equalisation scheme. BUPA left the market in late 2006, saying it could not compete under these conditions. In July 2008 a Supreme Court ruling on risk-equalisation ruled that it represented a distortion of market competition. This potentially paves the way for the breakdown of community rating. Some commentators welcomed it as a measure of making the market more competitive, while others see it as a path to higher insurance premiums for higher risk groups, principally older people. The implications of the ruling are currently under review by the government.

Bed designation and the public/private mix

A bed designation system in public hospitals began in 1991, arising out of the Commission's recommendations. The system designates beds as either private or public, while some beds remain undesignated (e.g. intensive care beds) and remain open to public and private patients. The system is intended to keep a check on the level of private use in public hospitals, and maintain a ratio of about 20 private beds for every 80 public beds. However, the Commission also recommended that a common waiting list be used for both public and private patients, which would have been a more radical move, meaning that medical need rather than ability to pay would determine who got access to hospital care in the fastest time. Wren argues that a bed designation system without a common waiting list had the effect of strengthening the inequitable two-tier system: 'by omitting a common waiting list, the government's legislation was providing private patients with designated private beds, which they could occupy even if public patients were in greater medical need. It offered public patients equitable access to public beds rather than equitable access to care' (Wren, 2003, pp. 88–9).

In addition, the proportion of private patients discharged from public hospitals actually far exceeds 20 per cent. The incidence and the extent to which this occurs varies between hospitals, and private activity in some hospitals has exceeded 40 per cent (Wiley, 2005). This occurs for many reasons. For example, private patients in general are younger and healthier and therefore need less complex treatment involving shorter hospital stays. Related to this, many older patients who are less likely to have insurance and who may be in need of 'step-down' care tend to stay in hospital longer in the absence of adequate convalescent facilities. In addition, private patients may simply end up in beds that are designated public, particularly when patients are admitted through accident and emergency. This 'crossover' can also occur in the opposite direction, but usually this happens to a much lesser extent (Nolan and Wiley, 2001). Furthermore, the growth of treatment in day beds, which did not come under the original designation system, became a new avenue for high levels of private patient treatment in public hospitals (Wren, 2003).

Overall then, the bed designation system has not succeeded in maintaining the public/private mix at the prescribed level. Furthermore, it appears that the trend of excess private utilisation of public hospitals has been increasing (O'Reilly and Wiley, 2007), despite the 2001 strategy acknowledging that 'the position of public patients in public hospitals relative to private patients … deteriorated' over the 1990s (Department of Health and Children, 2001a, p. 100). Other core elements of health policy effectively work against the bed designation system. These include the continued public subsidisation of private care in conjunction with rising levels of privately insured patients. For insurance companies, the cost of treating a subscriber in the public system is cheaper than in a private hospital and, consequently, as Wren (2003, p. 175) notes, 'more insured patients are treated in public hospitals than in private hospitals, even though 50 per cent of private beds are in the private sector'. As for the public hospitals, they are incentivised by the extra income gained to circumvent the bed designation system.

Waiting lists

As an alternative to a common waiting list, a waiting list initiative for public patients was introduced in 1993 and since then waiting list schemes seem to have become an embedded characteristic of the public system. As we saw in section one, action on waiting lists is not uncommon among healthcare systems over the last couple of decades. However, Irish initiatives have not been as successful as other countries in promptly reducing waiting list times (NESF, 2002a). The 1993 initiative sought to eliminate waiting times of over 12 months for adults for specific health problems, and 6 months for children. The initiative worked by allocating specific waiting list initiative funding to hospitals to carry out more elective procedures drawn from the waiting lists, and a further incentive was added in 2000 by granting extra funding to hospitals most successful in reducing waiting lists.

On the whole, however, the initiative proved relatively unsuccessful at reducing waiting lists, reflecting a lack of increased investment in public hospital capacity. While the numbers on waiting lists initially fell, they subsequently rose steadily until the late 1990s and eventually plateaued in 2001 (NESF, 2002a). The calculation of waiting times also came in for criticism. Much of the time spent waiting for hospital treatment was not actually counted as waiting. For example, it did not include the time spent waiting for a consultant appointment once one had been made upon visiting a GP. After visiting a consultant, waiting time for hospital treatment did not actually begin until three months after seeing the consultant. Therefore, official waiting lists did not begin until after a lot of waiting had already taken place.

The 1993 waiting list initiative worked by mobilising additional capacity as a temporary measure, which meant it was constantly responding to new build-ups in demand. The 2001 strategy promised to reduce waiting times with renewed vigour so that no person would be officially waiting more than three months for hospital treatment by the end of 2004. A more permanent measure of increasing public bed capacity was part of this plan, along with a National Treatment Purchase Fund (NTPF), which became the new focus of attention in 2002. This fund, which was initially proposed by the PDs who were in coalition government with Fianna Fáil, aimed to reduce waiting times through the purchase of private treatment for public patients from private hospitals in Ireland and from providers abroad, to meet the 2004 target. Fund activity was complemented by the creation of a new waiting list register in 2005. This register provides a database of waiting times for particular hospitals and particular treatments that can be accessed by GPs who can use this information to try to minimise waiting times for their patients. However, the method of discounting waiting times for consultants and the first three-month wait for hospital treatment still applies.

Both initiatives have proven more successful at reducing average waiting times than the original 1993 initiative. National average median waiting times for surgical procedures are now at 3.2 months (NTPF, 2008a); however, the 2004 target of *no* public patient waiting longer than three months remains elusive. In addition, the effectiveness of the fund on the grounds of efficiency and equity is questionable. Essentially, it involves the purchase of private care at the expense of investing in the public system. As the CPA (2007, p. 12) notes, 'while the NTPF reduces immediate pressures, it does not address the reasons behind the public system's inability to provide timely treatment in the first place, which should be the long term focus … Investing in public health services would gradually reduce the need for the NTPF to operate on its present scale'. Indeed in its annual report the NTPF prides itself in its 'sustained growth' (NTPF, 2008b, p. 3). In addition, the NESF (2002a, p. 88) points to the contradiction of 'turning to private suppliers to provide capacity for public patients, while dedicating some 20 per cent of existing public capacity to private patients'. While private patients can access private treatment at reduced cost in the public system, the public system is turning to purchasing private treatment elsewhere for public patients. Such a system also creates an incentive for consultants to convert public patient cases into private ones. If public patients have had to wait for three months or more, then the likelihood of their treatment being covered by the NTPF increases, which represents a gain in terms of private income for consultants – a point made generally about the nature of waiting lists by Bloor and Maynard (1992, in O'Reilly and Wiley, 2007).

Some changes to the waiting list system and the public/private mix are to be introduced on foot of new consultant contracts agreed in 2008. These new contracts represent the biggest change to the way consultants are contracted to work in the public health system since 1981. After protracted negotiations with the Irish Medical Organisation and the Irish Hospitals Consultants Association, lasting four years and involving issues such as salary, working hours and public versus private work, a new system is in the process of being implemented. This involves the creation of three categories, (1) consultants who work only in the public system and who therefore are paid a higher salary, (2) consultants who in addition to their public hospital work have limited private practice in public hospitals and co-located hospitals, working to an 80 per cent public and 20 per cent private practice ratio, and (3) consultants who, in addition to their public hospital work, can practice privately in private hospitals outside of the public hospital and co-located hospital system. All new consultants are to be appointed under the terms of these categories, while existing consultants may choose to remain on their existing contract or switch to a new one. The agreement also provides for a slightly longer working week, a longer working day and weekend work. Consultants are to work in teams and a new post of clinical director is to be created to manage consultant services and monitor a consultant's private practice so that it does not exceed 20 per cent. In addition, a common waiting list is to be implemented for outpatient diagnostic services, which should improve public patient access to this level of hospital service; however, it does not extend to in-patient services. Still in the process of being implemented, it remains to be seen if, in practice, the new contracts will modify the inequities of the two-tier system.

Public hospital capacity, private hospitals and co-location

The 2001 strategy promised to improve access in the public hospital system by expanding the number of hospital beds available. It acknowledged that the acute hospital sector could no longer improve productivity without an increase in capacity. While the number of acute beds remained at early 1990s levels, the throughput of patients had risen significantly. In all, 3,000 extra acute hospital beds were to be provided, 650 of these by the end of 2002 and the remainder by 2011. Of the initial 650 beds, 200 were to be provided by contracting them from the private sector for the purposes of reducing waiting lists. Again, because of the subsequent economic slowdown the initial target was not reached.

On the whole, it is difficult to assess how many extra beds have been provided. Progress reports on the 2001 strategy are vague on the number of new beds added to the system. The 2006 progress report, for example, states that 'the number of inpatient beds and day places available for use has steadily increased by an average of 300 beds per year' (Department of Health and Children, 2007, p. 19). However, Tussing and Wren (2006, p. 191) write that 'the government's claims about its progress in implementing the strategy's targets have been so confusing and so inconsistent with the data that it is difficult not to conclude that the government has been happy to obscure this issue'. In all, Tussing and Wren count 535 new in-patient beds provided by 2005. They also counted an increase of 475 day beds by 2005; however, the target in the original strategy was based on the need for 2,800 in-patient beds and only 200 new day beds in total. Furthermore, it appears that the definition of a day bed, or a 'day place' as the progress reports calls it, can be very flexible. From information obtained under Freedom of Information (FOI), Tussing and Dale found that the Department of Health and Children's definition of a day bed 'includes trolleys, recliners and couches, indeed anywhere a patient lies down, reclines or recovers "in the course of an elective day admission"' (Tussing and Wren, 2006, p. 195).

Going beyond attempts to increase capacity in the public system, increasing attention has turned towards the expansion of the private hospital system. The 2001 strategy stated, for example, that 'the Government is committed to exploring fully the scope for the private sector to provide additional capacity. Accordingly the extra beds in the period to 2011 will be provided by a combination of public and private providers ... the key objective is to provide the required extra capacity, whether this is in the public or private hospital sector' (Department of Health and Children, 2001a, p. 102).

Expanding the scope of the private sector began with the introduction of tax relief for private hospitals in 2001 and 2002. New private hospitals which have opened subsequent to this include the Galway Clinic opened in 2004 and the Beacon Hospital, Dublin, opened in 2006. More recently, the Minister for Health and Children announced a new co-location initiative, which involved the construction of private hospitals, again with tax reliefs, on the grounds of existing public hospitals. This was to become a new means of increasing capacity in the public sector as it is planned that this development will return 1,000 beds designated as private in public hospitals back to public beds in the public system. New co-located hospitals have been proposed at Beaumont and St James's hospitals in Dublin, as well as Limerick and Waterford regional hospitals, Cork University Hospital and Sligo General Hospital.

However, the plan has attracted enormous criticism because of the fear that it will result in the further residualisation of the public system. Private hospitals favour relatively uncomplicated elective surgery because this is the most profitable activity, and they rarely have Accident and Emergency departments for the same reason. It is feared that the most complex cases will be left to the public system, and that, as a result, the freeing up of 1,000 beds is not a straightforward, one-for-one exchange (Tussing and Wren, 2006). In addition, it is argued that this future capacity is not sufficient, given the needs of an ageing and growing population, which was underestimated in projections made for the 2001 strategy. There are also questions being raised about the viability of private hospitals, and that many may rely heavily on NTPF cases. There is also the concern that the cost of private insurance to cover treatment in these hospitals may rise, which, combined with the Supreme Court ruling on community rating, may lead to a decline in the level of private health insurance and greater use of public hospitals.

Looking at bed capacity from another angle, more recently, the HSE commissioned an Acute Hospital Bed Review in 2007 to examine acute bed needs until 2020, taking into account our ageing population in the ensuing decades. On the basis of that review the HSE felt vindicated in its stance that a major amount of additional acute beds are not needed and that the focus should be on primary care in particular: 'adding more and more acute inpatient beds to the hospital system is not in the interest of patients and not sustainable in the long term' (HSE, 2008, p. 20). Instead of continuing to build up the acute hospital system the HSE proposes to increase its efforts in the areas of primary care and chronic disease management, as well as increasing the efficiency of hospital services.

Primary care

The HSE is therefore turning more of its interest to the primary care system, which, historically, has been a neglected and poorly resourced sector. It consisted mainly of self-employed GPs and a fragmented network of other professionals, including midwives, physiotherapists, occupational therapists and social workers who either worked for the health boards or for voluntary agencies. The potential of primary healthcare has gained greater attention since the 1970s, coinciding with a growing interest in **health promotion.** In this context primary healthcare is understood as a means of keeping people well and preventing the escalation of health problems leading to more expensive and complex treatments in secondary care, that is, in hospitals. Its potential to improve health status and in particular to reduce health inequalities has also been noted. For example, the WHO (2008, p. 8) notes, 'health-care systems have better health outcomes when built on Primary Health Care'; by this it means a model:

> **Health promotion** is a concept which focuses on health improvement and optimal health, and the individual and social, economic and environmental conditions for its fulfilment.

> ... that emphasises locally appropriate action across the range of social determinants, where prevention and promotion are in balance with investment in curative interventions, and an emphasis on the primary level of care with adequate referral to higher levels of care ...

Something like this model of healthcare was proposed in the document *Primary Health Care – A New Direction* (Department of Health and Children, 2001b). It proposed the creation of inter-disciplinary primary healthcare teams comprising GPs, nurses and midwives, healthcare assistants, home helps, physiotherapists, occupational therapists and social workers, all working out of one location and serving populations of 3,000–7,000 people. In addition, a wider network of complementary professionals, such as speech and language therapists, community welfare officers and dentists, would serve a number of primary healthcare teams within a particular geographical area. This plan entailed significant investment in physical infrastructure and staffing, and it was envisaged that 400–600 primary healthcare teams would be needed by 2011, assuming a population size of 3.8 million people. Two interim targets of 20–30 teams by the end of 2003 and 40–60 teams by the end 2005 were set. While these were very welcome plans, their implementation has been very slow and targets have not been met, mainly due to inadequate resources in the HSE. By 2006, for example, only 10 teams were established. The social partnership programme *Towards 2016* made a commitment to establish 100 teams annually to meet a target of 500 by 2011. By 2007, 97 primary care teams were 'in various stages of development' (HSE, 2008, p. 30). Echoing the issue of how an acute bed is defined, the number of primary care teams which are fully operational is not clear (Burke, 2008). It would now appear that the healthcare system is caught between inadequate hospital bed capacity and inadequate primary care facilities in the context of a growing population.

Better primary care notwithstanding, access to it remains an issue. The CPA (2007), for example, raised concerns about how areas are targeted and prioritised for new primary care teams. This arises from the fact that poorer areas are not well resourced in terms of GP services (Layte et al., 2007). In addition, while the 2001 plan outlined a scheme of voluntary registration for primary care teams, the CPA recommends that registration with a primary care service should be mandatory. This would be particularly useful for groups who have difficulty registering for GP services, including Travellers, asylum seekers, homeless people, and refugees; groups which have a greater likelihood of poor health. Issues of eligibility for free primary care remain, as discussed earlier in relation to medical cards.

Health inequalities

Finally, and briefly, we consider health inequalities in the Irish context, which brings us back to the issues raised at the beginning of the chapter. The details of the inequities in the health system are part of a much broader context of health inequalities in Irish society, where differences in health status are marked by differences in socio-economic position in particular, and where other health differences, marked by ethnicity, geography and gender, are 'generated by underlying socio-economic inequalities' (Farell et al., 2008, p. 15). There have been some significant improvements in the health of the Irish people as a whole in recent years. For example, the standardised death rate per 100,000 of the population has been decreasing, especially since 2000, and the gap between Ireland and the rest of EU-15 in this regard has been declining (Eurostat, 2008). However, significant health inequalities within the population remain. As Kelleher (2007, p. 223) notes, 'as the economy has strengthened, we have replaced a traditional pattern of fairly universal disadvantage with a widening health inequality'. These inequalities can partly be attributed to problems with healthcare, particularly inequity of access: 'The inverse care law of inadequate provision for the most needy remains true' (ibid.). However, this is just one small aspect of a larger picture, where inequalities in health are the product of the broader inequalities in society, or the social determinants of health. As the WHO (2008, p. 26) states:

> Certainly maldistribution of health care – not delivering care to those who most need it – is one of the social determinants of health. But the high burden of illness responsible for appalling premature loss of life arises in large part because of the conditions in which people are born, grow, live, work and age ... Poor and unequal conditions are, in their

turn, the consequence of deeper structural conditions that together fashion the way societies are organized – poor social policies and programmes, unfair economic arrangements and bad politics ...

Therefore, good health depends on a range of factors, including the adequacy of housing, social security and education provision and, ultimately, levels of poverty and inequality within society. Poverty is literally 'bad for your health', as Barrington (2004) puts it. In addition, 'societies that are economically unequal have higher levels of poverty; and a strong relation has been found between the degree of income inequality in a country and poor health outcomes' (Burke et al., 2004, p. 13). Data on health inequalities in Ireland is relatively limited; however, the research that is available provides compelling evidence of unequal patterns of **morbidity**, and unequal **mortality rates**, across different socio-economic groups. In essence, those in the lower socio-economic groups are more likely to get sick more often and to die younger. Furthermore, health status is marked by a **social gradient**: better income is positively related to better health.

> **Morbidity** refers to sickness. The **morbidity rate** can refer to both the incidence and prevalence of sickness and disease within a particular group.

> **Mortality rate** refers to the death rate. The **mortality rate ratio** compares the death rate for one group with another.

> **Social gradient** refers to the relationship between health status and socio-economic group, whereby, for example, rising income or wealth is matched by improvements in health status.

Taking data on mortality first, Balanda and Wilde's (2001) study analysed CSO data on causes of death for all persons between 1989 and 1998 and compared mortality rate ratios. Their key finding was that if all causes of death are accounted for, the mortality rate in the lowest occupational class was 100–200 per cent higher compared to the highest occupational class. This unequal pattern was evident for the four main causes of death: for circulatory diseases it was over 120 per cent higher; for cancers it was over 100 per cent higher; for respiratory diseases it was over 200 per cent higher, and for injuries and poisonings it was over 150 per cent higher. In addition to the gap between the top and the bottom of the occupational hierarchy, their research also found a steep gradient across social groups.

Morbidity follows a similar pattern of inequality across social groups. The main source of evidence for this relationship is found in research that measures perceived health status, such as that conducted by Balanda and Wilde (2003) and Layte et al. (2007). Balanda and Wilde (2003) found, for example, that those on lowest incomes, those who were unemployed and those with no formal educational qualifications were much less likely to report positively about their general health status, their mental health, their overall satisfaction with general health and quality of life, and were more likely to have a limiting long-term illness. Layte et al. (2007) used the findings of the 2004 EU-SILC to analyse the relationship between poverty and ill health. Some of their more stark findings included the fact that 23 per cent of the general population report a chronic illness and that this rises to 38 per cent for the income poor and to 47 per cent for the consistently poor. A similar pattern emerges for self-reported good or very good health. Eighty-five per cent of the non-poor reported good or very good health; this declines to 66 per cent for the income poor and 57 per cent for the consistently poor.

Health inequalities in mortality and morbidity such as these raise serious challenges for the health service. While, as we already noted, equity in healthcare is but one part of the broader range of policy responses considered necessary to address health inequalities, in the Irish context the fact that healthcare is in many ways inequitable exacerbates the problem.

CHAPTER SUMMARY

▶ The first section of the chapter reviewed the main concepts associated with understanding health in a social policy context and which guide the development of health systems, namely health inequalities, equity and efficiency. This section also reviewed the main models or systems in which healthcare is delivered and the challenges facing all systems in recent decades. Of particular relevance is the tension between equity and efficiency in the context of rising costs.

▶ The second section of the chapter documented the development of the Irish healthcare system. This focused on the way the system evolved over time to produce a relatively unique mix of private and public healthcare and the various episodes in which opportunities to develop a more clearly defined social insurance-based or national health system failed to materialise.

▶ The consequences of this legacy for the contemporary healthcare system were discussed in section three. The issue of inequity of access has emerged as one of the most crucial issues in the Irish healthcare system in recent decades. This section analysed a number of policy developments and areas of the healthcare system which continue to be significantly challenged by health inequities, while the various trends towards greater privatisation of health services further exacerbate the problems in the public health system.

Discussion points

▸ Trace the historical reasons why Ireland does not have a free GP service for the entire population.

▸ Explain the public/private mix in the Irish healthcare system and evaluate recent attempts to modify this system.

▸ Weigh up the arguments for and against co-located hospitals.

Further reading

Barrington, R. (1987) *The Politics of Health and Medicine, 1900–1970*, Dublin: Institute of Public Administration.

Burke, S., Keenaghan, C., O'Donovan, D. and Quirke, B. (2004) *Health in Ireland – an unequal state*, Dublin: Public Health Alliance Ireland.

Graham, H. (2007) *Unequal Lives – Health and Socio-economic Inequalities*, Maidenhead, Berkshire: Open University Press.

Wren, M. A. (2003) *Unhealthy State. Anatomy of a Sick Society*, Dublin: New Island.

Useful websites

Department of Health and Children: www.dohc.ie

Health Service Executive: www.hse.ie

Institute of Public Health in Ireland: www.publichealth.ie

Public Health Alliance for the Island of Ireland: www.phaii.org

Notes

1 The sweepstakes continued until 1986, but its contribution to health funding diminished over the decades. It was replaced by the National Lottery, which has a much wider funding remit than the sweepstakes but does make a contribution to health services.

CHAPTER 9

EDUCATION POLICY

Going to school is one of the first milestone experiences we have in childhood. Most of us have memories of our first day in school and our education on the whole can be quite a subjective experience; we remember teachers, schools and subjects we especially liked or disliked; we have nightmares about messing up major examinations. Our achievements or otherwise in the formal education system play a key role in determining our life chances thereafter. This is why equality or, more precisely, equality of opportunity is highly valued in education policy; it is important that education systems are seen to offer everyone an equal chance of doing the best they can. Critics, however, argue that education systems are characterised by significant inequalities, which influence participation to the extent that it is not simply a matter of individuals doing the best they can or failing to do so. The concept of equality of opportunity and this debate are the starting points for this chapter, which aims to look at the key issue of equality in education, the particular way in which the Irish education system developed and the current key issues and challenges it faces.

CHAPTER OUTLINE

▸ Section one discusses the concept of equality of educational opportunity and examines its evolving influence in education policymaking.

▸ Section two examines the origins and development of education in Ireland, with particular reference to how the model of religious ownership with state funding evolved and how equality issues emerged and developed over time.

▸ Section three examines the contemporary Irish education system, with particular reference to equality of opportunity policy and the issues of disadvantage and diversity across the various education sectors.

SECTION 1: EQUALITY OF OPPORTUNITY AND EDUCATION POLICY

Equality of opportunity

In Chapter 5 we discussed the various meanings given to equality across the different political ideologies; in this chapter we apply these broader meanings to education. **Equality of opportunity** is the most commonly espoused concept associated with education policy. The concept has quite ambiguous and varied interpretations and perhaps for this reason, it manages to have a wide appeal.

> **Equality of opportunity** broadly refers to the notion that everyone is given an equal chance to succeed regardless of factors such as class, gender, disability, race or any other aspect of identity.

Equality of opportunity does not mean the same thing as equality; it is not a means of creating an equal society (however defined); rather it is a means of fairly allocating positions within society. This means that positions that confer wealth and privilege are not distributed according to ascribed characteristics such as gender or skin colour, but through acquired characteristics which everyone is given equal opportunity to obtain, such as educational qualifications. Therefore, 'when equality of opportunity prevails, the assignment of individuals to places in the social hierarchy is determined by some form of competitive process, and all members of society are eligible to compete on equal terms' (Arneson, 2008, p. 1). As is evident from Arneson's point, the concept implies an acceptance of the existence of a social hierarchy or inequality, or as Lynch and Baker (2005, p. 132) put it, equality of opportunity offers an 'equal opportunity to become unequal'. For some critics of equality of opportunity, including Lynch and Baker, this is the nub of the problem with equality of opportunity and they argue for alternative conceptions of equality.

Equality of educational opportunity fits broadly within a functionalist theory of education. Functionalist theory was dominant in sociology until the 1970s yet it continues to remain influential in education policymaking. Functionalism understands education as a force for 'fitting people in society'. On the one hand, the school acts as an agent of socialisation so that individuals can acquire the skills and learn the values needed to live successfully in society and perform in the economy. On the other hand, schools filter people or act as a selection mechanism, so that people end up in positions in society consonant with their abilities and performance in school. The outcome of this process is a **meritocratic society**.

> **Meritocratic societies** are those in which achievement and success reflect ability and effort rather than factors such as class, race, religion, gender or family background and connections.

The word meritocracy was first coined by Michael Young in 1958, who advanced the idea that IQ + effort = merit in his book, *The Rise of Meritocracy, 1870–2003: An Essay on Education and Equality*. While Young's aim was satirical, the concept quickly became established as a cornerstone of education policy internationally (Dench, 2006). Essentially, meritocratic systems function by responding to acquired characteristics rather than ascribed characteristics. Education therefore legitimates the inequality which exists in society. If it is accepted that everyone was given an equal chance in school, the subsequent inequality is seen as fair and a product of individual effort. Those who make the greatest effort in line with their intelligence are seen to deserve greater rewards in terms of money and status.

This functionalist focus goes hand in hand with liberalism when it comes to equality of opportunity. The basic idea underpinning liberal egalitarianism is 'that people should in some sense have an equal chance to compete for social advantages' (Baker et al., 2004, p. 25). This accommodates different perspectives and interpretations. The key difference is between a conception of equality of opportunity which interprets equality in a minimal or formal way and conceptions of equality which promote more generous interpretations of what constitutes minimum equality. The latter are known as maximalist or substantive interpretations of equality of opportunity. Despite these variations, because equality of opportunity is essentially about fair or equal ways of arriving at hierarchy or inequality in society, liberal conceptions of equality define equality in ways that, at most, permit incremental and reformist rather than radical change. Equality of opportunity in education is therefore a reflection of broader norms about equality and inequality in society, rather than a mechanism for radically transforming and equalising unequal social relationships; hence the common ground between a functionalist understanding of education and a liberal understanding of equality.

Formal/minimalist equality of opportunity

Formal equality of opportunity stresses the equal eligibility of citizens 'for all positions, posts and public employments in accordance with their abilities', as expressed in Article 6 of the 1789 French Declaration of the Rights of Man (cited in ibid.). The hallmarks of education policy built upon formal equality of opportunity are access and non-discrimination. As long as there are no discriminatory barriers that prohibit access to education or advancement within education, then, in this view, education functions in an equal opportunity way. Historically, examples of what would count as inequality of educational opportunity under this definition include the prohibition of Catholics from education under the penal laws, and the denial of access to higher education to women. Formal equality of opportunity policies tend to be favoured more by right-wing thinkers and governments, as a minimal conception of equality offers greater compatibility with the right-wing value of individual freedom.

Substantive/maximalist equality of opportunity

Substantive definitions of equality of opportunity go beyond the assurance of access and non-discrimination, arguing that these are not sufficient to ensure equality of opportunity. In this view formal opportunity is not the same as a genuine or real opportunity. For example, formal equality of access to university does not necessarily mean that a working-class child will have the same chance to attend as a middle-class child. Taking this kind of difference into account, 'a stronger form of equal opportunity insists that people should not be advantaged or hampered by their social background and that their prospects in life should depend entirely on their own effort and abilities' (ibid.).

The most well-known substantive formulation of equality of opportunity is John Rawls's notion of 'equality of fair opportunity'. This prevails when 'any individuals who have the same native talent and the same ambition will have the same prospects of success in competitions that determine who gets positions that generate superior benefits for their occupants' (Arneson, 2008, p. 7). The task of education policy to ensure equality of fair opportunity is to offset advantages of particular social groups through public measures. Here, equality of access is presumed and is extended along a continuum which includes equality of participation and equality of success or outcome (Lynch, 1999). Equality of participation focuses on the equal participation of all social groups at all levels of the education system, while equality of outcomes aims for equal rates of achievement for all social groups across the education system. Instead of simply focusing on non-discrimination, education policy is more likely to be concerned with educational disadvantage and seeks to address it by affirmative action. So, for example:

> If wealthy parents provide high-quality day care and nursery school and private tutoring for their children, society arranges public education practices so that children of non wealthy parents get the same or equivalent advantages ... The end result is that one can try to give one's own children a leg up in social competition, but whatever boost one provides will be met by a similar boost provided for other children whose native talent is the same as that of one's own children. (Arneson, 2008, pp. 7–8)

This approach to equality of opportunity is more typical of social democratic thinking. In general, policies that strive for substantive equality of opportunity involve extra resources for particular groups or geographical areas in an attempt to level the playing field. These are treated differently in a positive or affirmative sense to try to ensure equal participation or equal rates of achievement. Examples in the Irish context include the Early Start pre-school programme and *Giving Children an Even Break* programme at primary level.

Table 9.1   Key differences between formal and substantive interpretations of equality of opportunity

Minimal/formal equality of opportunity	Maximal/substantive equality of opportunity
Focus on equality of access	Focus on equality of participation and/ or equality of outcome
Concerned with discrimination	Concerned with educational disadvantage
Typical policies include formal statements stressing non-discrimination	Typical policies include positive discrimination, including targets, quotas, and extra funding for particular groups, or schools in particular areas

Critique of equality of opportunity: equality of condition

Critics of equality of opportunity argue that the concept is flawed because it assumes and accepts inequality, albeit inequality which is arrived at in a 'fair' way. Baker et al. (2004, p. 27) suggest that this fairness is simply a 'forlorn hope'. This is because 'major social and economic inequalities inevitably undermine all but the thinnest forms of equality of opportunity, because privileged parents will always find ways of advantaging their children in an unequal society' (ibid.). In other words, in an unequal society those with the greater resources will have the means and the power to find ways to stay ahead of any policy measures designed to equalise opportunity. Baker et al., therefore, propose an alternative form of equality called 'equality of condition'. This differs from liberal equality because it seeks to 'eliminate major inequalities altogether, or at least massively to reduce the current scale of inequality' (ibid., p. 33). Elsewhere, Lynch and Baker (2005, p. 132) define it as 'the belief that people should be as equal as possible in relation to the central conditions of their lives. Equality of condition is not about trying to make inequalities fairer, or giving people a more equal opportunity to become unequal, but about ensuring that everyone has roughly equal prospects for a good life.' Regarding education, this involves tackling inequalities both within and beyond the education system in order to challenge the key structures that reproduce inequality and oppression and impede real choices, including capitalism, patriarchy and racism.

However, a problem with the notion of equality of condition is that it is less well developed than the notion of equality of opportunity, particularly in terms of policy application (Lynch, 2000), and equality of opportunity has a much greater political appeal than equality of condition. Marxist, feminist and postmodernist critiques of equality and of education stemming from the 1960s onwards have all been influential in developing alternative conceptions of equality, and here we look at two in particular, equality of economic condition and equality of cultural condition or respect. Both of these demonstrate ways in which liberal equality of opportunity fails in an educational context.

Equality of economic condition

Equality of economic condition and its relevance to education stems from Marxist scholarship in the 1970s. This perspective argues that equality in education cannot be isolated from equality in other spheres of life; hence, equality of economic condition is necessary for education systems to perform in an egalitarian way. Equality of condition, therefore, 'aims at creating equality in the living conditions of all members of society. This refers to an ideal state where all goods, privileges and resources are distributed equally according to need' (Lynch, 1999, p. 39). In this context, educational institutions which pursue equality policies will not have their aims subverted by the groups with more resources and power to confer advantages on their children. As Lynch mentions, this is an ideal and, in practice, no education system operates within a society where equality of condition prevails. The closest approximation is in countries with relatively strong redistributive policies, most notably Sweden. This societal context parallels a strong egalitarian ethos in the Swedish education system (Dupriez and Dumay, 2006).

Equality of respect

Equality of respect refers to the cultural domain, and within education the concept illuminates ways in which education can perpetuate inequality through a cultural axis. Bourdieu and Passeron's (1977) work represented an early contribution to the importance of culture in education where they examined cultural transmission through the education system. Bourdieu (1986) developed the notion of 'cultural capital' which he used to show that it is not simply economic capital or resources that allowed certain children to succeed but also the cultural capital they have at their

> **Cultural capital** refers to attitudes and dispositions acquired within the family and community. It can include cultural goods such as books and formal academic qualifications.

disposal. Perception and appreciation of learning and education, role models and so on, may differ significantly within a middle-class milieu as opposed to a working-class one. This difference becomes a problem when education institutions are for the most part staffed by middle-class people and embody middle-class culture and values as the norm. For middle-class children, the transition to this environment is relatively smooth, whereas for working-class children this may not be the case. They are not 'at home' in this system and their ability to succeed in the system may therefore be hampered. Conversely, success for working-class students may be an ambivalent experience, representing a loss of a coherent, authentic sense of selfhood (Reay, 2001).

Issues of culture and respect were taken further by feminist and other theorists of identity. This work has drawn attention to the fact that school culture, including the curriculum, also transmits a gendered and racialised view of the world, couched within a white, settled, male, heterosexual perspective. This has a negative effect on minority groups within the education system, who are either rendered invisible or represented in stereotyped, negative ways. However, the need for equality of respect is being recognised somewhat in education systems in recent times through principles such as inclusion, integration and interculturalism.

Equality of educational opportunity and the development of education policy

In this part of the chapter we look briefly at the evolution of the concept of equality of opportunity and how it has broadly influenced education policy over time.

Ladders, talent pools and emerging debate about equality of opportunity

Prior to the twentieth century, there was little perceived need for a universal system of education once children had completed primary school. Further education was considered desirable only for an elite group of people with high intelligence, most of whom it was assumed already belonged to elite groups or the upper class. Post-primary education was made available to this group on a paid basis and was inaccessible to the lower classes who could not afford to pay. A limited number of scholarships were usually provided to facilitate the most able children of lower classes to continue their education at second level. Access to education via scholarships was compared to the rungs of a ladder, which only the most exceptional children of the lower classes had the ability to climb. The emergence of the use of the ladder as a metaphor for educational access is traced back to the 1870s when T. H. Huxley, who was greatly influenced by Charles Darwin's theory of evolution, proposed the notion of 'a great educational ladder, the bottom of which should be in the gutter and the top in the University and by which every child who had the strength to climb might, by using that strength, reach the place intended for him' (cited in Philpott, 1904, pp. 153–4 in Sanderson, 1987, p. 76).

The idea of educational ladders went hand in hand with other emerging ideas about intelligence and talents and developments in psychological testing which led to the idea that intelligence was about innate reasoning and abilities of comprehension which could be measured and quantified. Tied to this was the notion of talent pools, and 'the educational elite came to be known as the "pool" of talent, the nation's intellectual resources or the "pool of ability" (Evetts, 1970, p. 425). Membership of the talent pool was based on the possession of an IQ above a certain minimal threshold and it was assumed that the pool of talent among the working classes would not go to waste by facilitating a relatively small proportion of the most intelligent with an academic second-level education.

By the 1920s and 1930s, debates about equality and contributions from socialist theorists, such as R. H. Tawney, author of *Equality* (1931), advanced the more radical egalitarian notion of equality of condition leading eventually to a classless society. He forwarded the idea of equality not as 'equality of capacity or attainment, but of circumstances and institutions and the manner of life' (Tawney, 1931, p. 50). Using this notion of equality Tawney argued for universal access to second-level education. His ideas were enshrined in a pamphlet, *Secondary School for All*, which he wrote for the British Labour Party in 1922, and in which he advocated the abolition of secondary school fees and the introduction of free second-level education for all, which would in a generation abolish 'the vulgar irrelevancies of class inequality' (Tawney, 1922, p. 19). Arguments such as these influenced the universalisation of access to post-primary education which occurred during the mid-twentieth century.

Human capital and affirmative action

By the 1950s and 1960s ideas began to change about the notion of the talent pool. The fixed nature of IQ and the pool of talent were no longer accepted as immutable facts. The notion that these could be influenced by environmental or social factors and open to modification gained ground. For example, in a 1963 UK report entitled *Half Our Future*, Sir John Newsom argued that 'intellectual talent is not a fixed quantity ... but a variable that can be modified by social policy and educational approaches' (Newsom, 1963, p. 6 in Sanderson, 1987, p. 93). It followed that if improvements were made in educational provision, intelligence and ability might also be improved across the population.

This changing interpretation of the talent pool was bolstered by new thinking about the relationship between the economy and education emerging during the period of economic growth and industrial expansion from the 1950s onwards. If countries were to succeed in this expansionary phase then they would need to make the most of their workforce, and notions of fixed pools of talent did not help this cause. The concept of 'human capital' proposed by Schultz (1961) offered a new way of thinking about education and its relationship with the economy. In an article entitled *Investment in Human Capital* he encouraged economists and education policymakers to think about human abilities in terms of human capital, a factor of production increasingly significant to economic growth: 'although it is obvious that people acquire useful skills and knowledge, it is not obvious that these skills and knowledge are a form of capital ... that it has grown in Western societies at a much faster rate than conventional (non human) capital' (Schultz, 1961, p. 1). Consequently, at an OECD conference in Washington in the same year it was agreed to drop the concept of a pool of ability and take on board the significance of human capital in economic recovery and economic growth. Educational policies based on investing in human capital for the purposes of economic growth replaced the idea of working with a talent pool. As a result, 'from a preoccupation with genetically based "ceilings" of ability, concern was to be with talent as a consequence of social experience' (Evetts, 1970, p. 426). This had implications not just for the relationship between the economy and education, but also for the interpretation of equality of opportunity within education policy.

If talent or intelligence was now understood as a product, in part at least, of social experience then the onus was on educational opportunity policy to make the most of people's abilities. A shift occurred from defining equality of opportunity in formal terms to substantive terms, and during the 1970s focus shifted from equality of access towards equality of participation and achievement. Equality of opportunity now entailed policies such as the 'comprehensivisation' of secondary education so that all children would have the same education rather than being segregated between technical and academically oriented schools. Positive discrimination or affirmative action also became part of education policy. Evetts (ibid., pp. 427–8) noted that:

> Demands are now made, not for equal schooling, for with such unequal environments, this is a non-starter, but for positive discrimination in favour of educationally underprivileged children. The chief aim of compensatory education is to remedy the educational lag of disadvantaged children and thereby narrow the achievement gap between 'minority' and 'majority' pupils.

This new thinking also had an impact on the provision of higher education which began a process of 'massification' during the 1950s and 1960s. This meant that universities and newly created institutes of higher education were no longer the preserve of an elite few; they expanded to become part of a progression route for many on completion of second-level education. Mass access was accompanied by a process of diversification in the third-level sector. Influenced by the human capital perspective, it was argued that a new type of third-level education, based more on teaching and professional training than research, was needed to meet the needs of growing economies. These new institutions included the establishment of polytechnics in the UK and *Institutes Universitaires de Technologie* in France (Guri-Rosenblit et al., 2007).

Changes in the interpretation of equality of opportunity and the type of educational policy it implied did not occur without disagreement. For the Right, this represented steps too far in the interpretation of equality, to the extent that it interfered with liberty and amounted to a social injustice. From a more radical perspective, education provision was also subject to critique from the 1970s when issues of equality of condition and equality of respect became more prominent in debates about education. A key problem was the continuing inequalities in education systems, despite or perhaps because of equality of opportunity policy.

Knowledge capital, ladders of opportunity and the globalised 'race to the top'

Moving forward to the 1990s and 2000s the educational landscape has again changed and is going through another phase of realignment with economic imperatives, under the banner of economic globalisation. Human capital is now understood as knowledge capital and the central component of success in what are deemed knowledge economies. These economies signify the supposedly high-skill, high-wage transformations occurring in Western economies in the wake of industrial decline. In common with the 1960s there is again a shift in thinking about what counts as capital and what contributes to economic growth.

In the current era, brains and intelligence count most in what is regarded as human capital. Alan Burton-Jones, author of *Knowledge Capitalism* (1999), argues that 'knowledge is fast becoming the most important form of global capital – hence "knowledge capitalism" ... The central message is that we need to reappraise many of our industrial era notions of ... work arrangements, business strategy, and the links between education, learning and work' (Burton-Jones, 1999, p. vi). This reappraisal involves a blurring of the lines between learning and work, and we become individual 'knowledge capitalists' shaped by learning imperatives that require us to constantly innovate and update our skills through life-long learning. This line of economic thinking has been taken up by the OECD and the EU and applied to education policy. For example, in its 1996 report *The Knowledge Based Economy*, which was one of the first reports addressing the notion of the knowledge economy, the OECD describes education as a 'knowledge-intensive service sector' which is the key to future economic prosperity. Therefore:

> Governments will need more stress on upgrading human capital through promoting access to a range of skills, and especially the capacity to learn; enhancing the knowledge distribution power of the economy through collaborative networks and the diffusion of technology; and providing the enabling conditions for organisational change at the firm level to maximize the benefits of technology for productivity. (OECD, 1996, p. 7 in Peters, 2003a, p. 370)

The same themes are to be found at EU level. In a document called *Making a European Area of Lifelong Learning a Reality* (European Commission, 2001a), which was issued as a contribution towards the Lisbon goal of making the European economy the most competitive and knowledge-driven in the world, the competitive advantages to be gained from investing in people and upgrading knowledge and competences are identified as the key to economic success. In addition, educational investment in people is linked with social cohesion. Social exclusion is defined in terms of education; the socially excluded are those who don't have knowledge and the socially included are those who do. Investing in education or knowledge capital therefore fulfils both an economic agenda and a social agenda, combining economic efficiency with social justice.

In the context of national education systems, the UK provides a clear example of contemporary linkages between economic thinking and education policy and the shape equality of opportunity policy takes in this regime. The New Labour slogan of 'education, education, education' became well known when Labour entered government in 1997. Investment in education was at the centre of its policy agenda; it was seen as the main solution to problems such as unemployability and poverty. Furthermore, education became not so much a right as a responsibility, as individuals were charged with the duty to fulfil their potential through education. The notion of an educational ladder re-emerged in education discourse, this time as a 'ladder of opportunity', where access and effort are combined:

> ... I make no apologies for saying government has a responsibility for creating this new ladder of opportunity – a new ladder of opportunity

from the school to the workplace. That will allow the many, by their
own efforts, to benefit from the opportunities once open only to a few
(Brown, 1997, in Alexiadou, 2005, p. 105).

The ladder of opportunity which holds out opportunities in the knowledge
economy can be interpreted as a return to a more minimal form of equality
of opportunity, because once access is opened up individual effort is
emphasised. And once education delivers in terms of social cohesion, social
inequality is of lesser concern. There is no mention, for example, of the length
of this ladder of opportunity or how far the bottom is from the top. What
matters more is that everyone reaches their potential in the effort to make the
UK a highly skilled and therefore highly competitive knowledge economy.
Within such a frame of reference, the government has put a heavy burden of
expectation on education as a means to increase the competitiveness of the
workforce, and as a way of reconciling the objectives of competitiveness and
social justice through the provision of equal opportunities.

This hope of combining social justice and economic success within a
knowledge economy has become a common aspiration across European
countries and their education systems. This has implications in particular for
higher education, which as Peters (2003b, p. 153) remarks, 'has become the
new star ship in the policy fleet for governments around the world ... In short,
universities are seen to be a key driver towards the knowledge economy.'
Higher education institutions, particularly as they expand into fourth-level
education, are involved in 'a race to the top', because in knowledge capitalism
as Brown and Lauder (2006, p. 26) point out, the 'new rules of wealth
creation rest on "out smarting" economic rivals'. Universities therefore strive
to be identified as 'world class'. This has important implications for equality
of opportunity. Echoing New Labour's ladder of opportunity, equality in
education is no longer about equalising participation or outcomes but about
facilitating everyone to the best of their ability in a knowledge economy, with
access to university at the centre of attention.

However, Brown and Lauder are highly critical of this kind of policy
rhetoric. They argue that it downplays equality of opportunity policies, and
makes flawed assumptions about knowledge economies and the potential of
high-skilled high-wage employment for everyone. Furthermore, they
identify an intensification of elitism in higher education, as universities shift
their focus from 'massification' to competition for elite students. This is
occurring internationally, as a hierarchy of world-class universities compete
for the best students who in turn benefit from a 'winner takes all'
meritocratic system. The winner takes all thrust of meritocracy, as Lister
(2006, p. 234) points out, 'allows the meritorious few to streak ahead,
accumulating huge material rewards of various kinds, leaving the rest of the

field behind'. This in turn intensifies competition for the top-earning jobs, which are won by those who have the greatest competitive advantages in the globalising higher education system. Investing in knowledge capital, raising standards and exhorting everyone to grasp opportunities on the ladder of opportunity appear, therefore, to present a formula for increased levels of inequality despite the rhetoric of opportunities for everyone.

SECTION 2: THE DEVELOPMENT OF EDUCATION POLICY IN IRELAND

Pre-independence

In Ireland and elsewhere the earliest initiatives in education were voluntary in nature and usually motivated by religion. While the impetus for provision was voluntary, most education operated on a paid basis; thus, education was a private matter, accessible to the few who could afford to pay. Education was not of great importance in societies which were primarily agricultural, and where little changed from generation to generation. State intervention in education moved towards a mass system when industrialisation began to transform societies. In addition, the power of religious institutions in relation to knowledge production weakened. Across Europe, state intervention in education began in the latter half of the 1700s, with Prussia implementing compulsory attendance laws in 1763 which 'marked the first important move in the direction of national education' (Chitty, 1996, p. 250).

In the Irish case, the lack of industrial development obviated the need for mass elementary education. Irish education policy was shaped by the nature of the colonial administration. Britain was a late developer in terms of state intervention in education, as a laissez-faire attitude prevailed; however, in the case of Ireland, state intervention actually came about sooner because education was treated as an important tool of cultural control as opposed to industrial development.

Equality was not a major concern in nineteenth century Irish debates about education. For the most part, equality was mentioned in the context of equality between Catholics and Protestants in terms of access to education; equality in terms of gender or class was of relatively little concern. Second-level and third-level education were seen primarily as services for the middle classes, which were to be paid for, and widening access to the lower classes was not contemplated. As Coolahan (1981, p. 55) explains:

> Schooling was not viewed as a means of achieving greater social
> equality; rather the poor and the working classes were largely seen by

leaders of church and state as a self-perpetuating sector of society for whom a limited education in literacy and numeracy was deemed sufficient.

Education was also segregated in terms of gender. The same education was not seen as appropriate for men and women, particularly at second and third level. This gender divide was evident in terms of segregated curriculum, schools, teaching, administration, management and access to third level. As Harford (2008, pp. 1–2) notes, education was influenced by '… the doctrine of "separate spheres" which held that men and women should occupy different spheres. Men's sphere was the public world of work and commerce while woman's was the private world of the home, in her natural role as wife and mother.' This view was made all the more powerful by the Catholic Church whose male leaders were opposed to higher education for women in particular:

> The great Doctors of the Church affirm unanimously the inferiority of women in the intellectual order. This is by no means intended as a reflection of her dignity, as this inferiority arises from the *role* nature has destined her to fulfil in the drama of life. She eliminates the abstract from her intellectual activity, and seeks triumph in the sensible and the ideal, in which imagination plays the leading part. (O'Kane, 1913, cited in Pašeta, 1999, pp. 139–40 in Harford, 2008, p. 69).

Religious and state power intertwined in early provision. Colonial rule first concentrated on promulgating the Protestant faith and the English language by grant-aiding various schools with these aims, some of which 'out-churched the church' in their zeal to proselytise 'popish' children (Akenson, 1970, p. 33). For example, the Association for Discountenancing Vice and Promoting Religion received state grants to 'subsidise the schools where Protestant clergyman and teachers were striving to make the Irish more law abiding, industrious and temperate' (Goldstrom, 1972, p. 52 in McLaughlin, 2008, p. 44). Negative force was used from the late seventeenth century through the implementation of Penal Laws, which denied Catholics (or people of papist or popish religion, as Catholics were referred to in the legislation) the freedom to send their children abroad to be educated, to set up schools in Ireland and to teach Catholic children. Hedge schools or pay schools (clandestine schools teaching Catholic children) emerged under this regime, while wealthy Catholics still managed to emigrate for education despite the ban.

The Penal Laws were gradually repealed during the 1780s and 1790s and this period saw the flourishing of religious voluntary education provision. Many Catholic orders, which still play a prominent role in education provision, have their origins during this period. For example, the first Christian Brother school opened in Waterford in 1802. These schools charged relatively low fees, made possible by the Christian Brothers' very modest lifestyles and vigorous fund raising, and were traditionally associated with the education of the poor. Convent schools teaching girls were set up by groups such as the Presentation Sisters, the Loreto Sisters, the Dominicans and the Ursuline Sisters (Raftery and Nowlan-Roebuck, 2007).

Development of the primary school system

From the state's point of view this system was fragmented, with varying standards, and, more significantly, it posed a threat to colonial rule. As a result, Ireland got a state-supported national school system in 1831, while the equivalent in England did not occur until 1870 through the Forster Act. In Ireland, the 1831 initiative marks the origins of the contemporary primary school system and its main characteristics, in particular religious ownership of schools combined with state funding, can be traced back to this time. Thus, the reference to national schools refers to their nationwide presence rather than state ownership. Originally the aim was to teach children together for all subjects except religious instruction. The system was therefore envisaged as primarily a secular one which, it was hoped, would banish the proselytism associated with education up to that time.

A Board of Commissioners was created, made up of representatives of the main religious denominations. The board had the power to disperse funds for building costs and teacher salaries. It also had responsibility for the curriculum and appropriate textbooks. The textbooks commissioned by the board were devoid of references to anything Irish, such as Irish history and geography, and the Irish language itself was not recognised as a subject. This reflected the British policy of cultural assimilation for Ireland (Coolahan, 1981). The state promoted the idea of mixed denominational schooling, and funding was to favour joint applications from the different churches. However, the various religious groups objected, and, essentially, the system as it evolved ran on denominational lines, with each denomination applying for money for their own schools, either already in existence, including hedge schools, or new ones. Initially, schools which were not built under board funding would not receive funding; however, due to lobbying, especially from the Presbyterian Church, these schools became entitled to funding. This outcome benefited Catholic schools in particular, as they were in the majority. The system succeeded in expanding the primary school system, and in 1833 there were 789 schools educating 107,042 pupils and by 1860 this grew to 5,632 schools and 804,000 pupils (ibid.).

Development of the second-level system, including technical education

Provision of second-level education (known as intermediate education) was not as extensive as primary education in the nineteenth century. Again, early provision was dominated by religious groups, primarily the Church of Ireland, as most of the unofficial Catholic hedge schools did not provide education beyond primary level. Catholics who could afford to, emigrated to countries such as France and Italy where Irish colleges were established. Subsequently, when Catholic religious orders such as the Jesuits and the Holy Ghost Fathers began establishing secondary schools in the late eighteenth and early nineteenth century, this presented a new option for middle-class Catholics to attend these schools, which operated on a fee basis.

State intervention was prompted by inadequate financing as well as the problem of small numbers and poor standards, which left students who opted to continue to third level unprepared. In 1878 an Intermediate Education Act was passed. This provided for the establishment of an Intermediate Board comprising representatives of the main religious denominations. The board had the task of dispersing funds to second-level schools on the basis of examination results. The curriculum and examinations were oriented around academic subjects, including Greek, Latin, modern languages, English, natural sciences and mathematics.

During the preparatory stage of this legislation women were excluded by virtue of the fact that girls' schools were not included in the new examination system, which meant that they would not receive funds from the new board. This followed the Catholic Church's opposition to equal treatment of boys and girls in the intermediate system, which was guided by the idea that women had different roles and aspirations to men in society, and should not be subjected to competitive public examinations:

> … the American idea of educating girls on the same programme as boys and preparing them to compete for the same offices and professions should not be entertained for a moment in this country. (Dr Gilhooly the Bishop of Elphin, 1878, cited in O'Connor, 1981, p. 323 in Harford, 2005, p. 503)

However, a campaign spearheaded by women who were prominent in the provision of education for women, including Isabella Tod and Margaret Byers, was successful in altering the proposed legislation to allow women access to the intermediate examination system (Harford, 2005).

While the Intermediate Board ostensibly supported non-denominational schools, in practice, the schools operated along denominational lines. The second-level system continued as originally planned, with only minor modifications by the time Ireland gained independence, despite critical reviews and recommendations for change. Problems noted included the negative consequences of funding by results, a lack of trained teachers, poor pay and conditions for teachers, poor quality schools and poor standards. By independence, therefore, 'it was a rickety and run-down intermediate education machine which the new independent Irish Free State inherited' (Coolahan, 1981, p. 73).

Technical or vocational education at second level remained undeveloped in the nineteenth century. For the most part, it was provided by local philanthropic efforts, which opened individual schools and institutes for subjects such as art, design and mechanics. As Ireland was not industrialised there was little perceived need for this kind of education. In addition, the Catholic Church took little interest in it. Its development, therefore, proved the least controversial of all types of education. This provided the opportunity to devise a different administrative structure less hampered by religious issues. A Department of Agriculture and Technical Instruction was established in 1899, which liaised with local committees, and these committees developed technical education schemes funded by a combination of local and central monies. Demand for technical education was not as high as for intermediate education, as the status and employment opportunities flowing from intermediate education were regarded as superior to technical education and employment.

Development of third-level education

The establishment of Trinity College, the first university in Ireland, in 1591 predates any initiatives at first and second level. This is in line with developments across Europe, where universities were the first educational institutions to be established, usually under religious control (Collins, 2000). Trinity College operated as a fee-paying, residential institution, heavily imbued with a Church of Ireland ethos in terms of access, staffing and courses offered. Until 1793 it awarded degrees to Church of Ireland students only and women were not awarded degrees by Trinity until 1904 (Harford, 2008). By the mid-nineteenth century demand for third-level education suitable for middle-class Catholics grew. This was met with the establishment of non-denominational colleges in Belfast, Cork and Galway, all of which opened in the 1840s, with Queen's University as the awarding body for degrees offered by all three colleges. These colleges differed to Trinity, being non-residential, commanding lower fees and not quite so focused on the humanities.

Yet this was not the denominational education the Catholic Church wanted and it strenuously campaigned against these colleges. Debates about access for Catholics to third-level education overshadowed the issue of access for women, and the fact that women were not given access to these colleges was, as Harford (2008) notes, a peripheral issue. An alternative Catholic university was established by the Catholic Church in 1854, which subsequently became University College Dublin. Initially this university operated, with difficulty, on voluntary funding.

Higher education for women ran separately and women's colleges were opened by women from the two main religious denominations (ibid.). During the 1880s women were gradually admitted to the Queen's colleges. In 1879 a University Education (Ireland) Act was passed which dissolved Queen's university and replaced it with the Royal University of Ireland. This was a step forward for Catholic university education, as it awarded degrees to graduates of the Catholic university and offered funding in the form of scholarships.

By 1908, after decades of discussion and proposals, an Irish Universities Act, 1908, was passed and a new National University of Ireland (NUI) was established with three colleges, including the Queen's colleges at Cork and Galway, and the Catholic university in Dublin. Queen's College Belfast became Queen's University Belfast, and Trinity also remained outside of the NUI. The creation of the NUI largely facilitated Catholic control of third-level education (Inglis, 1998). The NUI also embraced Maynooth College in 1910, which was originally established in 1795 as a Catholic College mainly concerned with training Catholics for the priesthood. The 1908 Act also enabled local authorities to offer scholarships to students to attend university. However, a minority of students progressed to third level, only 5,000, for example, in 1914. University education continued to be an elite upper-class concern. It also remained predominantly male despite formal access being granted to women.

1920s–1950s

The education system changed very little in the first few decades of independence. The main thrust of policy was to leave it in the hands of the Church. The tense relationship the Catholic Church had with the colonial administration changed as the new state's goals for education were in tune with those of the Church. The new state now had the opportunity to promote cultural nationalism. This had been gaining momentum in the early twentieth century and essentially it meant building Irish national identity on native Irish culture. In this context, education became significant as a vehicle for a revival of the Irish language. Religious education also became highly important because of the connections made between religion and national identity (Williams, 1999).

Therefore, once the Free State was created, religious instruction and the Irish language took centre place in the curriculum, ensuring that it conformed to cultural nationalist ideals. Other subjects on the curriculum were also expected to promote Irish identity, and references to Anglo-Saxon culture were removed or minimised (Farren, 1995). This transformation in the content of education sought to reverse the policy of cultural assimilation put in place by the National Board of Education in 1831. A Department of Education was created in 1924. This replaced the Boards of National and Intermediate Education; however, the new department generally adopted the administrative and regulatory procedures already put in place by the boards. This meant that the tradition of decentralised school ownership and management continued while the state maintained strong centralised control of the curriculum, the inspection and examination process, and the financing of the system. In all, parents and teachers were afforded little or no involvement in governance at a local or central level (ibid.).

As for equality and access, while equality of opportunity 'as far as possible' (MacNeill, 1924, cited in ibid., p. 106) was mentioned as a guiding principle of education by Professor Eoin MacNeill, the Minister for Education in 1924, little was done to implement this principle in practice. Primary education remained the only form of education that was free, and only a small number of extra scholarships were granted for students to attend second level. Overall, developments from the 1920s to the early 1960s may be understood as operating within a 'theocentric paradigm', as put forward by O'Sullivan (2005). In this paradigm the purpose, ownership and control of education are understood within a framework of Christian principles about human nature, and the state maintains a subsidiary role.

Primary level

If anything, this new paradigm meant a turn for the worse in the primary school system. A new curriculum was introduced in 1922 which replaced the broad range and child-centred focus of the curriculum in place since 1901, with fewer subjects and instruction in Irish. As Walsh (2005, p. 259) comments, 'the Irish language was perceived as the panacea for all problems and, as it was for the good of the nation, it was necessary for the child.' In addition, the 1926 School Attendance Act, which made attendance in education compulsory for all those aged between six and fourteen, was 'promoted on the basis that a child needed to be in school to learn Irish' (ibid.). While enormous efforts were made to promote the Irish language in the education system, little attention was given to the negative effects of this curricular focus. The INTO, in particular, was critical of the system. In 1941 it published a report which found that 'the majority of infant teachers believed teaching through Irish inhibited the child intellectually, repressed his/her natural urge of expression and led to some children being mentally and physically damaged' (ibid, p. 260). Yet little effort was made to change the system and, with the exception of some relatively minor revisions and modifications, the curriculum stayed in place until the 1970s.

The proliferation of corporal punishment in the education system represented another negative development. Corporal punishment was enshrined as a right of parents in the 1908 Children's Act and while it was also permitted in schools, regulations issued by the Department of Education aimed to limit its use. Yet, as Maguire and Ó Cinnéide (2005, p. 639) point out, 'corporal punishment was widely used to maintain discipline in schools, and violations of the regulations were commonplace and, for the most part, ignored by the Department of Education.' Its widespread use and lack of departmental action can be related to the authoritarian control the Church exerted in schools. Walsh notes, for example, that one of the most influential figures in effecting curricular reform in the 1920s was Reverend Timothy Corcoran, a Jesuit Professor of Education, who 'espoused the doctrine of original sin prevalent in this period, whereby human nature was weakened and inclined towards evil. He further believed that strict authoritarian teaching was required to counteract this inherent failing in children' (Walsh, 2005, p. 258). Despite decades of opposition to this by parents, beginning in the late 1940s, the Department of Education did not abolish corporal punishment until 1982, which placed it about 50 years behind most other European countries (Maguire and Ó Cinnéide, 2005). Furthermore, it was not until the 1990s that the extent of abuse in schools in earlier decades was more fully exposed.

In regard to equality of opportunity, there was little emphasis on inequality or disadvantage. Programmes to ease the cost of schooling and deal with poverty, such as the provision of free school meals, free school books and the delivery of a school medical service, were kept to a minimum. The excuse of scarce resources provides only a partial explanation for this lack of services, because, as Coolahan (1981, p. 45) notes, 'underlying it also was the social conservatism of the body politic and of the churches at that period'. As an example of this, the new state did not have the courage of its own conviction about the provision of free primary education. When the first constitution was drafted in the 1920s, Article 10 on the right to free primary education was cleared with the Catholic Church for fear that the Church would object to this principle (Keogh, 1986, in Farren, 1995).

Second level

At second level, the overriding feature of the system during the early decades of independence was its academic, elitist and careerist focus, especially present in Catholic secondary schools (O'Sullivan, 2005). The influence of cultural nationalism also pervaded the second-level system. For example, Irish was made a compulsory subject and students were incentivised to use Irish by being awarded higher marks in examination papers if they answered them through Irish. This provision still remains in place.

Second level remained private and fee-paying and few scholarships were available to 'bright' children. The focus was on the preparation of middle-class children to compete for the middle-class jobs available in the civil service and semi-state companies like the ESB for boys, and teacher training and nursing for girls. Little attention was given to preparing students for other forms of work, and as Inglis (1998, p. 60) remarks, 'the accumulated effect of the classical curriculum was the production of an over-abundance of students who may have known how to decline the Latin word for a table, but had no technical skills as to how to go about constructing one'. Secondary schools also existed in a hierarchical relationship; the school one attended reflected class distinctions and influenced one's future career possibilities. Although referring to secondary schooling prior to independence, these class distinctions are well captured in James Joyce's *Portrait of an Artist as a Young Man*:

> ... Christian Brothers be damned! Said Mr Dedalus. Is it with Paddy Stink and Mickey Mud? No, let him stick to the jesuits in God's name since he began with them. They'll be of service to him in after years. Those are the fellows who can get you a position. (Joyce, 1972, p. 71 in Ledden, 1999, p. 333)

On the whole, second-level schooling remained inaccessible until the 1960s, and the proportion of scholarships available continued to be very low. In 1960, for example, only 3.4 per cent of students attending secondary schools were in receipt of scholarships (Coolahan, 1981). Some pupils were able to attend by virtue of relatively low fees or because of the policy of some schools to offer poor pupils with potential a second-level education, but not by virtue of a state equality of opportunity policy. In some families, only one or two children received a second-level education, as this was the limit of what could be afforded. Their social mobility was often significantly enhanced at the cost of the other children in the family.

Technical education

Probably the most significant change to occur in the first few decades of independence was in the area of technical education, which was made possible by the lesser involvement of the Church in this area. A Commission on Technical Education was appointed to review technical education in 1927 and the outcome was the Vocational Education Act, 1930, which, as O'Sullivan (2005, p. 133) points out, was 'the only major piece of legislation governing education enacted by the new state until the late 1990s'. This legislation facilitated the development of a network of vocational schools, and vocational education committees were created which managed these schools. This was the only second-level alternative to secondary schools until the 1960s, and the system was designed to prepare students for work in industry and agriculture, with the state reassuring the Catholic Church that the curriculum would not infringe on the secondary school curriculum (Farren, 1995). In any case, technical schools did not directly compete with the secondary schools because they came to represent preparation for lower status occupations and were therefore seen as less prestigious than secondary schools (O'Sullivan, 2005).

Third level

Few changes took place at university level once Ireland gained independence. Access remained very limited. There were, for example, only 214 local authority scholarships for entry to third level in 1962–3 and there was no major growth in student numbers from the 1920s to the 1960s (Coolahan, 1981). The numbers of women attending university grew only slightly, from 26 per cent of the full-time student body in 1938 to 30 per cent in 1960 (ibid.). Once issues of control and religious influence were settled in the 1908 legislation, a Catholic ethos pervaded the NUI universities. Catholic social thought, for example, was particularly evident in the content of subjects such as sociology and philosophy, which were frequently taught by members of the clergy. This Catholic ethos also extended to other subjects, as evidenced by UCC president O'Rahilly's contribution to a symposium on education in 1938:

> Here in Cork we have made some little headway. We have started a course in sociology – the papal encyclicals are for the first time prescribed as official texts. It is obligatory for students in commerce. It may be capable of extension so that all our students during their course may learn something about the living issues – family, state, communism, fascism and so on – on which they read about in the newspapers and see in the cinema … this year there has been another experimental innovation – the introduction of the 'elements of psychology, ethics and sociology' into the pre-medical year. It comes a bit early in the course, but it is the only place where it can be fitted (I am told that some of the parents resent it; their little darlings must not be diverted from bread and butter subjects). (O'Rahilly, 1938, p. 545 in Fanning, 2008, p. 84)

O'Rahilly's statement illustrates the presence of the theocentric paradigm at third level, not only in respect of the influence of religion in terms of course content, but also the subsidiary role of what would now be considered the 'consumers of education services', namely students. However, the reference to 'bread and butter subjects' also reveals the presence of what O'Sullivan (2005) refers to as the existence of a subordinate careerist strand within the theocentric paradigm. This careerist subtext became stronger in the 1950s as the demand for university education increased and the numbers of students at third level began to grow, to the extent that existing university facilities were unable to meet new demand and significant overcrowding occurred. The main form of expansion to take place was the building of the Belfield campus for UCD. This development was significant because it 'was by far the biggest single educational building programme ever financed by the Irish Government' (Sheehan, 1979, p. 67) at the time. It also signalled the beginnings of a major expansionist phase in Irish education in the 1960s and 1970s.

1960s–1980s

The 1960s witnessed a transformation in the thrust of education policy from an approach that was conservative, gradual and incrementalist to something briefly more radical and far-reaching. Yet, from another perspective, it could be said that Ireland was implementing changes that had already taken place in many European countries a decade or two earlier. These changes set about improving equality of opportunity by universalising second level and widening access to third level. They were primarily motivated by recognition of a changed world, as addressed by the new direction of Irish economic policy in the late 1950s and now impacting on education. If left unreformed the education system would risk the failure of Ireland's economic aspirations:

> The day of the unskilled worker, at any social level, is passing and with the development of modern science and technology, the future belongs to those who have trained themselves to meet its specific requirements in knowledge and skill (Lemass, 1965, in Walsh, 2005a, p. 157).

O'Sullivan (2005) suggests that a paradigm shift occurred from a theocentric to a mercantile education system. In this transformation, cultural nationalism, language revival and religious education all loosened their grip and the education system shifted its focus from a dual concern with earthly life and the after-life to a sole focus on life chances within this world. It also became more outward-looking, realising that students needed to be prepared for work in an economy that would become a member of the EEC (Peck, 1966). By the late 1960s, the preparation of employable citizens had taken over as a core aim of education. In the mercantile paradigm the state takes on a managerial role and manages 'on behalf of the users and funders of education – parents, tax-payers, industry, employers' (O'Sullivan, 2005,

p. 121). While the mercantile paradigm had its roots in the 1960s, it continues to unfold and develop in what O'Sullivan identifies as a predatory fashion, in that it has the power to dominate all aspects of education.

In the early 1960s some reforms took place during the period Dr Patrick Hillery was Minister for Education (1959–65), which involved a more interventionist role for the state. The most significant of these mirrored the international trend of comprehensivisation, as Hillery proposed the introduction of comprehensive and community schools. Initially they were relatively slow to progress because of prolonged negotiations with the Catholic Church and began as a pilot project, with the establishment of three schools in Cootehill, County Cavan; Shannon, County Clare; and Carraroe, County Galway (Walsh, 2005a). These schools sought to blur the academic–technical divide between secondary and vocational schools and shift the education system away from its heavy academic focus so that it would be more responsive to the new economic needs and opportunities emerging at the time. Their introduction was framed in pragmatic rather than ideological terms.

This had implications, in particular, for how concerns about equality were dealt with in the Irish education system. As Clancy (2007, p. 108) notes, there was no 'detailed exploration of egalitarian principles, which questioned the invidious status distinctions between the education offered for mainly middle-class children in secondary schools and mainly working-class children in vocational schools'. As a result, these new schools left existing hierarchical relations undisturbed: 'We retained the existing secondary and vocational schools (with their accompanying class divisions) and we added two additional types of school, comprehensive and community, which catered for a more balanced enrolment of all social groups' (ibid.). A segregated system remains at second level, which detracts from the development of substantive forms of equality of opportunity (Tormey, 2007; O'Sullivan, 2005).

Investment in education

The introduction of comprehensive schooling was a relatively minor development in comparison to what was to follow the publication of the *Investment in Education* report in 1965. This is described as the foundational document of modern education (Clancy, 1996) and 'a radical ideological departure in Irish educational thinking' (Brown, 1985, p. 250 in O'Sullivan, 2005, p. 129). This document paved the way for a fuller expression of equality of opportunity in the education system. The publication of this document originated in an OECD-organised conference held in Washington in 1961 which helped to disseminate the concept of education as human capital. The Irish delegates who attended the conference agreed to participate in an OECD pilot study to determine educational needs (Walsh, 2005a). The ensuing report was primarily a statistical assessment of the current system and an evaluation of future needs. Two major issues were highlighted: (1) there were large social-class and regional disparities in education participation rates and (2) the needs of the developing economy would not be met by the education system as it presently existed. These issues represented a dovetailing of equality of opportunity with economic necessity, and the document became the fundamental driver of major expansion and change in the education system.

Primary-level changes

Investment in Education highlighted the poor state of repair of many primary schools as well as inefficient use of resources between smaller rural and larger urban schools. Although subject to opposition, by the mid-1960s a policy of amalgamating rural primary schools had begun, and schools needing considerable physical upgrading were closed. More broadly, the social and economic changes of the 1960s prompted a review of the primary school curriculum and the 'realisation of the need for radical reform ... in congruence with the developing understandings of children and child development' (Walsh, 2005, p. 264). A new curriculum was introduced in 1971. The notion of childhood as a distinct phase of development informed the new curriculum as did new teaching methods intended to be more in tune with individual children's needs and abilities. In addition, subjects were to be taught in an integrated as opposed to a compartmentalised way. This also applied to religious instruction.

This became one of the catalysts for the emergence of an alternative multi-denominational model of schooling. In 1975, a group set up the Dalkey School Project which opened its own multi-denominational, co-educational and democratically managed school in 1978. A number of similar schools were opened by the early 1980s, and in 1984, Educate Together was set up as the coordinating committee for this type of school (Hyland, 1996). The growth of Educate Together was one part of a broader move towards diversity and greater democracy in the education system at the time. Other elements of this included the emergence of the Gaelscoil movement, which aims to provide primary and post-primary schools that offering education through the medium of Irish; as with Educate Together schools, these schools have become increasingly popular. Finally, the management structures of schools began to open up. In 1975, primary schools were obliged to set up boards of management that included representatives of parents and teachers, whereas previously schools were usually managed by a local member of the clergy. Yet religious control was maintained by virtue of the fact that the patron's (usually the bishop) nominees formed a majority of the board. Similar changes to management occurred in second-level schools in 1985.

Post-primary changes

The most significant educational reform to follow *Investment in Education* was the introduction of free, universal second-level schooling. As late as 1962 this was still considered 'unrealistic and utopian' by the Council of Education. Five years later, during the academic year 1967–8, free post-primary education was introduced by Donogh O'Malley, the Minister for Education (1966–8). This was done in conjunction with raising the compulsory school leaving age from 14 to 15. Over time this made progression to second level the norm, as, until then, many pupils simply remained in primary school until they were fourteen. In addition to the universalisation of second level, free transport was provided for those living three miles from school, and grants to offset educational cost were introduced on a means-tested basis. Much of the new demand was met by the creation of community schools, which also aimed to address the geographical inequalities in access to second-level education. The overall effect was quite far-reaching in terms of participation; access was no longer as hampered by inability to pay, families were no longer divided between those who could and could not attend second level on the basis of cost, and greater opportunities were open to people to realise ambitions in contrast to having to work in agriculture or as unskilled workers. Yet these changes did not have an equal impact across all social classes. Table 9.2, for example, documents increased participation levels, but also displays the unequal increases in participation across the different classes.

Table 9.2 Social group participation rates in full-time education, by
age in 1960–61 and 1980–1981

Year	1960–1961 15–19 years	1980–1981 15–19 years
Farmers	27.7	45.7
Professionals, employers, managers	46.5	76.4
Other non-manual	28.0	50.1
Skilled manual	17.3	47.7
Semi/Unskilled manual	9.8	30.5
All	29.8	55.9

Source: adapted from Breen et al. (1990, p. 132)

This pattern of unequal increases in participation supports O'Sullivan's (1989, p. 243) argument that the appeal to the concept of equality of opportunity during the reforms of the 1960s and beyond:

> ... was no more than an appeal to an unexplicated sense of 'fairness' and used to emotional rather than intellectual effect ... by specifically attempting to avoid ideology ... Irish educational planners have acted ideologically, i.e. in the interests of those social groups who benefit most from existing social and educational structures ...

One of the continuing inequalities in the system is the existence of private secondary schools. For secondary schools, the introduction of 'free fees' meant that the majority became non-fee paying, while the remainder retained their fee-paying system. Ten per cent of secondary schools opted to stay outside the free system (Sheehan, 1979). Yet, while these schools charge substantial tuition fees, they continue to have their teacher salaries paid by the state and, more recently, have also benefited from public money for capital needs. As Clancy (2007, p. 108) argues:

> These fee-paying secondary schools would appear to have the best of both worlds ... In most other countries private schools are fully financed by the fees paid by clients while in Ireland what have become private schools use tuition fees to supplement the state's contribution. It is in effect a state-subsidised private system.

In other words, those who can afford to attend private schools have the competitive advantages that this confers, enhanced by state support, which is contrary to any form of equality of opportunity.

Changes at third level

At third level the impetus of *Investment in Education* combined with the *Report of the Commission on Higher Education* (1967) served to expand the system and widen access, with the development of technical colleges at third level being particularly notable. Although occurring slightly later in Ireland, this mirrored the international trends of 'massification' and diversification at third level. Once universalisation of access to post-primary education had been achieved, equality of opportunity concerns shifted to third level, which was rapidly becoming the 'focal point of access, selection, and entry to rewarding careers for the majority of young people' (OECD, 1999, p. 20 in Clancy, 2001, p. 14). Not surprisingly, the *Report of the Commission on Higher Education* documented severe inequalities in third-level education, with participation heavily dominated by the middle classes.

A Local Authority (Higher Education Grant) Act was passed in 1968 which substantially expanded the amount of means-tested grants to attend third-level education. Greater emphasis was placed on technical education through the creation over the late 1960s and 1970s of Regional Technical Colleges (now Institutes of Technology), Dublin Institute of Technology and two National Institutes of Higher Education in Limerick and Dublin (now UL and DCU). Similar to developments at second level, participation increased substantially at third level (by 129 per cent from 1960–70 and 92 per cent from 1970–80). However, inequalities in participation between social classes remained very significant.

SECTION 3: EDUCATION SINCE THE 1990s

The last two decades have seen much activity in education. A greater number of reports, policy initiatives and pieces of legislation have appeared over the last two decades than in any other period since the 1920s. However, the state's greater involvement in the field of education has coincided with a strengthening of the predatory nature of the mercantile paradigm. The primacy of education as human capital in particular has become even more important since the 1960s, and the wave of reform beginning in the early 1990s was strongly tied to the needs of the economy, whether expressed as the need to produce more enterprising workers or workers more appropriately skilled for the knowledge economy. In the early 1990s, for example, the Minister for Education talked about the need 'to put an enterprise ethos into our system' (Brennan, cited in Bonel-Elliot, 1997, in O'Sullivan, 2005, p. 111), while by 2006 the then Taoiseach Bertie Ahern was emphasising that 'success in the future will be strongly dependent on growing the skills of our population' (Ahern 2006, in National Office of Equity of Access to Higher Education, 2008, p. 14).

Box 9.1 Key policy and legislative developments in education since the 1990s

1991 OECD Report, Review of National Policies for Education, Ireland
1992 Green Paper, Education for a Changing World
1995 White Paper, Charting Our Educational Future
1997 Universities Act
1998 Education Act
1999 White Paper, Ready to Learn
2000 Education (Welfare) Act

2000 White Paper on Adult Education Learning for Life
2004 OECD Report, Review of National Policies for Education: Review
      of Higher Education in Ireland
2004 Education for Persons with Special Needs Act
2006 OECD Report, Review of National Policies for Education, Review
      of Higher Education in Ireland

This activity in policy and legislation has been backed by greater investment in education, and since the 1990s Ireland ranks among the highest of those countries with the largest increases in educational expenditure, along with Greece, Hungary, Iceland and Korea (OECD, 2008c). However, much of this expenditure has been geared towards addressing basic deficiencies in the system rather than any overall enhancement. Expenditure levels are still below the average for the OECD as a whole (see table 9.3); this is manifested in class sizes, which are above average at primary level. In addition, at primary and secondary level there is an above-average ratio of students to teaching staff, and there is below average expenditure per student at primary, secondary and tertiary levels of the system (ibid.).

Table 9.3 Educational expenditure (both public and private) as a percentage of GDP in Ireland and the OECD mean, 1990, 1995, 2000, 2005

	1990	1995	2000	2005
Ireland	5.2	5.2	4.5	4.6
OECD mean*	5.2	5.5	5.3	5.6

Source: OECD (2000, 2008c)
*OECD mean refers only to mean of countries for which data is available

Within this overall context a number of key trends and issues can be discerned. The first of these is the expansion of the education system, most especially at third level. The scope of education has widened, as more attention is directed to lifelong and early childhood education. Alongside expansion, the problem of educational disadvantage has become a significant policy concern, and targeted programmes to address educational disadvantage have proliferated at all levels of the education system. Diversification and diversity have become more significant. Ireland is becoming less mono-cultural, due in particular to immigration over the past 10 years, and diverse needs and identities are gaining somewhat more recognition in the education system. The dominant model of Catholic-owned and -run schools is, to an extent, challenged by these trends. Going beyond culture, particular groups, such as children with special needs and lifelong learners, are also gaining a little more recognition within education provision.

Yet there are limits to these changes. For example, ever since 1831, religious ownership of schools continues to be the backbone of schooling at primary and second level, and any changes proposed continue to create debate and negotiation around issues such as the preservation of the religious ethos and the practicalities of religious instruction, which put a brake on change towards greater choice and diversity in the system. Furthermore, while equality of opportunity is placed at the core of education policy, in practice, this commitment is not always matched by adequate funding. More fundamentally, it could be said that the system suffers from the 'forlorn hope', as discussed in section one, of trying to produce 'fair inequality' from a system which is underpinned by inequalities that ensure that the advantaged in society continue to use and benefit from the education system in ways that perpetuate existing societal inequality. This section explores these trends and issues across the main areas of the education system as it currently operates.

Pre-school

Before compulsory school attendance at age six, children aged four to five attend infant classes at primary school, and it is estimated that all five-year-olds attend, and approximately 50 per cent of four-year-olds. Only 4 per cent of three-year-olds are enrolled, so overall access for three- to six-year-olds is estimated at 56 per cent, which is one of the lowest rates in Europe (OECD, 2006a). Outside of the primary school system, pre-school services have traditionally been run by the voluntary/private sector and these include play groups and pre-schools, such as Montessori, Steiner and Naíonraí (Irish language) pre-schools, all of which typically cater for three- to six-year-olds (Fallon, 2005). Access to these can be difficult for low-income families because of the fees charged, and low-income families tend to pay a greater proportion of their income on lesser quality services compared to middle-class families (Hayes, 2008).

Until recently, early childhood education was not a major issue owing to the attitude that the most appropriate place for young children was in the home, being cared for full-time by their mothers. Coinciding with the rise in the female labour force since the 1980s, state intervention in the pre-school sector has only begun to develop since the 1990s in terms of provision and regulation. The two main publicly funded pre-school programmes are targeted at children aged three to four from low-income families. These are the Early Start programme and pre-schools for Traveller children. Forty Early Start schemes are in operation and 46 Traveller pre-schools have been set up. The Early Start initiative was established in the mid-1990s but has not expanded since, and it is still referred to as a pilot project. A very limited number of pre-school classes are provided for children with special needs, mostly autism. On the whole, early childhood education in Ireland still lags behind the rest of Europe. Its organisation is fragmented, significant gains are still to be made in terms of quality of provision, and there is poor commitment to public provision, which compounds problems of access and affordability for low-income families.

Organisational and quality issues have been addressed somewhat in recent years. Following the White Paper *Ready to Learn*, a Centre for Early Childhood Development and Education[1] was established in 2002 to coordinate and develop provision, based on quality standards. The Office of the Minister for Children, established in 2005, attempts to coordinate the various Departments involved in early childhood services. However, despite these developments, Bennett (2007, p. 13) observes that the sector still suffers from the lack of recognition of the importance of early education and that it is treated as if 'it were a junior primary school, with a pedagogy and child staff ratios at odds with the natural learning strategies of young children'. These problems are compounded by an inadequate number of services, as Hayes (2007, p. 7) notes: '... there has only been a limited resolution of problems of access and affordability, with a large population of children who would benefit from early educational experiences unable to access them.'

This issue is important because of the high levels of child poverty in Ireland, as discussed in Chapter 11. As the OECD (2004b, p. 49) puts it, 'inequality at the starting gates of education remains a critical challenge for Ireland'. Early childhood education can make a significant contribution to reducing the risk of poverty in the long term by improving educational outcomes (Archer and Weir, 2005). The problem is that Early Start is a limited, targeted service that does not reach all children in poverty, and while it remains so it is subject to the problem that hampers targeted services, namely, that services for poor people become poor services. Issues such as these have led to recommendations from many quarters (OECD, 2004b, 2006a; NESF, 2005a; Hayes, 2008) that early childhood education be significantly developed towards a universal service, which would require major government expenditure.

Primary level and second level

Changes to the curriculum

At primary level, the *Revised Primary School Curriculum* was introduced in 1999 by the Department of Education and Science (as the Department was renamed in 1997). Revisions focused on the notion of the child as an active learner, and attempts have been made to introduce a greater variety of classroom teaching methods. The curriculum also contains a clear commitment to inclusion and diversity. While these changes were welcomed, doubts have been raised about how much change has actually taken place within the classroom (Murphy, 2005, in Smyth et al., 2007).

More far-reaching changes have taken place to the curriculum at second level, particularly at Leaving Certificate stage. This entailed the introduction of a transition year subsequent to completion of the Junior Certificate and two new senior-cycle programmes, the Leaving Certificate Vocational Programme (LCVP) in 1994, and the Leaving Certificate Applied Programme (LCAP) in 1995. In part, these new programmes were introduced as a result of greater numbers staying on at second level after compulsory school-leaving age since the 1980s. The content of the programmes was influenced by the belief that second-level schooling was too academic and that students should be prepared for the realities of the working world. Conversely, these programmes help to retain students at second level who are at risk of leaving school.

The human capital orientation of the 1991 OECD report, *Review of National Policies for Education, Ireland*, and the 1992 Green Paper *Education for a Changing World* influenced the debate about the academic nature of the traditional Leaving Certificate programme. These reports outlined a number of deficiencies in the education system relating to the predominance of factual knowledge over critical and entrepreneurial thinking and problem solving; and the failure to prepare students for the changing nature of work, particularly in terms of technology. Of the two Leaving Certificate programmes, the LCAP is considered the more radical innovation (Clancy, 2007), and its practical and applied nature allows students to progress on to post-leaving certificate courses but not higher education. Approximately 5 per cent of students take the LCAP and 25 per cent take the LCVP, demonstrating that the traditional or established Leaving Certificate is still the most common choice. However, this also depends on which Leaving Certificate programmes are offered in each school, as not all schools offer all programmes.

Early school leaving

Despite these initiatives, early school leaving remains an issue. While the scale of early school leaving is not as great as in earlier decades, the level of retention to Leaving Certificate level for students entering second level in 1999 was 83.7 per cent, which was a slight improvement on earlier cohorts in the 1990s (81.3 per cent in 1996, for example) (Department of Education and Science, 2008). Some early school leaving takes place prior to completing the Junior Certificate; with approximately 5.4 per cent leaving school before sitting this examination (ibid.). Early school leaving also occurs at the transition point between primary and post-primary school, where it is estimated that approximately 1,000 children per year do not transfer to post-primary schools (NESF, 2002b). The *National Action Plan for Social Inclusion 2007–2016* has set a target of ensuring that the proportion of 20–24-year-olds completing second level exceeds 90 per cent by 2013. This target may be difficult to reach, as borne out by earlier unmet targets. For example, the 1997 NAPS set out a target of a 90 per cent completion rate for the Leaving Certificate by 2000 and the same completion rate appeared in the 2003 partnership agreement *Sustaining Progress*, which was supposed to have been met by 2006.

Educational disadvantage

Early school leaving may be regarded as part of a wider problem of educational disadvantage. This concept entered into debates about education in the early 1990s (CMRS, 1992; Boldt et al., 1998) and has become a core feature of education policy and legislative developments. Educational disadvantage is strongly related to poverty, as students from lower social class groups are more likely to be at a disadvantage in terms of participation and achievement in the education system (Kellaghan et al., 1995; NESF, 2002b; CPA, 2003). Educational disadvantage is essentially an expression of inequality of educational opportunity. Acknowledgement of it as a problem, therefore, signalled a shift in approaches to educational opportunity from formally ensuring access to trying to ensure fair participation and achievement in a more substantive way.

Educational disadvantage was formally defined in the Education Act, 1998, as 'the impediments to education arising from social or economic disadvantage which prevent students from deriving appropriate benefit from education in schools' Section 32(9). Kellaghan (2001) argues that this definition is quite broad and non-specific. An alternative definition offered by Kellaghan (ibid., p. 5) suggests that:

> A child may be regarded as being at a disadvantage at school if because of factors in the child's environment conceptualized as economic, cultural and social capital, the competencies and dispositions which he/she brings to school differ from the competencies and dispositions which are valued in schools and which are required to facilitate adaptation to school and school learning.

In particular, Kellaghan focuses on the differences or discontinuities between a child's cultural and social capital and that required to succeed in school.

In practice, educational disadvantage programmes focus on improving equality of participation and achievement. Typically, programmes target extra resources to cover expansion of staffing levels, reduction of class sizes, increases in school budgets generally, funding of specific projects, and the involvement of other actors, such as parents, community groups, and the business community. The programmes do not, as such, address differences in families' economic circumstances, but aim to develop children's cultural capital, such as cognitive and language abilities; their social capital, by involving parents and the wider community; and their relationships, which benefit children's educational development.

Since the 1980s, extra funding was made available for schools in disadvantaged areas, using indicators of poverty such as number of families reliant on social welfare and social housing. Subsequently, more specific programmes and initiatives have been developed, including Early Start in 1994, as already discussed; the Home School Community Liaison scheme in 1990; Giving Children an Even Break in 2000; and the School Completion Initiative in 2002 (see Weir et al., 2005, for a detailed description of these programmes). In addition, the Education Act, 1998, provided the establishment of a committee to advise the Minister on strategies to combat educational disadvantage. The Educational Disadvantage Committee[2] was established in 2002. Aspects of educational disadvantage were also addressed in the 2000 Education (Welfare) Act through raising the minimum school leaving age to 16 or to the completion of three years of post-primary education, whichever is later, and by establishing a National Education Welfare Board in 2003 whose role is to ensure that every child receives a minimum education.

Over time, however, programmes have developed into a labyrinth of schemes and were criticised for a number of reasons, including for having little positive impact, being fragmented and unfocused, not providing enough resources and not comprehensively covering all schools in need (Educational Disadvantage Committee, 2003). In response, a new plan was unveiled in 2005 called *Delivering Equality of Opportunity in Schools* (Department of Education and Science, 2005). This is a five-year plan which aims to integrate existing schemes within a School Support Programme. The plan provides for treating the existing programmes in a more holistic manner in terms of how they apply to schools in disadvantaged areas, with a stronger focus on certain issues such as numeracy and literacy.

Programmes addressing educational disadvantage now seem to have become embedded in the education system. However, given the relationship between educational disadvantage and social class, it can be argued that the solutions are not to be found simply by pushing out the boundaries of equality of opportunity policy and reforming education policy. As discussed in section one, the general problem with equality of opportunity in terms of its acceptance of inequality is replicated in policies designed to address educational disadvantage. These policies remain detached from the bigger picture of inequality in society and the role that the education system plays in perpetuating that inequality or enhancing the educational advantages of some. As Derman-Sparks (2002, p. 52 in Tormey, 2007, p. 172) puts it, 'the meaning of advantage is the ghost that lurks within the meaning of disadvantage'. From an equality of condition perspective, the issue of educational disadvantage is more successfully tackled by addressing inequality in society at large which generates educational disadvantage within the more micro-context of education. Lynch (2001), for example, is particularly critical of the approach taken. She argues that:

> What policymakers too often forget is that inequality is a relational phenomenon. When the State targets a disadvantaged group, economically advantaged households generally use their superior resources to neutralise the effects of the public investment by increasing their private investment in their children, be it by investing in more selective schools, extra tuition, or by the increased resourcing of their children's schools, via voluntary contributions, donations, etc. Middle class families can and do make more choices about schooling, and they exercise more control over how it operates, than those from lower income backgrounds, not least because their resources permit it. (ibid., p. 399)

Recent manifestations of private investment in schooling include the growth of grind schools and the increasing numbers of students attending fee-paying primary and secondary schools (Lynch and Moran, 2006; Smyth, 2008). Both of these trends serve to undermine attempts at equality of opportunity within the education system and perpetuate a pattern of unequal educational outcomes.

Diversity, integration and segregation

Over the last decade greater awareness of, and commitment to, principles of inclusion, equality and rights are becoming evident in the education system (Lodge and Lynch, 2004). Central elements of this include the 1995 White Paper *Charting Our Education Future*, which set out the principles that should underpin education, namely, quality, equality, pluralism, partnership and accountability. Following this, the 1998 Education Act places an obligation on the Minister for Education and Science to make available the support services and the level and quality of education that will meet the needs and abilities of every person, including people with disabilities or special educational needs. The Act also requires schools to have an admissions policy and school plan which must provide for equal access and participation. The Equal Status Acts 2000 to 2004 prohibit discrimination in educational establishments in relation to areas such as admission and access to courses. However, exemptions apply, particularly in relation to the preservation of religious ethos. The Education for Persons with Special Needs Act, 2004, legally establishes the principle of inclusive education for children with special educational needs.

At the level of the curriculum, recognition of difference is becoming evident through the development of guidelines by the NCCA on **interculturalism** in the curriculum at primary and post-primary level (NCCA, 2005, 2006). In practice, a large shift has been taking place from segregated to integrated education, in

> **Interculturalism** in education is anti-discriminatory, based on respect for, and engagement with, cultural diversity, and the promotion of equality.

particular for children with special educational needs and for Traveller children. In addition to Travellers, participation by other ethnic minority groups in the education system has grown, owing to the scale of recent immigration to Ireland. Currently, immigrants make up 10 per cent of the primary school population and 7 per cent of the post-primary school population (Lenihan, 2008). Efforts towards the integration of a more diverse population of students have included investment in extra staffing for special needs assistants and English language support teachers.

Despite all of this, many shortcomings remain. Echoing the lack of debate about what equality means in the Irish education system, there is a similar absence of any real debate on recognition of difference. O'Sullivan (2005, p. 104) notes that 'the increasing uses of multiculturalism and interculturalism in education tend to be more by way of description, aspiration, advocacy and legitimation than as reflexive and analytical constructs.' A recent example of this is the handling of the issue of whether pupils have the right to wear the hijab in school. While the solution allows for flexibility by allowing individual schools to make a decision on this with the aid of guidelines issued by the Department of Education and Science, it highlights a reluctance to substantively debate difference in the education system and more widely in Irish society (see Mac Cormaic, 2008, and McGarry, 2008).

A particularly significant issue is the fact that the denominational model of education remains the dominant one, especially at primary level, and within that, Catholic schools are in the overwhelming majority. While Catholic schools are still in a majority, the Catholic Church may be gradually retreating from direct provision and handing over schools to trusts due to a decline in membership of religious orders. However, this does not detract from the fact that the Catholic Church is still a dominant actor in policymaking and uses this power to protect the denominational ethos of schools (Kissane, 2003). Here, it is in accord with the other main churches who similarly seek protection of their denominational ethos in their schools. In 2007 there were 3,279[3] primary schools, of which 3,039 were Catholic, 183 Church of Ireland, 14 Presbyterian, 1 Methodist, 34 multi-denominational, 5 inter-denominational, 2 Muslim, 1 Jewish and 1 Jehovah's Witnesses. Among these school types, Educate Together schools and Gaelscoileanna have seen significant growth since the 1980s. Some Gaelscoileanna operate under a Catholic patron and some are inter- or multi-denominational, while Educate Together schools are multi-denominational. The growth of these schools reflects growing demand for more choice in the education system.

The existence of greater choice and diversity in the education system does not necessarily lead to integration and inclusion. For example, there has been a long-standing practice at second level that parents make choices about schools beyond simply sending their children to the nearest available school, and this can contribute to a lack of diversity within the different school types at post-primary level (O'Sullivan, 2005). In addition, particular enrolment practices, such as the operation of waiting lists and the stipulation of residence within catchment areas, may contribute to subtle forms of rejection of certain pupils. Furthermore, with the shift towards the integration of Travellers and children with special needs into mainstream schools, there has been, as Tormey (2007, p. 185) points out, 'anecdotal evidence that some schools that welcome children from the Traveller community experience a decline in enrolments as parents avail of the market and "choose" to segregate the school system'. On foot of this, a school enrolment audit was carried out by the Department of Education and Science (2007) which has shown that while exclusionary practices are not widespread, in certain clusters, disparities in the enrolment of newcomer children, Traveller children and children with special educational needs do exist between schools.

An example of this exclusion and segregation came to light in September 2007 when it emerged that 90 pupils could not gain admission to the two existing primary schools in the Diswellstown area of Dublin 15 due to overcrowding. This area in West Dublin has seen significant population growth and much of it has been the result of immigrants settling in the area. The majority of the pupils who had no school place had parents who were not Irish, and it appeared that the existing Catholic national schools were enforcing religious requirements in their admissions policy (which they are entitled to do as a reflection of their ethos) as a way of dealing with potential overcrowding. Subsequently, the Archbishop of Dublin suggested that the future of Irish primary schooling might become more pluralist; instead of the Catholic Church providing nearly all schooling for Catholics and non-Catholics, it would turn more towards Catholic schools for Catholic children:

> The Catholic school will only be able to carry out its specific role if there are viable alternatives for parents who wish to send their children to schools inspired by other philosophies. The demand is there. The delay in provision of such alternative models has made true choice difficult for such parents and indeed for many teachers. It also makes it more difficult for Catholic schools to maintain their specific identity and bring their specific contribution to a pluralist society. (Martin, 2008, p. 7)

In some ways it now seems that the Catholic Church is making an argument for diversity and choice similar to the one being made by groups such as Educate Together since the 1970s.

As a starting point, the Department of Education and Science has established a new pilot model of school patronage for two new primary schools which opened in Dublin 15 in September 2008. These are referred to as community national schools which will be multi-denominational and come under VEC administration. This is a new departure at primary level because this is the first time that state-owned and state-run primary schools will exist. The fear, however, is that schools like these in areas of population growth where there are large immigrant communities would herald the emergence of a more segregated rather than diverse national school system, with immigrant children and children of non-Irish parents being ghettoised in these schools. In this way, a pattern of cultural segregation could emerge, similar to the way that elements of socio-economic segregation exist between fee-paying and non-fee paying schools, and between the different types of second-level school.

Third level

The third-level sector is currently undergoing a significant amount of reform and restructuring, and it is the part of the education system where the concept of the knowledge economy has had most impact. A recent OECD review of higher education in Ireland noted that 'tertiary education in Ireland is at a crossroads. It is recognised, perhaps more strongly than in almost any other country in Europe, that tertiary education is a key driver for the economy' (OECD, 2004c, p. 60). Higher education is seen as fundamental to the creation of a successful knowledge economy in Ireland, particularly in terms of innovation and the creation of knowledge capital in areas such as science and technology. At the same time, the 'race to the top', which is intrinsic to the globalised context of the knowledge economy, poses significant challenges.

Universities are now often described in economic rather than academic terms. For example, the Skilbeck report on the future of Irish universities described the university as 'a big, complex, demanding, competitive, business requiring large scale ongoing investment' (Skilbeck, 2001, p. 7). The OECD report recommended that if the higher education sector is to meet its strategic objectives more effectively, then research activity needs to be expanded and that this should include a significant expansion of 'fourth level' in the number of postgraduate students, including, for example, a doubling of PhD students and a doubling of the number of international students. The report also pointed to the need to broaden participation and improve life-long learning, both from an equal opportunity point of view and from an economic point of view. These points were reiterated in the 2006 OECD review, which also spoke of the need for further investment in third-level education. It warned that 'failure to invest further in the tertiary education system will put at risk its contribution to strengthening the knowledge economy and fully realising the climate of innovation it is keen to create (OECD, 2006b, p. 15). It is in this context that the re-introduction of third-level fees is now being considered, not so much in terms of equity but as an additional source of funding to drive the contribution of third-level education to the knowledge economy.

Protest against third–level fees, 2008. Source: authors' photograph.

Here we focus on some elements of this bigger picture of reform and re-structuring, namely access, participation and equality. Overall, participation in third-level education has grown significantly since the 1980s, and the non-university sector in particular has experienced major expansion in student numbers. In 1980 only one in five students entered third level (20 per cent), and by 2004 this had grown to just over one in every two students (54 per cent). A major policy change occurred in 1995 when third-level fees were abolished. This actually went against the grain of international trends at the time, where some third-level systems which were free were returning to some kind of fee-paying system (Eurydice, 2000). The government suggested that it would 'remove important financial and psychological barriers to participation at third level' (Government of Ireland, 1995, p. 101 in Clancy, 2005, p. 107), and the Minister for Education viewed third-level education as a universal service which should, therefore, be provided on a universal basis without having to pay. Others argued that this benefited the middle classes the most. Those who already could afford to pay were now getting the service for free. In effect, it acted as a subsidy to this group rather than making a significant difference financially to those who did not already pay fees.

Since the 1995 initiative more specific access and participation measures have been pursued. These began with the implementation of the 1997 Universities Act. This was the first major piece of university-related legislation since 1908 and, among other things, it clearly obliged universities to promote equity. Following this, the approach which has evolved has been one of targeting specific groups and addressing their under-representation, a task coordinated by the National Office for Equity of Access to Higher Education, which was established in 2003. The target groups include students from lower socio-economic groups and from other minority and non-traditional groups, including mature students and students with disabilities, but not students from ethnic minorities.

In its current action plan, the Office is conscious of the knowledge economy framework in which higher education now operates and sets an overall participation target of 72 per cent for the year 2020. Reflecting the interpretation of equality of opportunity in the context of the knowledge economy, which underscores the need to raise standards and facilitate everyone to achieve to the best of their ability, the action plan states that:

The term 'knowledge society' emphasises the fact that countries can no longer rely on elites to drive innovation and economic development. Increasingly, economic sustainability will depend on the learning achievements and skills of all citizens. This has added greater urgency to our pursuit of educational opportunities for all. (National Office for Equity of Access to Higher Education, 2008, p. 14)

Table 9.4 below presents a summary of targets set and achieved to date, as well as current targets.

Table 9.4 Third-level access targets from 2001 to 2013–20

Target group	Baseline 1998	Target for 2006	Outcome for 2006	Target for 2013–2020
Semi and unskilled-manual	23%	27%	33% (2004)	54% (2020)
Mature students	4.5%	10%	12.6% (2006)	20% (2013)
Students with disabilities numbers *	0.9%	1.8%	3.2% (2005)	Double

Source: data derived from National Office for Equity of Access to Higher Education (2008)

* The 2006 target was based on figures for students with all disabilities. The new target is based only on students with sensory, physical and multiple disabilities, and does not extend to students with specific learning disabilities or students with significant on-going illnesses. The rationale for this is that the former groups have particularly low participation rates. The target therefore is to double their number from 466 in 2006–7 to 932 by 2013–4.

While these targets are to be welcomed and represent greater commitment at realising a substantive form of equality of opportunity at third level, the broader picture of participation at third level is still one where significant patterns of inequality of opportunity exist. This is evident in the findings of a series of HEA-sponsored studies on participation at third level (Clancy, 1982, 1988, 1995, 2001; Fitzpatrick Associates and O'Connell, 2005; and O'Connell et al., 2006). This research focuses primarily on participation by socio-economic group, and Clancy in his earlier studies and the two more recent studies describe the pattern of entry into third level as one of continuity with change. On the one hand, more people are going to college and, for the most part, this includes more people from every socio-economic group, so that, to some extent, differentials are decreasing between groups. On the other hand, continuity is to be found by virtue of the fact that there are 'persistent social inequalities in access to higher education' (O'Connell et al., 2006, p. 136). This pattern is evident in terms of changes in participation rates between 1998 and 2004, set out in table 9.5 below:

Table 9.5 Estimated participation rates in higher education by father's socio-economic group 1998–2004

	1998	2004
Employers and managers	.65	.65
Higher professional	1.11	1.36
Lower professional	.63	.65
Non-manual	.29	.27
Skilled manual	.32	.50
Semi- and un-skilled	.23	.33
Own account workers	.39	.65
Farmers	.65	.89
Overall participation rate	.44	.55

Source: adapted from O'Connell et al., 2006, p. 49

With the exception of non-manual workers, all groups have increased participation. However, some groups have increased more than others. The biggest increases belong to higher professional, skilled manual workers, own account workers and farmers. The table also demonstrates which groups are over- or under-represented at third level in that their participation rate is above or below the overall participation rate of 55 per cent. Overall, semi- and un-skilled groups are under-represented, along with non-manual workers, whose participation actually declined slightly since 1998.

This pattern of inequality is not just evident in access to higher education but also within higher education institutions where, for example, 'the more prestigious the sector and field of study, the greater the social inequality in participation levels' (Clancy, 2001, p. 158). Thus, for example, participants in courses such as law, medicine and dentistry are more likely to come from higher professional groups. This is a reflection of the wider context of inequality of economic condition, where groups with superior economic and cultural capital can use the education system to their advantage and can subsequently benefit in terms of gaining the most advantageous positions in the labour market. While this remains the case, even though equality of opportunity has had a significant impact in opening up education and improving social mobility, its goal of giving people 'an equal chance to compete for social advantages' (Baker et al., 2004, p. 25) cannot be fully realised.

CHAPTER SUMMARY

‣ The opening section of this chapter examined the concept of equality of opportunity in education and considered critiques of this concept from an equality of condition perspective. A major criticism of equality of educational opportunity is that it cannot be realised without some sort of equality of condition within wider society. However, equality of opportunity has been a key influence in the development of education policy over time.

‣ The second section considered the development of education policy in the Irish context. Attention was given to how equality issues have evolved in the system and other significant characteristics of the system, most notably, the origins of a school system that combines private religious ownership with public funding were highlighted.

‣ The third section focused on the contemporary education system and discussed related policy issues, with particular reference to equality of opportunity. Equality of opportunity is now a core element of education policy and has contributed to the transformation of the education system, particularly at second and third level, from an elitist system to one where access has opened up and participation has grown significantly. However, this section also highlighted the limits of this achievement in a number of respects, most notably in terms of continued inequalities of participation across the education system, which are tied to wider inequalities of social and economic condition in contemporary Ireland.

Discussion points

‣ Think about the primary and post-primary schools you have attended. Consider who owns them, how they are funded, how long they have been in existence, the choice of subjects taught, and the extent to which the school population exhibited diversity or homogeneity when you attended the school.

‣ What are the differences between equality of opportunity and equality of condition?

‣ Consider the arguments for and against third-level education fees. Which seem more convincing in your opinion?

Further reading

Brown, P. and Lauder, H. (2006) 'Globalisation, knowledge and the myth of the magnet economy', *Globalisation, Societies and Education*, Vol. 4, No. 1, March, 25–57.

Lodge, A. and Lynch, K. (eds) (2004) *Diversity at School*, Dublin: IPA for the Equality Authority.

Lynch, K. (1999) *Equality in Education*, Dublin: Gill and Macmillan.

Useful websites

Department of Education and Science: www.education.ie

Notes

1   The Centre for Early Childhood Development and Education was abolished in 2008.

2   The Educational Disadvantage Committee was abolished in 2008.

3   Figures taken from http://www.education.ie/robots/view.jsp?pcategory =10861&language=EN&ecategory=41296&link=link001&doc=34229 (error in computation, sum should be 3,280)

CHAPTER 10

HOUSING POLICY

Housing is one of the most talked about topics in Irish society and it represents a microcosm of the changes that have taken place in Ireland over the last decade. While the recent housing boom may have been a sign of economic progress, housing is also, as Power (1993, p. 8) notes, 'the most conspicuous sign of inequality'. This is influenced by the fact that housing provision is delivered predominantly by the market, in contrast with other social services. For this reason Torgersen (1987) calls housing the 'wobbly pillar' of the welfare state. This means that while housing is a social need experienced by everyone, housing needs are more likely to be met through market provision. Buying or renting a home, therefore, represents more than the fulfilment of the need for shelter, it is also a source of profit to those in the housing industry, such as builders, estate agents and landlords. Housing as a commodity and as a means of making money generates inequalities between those who have acquired wealth from housing assets and those who have not, those who can purchase high-quality housing in good areas and those who cannot, and those who can afford to buy their own homes and those who cannot. Due to the problems generated by the housing market, state intervention also has an important role. The state intervenes in the market to modify some of these inequalities, to ensure that the housing market operates efficiently and to facilitate access.

There has been a long history of state intervention in the Irish housing market to facilitate people buying their own homes, which, measured in terms of owner occupation, has been very successful. Approximately 75 per cent of Irish housing stock is owner-occupied, which is high in comparative EU terms. While the cost of home ownership has dominated debates about housing in Ireland in recent years, housing policy and state intervention involve more than just addressing the issues raised by market provision of housing. The state is also a substantial provider of housing through the social housing sector, and it is involved in the regulation of a third sector, namely the private rental sector. However, in the Irish context these sectors have been overshadowed by the preoccupation with home ownership, to the extent that social housing has been left to play a residual role and private renting is dubbed the 'forgotten sector', whose occupants fare least well in terms of security and affordability.

CHAPTER OUTLINE

▸ The first section examines housing policy in general. It discusses key themes such as tenure structure and housing systems across Europe. It also looks at the role of the state and the market in the provision of housing, and the issues of access, affordability and social segregation.

▸ The second section charts the development of housing policy in Ireland from the nineteenth century to the 1980s. This section looks at the role of the state in housing over time and trends in housing provision, in particular the balance between social housing and private ownership.

▸ The third section examines current housing policy in Ireland from the 1990s and considers contemporary debates and challenges, drawing on themes explored in the first section of the chapter, including access, inequality and segregation. This section includes a discussion of housing need and homelessness, segregation in the housing system, issues in relation to affordability, and the future sustainability of contemporary housing patterns.

SECTION 1: AN OVERVIEW OF HOUSING POLICY

Housing tenure: owner occupation, private renting, social renting

Tenure comes from the verb *tenir* meaning 'to hold'. Variations in tenure status refer to the ways in which people occupy or possess their houses, with varying levels of rights and security.

Housing is divided into different tenure types, and housing provision across countries varies according to **tenure** structure. The three main forms of tenure are owner occupation, private renting and social renting.

Owner-occupied housing

Owner-occupied housing refers to housing owned by the occupier and it is usually paid for by acquiring a mortgage from a bank, building society or local authority. As this is privately owned property it is generally associated with a high level of security, choice and control, provided that the owner can afford the property. Over much of the twentieth century the tendency has been for the poorer European countries, including Ireland, Portugal, Greece and Spain to have high levels of owner occupation. Newer members of the European Union since 2004, including Central and Eastern European countries, have even higher levels of owner occupation. This has occurred in the context of rapid privatisation of formerly state-owned housing stock since the 1990s. Some suggest that the desire to own one's own home is a natural instinct and that over time the typical pattern is to see owner occupation grow at the expense of renting (Saunders, 1990). However, this is a contested idea and something which we will return to later, with reference to Irish housing policy in particular.

Private rented housing

Private rented housing refers to accommodation rented from a 'for-profit' landlord on the open market. This is generally considered the least secure tenure type. However, levels of security can vary from country to country with regard to issues such as tenancy rights and regulation of rents and leases. In the case of both owner occupation and private renting, access and the type and quality of accommodation will be determined by individual ability to pay.

Social renting

Social renting refers to renting in the social housing sector, where accommodation is provided by government, usually through local authorities, and other non-profit organisations. Social renting is generally associated with a high level of security. Prior to the 1980s the term public housing was more commonly used and it referred to state-provided housing alone. The term social housing refers to both local authority housing provision and housing provided by other non-profit providers. Access to local authority housing is usually determined by bureaucratic allocation mechanisms to distribute housing to those most in need. Criteria for assessing need may include income level, evidence of living in overcrowded or unfit accommodation, family size and so on. Applicants are usually placed on a waiting list before receiving accommodation. Other non-profit providers include housing charities/ associations, limited dividend companies and housing cooperatives. This type of provision may be state-sponsored, as many of these providers are funded by government, but the housing provided is not state-owned or managed. Non-profit providers may concentrate on providing housing for a particular group such as older people, people with disabilities or the homeless. There is a relatively high level of social housing provision by non-state providers in continental countries; however, in Ireland only a very small proportion of social housing is not provided by the state. In the Irish context, the main voluntary providers of housing are the Iveagh Trust, St Vincent de Paul, Focus Ireland and Respond!

Housing: a commodity, a social right, a matter of access?

One of the main ways in which housing systems differ across countries is in the balance between these three tenure types. This diversity can be due to historical, socio-economic and policy factors, and not necessarily the level of wealth or prosperity in a particular country. In policy terms, the diversity may be understood as a contrast between policy approaches which treat housing primarily as a commodity provided by the market, and approaches which treat housing as a social right, provided by the state. In market-dominated housing systems, such as the US system, housing is treated primarily as a commodity to be bought in accordance with income, and only a very minimal amount of social housing is provided. Such a system results in high levels of owner occupation but also high levels of homelessness and accessibility and affordability problems (Paris, 2007). By contrast, the treatment of housing as a social right formed the basis of Eastern European housing policy prior to 1989, where the majority of people were housed in accommodation provided by the state. However, in practice, there were problems with this model as states did not necessarily allocate housing according to need and housing standards were relatively low (Hegedüs and Tosics, 1996). The majority of Western European countries fall between the two extremes, and while a right to housing is not guaranteed, most countries develop their housing policies around the right of access to adequate housing (Edgar et al., 2002). As such, there is a greater mix between tenure types, and practically all housing is subsidised in some way so that access to owner occupation is not left purely to market forces.

European housing regimes

Overall, it is difficult to identify clear housing regimes. Across Europe there are diverse patterns of housing tenure, and as Edgar et al. (2002, p. 8) point out, 'one cannot easily read ... across from the four European social welfare models to models of housing policy and find a congruent match'. However, work by Kemeny (1995, 2006) helps to distinguish between systems which are primarily market-oriented and systems which are more concerned with access. His typology is based on the variations in the rental system in different countries. He suggests that social renting and private renting should not be treated as two entirely distinct housing tenures. Instead, he identifies two different systems, which he calls dualist and integrated rental systems. The dualist system keeps private and social renting separate, and social rented accommodation is provided for those with low incomes only, through means-testing. Provision is primarily through the state via local authorities. The integrated system allows for competition between private and social renting, with both private landlords and local authorities providing social rented accommodation, as opposed to mainly or only the state in the dualist system. Generally, social renting is accessible to all regardless of income and the effect is to dampen market rental levels, as private landlords have competitors that are absent in the dualist system. The standard of accommodation is kept quite high as a result of competition. However, a problem is that the providers, especially the non-government ones, may express a preference for the more middle-class renters with stable jobs and incomes, and the poorer renters are left to the state-provided houses or drift to the private sector to cheap, low-quality accommodation. Thus, social housing in this system may not adequately meet housing need, but concentrate on the needs of middle-income households (Kleinman, 1996). According to this typology, Germany, Sweden, Denmark, the Netherlands, Switzerland and Austria have integrated systems, whereas the UK, Ireland, Norway and Finland display dualist systems. In terms of welfare regimes, the dualist system is more common in liberal welfare states, while the integrated rent system is more likely to be found in corporatist and social democratic welfare states.

Recent reforms of housing policy in Europe

We now turn to look briefly at housing policy in the context of welfare state reform over the last two decades or so, and in particular we look at the problems generated by a market-dominated housing policy system. The 1950s and 1960s were the heyday of social housing provision in Europe (Priemus and Dieleman, 1999). States invested heavily in housing in response to severe housing shortages in the decades after World War II and large-scale housing provision was seen as a legitimate state activity. The term mass housing is used to refer to the large social housing estates that were built, where an emphasis on quantity superseded concerns with quality. As described by Power (1993, p. 5):

> Mass building to minimal standards was undertaken everywhere, often state-sponsored but often actually provided through non-state bodies. Careful planning and environmental issues were luxuries that simply could not be afforded. Much early post-war housing was monotonous, minimal, dense and 'public' in character. 'Mass housing' is an inexact term used to describe post-war, publicly sponsored, industrially built, large scale housing estates for moderate-to low-income households.

While not a uniform trend, there has been a decline in the share of social housing across Europe since the 1970s. Several factors influenced this decline. To begin with, there was a sense that the housing provision of the 1950s and 1960s had served its purpose and that the needs of this era had been fulfilled. In addition, incomes rose in the long period of economic prosperity following World War II, and this fuelled a preference for home ownership which, it was assumed, would be best served by private market provision (Edgar et al., 2002). As a result, housing construction activity switched from the production of high-rise mass social housing estates to the production of single family houses, destined for owner occupation. This process saw the exit of wealthier families from both the private rented and the social rented sector. The declining share of social housing must also be seen in the context of the wider fortunes of welfare states since the 1970s, which are marked by the so-called fiscal crisis and the assertive rise of neo-liberal thinking. As a result, the legitimacy of governments spending large amounts of money on building and managing housing was called into question. Since then, in comparison to other social services, Edgar et al. (2002) suggest that housing policy has actually seen the most fundamental transformation in the context of welfare reform, with the state withdrawing from provision and letting market solutions prevail.

Consequently, the provision of houses has been replaced by alternative policies which stress market-based solutions to housing issues. These include a switch in state housing expenditure from object to subject subsidies. In other words, instead of investing in bricks and mortar (social housing), the state gives housing allowances to individuals to access housing in the private market. This policy was followed in France, for example, from 1979 onwards. The privatisation of social housing by giving tenants the option to buy their house at below-market prices is another version of the shift from object to subject subsidies. The enactment of the 'right-to-buy' legislation in Britain in 1980 is a notable example of this policy. The allocation of the remaining social housing is much more targeted. The focus of social housing provision is now on those most in need and therefore with the lowest incomes, such as the unemployed and one-parent families, and, as such, social housing has assumed a much more distinct welfare role than in the past.

A shift in housing provision and management from the state to other non-profit providers is another example of state withdrawal from housing. This is evident in the UK and to a lesser extent in Ireland. However, in other countries with a stronger tradition of non-state social housing, a shift away from the social market towards open-market based structures can be observed. Reforms in France and Germany, for example, allowed non-profit providers to act as private landlords and to exit social renting (O'Connell, 2005a).

Key problems and responses in contemporary housing policy: residualisation, social segregation, accessibility and affordability

The reforms discussed in the previous section represent trends towards the treatment of housing primarily as a commodity. This policy shift has also resulted in the stronger presence of problems such as residualisation, social segregation, lack of access and affordability, which are typically associated with a policy regime which treats housing first and foremost as something to be bought and sold. In this section we look broadly at how these problems are manifested and some of the attempts made to solve them.

Social housing

Initially regarded as a 'visionary solution', mass housing estates came to be thought of as potential ghettoes (Power, 1993, p. 389). A major problem with social housing from the 1970s on is captured in the term **residualisation**, which refers to a number of trends. These include the reduction in the size of the tenure and in the quality of social housing dwellings and estates, as houses not bought by tenants tended to

> **Residualisation** primarily refers to the marginalisation of social housing within housing policy and provision, and the social exclusion of tenants of social housing.

be those in the poorest condition and in the least preferred areas. Residualisation also refers to the way in which the role of social housing provision becomes a residual one in solving housing problems, as more housing needs are channelled through market-based policy instruments. Finally, residualisation also refers to the way in which the social profile of tenants becomes more and more concentrated in terms of poverty and disadvantage.

Residualisation, in turn, is connected with the marginalisation of social housing tenants and more intense patterns of spatial segregation (Murie, 1997). Tenants who may have already been marginalised and socially excluded due to unemployment and poverty through labour market restructuring found themselves further marginalised by the stigma associated with living in social housing estates where a number of social problems were spatially concentrated. In addition, demand for social housing from other disadvantaged groups that were growing in number, such as one-parent families and ethnic minorities, contributed to the concentration of inequality. Centralised and bureaucratic management systems were ill-equipped to deal with issues in housing estates stemming from marginalisation and social exclusion, such as ethnic tensions, drug abuse and general disorder.

Recent developments in social housing, including regeneration and an emphasis on local estate management and tenant participation projects, have tried to tackle residualisation. Areas with high concentrations of social housing have also been targeted through area-based social inclusion programmes. Regeneration and 'rescue' programmes became popular in the 1980s, with investment focused on up-grading existing social housing stock. By the 1990s attention turned again to shortages in social housing stock. However, the emphasis now is on smaller estates, and social housing provision remains more limited and targeted than the mass housing projects of the 1950s and 1960s.

Private renting

In the private rented sector the influence of a strong market-based housing policy leads to problems of **segregation** in particular, with clear divisions between high, middle and low segments of the market. The lower end of the rental market becomes concentrated in areas where cheap, low-quality accommodation is rented

> **Segregation** in housing refers to the division of areas by tenure, social groups and social classes in particular.

to low-income households and where minority ethnic groups in particular may cluster, accessing what may be the only accommodation option open to them. This is especially the case with new migrants (Özüekren and van Kempen, 2003). In addition to migration, urban-related trends such as a return to inner-city living, demographic change, changing household composition, and the transition from industrialisation to post-industrialisation have meant that there has been a resurgence in private renting in recent years. Private renting is recognised as an important source of relatively cheap and flexible accommodation in post-industrial cities with higher levels of labour mobility than in the past. State encouragement of the sector has also been evident through tax incentives and direct subsidies.

Owner-occupied housing

For reasons similar to those related to private renting, owner occupation is also subject to problems of segregation and accessibility, where the market responds not to need but ability to pay. Differences in the ability to pay for housing is manifested as spatial segregation, whereby private housing divides into high quality homes in good locations and poorer quality housing in less desirable and less

> **Gentrification** refers to the redevelopment of areas and replacement of low-income housing by more expensive housing. This tends to attract higher income groups, thus 'crowding out' lower income households.

accessible locations. The phenomenon of segregation is exacerbated by the processes of displacement and gentrification, as urban areas where the poor may have traditionally resided are redeveloped or '**gentrified**' and become areas that attract high-income home owners. As Lyons (2003, p. 307) notes:

> Over the past 40 years, all major cities have experienced gentrification and rises in property values which have, on average, out-paced the increases in consumer price indices … The outcome has been a gearing-up of incomes of home owners in such cities, and increasing barriers to entry into the housing market for people on lower incomes.

Despite the barriers to home ownership, the drive to own one's home remains very strong in market-oriented systems due to the lack of viable alternatives. As Kemeny (2006, p. 13) notes:

> The choice for most households ... is between profit-driven rental dwellings with high rents and weakened rights to retain their contract on the one hand, and home ownership on the other. Thus it is not strange that most households choose to own their own home and that in these countries we find large amounts of slum housing.

In other words, the emphasis on home ownership pushes people to buy what they can afford even if this is unsuitable poor-quality accommodation and thus the trend of segregation continues.

In market-based systems, problems of accessibility and affordability become particularly acute during housing booms. Rising prices mean that the housing market becomes inaccessible or unaffordable for those earning insufficient incomes to generate large enough mortgages. As the private market grows, the main concern of housing policy becomes one of facilitating access to the market, assisting people to purchase their own homes, and, consequently, the concept of affordability has entered the language of housing policy, not just in Ireland but across European housing systems (Paris, 2007).

Government assistance towards owner occupation has also changed in response to this problem, with subsidies and support becoming less universal and targeted more towards those on lower incomes trying to access owner-occupied housing. In some countries, notably Ireland, the concern with affordability has overshadowed the more traditional concern with housing need and social housing provision. More broadly, this represents a shift, as Gibb (2002, p. 331) has noted, towards 'efficiency and effectiveness criteria superseding social justice and bureaucratic norms' within European social housing policy.

SECTION 2: THE DEVELOPMENT OF HOUSING POLICY IN IRELAND

Pre-independence

The history of state intervention in the area of social housing is tied to issues such as poverty and public health problems, which coincided with poor housing conditions. In Ireland, social unrest was another factor, particularly in the case of rural housing provision. This meant that social housing in Ireland started sooner and therefore has a longer history than most other European countries (O'Sullivan, 2004). Fahey (2001, pp. 120–21) argues that the origins of local authority housing in Ireland were a 'side effect of agrarian agitation and land reform in the late nineteenth century'. The process of land reform saw tenant farmers gaining their own farms. This did not extend to farm labourers for whom improved housing conditions served as a compensatory measure. In addition to rural agitation, Cullen (2001) argues that concern with public health was a factor in the drive to provide rural housing. For example, inspections by sanitary officers carried out under the Public Health (Ireland) Act, 1878, revealed the poor living conditions of agricultural labourers which contributed to ill health and served as another trigger to improve housing conditions.

Generous provisions for the construction of local authority cottages for agricultural labourers began with the Labourers (Ireland) Act, 1883. This Act enabled boards of guardians to provide houses for rent to labourers. The 1906 Labourers Act provided more generous subsidies to rural local authorities (which had replaced boards of guardians in the 1898 Local Government Act) for the provision of housing for agricultural labourers. By the time Ireland gained independence a substantial local authority housing stock had been built under the Labourers Acts, amounting to 48,000 houses (Fahey, 2001). Instead of dealing with private landlords, labourers now dealt with local authorities, and 'no longer were they at the mercy of a tyrannous landlord who could evict them whenever and for whatever reason suited, they were now protected by the State and as long as they avoided trouble and paid their rents they had nothing to fear' (Cullen, 2001, p. 54). These houses offered a security of tenure not previously experienced by agricultural labourers.

However, state support for housing did not extend as generously to urban areas. This can be attributed to a number of factors. As outlined by Daly (1985, p. 122), reasons such as 'the relative political weakness of Irish cities; their stagnation during the nineteenth century, and an undefined feeling that the city was somehow alien to the true Irish identity' all played a part. Another element was the fact that 'Dublin housing lacked the powerful sympathies of the Roman Catholic clergy, in marked contrast to the land question' (ibid.). State intervention in the provision of rural housing could be justified on the grounds that the Irish case was exceptional and similar claims in England could be resisted. However, urban housing was treated as a different matter. The government was fearful that support for urban housing in Ireland would set a precedent for local authorities in other parts of Britain to follow.

The working class and the poor in urban areas lived in tenements which were large houses inhabited by a number of families and were a particular feature of late nineteenth and early twentieth-century Dublin. Slums were areas which had large numbers of tenements in such poor condition that they were unfit for human habitation. Tenements were formerly the homes of the upper classes who moved from the centre to high-status suburbs when Dublin went into economic decline in the nineteenth century. Their condition over time declined as they were let to the poor who could only afford the most basic accommodation and many were continuously sub-divided. As a result, severe overcrowding, ill health and high death rates were the norm for tenement Dublin, and one-third of the population lived in one-room tenements (Aalen, 1985). Sean O'Casey's work, for example his play *The Plough and the Stars*, offers an insight into the living conditions prevailing in Dublin at the time.

State support for the building of social housing in urban areas originates in the 1866 Labouring Classes (Lodging Houses and Dwellings) Act which provided loans to urban local authorities and private companies towards the cost of constructing houses. Further financial assistance was provided by the 1875 Artisans and Labourers Dwellings Improvement Act. At this time social housing was more likely to be built by private bodies. These included three types, philanthropic bodies, semi-philanthropic bodies, and companies building housing for their workers. Company housing was relatively rare as Irish cities did not have a large industrial base; however, some housing was built by brewery companies such as Guinness and Watkins, and by Pims, a Quaker textile company. Semi-philanthropic bodies were more active, particularly the Artisans Dwelling Company, established in Dublin in 1876. In total, it built 3,081 dwellings up until 1907. Most of its houses were built on new land on the then outskirts of Dublin, such as Coombe, Rialto and Stoneybatter. Houses were built in parallel rows, and were typically single-storey terraced cottages or two-storey terraced houses, with small yards at the back. These houses were let to the more secure workers, at rents higher than those in the tenements or for housing provided by the council. In Cork, a company called the Improved Dwellings Company built houses in schemes such as Prosperity Square, Industry Place and Prosperous Place. These names were suggestive of the attributes of the 'respectable working class' who were to be housed there on land which was previously occupied by slums particularly prone to diseases such as typhus, smallpox and cholera (Cronin, 2006; Keohane, 2002).

An example of a philanthropic body active in the provision of housing was the Guinness Trust (later the Iveagh Trust). This was founded in 1890 and became involved in the provision of housing for the poorer sections of the working class, building tenements up to five storeys high in inner city Dublin locations, particularly around St Patrick's Cathedral. The Iveagh Trust still operates as a philanthropic body and 'is the oldest and largest, non-governmental housing body in Ireland' (Williamson, 2000, p. 642). Council housing built under the 1866 Labouring Classes (Lodging Houses and Dwelling) Act fared less well, one- and two-room dwellings built in areas where uninhabitable slum housing had been cleared were not popular with intended tenants, and the council's poor management of the housing meant that much of this early strand of social housing simply replicated the slums it had replaced. In Cork, the council began to build small numbers of terraced houses in schemes such as Maddens Buildings (1886) and Barrets Buildings (1888), both on the north side of the city, and Horgans Buildings (1891) on the south side of the city. However, the rents charged for the new houses were beyond the reach of poorer tenants whose housing problems therefore remained unresolved (Cronin, 2006).

Iveagh Trust Housing, Ross Road, Dublin.
Source: author's photograph.

Local authority provision was strengthened by legislation in the late nineteenth and early twentieth century by the 1890 Housing the Working Classes Act and more especially by the 1908 Housing Act. These acts provided more generous financing and the 1908 Act was significant because it provided for an Irish Housing Fund to be used to subsidise the provision of urban housing. The 1908 Act emerged in response to the pressure put on the British government by urban nationalist politicians who wanted action on housing for the working classes in urban areas similar to housing supports for rural labourers. The legislation strengthened local authority provision, putting its output ahead of other social housing providers, for whom it was becoming less financially viable to continue providing houses. This trend ran contrary to many other European countries (Norris, 2005) and it was not until the 1990s that non-profit housing organisations re-emerged as significant providers of social housing (O'Sullivan, 2004). While local authority housing output did improve, it failed to meet the scale of need in Dublin. A 1914 Housing Inquiry revealed that 14,000 houses were needed urgently to relieve congestion in the slums. Daly (1985, p. 122) suggests that this inquiry marked the first time there was any urgency felt about the housing problems in Dublin and that 'it would not be implausible to trace a growth in interest in Dublin housing to the threat of socialism and the aftermath of the 1913 lock-out'. However, action on foot of this inquiry was stalled by the restrictions on spending during World War I and the general situation of political unrest in Ireland as the decade went on.

1920s and 1930s

After Ireland gained independence state action on housing was a significant feature of social policy development. This action occurred on two fronts, on the one hand, there was a significant social housing output, especially from the 1930s onwards, and on the other hand, substantial amounts of money were channelled towards the support of privately owned housing. As noted by O'Sullivan (2004, p. 332), 'the progress made in providing housing either directly by the State or indirectly via grants and subsidies in the first 40 years since independence, was remarkable in the context of the development of other welfare services and contributing largely to the predominance of owner-occupation.' This is not to say that all housing problems were resolved; however, in comparison to other areas of social policy such as social security, health and education, which were either left underdeveloped or in the hands of the Catholic Church, housing represented a particularly active area of state intervention.

The first initiative in the area of social housing was the Million Pound scheme in 1923. This provided new funding for urban local authority house construction, where local authorities were required to provide one pound for every two pounds of funding received from central government. Councils aimed to build inner-city cottages which were what people wanted after slums were torn down. The biggest development in the 1920s was the completion of 1,000 cottages in Marino, Dublin. This and other smaller schemes were not new ideas, but the fulfilment of proposals put forward before World War I. The Marino development was significant because it embodied some of the ideals of the town planning movement which was active in Dublin at the time, namely the idea of a garden city with a mixture of house designs and central open spaces with roads radiating off.

Over time, the general pattern of development involved the spread of cottages in the suburbs, with a predominance of blocks of flats in more central locations. In the early 1920s in Cork, garden city ideas were manifested in the Council's building of MacCurtain's, MacSwiney's and French's Villas. The former two consisted of two-storey houses in short terraces with gardens front and back, while French's Villas were semi-detached, following the middle-class standard of housing established in the nineteenth century (Hourihan, 2006). Private house building got a major boost by the Housing (Building Facilities) Act, 1924, which provided generous grants for private housing. The grants tended to favour the financially better-off house builders who were in a position to build larger houses (O'Connell, 2005b), which they did mostly on the outskirts of cities.

The housing problems of the urban poor did not receive attention again until 1929 when a survey revealed the need for 40,000 new dwellings in urban areas in the wake of further slum clearance. When compared to the 1914 Inquiry, the Dublin housing situation had worsened, the survey revealing that there were 15 per cent more unfit houses (Daly, 1985). These findings were addressed in legislation introduced by the new Fianna Fáil government entitled the Housing (Financial and Miscellaneous Provisions) Act, 1932. This legislation paved the way for a significant increase in local authority housing activity through the provision of funding to construct dwellings for those who had been dislocated by slum clearance throughout the 1930s, 1940s and 1950s. In Dublin, residents were either re-housed in new city centre flat complexes or new local authority suburban housing estates in the then 'wilds of the countryside' (Fahey, 2001, p. 123), in places such as Cabra and Crumlin.

Growth of the suburbs increased the separation of workplace and residence for many and, over time, contributed to the rise of car ownership, which in turn prompted the further spread of urbanisation (Horner, 1985). In Cork, relatively large developments were built in Gurranabraher and Farranferris in the 1930s, but they were more compact in terms of density and layout compared to the Council's developments in the 1920s (Hourihan, 2006). Local authority output grew as a result of this legislation, and together with continuing provision under the Working Classes and Labourers Acts between 1933 and 1943, a total of 48,875 local authority houses were completed in contrast to 9,994 in the previous decade. Yet this output was in many ways catching up with long-standing problems which could be traced back at least as far as the 1914 Inquiry.

At the same time, the push to enable private ownership did not decline. The 1932 legislation provided further subsidies for private housing. Other measures were also introduced to encourage private ownership, including a strengthening of the right of local authority tenants in rural areas to purchase their local authority houses. This option had been in existence since 1919 but did not become universally established until the 1936 Labourers Act which obliged local authorities to sell off labourers' cottages at generous discounts. This turned out to be an extremely successful scheme and O'Connell (2005b, p. 30) suggests that overall tenant purchase of local authority housing 'could accurately be described as one of the most sustained and long running programmes of privatisation ever undertaken by the State in Ireland'. By 1964 80 per cent of rural local authority housing had been purchased (Fahey, 2001).

1940s and 1950s

A 1948 White Paper entitled *Housing: A Review of Past Operations and Immediate Requirements* estimated that a further 100,000 new houses were needed in the ensuing decade. It divided this into 60,000 social houses and 40,000 private sector houses. A 1948 Housing (Amendment) Act provided for increased funding for local authorities to meet the target set out in the White Paper, and social housing output increased substantially over the following decade. Examples of these social housing developments include Ballyfermot in Dublin and Ballyphehane in Cork. However, social housing output was outpaced by the growth in private housing, which far exceeded predictions. The growth in private housing was assisted by provisions in the 1948 Act and subsequent amendments which provided for further financial assistance to private house builders. O'Connell (2005b, p. 26) argues that the 1948 White Paper set in train the 'institutionalisation of owner occupation as the dominant tenure'. The White Paper noted that housing for the working classes was proceeding quite well as a result of continuing slum clearance, but the middle classes living in cities were mainly living in poor-quality rented housing. This problem was to be remedied not by providing social housing for the middle classes but by encouraging more owner occupation. Table 10.1 below shows the growing share of owner occupation from the 1940s (when the nature of housing occupancy was first recorded in the 1946 census) to the early 1980s and the impact this had on the other tenures, with the tenure share of private renting and social renting both declining.

Table 10.1 Housing tenure and housing stock, 1946–81

	1946	1961	1971	1981
%				
Local authority rented	n. av.	18.4	15.5	12.5
Private rented	42.7*	17.2	13.3	10.1
Owner occupied	52.7	59.8	68.8	74.4
Other**	4.6	4.6	2.4	3.0
Total	100.0	100.0	100.0	100.0
000s:				
Local authority rented	n. av.	124.6	112.6	111.8
Private rented	282.7*	116.3	96.7	90.3
Owner occupied	348.7	404.6	499.7	667.0
Other**	31.1	30.9	17.4	27.0
Total	662.5	676.4	726.4	896.1

Source: CSO, Census of Population, various years

Notes:

n. av.   not available

* Local authority renting figures were included with privately rented dwellings in the 1946 census.

** 'Other' refers to situations where households were living in employer-provided accommodation, caretaking a property, renting from a non-profit provider other than a local authority or not paying any rent.

1960s and 1970s

While the output of social housing increased in these decades, the role of social housing declined in favour of a greater emphasis on owner occupation. Much of the legislative and policy developments in this period contributed to this trend. The main piece of housing legislation was the 1966 Housing Act. This rationalised and reformed much of the existing housing legislation, setting out the powers and duties of local authorities in relation to housing provision and ending the tradition of separate legislation for urban and rural housing. As a consequence, the right of urban tenants to purchase their local authority houses was established. This took off particularly in the 1970s, when the incentives to do so were increased. This contributed to the growing share of owner occupation in urban areas, which until then fell well behind rural areas. Owner occupation in urban areas rose from 38 per cent in 1961, to 52.5 per cent in 1971, to 65.6 per cent in 1981. Increasing urbanisation was also a factor.

Social housing continued to be built and actually expanded in a major way by the 1970s. This was triggered in part by incidents in Dublin in the early 1960s that revealed the poor and unsafe conditions of much of the housing stock, as slum buildings still had not been completely eradicated by previous initiatives. These incidents included the death of an elderly couple caused by the collapse of a tenement house in Bolton Street in 1963 and the death of two children caused by the collapse of two houses in Fenian Street two weeks later. A 1964 White Paper entitled *Housing Progress and Prospects* considered tens of thousands of houses in the country to be unfit for human habitation. What followed was large-scale investment in the building of public housing which resulted in the development of large housing estates on the peripheries of towns and cities, including Tallaght, Clondalkin and Blanchardstown, where the tradition of low-density, low-rise houses continued. The only high-rise development built was Ballymun.

While the scale of public housing developments was unprecedented during this period, the construction of owner-occupied dwellings far outpaced social housing output. As the main cities developed, the separation of areas into public and private housing became more defined. Private housing boomed in particular during the 1970s. Demand was accelerated by population growth, and the drive to encourage individuals to purchase their own houses was reinforced more strongly than ever. A housing policy document entitled *Housing in the '70s* expressed the concern that private ownership was still not favoured enough over renting from local authorities. Accordingly, incentives to purchases one's own home were increased, particularly for first-time buyers.

During this house building boom, the quality of developments both in the private and public sector left a lot to be desired. In the private sector, as Hourihan (2006, pp. 282–3) points out:

> Economics was the overriding influence on the middle class estates of the 1960s and 1970s ... It was a time of high inflation, particularly of house prices, and the result was suburban estates that were built as cheaply as possible. Roads were long and straight, as this saved on road length per house and the cost of utilities. Economies were also achieved through building large estates, sometimes of hundreds of houses, and of standardising the styles as much as possible ... The space between buildings became progressively smaller, so that even detached houses were separated by only a few feet in some cases and

garden sizes became diminutive in order to save on site costs. The quality of materials also dis-improved, with items like cavity blocks and untreated window frames that rotted after only a few years.

In the public sector, by contrast, the layout of housing estates tended to be superior as there was not the same pressure to utilise all available space in order to maximize profits. Yet, many were built in a way that limited access to and from the estates so that developments were physically and socially isolated from surrounding areas. For example, writing about North Clondalkin, which has a heavy concentration of local authority estates built in the 1970s, Bartley (1998, p. 144) notes that 'it requires a special effort to enter North Clondalkin. The structure of the roads network hierarchy is such that anybody who does not need to visit the area for a specific purpose will automatically bypass it.' The quality of construction was similarly poor. Many new social housing developments were constructed with pre-fabricated units and had central heating but no chimneys. As a result, ventilation problems quickly gave rise to dampness and condensation (Hourihan, 2006). The physical decline of many of the new social housing estates was rapid. The encouragement of owner occupation was further enhanced by the sale of local authority housing to tenants. As a result, the stock of social housing fell, with the majority remaining being the least desirable to own and located in the least desirable areas.

1980s

By the 1980s social housing became increasingly residualised. As Fahey (2001, p. 127) explains:

> … as affluence grew among the upper working class and the lower middle class, they began to turn their backs on social housing and make their way into owner-occupation. This process was hastened in Ireland by the eagerness of the authorities to sell public housing to tenants. The better-off segments of the traditional clientele for social housing thus turned towards other tenures. In consequence, social housing shifted downmarket. More and more it came to be associated with the poor and marginalised both in fact and in public perception.

Local authority housing estates became the physical receptors of many of the problems of the 1980s, such as long-term unemployment, homelessness, and a rise in drug abuse; and the tenure's image as problematic and residual grew. Power (1993, p. 372) notes that the Irish pattern of social housing created 'intensely segregated and run-down social rented housing estates.

Irish social housing was more marginal than in any other country.' Added to these problems, the poor economic climate of the 1980s meant investment in social housing declined so that social housing output fell sharply (see table 10.2). Attention shifted to making the most of existing social housing stock, and renewal schemes began in 1985. The schemes concentrated on the physical improvement of buildings, addressing the problems emerging from the poor standards of construction. However, this initiative was quite small in scale given the budgetary constraints governments were experiencing at the time.

Table 10.2 Housing activity in the 1980s: numbers of local authority and private houses completed, numbers of local authority houses sold to tenants

Year	Local authority house completions	Private house completions	Local authority houses sold to tenants
1980	5,984	21,801	4,949
1981	5,681	23,236	4,426
1982	5,686	21,112	3,492
1983	6,190	19,948	3,492
1984	7,002	17,942	2,734
1985	6,523	17,425	1,550
1986	5,516	17,164	533
1987	3,074	15,376	1,443
1988	1,450	14,204	4,816
1989	768	17,300	18,166

Source: Department of the Environment, Heritage and Local Government, Annual Housing Statistics Bulletin, various years

A Surrender Grant, introduced in 1984, was another policy aimed at making the most of existing stock; however, it actually contributed to the residualisation of social housing. The grant was given to local authority tenants who opted to leave their local authority house and purchase a dwelling in the private market. The logic was that this would be an efficient way of increasing social housing stock and targeting it at the most needy. However, the result was the loss of the more well-off tenants who were replaced by tenants with lower incomes and who were often vulnerable in other ways, through having recently been homeless, for example, and who needed more support than local authority housing departments traditionally offered. The initiative had a negative economic and social impact on local communities (Threshold, 1987) and the policy was abandoned in 1987. However, a new tenant purchase scheme was subsequently established, which accounts for the dramatic rise in local authority houses sold to tenants in 1989 (see table 10.2).

The 1980s also saw difficult times for some owner occupiers. Ability to service mortgages became a significant issue because of the escalation of interest rates in the late 1970s and early 1980s, which peaked at 18 per cent. An indication of the difficulty this caused is the rise in rent and mortgage supplement payments made under the Supplementary Welfare Allowance scheme which grew from 1,300 to 8,800 between 1980 and 1987 (Blackwell, 1990). The housing boom of the 1970s turned to a slump as output declined and new house prices fell by 27 per cent in real terms between 1980 and 1987 (ibid.).

The introduction of the 1988 Housing Act was another notable development in the 1980s, particularly with respect to homelessness. Until the 1980s the issue of homelessness was of little official concern and detached from the larger housing policy context. Homelessness was primarily understood as a personal condition. As Harvey (1995, p. 76) noted, 'homeless people were seen as drop-outs, vagrants, tramps, anti-social people, for the most part unwanted elderly men.' The main form of accommodation offered was a bed in a county home, with voluntary agencies such as the Society of St Vincent De Paul also offering emergency accommodation. Newer voluntary agencies – such as the Simon Community, operating in Dublin from 1969, and Focus Point (now Focus Ireland), which was set up in Dublin in 1985 – sought both to provide services and to challenge the state on its inaction (Harvey, 2008). The 1980s marked a change, with research initiated by voluntary agencies indicating that homelessness had been on the rise since the 1970s and that the traditional perception of homelessness obscured the fact that it was a structural problem that affected both men and women, and people of all ages, including children (O'Sullivan, 2005a, 2008).

The 1988 Housing Act gave local authorities responsibility for homelessness, which previously had been the remit of health authorities under the 1953 Health Act. Yet, while the 1988 legislation gave local authorities statutory responsibility in terms of assisting the homeless, it did not oblige them to house homeless people. An obligation to carry out periodic assessments of homeless people and, more broadly, housing need was also included in the Act. These assessments began in 1989 and are carried out every three years. The legislation is notable also for the inclusion of a statutory definition of homelessness. In section 2 of the Act a person is defined as homeless if:

> ... there is no accommodation available which, in the opinion of the authority, he ... can reasonably occupy or remain in occupation of, or he is living in [an] institution, and is so living because he has no accommodation ... and he is ... unable to provide accommodation from his own resources.

This definition was well received because it highlighted homelessness as a problem linked to lack of accommodation, thus privileging structural factors over individual ones (Phelan and Norris, 2008). Yet, implementation of the legislation was patchy at local level (Harvey, 1995) and homelessness actually grew over the 1990s.

SECTION 3: IRISH HOUSING POLICY SINCE THE 1990s – CONTEMPORARY ISSUES AND DEVELOPMENTS

Box 10.1   Key housing policy developments since the 1990s

1991 A Plan for Social Housing
1995 Social Housing – the Way Ahead
2000 'Part V' of the Planning and Development Act
2000 Homelessness – An Integrated Strategy
2001 Youth Homeless Strategy
2002 Homelessness Preventative Strategy
2004 Residential Tenancies Act
2007 Delivering Homes, Sustaining Communities
2008 The Way Home: a strategy to address adult homelessness in Ireland 2008–2013

The most recent period of Irish housing policy has been dominated by the housing boom that lasted from the mid-1990s to the mid-2000s. This is now being followed by an emerging housing bust. House prices began to increase from the mid-1990s onwards and a new housing boom emerged which was much larger in scale than the previous boom of the 1970s, and unprecedented in the wider European context (Redmond and Norris, 2005). Much has been written about the causes and the impact of the boom, with critics suggesting it has exacerbated housing inequalities. Drudy and Punch (2005, p. 41) suggest, for example, that 'market ideologies have become the dominant forces underlying recent policy evolution in Ireland', which has intensified the lack of access. Fitzgerald and Winston (2005) maintain that the housing system has contributed to the overall inequalities in Irish society. They argue that government intervention in the housing market combined with the 'house price inflation since the mid-1990s has effected a silent redistribution of wealth in favour of home owners and owners of development land at the expense of those trying to enter the housing market' (ibid., p. 224).

Overall, the key problems of residualisation, social segregation, lack of accessibility and affordability, already reviewed in the broader context of European housing reform, are repeated in the Irish context. This is not to say that these problems did not exist before the 1990s, but this section shows how they have become particularly critical since then. This section reviews each sector and the issues associated with it individually, before briefly considering the issue of the emerging housing bust which, as a product of housing policy reliant on the market, has the potential to further exacerbate problems such as affordability and inequality. First, we set the section in context, with an overview of tenure patterns since the early 1990s.

Table 10.3 Housing tenure and total housing stock, 1991–2006

	1991	2002	2006
Housing tenure %			
Local authority rented	9.7	6.9	7.2
Private rented	8.0	11.1	13.4*
Owner occupied	79.3	77.4	74.7
Other	3.0	4.6	4.7
Total	100.0	100.0	100.0
Housing stock** 000s	1,176	1,506	1,804

Source: CSO, Census of Population, various years

Notes:

* The 2006 census distinguished private renting from renting from voluntary bodies for the first time. When separated, private renting amounted to 9.9 per cent and voluntary bodies to 3.45 per cent.

** Total housing stock figures include both occupied and unoccupied residences.

Housing stock grew by 53.4 per cent from 1991 to 2006. This increase was partially due to population growth and to changes in household size, which had been gradually getting smaller since the 1920s. In 1926, the most common household size was six persons or more; by 2006, this was the least common size. Two-person households are now the most common. Another important trend was the gradual shift in tenure trends that had prevailed for the previous 50 years. The share of owner-occupied housing reached a peak in 1991, amounting to 79.3 per cent of all housing; however, this declined to 74.7 per cent by 2006. This brought its share back down to its early 1980s level. The rise in house prices may have been a factor in this trend. By contrast, the share of private renting increased, which mirrors the resurgence of private renting across Europe. Private renting grew from its lowest point of 8 per cent in 1991 to 13.4 per cent in 2006, yet this is still far below the levels prevailing in the mid-decades of the twentieth century. Finally, table 10.3 displays a very slight growth in the share of social housing, which has been the first rise since 1961.

Social housing

The lack of investment in social housing stock, which accumulated over the 1980s, resulted in longer waiting lists. Consequently, attention began to return to larger building programmes in the 1990s, but not on as large a scale as during previous decades. Policy towards the design and planning of social housing changed as well, in an effort not to repeat some of the mistakes of the past, particularly in relation to social segregation.

New policies were published in the early 1990s, namely *A Plan for Social Housing*, 1991 and *Social Housing – the Way Ahead*, 1995. Both sought to address the shortage of social housing, to improve access to housing generally, and to deal with the divisions between private and social housing. These aims were to be achieved by implementing policies such as ending the building of large local authority housing estates, building mixed tenure estates, facilitating greater involvement of other non-profit providers in the sector, and enabling tenant participation in the running of local authority housing estates. In addition, these policies aimed to facilitate a greater range of housing options for lower income households through improvement of the terms of tenant sales and the introduction of shared ownership housing, a Low Cost Housing Sites Scheme and a Mortgage Allowance Scheme to encourage social tenants to buy in the private sector.

However, the overall objectives of policy in relation to social housing did not change. Owner occupation remained the key focus on the grounds that this would allow government to target social housing at the most needy. For example, *Social Housing – the Way Ahead* states that:

Government policy seeks to promote home ownership, not only because it is the preferred form of tenure for most people, but also because extending the ownership option to those who would otherwise not be able to afford it reduces the demand for rented social housing. This helps concentrate resources on those in the most acute need. (Department of the Environment, 1995, p. 25)

In essence, social housing still remains a residual sector in terms of overall size.

Since the early 1990s there has been a slow increase in social housing output (table 10.4), but this has not matched the growth in housing need, particularly of people who are unable to afford their existing accommodation. This category grew from 13,328 households in 1999 to 25,045 households in 2005. In addition, social housing output in recent years is still much lower than the output in the early 1980s when fewer resources were available and housing waiting lists were actually lower.

Table 10.4 Social housing output and local authority houses sold, 1990–2007

Year	Local authority housing completions	Local authority houses acquired*	Voluntary/ non -profit houses**	Local authority houses sold
1990	1,003	–	–	5,600
1991	1,180	–	–	3,143
1992	1,482	–	–	1,332
1993	1,200	369	890	613
1994	2,374	467	901	505
1995	2,960	882	1,011	950
1996	2,676	897	917	2,284
1997	2,632	585	756	2,139
1998	2,771	511	485	2,006
1999	2,909	804	579	2,256
2000	2,204	1,003	951	1,844
2001	3,622	1,400	1,253	1,411
2002	4,403	671	1,360	1,195
2003	4,516	456	1,617	1,567

Year	Local authority housing completions	Local authority houses acquired*	Voluntary/ non -profit houses**	Local authority houses sold
2004	3,539	971	1,607	1,652
2005	4,209	918	1,350	1,738
2006	3,968	1,153	1,240	1,855
2007	4,986	2,002	1,685	1,231

Source: Department of the Environment, Heritage and Local Government, Annual Housing Statistics Bulletin, various years

Notes:

* Prior to 1993 the number of local authority houses acquired was relatively small and recorded under local authority housing completions.

** Numbers of voluntary and non-profit houses recorded are those completed as a result of new funding arrangements introduced in 1991.

Other developments following from the policies of the early to mid-1990s include the attempt to encourage more voluntary provision of social housing. Under the *Plan for Social Housing* improved funding arrangements were put in place for voluntary providers, with the intention that they would play a greater role in providing and managing mainstream social housing for low-income families. This would mean that local authorities would no longer be the sole provider in the case of housing need. This change has contributed to the expansion of output, yet not to the extent that the Department of the Environment, Heritage and Local Government intended. For example, an annual target of 4,000 voluntary and cooperative houses by 2006 was set in the *National Development Plan 2000–2006*. Reasons for this target not being met include the escalation of house building costs, difficulties with raising money to meet costs not covered by government funding, and administrative difficulties with the provision of funding (Williamson, 2000; Brooke and Clayton, 2005).

Local authorities have also continued to promote home ownership, particularly among lower income households, so that they can get on the 'housing ladder'. This occurs both through the traditional method of the sale of local authority houses to tenants, and through new schemes which have come on stream since the 1990s, including shared ownership and affordable housing. While the sale of local authority houses continues, the numbers have declined in contrast to previous decades (see tables 10.2 and 10.4). This may be due to the poor quality and the overall residual nature of remaining stock and also the lack of affordability for current tenants whose incomes have been declining relative to the rest of the population (Norris et al., 2007).

The shared ownership scheme was introduced under the 1991 *Plan for Social Housing*. Under the scheme a person who qualifies on the basis of having an income under a certain threshold buys 50 per cent of a property with a mortgage, rents 50 per cent from the local authority and buys out the local authority share within 25 years. This was introduced as an attempt to diversify tenure on housing estates and facilitate a greater mix between owner-occupied and social housing. However, the scheme has not proven very popular, with transactions peaking at 1,686 in 2002 and declining to 180 by 2007, and it is actually quite expensive for low-income households to access a house via this route. In general, such schemes also have the effect of further residualising the remaining local authority population as they 'cream off' the top tier of housing applicants (Fahey and Watson, 1995, p. 10).

This brings us to an enduring issue with social housing, which is the continuing residualisation of the sector. The problem of residualisation has been exacerbated by the polarising effects of the recent economic and housing boom. It is also an inevitable effect of housing policy which targets only the most needy for social housing and encourages those with sufficient incomes to purchase their local authority house or leave the sector. Despite Ireland's period of economic prosperity, the profile of local authority tenants has worsened from the 1980s to the 1990s in terms of poverty, unemployment and lack of educational attainment, particularly in the case of urban local authority areas (Nolan et al., 1998; Nolan and Whelan, 1999). In an analysis of relative poverty by housing tenure, Fahey et al. (2004) found that social renters have by far the highest level of poverty, with 60 per cent of social renters relatively poor after housing costs are taken into account, compared to 27·5 per cent of private renters and 13 per cent of owners of mortgaged private housing. Furthermore, social housing estates are still highly spatially segregated. As Drudy (2006, p. 263) points out, 'this is particularly obvious in the main urban centres and on the periphery where some estates contain up to 90 per cent Local Authority mainly low-income tenants.' Dublin is particularly spatially segregated. For example, a research project which compared seven European cities found that Dublin and London had the highest levels of segregation; Scandinavian cities such as Helsinki and Umeå had the least; and the continental cities of Lisbon, Toulouse and Turin had intermediate levels (Bertaux et al., 2002). The locations of the most deprived areas in Dublin and London were found mainly in the inner city, but also in the periphery, which is a pattern similar to spatial segregation in American cities, but not to the same degree (ibid.). The effect of high levels of spatial segregation is to 'divide, isolate and exclude rather than integrate urban communities' (Corcoran, 2000, p. 77). This has a negative effect on the quality of life of local authority tenants. This is especially the case for particularly troubled 'difficult to let' and 'difficult to manage' estates, though these are relatively small in number (Fahey, 1999).

These problems are being addressed somewhat by the changes in the management role of local authorities instigated by the Housing Act, 1992, which required local authorities to develop housing management plans for their areas. Local authorities' powers were also augmented by the Housing Act, 1997, which enables them to evict tenants on the grounds of anti-social behaviour. The existing style of local authority management was criticised for being remote and inefficient and was seen as part of the problem. The new approach encourages practices such as tenant involvement in dealing with estate management, including, to some extent, housing allocation and anti-social behaviour. However, as Redmond (2001, p. 302) notes, this emphasis on improving management effectively sidelines 'any serious engagement regarding the structural socio-economic position of tenants', which is at the heart of the residualisation of the sector.

Owner occupation

The owner-occupied sector has seen the most dramatic changes over the last decade, most clearly evident during the housing boom, 1996–2006, when there was an unprecedented level of private housing construction and house price escalation. Various factors gave rise to increased demand, such as an increasing population, and, in particular, an increase in the population of young adults; smaller households; increasing wealth; and easier availability of mortgages combined with lower interest rates. As prices rose, houses and land became more lucrative commodities and speculative demand drove prices even higher. This, in turn, contributed to increasing inequality, as the housing market boom allowed developers and speculators to accrue 'unearned profits' on the basis of price rises. As the NESC (2004, p. 2) notes, 'rapidly rising property prices have been an independent source of significant change in the distribution of wealth and income in Irish society'. Nationally, new house prices increased, on average, by 250 per cent between 1996 and 2006, and by 333 per cent for second-hand houses over the same period. Prices in Dublin rose even higher due to factors such as the more limited availability of development land and higher demand for houses. Therefore, in Dublin over the same period, new house prices rose by 318 per cent, on average, and second-hand ones by 390 per cent.

Affordable housing

The problem of affordability became a major issue by the late 1990s. As wages did not increase in line with house prices, many socio-economic groups who traditionally would have bought a house in the owner-occupied sector found themselves priced out and having to rely on the private rented sector or apply for social housing. Affordability, as Fahey et al. (2004, p. 14) recognise, is a 'slippery concept' given variables such as gross and net income and mortgage interest rates. The government defines affordability by setting a threshold of 35 per cent of disposable income going on housing costs, as stipulated in Part V of the Planning and Development Act, 2000.

The government response to the housing boom and the problem of affordability mainly centred on an attempt to maintain the efficiency of the housing market, working on the assumption that ownership was still the preferred tenure, and steering those who had found the market difficult to access towards it. However, as the NESC suggests (1999, p. 501), the 'steering of households towards owner occupation in turn creates a consumer "preference" which in turn leads to policy to encourage it'. Relatively minor efforts were made to dampen house price inflation in the late 1990s in response to a series of commissioned reports about the housing boom produced by the economist Peter Bacon. However, the limited attempts to try to assist people in purchasing homes, such as reductions in stamp duty, had the opposite effect of fuelling house prices even further (Memery, 2001). The focus from the late 1990s onwards turned towards the provision of 'affordable houses' to first-time buyers whose income fell below a certain threshold and who had little chance of buying a house on the open market.

The first 'affordable housing scheme' was launched in 1999. This scheme allows local authorities to build housing and sell it at cost to private buyers whose household income is below a certain threshold. The house is paid for by means of a low-interest mortgage made available by the local authority. The scheme was developed further under the provisions of Part V of the Planning and Development Act, 2000. This Act required property developers to transfer, at cost price, 20 per cent of dwelling land, sites or finished houses to local authorities as a condition of planning permission, and this portion was to be provided as affordable, social and voluntary housing. In the Irish context, this was a radical and progressive piece of legislation. It was in part an attempt to intervene and halt the escalating price of development land and the excessive profits generated from it. It also allowed local authorities and voluntary providers to access land for housing provision in urban areas, which had become prohibitively expensive over the 1990s.

However, the legislation was very strongly opposed by property developers who resisted the idea of mixed tenure estates and argued that the legislation was unworkable and would damage them economically (Redmond, 2003). Their successful lobbying led to the Planning and Development (Amendment) Act, 2002, which allowed property developers to compensate local authorities with an equivalent monetary value of the sites, land or dwellings or to provide these in an alternative area, or to combine both. The monetary contribution made by developers has risen significantly, from €0·8 million in 2003 to €35·4 million in 2006 (Department of the Environment, Heritage and Local Government, 2007a). The provision of alternative land has also been commonly used, with the result that little affordable housing is provided in urban areas where demand is highest. Overall, housing provision under Part V has been slow to develop; however, output has improved since 2005 (see table 10.5). A third affordable housing scheme was introduced under *Sustaining Progress*, the social partnership agreement of 2003. The agreement contained a special initiative on housing and accommodation, to further increase the supply of affordable housing by 10,000 units, although this target has not yet been achieved.

Table 10.5 Affordable housing output 1999–2007

	1999	2000	2001	2002	2003	2004	2005	2006	2007
1999 scheme	40	86	272	882	1,524	860	857	743	869
Part V	–	–	–	46	88	374	962	1,600	2,063
AHI	–	–	–	–	–	–	124	501	241

Source: Department of the Environment, Heritage and Local Government, Annual Housing Statistics Bulletin, various years

Affordability

Research suggests that, in general, the levels of unaffordability among owner occupiers are relatively low, and it appears that those assisted into home ownership through various government schemes are actually those who subsequently experience the biggest problems with affordability. For example, Fahey and Duffy (2007) found that in 1999/2000 only one per cent of owner occupiers exceeded the threshold of 35 per cent of household expenditure on housing costs. They also looked at actual outgoings on mortgage payments since the early 1970s to 2000, and this data reveals that as a percentage of household expenditure they have been quite consistent for owners with mortgages (between 7·4 per cent and 9·6 per cent). However, research by Norris et al. (2007) suggests that among owner occupiers, it is those whose ownership has been facilitated by government-sponsored schemes who fare the worst in terms of affordability.

Table 10.6 Households spending more than 35 per cent of gross weekly income on rent or mortgage payments 1990–2003

Scheme	Percentage of households spending 35 per cent or more of gross weekly income on rent or mortgage payments
Tenant purchase	32
Mortgage allowance	33
Local authority loan	40
Shared ownership	52
Affordable housing	33

Source: Norris et al., (2007, p. 352)

This would suggest that there are limits to private ownership, and emphasising it as the preferred tenure results in severe financial problems for low-income households struggling to own their own homes.

Private renting

This tenure type has increased in recent years. The amount of private rental housing stock has grown dramatically, resulting in its growing tenure share (see table 10.3). Cities in particular have been transformed by apartment developments, of which a large share has been sold to the investor market and privately rented. Data from the 2006 census indicates that there are a total of 109,866 flats and apartments in purpose-built blocks in the state and that 62,084 of these have been built in the ten-year period from 1996 to 2006. The proportion which is privately rented is 35·9 per cent, which is much higher than the proportion of all dwelling types privately rented (9·9 per cent). This increase is mirrored in the rise of private investors in property, which became a growing phenomenon over the 1990s. Research by Memery and Kerrins (2000, in Memery, 2001) showed that 70 per cent of the landlords surveyed first entered the private rented sector in the 1990s. This is also the sector where the inequalities in Irish housing are sharply evident and the system is tiered, between upper-middle class, middle class and low-income households who pay 'relatively high rents for low-quality dwellings' (Drudy and Punch, 2005, p. 81). Low-income households who rent are also affected by the affordability problems in the owner-occupied sector, as households who postpone house purchase and rent instead, create a 'crowding-out' effect and reduce access for low-income households. Properties which were traditionally rented by low-income households may also be subject to a process of gentrification. This means that they are refurbished and let for a higher return, leading to a diminishing number of affordable properties for the low-income renters (Punch, 2005).

In policy terms, private renting was neglected for many years and deemed 'the forgotten sector' (O'Brien and Dillon, 1982). This neglect has gradually been addressed, both in terms of supply and demand. However, on balance, it would seem that investors have been the main beneficiaries. Measures to boost supply can be traced back to Section 23 of the Finance Act, 1981. This provided financial incentives in the form of very generous tax relief to people who invested in accommodation for sale and for letting in 'designated areas'. The scheme granted landlords or owner occupiers tax allowances equivalent to the cost of the property minus the site value over a period of ten years. Landlords could offset the cost of purchasing, converting or refurbishing a property against the rental income earned from the property as well as rental income from any other rental properties they owned. This type of tax relief has continued in various Finance Acts since 1981 and it took off in particular in the 1990s (Galligan, 2005). The scheme is used to incentivise development in areas identified as in need of investment. In the past, these included the Temple Bar area in Dublin and various seaside resorts, and, more recently, park and ride facilities and student accommodation schemes. While this relief has been successful at boosting and improving the supply of housing stock in areas where there may have been little incentive to do so, it is quite regressive in terms of its tax impact. One has to be sufficiently wealthy in the first place to invest in property in order to avail of the tax incentives associated with this type of investment. Tax relief for renters is minor in comparison. The only tax relief a private renter can avail of is 20 per cent of rent paid, subject to a maximum of €2,000 for a single person and €4,000 for a married couple (2008 figures).

Tax relief to renters was introduced in the early 1990s, along with a series of other measures giving a little more security to renters than heretofore. These measures were contained in the Housing (Miscellaneous Provisions) Act, 1992. This Act provided that a minimum period of written notice (28 days) to quit must be given to a tenant, it also provided for the making of regulations regarding standards of accommodation, the provision of rent books and registration by landlords. However, compliance with the provisions of the legislation has been poor. For example, in 2006 a total of 9,835 inspections were carried out on standards; 1,697 accommodation units were found to be sub-standard (17.25 per cent). Legal action was taken in only 36 cases.

Further attention was paid to the rented sector by the Commission on the Private Rented Residential Sector (2000). This was set up in 1999 to address issues such as tenant security, and the rights and responsibilities of landlords and tenants. The commission included representatives of property owners, auctioneers, etc., as well as tenants. These competing interests meant that the commission's deliberations were conflictual and the outcome was one of compromise rather than consensus on how to proceed. The main recommendations included improving security of tenure by entitling a tenant to occupy a dwelling for three and a half years, once a minimum continuous period of six months' renting had passed. An 'open market rent' was recommended, subject to review not more than once per annum. The establishment of a Private Residential Tenancies Board was also recommended, which would deal with disputes, with registration of landlords and with the promotion of good practice. These recommendations were legislated for in the Residential Tenancies Act, 2004. However, the provisions are still quite weak in relation to tenant's rights. Security of tenure is diminished by the inclusion of situations which allow landlords to regain the property, such as needing it for self-occupation or for a member of the landlord's family. The regulations in relation to rent are also weak. Renters who rely on rent allowance also face discrimination when advertisements for rental vacancies can openly stipulate that rent allowance is not accepted, and this form of discrimination is not covered under equality legislation.

Besides issues of security in this tenure, affordability is also a problem. Yet it is relatively neglected compared to the attention given to the issue in the owner-occupied sector. The neglect of this issue strengthens the view that private renting is still predominantly regarded as a transient and inferior option, prior to either owning one's own home or acquiring social housing for a lower rent. Fahey and Duffy (2007) found that in 1999/2000, 20 per cent of private renters exceeded the 35 per cent of household expenditure threshold. In addition, looking at outgoings on rent from the 1970s to 2000, they found that private renters have seen a large increase in expenditure since 1987 (from 12·5 per cent in 1987 to 21 per cent by 1999/2000). Another indication of the affordability problems in this sector is the fact that private renters are more likely to experience consistent poverty compared to home owners and social renters (Fahey et al., 2004).

While the increase in rent costs is due in part to rents tracking the rise in house prices during the housing boom (Drudy and Punch, 2005), the fact that rents started to increase from 1987 suggests that the rise is also in part an effect of the cutbacks in social housing at this time (Fahey et al., 2004). This is because individuals who qualified for social housing but who could not be housed had to turn instead to the private rental sector and finance their accommodation with rental supplements, which were available through the Supplementary Welfare Allowance scheme to people not in work. In

2006, there were 59,861 recipients of rent supplement, and 53 per cent of these were in receipt of the payment for over 18 months (Department of Social and Family Affairs, 2007). Costs have escalated from 7.8 million in 1989 to 388 million in 2006. The increasing use of this mechanism to meet housing needs has meant that a segment of the private rental sector has taken on a social housing or welfare role. A new Rental Accommodation Scheme is being implemented for those on rent supplement long-term. This scheme aims to allocate social housing to long-term recipients of Supplementary Welfare Allowance or to secure long leases in the private rented sector for them. By the end of 2007, local authorities had transferred 11,096 households. However, this acts as a support for those on welfare only; it ignores the affordability problems of private renters on low incomes in work. As Fahey et al. (2004) argue, the focus on affordable home ownership has completely overshadowed problems with affordability in the private rented sector, and greater attempts should be made to make private renting a viable and affordable tenure choice for low-income families and for those at the early stages of adulthood.

Homelessness

Homelessness grew substantially over the late 1990s and early 2000s and has since fallen back (see table 10.7). However, it must be noted that there are significant definitional and methodological issues that can affect the results obtained, and voluntary agencies dealing with homelessness regularly disagree with the findings produced by the homeless assessments (Brownlee, 2008). A series of policies were developed in the early 2000s to tackle existing and prevent further homelessness. These were *Homelessness – An Integrated Strategy* (2000), *Youth Homeless Strategy* (2001) and *Homelessness Preventative Strategy* (2002). These policies signalled a greater effort to tackle and prevent homelessness on the part of statutory services in partnership with voluntary services. The reference to integration in the first strategy referred to the need to integrate the efforts of both sectors and to focus on a continuum from emergency to long-term responses, as well as responding to needs in the areas of health, education and employment. Part of the solution proposed in the strategy was to create Homeless Fora in all local authorities, comprising statutory and voluntary representatives who are responsible for creating homeless action plans for their area. In Dublin, the homeless forum has been replaced by the Homeless Agency. The implementation of these policies seems to have been effective in reducing homeless numbers, particularly in Dublin. However, Phelan and Norris (2008) argue that this phase in policy has coincided with a shift back to understanding homelessness in mainly personal terms in the way services are organised. Consequently, homelessness is detached from wider problems such as lack of access to housing. Recognising the wider housing issues associated with homelessness, the Simon Community, for example, proposes a 'settlement first' solution, which focuses on providing adequate housing first and then providing the relevant support services.

Table 10.7 Homeless persons in housing assessments 1991–2005

Year	Number of homeless persons
1989	1,491
1991	2,751
1993	2,667
1996	2,501
1999	5,234
2002	5,581
2005	2,399

Source: Department of the Environment, Heritage and Local Government, Annual Housing Statistics Bulletin, various years

In July 2008 a new homelessness strategy was published, entitled *The Way Home: a strategy to address adult homelessness in Ireland 2008–2013* (Department of the Environment, Heritage and Local Government, 2008a). This strategy appears to address some of these issues. It has three main aims: to eliminate long-term occupation of emergency services (defined as a stay of more than three months), to eliminate the need to sleep rough, and to prevent the occurrence of homelessness. The strategy proposes to meet the first two aims by 2010, as previously agreed under the social partnership agreement, *Towards 2016.* These aims are to be principally achieved by placing greater emphasis on long-term solutions and mainstream housing, including both social housing and the rental accommodation scheme, for persons moving out of emergency accommodation. In addition, emphasis is placed on settlement and other support services for people moving on from emergency accommodation. While these targets represent very positive developments in homeless policy, their realisation seems doubtful currently, given the changing economic context in which the report was published. As Brownlee (2008, p. 39) comments, 'with each passing day the prospect of ending long-term homelessness or the need to sleep rough by 2010 seems ever more remote, while a funding crisis for homeless services now appears to be upon us.' It therefore remains to be seen whether the new strategy will realise its aims.

A sustainable, affordable future or boom to bust?

For many years, in successive strategy statements, the broad aim of housing policy has been 'to enable every household to have available an affordable dwelling of good quality, suited to its needs, in a good environment and, as far as possible, at the tenure of its choice' (Department of the Environment, Heritage and Local Government, 2005, p. 44). As we have seen in this chapter, this overall aim of housing policy has failed on many fronts, with the pursuit of a market-oriented system based on home ownership creating many problems in areas such as accessibility, affordability and integration. A more recent issue and challenge is sustainability. Yet, here again, it can be said that Irish housing policy has not followed an environmental and socially sustainable path of development. This applies very much to the intense period of housing activity since the mid-1990s and its 'patterns of settlement, neighbourhood design and density' (NESC, 2004, p. 2) which, as NESC argues, 'are storing up significant social, environmental, budgetary and economic problems in years to come'.

A new housing policy document entitled *Delivering Homes – Sustaining Communities* was published in 2007. This publication indicates that sustainable development is becoming more central to housing policy developments. Sustainable communities are defined as:

> ... places where people want to live and work, now and in the future. They meet the diverse needs of existing and future residents, are sensitive to their environment, and contribute to a high quality of life. They are safe and inclusive, well-planned, built and run, and offer equality of opportunity and good services for all. (Department of the Environment, Heritage and Local Government, 2007b, p. 7)

However, home ownership is still strongly pursued as one of the main components of government housing policy within this document. The document specifically links the notions of stability and sustainability with home ownership:

> The government believe that home ownership should be available to as many people as possible where this is their preferred option. Home ownership can be an important factor in underpinning social stability and promoting good civic values. (ibid., p. 43)

The specific actions underpinning these statements include various targeted interventions designed to increase access to housing for first-time buyers. In this regard, the sale of local authority flats to their tenants is to be initiated as well as new schemes to allow tenants of voluntary housing association accommodation to purchase their homes and social housing tenants to purchase a portion of their house at the allocation stage and to increase this portion over time. These new developments suggest that the role of social housing will continue to be a residual one and such developments do not address the fact that people who become home owners through such schemes experience the greatest problems with affordability.

However, this document addresses quality of housing and its contribution to overall quality of life. It focuses on issues such as housing design which is energy efficient and adaptable to changing needs over the life course, and the creation of local communities which promote social inclusion. Some of these issues will be discussed in greater detail in Chapter 13, which deals with sustainable development more broadly.

The immediate opportunity to implement the type of housing envisaged in these policy documents comes in the form of the most recent National Development Plan 2007–2013, which is subtitled *Transforming Ireland – A better quality of life for all*. This plan aims to build 6,000 voluntary and cooperative houses over the period 2007–9. Social housing is also set to rise substantially. It is envisaged that 27,000 new social homes will have commenced or been acquired between 2007 and 2009 and that a target of 60,000 in total will have been achieved by 2016. However, given the plans for the sale of such houses to tenants, the overall effect on the stock of social and voluntary housing may be minimal. Affordable housing is also set to rise substantially; 17,000 units are planned for the period 2007–9 and a total of 40,000 are planned over the full duration of the National Development Plan.

These plans are beginning to be implemented at a critical juncture in Irish housing. By 2007 it became evident that house prices were beginning to fall substantially. From the first quarter of 2007 to the first quarter of 2008 the average price for new houses nationwide declined by 3.1 per cent and by 5.4 per cent for second-hand houses. In Dublin, the decline in prices has been greater, at 4.8 per cent for new houses and 10.4 per cent for second-hand houses over the same period (Department of the Environment, Heritage and Local Government, 2008b). House completions are also declining from their peak in 2006 of over 88,000 houses to over 71,000 in 2007, and an output of 12,679 (ibid.) for the first quarter of 2008 would suggest a sharp drop in 2008 overall. The continuation of these trends will give rise to a new set of challenges, particularly the prospect of **negative equity**. Recent house buyers, particularly first-time buyers, are vulnerable to this risk, especially younger buyers who may have bought a house or an apartment which is not designed for long-term family living. Such people

Negative equity refers to the situation where the market value of a house is lower than what is owed in the mortgage taken out to pay for the house.

suffer the consequences of housing policies which treat houses primarily as commodities without regard for need or sustainability. The notion of building sustainable communities will be particularly challenging in the current shift from housing boom to housing bust.

CHAPTER SUMMARY

▸ The first section outlined tenure trends across Europe and showed that while there are different approaches to housing policy and provision, the levels of owner occupation across countries have risen over time. This was connected to wider policy developments which have seen states lessen their involvement in the provision of social housing and turn towards greater use of market-oriented solutions to housing provision. However, it was also shown that this tends to exacerbate problems such as housing inequality, social segregation, lack of access and affordability.

▸ The second section charted the origins and development of Irish housing policy and development. Since gaining independence Irish housing policy has promoted a shift from renting, both in the private or social housing sector, to owner occupation. While the state did play a substantial role as a social housing provider, the gradual privatisation of this sector has meant that it has become residualised and this process has diminished the status of the sector.

▸ The final section profiled developments and challenges in each of the main Irish housing sectors since the 1990s. The section showed how housing problems such as inequality, affordability and lack of access, as discussed in section one, are manifested and continue to pose significant challenges in the contemporary Irish context.

Discussion points

▸ Think about the accommodation you live in. Consider who owns it, how it is or was paid for, and what financial assistance from the state may have applied in the past or may apply currently. Assess the design of the building and the surrounding area in relation to your needs and quality of life.

▸ Select what you would consider the most significant influences on the development of Irish housing policy and analyse their impact.

▸ Assess the impact of a housing boom on the various housing tenures in the Irish housing system.

▶ Assess the impact of a housing bust on the various housing tenures in the Irish housing system.

Further reading

Drudy, P. J. and Punch, M. (2005) *Out of Reach – Inequalities in the Irish Housing System*, Dublin: Tásc at New Island.

Norris, M. and Redmond, D. (eds) (2005) *Housing Contemporary Ireland, Policy, Society and Shelter*, Dublin: IPA.

O'Connell, C. (2007) *The State and Housing in Ireland: ideology, policy and practice*, New York: Nova Science.

Useful websites

Department of the Environment, Heritage and Local Government: www.environ.ie/en

FEANTSA, the European Federation of National Organisations working with the Homeless: www.feantsa.org

PART IV

ANALYSING IRISH SOCIAL POLICY II: SOCIAL GROUPS AND QUALITY OF LIFE

The final part of this book focuses on a number of wider themes and issues that impact on people's overall well-being and quality of life. Attention is first given to a number of different social groups and their position in terms of social policy. Presented across two chapters, the needs, rights and recognition of particular social groups are considered. The role of social policy in responding to the needs and rights of children, older people, people with disabilities and carers is critically examined in Chapter 11. The analysis hinges on the ways in which social policy can act to problematise or challenge perceptions of difference that exist with regard to different social groups. Chapter 12 also discusses these issues with reference to particular social groups for whom rights and recognition have been delayed, partially granted or problematised in various ways. The positions of the Travelling community, immigrants, and gay, lesbian and bisexual people are considered, and issues of diversity and discrimination provide a particular focus. These two chapters demonstrate the expanding scope of social policy in which debates about conventional forms of social policy provision and analysis are challenged and re-conceived. The final chapter takes this theme further by looking at how the boundaries of social policy have also been shifted by the growing concern with sustainable development and quality of life.

▶ Chapter 11 considers the role of social policy in responding to the needs and rights of various social groups in Irish society. Focus is centred on groups for whom acknowledgement of differentiated needs and recognition of their rights is a central concern. The chapter considers the positions of children, older people, people with disabilities, and carers, in terms of social policy; and some of the main challenges and contemporary areas of debate are highlighted.

▶ Chapter 12 is also based on the theme of social groups and social policy. It focuses on groups whose identity has met with lack of recognition and who consequently may experience discrimination and exclusion. The chapter discusses immigration and social policy issues arising for migrant workers, refugees and asylum seekers. The chapter also includes groups whose identity and specific needs have gone unrecognised over a long period of time, namely Travellers, and lesbian, gay and bisexual people.

▸ Chapter 13 discusses the links between social policy, sustainable development and quality of life. The evolution of sustainable development policy and the attempt to link economic, environmental and social development in order to improve quality of life in a time of rapid economic transformation is considered in the Irish context. Particular attention is given to transport policy, which serves as an example of the need to link economic, environmental and social development, and which presents challenges in terms of social cohesion, social equity and disparities in quality of life.

CHAPTER 11

SOCIAL GROUPS AND SOCIAL POLICY: NEEDS, RIGHTS AND RECOGNITION

Many welfare issues arise with regard to the realisation of social rights in contemporary Ireland. This chapter explores the positions of children, older people, people with disabilities and carers with reference to the development of social policy in Ireland. Recognition of these groups in policy terms marks an important acknowledgement of the differentiated needs and risks we experience throughout our lives. This is important because the construction of citizenship and the social rights afforded to all of these groups are crucial to overall well-being and quality of life, and should be seen in tandem with the wider issues of equality and redistribution discussed in part three of the book. The examination of particular groups undertaken here seeks to highlight the needs and experiences of various and interrelated groups and issues as attended to in Irish social policy.

CHAPTER OUTLINE

▶ This chapter maps social policy developments as they relate to the citizenship rights of different social groups in Ireland. In this context, the main contemporary issues arising in the recognition of the differentiated needs of these groups and the realisation of their social rights are critically examined.

▶ The chapter is divided into four sections which examine the positions of children, older people, people with disabilities and the experiences of carers and caring in Ireland. Relevant issues are explored in order to further understand the challenges that relate to both appropriate policy design and the wider importance of recognition and rights for these groups.

SOCIAL GROUPS, RECOGNITION AND CITIZENSHIP

The maturation of welfare capitalism and the concurrent development of social policy over the course of the twentieth century, while noteworthy in terms of the extension of citizenship rights in overall terms, re-enforced a particular social order with regard to the position of particular social groups in society. The status of women is a case in point, as highlighted in various places throughout the book. This argument can also be made in respect of a number of other social groups for whom the social construction of their difference resulted in different and often less favourable treatment. As Christie (2004, p. 149) puts it:

> Differences tend to be constructed on the basis of what is assumed to be 'normal'/'natural' and what is thereby constructed as 'abnormal'/ 'unnatural'. Those defined as different are often made inferior and such groups may be defined as *having* problems or *being* problems so that a social policy response is required. Social policy both reflects and potentially challenges 'common-sense' notions of difference depending on how it formulates the social 'problem' and a policy response to it. The processes of differentiation that are part of social policy practice highlight the needs and abilities of groups, but often in ways that continue to privilege the needs of the dominant group.

There has been a long-standing tendency in the history of social policy to categorise people, as illustrated in Chapter 1. Seen from the vantage point of the twenty-first century, this differentiation has had negative consequences for developing an inclusive framework of social rights. The path of citizenship rights initially developed in a way that catered most efficiently for the needs of able-bodied, adult, working men. The latter part of the twentieth century has seen a significant challenge mounted to this historical bias in social policy.

Chapter 4 discussed Marshall's model of citizenship, which theorised the development of social citizenship in the context of the post-World War II national welfare state. Marshall's account connected the nation state with social citizenship and proposed the welfare state as a community of belonging or the creator of a 'great community' with a supra-local, supra-class and supra-ethnic vision of national consciousness (Wolfe and Klausen, 1997). Dwyer (2004b, p. 37) notes that 'the notion of a national society within specified geographical boundaries with an imagined homogenous cultural, linguistic, racial and ethnic community was increasingly the backdrop against which the social element of citizenship developed.' The 'false universalism' of this model was also discussed in Chapter 4 in relation to the changing nature of society over the last decades of the twentieth century and into the twenty-first century, when both hidden and new identities challenged this notion of citizenship and prompted new debates about citizenship rights and recognition. The challenge, as Williams (1992, p. 214) puts it, is to 'catch some understanding of the relationship between diversity and power, between the individual, their identity, their landscapes of choice, and risk and the ways these are structured by societal relations of power and inequality'.

At a practical level, there is now greater awareness of the social exclusion, marginalisation and discrimination that can be experienced by different social groups. This chapter and the next attend to these issues in a contemporary context as they apply to various groups in Irish society. The level of recognition enjoyed by different groups varies; the point here is not to set groups in opposition but rather to acknowledge the reality of diversity of need, to explore the differing struggles for recognition and to examine the vindication of social rights in the Irish context. It is important to note in this context, however, that there exist, in reality, many cross-cutting issues; a person may be older and have a disability, for instance; a Traveller child may experience exclusion owing to the lack of recognition of their cultural identity and their specific needs in childhood.

Our focus here and in Chapter 12 is to present an account of the main social policy issues that arise in respect of different social groups for whom the contested nature of social rights in Ireland can present particular difficulties. Disability activist Donal Toolan (2003, p. 175) provides one insight that challenges us to consider the issues that arise: 'Modern Ireland's engagement with the concepts of rights seems at best uncomfortable. Any resolution of that discomfort seems to have been arrived at through the efforts of a perceived minority and their capacities to ultimately rely upon external forces to vindicate their lonely position.' The notion of 'struggle' and having to 'fight' for recognition and rights has been a consistent theme in the history of social policy for many different social groups, especially where difference has been problematised, ignored, or both.

SECTION 1: CHILDREN – FROM INVISIBILITY TO RECOGNITION

Historically, the position of children was seen, generally speaking, as a matter of private responsibility, with parents considered the sole and duty-bound providers of care and protection of their children. Broader policy reflected the "familialisation" of children' (Ridge, 2008, p. 380), whereby 'historically, children's needs and interests have remained hidden within the private sphere of the family and as a result they have tended to be invisible in the policy process' (ibid.). This has been a significant feature of the social policy approach to children. Richardson (2005, p. 160) refers to 'the principle of family autonomy' that in a sense informed the overall perspective on the position of children in society for much of the twentieth century. The Irish Constitution, 1937, for example, reinforced the primacy of the family as the 'primary and fundamental unit group of society' in which parents have 'inalienable and imprescriptible' rights (in ibid.). Paradoxically, given its constitutional standing, the overall approach was actually one of limited state support for the family and the position of children in that domain. Apart from the introduction of Children's Allowance during the 1940s, state support structures for the family remained weak. This was in keeping with the overall welfare approach of the first half of the twentieth century, which sought to minimise state intervention as far as possible. Furthermore, the dominant notion of the family was the traditional married nuclear family and, apart from the recognition of widows and orphans in the social welfare system, there was little acknowledgement of the rights of other family forms, as illustrated in Chapter 2. The position and recognition of the child within and outside of the family remains a central aspect of the contemporary debate around realising the rights of children.

Child protection and child welfare

Changes in thinking during the late nineteenth century led to an acknowledgement of the need to provide some protection to children. Thus, early legislation such as the Cruelty to Children Act, 1889, criminalised cruelty to children, and the introduction of the Children Act in 1908 allowed for children to be removed from their parents where neglect or abuse was confirmed (Richardson, 2005). This remained the overarching framework for child protection until the 1990s, although the *Report on the Reformatory and Industrial Schools System* (known as the Kennedy Report), published in 1970, did mark the beginning of a new phase of childcare policy. The Kennedy Report recommended that taking children into care should be the last resort and that the focus should be on preventing problems of family breakdown in the first place, as a result of which many of the larger reformatory and industrial schools were finally closed. Other developments, including the growing awareness of child abuse during the 1970s and the professionalisation of social work in Ireland (ibid.), demanded a radical improvement in the policy and legislative framework of child welfare and protection in Ireland.

The Child Care Act, 1991, emerged as a landmark legislative development for the protection and welfare of children and set the tone for a decade of much greater consideration of the needs and rights of children.

The implementation of this Act, which took a number of years, coincided with a much more public confrontation of child abuse during the 1990s. The shortcomings of the child protection system were brought into acute focus and attention to the neglected position of children in Irish society was heightened, as discussed in Chapter 3.

The Child Care Act, 1991,[1] continues to provide the legal framework for the operation of the child protection system and as such it is a crucial element of children's social policy in the vindication of the most basic of rights, that of protection. The Act is significant not least because it places a duty on the HSE (previously the health boards) to respond to children not receiving adequate care and protection. In so doing the welfare of the child is to be central and 'must regard the welfare of the child as the first and paramount consideration, have regard to the rights and duties of parents, give due consideration to the child's wishes and have regard to the principle that it is generally better for children to be brought up in their own families' (Barron, 1995, p. 10). The Act also covers childcare emergencies and various care proceedings, children in the care of the HSE, regulation of pre-school services and the registration of children's residential centres (ibid.). In addition, the legislation requires the HSE to provide accommodation for children who are homeless.

It is worth noting that despite such a substantial updating of the statutory approach to child protection in the early 1990s, mandatory reporting of child abuse was not introduced. Proposals contained in the original Child Care Bill were excluded from the final legislation, having been defeated in Dáil debates (Ferguson, 1995). This remains the position despite many calls for mandatory reporting of child abuse over the years. Specifically with regard to child protection procedures, national guidelines were published in 1999, *Children First: National Guidelines for the Protection and Welfare of Children*, and a review of compliance with these guidelines was completed in 2008 (see Office of the Minister for Children and Youth Affairs, 2008).

Box 11.1 Key legislative and policy developments with regard to children

1991 Child Care Act

1992 Irish ratification of the UN Convention on the Rights of the Child

1999 White Paper on Early Childhood Education (Ready to Learn)

1999 Establishment of the Social Services Inspectorate (SSI)

1999 Children First: National Guidelines for the Protection and Welfare of Children

2000 The National Children's Strategy: Our Children – Their Lives

2001 Children Act

2001   Establishment of the National Children's Office (NCO)
2001   Establishment of the Centre for Early Childhood Development and
       Education
2001   Youth Homelessness Strategy
2003   Ombudsman for Children Act
2004   National Play Policy (Ready, Steady, Play!)
2005   Establishment of the Office of the Minister for Children (into which
       the NCO was subsumed)
2006   Establishment of the Irish Youth Justice Service
2007   Child Care (Amendment) Act
2007   National Recreation Policy for Young People (Teenspace)
2007   Establishment of the SSI on a statutory basis with extended powers
       within the Health Information and Quality Authority (HIQA),
       known as the Office of the Chief Inspectorate for Social Services
2008   National review of compliance with Children First: National
       Guidelines for the Protection and Welfare of Children
2008   National Youth Justice Strategy 2008–2010

Developing a framework of social policy for children

The 1990s undoubtedly marked a watershed in the recognition of the needs
of children. Since the introduction of the Child Care Act, 1991, there has
been a substantial opening up of the debate about the position of children
in society, their recognition and their rights. The ratification of the *UN
Convention on the Rights of the Child* by Ireland in 1992 is also significant.
The Convention was agreed in 1989 and it sets out an international legally
binding framework for delivering and realising the rights of children.
Periodic reports[2] are delivered to the UN Committee on the Rights of the
Child[3] which monitors the implementation of the Convention in individual
countries. The report issued on Ireland during the mid-1990s was critical of
'the absence of a focused Governmental approach to the needs of children'
(Langford, 2007, p. 251) and this is an issue which subsequent policy
developments have sought to address.

The growing recognition of children in social policy is evident in a number
of other developments since the 1990s. A dedicated Minister of State for
Children was appointed in 1994, and in 1997 the Department of Health was
renamed the Department of Health and Children. The first ever National
Children's Strategy was published in 2000 following consultation and input
from 2,500 children and young people. The adoption of 'a whole child
perspective' in the strategy (2000, p. 24) is significant in its acknowledgement
of children's own capacities, the recognition of various dimensions of
children's development and the identification of the range of supports, formal

and informal, on which children are reliant. The overall vision of the strategy seeks: 'An Ireland where children are respected as young citizens with a valued contribution to make and a voice of their own; where all children are cherished and supported by family and the wider society; where they enjoy a fulfilling childhood and realise their potential' (National Children's Strategy, 2000, p. 4). Three national goals were identified:

- Children will have a voice in matters which affect them and their views will be given due weight in accordance with their age and maturity.
- Children's lives will be better understood; their lives will benefit from evaluation, research and information on their needs, rights and the effectiveness of services.
- Children will receive quality supports and services to promote all aspects of their development. (ibid., p. 11)

The National Children's Office (NCO) was established in 2001 to oversee the implementation of the strategy, with lead responsibility for goals one and two above. Goal three implies ongoing responsibility from a range of government departments. The appointment of the first Ombudsman for Children[4] in March 2004 and the activities engaged in by her office, and the establishment of Dáil na nÓg (Youth Parliament)[5] and Comhairle na nÓg (Youth Councils) provide new fora for children to participate and voice issues that concern them. In December 2005 a decision was taken to strengthen the position of the Minister of Children, commonly referred to as a 'super-junior' ministry in which the Minister attends all cabinet meetings, with responsibility for what is now the Office of the Minister for Children and Youth Affairs (OMCYA). The NCO was subsumed into the new Office of the Minister for Children (OMC),[6] also bringing together a range of relevant policy units from various departments, including Early Childhood Education, Child Care Policy Unit, Youth Justice Service and the Childcare Directorate (Lenihan, 2005).

Arguments had long been made that closer coordination of the various elements of social policy relevant to children was essential to the effective functioning of policy and its implementation. The lifecycle approach endorsed by the social partnership agreement *Towards 2016* establishes key policy goals with respect to children and 'encourages a collaborative, cross-sectoral way of working, which is the *modus operandi* of the OMC' (Langford, 2007, p. 253). The benefits of the longer-term framework of *Towards 2016* are also highlighted by the first Director General of the OMC, Sylda Langford (ibid.), particularly with respect to social policy and children: 'Having a longer timeframe forces us to think differently about policy and makes a focus on achieving better outcomes more realistic. In some contexts, there is a tendency to think that our aspirations for children and children's services are almost impossible to achieve, but if there is a stable ten-year horizon, they can seem possible.'

It is clear that over the last decade there has been notable development of government/state structures which focus more particularly on meeting the needs of children. Increased investment in services and the support of research on children (e.g. the National Longitudinal Study of Children in Ireland), along with policies designed with children's input into their needs (e.g. Ready, Steady, Play! and Teenspace), represent advances in giving recognition to the distinct needs and voices of children in recent years. The right of children to be heard has undoubtedly been enhanced by the activities of the Ombudsman for Children. The challenge now is to establish the precise basis of children's rights, and to consider the ways in which social policy can respond to address existing shortcomings.

Challenges to realising the rights of all children

For all of the policy innovations brought forward in recent times there remain a number of significant problems that have clear implications for the vindication of the rights of children in Ireland. These include issues such as the persistence of child poverty, the variable quality and availability of childcare and pre-school services (for a wider discussion of education services see Chapter 9), and problems with timely access to certain social and family support services. Problems also arise in relation to the level and types of support available for children and young people in and leaving the care and youth justice systems, and the persistence of child and youth homelessness. These issues are briefly considered below.

Child poverty

Child poverty continues to be a very significant problem in Ireland, with children exposed to a higher than average risk of both consistent and relative income poverty (see Chapter 7 for an explanation of these measurements). Poverty data from 2006 (EU-SILC) indicates that 10.8 per cent (69,000) of children experience consistent poverty as compared with 6.9 per cent of the population as a whole, and that 22.4 per cent (282,000) of children are at risk of poverty (CPA, 2008). This data raises substantial questions about how best to deal with, and respond effectively to, the poverty experienced by children. Significant increases in Child Benefit over the period 2000–2007 and the introduction in 2006 of the Early Childcare Supplement (paid in respect of children up to the age of five years) mark important developments in the financial support made available for children. However, this has not been matched by adequate attention to targeted payments for low-income families, most notably the Qualified Child Increase (formerly known as the Child Dependent Allowance). The payment rate of the Child Dependent Allowance, a payment which arguably would provide more targeted support for children at risk of poverty,[7] remained frozen for over a decade (1994–2006), resulting in a significant drop in its real value (Sweeney, 2007). It is widely recognised that children who experience sustained poverty are disadvantaged as a result, which can also impact negatively on their opportunities and life chances in adulthood.

Childcare

The strong male breadwinner model of welfare provision, most noted for its impact on the position and opportunities available to women, has also left its mark on the development of services for children. Attention to, and investment in, childcare and early childhood services and associated supports do not have a long history in Ireland. As Rush et al. (2006, p. 155) suggest, 'Ireland has traditionally subscribed to the "maximum private responsibility" model of childcare'. This means that the state takes minimal responsibility and targets support at children in poverty or at risk.

The first examinations of the issue of childcare in Ireland were conducted in the 1980s (e.g. *Report of the Working Party on Child Care Facilities for Working Parents*, 1983), but it was not until the 1990s that the issue was attended to in any serious way. As Langford (2007, p. 258) points out, 'the history of Government intervention in the sphere of the provision of childcare services in Ireland spans little more than a decade.' The growing participation of women in the formal labour market during the course of the 1990s heightened awareness of the demand for childcare, and increasing pressure was brought to bear on the government about the need to address the issue. A number of initiatives have developed since the mid-1990s to improve the availability of childcare, and greater attention has also been given to the area of early childhood care and education.

Initiatives include the Early Start Pre-school Project in 1994, the National Childcare Strategy (1999) and the Equal Opportunities Childcare Programme (EOCP). The EOCP aimed to provide quality childcare for parents pursuing education, training and employment. It created 34,000 new childcare places and 25,000 existing places were also funded through the programme by the end of 2006 (OMC, 2007). The formation of City and County Childcare Committees as part of the National Development Plan 2000–2006 (co-funded with EU structural funds), the establishment of a National Forum on Early Childhood Education in 1998, the White Paper on Early Childhood Education, *Ready to Learn* (1999), and the setting up of the Centre for Early Childhood Development and Education (CECDE)[8] in 2001 (Duignan and Walsh, 2004; Hayes and Bradley, 2006), are among the other notable developments in this area. The National Childcare Investment Programme 2006–2010 (replacing the EOCP) aims to create

50,000 new childcare places, with significant capital investment (€357m) and an allocation for current spending (€218m) and capital grants, which are open to community-based and private childcare providers (OMC, 2007).

However, while the supply of childcare has increased and has seen much-needed investment in recent years, the issue of affordability remains a very significant one. In addition, the quality of childcare to which children are entitled is another critical consideration that is often overlooked. Hayes and Bradley (2006, p. 166) note that 'the long-standing neglect of childcare services has meant that families have limited and costly choices and children are subject to services of variable quality with little guarantee of appropriate developmental care, education and support.' In addition, the inadequate implementation of policy in this important area (see NESF, 2005a) means that problems persist for children, parents and providers. In short, the market imperatives which have provided much of the impetus for increased childcare provision from an exceptionally low base since the 1990s need to be matched with attention to the needs of the child. In the view of one submission to the NESF (ibid., p. 38), 'children have needs and rights of their own separate from that of the labour force and … we need to act on what we know currently is in children's best interests when designing how services will develop into the future'. Fine-Davis (2004, p. 52) also notes that 'childcare is not just about finding places for workers' children so as to provide workers for the labour market. It is also very much about children's developmental and social needs and the long-term social, and indirectly, economic effects for society.' This is an issue to which we return in the context of the recognition afforded to caring activity in Irish society more generally.

Finally, given that childcare developments were primarily brought about as a response to economic (rather than welfare or equality) considerations in Ireland, it is worth noting a wider but related shift in thinking about children in terms of 'tomorrow's future'. While at a general level this observation is not new, the increasing tendency to justify investment in children's services in terms of their future economic return, is noteworthy. This has been evident, in particular, in the 'Third Way' approach to social policy. Addressing the broader issue of education in Britain, the Commission on Social Justice (1994, p. 311 in Daniel and Ivatts, 1998, p. 14) states: 'Children are not a private pleasure or a personal burden; they are 100% of a nation's future … the best indicator of the capacity of our economy tomorrow is the quality of our children today.' This translates in particular into the education of children as the production of human capital or knowledge capital as discussed in Chapter 9. While the notion of 'social investment' in children is clearly beneficial at many levels in terms of enhancing the lives of children overall, certain questions do arise. Ridge (2008, p. 381) explains that improvements notwithstanding, 'there is a tension between policies that focus on children as future adults and the quality of life that they experience in childhood.' The question is whether, in such a context, children are being approached as 'beings' in the present or 'becomings' for the future (Fawcett et al., 2004, p. 17).

Vulnerable children

We now briefly turn our focus to some of the most vulnerable groups of children in order to draw attention to some of the most pressing issues that arise in the context of promoting the realisation of rights for all children. A report completed for the Ombudsman for Children in 2007, *The Barriers to the Realisation of Children's Rights in Ireland* (Kilkelly, 2007), examines the ways in which particular groups of children experience many breaches of their rights in the context of the principles of the *UN Convention on the Rights of the Child*. Against this benchmark the findings raise very serious questions about the adequacy of services and supports available at present. In particular, the position of children in the care system, children in the criminal justice system, homeless children, immigrant and asylum-seeking children, Traveller children and children at risk of abuse and neglect, are examined and the multiple barriers that present as obstacles to the realisation of their social rights are identified. Kilkelly (2007, p. 19) finds that these children:

> ... have not, to date, benefited from coherent policy or targeted intervention, supports or services. They also suffer marginalisation and, in some cases, discrimination. Many such children face the additional obstacle of being isolated from their families and friends, without advocacy or support or anyone to lobby on their behalf.

Other children also experience difficulty in the realisation of their rights, including sick children and children with disabilities, mental health problems and drug and alcohol abuse difficulties (ibid.).

There has been an increase in the number of children in the care of the state in recent years. While there undoubtedly have been improvements in the monitoring of the care provided, as seen, for example, through the work of the Social Services Inspectorate, there are continuing obstacles facing these children and young people. Apart from the need to work in a more preventive way to minimise the number of children going into care in the first place and to ensure that, wherever possible, this is as short-term as necessary, Kilkelly identifies other problems that arise for these children. These include issues such as the support available to foster carers; the position of adoption; problems in residential care; the risk of stigma, stress and bullying; the lack of input from children about decisions that affect their lives; and the right to be kids (ibid.). In addition, the level of support made available to young people leaving the care system as adults, known as aftercare, is discretionary and variable by region. Calls have been made for young people to have a statutory right to aftercare to support their transition to independent living (Focus Ireland, 2008).

The preponderance of disadvantaged children and young people coming into contact with the justice system has long been identified as a problem but, as Kilkelly (2007, p. 26) points out, 'such young people enter a system which currently gives them few opportunities to have their problems addressed.' Langford (2007, p. 257) also highlights this as an issue of concern, pointing out that 'a major objective for the OMC is to bring about a more coherent system for meeting the needs of this very vulnerable group of children and young people.' The present reform of the youth justice system (through the implementation of the Children Act, 2001, and the establishment of the Youth Justice Service in 2005) is noteworthy in terms of current plans for improving the services in this area. However, concerns are raised by Kilkelly (2007) about present shortcomings, such as the lack of appropriate court room facilities or training for lawyers and judges, under-resourcing of the Garda Diversion Programme, the poor condition of detention facilities, the lack of appropriate education or care plans, and the poor access to complaints mechanisms for these young people.

The position of the Travelling Community and that of migrants and asylum seekers is dealt with in detail in the following chapter but Kilkelly's identification of the breaches of the rights of these children is also of note here. The vulnerable position of immigrant and asylum-seeking children has been a particular source of concern in recent times (see Fanning et al., 2001; Fanning and Veale, 2004). The particular problems of poverty and social exclusion arising out of the system of direct provision and the denial of Child Benefit to asylum-seeking children (see Chapter 12 for details) raise major questions about the prospect of social inclusion for these children and their families.

The nature of the support services available to separated children seeking asylum has also come in for particular attention and concern (see Christie, 2003; Veale et al., 2003; Mooten, 2006). The asylum process has paid insufficient attention to making the system more child-focused, and there is a need for more specialist training for officials and interpreters (Mooten, 2006; Kilkelly, 2007). In addition, problems with the adequacy of child-support measures, the availability of social workers and the provision of appropriate accommodation and supervision for these children are issues of particular note (Veale et al., 2003). The numbers of these children going missing from HSE care in recent years has also been a cause for considerable concern (Mooten, 2006; Corbett, 2008). The issue of child trafficking has been highlighted as an area requiring urgent attention, particularly with regard to legislation, the asylum process, and safe accommodation for, and the monitoring of, such children in HSE care (Mooten, 2006; Kilkelly, 2007).

The issue of homelessness as it relates to children (whether on their own or with their families) presents a series of difficulties quite apart from the emotional trauma, including shortcomings in the appropriateness of emergency accommodation (e.g. where B&Bs are used and have to be vacated during the day) and a shortage of medium and long-stay accommodation (ibid.). Mayock and O'Sullivan (2007), for example, document the real-life experiences of young homeless people in Dublin and while this study does not focus primarily on children it is clear that many of the problems that contribute to young people becoming homeless occur in their childhood years. As the authors point out, many of the young people in their study 'were known to various agencies of the State – including the childcare, youth homeless and criminal justice systems – from a young age and over an extended period. This finding points to failures within numerous systems of intervention and at various junctures in children's and young people's lives' (ibid., p. 267). The consequences of inadequate support and/or services for children have a much longer-term impact, as demonstrated here.

With regard to children at risk of abuse or neglect, as Buckley (2002, p. 2) notes, 'While both the implementation of the Child Care Act, 1991 and the increased focus on the safety and welfare of children have been unequivocally welcomed, some of the concurrent effects have been viewed less positively.' Pointing to a number of examples, such as the tendency to utilise more resources in investigating suspicions of child abuse rather than in strategies to prevent it from occurring, she argues that 'there is no room for complacency ... and it is clear that some sort of equilibrium between protective and preventive services needs to be reached before the system can be considered adequate' (ibid., p. 3). Kilkelly (2007), too, notes a number of shortcomings in both the prevention and response strategies in place at present. In terms of prevention, the lack of implementation and enforcement of the Children First Guidelines in certain cases, the absence of a sex offenders register, shortcomings in the notification system related to sex offenders, the lack of an effective system of vetting, and the lack of treatment services or assessment of sex offenders are of particular concern (ibid.). Impediments to responding effectively to abuse and neglect include the lack of universally agreed criteria for identifying risk and the use of social work time (Buckley, 2005). Problems with cooperation between agencies and professionals, the lack of resources (e.g. waiting lists for assessments), and the need for an out-of-hours social work service (despite numerous calls for its introduction) highlight other major shortcomings in the supports available to families, particularly those in crisis. The decision taken by the HSE in

2008, for example, to defer the introduction of an out-of-hours service has been roundly criticised (e.g. Barnardos, 2008). In short, considerable concerns have been raised about the capacity of the system to respond effectively to children at risk.

In overall terms, therefore, while considerable improvements have been made in recognising the distinct needs of children in Ireland since the 1990s, substantial issues remain to be resolved in ensuring the full vindication of their rights. The challenge now, as Richardson (2005, p. 183) explains, 'is for adequate resources to be made available on a continuous basis in order that the full potential of the frameworks and policies developed can be realised. Policies must now be proactive rather than reactive and driven by a real political commitment to enhancing the position of children in Ireland.' An amendment to the constitution to give full expression to the rights of children, recommended by the McGuiness Report (1993), is now widely regarded as necessary (Children's Rights Alliance, 2008; Ombudsman for Children, 2006; Richardson, 2005; Kilkelly, 2007). A commitment to amend the Irish Constitution given in the Programme for Government (Government of Ireland, 2007a) is currently under review by the Joint Committee on the Constitutional Amendment on Children.[9] The state–family relationship and the position of children both within that domain and as individuals in their own right are issues that will have to be teased out in order to fully recognise children as citizens in their own right.

SECTION 2: OLDER PEOPLE – EARLY RECOGNITION AND DELAYED RIGHTS

One of the main challenges faced by older people is the existence of ageism in society,[10] which in basic terms refers to discrimination experienced by people on the grounds of age. In terms of older people this is often manifest in pervasive stereotypes and particular assumptions made about their roles and capacities by other members of society. This is sometimes reflected in policy discourse too. For example, the growing numbers of older people is frequently presented as a significant economic problem and social burden which largely ignores the 'demographic bounty' (O'Shea, 2006) that greater numbers of older people present. The offensive term 'bed blockers' used in the healthcare debate during the 2000s offers another pointed example, where, as Edwards (2004) puts it, 'They are called "bed blockers" as if they are to blame for a healthcare system which fails older people who are ill.' Such views re-enforce negative stereotypes of older people which ultimately undermine them and their right to recognition on the basis of respect. In addition, Bytheway's (1995) argument that the categories used to describe ageing are socially constructed and often serve to undermine or restrict resources and opportunities on the basis of chronological age, presents considerable challenges to policymakers and to the attitudes of society at large.

In terms of policy attention, the equality legislation introduced since the 1990s has been important for older people in outlawing age discrimination, although the work of the Equality Authority demonstrates the ongoing challenges in this area. In 2007, for example, 24 per cent of the Employment Equality Acts cases under review by the Authority related to the issue of age (Equality Authority, 2008). Many of these cases involved, 'allegations of discrimination by older workers. Age limits in the workplace are the focus for many of these allegations including fixed retirement ages. It is clear from the casefiles that there are significant numbers of older people who do not want to be forced to retire' (Crowley, 2008). While there is no set statutory retirement age in Ireland, age 65 is commonly applied and employers can set the retirement age for employees. The adoption of a more flexible approach to work and retirement may well provide a solution to these issues and be more in line with the preferences of older people (see Fahey and Russell, 2001).

The historical development of social policy for older people in Ireland could best be described as piecemeal and somewhat fitful. Recognition of the income needs of older people, in the form of the social assistance-based Old Age Pension, introduced in 1908, marked a crucial early income entitlement for older people in Ireland. However, there has been patchy rather than complete recognition of the needs and rights of older people since then. In overall terms, key aspects of social service provision for older people, particularly health and social care, reflect the very mixed economy of Irish welfare, with the family, the private sector, the voluntary sector and the state all involved. In this brief section some of the main policy developments are highlighted in order to provide some insight into the issues that arise around recognition and rights for older people in Ireland at present.

Box 11.2 Key legislative and policy developments with regard to older people

1990 Health (Nursing Homes) Act

1994 Shaping a Healthier Future: A Strategy for Effective Healthcare in the 1990s

1998 Health Promotion Strategy for Older People: Adding Years to Life and Life to Years

2001 Health Strategy: Quality and Fairness: A Health System for You

2001 Introduction of universal entitlement to a medical card for all persons over age 70
2002 Report of the Working Group on Elder Abuse: Protecting Our Future
2003 Law and the Elderly (report from the Law Reform Commission)
2003 Establishment of the Elder Abuse National Implementation Group
2007 Health Act
2008 Announcement of the establishment of the Office for Older People
2008 Publication of the Report of the Interdepartmental Working Group on Long Term Care (completed in 2006)
2008 Nursing Home Support Scheme Bill
2009 Removal of universal entitlement to a medical card for persons over age 70

Income, poverty and older people

Income for older people is derived from a number of sources (e.g. the state pension, occupational pensions, returns on savings, continuing in employment, etc.). In reality, the state pension continues to be the primary income source for older people. Hughes and Watson (2005) found that the state pension provided 56 per cent of overall income for older people, occupational pensions 21 per cent, earnings 13 per cent, and income from investment 9 per cent. The state pension (along with the other social transfers), therefore, plays a vital role in minimising the risk of poverty for older people. The risk of income poverty grew significantly for older people during the 'celtic tiger' years although this risk saw a welcome reduction to 13.6 per cent in 2006. Consistent poverty and deprivation has been lower for older people than for the population overall. However, there is a greater prevalence of housing deprivation among older people (Layte et al., 1999; Prunty, 2007). Some older people are more vulnerable to poverty, including those living alone, rural dwellers, those in the BMW region and women (although the gap has narrowed) (Prunty, 2007). Maintaining the real value of the state pension over time will remain a critical element of income adequacy for older people. In addition, access to second-pillar occupational/personal pensions is uneven at present, and the outcome of the deliberations on the Green Paper on Pensions (2007) should indicate the longer-term orientation of the Irish pension system. This policy needs to be developed with reference to wider issues regarding the income needs and work preferences of older people. McCashin (2007, p. 164) advocates 'greater policy integration' around income supports for older people, noting the need to hear the views of older people and given developments such as the lifecycle approach adopted in *Towards 2016* and the activation trend that has been in evidence in social security policy more generally over the last decade. Such an integrated approach will be important in the development of any future strategy for the well-being of older people in Ireland.

Care supports for older people

Home and community-based care

The care needs and preferences of older people vary significantly (Garavan et al., 2001). Despite a common misconception to the contrary, the vast majority of older people continue to reside in their own home, and government policy since the publication of *The Care of the Aged Report* (1968) has been to support and realise the preference of older people in this regard. Subsequent policy, namely *The Years Ahead: A Policy for the Elderly* (1988) has continued to emphasise the role of the family and the voluntary sector in this endeavour (O'Loughlin, 2005). However, the role of the state in, and access to, home care provision has developed in an ad hoc and discretionary way. Section 61 of Health Act, 1970, allowed for home help, with the CEO to determine eligibility and, discretion notwithstanding, the provision of state-funded home care did expand from the late 1970s onwards (Timonen and Doyle, 2008). However, differences in the extent and type of help available, in the eligibility criteria applied and the practice of charging (in some areas) illustrate the variable nature of home care arrangements that have developed in Ireland (ibid.).

The introduction of the Home Care Package Scheme[11] in 2001 and its subsequent expansion (11,565 home care packages were made available over the course of 2007; HSE, 2008) represent the most recent development in the area of home care for older people. The scheme involves the provision of home care based on the specific needs of the person and can comprise nurses, home care assistants, home helps and services from physiotherapists and occupational therapists (Department of Health and Children, 2008a). However, while there has been considerable investment in this scheme in recent years, as the Department itself states, the Home Care Support Scheme 'is not yet a national scheme and is not established in law. As it is an administrative scheme, you neither have an automatic right to the Scheme, nor to avail of services under the Scheme' (ibid.). Apart from the obvious lack of clarity around entitlement to this scheme, Timonen et al. (2006) note other difficulties with the Irish 'cash-for-care' model, including issues with adequacy of the grants (with many having to supplement the actual costs through private means or informal care), the differing approaches to delivering grants (some are up-front payment, while others are retrospective) and the lack of regulation of the supervision or training provided by private care agencies. On the latter point, Timonen and Doyle (2007, p. 265) stress that 'public policies and regulation are urgently needed to safeguard the rights of the care workforce and to monitor the quality of care delivered by formal domiciliary service providers in Ireland.' In short, the home care services provided through this scheme are not accessible to all older people and it is not regulated to the same standard as institutional care. The discretionary approach to the delivery of home care provision continues, with greater reliance on a poorly regulated private sector in the absence of more extensive statutory provision.

The NESF (2005b) report *Care for Older People* notes the overall shortcomings inherent in the present approach to delivering care for older people in Ireland:

> There is strong evidence that older people want to remain living in their own homes and communities as independently as possible for as long as possible. This preference has been accepted by successive Governments as a key policy objective. Yet this objective is nowhere near achievement. This is reflected in our under-developed community care system, which is crisis driven, lacks sufficient co-ordination and resources and does not afford older people the choice, independence and autonomy they seek and deserve. (ibid., p. iv)

A number of key barriers to the implementation of this policy objective are identified by the NESF: the relatively low level of spending on services for older people, the fact that funding is not targeted at the primary policy objective (i.e. a lot of resources are taken up with the residential elements of care for older people), the need to fully address equality for older people, the lack of clarity around service entitlement and the need for an updated strategy for older people.

The result of the continuing discretionary nature of community care provision for older people means that 'although Ireland is characterised by a mixed economy of social care, the existing model ... places the family firmly at the centre of social care provision' (Pierce, 2006, p. 195). The viability of such an approach has come under increased pressure as the assumptions underpinning such a basis for the provision of care fail to take account of significant social change impacting on the availability of informal care and the preferences of older people in this regard. In terms of the family, as O'Shea (2002, p. 89) notes in a review of the nursing home subvention scheme, 'the main problem is not families' continued willingness to care, which remains intact, but the fact that families are being asked to do too much without adequate support from the statutory sector. This is where the attrition on families' willingness to care is occurring.' The weaknesses in primary healthcare are particularly evident with regard to the availability of services for older people and their families. This is compounded by the fact that there has been little public debate about how these issues should be addressed. For example, the implication of the approach taken in the home care scheme, as outlined earlier, suggests a greater role for private providers in the future, although the supporting and regulatory structures remain underdeveloped. Timonen and Doyle (2008, p. 86) explain the nature of the challenges:

> ... the Irish care regime is yet to make the transition to a state of joined-up thinking about the different components of this regime. Formal and informal care are still viewed as opposites, rather than complementary areas that should be able to interact in a manner that eases the transition between the home and institutional care for the older person in need of care. Informal carers are still taken for granted, and provided with little monetary recognition of their work; the carer's allowance retains its safety-net and residual character ...

The shifting, yet discretionary, welfare mix in care supports for older people in the community needs to be the subject of much more sustained public debate to inform a coherent national policy strategy in this area.

Residential care

In terms of older people in need of long-stay/nursing home type care, this system continues to evolve. While the Nursing Home Subvention Scheme, which developed over the course of the 1990s, undoubtedly increased capacity (with greater numbers of private nursing homes), its overall effectiveness has been hampered by rising costs and a lack of consistency in the eligibility requirements applied and in the levels of subvention granted to individuals (Mangan, 2002; O'Shea, 2002). In 2006 an announcement was made to overhaul the long-term nursing home system by way of the introduction of a 'Fair Deal' scheme. The anomalies in the existing system were highlighted by the Minister for Health and Children (Harney, 2006), with reference to issues of cost and the problem of using 'imputed income' as a method of calculating subvention entitlement, which caused anxiety among older people and their families.

The Nursing Home Support Scheme Bill, 2008, proposes to give effect to the government position that people should make a contribution towards such care. People will be required to pay 80 per cent of their assessable income and 5 per cent of the value of any assets (above €36,000 for an individual), which will only be collected posthumously, in the settlement of their estate. At this time contributions based on the value of a home will not exceed 15 per cent of its value. Furthermore, the Bill proposes that all medical needs and financial circumstances will be assessed in the same way by the HSE (Department of Health and Children, 2008b). Announcing the publication of the Bill the Minister for Health and Children (Harney, 2008), noted that 'for the first time, it will make the arrangements for financial support for people who need long term care comprehensive, clear and coherent.' The scheme is intended to cover all persons in need of long-term care and both public and private nursing home facilities. The legislation to give effect to the Fair Deal scheme is soon to go through the Oireachtas, at which stage the detail of the scheme should emerge. The overhaul of the subvention system has been widely welcomed, although questions do remain about the wider and long-term implications of the 'beyond the grave' payment for such a service. At the least, it marks the introduction of an unprecedented charging structure within the Irish health service.

Elder abuse

Attention to the issue of elder abuse is relatively recent in the Irish context. Following an exploratory study conducted by the National Council on Ageing and Older People (NCAOP) in 1998, the Department of Health and Children established a Working Group to examine the matter. Its report, *Protecting Our Future, Report of the Working Group on Elder Abuse* (Working Group on Elder Abuse, 2002), made a series of recommendations. The Elder Abuse National Implementation Group was subsequently set up to advise on the implementation of the recommendations contained in the report. The establishment of an Elder Abuse service within the HSE, the appointment of Senior Case Workers, a dedicated information line for persons concerned about elder abuse and the promotion of public awareness are notable service developments in this area in recent years. The extent of elder abuse is not fully known, but figures from the HSE show that 523 cases were dealt with during the first four months of 2008, compared to 927 for 2007 (Age Action Ireland, 2008). Eighty-three per cent of the referrals related to people living in their own home, with 96 per cent of these cases alleging abuse by family members (ibid.). Age Action Ireland believes that 'this is just the tip of the iceberg' and that 'the figures shine a light on one of the largely hidden and greatly under-reported forms of abuse which is widespread in Ireland' (Timmons, in Age Action Ireland, 2008).

An 'age-friendly' society

The care needs and rights of older people, while gaining greater attention in recent years continue to lack an official statutory entitlement to an equal assessment of need. These shortcomings mean that access to the available services is not secure on an equal basis for all older people. A commitment to a national strategy is contained in the current *Programme for Government*.

In their position statement *An Age Friendly Society*, the NCAOP (2005, p. 42) points to the major weakness of the current model of social care delivery for older people: 'Over many years, the Council has advocated the development of a legislative framework governing the provision of these essential services to older people as entitlements rather than – as at present – on a discretionary and unequal basis.' Apart from the anomalies highlighted with regard to home care provision and entitlement, there are areas to which upper-age limits are applied, including age-related requirements attached to driving licence applications and age limits associated with membership of some state boards (Citizens Information, 2008). The age limits of 50–64 attached to the HSE Breast Check Screening Programme have come in for particular criticism from older people's groups.

In overall terms, the realisation of an 'age-friendly society' in Ireland will require much more sustained focus on the rights of older people and how best to deliver them. The NCAOP (2005, p. 42) provides a clear articulation of the benefits of an age-friendly society:

> In calling for an age friendly society in Ireland, the Council does not seek preferential treatment for older people. Rather it reiterates the UN call for a society for all ages. In such a society, parity of esteem with other citizens will be accorded to older people. They will be treated with equal dignity and respect by the organs of the State, as well as by their fellow citizens. Their independence will not be compromised by inequality of opportunity and their participation in the activities of society will not be denied by differential conditions of access based on age.

The political voice of older people was demonstrated to significant effect during the medical card controversy in late 2008 and perhaps a marker has been laid about the potential clout of this group.

SECTION 3: PEOPLE WITH DISABILITIES – THE BATTLE FOR RESPECT FOR DIFFERENCE

Institutionalisation, segregation and the widespread neglect of the rights of people with disabilities throughout the nineteenth and most of the twentieth century (see Finnane, 1981; Robins, 1986; and Malcolm, 2003, for historical accounts) represent a most salient illustration of how the social construction of difference can have massive implications for the lives and well-being of different social groups. Developments in thinking during the twentieth century have rejected the shortcomings of an approach which largely marginalised and denied the individual rights of people with disabilities. The move towards de-institutionalisation, in particular, marked the beginning of a long road in the struggle to challenge long-held assumptions about 'disability'. The move away from institutionalised provision for people with disabilities began in the US in the late 1960s, and the emergence of a disabilities rights movement began to challenge the conventional assumptions about disability, and promoted independence, rights and a greater awareness of the segregation and exclusion experienced by people with disabilities.

Different approaches to disability have since been identified (see Oliver, 1996), which provide an important way of appreciating how perspectives can shape or challenge prevailing attitudes and understandings. The **medical model of disability** approaches disability in individual terms, diagnosing 'conditions', 'impairments', etc., that have the effect of defining an individual by these traits. The **social model of disability**, in contrast, sees society as contributing to disability through its inability to accept and give recognition to difference. The lack of appropriate design of buildings and other public spaces, which impede access, or fail to provide appropriate facilities for people with disabilities, is but one simple illustration of how society can fail to take account of differing needs and thus contribute to the exclusion of people with disabilities. Seen in this way there is an absence of respect for difference. The approach to equality that promotes 'sameness' of treatment has shortcomings in terms of allowing that people be recognised as both 'different and equal'.

> **The medical model of disability** refers to an approach to disability which tends to focus on individual conditions/impairments. This approach was dominant in the past but it has been challenged by the **social model of disability** which highlights the wider structural forces that contribute to the exclusion/disadvantage of people with disabilities in society.

Taking the case of education, for example, in the past, people with disabilities did not enjoy anything like full access to education provision. Historically, little emphasis was placed on the value of education for people with disabilities and the system did not acknowledge their needs or difference. During the 1960s the state began to examine the issue, as demonstrated in the publication of the White Paper, *The Problem of the Mentally Handicapped* (1960) and the *Report of the Commission of Inquiry on Mental Handicap* (1965). The report recommended the creation of additional special school day places for children and an increase in the number of residential places. While the report sought to improve education provision it did not challenge the segregation of children with intellectual disability (Griffin and Shevlin, 2007). The number of special schools (and special classes in mainstream schools) grew in subsequent years, although, in keeping with the wider structures of the Irish education system (see Chapter 9), this was achieved mainly through religious and voluntary effort, and assessment and timely access to education services remained problematic (ibid.). In addition, appropriate provision in post-primary education remained underdeveloped (McDonnell, 2003).

The Green Paper on *Services for Disabled People, Towards a Full Life* was published by the Department of Health in 1984, which demonstrated a broadening perspective on disability issues. Reference was made to the need to improve public transport and public buildings and to promote access to employment and to fuller participation in society in general. The move away from institutional to community-based care, as recommended in *The Psychiatric Services: Planning for the Future* (1984), marked another important policy step in moving away from the institutional approach of the past. However, while it was noteworthy for its endorsement of community-based provision, it failed 'to challenge the dominant medical model and the way mental illness is constructed and treated within this model' (Sapouna, 2006, p. 91). This shift towards community-based services was important in establishing a less exclusionary type of recognition, although shortcomings in the implementation of the plan led to difficulties for some service users. In short, while there was growing attention to the position of people with disabilities in Ireland it has taken a long time to challenge the dominant medical/care model and move to one that sees persons with disabilities as individuals with rights and entitlements in their own right.

Box 11.3 Key legislative and policy developments with regard to people with disabilities

1991   Needs and Abilities: A Policy for the Intellectually Disabled

1992   Green Paper on Mental Health

1993   Report of the Special Education Review Committee

1996   Report of the Commission on the Status of People with Disabilities: A Strategy for Equality

1998   Education Act

1998   Employment Equality Act

1999   Towards Equal Citizenship: Progress Report on the Implementation of the Recommendations of the Commission on the Status of People with Disabilities

1999   Establishment of the National Educational Psychological Service

2000   Establishment of the Equality Authority

2000   Establishment of the National Disability Authority

2000 Equal Status Act
2001 Mental Health Act
2001 Report of the Task Force on Autism
2002 Report of the Task Force on Dyslexia
2002 Establishment of the Mental Health Commission
2004 Education for Persons with Special Educational Needs (EPSEN) Act
2004 National Disability Strategy
2005 Establishment of the National Council for Special Education
2005 Disability Act
2006 A Vision for Change: Report of the Expert Group on Mental Health Policy
2007 Citizens Information Act

Policy development since the 1990s

The 1990s witnessed something of a watershed in acknowledging the extent to which the recognition of people with disabilities had fallen short. In 1996, the Commission on the Status of People with Disabilities: A Strategy for Equality stated that:

> People with disabilities are the neglected citizens of Ireland. On the eve of the 21st century, many of them suffer intolerable conditions because of outdated social and economic policies and unthinking public attitudes. Changes have begun to come about, influenced by international recognition that disability is a social rather than a medical issue, but many of those changes have been piecemeal. Public attitudes towards disability are still based on charity rather than on rights, and the odds are stacked against people with disabilities at almost every turn. Whether their status is looked at in terms of economics, information, education, mobility, or housing they are seen to be treated as second-class citizens. (ibid., p. 5)

The relative invisibility of people with disabilities in the past is pointedly illustrated in the absence of relevant data collection in the census between 1911 and 2002 (see Doyle, 2003). In addition, the notable absence of state provision of services meant that there has been large-scale reliance on the voluntary sector as the main provider of services for people with disabilities throughout the twentieth century (see Colgan, 2006; Woods, 2006). Given their importance as service providers, such organisations 'have also played a key role as pressure groups, trying to keep the issues of people with disabilities on the political agenda' (Quin and Redmond, 2005, p. 150). It is against this backdrop that the commission highlighted the substantial work to be done in recognising the needs and rights of people with disabilities (it issued 402 recommendations), and it does appear to have been influential in the policy development that has since followed in this area.

Major policy developments over the last decade include the Employment Equality Act, 1998, and the Equal Status Act, 2000. In addition, the Education Act, 1998, the establishment of the National Disability Authority in 2000, the Mental Health Act, 2001, the Education for Persons with Special Educational Needs (EPSEN) Act, 2004, the announcement of the Disability Strategy in 2004 and the introduction of the Disability Act, 2005, have all been significant.

Education

Returning to education, the 1990s marked the beginning of more sustained state attention to this neglected area, with the introduction of a pilot educational psychological service for schools in 1990 and the publication of the *Report of the Special Education Review Committee* in 1993, which highlighted many shortcomings in provision, access and resources and sought substantial development of appropriate services (Griffin and Shevlin, 2007). It took a somewhat guarded approach to the issue of integration: 'we favour as much integration as is appropriate and feasible with as little segregation as is necessary' (SERC Report, 1993, p. 22, cited in ibid., p. 52). Nevertheless, it had a significant impact on the development of policy in this area in subsequent years. The Commission on the Status of People with Disabilities (1996, p. 171, cited in McDonnell, 2003, p. 259) made clear that in terms of education, the participation of people with disabilities 'is significantly below that of the population in general'. Against this backdrop, the Education Act, 1998, the Education (Welfare) Act, 2000, the Education for Persons with Special Educational Needs (EPSEN) Act, 2004, and the Disability Act, 2005, have come to provide the current legislative framework for the educational rights of people with disabilities. The legislative developments of recent times are highly significant, if not long overdue, in establishing recognition of the educational entitlements of people with disabilities in Ireland. According to the preamble to the Education Act, 1998, it is: 'An Act to make provisions in the common good for the education of every person in the state, including any person with a disability or who has other special educational needs.' However, the medical definition of disability used in the 1998 Act has been noted (see McDonnell, 2003; Griffin and Shevlin, 2007). McDonnell (2003, p. 262) explains the consequences of this 'psycho-medical model of disability' in terms of education where:

> ... 'disability' has been deprived of its meaning as a socio-political indicator of inequality and discrimination, while the term 'special

needs' directs the professional gaze towards the pupil rather than towards professional practices or organisational structures. In other words ... the focus of attention remains fixed on the particularities of the individual's body or mind rather than on the marginalizing and exclusionary practices and structures of society ...

A marked shift is evident in the definition of disability applied in the more recent EPSEN Act, 2004, which also outlines more explicitly the principle of inclusion to be followed (see Griffin and Shevlin, 2007, for details). In addition, the Act details the procedures for the assessment of special needs and the drawing up of individual education plans. The policy of inclusion has been backed up in practical terms with the establishment of the National Council for Special Education and the appointment of greater numbers of special needs assistants and resource teachers (Department of Education and Science, 2004, cited in Ring and Travers, 2005).

In short, much change has come about in a relatively short space of time in terms of legislation and increased resource provision in the area of education. While this policy development is of course welcome and represents a radical improvement in the level of services available, there remains an argument that it has fallen short of what is actually required to ensure the educational rights of all persons with disabilities in Ireland. The substantial investment and improvement come from a remarkably low base at a time when demand for such educational rights is rising. Over the last decade, the number of parents who have sought to vindicate, through the courts, the rights of their children to an education demonstrates 'the battle' that securing an appropriate education can still be. The Supreme Court judgement that the state's responsibility to provide free primary education does not extend beyond the age of 18, delivered in 2001, provoked much public debate regarding the rights of people with disabilities in Ireland. The *Disability Strategy* announced in 2004 and the provisions contained in the Disability Act, 2005, notwithstanding, the needs and rights of *all* persons with disability to access education remains problematic.

The Disability Strategy, 2004

The *Disability Strategy* was launched in 2004 and had a number of components: the Disability Bill, 2004, the Comhairle (Amendment) Bill, 2004, sectoral plans and a commitment to a multi-annual investment programme in current and capital expenditure for disability services. Taken together these have the capacity to make a notable impact on the quality of service provision. The implementation of the strategy is still in progress; the legislation has been enacted and the sectoral plans are significant in their potential to 'mainstream' disability policy priorities. Key elements of the

Disability Act, 2005, include the delivery of an individual assessment of health and educational needs and the provision of a related service statement. The Act also places obligations on public bodies with regard to access to public buildings, services and information. Sectoral plans outlining how the needs of people with disabilities are met and plans for the future must be developed by six named government departments. Part five of the Act gives legal status to the 3 per cent target for the employment of persons with disability in the public service (Department of Justice, Equality and Law Reform, 2005a).

However, for all of the progress achieved, many have expressed concern and disappointment about the lack of an overtly **rights-based approach** to meeting the needs of people with disabilities. De Wispelaere and Walsh (2007, p. 535), for example, argue that 'the Disability Act 2005 fails to meet the conditions for robust rights-based legislation in relation to disability services. The failure to provide secure access to public services is exacerbated by the fact that there is no genuine right to challenge assessment, service delivery or even the wider policy context, particularly resource commitments.' The full implementation of the Act is not due for some time and the announcement to delay the introduction of the advocacy support service has been a setback (Inclusion Ireland, 2008). In this context, as Quin notes (2006, p. 187), 'the fact that personal social services are subsumed under health makes them vulnerable to under-resourcing and cutbacks in relation to many aspects of health care – particularly acute care – with which they must essentially compete for funding.' This is a point which may take on even greater significance in the current economic climate, in which cutbacks appear to be the order of the day.

> **A rights-based approach** is one which advocates a guaranteed level of social provision as a matter of right and entitlement. Inequities that often arise in discretionary and variable levels of social supports are thereby removed.

Mental health services

It is important to point out some of the other enduring deficiencies in the service provision for persons with disabilities and their families in Ireland. Taking the case of mental illness, the associated services are widely regarded as the 'Cinderella' of the health services in terms of current resources and capital investment. The share of overall public health funding spent in this area has declined from almost 14 per cent in 1984 to 7.76 per cent in 2007 (MHC, 2008), and service provisions for persons experiencing mental illness continued to display shortcomings in the first decade of the twenty-first century (see Crowley, 2003). At a broader level, wider public attitudes continue to indicate very varying perceptions of mental health problems and their impact (HSE, 2007b).

On the other hand, the implementation of the Mental Health Act, 2001, the establishment of the Mental Health Commission and the publication of *A Vision for Change: Report of the Expert Group on Mental Health Policy* (Expert Group on Mental Health Policy, 2006) point to increased policy attention to this area in recent years. The updating of mental health legislation has been widely welcomed, particularly with regard to changes in the legal rights of persons admitted to psychiatric hospitals. The full implementation of *A Vision for Change* (which is envisaged to take seven to ten years) will, if delivered, represent radical progress in the area of mental health services.

These policy developments notwithstanding, recent evidence suggests that problems persist in accessing appropriate and timely services for mental health difficulties. For example, over 3,600 children are presently awaiting assessment by a psychiatrist, over 1,000 of whom are expected to have to wait at least one year for their appointment (O'Brien, 2008). A recent study on support services for families with mental illness, conducted by Kartalova-O'Doherty et al. (2006, p. 198), finds, 'that not only are formal and comprehensive family support resources lacking, but also that the existing support resources are not consistent and vary dramatically across catchment areas, public and private sectors, individual hospitals, units, and community residences, and various parts of the country'. In terms of the quality of services, the Inspector of Mental Health Services (MHC, 2008, pp. 84–5) has noted that despite the improvements brought about by the implementation of the Mental Health Act, 2001, some significant problems remain:

> The staffing of mental health teams continued to be painstakingly slow. The HSE embargo on recruitment further delayed the appointment of key mental health staff, with the decades-old goal of multidisciplinary community and specialist teams – such as mental health services for elderly, forensic services and rehabilitation services – remaining unattained. In many areas, service users are still unable to access basic mental healthcare. Mental health services for people with intellectual disability are practically non-existent.
>
> Conditions in large psychiatric hospitals continue to be poor, with only minimum maintenance being provided. A number of wards have closed, but there are still over 1,100 residents in psychiatric hospitals, mostly in unsuitable buildings. In total, more than 2,600 people with enduring mental illness continue to be cared for with 24-hour supervision in community residences or in long-stay psychiatric wards, with minimal or non-existent rehabilitation services.

Taken in these terms, the implementation of *A Vision for Change* would radically improve the current situation for all service users of the mental health services in Ireland.

Persisting barriers to social inclusion

Given the foregoing, it not surprising that concerns about the social exclusion experienced by people with disabilities continue to be relevant. Findings from the National Disability Authority (2005, p. 96) report suggest that:

> ... in Ireland people with disabilities live unequal lives and are at higher risk of social exclusion compared to others. People from poorer social backgrounds are at greater risk of becoming disabled, and in turn disability is associated with earlier school leaving, poorer qualifications, lower employment, lower incomes, higher poverty risk, and a more restricted social life. Socio-economic disadvantage and disability are intertwined, but each separately serves to reduce participation in the workforce and in social life outside the home.

In addition, a recent study entitled 'The Experience of Discrimination in Ireland' found that people with disabilities reported more incidents of discrimination and that disability was one of the strongest indicators of discrimination risk (Russell et al., 2008). The findings of an OECD (2008c) study confirm that the employment rates of people with disabilities in Ireland are among the lowest in the OECD. Only approximately one in three persons with a disability is in employment; dependence on long-term disability benefits has increased; and the incidence of poverty is two to three times higher than for the population at large (Martin, 2008b). These are issues that have gained greater attention in recent policy developments, in line with the approach advocated by the Developmental Welfare State (NESC, 2005) endorsed in *Towards 2016* and in the NAPSInc, which aims to increase the employment rates of people with disabilities (Fitzgerald, 2007). Efforts to improve access to employment are vital to promoting the opportunities of this group overall, but this approach must take due cognisance of the fact that some people with disabilities will remain outside the labour market. As Fitzgerald (2007, p. 253) notes: 'Adequate levels of welfare payments, which track other incomes in society, will remain the cornerstone of anti-poverty policies for this group.' This point is particularly significant in light of the growing discourse of activation that surrounds social security and welfare reform discussed in Chapter 7. Taking the situation of people with disabilities overall, it is clear that while important advances have been made, the persistence of significant social exclusion requires a redoubling of effort to tackle the issues that have endured.

SECTION 4: CARING AND CARERS – WORKING FOR RECOGNITION

While the nature and types of welfare provision have long been debated, attention to issues of care and caring have a much shorter history in social policy. Due in the main to the emergence of specific feminist scholarship on the subject, attention has been drawn to this long-neglected aspect of welfare. Issues such as the poor working conditions and levels of support available to carers in the informal sector have come in for greater scrutiny since the 1980s. The feminist development of 'an ethic of care' (see Chapter 5) has been central to enhancing our understanding of the issues that arise in this area. Williams (2001), for example, advocates the development of a new ethic of care which could balance the long-established ethic of work as a new basis for welfare citizenship. Acknowledgement of the interdependence that is central to care is also key. For this to be realised in terms of citizenship means complementing the 'rational economic actor model of the citizen' (Lynch and Lyons, 2008, p. 182) with a 'Care-Full model of the citizen, one that recognises the centrality of care and love relations to the mental health and well being of all members of society' (ibid., p. 183).

Historically, the assumed role of the family and in particular women has meant that while social policy developed in a broad range of areas over the course of the twentieth century, care and caring were largely taken for granted, as something that would just happen in the context of the family. This belief has been challenged in terms of the assumptions underpinning the development of the welfare state itself (see Chapter 4), in which the male breadwinner model of welfare was built on the notion of a male 'earning'/female 'caring' dichotomy. Apart from undermining the equal right to care of both men and women, this model has, to varying degrees, imposed a system in which women were 'dependent' and largely defined in terms of a predetermined caring role. Seen in this way, women were denied choice regarding the basis of their participation in society; an issue which the feminist movement subsequently challenged. This is not to say that women did not want to care or did not value it, rather what feminists seek is that this activity is recognised and valued in a meaningful and respectful way. In fact, what is increasingly argued for is the right to care; both in the sense of providing and receiving care, as a critical element of all our social rights.

The consequences of the long-standing neglect of the issue of caring is particularly evident in the Irish context. The trajectory of welfare state development reflected a particular view of the sanctity of the family and the primary position of women in the home, as in the Irish Constitution, 1937, discussed in Chapter 2. This was re-enforced by legislation which consolidated this role for women. As Fanning (2006, p. 15) notes, 'the emphasis on the unpaid role of women as carers within the Irish welfare economy was sustained in part by discrimination.' The recognition afforded in the constitution was provided without reference to the choices, autonomy or social rights of women, drawn up as it was without consideration of the notion of gender equality.

Box 11.4 Key policy developments with regard to carers and care

1990   Introduction of the Carer's Allowance
2001   Introduction of the Carer's Benefit
2006   Introduction of the Early Childcare Supplement
2006   Commitment to the development of a National Carers' Strategy

---

Policy development

The long tradition of informal care coupled with the considerable role played by the voluntary sector (including the Church) in the provision of many of the personal social services, has meant that, in overall terms, there is a long history of leaving 'care work' to the informal and voluntary sectors. In fact, policy strategies on the care of older people, for instance, have long sought 'to encourage and support the care of older people in their own community by family, neighbours and voluntary bodies' (Department of Health, 1994, p. 67 in Timonen and McMenamin, 2002, p. 22). It is not surprising then that few policies have attended to this issue, until more recent times.

The first acknowledgement of informal carers in the social security system came in the late 1960s. The Prescribed Relative Allowance, for example, was payable to persons aged over 70 years requiring full-time care. The terms of the payment, while altered, remained very restrictive (Cousins, 1994). The introduction of the Domiciliary Care Allowance in 1973, through the Department of Health, provided a payment in respect of children age 2 to 16 years who, owing to a disability, required full-time and constant care. This allowance remains in place. The introduction of the Carer's Allowance in 1990 replaced the Prescribed Relative Allowance and the terms of eligibility have since been broadened (allowing a number of hours of paid employment, for example). It remains a means-tested payment and, as Murphy (2007, p. 113) notes, 'while in some ways all such changes are laudable, it has to be asked whether women (by far the primary recipients of carer's allowance) are being pushed towards a triple burden of childcare, adult care and paid employment and how this is related to the mental and physical health of these women.' A social insurance-based Carer's Benefit was introduced in 2001 and it provides for persons to take time off work (up to a maximum of 104 weeks) to provide full-time care. The Carer's Benefit is payable to the carer during this period. The take-up of this benefit has been very low to date; there were 2,080 recipients in 2007 (DSFA, 2008b).

Counting carers and the pursuit of recognition

The long-standing invisibility of this group is illustrated by the fact that little official data was collected about them until relatively recently. The first census data generated on the level and extent of caring in Ireland was gathered in Census 2002 and a similar question was included in Census 2006. The census question referred specifically to 'a friend or family member with a long-term illness, a health problem or a disability' (including those associated with old age). This found that 4.8 per cent of persons over the age of 15 years (almost 161,000) were engaged in regular unpaid caring activities in Ireland in 2006 (CSO, 2007a). Over one-quarter of these provided more than 43 hours' care per week, and two-thirds of this group were women (ibid.).

Carers have recently had an opportunity to voice their views through a series of consultation seminars about their experiences of caring held during 2007. This process is part of a policy commitment contained in *Towards 2016* to develop a National Carers' Strategy (due at the end of 2007 but not published at the time of writing). The findings of this consultation are contained in *Listen to Carers: Report on a Nation-wide Carer Consultation* (Carers Association et al., 2008). This report documents the key issues that arise for carers and provides an insight into the impact of neglect on this group and the scale of the challenges that need to be confronted. The report highlights 'an urgent need for action' (ibid., p. v) and the overarching message is '… that carers in Ireland are seeking and need a whole new relationship and interface with the state and support services to maintain them in their caring role' (ibid.).

A three-pillar approach is advocated for the strategy, based on a fair shouldering of the caring responsibility by the state, adequate income support for carers and a range of supports that target and meet carers' needs. For this to be realised, a substantial overhaul of current social care practices will be required. Inadequate availability of home and community care services and the tendency to take the availability of family care for granted were noted. The '"arms length" approach' (ibid., p. 5) to carers is evidenced by the poor availability of information, long delays, fragmentation and lack of coordination, and lack of respect for carers. The lack of recognition and respect for carers was found to be a common experience. In terms of the needs of carers, a series of recommendations were made with regard to the development of services and supports (e.g. training for carers, respite, needs assessment for carers), income supports (e.g. adequate financial recognition, security for the future), employment and work/life balance, and social inclusion.

Taking the issue of income support as an example, strong dissatisfaction was reported with the means-testing aspect of the Carer's Allowance and that if means-testing is not removed it should not continue to take into account the income of spouses, as is the case at present. In the view of one participant, 'it is unjust to tie any funding to private resources rather than the value of the work that is being performed' (ibid., p. 18). However, Timonen and McMenamin (2002, p. 28) argue that 'it is very unlikely that the means testing of carer's allowance will be abolished despite repeated calls for "universalization" by interest groups such as the Carers' Association. In other words, the carer's allowance remains an income support mechanism rather than a payment for caring.' Issues such as these are fundamental to the value that is placed on caring activity and the wider contribution that is made to society. There is a long way to go in realising the objectives outlined in the consultation report; the content of the forthcoming strategy and the plans for its implementation will be critical. The case for 'a more carer-friendly society' (ibid., p. 27) has again been made, the response to which is relevant to us all.[12]

The approach to care, more broadly defined, raises yet more issues for consideration. For instance, the census information on caring excludes one of the most common caring activities, that of caring for children. Addressing this point and drawing on another data source, Lynch and Lyons (2008, p. 170) argue that:

> Even though it is no doubt unintentional, the failure to collect data on hours spent on child care work in the Census, means that child care, which is *the* major form of care work in Irish society, is not counted in terms of work hours. Yet it is the form of care work that women of all social classes and ages are significantly more likely to undertake than men. There is a deeply patriarchal set of assumptions hiding women's unpaid work in the household in this way; it is a form of institutionalised sexism that needs to be addressed.

Other figures relating to children in non-parental care in 2002, for instance, indicate that 31.2 per cent of these pre-school age children and 46.1 per cent of school age children were cared for by unpaid relatives (Department of Justice, Equality and Law REform, 2004, p. 7 in O'Sullivan, 2007, p. 280). There is, therefore, a huge reliance on the extended family to support the caring of children, but this reality is largely neglected in the formal policy domain. It is clear from these figures that a massive contribution is made by grandparents, aunts, etc., to the care of children, for which there has been little official recognition to date.

In sum, demographic and social change means that the old assumptions around the availability of care no longer hold. The unpaid army of women that provided the bedrock of the care infrastructure in Ireland are increasingly occupied in the formal labour market. Family forms have also changed and people tend not to live as close to their extended family as previously. It is clear that the carers of today, very many of whom are women, are not adequately recognised or supported in their activities. We are now faced with what Fanning and Rush (2006, p. 4) refer to as a 'social care infrastructure deficit', in which policy has struggled to keep pace with the challenges that arise. Rush (2006, p. 53) points to a wider policy tension evidenced in the Developmental Welfare State (NESC, 2005), in which the care deficit is identified although ultimately it 'reiterates a commitment to an expanding labour market without providing a convincing strategy to support the diminished capacity of families to provide care'. Taken together, these realities and tensions suggest that the unplanned 'muddling through' approach to an issue as fundamental as care cannot continue. Addressing this requires that the priorities of the Irish welfare state are made explicit and include recognition of, and a vision for, the place of care in contemporary Irish society.

CHAPTER SUMMARY

▸ This chapter examined the ways in which social policy attends to the needs and rights of various social groups in society. The approach to difference and differentiated need has historically been problematised. Recognition and respect are critical to the realisation of rights. Issues of redistribution also arise.

▸ Social policy for children has seen substantial development and innovation over the last two decades. The challenge now is to consider the impact of persisting impediments (such as child poverty), social service shortcomings (particularly in meeting the needs of vulnerable children) and constitutional reform to protect the rights of children living in Ireland in the twenty-first century.

▸ Despite the early recognition of older people in social security terms, contemporary social policy is marked by a number of challenges. The existence of ageism and the lack of clarity around certain aspects of care support or a coherent vision for these services, present as challenges to achieving a more 'age-friendly society'.

▸ The marginalisation and segregation of people with disabilities in the past have been significantly challenged. Considerable advances have been made, although there are some serious issues that remain to be overcome, including the persistence and pervasiveness of poverty and social exclusion experienced by people with disabilities.

▸ Caring remains one of the most vital yet neglected aspects of human well-being. The position of carers has largely been taken for granted in the past. Old assumptions are increasingly being challenged by circumstance and by the growing demands for carers to be recognised. That particular battle for recognition continues.

Discussion points

▸ Discuss the norms on which citizenship rights have traditionally been based. How have these influenced the development of welfare provision in Ireland?

▸ Analyse the notion of a 'rights-based' approach to welfare provision and discuss its implications with reference to a particular social group.

▸ Examine the implications of the 'familialisation of children' for the vindication of their rights.

▸ What is ageism? Identify the issues that arise in social policy terms.

▸ Discuss the impact of the lack of respect for difference evident in the approach taken to people with disabilities in the past.

▸ What is your assessment of the status and recognition of care and caring in Irish social policy at present?

Further reading

Fanning, B., and Rush, M. (eds) (2006) *Care and Social Change in the Irish Welfare Economy*, Dublin: UCD Press.

Kilkelly, U. (2007) *Barriers to the Realisation of Children's Rights in Ireland*, available from: http://www.oco.ie/policyResearch/research.aspx

National Economic and Social Forum (2005) *Care for Older People*, NESF Report No. 32, Dublin: NESF.

Quin, S. and Redmond, B. (eds) (2003) *Disability and Social Policy in Ireland*, Dublin: UCD Press.

Useful websites

Equality Authority: www.equality.ie

Consult websites of relevant organisations for useful policy position statements, research reports and campaigns.

Notes

1 See Ferguson and Kenny (eds) (1995) for a comprehensive overview of the main features of the Act and its implications for child protection practices in Ireland. Buckley (2002) and Burns and Lynch (eds) (2008) provide more recent reviews of the issues and challenges that arise.

2 A link to all of these reports is available on the Department of Foreign Affairs website: http://www.dfa.ie/home/index.aspx?id=319

3 See http://www2.ohchr.org/english/bodies/crc/ for details.

4 See www.oco.ie for details of the work and functions of the Ombudsman for Children.

5 See www.dailnanog.ie for information.

6 OMC refers to the Office of the Minister for Children for the purposes of this chapter only. The OMC has since been re-named the Office of the Minister for Children and Youth Affairs (OMCYA).

7 See the Combat Poverty Agency (2005) and Sweeney (2007) for comprehensive assessments of these issues.

8 The Centre for Early Childhood Development and Education was abolished in 2008.

9 See http://www.oireachtas.ie/viewdoc.asp?fn=/documents/Committees 30thDail/J-ConAmendChildren/Homepage.htm for relevant details and updates.

10 The work of the National Council on Ageing and Older People (2005), the Equality Authority and the Older and Bolder campaign (www.olderand bolder.ie) are of particular note in the Irish context.

11 An evaluation of the scheme is underway; see the Department of Health and Children for updates.

12 See also a report produced by the Equality Authority (2005), *Implementing Equality for Carers*, which provides an overview of the position of carers in Ireland and offers a comprehensive set of recommendations related to the pursuit of equality for carers.

CHAPTER 12

SOCIAL POLICY AND SOCIAL GROUPS: ISSUES OF DIVERSITY AND DISCRIMINATION

This chapter continues the focus on social groups and social policy begun in the previous chapter. Here the focus is on groups whose identities contribute to the diversity of Irish society, but whose recognition and realisation of rights has been problematic, and issues of discrimination arise for all groups in varying ways, through, for example, racism and heterosexism. The greater part of the chapter concentrates on the issue of immigration and the policy responses to the unprecedented growth of immigrant groups and ethnic diversity in Irish society. The chapter also discusses the position of Travellers in Irish society as an indigenous ethnic minority, and the position of lesbian, gay and bisexual (LGB) people who were largely invisible minorities until the 1970s.

All of these groups pose challenges to the dominant construction of Irish identity and citizenship that reflects a homogeneous nation built on being white, settled and heterosexual. They draw attention to how citizenship creates boundaries which include and exclude. As groups and identities with greater diversity and difference have become more visible in Irish society and, to varying degrees, have campaigned for rights and recognition, institutional structures and policies have grown around issues of equality, racism, integration and interculturalism. In particular, these issues have influenced the language and design of social policy and social services. However, issues of inequality, exclusion, racism and heterosexism continue to be serious problems in various ways for the groups discussed in this chapter.

CHAPTER OUTLINE

▸ Section one focuses on the evolution of immigration policy and the treatment of immigrants as migrant workers, asylum seekers and refugees. The issue of differential treatment and its effects, both across and within these groups, in relation to social policy, integration and citizenship is examined.

▸ Section two considers the concept of ethnicity in relation to Travellers and the development of policy in relation to their position in Irish society. Their lack of recognition as an ethnic minority and the consequent discrimination and inequality Travellers experience in relation to social policy provision and within Irish society generally are discussed.

▸ Section three considers the concepts of heterosexism and heteronormativity before going on to examine issues regarding LGB rights and recognition in Irish society and in relation to particular legislative and social policy developments.

SECTION 1: IMMIGRATION AND IRISH SOCIAL POLICY

Immigration and diversity

Since the mid-1990s Ireland has experienced a period of significant transformation. A substantial part of this is related to **migration**, specifically immigration. We have become a 'migration nation', as the recent statement from the Office of the Minister for Integration (2008) puts it. Migration, as Drake (2001, p. 102) notes, is a key factor in social change and Ireland's recent experience is part of a wider pattern:

> **Migration, immigration, emigration**: migration refers to movement from one country to live in another; immigration refers to movement into a country; and emigration to movement from a country.

Perhaps one of the most important contributions to social diversity has been the growing mobility of populations. The twentieth century has seen increasing flows of labour, not only within states but across national boundaries. This mobility was accelerated by colonisation, by disasters such as war and famine, and by demand for workers in industrialised nations … migration has fostered greater ethnic, social and cultural diversity.

Recent immigration does not spell the first instance of diversity and difference in Irish society. This is evident in the issues raised in discussions about other social groups in both this and the previous chapter; however, the scale of immigration brings a new dimension to issues of difference, diversity and racism. When large-scale immigration occurs quite rapidly and difference becomes more readily visible, this prompts greater questioning of issues such as Irish citizenship, who is Irish and who can be an Irish citizen, and what rights and entitlements are afforded to non-citizens. Differential treatment can pave the way for racist patterns of discrimination which can emerge in multiple forms, where immigrants en masse, or particular categories of immigrants, such as asylum seekers or particular nationalities or ethnic groups, are treated in racist ways. Racism may be defined as 'a specific form of discrimination and exclusion faced by minority ethnic groups. It is based on the false belief that some "races" are inherently superior to others because of different skin colour, nationality, ethnic or cultural background' (Watt and McCaughey, 2006, p. 169). The notion of racialisation is an important element in understanding contemporary patterns of racism. Racialisation refers to the processes by which particular groups are ascribed physical and cultural differences. The concept accounts for the racism experienced by particular groups despite the scientifically spurious nature of race (Barot and Bird, 2001).

As profiled in part one of the book, Ireland has had a long history of emigration. The large waves of emigration in the 1950s and 1980s contributed to the growth of social diversity in other countries such as the UK where Irish migrants, among others, fulfilled the demand for workers. However, emigration created greater cultural homogeneity in Ireland than might have otherwise been the case, as some people chose to emigrate as much for social and cultural reasons as economic ones. These included groups such as single women, single mothers, and gays and lesbians who were all, in various ways, denied social rights, equal treatment, recognition and respect in Catholic conservative Ireland (Clear, 2004; O'Carroll and Collins, 1995).

Until recently, Ireland's experience of immigration has been less well documented. As Mac Éinrí (2001) notes, prior to the 1990s immigration flows into Ireland were relatively small and did not produce a significant increase in diversity. The main groups that immigrated to Ireland were returning Irish emigrants, small numbers of high-skilled migrants, primarily working in the multi-national sector, and people coming from continental Europe and the UK for counter-cultural reasons or to retire. In addition, very small numbers of programme refugees[1] came to Ireland, including Hungarians in the 1950s, Chileans and Vietnamese in the 1970s, and Iranians in the 1980s (Fanning, 2002). With the exception of the programme refugees, for the most part these forms of immigration consisted mainly of people who were not significantly 'different' to the existing Irish population. Their presence did not challenge existing interpretations of Irishness and Irish culture as white and Catholic; there were no major increases in demand for social services, and user groups remained relatively homogenous.

By the mid- to late 1990s new immigration flows changed this equilibrium. To appreciate the scale of these changes the Irish experience of immigration can be contrasted with other European countries. As the NESC (2006, p. 21) points out, 'Ireland was the last member of the EU-15 to become a country of net immigration. Despite this, the country has caught up quickly and now has one of the highest immigration rates in the European Union: in 2003, the increase stood at 7.1 migrants per 1,000 of the population, against an EU-15 average of 4.1 …' Net migration levels peaked in 2006 when 107,800 immigrants came to Ireland and 36,000 emigrants left the country.[2] The most noticeable change in the nationality of immigrants has been the emergence and relative size of the EU-12 category. This includes the 10 countries that joined the EU in May 2004, including Poland, Latvia, Lithuania, Hungary, Slovakia, Slovenia, Malta, Cyprus, Czech Republic and Estonia, and the two countries that joined the EU in January 2007, namely Bulgaria and Romania. Since 2004, these countries have accounted for the majority of migrants coming to Ireland, followed by returning Irish emigrants and people from the 'rest of world' category, which is mainly African and Asian countries.

Labour migration accounts for the bulk of this rise in immigration. The relatively small high-skills category of immigrants prior to the 1990s has been significantly augmented by large numbers of both high- and low-skilled labour migrants coming to Ireland in response to labour shortages arising during the economic boom. The other main change in immigration is related to asylum seeking, which by the late 1990s rose from a very small base.

The result is that the composition of the Irish population has changed, with significant growth in the numbers whose nationality is not Irish. In the 2002 census, for example, 92.9 per cent were of Irish nationality and 5.8 per cent were of non-Irish nationality. By 2006, 88.8 per cent of the population were Irish and 10 per cent were non-Irish. If citizenship denotes formal membership of a country together with a shared national culture or identity, immigration potentially disrupts this way of understanding citizenship. Membership of Irish society has been predominantly based on being born in Ireland within a stable, homogeneous population. Irish citizenship was therefore based on what are assumed to be universal traits in the population: more or less everyone is assumed to be white and Catholic and to share the same culture, and these traits remained relatively static over time. These assumptions about citizenship, rooted in the Marshallian model as mentioned in the previous chapter, are now open to question. As Joppke (1999, p. 629) points out:

> Immigration is one reason why Marshallian citizenship universalism is no longer plausible today. The movement of people across states revealed that citizenship is not only a set of rights, but also a mechanism of closure that sharply demarcates the boundaries of states

... As a mechanism of closure, citizenship (commonly ascribed at birth) is like a filing mechanism, distributing people to just one of the world's many states ... for those who manage to enter the territory of another state, access to this state's citizenship is generally denied, and available only if demanding (residence and personal) characteristics are fulfilled, which are differently conceived in different states.

Therefore, when immigrants become a significant part of the population, issues of citizenship come to the fore. If citizenship is the basis of a 'right to rights' (Arendt, 1961, p. 294 in Fanning, 2007a, p. 10), what rights and entitlements are afforded to non-citizens? Who can become a citizen and how? What impact do rights and regulation of immigrants have on equality, integration and racism? In cases where immigrants and new ethnic groups do become citizens, this can potentially pose a further set of issues which have to do with recognition and respect and the degree to which citizenship accommodates cultural diversity. Again, as Joppke (1999, p. 630) points out:

There is a second way in which immigration has stirred up the Marshallian citizenship orthodoxy. Even if immigrants have acquired the citizenship of (or, at least safe membership status in) the receiving state, they are often not content with enjoying equal rights. As carriers of ethnic difference, immigrants notice that even liberal states, which are philosophically indifferent to the cultural preferences of their members, are couched in distinct cultural colours – its official language, holidays, or church relations cannot but privilege the ethnic majority population over the immigrant minorities.

Therefore, while gaining citizenship might mean formally gaining inclusion and social rights, ethnic minority citizens may still be excluded and subject to racist discrimination in a country that privileges particular majority cultural norms. Similar issues arise for indigenous ethnic minorities, such as Travellers who are discussed in the next section of this chapter.

With respect to immigrants we can begin to look at these questions by examining various administrative categorisations used to manage and regulate immigration to Ireland. Across the board, the rights and entitlements of immigrants, whether as workers, asylum seekers or refugees, are calibrated and categorised, creating grades of exclusion, inclusion or integration in Irish society. Much of this rests on the degree to which various immigrant groups are considered compatible with our national economic interests (Boucher, 2008) and the degree to which they **assimilate** into our predominantly monocultural tribal notion of Irishness (Mac Éinrí, 2007). The remainder of this section of the chapter firstly reviews the development

> **Assimilation** refers to the absorption into a dominant majority of a usually smaller minority group, which, as a result, loses its group specificity and awareness of itself as a group.

of administrative categories and associated rights and entitlements in relation to migrant workers and how this impacts on the experiences of various migrant groups. This is followed by an examination of these issues in relation to other migrant categories, namely asylum seekers and refugees. The section also looks at developments in relation to Irish citizenship legislation and integration policy prompted by the recent rise in immigrant communities in Ireland.

Box 12.1   Key legislative and policy developments with regard to immigration

1996   Refugee Act
1997   Establishment of the National Consultative Committee on Racism and Interculturalism (NCCRI)
1999   Integration: a two way process
2000   Dispersal and Direct Provision Scheme
2003   Immigration Act
2004   Habitual Residence Condition
2004   Citizenship Act
2005   National Action Plan Against Racism
2006   Immigration Act
2007   Establishment of the Office of the Minister for Integration
2008   Immigration Residence and Protection Bill
2008   Migration Nation Statement on Integration Strategy and Diversity Management
2008   Abolition of the National Consultative Committee on Racism and Interculturalism

---

Immigration policy and labour migration

Irish immigration policy is primarily concerned with border control and law and order, including the regulation of migrants' movement in and out of the state, and their residence within the state. The Aliens Act, 1935, was one of the early pieces of immigration legislation in which migrants were referred to as 'aliens'. More recently, with the passing of the Citizenship and Nationality Act, 2001, the term 'aliens' has given way to the term 'non-nationals'.

Specifically regarding labour migration, Ireland's entry to the EEC in 1973 changed the status of immigrants from other EEC countries due to the right to freedom of movement of workers that came with EEC membership.

Freedom of movement was widened to citizens of the European Economic Area (EEA) countries in 1992. The EEA includes all EU member countries, Iceland, Norway and Liechtenstein. In 1993 the Maastricht Treaty introduced the right to freedom of movement of all citizens of the EU. Further change came with the expansion of the EU in May 2004 to include 10 new member countries. People from eight of these countries (Malta and Cyprus excepted) were not given the automatic right to work in other EU countries. Existing member states were given the option to impose employment restrictions for up to seven years. Ireland, along with the UK and Sweden, were the only countries to immediately extend the right to work to citizens from the new member states. The right to work was not extended to citizens of the new 2007 EU member states, Romania and Bulgaria.[3] In general, EU citizens resident within Ireland have the same rights as Irish citizens to social services such as healthcare, education, housing and social security. The next section looks at the distinctions made between two main categories of non-EEA immigrants: work-permit holders and green card holders. It analyses their overall position with regard to rights and entitlements and issues arising regarding their experiences within the Irish labour market and Irish society.

Immigration policy and non-EEA migrant workers

In the past, Ireland was considered to have an ad hoc, liberal and employer-led approach to economic immigration (Mac Éinrí, 2001; Ruhs, 2004). Employers were given the freedom to recruit, through work visas and work permits, as many non-EEA workers as they needed for whatever job. However, as several authors (Loyal, 2003; Garner, 2004; Hayward and Howard, 2007) have noted, recruitment drives sought out workers who looked and sounded like Irish people and who may have been descendants of previous Irish emigrants. It was assumed that these groups would more easily assimilate into Irish society during their stay, which was assumed to be temporary. In anticipation of EU enlargement the state began to develop a more interventionist role, which, as Allen (2007) argues, has seen a gradual tightening of regulations with respect to labour migration. In addition, immigration policy is becoming more finely tuned in response to global competition for workers with particular skills. This has led to greater restrictions on low-skilled labour migration and greater distinctions between conditions and rights for high-skilled versus low-skilled workers.

Work permits

Ireland has generally relied on a work-permit scheme. This means that an employer must demonstrate that he or she has a particular need for the worker in question. Before February 2007 the permit system operated by granting a permit to an employer for a worker after a labour test to show that no person within the EEA could be found to do the particular job. The worker was not free to sell his or her labour on the open labour market. The employer, not the prospective employee, applied for the permit. The work permit lasted for one year and could be renewed on a yearly basis. After one year, work-permit holders were entitled to apply for family reunification provided they could support their family.

Conroy and Brennan's (2003) research for the Equality Authority found a very negative picture of the situation of migrant workers. This was especially the case for work-permit holders working in low-paid sectors of the economy, where the majority are employed, in areas such as hotel and catering services, agriculture, construction and care work. Many breaches of labour law were found, including, for example, non-payment or delayed payment of wages, pay rates below the minimum wage, excessive working hours, and difficulties with leaving exploitative work conditions because the employer held the work permit of the employees. A number of high-profile cases of exploitative work conditions, such as the case of the Turkish construction company Gama, brought the exploitation and discrimination being faced by migrant workers to the fore of the social partnership deliberations for the *Towards 2016* agreement in 2006.

Subsequently, in February 2007, some changes were made to the work-permit scheme as a result of the implementation of the Employment Permits Act, 2006. While these changes responded to some of the criticisms of the existing system, restrictions on low-skilled immigration have tightened. For example, work permits are now issued to the worker not the employer and last for two years. However, the number of eligible occupations has been further restricted and salary conditions apply. The rules regarding family reunification remain the same as those in place prior to 2007. This means that there is no automatic right to family reunification; it is granted at the discretion of the Minister for Justice, Equality and Law Reform.[4] In addition, many EU countries have a wider interpretation of who counts as family for reunification purposes (Pillinger, 2008). Family reunification is a particularly acute issue for work-permit holders, as applications are frequently refused (Migrant Rights Centre Ireland, 2006a).

Since 2007, work-permit holders' dependants are entitled to work under a spousal/dependant work permit. However, this only applies if these individuals are legally resident in the state, which means that it depends on a successful family reunification application. The 2007 changes do aim to prevent some aspects of potential exploitation in the system. It prohibits employers from deducting recruitment expenses from employees' wages and the employer may not retain an employee's personal documents. In addition, a National Employment Rights Authority was established in 2007 to promote knowledge and enforcement of employee rights and employers' responsibilities, and heavier fines and imprisonment terms were introduced for breach of labour law.

Green cards

Prior to 2007, work visas and work authorisations[5] were designed to facilitate the recruitment of suitably qualified people from non-EEA countries for designated sectors of the labour market where skill shortages existed. The conditions attached were generally more favourable than those attached to work permits. In 2007, following implementation of the Employment Permits Act, 2006, the green card scheme replaced work authorisations and visas, and generally the rights and entitlements of these workers have been enhanced under the new regime. This scheme applies to all workers earning over €60,000 and to workers in areas with skill shortages, such as health, financial services, IT, and science and technology, who earn between €30,000 and €60,000. The green card lasts for two years and after this period the holder has the right to apply for permanent residency. Green card holders are entitled to immediate family reunification and their dependants have the right to work with a spousal/dependant work permit.

Discrimination and social rights

Despite these changes, issues of inequality and racism as well as gendered patterns of discrimination continue to mark the experiences of migrant workers in the Irish economy. The broad thrust of the findings of Conroy and Brennan's (2003) study has been replicated in subsequent research (Migrant Rights Centre Ireland, 2007; O'Connell and McGinnity, 2008). In general, migrants fare less well than Irish nationals when it comes to levels of pay, unemployment levels, access to professional and managerial occupations, and in relation to discrimination experienced when looking for work and in work. Furthermore, certain minority ethnic groups and female migrant workers fare less well. O'Connell and McGinnity (2008), for example, found that while non-Irish nationals are three times more likely than Irish nationals to experience discrimination when looking for work, this becomes seven times more likely for Black people. Across the board, groups who bear the greatest resemblance to Irish workers, that is, those who are white and come from English-speaking countries, generally fare better. When it comes to pay, non-Irish nationals are generally less well paid, and female migrants fare less well than male migrants, earning on average 15 per cent less. In addition, Pillinger (2006) documents other areas of gender-based discrimination for female migrant workers, especially denial of rights and entitlements in relation to pregnancy. This problem is compounded by the general problem migrant workers have with accessing services and realising entitlements because of a lack of information.

Social rights and the habitual residence condition

All workers, Irish, EEA and non-EEA, have the same protection and entitlements under labour law regarding rights such as maternity leave, parental leave, the minimum wage, working time and holiday entitlements, redundancy payments, etc. Distinctions and gradations begin to apply when it comes to entitlements to social services. Non-EEA workers, for example, are not entitled to apply for social and affordable housing, but they do have access to publicly provided healthcare, and children of all migrants have the same access to education as Irish children under 18 years of age. Access to social security became particularly restricted on foot of EU enlargement in 2004, with the introduction of the Habitual Residence Condition (HRC). It was introduced to prevent the perceived risk that people would move to Ireland to avail of the social welfare system rather than to take up employment. This is referred to as 'welfare tourism' or 'social welfare shopping'. Mary Coughlan, the Minister for Social and Family Affairs at the time, declared that:

> I will not allow our social welfare system to become overburdened and I will be taking the precaution of ring fencing that system of social protection ... We need to ensure that our social welfare system and other public services are not open to abuse. (Department of Social and Family Affairs, 2004)

However, there is little evidence of immigration linked to 'welfare tourism'. The experience of Sweden since EU enlargement in 2004 bears this out. Along with Ireland and the UK, it allowed EU-10 workers to come to Sweden but did not restrict access to welfare as the UK and Ireland did. Doyle et al. (2006) found that the level of immigration to Sweden by EU-10 migrants has been much lower than Ireland. The main reason for the difference seems to be employment related, as far fewer employment vacancies were available in Sweden. The fact that English is the vernacular language in Ireland may also have been a factor. In any case, the change did not have an effect on the Swedish welfare system; the number of applications for social assistance in 2004 remained similar to that in 2003.

The HRC stipulates that all applicants, regardless of nationality, have to satisfy a residency condition for a number of social assistance payments.[6] In general, an applicant who has been present in Ireland for two or more years, who works there and intends to make it his or her permanent home satisfies the condition. It is presumed that the applicant is not habitually resident until the contrary is proven, therefore, the onus is on the applicant to prove that he or she is habitually resident. In effect, with the introduction of the HRC, social welfare became a tool of immigration policy and the restrictions downgraded entitlement to assistance-based and universal social welfare payments for everyone.

Amendments were made to the system after the EU Commission found that the condition contravened EU law. Consequently, EEA citizens working in Ireland and who have 'a history of working in the state' but not necessarily fulfilling the HRC became re-eligible for Supplementary Welfare Allowance and family payments, that is, Child Benefit and One Parent Family Payment. However, as the Migrant Rights Centre Ireland (2006b) points out, no definition of a 'history of working in the state' has been developed. In addition, needing a history of working in the state means that EEA nationals who are job seekers and who have not yet found a job do not benefit from the amendments.

The amendments do not apply to all other migrant workers, and the system can have a particularly negative impact on work-permit holders. It can lead to workplace exploitation by locking a person into an undesirable job when there is no alternative but unemployment and no social welfare support. Work-permit holders who cannot work due to illness or injury are also particularly vulnerable, and those without work are at high risk of homelessness. Furthermore, homeless services were also interpreted to come under the remit of the HRC (Sheehan, 2007). Overall, as the Migrant Rights Centre Ireland (2006b, pp. 17–18) notes, 'migrant workers' lives can fall apart very quickly without state support'. The condition has also had a very negative impact on asylum seekers which is discussed further below.

Asylum seekers and refugees

Defining asylum seekers and refugees

An asylum seeker is a person who seeks to be recognised as a refugee in accordance with the terms of the 1951 UN Convention relating to the Status of Refugees. If an asylum seeker's claim for refuge is recognised then that person's status moves from an asylum seeker to a refugee. A refugee:

> … is a person who owing to a well-founded fear of being persecuted for reasons of race, religion, nationality, membership of a particular social group or political opinion, is outside the country of his nationality and is unable, or owing to such fear, is unwilling to avail himself of the protection of that country; or who, not having nationality and being outside the country of his former habitual

residence, is unable or owing to such fear, is unwilling to return to it.
(Article 1 of the Geneva Convention, 1951)

Initially the Convention referred to Europe only and, as Mac Éinrí (2006, p. 359) points out, 'it reflected a post-WWII Cold War perspective which tended to see refugees in Europe … as heroic individuals fleeing from Communism'. Ireland's first experience of refugees under the Convention conformed to that impression. Hungarian refugees coming to Ireland in the 1950s following the Hungarian revolution were initially welcomed as it was assumed that these were primarily Catholic people fleeing communism (Raftery, 2006). The initial enthusiasm quickly wore off and, as Fanning (2002) suggests, the episode left a legacy of discriminatory and exclusionary practices towards asylum seekers and refugees.

Over time, as Mac Éinrí (2006) notes, reasons for asylum seeking and the origins of asylum seekers began to change. By the 1990s, asylum-seeking trends were more strongly related to movement from underdeveloped Southern countries to wealthy Northern countries. As well as fleeing situations of war and conflict, reasons for leaving included poverty, famine and environmental disasters, which are situations not covered under the original Convention. In some cases these reasons overlapped with economic reasons as they involved situations where it was impossible to maintain a livelihood. However, economic refugees were not recognised under the Convention. While reasons for seeking asylum have grown over time and in many cases are quite complex, policy developments run counter to these trends. States, as Mac Éinrí (ibid., pp. 359–60) notes, have 'gradually imposed new barriers designed to make it administratively difficult, if not impossible, for many would-be refugees to apply for asylum'. Moreover, as Lentin and McVeigh (2006, p. 43) argue:

> States insist on making a distinction between 'asylum seekers' and 'refugees' even though this does not exist in the Geneva Convention. The notion of an 'asylum seeker' is invented by states in order to deny refugee status to many people who say they are refugees. Thus there are many people who may meet the UN definition of being a refugee and yet are denied recognition as such by states employing their own restricted and limited definitions of what constitutes a refugee.

This tightening of policy towards asylum seeking occurred over the course of the 1990s and into the 2000s as the numbers seeking asylum in Ireland increased in an unprecedented way from 39 applicants in 1992 to a peak of 11,634 by 2002. Since 2002 the number of applicants has been falling; in 2007, for example, a total of 3,985 people applied for asylum in Ireland.[7]

Asylum and refugee policy

A Refugee Act was published in 1996 and had the agreement of all parties in the Dáil as well as many NGOs. It was 'hailed as progressive ... because it broadened the 1951 Geneva Convention definition of "refugee" to include "membership of a particular social group" extending to membership of a trade union, being either male or female, or having a particular sexual orientation' (ibid.). However, its implementation was delayed and it was subsequently amended in a series of other Acts in the midst of what was termed an 'asylum crisis' in the late 1990s and early 2000s. The proposed broadening of the definition of a refugee never occurred and, instead, the Immigration Act, 1999, the Illegal Immigrants Trafficking Act, 2000, and the Immigration Act, 2003, signalled a more restrictive approach to asylum seeking, as the state aimed to curb the numbers coming to Ireland seeking asylum. These acts deal with issues such as the state's powers in relation to deportation, the finger printing of asylum seekers, and the designation of 'safe countries' from which applications for asylum are disallowed.

Furthermore, increasing emphasis is placed within legislation and in political discourse on the need to distinguish between 'genuine' refugees versus 'bogus' or 'illegal' asylum seekers. This has had the effect of criminalising asylum seekers, all of whom under the Geneva Convention have a legal right to seek asylum, and the 'genuine' are only deemed genuine once they have been recognised as refugees. A very small proportion of asylum seekers are successful in their application to be recognised as refugees and it is particularly significant that a greater number are recognised on appeal than in the first instance, signifying the restrictive basis on which decisions are made. In 2005, for example, a total of 455 applicants were recognised as refugees in the first instance and a further 511 were recognised on appeal.[8] Research on asylum-seeker experiences carried out by the Irish Immigrant Support Centre (NASC, 2008) found that asylum seekers felt that the interview process is primarily based on questions designed to find reasons, however small, to refuse refugee status. This research also highlighted problems with the quality of translation and interpretive services provided for interviews, which potentially have a negative impact on applicants' cases.

Social policy provision for asylum seekers

Asylum seekers are at the bottom of the hierarchy when it comes to how migrants are categorised in relation to social rights and social policy provision. Their needs are addressed in the most minimal way, and social policy has essentially become a tool to deter asylum seeking. Prior to 2000, relatively generous conditions were in place as asylum seekers had access to Supplementary Welfare Allowance and rent supplement to meet their basic needs, and for a brief period were given the right to work. However, concerned that the social welfare system was operating as a 'pull factor for non-genuine asylum seekers' (Minister for Justice, Equality and Law Reform, 1999, in O'Connor, 2003a, p. 8) the Minister introduced the Dispersal and Direct Provision scheme for all asylum seekers in April 2000. This scheme is administered by the Department of Justice, Equality and Law Reform through the Reception and Integration Agency (RIA).

Under the scheme asylum seekers who have made a claim for asylum are initially housed in a reception centre in Dublin for a short period of time. They are then 'dispersed' to accommodation centres around the country. Asylum seekers are provided with full board, and the only monetary payment they receive is an allowance of €19.10 per week per adult and €9.60 per week per child. These rates were introduced in 2000 and have not been raised since. Full board means that individuals are not allowed to cook their own meals (with the exception of six self-catering centres). The majority of accommodation centres are run on a contract basis by private interests such as hotel and guest house owners for the RIA. There are currently 58 centres in operation, which are subject to inspection by the RIA. However, inspections appear to be minimal and inadequacies related to heating, recreational facilities, cleanliness, food and overcrowding have been overlooked (Mac Cormaic, 2007).

The day-to-day experience of the system for asylum seekers is overwhelmingly negative. As O'Connor (2003a, p. 40) points out, it 'often leaves asylum seekers bored, isolated, socially excluded, impoverished, deprived of services, unaware of their entitlements, demoralised, deskilled and institutionalised' and has a detrimental effect on their human rights. Fanning and Veale (2004) highlight the particularly damaging effects of the scheme on the lives of children growing up in such an environment; they live in extreme poverty and deprivation, and their parents are prohibited from basic elements of caring and parenting, such as cooking meals for their children. In addition, the type of food provided bears little or no relation to ethnic preferences, which affects asylum-seeker well-being, particularly children and breastfeeding mothers (Manandhar et al., 2006).

This restrictive approach is reinforced by the denial of rights across the social services, other than basic education and healthcare. Asylum seekers are entitled to health services under the medical card scheme and asylum-seeking children are entitled to education until they reach 18 years of age. Asylum seekers are not entitled to participate in any other form of education or training course and are not entitled to work. If asylum seekers move out of the accommodation centres, they are not considered to have an accommodation need and do not qualify for rent supplement. They are entitled to apply for exceptional needs payments under the Supplementary Welfare Allowance scheme for extra essential expenditure, but payment is at the discretion of a community welfare officer. The HRC had a particularly detrimental effect on asylum seekers because it removed the universality attached to Child Benefit. Consequently, since 2004, denied asylum seekers are not entitled to the main social welfare payment they had been able to claim. While a person is applying for refugee status they are not considered habitually resident in Ireland; therefore they do not comply with HRC regulations (Visser, 2005).

Social policy provision and refugees

Once asylum seekers are recognised as refugees their social rights and entitlements are similar to those of Irish citizens. In addition, they are exempt from the HRC. They are entitled to apply for family reunification, but as in the case of migrant workers, this is granted at the discretion of the Minister for Justice, Equality and Law Reform. They are entitled to apply to become an Irish citizen through naturalisation three years after the date of their asylum application. However, Lentin and McVeigh (2006, p. 44) make the point that although refugees can eventually become citizens, they tend not to be seen in that light; 'state agencies … continue to dub them "refugees" in talking about their "integration", long after granting them status.' Also, their prior experience as asylum seekers can have long-term negative effects for their integration into Irish society. Making the transition from direct provision, where their lives are kept on hold, to trying to live a normal life in Irish society can be difficult (Faughnan and Woods, 2000).

Immigration and citizenship

For the most part, labour migration has been treated as a temporary phenomenon, and the majority of migrant workers, especially those with work permits, are treated as temporary guest workers for whom the issue of citizenship is not relevant. High-skilled migrants, in contrast, are more highly valued and there is greater access for these groups to long-stay residence in Ireland, with similar rights and entitlements as Irish citizens. Their long-term presence also gives them the option to apply for Irish citizenship through naturalisation; however, on the whole, their presence and access to social services is not problematised and does not evoke discussions about threats to Irish citizenship. When it comes to asylum seekers, however, the opposite has been the case. This has led to changes in Irish citizenship laws, making entitlement to Irish citizenship more restrictive than heretofore and a mechanism to separate the 'deserving' from the 'undeserving' immigrant.

The problematisation of Irish citizenship emerged in 2003 when changes were made to the right to residence of migrant parents of children born in Ireland. According to Irish citizenship rules at the time all children born on Irish soil were automatically entitled to Irish citizenship. In 1989 a Supreme Court case known as the 'Fajujonu ruling' allowed migrant parents of children born in Ireland to remain in Ireland to provide them with 'company and protection'. This meant that asylum seekers could apply for residency as opposed to refugee status on this basis and, as Garner (2007) suggests, many asylum seekers were advised to do this because of the length of time it took to process asylum-seeking applications. In 2003 the Minister for Justice, Equality and Law Reform challenged the 'Fanjujonu ruling' in the case of two families of Czech, Roma and Nigerian origin who were to be deported. This time the Supreme Court held that 'non-national' parents no longer had a case to reside in Ireland to bring up their child; the State's right to deport took precedence. In February 2003, the Minister decided to retroactively abolish the process whereby migrant parents could apply to remain in Ireland on the grounds of having a child citizen (Lentin, 2005). Every case before that date was to be decided individually. In July 2005 the Minister reversed this decision and allowed parents of Irish-born children before 1 January 2005 to apply for leave to remain,[9] possibly due to the costs involved in potential court cases.

More far-reaching changes were instigated by the Minister for Justice, Equality and Law Reform in 2004. Irish citizenship was largely based on *jus soli* or soil-based rules, meaning that anyone born on Irish soil had automatic entitlement to Irish citizenship. The Minister claimed that this was unsatisfactory in a number of ways, principally because migrants, specifically women in the late stages of pregnancy were coming to Ireland as 'baby tourists' to take advantage of the system. Furthermore, the Minister argued that citizenship was being too easily granted to people with no cultural or historical ties to the country. The Minister proposed that a residency requirement of three years be applied to non-national parents before their Irish-born child would become entitled to Irish citizenship. Though many of the Minister's claims were not adequately substantiated and very much open to question (Brandi, 2007; Garner, 2007), the proposal was accepted by 80 per cent of those who voted in the 2004 Citizenship Referendum. The Irish Nationality and Citizenship Act, 2004, was subsequently passed. With this Act there has been a move from 'unconditional to conditional *jus soli*' (Joppke, 2008, p. 8). This is part of a wider move 'not toward abandoning *jus soli* in total, but making it contingent on legal residence requirements of a parent' (ibid.), which is occurring in immigrant-receiving states.

From January 2005, therefore, in order to be entitled to Irish citizenship a person must have a parent who is one of the following:

(a) an Irish citizen or entitled to be an Irish citizen
(b) a British citizen
(c) a non-national entitled under the immigration laws of the UK to reside in the UK without any restriction on his/her period of residence

(d) a non-national who satisfies the 'reckonable residence' requirement
at the time of the child's birth. The reckonable residence period
usually amounts to at least three out of the four previous years.

The new rules strengthened the principle of citizenship by descent or the
principle of *jus sanguinis*, and as Garner (2005, p. 80) puts it, 'what the
change in Irish law does is convey the message that in order to be Irish it's
a very good idea to be Irish to start with.' Besides citizenship by birth on
Irish soil and citizenship by Irish descent, citizenship can also be acquired
through naturalisation and by marriage. Individuals may apply to the
Minister for Justice, Equality and Law Reform for a certificate of
naturalisation, which is granted at the Minister's discretion after criteria
based mainly on character and length of residence are satisfied. Until 2005
post-nuptial citizenship was granted by making a declaration. Now post-
nuptial citizenship may only be granted at the Minister's discretion.
Therefore, neither of these avenues to citizenship are automatic rights, and
criteria for applying, especially in the case of citizenship through marriage,
have become more restrictive.

In addition, as Lentin (2005), Lentin and McVeigh (2006), Fanning
(2007a) and Garner (2007) point out, moves such as the Citizenship
Referendum and Citizenship Act have racialised particular immigrant
groups. Far from the sentiment behind the 1951 Convention, asylum seekers
as a whole have been ascribed particularly negative cultural traits, such as
taking advantage of the welfare system and 'abusing' Irish citizenship laws.
The primary thrust of policy has become deterrence not asylum.

The effects of this racialisation is borne out in studies on racism and
discrimination in Ireland, where the most negative attitudes are harboured
against asylum seekers (McGinnity et al., 2006), in common with Travellers,
another group that experiences high levels of racism (Citizen Traveller,
2000), as discussed in section two below.

Immigration and integration

While the discussion of immigration has so far concentrated on issues of
differential rights, deterrence and discrimination, the concept of integration
and the development of integration policy has also become a notable element
of state activity in relation to immigration since the late 1990s. There are,
however, many problems with how integration policy has evolved. At the
broadest level, several authors (Boucher, 2008; Fanning, 2002, 2007a;
Feldman, 2008; Mac Éinrí, 2007) have pointed out the stark contradiction
of a state which, on the one hand, expresses a desire for integration,
cohesion, and anti-racism in relation to immigrant and new ethnic groups,
and, on the other, categorises, discriminates, racialises, excludes and
impoverishes these groups to varying degrees. If integration as a process is

defined as flowing 'from the totality of policies and practices that allow societies to close the gap between the rights, status and opportunities of natives and immigrants and their descendants' (OECD, 2007, p. 13 in Feldman, 2008, pp. 1–2), then it is clear that, in practice, policy in Ireland has in many instances widened the gap and reduced the potential for integration. In addition, integration is quite a vague concept and models of integration can vary. The Irish model, for example, seems to rest on the concept of interculturalism, while little mention is made of equality, social justice or social rights.

The idea of integration policy materialised with the publication of *Integration: a two way process* (Department of Justice, Equality and Law Reform, 1999). The report defined integration as 'the ability to participate to the extent that a person needs and wishes in all of the major components of society, without having to relinquish his or her own cultural identity' (ibid., p. 9). Reflecting immigration trends of the late 1990s, the policy only applied to refugees and people granted leave to remain and did not include asylum seekers or migrant workers. The exclusion of asylum seekers from any form of integration policy has continued. The report made four broad recommendations, including the need to identify an organisational structure for coordinating and implementing integration policy, to raise public awareness, to make mainstream services more accessible and to conduct research. Subsequently the RIA, established in 2001, became the organisation responsible for the integration of refugees. Its activities are still broadly influenced by the 1999 report in that it clearly makes a distinction between asylum seekers and refugees in terms of restricting its integration responsibilities to the latter group.

In 2005 the government produced a *National Action Plan against Racism* (NPAR) (Department of Justice, Equality and Law Reform, 2005b). This plan, running between 2005 and 2008, adopted a more comprehensive approach to integration and connected it more clearly to anti-racist and intercultural policies. However, for the most part, policies are still targeted at particular groups, and this time Travellers and migrants (meaning primarily migrant workers) are included as well as refugees. The idea of integration as a two-way process was again articulated and the plan mentioned the obligation of both cultural and ethnic minorities and the state to create a more inclusive society and intercultural society.

The plan is underpinned by 'an intercultural framework' which is based on protection (against racism); inclusion (economic inclusion and equality of opportunity); provision (accommodation of diversity in service provision); recognition (diversity awareness); and participation (full participation in Irish society). The plan contained relatively detailed consideration objectives, implementation measures and anticipated outcomes under these four elements over the duration of the plan. However, it did not consider the differential rights and entitlements of migrant groups which cause barriers to intercultural integration, or, as Fanning (2007b, p. 237) puts it, create state-sanctioned 'internal borders' in Irish society. Therefore, contrary to the anti-racist sentiment of the plan, Fanning (2007a) points out the ways in which differential rights contribute to both structural and institutional racism. Structural racism occurs through the exclusion of non-citizen groups such as asylum seekers from social services and anti-racist initiatives. Accommodation of diversity in service provision, therefore, means little if access to a service is denied. Institutional racism, which is only briefly acknowledged in the NPAR, contributes to a situation where unequal access to social services and unequal outcomes prevail for ethnic minority citizens despite formal entitlement to services and inclusion in policy initiatives such as anti-poverty and anti-racism policies.

In 2007 the notion of integration gained greater attention with the appointment of a Minister of State for Integration and the creation of an Office of the Minister for Integration (OMI). In 2008 the OMI published *Migration Nation Statement on Integration Strategy and Diversity Management* (OMI, 2008). The document outlined a number of principles and future actions on integration and diversity. It states that 'the key challenge facing both government and Irish society is the imperative to integrate people of much different culture, ethnicity, language and religion so that they become the new Irish citizens of the 21st century' (ibid. p. 8). With that the statement outlines the need to **mainstream** integration policy so that it goes beyond **targeted initiatives** for particular groups, and in that regard an intercultural approach to core social services is highlighted. The statement seems particularly conscious of the need to avoid the risk of creating 'parallel societies, communities and urban ghettoes' (ibid., p. 10) and the need to bypass the negative

> **Mainstreaming** refers to bringing a particular issue or concept into the generally recognised and accepted way of thinking about and doing things. In policy terms, it means integrating, for example, gender-related, intercultural, socially inclusive and LGB perspectives into the design, implementation and evaluation of policy.

> **Targeting**, in tandem with mainstreaming, refers to the design and delivery of specific services for a particular minority, for example, Traveller-specific healthcare services.

experiences other European countries have had in relation to the marginalisation of second- and third-generation ethnic minority communities. In this regard the statement endorses the proposal in the Immigration and Residence Protection Bill, 2008, to introduce a language requirement for those applying for long-term residence and proposes that it also be required for those applying for citizenship. This follows the shift towards a 'civic integration' (Joppke, 2008) approach now being adopted at EU level and by other European countries. However, others interpret this as a weakening of integration as a two-way process and the emergence of 'neo-assimilationism' (Shierup et al., 2006, p. 47, in Boucher, 2008, p. 5).

While awareness of the importance of mainstreaming integration policy is significant, the traits of previous policies remain. The lack of recognition of the effects of a differential approach to rights and the issues of structural and institutional racism continues. In addition, the vision of new Irish citizens seems biased towards skilled migrants and the pursuit of 'Immigration Laws that control and facilitate access to Ireland for skilled migrants with a contribution to make' (OMI, 2008, p. 9). These groups are more likely to succeed economically and integrate into Irish society in their own right (Boucher, 2008). For other immigrant groups, the risk of segregation and 'parallel societies' feared in the statement remains. For example, issues of segregation have begun to emerge in the education sector as discussed in Chapter 9. In addition, the trend, noted across other European countries in Chapter 10, for migrants to cluster in areas where relatively low-cost private rented accommodation is available, is at risk of being replicated in the Irish context in a way that 'may exacerbate existing spatial concentrations of disadvantage' (NCCRI, 2008, p. 11). Furthermore, 'non-nationals' as a whole are at a substantially higher risk of poverty than Irish nationals. In 2006, for example, Irish nationals had an 'at risk of poverty' rate of 16.6 per cent, while the rate for 'non-nationals' was 23.5 per cent (CSO, 2007b). The impact of a two-tier labour migration policy together with an approach to social policy which differentiates and discriminates between various migrant groups ultimately risks creating a situation of long-term ethnic minority disadvantage which overpowers integration policies which do not adequately address these issues.

SECTION 2: TRAVELLERS AND IRISH SOCIAL POLICY

Travellers and ethnicity

Travellers are a minority ethnic group who occupy an unequal position in Irish society. Their status as Irish citizens is ascribed at birth, yet their realisation of citizenship rights has been for the most part denied. As a result:

Travellers fare poorly on every indicator used to measure disadvantage: unemployment, poverty, social exclusion, health status, infant mortality, life expectancy, illiteracy, education and training levels, access to decision making and political representation, gender equality, access to credit, accommodation and living conditions. (O'Connell, 2002, p. 49)

The issue of Travellers' position in Irish society and their access to social rights is contested. Much rests on whether Travellers are recognised as an ethnic group commanding rights and respect on the basis of their ethnic identity, or whether they form a sub-culture of poverty who should be absorbed back into mainstream, settled, Irish monocultural society where they can avail of rights and services in the same way as the majority population. The perception of Travellers as a sub-culture of poverty suggests that their problems are primarily economic ones, to be addressed by absorption back into mainstream society and mainstream social policy. For Travellers, however, the issue is primarily one of culture and identity, and the denial of ethnic identity generates anti-Traveller racism which has material effects such as poverty and health inequality. As Pavee Point (2006, p. 1) puts it:

A key issue in shaping social policy and practice has been the way in which Travellers' identity is conceptualised: who the Travellers are and what their place is in Irish society, in the eyes of policy makers, service providers and the majority population; and how Travellers themselves assert their identity.

The concept of ethnicity is itself complex and contested (Ratcliffe, 2004) and the notion of Travellers as an ethnic group has also generated debate (Equality Authority, 2006; McCann et al., 1994; McVeigh, 2007). The concept of ethnicity first came into use during the 1950s and replaced the flawed assumption that distinct racial groups exist. However, theories about what constitutes ethnicity change over time and while, on the one hand, ethnicity and ethnic group formation have an elusive quality, on the other hand, there is also a problem with attributing essential qualities to ethnic groups that 'freeze' them over time, and make it difficult to see issues in common; 'difference' becomes everything (Ratcliffe, 2004).

The core aspect of ethnicity is that it 'is a self-conscious and claimed identity' (Platt, 2008, p. 370); in other words, it is based on how an ethnic group understands itself, not on characteristics attributed to it by others. Cornell and Hartman (1998, p. 19) suggest that ethnic groups are based on three kinds of claims: 'a claim to kinship, broadly defined; a claim to a common history of some sort; and a claim that certain symbols capture the core of the group's identity'. Claims about common ancestry need not be founded in fact, and there are, for example, various accounts of the historical origins of Irish Travellers. Furthermore, cultural claims do not have to be premised on actual practice. Travellers, for example, identify with a culture of nomadism, but not all Travellers are necessarily nomadic.

According to McDonagh (2000), Travellers see themselves as an ethnic group based on the grounds that they are biologically self-perpetuating, share fundamental cultural values, make up a field of communication and interaction, have a membership that defines itself and is defined by others, and are subject to oppression. The notion of oppression is important for understanding Travellers' unequal position in Irish society and in relation to social policy and social rights. They are a minority, not just numerically (the 2006 Census counted 22,435 Travellers), but also in terms of power relations in Irish society. This is expressed through anti-Traveller prejudice or anti-Traveller racism. Travellers as a group are racialised in the sense that they are associated with a raft of negative traits and considered inferior to the majority settled population.

Travellers in Irish society and Irish social policy prior to the 1960s

Nomadism was the norm rather than the exception for many groups of people in pre-modern Ireland. Helleiner (2000, p. 31) notes, for example, that 'learned classes such as poets, bards, and doctors, as well as lower status groups such as jesters, gamblers, musicians, merchants and craftsmen' were all mobile by occupation. Furthermore, pastoralism rather than agriculture was the norm in how land was used. This again normalised mobility. Helleiner suggests that this mobility, interpreted as 'uncivilised' behaviour, was initially suppressed by 'English colonial discourse and practice from the second half of the sixteenth century' (ibid.). Colonial discourse, therefore, associated settlement with civility. Accordingly, early houses of industry, as discussed in Chapter 1, were designed to punish various groups of vagrants, and Travellers would not have been distinguished from the larger mass of the wandering poor under colonial rule (Hayes, 2006).

Moving forward to the late nineteenth and early twentieth century, nomadism was again discouraged and marginalised, but this time, as MacLaughlin argues, from a nationalist and nation-building perspective. 'Nomadism and "tinkers" in Ireland were regularly perceived as a threat to national progress by propertied sectors in Irish society ... Travellers, like Gypsies in mainland Europe, were considered inferior to the propertied classes because they literally had no territorial stake in the nation-state' (MacLaughlin, 1999, p. 137). MacLaughlin suggests therefore that the nation state in the early decades of independence was constructed out of a series of 'exclusions and dominations, a place where the patriarchal values of the rural bourgeoisie occupied a pride of place, a place where Travellers were scarcely considered as citizens of the state' (ibid., p. 138).

Thus, Travellers were excluded from the very gradual expansion of social provision. Their lack of fixed abode precluded them from locally administered services, such as local authority housing and Home Assistance. Lack of attendance at school was not considered a problem and compulsory attendance was not enforced when it came to Traveller children. Their existence was occasionally debated in terms of issues such as the threat it posed to rural class relations (Helleiner, 2000), and to public health (Breathnach, 2006), but for the most part concerns were not acted upon. Travellers' exclusion from Irish society and their lack of access to social services, such as they existed, were not seen as problems to be solved.

For the most part, Travellers in need relied on charitable assistance from voluntary organisations such as the St Vincent de Paul and the Legion of Mary (Breathnach, 2006). In many respects lack of official concern about Travellers worked to their advantage; they occupied a niche position and relations with others were not overly negative. Breathnach (ibid.), for example, suggests that the growth of state intervention and regulation of society and social policy had the effect of more clearly demarcating Travellers as a non-conforming minority, while McVeigh (2008, p. 93) suggests that 'arguably for ethnic nomads, being neglected by the state is often far less oppressive than being "protected" or "respected" by it'. The deterioration of relationships between Travellers and the rest of the population and an increase in anti-Traveller racism can be traced back to the early 1970s when state intervention grew (Mac Gréil, 1977).

Box 12.2 Key legislative and policy developments with regard to Travellers

1963 Commission on Itinerancy
1983 Travelling People Review Body
1995 Report of the Task Force on the Travelling Community
1996 National Strategy for Traveller Accommodation
1998 Housing (Traveller Accommodation) Act
2002 Traveller Health Strategy 2002–2005
2002 Housing (Miscellaneous Provisions) Act
2006 Report and Recommendations for a Traveller Education Strategy

---

1963 Commission on Itinerancy

Why did the state begin to turn its attention towards Travellers in the 1960s? The 'problem of Travellers' had been occasionally raised in the Dáil over previous decades, and measures were sought to control their nomadism, but action targeting Travellers never transpired as a result. Breathnach (2006) notes that by the 1950s complaints about issues such as trespass and wandering horses, and the siting of campsites increasingly came from urban TDs. This was the context in which the Taoiseach Sean Lemass decided in 1960 to establish a Commission on Itinerancy. This commission, which reported in 1963, 'marked the beginning of an explicit settlement policy' (McVeigh, 2008, p. 94).

The commission clearly reflected the prevailing view of the time that Travellers were a social problem, to be solved by absorption into the rest of the population to live 'a better way of life'. This absorption was possible because the commission was of the view that there was nothing distinctive about them as a group, and specifically that they were not a distinct ethnic group.

This view, as Hayes points out (2006, p. 143), is connected to the construct or myth of Traveller identity as '"falling out" of Irish society as a consequence of colonial expansion and colonial violence in Ireland', which became the dominant interpretation of Travellers' origins and position from the 1960s onwards. If Travellers are assumed to have 'dropped out' then re-assimilation becomes the obvious policy response and a 'righting of the past wrongs perpetrated on fellow Irish citizens by colonial oppressors' (ibid., p. 144).

Self-reform, rehabilitation and settling down was the ultimate vision of the commission: 'itinerants, by an improvement in their behaviour pattern and therefore in their public image and by settling in a district would come to be accepted more quickly by the settled community' (Commission on Itinerancy, 1963, p. 103). The crux of the commission's recommendations rested on permanent settlement, whether in houses supplied by local authorities or in official campsites. This would become the foundation for availing of the same opportunities as settled people, including social services and conventional employment. In other words, as Fanning (2002, p. 153) puts it, 'Travellers were not to have equal rights to welfare unless they first ceased to be Travellers. The price of social citizenship, within the assimilation logic of the social policies which emerged to address the "problem of itinerancy" included the surrendering of identity and difference.'

In the event, the assimilationist thrust of the commission's recommendations failed. There were two key problems. Settled people remained hostile and resistant to Travellers regardless of whether they were settled or nomadic. Consequently, local provision of services proved politically unfeasible. Secondly, the majority of Travellers did not want to be permanently settled. Voluntary organisations continued to be the main providers of services to the Travelling community. The commission recommended the local voluntary committees who would 'bridge the gap' (Commission on Itinerancy, 1963, p. 107) between Travellers and their becoming accustomed to a settled way of life. Following this, the Itinerant Settlement Committee was formed in 1965. According to Ní Shuinéar (1998, p. 8), it 'had a great deal to show for its efforts: from a starting point of zero in the mid sixties, Traveller-specific provision in 1982 included forty-one social workers, thirty preschool classes, seventy "special" (primary) classes, four "special" schools, and two residential care units'. However, provision was primarily charitable rather than rights-based, with an emphasis on 'special' or segregated provision.

1983 Travelling People Review Body

This was the second official review of Travellers in Ireland. The main issue was reframed: Travellers were no longer the problem requiring a solution, the key issue was the social problems or social deprivation Travellers experienced. In addition, the review seemed to have moved on from a policy of assimilation: 'in light of experience and current knowledge the concept of absorption is unacceptable ... it is better to think in terms of integration' (Travelling People Review Body, 1983, p. 6). However, it is clear from the report that those who remained nomadic were understood as a group who were choosing not to conform to the settled norms on which social services were delivered and were thus putting themselves at a disadvantage. Again, social citizenship and social rights were only accessible if Travellers shed their difference and became the same as the settled population. The choice to be nomadic was considered an inferior one. Therefore, while the report offered a definition of Travellers which recognised their cultural distinctiveness, this did not have any bearing on the nature of social services and their accessibility to diverse groups of people. For example, in terms of accommodation, the report's recommendation was for the provision of 'a house for all Traveller families who desire to be housed. Travellers who are not so accommodated cannot hope to receive an adequate education. Nor can they avail satisfactorily of services such as health and welfare which are of such significance in the life of all people' (ibid., p. 15).

Subsequent legislative developments for Travellers include the Housing Act, 1988, which was the first piece of legislation to specifically make reference to Travellers (Crowley, 2005). This was in the context of Local Authority responsibility for providing halting sites. In 1989, the Prohibition of Incitement to Hatred Act included 'membership of the Travelling community' as a ground on which incitement to hatred is prohibited, but only after Traveller groups campaigned for inclusion in the legislation (McVeigh, 2007). However, this legislation has been largely symbolic for the groups mentioned in the Act. The grounds for prosecution have proven very ineffective, particularly in relation to proof of intent. While the government promised a review of the legislation in 2000 no review has been completed.

More broadly, as Ní Shuinéar notes (1998, p. 14), 'sea changes took place between the 1983 publication of the Review Body Report and the setting up of the Task Force in 1993.' These changes can largely be attributed to the rise of the Traveller movement or the politicisation of Travellers (Breathnach, 2006; McVeigh, 2008). In particular, the Irish Traveller Movement and Pavee Point have been significant in affording Travellers their own voice and facilitating participation in policymaking processes, such as the 1995 Task Force and subsequent policy developments.

1995 Report of the Task Force on the Travelling Community

This report seemed to represent a definite move forward in terms of understanding Traveller issues. Here, for the first time, the issue of discrimination was given some attention. The report stated, for example, that:

> The 'Settled' community will have to accept that their rejection of Travellers is counter-productive and that incidents of social exclusion and discrimination against the Traveller community, such as the refusal of service in hotels, public houses and other establishments and the segregation of Travellers in the provision of facilities, must end. (Task Force on the Travelling Community, 1995, p. 58)

In addition, the report linked discrimination to inequalities experienced by Travellers – 'the recognition of the importance of concepts of culture, ethnicity, racism and discrimination has entered in the debate about the situation of Travellers. This has resulted in a redefinition of the Traveller situation in terms of cultural rights as opposed to simply being a poverty issue' (ibid., p. 63). However, the main report did not go so far as to recognise the claims of Travellers as a specific ethnic group and this has remained the case at official state level. Nevertheless, the report envisioned the development of an intercultural framework for the future development of social services in relation to Travellers.

Yet, an addendum to the main report signed by four members of the Task Force reflected views that remained much closer to the thrust of the 1963 and 1983 reports. These members felt it was still inevitable that Travellers would be integrated into the settled community over time and that a nomadic lifestyle is unsustainable. In this regard, the nomadic lifestyle was represented as 'inordinately expensive on the taxpaying community to maintain for the questionable benefit of a small section of the population' (ibid., p. 289).

The main report, however, took a different view. The report was quite comprehensive in how it addressed policy and issues concerning Travellers. It dealt with relationships between Travellers and the settled community, culture, discrimination, accommodation, health, education and training,

Traveller economy, Traveller women, and disability. Across the range of issues, the Task Force emphasised the need to respect Traveller culture. The bulk of the Task Force recommendations concerned education. The Task Force outlined a number of principles and objectives, including equality of access, acknowledgement of cultural diversity, and the principle of integration. Accommodation was also at the core of the report. The Task Force did not express a preference for particular forms of accommodation, but recommended further provision of both standard housing and Traveller-specific accommodation as indicated by Traveller preferences. Regarding relationships between Travellers and the settled community, the Task Force recommended action on increasing awareness and improving relationships between settled and Traveller community. Out of this came the Citizen Traveller campaign run by Traveller organisations with the aim of generating recognition and respect for Travellers in Irish society.

Policy and problems since the 1995 Task Force on the Travelling Community

For the most part the report was treated positively. McVeigh (2008, p. 91), for example, speaks of it as the highpoint of interculturalism which pointed to a future 'of gentle if limited reformism and reform in state policy towards Travellers'. This was bolstered by the passing into law of the Employment Equality Act in 1998 and the Equal Status Act in 2000. Both of these pieces of legislation included being a member of the Travelling community as a ground for recognising discrimination, but as a separate category to the race ground. The Equal Status Act defined the Travelling Community as follows:

> 'Travelling Community' means the community of people who are commonly called Travellers and who are identified (both by themselves and others) as people with a shared history, culture and traditions including, historically, a nomadic way of life on the island of Ireland. (Section 2, Equal Status Act, 2000)

This definition contains elements of ethnic identification yet, officially, Travellers are not recognised as such by the Irish state, with the government being until recently 'formally agnostic' on this issue, as the Equality Authority (2006, p. 36) puts it. However, more recently, the governmental stance has changed to one of denial (McVeigh, 2007, 2008), an issue returned to later in this section. A monitoring committee established to periodically examine progress on the Task Force recommendations reported in 2000 and 2005, and both times was generally quite pessimistic about improvements made since the Task Force report. In 2000 it observed that 'five years after the publication of the Task Force report there is lack of real improvement on the ground' (Committee to Monitor and Co-ordinate the Implementation of the Recommendations of the Task Force on the Traveller Community, 2000, p. 8), while in 2005 it stated that:

> The bottom line is that despite the allocation of considerable financial and staff resources and some progress being achieved, Travellers continue to have lower life expectancy, lower education qualifications and, in may cases, unacceptable accommodation. Traveller culture is under threat, both from lack of recognition by the settled community, but also from internal changes within the community. (Committee to Monitor and Co-ordinate the Implementation of the Recommendations of the Task Force on the Traveller Community, 2005, p. 6)

Here we look briefly at some of the limited progress and continuing problems with regard to accommodation, education and healthcare for Travellers since the 1995 Task Force report.

Accommodation

With regard to accommodation, a National Strategy for Traveller accommodation was published in 1996 and this was followed by the Housing (Traveller Accommodation) Act in 1998. The purpose of the Act was to provide a legislative framework within which Traveller accommodation could be provided. The Act requires local authorities to produce five-year programmes on meeting existing and projecting future Traveller accommodation needs. The legislation also provided for the creation of the National Traveller Accommodation Consultative Committee on a statutory basis and for the creation of Traveller accommodation consultative committees within local authorities. Traveller accommodation includes standard houses and accommodation which is Traveller-specific, that is, group housing schemes, halting sites and temporary sites. However, the provision of Traveller accommodation remains a problem. Though the Act put greater responsibility on Local Authorities and involved more direct Traveller participation, outcomes have not been satisfactory.

Progress has been slow, and significant but declining numbers of Travellers still live on the side of the road. Many of the halting sites lack adequate amenities or are located in inappropriate places which are dangerous and unhealthy. Norris and Winston (2005) note a paradox in how accommodation provision has been unfolding. There has been a trend towards more assimilationist forms of provision since the 1995 Task Force, which at a conceptual level made an effort to recognise the cultural specificity of Travellers' needs and rights. A greater proportion of Traveller-specific accommodation was actually provided from the 1960s to the 1980s when, at an official level, assimilationist thinking was much stronger. This trend is continuing. The number of Traveller families housed in standard local authority housing continues to grow and has risen from 2,395 families (44 per cent) in 2002 to 3,071 (51 per cent) in 2007. By contrast, the number of families in Local Authority halting sites and on unauthorised sites is declining. Travellers on unauthorised sites, such as on the roadside, have fallen from 939 families (17 per cent) in 2002 to 594 families (10 per cent) in 2007 (Department of Environment, Heritage and Local Government, 2008b).

However, for the Traveller families who continue to live at unauthorised sites their presence was criminalised under the introduction of the Housing (Miscellaneous Provisions) Act, 2002, which made trespass illegal. This legislation directly impacted on Travellers and was criticised by a number of Traveller groups for being racist. The Citizen Traveller campaign, for example, ran an advertisement against the Act, describing it as 'racist and unworkable' (The Traveller, 2002, p. 11 in McVeigh, 2008, p. 95) and was 'wound up' (ibid.) soon after for its efforts.

Education

With regard to education, the general move has been to end segregated education, whether in schools catering for Travellers only or in special classes in mainstream schools. At the same time, mainstream education, in theory at least, is to become much more intercultural so that cultural diversity and all ethnic groups are respected. The 1995 White Paper on Education set participation targets for Traveller children. These included a target of 100 per cent completion rate at primary level to be reached within five years, a target of a 100 per cent completion rate at Junior Certificate level, and a 50 per cent completion rate at senior cycle to be reached within 10 years. In 2002, *Guidelines on Traveller Education in Primary Schools* and *Guidelines on Traveller Education in Second-level Schools* were published. Both emphasise an intercultural approach to education and the full integration of Traveller children in mainstream schooling. However, improvements and progress have been limited. Travellers do not have equality of opportunity in the Irish education system; in various ways they continue to experience inequality of access, participation and outcome.

Full participation at primary level was more or less achieved by the mid-2000s and segregated classes in primary schools were fully phased out by 2004; however, outcomes regarding literacy and numeracy are poor. At second level, while progression rates from primary level have increased, retention and attainment remain problems, and the 1995 targets have not been met, although participation has been gradually increasing. Eleven years after the Report of the Task Force on the Travelling Community (1995), the targets with regard to second level still remain recommendations in the Report and Recommendations for a Traveller Education Strategy

(Department of Education and Science, 2006a). Issues of segregation and discrimination are still very real (Lodge and Lynch, 2004; see also Chapter 9). For example, the bulk of Equality Authority casework regarding discrimination in education involves discrimination against Travellers. This includes issues such as being refused enrolment, being withdrawn from core subjects, being given art work while other students study core subjects and being harassed by other pupils on the grounds of being a Traveller (Department of Education and Science, 2006b).

Despite several reports and the issue of guidelines, intercultural education is still not embedded in the education system. Teacher training in interculturalism is limited; for example, modules on interculturalism, equality and diversity are not compulsory in teacher training. Outside of the primary and post-primary system, education remains segregated for Travellers at pre-school level and for Travellers who leave school early. Forty-six Traveller pre-schools and over 30 Senior Traveller Training Centres exist. Senior Traveller Training Centres cater for Travellers from the age of 15 onwards and many leave post-primary school early to attend a Training Centre. The Report and Recommendations for a Traveller Education Strategy (Department of Education and Science, 2006a) recommended that this provision be integrated into mainstream education structures so that education services across the board are inclusive of all children. Pavee Point (2006) has endorsed this recommendation. However, a Traveller Education Strategy has yet to be published and no move has been made to implement this recommendation. As for third-level education, participation by Travellers is very limited; in 2004, for example, it was estimated that 28 Travellers were enrolled in higher education (Department of Education and Science, 2006a). Citing a lack of data, targets were not set to increase Traveller participation (along with other ethnic minority groups) at third level in the National Action Plan for Equity of Access to Higher Education (National Office for Equity of Access to Higher Education, 2008).

Health

Travellers bear the brunt of severe health inequality. Two studies carried out on the health status of Travellers in the late 1980s (Barry and Daly, 1988; Barry et al. 1989) found stark health inequalities among Travellers compared to the rest of the population. Principally, these related to stillbirths, which were twice the national rate, a rate of infant mortality which was three times the national rate, and life expectancy levels ten and twelve years below settled men and women, respectively. In terms of policy developments since the Task Force report, a Traveller Health Advisory Committee was established in 1998 which includes representatives from the Department of Health and Children, Traveller organisations and the HSE. At regional level, Traveller health units have been set up. In the revised NAPS 2002 specific targets in relation to Traveller health status were adopted. These involved reducing the life expectancy gap between Travellers and settled people by at least 10 per cent by 2007. The advisory group had input into the publication of *Traveller Health: A National Strategy 2002–2005*. The strategy focused on the need to have both a mainstreaming and targeted approach when dealing with Traveller health issues. The targeted approach has primarily involved a Traveller-specific model of primary healthcare, with a high degree of participation from Travellers, including training Traveller women as primary care workers for their community. As regards the provision of mainstream health services, mainstreaming, as Fay (2001, p. 109) notes, 'does not mean integration into existing services, it means that services change so that they are relevant and accessible to both Travellers and other minority ethnic groups, as well as to the majority population. It means that we have ethnic pluralism in health where health provision is intercultural.' In 2007 the HSE published a *National Intercultural Health Strategy 2007–2012* (HSE, 2007c). This contains recommendations for the further development of an intercultural approach to health policy design, access and delivery, as it pertains to Travellers, other minority ethnic groups, and immigrants.

However, Traveller utilisation of health services continues to be an issue, especially where mainstream services lack an intercultural ethos and poor relationships with health professionals, such as GPs and midwives, hamper access and affect the quality of care Travellers receive (Hodgins et al., 2006; Reid and Taylor, 2007). The problem of health inequalities among Travellers is also hampered by a lack of data. Despite frequent recommendations for systematic data collection with respect to Traveller health, is was not until 2007 that an all-Ireland Traveller health study got underway, which represents the first nationwide survey of Traveller health since the late 1980s. In the meantime, other studies have highlighted particular health issues among the Travelling community, such as depression, particularly among Traveller women (National Traveller Women's Forum and Pavee Point, 2002), and suicide, particularly among young Travellers (Tallaght Travellers' Youth Service/NEXUS, 2006). Travellers continue to have a significantly shorter life expectancy compared to the rest of the population. This is indicated by findings from the 2006 Census, which show that 2.6 per cent of the Traveller community were 65 years or over compared to 11 per cent of the total population.

In short, across the social services reviewed here and in other policy areas such as equality and anti-racism policy, the situation may be summarised, as McVeigh (2008, p. 99) puts it, as 'reformism without much reform'. The range of new policies, consultative structures and organisations pertaining to Travellers significantly outweighs tangible outcomes for Travellers in terms of services. In addition, there is a disconnection between policy discourse on issues such as interculturalism and anti-racism and the state of relationships between Travellers and settled people. As Breathnach (2006, pp. 146–7) notes, 'the daily relationship between Travellers and settled people remains unaffected by wider debates about cultural difference and tolerance. While Travellers now have a political voice, settled people have become more adamant in their refusal to countenance their rights as citizens.' This disconnection does not just occur between Travellers and settled people, the state, as McVeigh (2007, 2008) suggests, has become more trenchant in its anti-Travellerism in recent years, the culmination of which is evident in its explicit refusal to recognise Travellers as an ethnic minority in its periodic reports to the UN Committee on the Elimination of Racial Discrimination, despite being called upon by the Committee to do so.[10] This 'ethnicity in denial', as McVeigh (2008) calls it, has far-reaching consequences, because it obviates the grounds for recognising anti-Traveller racism and for respecting Travellers ont he basis of their cultural difference.

If this is the case, then it would appear that little progressive or deep-seated change has occurred since the state first turned its attention to Travellers in the 1960s.

SECTION 3: LESBIANS, GAYS AND BISEXUALS AND IRISH SOCIAL POLICY

Heterosexism, heteronormativity and sexual citizenship

The heterosexual assumptions underpinning social policy are rarely highlighted. Issues relating to sexuality in Irish society have been dominated in recent decades by issues relating to abortion, divorce and contraception (see Chapter 3), all debated within an implicit heterosexual framework. Until the 1990s, homosexuality and issues of discrimination and rights in relation to the LGB community garnered less attention. This is reflective of social policy and sexuality generally; sexuality is usually ignored in policy analysis (Carabine, 1998) and 'sexuality tends to make an appearance when it is perceived as a problem – as in the case of homosexuality, lone motherhood, teenage pregnancy, under-age sex, prostitution, divorce, sexually transmitted infections (STIs) and sexual offences' (Carabine, 2004, p. 2). The problematisation of sexuality is built upon the construction of what is assumed to be normal sexuality. This privileges an ideal of heterosexual, monogamous, married relationships, which also becomes the privileged site of reproduction and childrearing. This assumption of normalcy is so pervasive that it goes without question. As Dunphy (2000, in ibid., p. 17) puts it, 'We inhale heterosexuality with the air we breathe.' Other expressions of sexuality and sexual relations are rendered invisible or are treated as deviant to varying degrees.

This position has been framed by the concepts of heterosexism and heteronormativity. Heterosexism is defined as 'the system by which heterosexuality is assumed to be the only acceptable and viable life option' (Blumenfeld and Raymond, 1993, p. 244 in Wilson, 2001, p. 121). Heterosexism results in discrimination against non-heterosexuals. This may be 'discrimination by neglect, omission and/or distortion, whereas often its more active partner – homophobia – is discrimination by intent and design' (Blumenfeld and Raymond, 1993, p. 245 in ibid.). Heterosexism, therefore, focuses on ways in which non-heterosexuals may be discriminated against in areas such as social security policy and family policy which is built upon heterosexual coupledom. Homophobia can be manifest in outright denial of rights, bullying, harassment and physical attacks.

However, it is important to focus not just on how non-heterosexuals are excluded and discriminated against, but also to critically interrogate the norms upon which heterosexuality and the heterosexual world is built. Work on the social construction of sexuality by historians and theorists such as Jeffrey Weeks, Michel Foucault and Ken Plummer demonstrates that norms associated with sexuality are not 'natural' and that deviancy is not 'sinful', but that normalcy and abnormalcy are both social constructs, created over time and tied into, and promoted by, the interests of religion and capitalism, and by states in nation-building exercises.

Adrienne Rich's (1980) concept of 'compulsory heterosexuality' and the concept of 'heteronormativity' coined by Warner (1991) illuminate the social construction of sexuality by critiquing heterosexuality as an institution or as an order. Instead of focusing on gay men and lesbians as the invisible minority groups, the overarching norm of heterosexuality, which implicates everyone, is questioned and challenged by queer politics. As Warner (1991, p. 6) puts it:

> Because the logic of the sexual order is so deeply embedded by now in an indescribably wide range of social institutions, and is embedded in the most standard accounts of the world, queer struggles aim not just at toleration or equal status but at challenging those institutions and accounts. The dawning realization that themes of homophobia and heterosexism may be read in almost any document of our culture means that we are only beginning to have an idea of how widespread those institutions and accounts are.

This implicates things that, on the surface, are not about sexuality. Warner provides the example of caring and, specifically, caring for older people, which he says 'does not initially seem to be an issue of sexuality. But a society that relegates care systematically to offspring and spouses leaves elderly lesbians and gays with a disproportionately high likelihood of neglect' (ibid., pp. 7–8).

More recently, sexuality has been discussed in the context of citizenship, and debates have emerged around the notions of sexual citizenship and sexual rights (Lister, 2002; Richardson, 2000a, b). However, the meaning of sexual citizenship and what constitutes sexual rights is open to debate and not easily defined. Regarding citizenship rights, Lister (2002) suggests that LGB people may be understood as 'sexual minorities' who are treated as second-class citizens or who have partial citizenship. Their access to various citizenship rights has been hampered because of the way sexuality determines the allocation of citizenship rights. Rights are therefore shaped by particular notions of sexuality as well as being racialised and gendered. Richardson (2000a) suggests that sexual rights may be understood in three forms: claims to rights centring on sexual practice, broadly involving the right to have sex; claims to rights centring on rights of self-definition and identity, for the right to be gay, to be recognised as such and not discriminated against for it; and claims to rights within social institutions, such as the validation of same-sex marriages. This partly mirrors the progress of gay and lesbian politics, from the decriminalisation of homosexuality and legalisation of same-sex activity, to identity politics and anti-discrimination legislation, through to demands for the right to be married and benefit from the rights and entitlements associated with marriage. These rights and entitlements relate to social security, pensions, taxation, inheritance, and, in relation to children (e.g. guardianship, adoption, fostering, fertility treatment), parenting. These rights are being realised to varying degrees in some countries, either through the legal recognition of same-sex marriage or some form of civil partnership.

However, these developments have provoked debate about what they mean for citizenship and heteronormativity and whether the basis on which these claims are made and met radically challenge heteronormativity or conservatively represent a form of assimilation into heterosexual norms and culture. These claims, as Richardson (2004) notes, tend to be made on the basis of sameness and of presenting the notion of the normal or 'good' lesbian/gay citizen who conforms to the notion of stable coupledom and who values family life. On the other hand, the move can also potentially be interpreted as transformative. In this view, claims for equal rights may have 'the potential for reimagining concepts of marriage, family and citizenship, as new forms of knowledge about intimate relationships and "families of choice" enter the mainstream' (ibid., p. 399). These issues remain open to question and may not be, as Richardson suggests, a question of either/or but of an uneven, complex process.

Lesbians, gay men and bisexuals in Irish society: from criminalisation to activism for equal rights

Sex between men was first criminalised in Ireland under 'An Act for the Punishment of the Vice of Buggery' in 1634. As part of the colonial project to civilise Ireland, one of the first individuals to receive the death penalty in Ireland under the Act was John Atherton, the Bishop of Waterford and Lismore, who actually campaigned to have the law implemented in Ireland (Lacey, 2008). In the 1861 Offences against the Person Act, punishment for buggery was altered to a prison sentence, lasting anywhere from 10 years to life imprisonment. In the 1885 Criminal Law Amendment Act the scope of illegal male homosexual activity was broadened from buggery to all sexual acts, referred to as 'gross indecency'.

In the early decades of independence these laws were mainly only applied in cases where minors were involved. However, homosexuality was cast as something foreign to Irish identity, with nationalist discourse displaying something of the same homophobia as colonialist discourse (Conrad, 2001). Hence, gays and lesbians were largely invisible in the construction of Irish citizenship. Sexual difference, like ethnic difference, was not acknowledged in the homogenous construction of nationhood and Irish identity. LGB people were, for the most part, invisible, with Crone (1995, p. 61), for example, describing lesbians (while never criminalised) as 'an underground minority, a subculture whose members have been unwilling or unable to court publicity, because to do so may have invited violence, rape or even death'.

The birth of the gay and lesbian movement in Ireland was part of a wider international movement, which had its roots in the Stonewall riots in New York in 1969. Stonewall refers to the Stonewall Inn, a transvestite bar in Greenwich, New York, which the police regularly raided. On 28 June 1969 people in the inn resisted and took their protest on to the streets. A movement for gay and lesbian liberation spread to other countries and the Irish Gay Rights Movement was founded in 1974. The lesbian movement became more formally organised after a conference in 1978, out of which Liberation for Irish Lesbians was formed (Rose, 1994). Gay and lesbian activism in Ireland also emerged in the context of the women's movement, although issues related to sexuality and sexual liberation were not at the core of Irish feminism at the time (Connolly and O'Toole, 2005).

> ## Box 12.3   Key legislative and policy developments with regard to lesbians, gays and bisexuals
>
> 1993 Criminal Law (Sexual Offences) Act, 1993
> 2002 Equality Authority – Implementing Equality for Lesbians, Gays and Bisexuals
> 2003 NESF – Equality Policies for Lesbian, Gay and Bisexual People
> 2006 Irish Human Rights Commission – The Rights of De Facto Couples
> 2006 Law Reform Commission – Rights and Duties of Cohabitants
> 2006 All-Party Oireachtas Committee on the Constitution – Tenth Progress Report: The Family
> 2006 Working Group on Domestic Partnership – Options Paper
> 2008 Heads of Civil Partnership Bill

A core element of the gay rights movement during the 1970s and 1980s was the push to decriminalise homosexuality, or to claim rights around sexual practice or sexual conduct. This formally began with the establishment of the Campaign for Homosexual Law Reform in 1976. This led to a case being taken by David Norris (with Mary Robinson as his Senior Counsel) to the High Court in 1977 in which criminalisation was legally challenged as unconstitutional, breaching his rights to bodily integrity, to privacy and to his equality before the law, freedom of expression and freedom of association. An unsuccessful outcome at the High Court led to an appeal to the Supreme Court, which decided 3:2 against his case. The majority were in agreement with the judgement of O'Higgins C. J. on the case:

(1) Homosexuality has always been condemned in Christian teaching as being morally wrong. It has equally been regarded by society for many centuries as an offence against nature and a very serious crime …

(4) Male homosexual conduct has resulted, in other countries, in the spread of all forms of venereal disease and this has now become a significant public health problem in England.

(5) Homosexual conduct can be inimical to marriage and is *per se* harmful to it as an institution.

(Norris v. Ireland, 1984, p. 63 in Flynn, 1997, p. 495)

This judgement demonstrated that Ireland in the 1980s still reflected the view that homosexuality was deviant, sinful and disruptive of what was taken as the natural order of marriage, or the heteronormative order.

David Norris took his case to the European Court of Human Rights where he was successful in 1988. This decision prompted a renewed wave of gay and lesbian activism to influence the legislative reform that would ensue in Ireland. An umbrella group, Gay and Lesbian Equality Network (GLEN), was set up and it was agreed that 'demands should be for equality in the criminal law and for anti-discrimination legislation' (Rose, 1994, p. 40), which, as Rose (ibid.) puts it, 'were bold and radical demands at a time when the Right seemed invincible'. Other groups acted in solidarity, including the Irish Council for Civil Liberties (ICCL), the trade union movement, and various women's, Traveller and disability groups (Flynn, 1997). Against them were conservative Catholic groups, principally Family Solidarity, which were opposed to decriminalisation of any sort. In the event, when homosexuality was finally decriminalised in the Criminal Law (Sexual Offences) Act, 1993, a favourable outcome was attained. This included a full repeal of existing legislation outlawing homosexuality and giving homosexuals an equal footing with heterosexuals in relation to sexual rights such as age of consent and privacy codes, all of which were framed in the language of needing 'to recognise, respect and value difference' (Minister for Justice, 1993, in Rose, 1994, p. 57).

Since that time LGB groups and individuals have gained greater visibility in Irish society and have made gains in terms of equal treatment in various pieces of legislation. Having gained equal rights to sexual practice, the focus turned more firmly towards anti-discrimination and equal treatment in relation to identity or sexual orientation. In 1995, GLEN published a survey on discrimination and its impact on poverty and exclusion among the gay and lesbian community. It showed that fear of discrimination in particular was high in relation to, for example, work and accessing services. In addition, 41 per cent of respondents reported being threatened by violence because they were assumed to be gay or lesbian (GLEN/NEXUS, 1995). The first piece of legislation to specifically refer to sexual orientation preceded the transformative events of 1993, namely the 1989 Prohibition of Incitement to Hatred Act. However, in common with the Travelling community, the inclusion of sexual orientation was only achieved after action on the issue. Fuller recognition of sexual orientation in relation to discrimination appeared in the Employment Equality Act, 1998, and Equal Status Act, 2000, where sexual orientation, interpreted as 'heterosexual, homosexual or bisexual orientation' is included as a ground on which discrimination is prohibited. Other forms of recognition of equal treatment included the Health Insurance Act, 1994, which prohibits loading premiums on the grounds of sexual orientation.

In the early 2000s, both the Equality Authority and NESF published reports focusing on equality issues for LGB people. Both reports focused on the need for greater attention to LGB needs in mainstream services and greater attention to the impact of decisions made in government departments and agencies on LGB people. The Equality Authority, for example, drew attention to the need to 'mainstream LGB people's situation, experience and identity into the design, delivery and implementation of social policy and services' (Equality Authority, 2002, p. 4). This is to be achieved by routine equality proofing of decisions for their impact on LGB people in so far as legislation extends equal treatment to the LGB community. The NESF report focused on the barriers and challenges to the mainstreaming equality focus in the Equality Authority report. It noted, for example, 'the tendency for sexual orientation to be either glossed over or overlooked in the proofing process' (NESF, 2003, p. 3), and the problem of lack of data for effective monitoring. It also drew attention to economic disadvantage in the LGB community and recommended direct targeting of these groups in anti-poverty and social inclusion initiatives. Both reports also drew attention to the need to recognise same-sex partnerships with regard to issues such as parenting, inheritance, property, healthcare and illness, pensions and immigration.

Equal rights for same-sex couples

Since the mid-2000s equality and rights discourses in relation to LGB people have shifted more firmly to the third form of sexual citizenship rights, as identified by Richardson (2000a), namely claims to rights within social institutions, such as the validation of same-sex marriages. Building on the recommendations of the Equality Authority and the NESF reports, the issue has also been progressed, along with issues relating to opposite-sex cohabiting couples, by reports issued by the Irish Human Rights Commission (2006), the Law Reform Commission (2006) and the Working Group on Domestic Partnership, established by the Department of Justice, Equality and Law Reform in 2006. These reports discuss various options and issues regarding the recognition of same-sex partnerships, and the rights and duties that recognition would entail.

In a related vein, 2006 saw the publication of the tenth progress report of the All-Party Oireachtas Committee on the Constitution, which reviewed Article 41 relating to the family. A re-definition of the family in the constitution would have enormous strategic importance in terms of equal rights for family forms not based on heterosexual marriage. As it stands, Article 41.3.1 states that 'the State pledges itself to guard with special care the institution of Marriage, on which the Family is founded, and to protect it against attack.'

The committee received a raft of submissions, which demonstrated 'that there is no unanimity as to what comprises a family. Definitions include the family based on the Catholic sacrament of matrimony, families formed subsequent to divorce and remarriage, as well as families not based on marriage' (All-Party Oireachtas Committee on the Constitution, 2006, p. 49). Submissions received which commented on the issue of same-sex marriages were particularly revealing of the depth of conservative heteronormative attitudes and the gulf between the groups who espoused these views versus the groups who argued for the recognition of same-sex couples. For example, those who argued against the recognition of same-sex marriages suggested that it would attack, devalue and destroy marriage as it currently exists; that marriage is a natural institution, not a social or cultural construct; and that same-sex marriage is an absurdity or impossibility. Those who argued for recognition did so on the basis of equal rights and fairness, arguing that the current arrangements unfairly discriminate against same-sex couples financially and in terms of equal rights in relation to sexual identity.

The committee ultimately decided that the constitutional interpretation of the family should be left undisturbed:

> ... an amendment to extend the definition of the family would cause deep and long-lasting division in our society and would not necessarily be passed by a majority. Instead of inviting such anguish and uncertainty, the committee proposes to seek through a number of other constitutional changes and legislative proposals to deal in an optimal way with the problems presented to it in the submissions.[11] (ibid., p. 122)

Meanwhile, a High Court Case was taken by Katherine Zappone and Ann Louise Gilligan in 2006, a lesbian couple who married in Canada in 2003. The couple sought to have their marriage recognised in Ireland and to be treated by the Revenue Commissioners as a married couple for taxation purposes. They argued that the constitutional definition of marriage did not specify whether it is same-sex or opposite sex. However, the High Court decided against their case, arguing that the traditional view of marriage assumes opposite-sex couples. The case has subsequently been appealed to the Supreme Court.

These various reports and the High Court case culminated in the introduction of legislation to recognise civil partnerships, to rectify the 'second-class citizenship' of LGB people, as former Taoiseach Ahern (Law Reform Commission, 2006, p. 19) put it. In June 2008 the government published the heads of the Civil Partnership Bill, which proposes to introduce legislation recognising civil partnership status for gay and lesbian couples and opposite-sex cohabiting couples. However, the extent to which partnership status will entail full equality with heterosexual couples with regard to rights related to social welfare, taxation and inheritance is as yet unclear until the Bill is published in full. In addition, equal rights are not extended to issues such as same-sex parenting and adoption, and, ultimately, partnership registration falls short of the right to marry. For some gay and lesbian groups campaigning on the issue of marriage, such as LGBT Noise and Marriage Equality, the Bill does not go far enough, and offers an inferior form of relationship status. For others, such as GLEN, the proposed Bill has been largely welcomed, with the exception of its implications for same-sex couples who are co-parenting children, as no joint legal rights in relation to children are currently proposed.

Issues of heterosexist discrimination in relation to family life and parenthood have been particularly problematic, especially for lesbian mothers, as O'Connell (2008) points out. For example, fertility clinics in Ireland often exclude same-sex couples on the grounds that they offer infertility treatment only. While the Commission on Assisted Human Reproduction (2005) recommended that under equality legislation lesbian women should be afforded the same access as heterosexual women, no action has been taken. In addition, the non-biological parent of children in a same-sex family is legally treated as a stranger to them. They have no rights in relation to guardianship, and children in this situation have no automatic claim to their non-biological parent's estate after death. Furthermore, while same-sex couples can foster children, they cannot adopt. Finally, there is the continued battle with groups (such as the Iona Institute) who argue against the recognition and rights of same-sex families and bring to bear arguments such as the instability of such families, and the negative effects on children of not having parents of both genders, and not having a father in particular.

On a broader level there are questions about how deeply embedded equality and anti-discriminatory attitudes are. For example, Connolly and O'Toole (2005, p. 173) comment that:

> Although there has been a sea-change in Irish attitudes to the LGBT community in the past 20 years, some of the old prejudices still pertain, particularly for women. So for example, although current equality legislation guarantees protection against discrimination on the grounds of sexual orientation, there have been few cases so far involving lesbians. To make such a case involves taking a public stand, and clearly few lesbians are ready to take this step.

In addition, NESF (2008), commenting on progress made with regard to equality for LGB people since its 2003 report on *Equality Policies for Lesbian Gay and Bisexual People*, notes that while great strides have been made, 'members of this community have good reason and cause for concern in not making their sexuality known in public' (NESF, 2008, p. 49). It cites, for example, a Gay Community Market Report (2007 in ibid.) which found that only 50 per cent feel they can be open about their sexuality at work.

While not directly comparable, 12 years earlier the GLEN/NEXUS (1995) study found that 42 per cent were completely 'out' in their workplace. In addition, homophobia within schools, especially second-level schools (Minton et al., 2008) is a particular problem. While much attention has been given recently to progress achieved on the issue of recognising same-sex couples, the desire to live as 'ordinary' citizens remains unfulfilled when, at base, issues such as these continue to exist.

CHAPTER SUMMARY

▸ This chapter focused on rights and recognition issues for groups who, in various ways, have been excluded from full and equal participation in Irish society, based on their difference from the established norms of Irish identity and citizenship.

▸ The chapter broadly discussed the theme of immigration, diversity and racism, and the differential rights afforded to various categories of immigrant. The implications of this differential treatment in social policy, integration policy and formal citizenship status were examined.

▸ Travellers were discussed as an indigenous ethnic minority, also treated in racist ways by state and society, and whose inclusion in Irish society, commanding respect and equal rights, still remains a significant challenge.

▸ The position of lesbians, gays and bisexuals as minority groups in Irish society was examined in the final section of the chapter. This charted the gradual gains in terms of equal rights for these groups; however, challenges remain in the sense that heterosexist and homophobic discrimination has not vanished and, in particular, debates regarding marriage, family and parenthood still reveal the deep-seated heteronormative order by which society operates.

Discussion points

▸ Discuss the notion of the 'deserving' versus the 'undeserving' immigrant. How is this manifest in Irish immigration policy?

▸ Identify and discuss ways in which Irish social policy is used as an instrument of exclusion in relation to minority groups in Irish society.

▸ What is anti-Traveller racism and why does it continue to be a problem in contemporary Irish society?

▸ Discuss reasons for and against changing the definition of the family in the Irish Constitution.

▷ Discuss what it means to both mainstream and target social services in relation to minority groups.

Further reading

Fanning, B. (ed.) (2007) *Immigration and Social Change in the Republic of Ireland*, Manchester: Manchester University Press.

Fanning, B. (2002) *Racism and Social Change in the Republic of Ireland*, Manchester: Manchester University Press.

McVeigh, R. (2008) 'The "Final Solution": Reformism, Ethnicity Denial and the Politics of Anti-Travellerism in Ireland', *Social Policy and Society*, Vol. 7, No. 1, (January) 91–102.

Rose, K. (1994) *Diverse Communities, the evolution of lesbian and gay politics in Ireland*, Cork: Cork University Press.

Useful websites

Translocations: Migration and Social Change – An Irish Inter-disciplinary Open Access E-Journal: www.translocations.ie

Consult websites of relevant organisations for useful policy position statements, research reports and campaigns.

Notes

1   A programme refugee is a refugee invited to Ireland by the government, who is already recognised as a refugee (that is, does not have to go through the asylum-seeking process once in the country), usually on the basis of a humanitarian request.

2   See the CSO, www.cso.ie, for more detailed data and updates on population and migration estimates.

3   Currently, Romanians and Bulgarians have the right to remain in Ireland for three months, and for longer periods they must be self-employed or working under a work permit.

4   Ireland, along with the UK, were the only two EU countries to opt out of an EU Council Directive in 2003 which permits family reunification of one's spouse and dependent children if one is legally resident (with the exception of asylum seekers) in an EU country (IOM, 2005).

5   Work authorisation was granted to persons from countries where visas are not required to enter Ireland and work visas were granted to persons from countries where visas are required to enter Ireland.

6   These payments initially included Unemployment Assistance, Old Age Non-Contributory Pension, Blind Pension, Widow(er)s' and Orphans' Non-Contributory Pensions, One-Parent Family Payment, Carer's

Allowance, Supplementary Welfare Allowance (other than once-off exceptional needs payments) and Child Benefit.

7   See the Office of the Refugee Applications Commissioner, www.orac.ie, for data related to asylum-seeking trends.

8   See the Irish Refugee Council, www.irishrefugeecouncil.ie, for data relating to asylum seekers recognised as refugees.

9   Leave to remain is a status conferred on an asylum seeker at the discretion of the Minister for Justice, Equality and Law Reform, where the asylum seeker does not fulfil the conditions of the 1951 Geneva Convention but is granted leave to remain in the country on humanitarian grounds.

10   Ireland ratified the UN Convention on the Elimination of All Forms of Racial Discrimination in 2000.

11   A minority of the committee did recommend changing the constitution based on recognising and respecting a right to family life not based on marriage.

CHAPTER 13

SOCIAL POLICY, SUSTAINABLE DEVELOPMENT AND QUALITY OF LIFE ISSUES

The previous two chapters indicated how a focus on particular social groups demonstrates the expanding scope of social policy beyond traditional social service areas. This chapter also looks at how the boundaries of social policy are changing, this time as a result of the challenges posed by green thinking and growing concern with environmental issues and the need for sustainable development. Traditionally, social concerns and environmental concerns have been interpreted as being irreconcilable (Eames, 2006). Green arguments challenge economic thinking based on continued economic growth that equates welfare with consumption. The implications of this, as Barry (1998, p. 224) points out, are potentially 'dramatic for social policy, given that one of the central justifications for social policy is to reduce socio-economic inequality via the redistribution of income, goods and services generated from a growing economy'. However, environmental concerns and environmental politics are increasingly moving from the margin to the mainstream, and are beginning to exert greater influence over policy debates and reform, not just in relation to environmental protection policies but also in relation to social and economic policy. This chapter looks at the relationship between sustainable development and social policy as a two-way challenge or relationship. On the one hand, the increasingly accepted need for sustainable development challenges mainstream social policy in terms of its reliance on continued economic growth for the realisation of social goals, and in terms of models and forms of welfare provision that do not take account of their environmental impact. On the other hand, the core concerns of social policy in relation to inequality and equity challenge the design of environmental policies in terms of their impact on different groups in society.

CHAPTER OUTLINE

▸ Section one explores some of the links between the discipline of social policy and environmental concerns. In particular, the evolution of the concept of sustainable development is examined and connected with concepts such as quality of life and social sustainability. Some of the models and debate around the concept of sustainable development are also examined.

▸ Section two outlines the rise of environmental concerns in Ireland. The evolution of economic policy and the tension between it and environmental protection are important for understanding contemporary problems with sustainable development in Ireland since its official endorsement in 1990. This section looks at how progress towards sustainable development has been hampered by economic concerns, while little or no attention is given to social concerns such as environmental inequalities.

▸ Section three briefly examines the consequences of this approach. Transport policy is taken as one particular example of issues related to sustainable development and quality of life in contemporary Irish society. Travel and transport policy is an area which goes beyond the conventional boundaries of social policy; however, by focusing on it, the aim is to demonstrate some of the connections between social policy and environmental concerns, which need consideration if the three pillars of sustainable development, namely social, economic and environmental concerns are to be fully integrated.

SECTION 1: SOCIAL POLICY AND ENVIRONMENTAL CONCERNS

Social policy and the environment

Concern for the environment is often considered to have emerged during the 1960s and 1970s. However, it actually has a much longer history, which has parallels and connections with the emergence of social policy. As Cahill (1991, p. 19) suggests, social policy 'was born out of a dissatisfaction with, and documentation of, the damage wrought to individuals by industrialism'. This damage included poverty, ill health, poor housing, child labour and poor factory conditions. These problems intensified as industrialisation coincided with urbanisation, which saw large populations concentrated in small areas. Early environmental concerns had similar origins. Industrialism was criticised for damaging nature or the countryside, particularly in terms of the use of raw materials and the rise in pollution, while the growth of urbanisation was criticised for being 'unnatural' and inhumane, and the cause of problems such as ill health, and the spread of disease and pollution (Macnaghten and Urry, 1996).

These problems led to both the development of modern social policy and many of the first 'environmental' groups. In many cases concern for the welfare of species and habitat preceded concern for human welfare. Furthermore, many reformers and activists were members of both early environmental groups and social policy groups (Parry and Parry, 2000), suggesting that they did not perceive major differences in being concerned about human welfare and the environment. One of the first examples of these types of groups is the Society for the Prevention of the Cruelty to Animals, founded in the UK in 1824. William Wilberforce was a prominent member who was also active in campaigning for the abolition of human slavery. An American Society for the Prevention of Cruelty to Animals was founded in 1866, and legislation for the prevention of cruelty to animals was used to try the first case of child abuse taken to court in the US in the absence of legislation on child abuse. Societies for the Prevention of Cruelty to Children came later – 1884 in London and 1885 in New York – and used methods 'consciously similar to that of the RSPCA' (ibid. p. 165). Edwin Chadwick, one of the early members of the Society for the Prevention of Cruelty to Animals, became well known for his later efforts in the public health movement. In 1842 he published a *Report of the Sanitary Conditions of the Labouring Poor*, providing an account of the damage industrialism and urbanisation had wrought on the health and living conditions of the poor. He drew attention to the 'environmental bads' affecting the life of the poor, 'atmospheric impurities', bad housing, lack of light, poor ventilation, lack of clean water, build up of waste and overall poor sanitation. This led to reform of governmental responsibility for 'environmental goods', such as clean water, clean air, safe food and general sanitation, which were first legislated for in the 1848 Public Health Act. The mid-nineteenth century public health movement, as Dean (2002) notes, can be considered the first articulation of the environmental rights of citizenship, preceding the concerns of the 1970s discussed below.

However, over time it could be argued that mainstream social policy lost its connection with environmental concerns and became more firmly 'anthropocentric', which meant that a boundary formed between concern for humans and concern for wider environmental issues such as the use of natural resources, the physical environment, animal welfare and so on. As Ferris (1991, p. 26) notes, 'post-enlightenment liberalism and socialism which shape the parameters of contemporary thinking about social policy were both premised on the conquest of nature'. Within social policy, human nature and its fulfilment, whether in liberal or socialist terms, is perceived by what is economically and technically feasible, and therefore detached from ecological limits that were applied to the non-human organic world (Hewitt, 2000). Social policy and well-being, whether coming from a right- or left-wing perspective, are wedded to the logic of industrialism and the assumption that economic growth is open-ended and living standards will continuously improve. Within social policy, the outcome is the subject of distributive struggles: whether governments intervene in the standards of living so that different groups benefit relatively equally or whether one's standard of living is left mainly to market mechanisms with a minimal state-based safety net.

Furthermore, as Fitzpatrick (1998) points out, welfare or well-being is promoted in very economistic or 'productivist' terms, which reduces what is meant by quality of life to materialistic terms. Productivism is based on a number of core ideas. These include the employment ethic, which is the idea that 'jobs should be the principal means by which income and status is distributed to the vast majority of people' (ibid., p. 14), and so essential is the wage contract to our sense of self-worth and self-esteem that it is difficult to envisage anything else. A second element is what Fitzpatrick terms 'the accumulative impulse', which is 'the notion that welfare equals material affluence' (ibid., p. 15). In other words, one's perception of quality of life is equated with one's material standard of life; 'in personal terms this comes down to the common instinct that our individual worth should be measured against a materialist yardstick' (ibid.).

By the 1960s and 1970 things were happening outside the discipline of social policy which challenged these assumptions and ways of achieving well-being. The environmentally disruptive effects of the growth model were becoming increasingly apparent and the modern green movement emerged in response to problems such as the loss of wilderness in the US, pollution such as acid rain, the impact of chemical pesticides, and the damaging effects of nuclear energy. In addition to these often quite localised environmental problems and movements, the notion that the world was in environmental crisis gained centre stage due to a number of pivotal reports. These included the Club of Rome report, *The Limits to Growth* (Meadows et al., 1972). This report argued that 'if the present growth trends in world population, industrialisation, pollution, food production and resource depletion continue unchanged, the limits to growth on this planet will be reached sometime within the next one hundred years. The most probable result will be a rather sudden and uncontrollable decline in both population and industrial capacity' (ibid., p. 23).

In a special issue of the ecologist magazine, *Blueprint for Survival*, another report was published in 1972 with a similar message, which gained a lot of attention. This argued that 'continued economic growth would end either against our will, in a succession of famines, epidemics, social crises, and wars, or because we want it to … in a series of thoughtful, humane and measured changes' (Goldsmith and Allen, 1972, p. 15). Both reports supported the idea of limits to growth. This assumes that there is a trade-off between environmental protection and economic growth and one can only be achieved at the expense of the other. These reports provoked a lot of criticism and eventual backlash against environmental thinking. They were accused of being overly pessimistic, apocalyptic, and lacking in concern for human welfare, but they did stimulate the beginnings of a debate, resulting in the emergence of the concept of sustainable development and its growing recognition and acceptance, though what it means is open to interpretation.

Social policy and modern environmentalism

For the most part, however, this thinking occurred outside the discipline of social policy, which was slow to react to the implications of environmental thinking. In this sense social policy perhaps shared the traditional left-wing sceptical response to environmentalism, which held that it was a middle-class **post-materialist** concern, typically about conservation, and that it posed a threat to improving the living conditions of the poor in both the developed and developing world (Foley, 2004; Yearley, 1991). However, by the 1990s and early 2000s several strands of research within social policy had emerged to address environmental issues. These included consideration of the 'greening of social policy' and the connections between social policy and sustainability (Cahill, 1991, 2002), and the implications of the green critique for social policy, involving an examination of ways in which social policy had not been 'green' in its development (Fitzpatrick, 1998). Another strand of research focused on the sectoral areas of social policy, such as health and housing, from an environmental perspective (e.g. Huby, 1998); while resource issues, such as water, food, energy, and transport, which had not been part of mainstream social policy analysis were now also being analysed from a social policy perspective (Cahill and Fitzpatrick, 2002; Healy, 2003; Huby, 1998, 2001). This entailed, for example, asking questions about the impact of policy in these areas on poor and vulnerable groups such as older people and people with disabilities. In this sense, the concepts of social inclusion and exclusion widened to incorporate environmental issues that affect quality of life, such as 'water poverty', 'travel poverty' and 'fuel poverty'.

> **Post-materialism** is an idea primarily associated with the work of Inglehart (1977) that suggests that once people have attained material security, their priorities change and they become more concerned with values such as self-expression and quality of life.

A related area involves research about the environmental concerns of disadvantaged groups (Burningham and Thrush, 2001) and issues of **environmental justice** and environmental inequalities (Adebowale, 2008). In some respects these have parallels with issues arising in other contexts, such as Guha and Martinez-Alier's (1997) research on the 'environmentalism of the poor'.

This looks at the materialist environmental basis for many development-induced conflicts in countries such as India, including water and land pollution, which threaten the livelihoods of the poor. In addition, in the US, the emergence of a grassroots environmental justice movement

> **Environmental justice** highlights the fact that poor and minority groups suffer disproportionately from environmental 'bads' such as pollution and poor quality living environments. Environmental justice seeks fairness in relation to the distribution of environmental 'goods' and 'bads', and equal access to, and participation, in environmental decision-making.

has seen a convergence of environmental concerns and social justice based on the fact that minority groups such as Black people, Hispanics and the poor are at greater risk of environmental contamination and nuisances (Sarokin and Schulkin, 1994). More recently, at an official level in the UK, sustainable development policy has also given more attention to issues of environmental inequalities, or the theme of 'environment and social justice', noting, for example, that 'problems of environmental injustice afflict many of our most deprived communities and socially excluded groups. Both poor local environmental quality and differential access to environmental goods and services have a detrimental effect on the quality of life experienced by members of those communities and groups' (Lucas et al., 2004, in Eames, 2006, p. 5).

As debate such as this has unfolded, thinking has progressed from the traditional scepticism about the implications of green thinking for social issues such as poverty and inequality. The common ground between these various strands of research is the general point that if environmental issues are to be fully understood and addressed, they cannot be divorced from social issues. Within social policy, this may be understood as something of a two-way relationship. On the one hand, the environmental critique poses a challenge to social policy for its contribution to unsustainable development. As Hoff and McNutt (2000, p. 461) point out, 'traditional models of social welfare, based on models of the economy that do not take into account the key role of the resource base, have outlived their usefulness for guiding social policy making.' This invokes the need for the 'greening' of social policies. On the other hand, the discipline of social policy can contribute to the integration of social and environmental issues, by bringing issues of inequality and equity to attention, which is a vital part of achieving sustainable development (Fitzpatrick, 2003). The next section examines some of these points by looking at the evolution of thinking about sustainable development and the continuing issues, conflicts and challenges in this domain.

The evolution of the idea of sustainable development and its relationship with social justice, quality of life and social sustainability

A UN Conference on the Human Environment, called *Only One Earth,* was held in Stockholm in 1973. This was the 'first major attempt to involve the nations of the world in a concerted, constructive response to environmental problems' and 'it is generally regarded as a milestone in the development of global responses to environmental issues' (Reid, 1995, p. 36). Of major concern to the conference was how to manage resources at a global level in order to tackle the mounting problems of pollution beyond 'harmless' dispersal, which was the taken-for-granted way of dealing with pollution. However, this concern did provoke some conflict as it was felt to reflect the interests of the Northern participant countries and to put obstacles in the way of the development priorities of Southern countries. These countries considered themselves to be suffering from the '**pollution of poverty**', an idea first articulated at this conference. For countries coming from this perspective, measures to

> The **pollution of poverty** refers to the environmental problems that arise from a lack of development, such as poor water quality, poor housing, malnutrition and disease.

tackle pollution would be a luxury, something to attend to once higher living standards had been attained.

Little headway was made in resolving this conflict at the conference; 'while it was clear that environment and development should be integrated, it was unclear as to how this should happen' (Elliot, 2005, p. 33). However, the conference did produce a document called the *Stockholm Declaration on the Human Environment* which contained a number of important principles. These principles added environmental concerns to the idea of rights and the idea of equity. The declaration, as Hayward (2005, p. 55) notes, was 'the first authoritative statement supporting the idea of environmental human rights' and, though not legally binding, its thinking became widely diffused and accepted in subsequent agreements and reports. Principle 1 of the declaration stated that:

> Man has the fundamental right to freedom, equality and adequate conditions of life, in an environment of a quality that permits a life of dignity and well-being, and he bears a solemn responsibility to protect

and improve the environment for present and future generations. (cited in ibid.)

In this principle the language of rights and responsibilities was extended to the environment. The right to an environment of good quality became an important component in thinking about human rights alongside civil, political and social rights, and the duty of governments was extended to protect and improve the environment for both present and future generations. This contrasts, as Aiken (1992) notes, with the 1966 UN International Covenants on Civil and Political Rights and on Economic, Social and Cultural Rights, which treated the environment as a resource and declared that it was a right of all people to make full use of their natural wealth and resources. The understanding of the environment, therefore, changed from being seen solely as a form of capital to exploit in order to improve people's lives to something to protect in order to improve people's lives. From a social policy perspective, this concern with environmental protection as a human right can also be understood in part as the 'greening of citizenship', entailing a 'discursive reframing of "Public Health" legislation as "Environmental Protection" legislation' as Dean (2002, p. 24) notes. In this respect, certain basic social goods and social rights, such as collective provision of clean water, are reclassified as an environmental right to an environmental good.

The reference to future generations in the principle is based upon the notion of inter-generational equity, which means equity between generations. This contrasted with the prevailing understanding of equity, which is intra-generational, meaning equity within generations. Inter-generational equity changes the temporal frame of reference of present trends and policies and projects their consequences over many generations (Fitzpatrick, 2002). In the Stockholm Declaration inter-generational equity is conceived as the responsibility that the present generation has towards future generations, and 'conserving Nature was no longer in opposition to human welfare; it was a claim future generations had against us' (Aiken, 1992, p. 193). In addition to producing the declaration, the conference resulted in the establishment of the UN Environment Programme, and at national level a number of countries began to treat the environment as a separate area of government, entailing new institutional structures. Several countries' environmental protection agencies and separate ministries of the environment were established in the early to mid-1970s, such as the US Environmental Protection Agency in 1970. A number of environmental NGOs were established at this time as well, such as Greenpeace in 1971.

One of the first reports to use the term sustainable development was the *World Conservation Strategy*, published by the World Conservation Union in 1980. However, it primarily concentrated on the conservation of living resources and this, as Baker (2006, p. 18) points out, limited its focus because it mainly addressed 'ecological sustainability, as opposed to linking sustainability to wider social and economic issues'. The report was also criticised for placing too much emphasis on poor people as the cause of environmental damage (Langhelle, 1999). The concept of sustainable development gained much wider recognition after the publication in 1987 of *Our Common Future*, also known as the Brundtland Report. This report was the product of a UN Commission called the World Commission on Environment and Development, which was established after the UN held a Stockholm +10 conference in Nairobi in 1982. The commission was given the task of proposing long-term environmental strategies with an international cooperative focus between developing and developed countries.

The report was something of a breakthrough document in terms of environmental thinking and environmental policymaking. It changed the way of thinking about the relationship between the economy, society and the environment, seeing them as the three pillars of sustainable development. In institutional terms, it urged the replacement of environmental policy as a discrete area of government with the integration of environmental, social and economic policy. Compared to the reports of the early 1970s, it did not convey a message of doom and it modified to some extent the limits to growth thesis. This is perhaps one of the reasons why the concept of sustainable development became so attractive and endorsed by interests and groups coming from very different starting points regarding social, economic and environmental issues. The report began by declaring that:

> Our report, *Our Common Future*, is not a prediction of ever increasing environmental decay, poverty, and hardship in an ever more polluted world among ever decreasing resources. We instead see the possibility for a new era of economic growth, one that must be based on policies that sustain and expand the environmental resource base. (World Commission on Environment and Development, 1987, p. 1)

Its much-quoted definition of sustainable development is 'development that meets the needs of the present without compromising the ability of future generations to meet their own needs' (ibid., p. 43). This definition is informed by two key ideas: needs and limitations. With respect to needs, it prioritised 'the essential needs of the world's poor', while its reference to limitations meant 'the idea of limitations imposed by the state of technology and social organization on the environment's ability to meet present and future needs' (ibid.).

The report suggested that some limits could be expanded and that the carrying capacity of the earth's resource base could be enhanced by growth in knowledge and technology. However, this was not to detract from the need for equitable access to resources or from recognition of the fact that ultimate ecological limits do exist. The report therefore proposed the idea of changing the quality of growth. It suggested that Southern countries needed growth to eradicate poverty and to develop in ways that are not destructive to the environment, which is what tends to happen in situations of extreme poverty. However, if this growth were to be a duplication of the model pursued in developed countries then further environmental destruction would ensue. All countries needed to change the quality of their growth, by making it 'less material- and energy-intensive and more equitable in its impact' (ibid., p. 52). Northern countries, in particular, needed to change the quality of their growth by more efficient use of materials and less use of energy. The report's reference to social organisation, therefore, involved an equitable distribution of resources. This means striving for intra-generational as well as inter-generational equity when it comes to issues of poverty, consumption and living standards:

> A world in which poverty and inequity are endemic will always be prone to ecological and other crises. Sustainable development requires meeting the basic needs of all and extending to all the opportunity to satisfy their aspirations for a better life. Living standards that go beyond the basic minimum are sustainable only if consumption standards everywhere have regard for long-term sustainability ... sustainable development requires the promotion of values that encourage consumption standards that are within the bounds of the ecological possible and to which all can reasonably aspire. (ibid, pp. 43–4)

This challenged the high consumption countries of the North in particular, which consume a far greater share of the world's resources in proportion to their population size. Addressing this inequality within ecological limits requires redistribution. Living standards in poorer nations need to rise in order to meet basic needs and eradicate absolute poverty and the range of associated problems, such as malnutrition, ill health and slum housing. For this to occur in an environmentally sound or sustainable way, the challenge, as Baker (2006, p. 20) points out, is for the 'industrialized world to keep consumption patterns within the bounds of what is ecologically possible and set at levels to which all can reasonably aspire'. The

> **Ecological footprint** is a measure of human impact on the environment. It represents the land required for a particular population to maintain its current levels of consumption and waste disposal.

concept of the **ecological footprint** has probably become the most well-known way of understanding unequal use of resources, or of going beyond ecological limits (Littig and Grießler, 2005). Living within ecological limits, or within our ecological footprint involves social change or 'changes in the understanding of well-being and what is needed to live a good life. This change allows necessary development in the South' (ibid., pp. 20–21).

The Brundtland Report and sustainable development policy

Since the early 1990s, policy developments which are attempting to realise sustainable development in practice have gathered pace. The Brundtland Report and the concept of sustainable development it articulated became a catalyst for the mainstreaming of green thinking and environmental policy. Sustainability has permeated every level of governance and policymaking. At a global level the trajectory of sustainable development can be traced through UN earth summits, the main ones being held in 1992 and 2002. The idea of holding an earth summit was recommended in the Brundtland Report to progress the implementation of sustainable development globally, and the first one took place in Rio de Janeiro. It led to the endorsement of the concept of sustainable development by 150 nations and a number of agreements, including Agenda 21 and the UN Framework Convention on Climate Change (UNFCCC). Agenda 21, signed by 173 nations, amounts to a comprehensive local action plan to implement sustainable development in a way that emphasises local community participation in particular. The Agenda requires local authorities to produce a local plan to promote sustainability and this is known as Local Agenda 21. The UNFCCC involves nations signing up to a declaration that serious action is needed to reduce greenhouse gas emissions in order to tackle climate change. Subsequently, negotiations in 1997 in Kyoto led to the Kyoto Protocol that set targets for industrialised countries to reduce their greenhouse gas emissions over the period 2008–12.

In 2002 a World Summit on Sustainable Development was held in Johannesburg to review what had happened since the Rio summit and to push forward efforts to achieve sustainable development. The review of the preceding 10 years was overwhelmingly negative. Unsustainable production and consumption, coupled with problems of pollution and depletion of natural resources, continued to be very serious issues. Furthermore, sustainable development was not sufficiently embedded into other policies, the implementation of Local Agenda 21 was uneven, and there was little cooperation between developed and developing countries to progress a common sustainable development agenda. At this stage as well the US had signed up to the Kyoto Protocol in 1998 but refused to ratify it in 2001. One of the main outcomes of the summit was the continuation of the Local Agenda policy and processes through a new version called Local Action 21.

This stressed the social dimension to sustainable development in particular and focused on issues such as poverty and social exclusion as obstacles to sustainable development and the need to create sustainable communities and cities. On the whole, however, the Johannesburg summit is thought to have been less successful; conflicting national interests dominated discussions and its outcomes were not as decisive as the Rio Summit (Baker, 2006). Opinion is divided on the significance and effectiveness of the earth summits and their outcomes.

Sustainable development and quality of life

Conceptual developments related to sustainable development have also progressed since the publication of the Brundtland Report. The notion of changing our understanding of well-being and what is needed to live a good life invokes the concept of quality of life which was central to the definition of sustainable development in another environmental report published subsequent to the Brundtland Report. In *Caring for the Earth*, a follow-up to the 1980 *World Conservation Strategy*, sustainable development is defined as 'improving the quality of life while living within the carrying capacity of supporting ecosystems' (World Conservation Union, 1991, p. 10). The notion of improving quality of life has become an increasingly popular way of addressing the issue of sustainable consumption in developed societies. Quality of life, as Jacobs (1997, p. 51) suggests, focuses:

> ... not on what consumers will *lose* as a result of environmental policies, but on what they will gain. Such policies improve the environment: they lead to lower *greenhouse* emissions, reductions in pollution and traffic congestion, protection of countryside and natural habitats and so on. The argument then is that these things *make people better off.*

They do this in a collective way; expenditure on policies which improve quality of life do not raise individual living standards, understood as income, but focus on environmental goods which improve well-being. Environmental goods, defined in the broadest sense as 'any aspect of the environment to which a positive value may be attached, whether a natural feature, a species of animal, a habitat, an ecosystem or whatever' (Miller, 1999, p. 152), are, therefore, as Jacobs (1997) argues, social goods. Like basic social services, such as public health, environmental goods such as clean rivers, clean air, open spaces and low traffic levels, are shared and are provided collectively rather than through individual purchase. Providing and protecting these goods involves public expenditure, which, through taxation, reduces personal expenditure, but, from a quality of life perspective this loss of income does not reduce but rather enhances quality of life. Quality of life has become a core element in governments' sustainable development strategies; for example, in the UK, the Labour government has 'headlined its sustainable development strategy a plan for improving quality of life' (Cahill, 2003, p. 559). Similarly in Ireland, the notion of quality of life is more frequently invoked in policy developments, including the current National Development Plan 2007–2013, *Transforming Ireland – A Better Quality of Life for All* (Government of Ireland, 2007c).

Social sustainability

Quality of life may also be understood as a component of another concept which is being more frequently referred to in political discourse and social policy objectives since the late 1990s. This is the promotion of social sustainability, sometimes also referred to as sustainable communities and sustainable cities. This concept adds to sustainable development discourse by suggesting that it is not just the environment that needs sustaining but also societies and communities. As Littig and Grießler (2005, p. 67) note, the concept is derived from:

> … the conclusion that human needs cannot be sufficiently met just by providing an ecologically stable and healthy environment, but that – if a society is indeed committed to sustainability – the equally legitimate social and cultural needs ought to be taken care of as well. Economic, social, and cultural conditions, efforts, and values are deemed to be resources that also need to be preserved for future generations.

This concept also reflects the move to greater consideration of the social dimension or pillar of sustainable development. During the 1970s and 1980s the major concern was with environmental damage and how economic growth was contributing to this. Re-conceiving the relationship between the economy and the environment was therefore a matter of urgency. Focus on society came later, especially on foot of implementing Local Agenda 21, which depends on local participation to work. Social sustainability can be defined as:

> Development (and/or growth) that is compatible with harmonious evolution of civil society, fostering an environment conductive to the compatible cohabitation of culturally and socially divisive groups while at the same time encouraging social integration, with improvements in the quality of life for all segments of the population. (Polese and Stren, 2000, pp. 15–16 in Colantonio, 2007, p. 5)

The concept emphasises the importance of social integration or social cohesion as a feature of sustainable societies. From a policy perspective, this is achieved by meeting social needs, creating equity and improving quality of life. The benefits, among other things, are that social sustainability and environmental sustainability are mutually reinforcing.

Models and diverse interpretations of sustainable development

So far, this section has looked at the main concepts associated with sustainable development, emphasising the social aspects of sustainable development and briefly outlining how policy has evolved. It is also necessary to consider the politics of sustainable development and the debates around what sustainable does or ought to mean. In other words, sustainable development needs to be situated in the wider context of green thinking and ideology as discussed in Chapter 5. At a surface level sustainable development is a concept that has gained widespread recognition and acceptance as something to favour. As Cahill (2003, p. 558) puts it, 'employers, government agencies, and pressure groups have all sprayed "sustainable" onto policies and titles.' Sustainable development provides a 'common language', but different groups give different meanings to the concept.

Investigating these differences, Jacobs (1999) suggests that the concept is contested around at least four different areas or fault lines. These fault lines reflect the broader differences in environmental thinking as discussed in Chapter 5, from the weakest of technocentric perspectives on the environment to the strongest or most radical eco-centric perspectives. The four fault lines are environmental protection, equity, participation and scope. At one end are the technocentrics whose position on these issues amounts to a weak model of sustainable development. Here, sustainable development is understood in a procedural and practical manner, and normative issues such as equity are considered largely irrelevant to its successful implementation. This model is less stringent about environmental protection; equity gets limited or no attention, especially when it comes to the consumption patterns of Northern countries; participation is limited to consultation with key stakeholders, and a centralised top-down model of decision-making is employed; the scope of policy remains wedded to more traditional environmental policy areas, and the notion of quality of life, for example, tends to be limited to the idea that a clean or good environment is an important factor in enhancing quality of life.

For proponents of the strong approach, 'sustainable development *is* increasingly taking on the mantle of an ideology: a comprehensive set of values and objectives, an analysis of the operation of the political economy, and a strategy for political change' (Jacobs, 1999, p. 30). Here, environmental protection is much more strongly informed by environmental limits, such as the 'carrying capacity' of the eco-system; concern about equity remains close to the original Brundtland concern about intra-country social justice and redistribution; a 'bottom-up' model of participation is emphasised, whereby local communities have direct involvement in sustainable development involving environmental, social and environmental goals for their area; finally, this implies a much broader scope, extending the remit of sustainable development to far-reaching social transformation, taking in, for example, all areas of social policy and having a much fuller conception of quality of life. In this version, sustainability 'is applicable not just to the environment or environmental economy, but to society itself' (ibid., p. 37).

Taking the contested nature of sustainable development further, Baker (2006) identifies four models on what she calls a sustainable development ladder. This ladder includes four forms of sustainable development: pollution control, weak sustainable development, strong sustainable development and an ideal model of sustainable development. These forms or approaches to sustainable development involve different political scenarios and practical policy options and are underpinned by differing attitudes towards nature and the relationship between human beings and nature. At the foot of the ladder is a minimal approach to environmental protection involving pollution control policies. On the next rung of the ladder is a weak model of sustainable development, which aims to integrate environmental concerns into the capitalist economy by economic instruments. By pricing environmental goods and bads, environmental problems are managed by market solutions and market-based interventions such as taxes and tradable quotas. A strong model of sustainable development is further up the ladder and it gives more serious attention to environmental protection, understanding it as a necessary condition of economic development, with greater emphasis on the protection of natural

> The **precautionary principle** refers to the idea that the absence of scientific certainty should not be taken as a reason for failing to respond to, or to take precautionary measures against, the occurrence of environmental risks.

resources and adopting the **precautionary principle** in the face of scientific uncertainty and risk. Market solutions alone are not seen as the answer to environmental problems and this model invokes stronger government intervention. This model involves the participation of everyone in society in adopting environmentally friendly behaviour and consumption patterns that will result in a better quality of life and not just relying on market signals to change behaviour. At the top of the ladder is what Baker (2006) refers to as the ideal model of sustainable development. For some of its proponents this involves a rejection of the concept of sustainable development, or at least the mainstream models of sustainable development. This model espouses something more radical and transformative, reflecting eco-centric principles, as discussed in Chapter 5, where the capitalist economic model is rejected, as is the anthropocentric attitude towards nature.

Box 13.1 The Ladder of Sustainable Development

	Ideal model	Strong sustainable development	Weak sustainable development	Pollution control
Normative principles	Principles take precedence over pragmatic considerations (participation, equity, gender equality, justice, common but differentiated responsibilities)	Principles enter into international law and into governance arrangements	Declaratory commitment to principles stronger than practice	Pragmatic, not principled approach
Type of development	Right livelihood; meeting needs not wants; biophysical limits guide development	Changes in patterns and levels of consumption; shift from growth to non-material aspects of development; necessary development in Third World	Decoupling; reuse, recycling and repair of consumer goods; product life-cycle management	Exponential market-led growth
Policy integration	Environmental policy integration; principled priority to environment	Integration of environmental considerations at sector level; green planning and design	Addressing pollution at source; some policy coordination across sectors	End of pipe approach to pollution management

	Ideal model	Strong sustainable development	Weak sustainable development	Pollution control
Policy tools	Internalization of sustainable development norms through on-going socialization; reducing need for tools	Sustainable development indicators; wide range of policy tools; green accounting	Environmental indictors; market-led policy tools and voluntary agreements	Conventional accounting
Civil society–state relationships	Bottom-up community structures and control; equitable participation	Democratic participation; open dialogue to envisage alternative futures	Top-down initiatives; limited state–civil society dialogue; elite participation	Dialogue between the state and economic interests

Source: adapted from Baker (2006, pp. 30–31)

These models and fault lines point to the difficulties with sustainable development in a political and practical context. Sustainable development is still very much an aspiration rather than an achievement. Limiting environmental policy to pollution control policies was typical of the 1970s, and since then in many countries the tension in practice has been between weak and strong models of sustainable development. As for Ireland, although sustainable development has been endorsed in policymaking since 1990, at best it can be said that policy as it has evolved has adopted a weak approach to sustainable development (Pepper, 1999). The concept is frequently morphed into the notion of sustainable growth, or sustainable economic development, with the emphasis on the sustainability of economic growth alone, or, as Taylor (1998, 2001) puts it, the primary concern is to 'conserve the emerald tiger'. The next section examines the evolution of the tension between the economy and the environment in the Irish context, leading to a very economistic or weak version of sustainable development. The discursive commitment to integrating environmental concerns with economic and social concerns is weakened by the dominance of economic priorities, creating a cycle which makes sustainable development more difficult to achieve as pressures on the environment and environmental damage grow. However, while reference is made to the need for social cohesion and sustainable communities within sustainable development discourse, little or no reference is made to social policy concerns, such as equity and social justice, or to the notion of environmental inequalities. In other words, the two-way relationship between social policy and the environment is largely unacknowledged in the Irish model of sustainable development.

SECTION 2: SUSTAINABLE DEVELOPMENT IN THE IRISH CONTEXT

Environmental conflict and the beginnings of Irish environmental policy

Prior to the 1970s environmentalist activity in Ireland was primarily associated with conservation and regeneration. For example, An Taisce was established in 1948 and the Irish Georgian Society was founded in 1958. Both of these organisations focused on preserving Ireland's architectural heritage and physical environment. Meanwhile, protests over poor housing and the decay of inner-city Dublin were also occurring, which might be understood as a reaction against environmental inequality, although such a concept was not in use at the time. A housing action campaign sought inner-city regeneration, which emphasised development to meet basic needs and to provide a safe, healthy environment in which to live. Protest more directly related to the environmental consequences of industrial development can be traced back to opposition to a state project to build a nuclear power station in the 1970s (Baker, 1990). At that time, nuclear power was mooted as an option for meeting the increasing energy demands anticipated with the growth of newly establishing industries since the opening up of the Irish economy in the 1960s. The opposition to the siting of a nuclear power plant at Carnsore Point in Wexford proliferated into numerous other protests, not least protest against chemical companies, centring particularly on the issue of toxic waste disposal (Allen and Jones, 1990; Baker, 1987, 1990; Keohane, 1989).

With regard to planning in general, Bartley (2007) identifies a shift in governments' approach to planning from a pre-industrial or minimal planning phase, which prevailed from independence until the 1960s, to a phase, lasting from 1960 to the mid-1980s, which he refers to as an industrial modernisation phase. Prior to 1960 a laissez-faire attitude prevailed and little thought was put into planning. The core element of the industrial modernisation phase was the introduction of the Local

Government (Planning and Development) Act, 1963. This designated local authorities as planning authorities and obliged them to develop spatial development plans, which were to be reviewed every five years, setting out future development required in relation to land, transport and sanitary services and so on. Local planning was to be complemented by an approach to regional planning recommended by the Buchanan Report, 1968, based on promoting the growth of a number of urban centres outside Dublin, to counterbalance development in the capital. However, these planning initiatives proved largely ineffective in delivering development that balanced economic with environmental concerns. Overall, environmental control policies, particularly in relation to planning, were increasingly shown to be weak in numerous areas, such as resourcing; inadequate imposition of sanctions; gaps in coverage, particularly in relation to state activities, both national and local; and lack of any incentives to encourage environmentally benign behaviour (Clarke, 1979; Convery, 1982).

The first policy review solely devoted to the environment, entitled *Towards an Environment Policy*, was carried out by the Environment Council which was established in 1978. It highlighted the planning process as especially inadequate. The review argued that:

> Many environmental problems resulting from development arise because of thoughtlessness or an inadequate understanding of the consequences of particular actions. The adverse effects are shown in increasing pollution of the air, water and land, by over-exploitation of non-renewable natural resources and by developments which are ill-conceived, unsympathetic to the environment and of poor quality (Environment Council, 1979, p. 7).

The review was particularly critical of local development plans arising out of the Local Government (Planning and Development) Act, 1963. The Environment Council suggested that these 'would appear to reflect the attitude that they are a statutory requirement to be fulfilled rather than an opportunity for directing future development in a positive way and as part of an ongoing process of forward planning, monitoring, development control and review' (ibid., p. 11).

Towards an Environment Policy and a subsequent report, *A Policy for the Environment* (Environmental Council, 1980), provide an indication of emerging thought on environmental policy in Ireland; particularly in terms of how industrial development and the rise of environmental concerns over the previous decade were assessed and how a more coherent environment policy might deal with the two. While the council recommended that an overall environmental policy would facilitate better consideration of the links between environmental and other national aims, it ultimately perceived the interaction between environmental and economic policy as a matter of trade-offs. The council therefore suggested that 'an environment policy must be conceived in such a way as to minimise the conflicts with other areas, and trade-offs with objectives and goals of other policies must be consciously accepted' (Environment Council, 1979, p. 10).

The first report (though subject to many information gaps) on the state of the environment was published in 1985 (Cabot, 1985). It profiled, in a more comprehensive way, the pressures arising out of Ireland's rapid phase of economic growth. Although the 1980s were a time of economic recession, the decade also marks the end to what Tovey and Share (2000, p. 436) identify as 'ascetic developmentalism' and the gradual transition to a high-consumption society. Reflecting this, the report documented a range of environmental pressures, including rapid population growth, urbanisation, and changed expectations, relating in particular to consumption. The report also noted that governmental policy was ill-equipped to deal with these trends, which was manifest in inadequate infrastructure, including transport, communications and sanitary services, along with problems meeting increased energy demands and dealing with waste disposal. Furthermore, as the government itself later admitted, 'in practice, the need to achieve a balance between environment and development did not exert a strong influence on policy formation in many sectors during the 1980s' (Department of the Environment, 1997, p. 22).

Trends related to urbanisation and suburbanisation were particularly problematic. The recommendations of the Buchanan Report were not implemented and Dublin grew at the expense of other urban regions, in a largely unregulated manner. As Bartley (2007, p. 35) notes:

> Reliance was placed almost entirely on the private sector to develop all aspects of settlement apart from necessary infrastructural development and social housing ... planning presided over rapid and extensive provision of public and private residential accommodation as settlement policies persisted with suburban housing estates as the appropriate response to continuing urbanisation trends.

Inner-city areas also suffered under this trend. As people migrated to the suburban edges, city centres were emptied out of both people and businesses, and the built environment was neglected.

The emergence of sustainable development policy in the 1990s

Reflecting international developments, including the Brundtland Report and the endorsement of sustainable development by the EU, by the 1990s, all things environmental came into sharper focus in Ireland. The tension between the environment and economic development was being replaced by the belief that integrating the environment with economic concerns posed opportunities for still urgently needed economic growth, as opposed to posing a threat to it. The publication of *An Environmental Action Programme* (Department of the Environment, 1990) represented the first official recognition of sustainable development in Ireland (Convery, 1992). The programme's reference point was to a 'new enlightened approach to environmental management' and based itself on three considerations: (1) the concept of sustainable development, defined as 'a reasonable balance in man's interest between development and nature' (2) the precautionary principle and (3) the 'integration of environmental considerations into all policy areas' (Department of Environment, 1990, pp. 1–2). However, integration was still primarily understood in terms of linkages between the economy and the environment, not society or social policy.

Among the several areas and actions proposed in the programme, including, for example, environmental awareness, air quality and climate change, a significant aspect of its proposals for industry involved the role of a new Environmental Protection Agency (EPA). This was legislated for in the 1992 Environmental Protection Act, and was established in mid-1993 as an independent body responsible for pollution control in Ireland, and for supervising Local Authority's environmental responsibilities (Coyle, 1994). Mary Harney, the Junior Minister for Environmental Protection, firmly placed the role of the EPA as one of ensuring a balance between providing environmental protection and providing 'sustainable economic development' (Harney, 1992, p. 31). Furthermore, she saw this balancing role, as one not of tension, but of mutual enhancement, particularly in terms of the environment serving as a potential source of jobs. She argued that:

> Much of our recent economic recovery can be attributed to industries which are dependent on a clean environment, for example food, agriculture, electronics and tourism. Continued economic growth, I believe, will depend more and more on the perception abroad that Ireland is 'environmentally friendly'. ... In the 1990s we look forward to jobs because of the environment. (ibid., p. 32)

The influence of European developments and the concept of ecological modernisation on the growth of sustainable development in Ireland

While the EEC made a declaratory commitment to improvements in quality of life and environmental protection as far back as 1973 (Liberatore, 1991), its power in the area of environmental regulation was not augmented until the Single European Act, 1987. The main impetus for this sprung from the varying standards of environmental protection in the member states. In particular, countries with high levels of environmental protection, principally the Scandinavian member states, were potentially incurring greater production costs (Williams and Bjarnadottir, 1998). Environmental regulation and sustainable development measures were therefore needed to level the economic playing field.

In 1997, after much deliberation, the Treaty of Amsterdam added sustainable development to the EU's central objectives, and with it, the principle of integrating the environment into other policies. The particular way in which the EU has pursued sustainable development policy is described as an ecological modernisation approach. This focuses on particular aspects of the Brundtland formulation of sustainable development, principally the notion of changing the quality of economic growth. Ecological modernisation may be defined as 'the ecological restructuring process of production and consumption' (Spaargaren and Mol, 1992, p. 335). The ecological restructuring of production, in policy terms, means that the development of economic and environmental policy, in general, is underpinned by the belief that, qualitatively, a different kind of economic growth is possible. This growth is one that allows productivity gains to be made above and beyond the rate of growth (Jacobs, 1999) and to which stronger environmental protection can make a contribution (Young, 2000).

The ecological modernisation position involves a number of distinct, but related, arguments. It is argued that economic growth is not synonymous with the increased use of non-renewable resources. What is important, therefore, is not reducing economic growth, measured in terms of GNP, but in making sure that growth is sustainable. This sustainability is to be achieved, in part at least, through technological developments. According to this perspective, not only does environmental protection not hinder economic growth, it can also be a source for future growth. This, it is argued, will be achieved through the production of low-polluting goods – 'clean' cars, CFC-free aerosols, and so on – which consumers are increasingly demanding. In addition, pollution-control technology itself has the potential to become an important source of economic wealth. In these ways economic growth can 'de-couple' from environmental degradation, while more efficient production processes mean less use of materials for the same level of output, known as 'dematerialisation'.

Young (2000) suggests that the emergence of ecological modernisation is best understood as 'a late twentieth century strategy to adapt capitalism to the environmental challenge, thus strengthening it'. At the same time, as Spaargaren and Mol (1992, p. 336) note, since ecological modernisation 'highlights the industrial rather than capitalist character of modern society...

the capitalist character of modern society is hardly questioned ... [and] seen as not relevant to overcoming the ecological problem'. This element of ecological modernisation, according to Hajer (1995), is one of the reasons why governments might find ecological modernisation appealing in handling environmental problems. As he sees it, 'ecological modernisation explicitly avoids addressing basic social contradictions that other discourses might have introduced' (ibid., p. 32). Remedying environmental change is seen as a 'positive sum game': environmental damage is not an impediment to growth, quite the contrary, it is the new impetus for growth. As Garner (1996, pp. 32–3) notes, because of this positive sum view, 'governments were able to take action on environmental problems without fearing an economic backlash'.

In practice, EU sustainable development policy has evolved through periodic environmental action programmes and, currently, the Sixth Environmental Action Programme, 2000–2010, *Environment 2010: Our Future, Our Choice*, is in the process of being implemented. Each action programme focuses on particular areas of environmental concern and in the sixth programme climate change, nature and bio-diversity, environment and health, natural resources and waste are the areas addressed. The programme clearly reflects the aims and reasoning of ecological modernisation:

> A healthy environment is essential to long term prosperity and quality of life and citizens in Europe demand a high level of environmental protection. Future economic development and increasing prosperity will put pressure on the planet's capacity to sustain demands for resources or to absorb pollution. At the same time, high environmental standards are an engine for innovation and business opportunities. Overall, society must work to de-couple environmental impacts and degradation from economic growth. Business must operate in a more eco-efficient way, in other words producing the same or more products with less input and less waste, and consumption patterns have to become more sustainable. (European Commission, 2001b, p. 3)

Ecological modernisation is also associated with new environmental policy instruments, which mark a shift away from regulatory policies common in the 1970s to market-based instruments. These were initially promoted by the OECD in the mid-1970s, endorsed by the Brundtland Report and further encouraged by the EU since the 1990s. Two main instruments are used: tradable quotas and green taxes or **ecological tax reform**. Both of these have been implemented to

Ecological tax reform refers to reform of tax systems, towards taxation based on the use of natural resources, such as oil and water, and the use of polluting products such as cars.

some extent in relation to pollution. The EU's response to the Kyoto Protocol, for example, has been to institute an EU Emissions Trading Scheme (EUETS) for greenhouse gases, while Scandinavian countries and the Netherlands are the leaders in terms of green taxes, as illustrated by the recent introduction of carbon taxes and landfill taxes.

From an Irish point of view, there has been a significant 'Europeanisation' of national environmental policies, as Connaughton et al. (2007) notes. A number of European Directives have significantly influenced policy regarding issues such as waste, water, environmental impact assessments, emissions ceilings and special areas of conservation. Yet, as Connaughton et al. (ibid., p. 77) observe, 'the rhetoric of strategy has taken precedence over the reality of action when it comes to assessing the progress in EU member states ...', and this is especially true in the Irish case. This is part of the bigger picture in which environmental policies and sustainable development policies have evolved in circumstances where a weak model of sustainable development and ecological modernisation have been used to legitimate a strong emphasis on economic growth and competitiveness. Therefore, whereas social policy has generally been subordinate to economic policy, now environmental policy is also sharing that relationship in Ireland. In reality, the rhetoric of integrating the three pillars of sustainable development is translated into subordinating the environmental pillar while scarcely recognising the social pillar.

The influence of the EU and ecological modernisation thinking are particularly evident in *Sustainable Development: A Strategy for Ireland* (1997), which represents the most comprehensive document on environmental policy to date. It set out the government's elaboration of the concept of sustainable development and suggested that more strategic or systematic action was needed on the environment, particularly in the context of an increased awareness of the pressure that economic success had placed on both society and the environment.

In contrast to the earlier *An Environmental Action Programme* (1990), the 1997 document defines sustainable development in broader quality-of-life terms and suggests that the meaning of sustainable development 'seeks an acceptable quality of life for present and future generations, recognising that the actions of the present affect the inheritance of future generations' and that it is 'an inclusive concept bringing environment to the heart of economic growth and quality of life concerns, and requiring the active participation of economic operators and the public, as well as all levels of Government' (Department of the Environment, 1997, p. 20).

Despite references to quality of life, sustainable development policy is elaborated in economistic terms, with the main form of integration envisaged in terms of economic and environmental policy. Social policy and social concerns received scant reference, except in the context of the Rio Declaration, where mention is made, for example, of fair access to a clean and healthy environment and equity in the use of environmental resources. These references to equity and access did not influence any other aspect of the strategy. The elaboration of the principle of integration in the strategy highlights the move towards an ecological modernisation approach, based on the idea that Ireland's economic growth is at a transition stage to a state where it would be qualitatively transformed, and therefore be more efficient and less demanding on natural resources. This transformation is to stem from an increasing share of economic activity being represented by the services sector and the deployment of more efficient methods of production, both of which represent moves towards the de-materialisation of the Irish economy. Thus, integration of environmental and economic policy is not perceived to involve costs or compromises, but is a means, the strategy argued, of 'decoupling ... economic growth and environmental degradation; it promotes economic and environmental efficiency through reduced materials and energy use, waste prevention and minimisation, re-use and recycling and it assists the realisation of economic advantage founded on environmental quality' (ibid., p. 27). In this way a relatively weak model of sustainable development is espoused. This is evident in the manner in which issues such as equity are not seriously considered; sustainable development is to be achieved through largely technical means and no contradictions are perceived between continued economic growth and environmental protection.

More recent statements regarding sustainable development contain greater reference to the social dimension of sustainable development, as mention is made of social cohesion or social inclusion as part of an environmentally friendly society. However, the imperative of economic growth remains and is reinforced by increasing mention of the necessity for economic competitiveness, in which sustainable development is seen as having an integral role. In *Towards 2016*, for example, the overall goal is to enhance 'Ireland's competitive advantage in a changing world economy and [build] sustainable social and economic development' (Government of Ireland, 2006, p. 6). Connections between environmental and social policy are forged with the aim of creating a 'socially inclusive and environmentally friendly society' (ibid., p. 14), while 'environmental sustainability' is perceived as a 'strategic asset' and a source of 'competitive advantage' (ibid., p. 32). This line of thinking is also evident in two other documents the Department of the Environment, Heritage and Local Government has produced since the publication of *Sustainable Development: A Strategy for Ireland (1997)*.[1] These are *Making Ireland's Development Sustainable* (2002), which reviewed progress since the 1997 strategy in a report prepared for the World Summit on Sustainable Development in

Johannesburg; and *Ireland's Progress Towards Environmental Sustainability* (2007), which reviewed developments in the context of achievements made over the course of the National Development Plan 2000–2006, and the key challenges for the National Development Plan 2007–2013. The 2007 document, in particular, reinforces the dominance of the economic pillar in sustainable development and reiterates the smooth compatibility between the environment and the economy, remarking that 'environmental protection and economic progress go hand in hand' (Department of the Environment, Heritage and Local Government, 2007c, p. 2). The rationale for environmental protection is narrowed to particularly economistic and productivist terms, and quality of life, while mentioned, is confined to the state of the natural environment only. 'In an increasingly competitive world, the quality of the air we breath, the purity of the water we drink, the cleanliness of our beaches and the beauty of our countryside will operate as a competitive advantage for Ireland winning investment, encouraging others to do business with us and attracting tourists. Above all, a good clean environment underpins the high quality of life we all expect and deserve' (ibid.).

SECTION 3: SOCIAL POLICY, TRANSPORT AND THE ENVIRONMENT

Transport trends and problems

This section moves from the broad critique of sustainable development policy in Ireland to looking at the specific issue of transport policy and travel patterns. Transport and transport policy is clearly a matter of environmental concern. Transport has been a major factor in the increase in greenhouse gas emissions in Ireland. In overall terms, Ireland is failing to meet its obligations under the Kyoto Protocol to limit emissions to 13 per cent above 1990 levels by 2012. Currently, emission levels are 10.2 per cent above that target. While the major contributing sectors to greenhouse gas emissions are agriculture, energy and transport, the transport sector accounts for the largest increase in CO_2 emissions. Due to the increased levels of car ownership and goods vehicles, emissions from transport sources increased by 178 per cent between 1990 and 2007 (EPA, 2008a). Car ownership, as the EPA (2008b, p. 17) notes, 'has changed dramatically, with the proportion of households with multiple vehicles increasing substantially'. New car registrations were 15 per cent higher in 2006 than in 2002 and 'there is a continuing trend to purchase cars with larger engine sizes.' Overall, the number of cars per 1,000 of the population has increased considerably in a decade; in 1996 there were 382 cars per 1,000 adults and in 2006 this increased to 528 per 1,000 adults (Department of Transport, 2008).

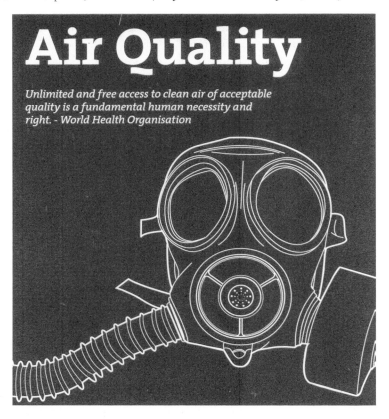

Air Quality

Unlimited and free access to clean air of acceptable quality is a fundamental human necessity and right. - World Health Organisation

Image from an Enfo leaflet on air quality. Source: www.enfo.ie

Transport is also a major contributor to poor urban air quality and therefore to health risks associated with poor air quality. Cork and Dublin are the main areas in Ireland where air quality is most at risk of pollution and exceeding standards set by the EU Directive on National Emissions Ceilings (EPA, 2008b). Two pollutants in particular are associated with road traffic, particulate matter (PM_{10}) and nitrogen dioxide (NO_2). The inhalation of small particles is associated with respiratory and cardiopulmonary disorders, such as asthma, heart disease and lung cancer. Children and older people are particularly vulnerable to health problems due to exposure to air pollution. Low-income groups generally also bear the brunt of environmental inequalities associated with road traffic (Baeten, 2000). They are, for example, more likely to live near busy roads, and thus have greater exposure to air pollution and to noise pollution, and they are also more vulnerable to accidents because of where they live and their greater likelihood to walk or to cycle (Lucas et al., 2001).

A major problem is the increasing volume and usage of motor cars which counters gains made in cleaner car technologies. As the EPA (2008b, p. 54) notes, 'while new standards for car emissions and the resultant cleaner technology have curbed emissions from individual vehicles, this has been offset by the increasing number and bigger engine sizes of vehicles on Ireland's roads.' In other words, transport growth has not been decoupled from its environmental impact in a way that ecological modernisation intends. This problem is not exclusive to Ireland; across industrial countries, behavioural trends involving higher levels of car ownership and greater use is outstripping the mitigating effects of technological improvements to cars (Steg and Gifford, 2005).

In the Irish context, traffic volume and car use patterns are also directly connected with the ways in which land use and settlement patterns have evolved. In particular, the manner in which suburbanisation has unfolded poses serious environmental challenges due to the intensification of low-density urban sprawl throughout the housing boom of the mid-1990s to the mid-2000s. During that time there has been a proliferation of detached houses, which create larger ecological footprints than other housing types, and which are spread out over wide areas. Noting this trend, the European Environment Agency (2006) points to Dublin sprawl (along with Istanbul and Madrid) as 'a worst-case scenario' of urban planning and something that newer less well developed EU member states should refrain from emulating. Rural settlement patterns are similarly typified by sprawl, as one-off houses are being built in a widely dispersed or scattered manner. The legacy of weak planning policies has continued to be influential in this regard, despite a new focus on sustainable development in the Planning and Development Act, 2000, which obliges local authorities to produce six-year sustainable development plans. Public transport has not developed in tandem with housing sprawl and is more costly to provide in comparison to transport which serves compact settlement areas. Consequently, 'Ireland is unique by Western European standards in that 15% of people say they live more than 20 minutes from public transport compared with less than 5% in most other countries' (European Foundation for the Improvement of Living and Working Conditions, 2003, p. 31 in Winston, 2007, p. 66). The upshot of this is increased commuterisation and a growth in the distances travelled to work for all commuters, especially rural dwellers, as shown in table 13.1 below.

Table 13.1 Average distance from work (km), 1991, 1996, 2002, 2006

	State	Urban	Rural
1991	7.7	7.0	8.5
1996	10.7	9.1	13.1
2002	15.7	12.5	21.3
2006	15.8	12.8	20.9

Source: CSO (2007c)

A long-standing trend has been increasing car dependency as a means of travel to work, as evident in table 13.2 below. Travel by car has grown at the cost of travel on foot, bicycle, and bus, all of which have less environmental impact. Travel by train has increased slightly and this is primarily attributable to the introduction of the DART and the LUAS in Dublin.

Table 13.2 Means of travel to work 1991, 1996, 2002, 2006 (percentage of total)

Means of travel	1991 %	1996 %	2002 %	2006 %
On foot	11.1	11.5	11.4	10.9
Bicycle	4.4	3.6	2.1	1.9
Bus	7.7	7.6	6.7	6.1
Train	1.7	1.7	2.1	2.9
Motorcycle	1.1	0.9	1.1	0.7
Motor car driver	38.9	46.3	55.1	57.1
Motor car: passenger	8.0	8.7	6.7	5.5
Lorry/van/other	4.0	4.3	7.1	7.8
None	19.8	12.3	6.1	5.6
Not stated	3.2	3.1	1.7	1.6
Total*	100	100	100	100

Source: CSO (2007c)

Note:
* Totals are rounded figures.

Transport inequalities, travel poverty and social exclusion

Transport policy is primarily concerned with mobility as physical movement, and on improving the movement of those who are already mobile. This focus obscures the fact that transport is integral to social goals, such as social inclusion and improving quality of life. Those who don't have cars and whose access to public transport is non-existent or very limited are socially excluded. People who are **travel poor** experience

> **Travel poverty** refers to a lack of mobility which exacerbates social exclusion.

social exclusion through lack of access, whether this be access to commercial goods and services, employment opportunities, social and leisure activities, or social services such as healthcare (Lucas et al., 2001). The need for transport to access healthcare and other social services is compounded when public services are in retreat (Nutley, 2000), such as the centralisation of hospital services. The spatial positioning of services is also determined by transport policy, as services tend to follow new roads, and therefore become located along major road networks and out-of-town centres. As a consequence, local communities lose localised services, such as doctor surgeries, banks, post offices and shops, which were more easily accessible for those without cars. Transport policy which assumes car ownership and is based on ease of movement for car drivers detracts from rather than enhances social sustainability and sustainable communities.

The social dimension of transport is not just about social exclusion, but quality of life and social capital (Currie and Stanley, 2008; Steg and Gifford, 2005). Mobility and transport can contribute to 'social capital and the building of networks and relationships between people, feelings of trust and mutual assistance or reciprocity' (Stanley and Lucas, 2008, p. 37). Mobility and access to transport give 'people greater access to a wider range of interests and activities and [allows] them a higher degree of engagement with other like-minded members of the various communities to which they belong, thus enriching their lives and contributing to social and economic vitality' (Troy, 1996, p. 208 in Lucas, 2004a, p. 10). On the whole, however, the role of transport in enhancing quality of life has been scarcely explored, and quality of life in debates about transport tends to be reduced to an economistic notion of time saving, particularly for workers.

Travel poverty not only refers to those who don't own cars and who have little or no access to public transport, it is also concerned with those on low incomes who are dependent on cars for mobility. These people are 'forced' to own cars (Lucas et al., 2001), or are 'structurally dependent' on cars (Roberts et al., 1999, in McDonagh, 2006). This means that in the absence of suitable public transport these people have little choice but to own a car to meet their essential needs such as access to employment, healthcare and shopping. This explains why there is still a high level of car ownership within low-income families. This is especially the case for low-income families who live in isolated rural areas; who work in shifts and/or at isolated locations on the edge of cities; or who have to make multi-purpose trips under time constraints, which applies to women as mothers and carers in particular (Lucas, Grosvenor and Simpson, 2001). In addition, car ownership among low-income households to an extent exacerbates their poverty and social exclusion (Wickham, 2004), as sacrifices are made in order to be able to run a car, and in comparison with wealthier car owners, fewer and shorter trips are made (Lucas, Grosvenor and Simpson, 2001).

Regarding rural transport and travel poverty, although car dependency is very high in rural Ireland and rural car ownership is higher than urban car ownership (CSO, 2007d), this obscures the problems experienced by those living in rural areas without access to cars. This includes people with disabilities, older people, women and younger people (McDonagh, 2006). Cloke (1993, in McDonagh, 2006) found, for example, that these people feel 'trapped either at home or away from home' because of their dependency on very limited public transport services or depending on neighbours for lifts. Furthermore, lack of transport is a significant factor contributing to the loneliness of older rural dwellers (Drennan et al., 2008). In addition, a study by McGrath (1999) comparing travel patterns of urban car owners versus rural car owners shows that the quality of rural life is not necessarily enhanced by car ownership. He found that rural dwellers spend far more time in their cars, often making trips to meet the needs of passengers such as other family members, in the absence of public transport and general lack of accessible amenities in the countryside. As for travel poverty in urban areas, lack of public transport contributes to the social segregation of particular areas; especially areas with high levels of social housing. Wickham (2004), for example, cites the example of Jobstown, an area of high unemployment with a high proportion of social housing but very poor public transport links to other areas in the city. '... in Jobstown, those without a car were isolated: getting a job or even doing the shopping became major and sometimes insuperable logistical problems' (ibid., p. 13).

Challenges for the development of sustainable transport policy

Transport policy has primarily been influenced by transport economics, and decisions and evaluation have been based primarily on the cost of providing transport, while benefits are primarily measured in time gained for people on the move. As Lucas (2004a, p. 11) notes:

Decisions about how the state spends money on transport have traditionally been made on the basis of cost benefit analysis ... there is a tendency for [cost benefit analysis] to favour transport projects that bring small journey-time savings to a large number of travellers. Traditionally, therefore, transport-spending decisions have tended to favour road-building projects over public transport services and cycling and walking amenities.

Furthermore, transport policy has traditionally been based on a 'predict and provide' model, which means building and up-grading roads on the basis of future projections of demand for road use based on car driving patterns. As environmental and sustainable development concerns have increasingly entered policy discourse, the notion of sustainable transport policies has come to the fore. In common with the concept of sustainable development, the meaning of sustainable transport is open to diverse interpretations. As Steg and Gifford (2005, p. 60) note, 'it is generally accepted that ... sustainable transport implies finding a proper balance between (current and future) environmental, social and economic qualities ... it is less clear which environmental, social and economic qualities should be guaranteed and balanced.' In practical terms, sustainable transport policy involves a shift from a predict and provide model to a demand management model, based on curbing escalating car use, and providing and encouraging alternative modes of transport which have a lesser impact on the environment. In the Irish context, where planning and transport policy are very heavily based on mobility by car, the transition to sustainable transport is a huge challenge. It is very difficult and costly to reverse decades of policy and provision based on urban sprawl, rural dispersion and car dependency. In addition, it is evident that minimal attention is given to social concerns in the evolution of sustainable transport policy in the Irish context.

One of the major challenges sustainable transport has to address is the residualisation of public transport. As noted earlier, travel by bus accounts for a very small proportion of travel to work patterns and has been in slow but consistent decline. In addition, travel by bus is not perceived as a viable option for travel, but more of a safety-net service. For example, a survey carried out by the Dublin Transport Office in 2006 found that half of all car drivers in the greater Dublin area would not switch to travelling by bus even if services were improved. Reasons for not choosing buses included unreliability, poor connections and long waiting times. Buses were perceived as a service for older people and for people with no other transport choices (Cullen, 2006). While travel by rail has increased, in the overall scheme of things it accounts for a very small proportion of the means of travel. Furthermore, as Wickham (2004, p. 11) notes, 'in car dependent cities, public transport initiatives tend to be isolated and often prestigious projects.' This is particularly the case in Dublin, exemplified by the DART and LUAS.

The DART, for example, primarily serves wealthier areas in Dublin. In addition, as isolated initiatives, they have the effect of improving access for particular city areas – which in turn increases the value of property in those areas – and of crowding out lower income householders and making services less accessible to them.

Initiatives based on improving public transport, such as quality bus corridors, more frequent services, and integrated ticketing should benefit those who already use these means of travel, such as older people, younger people and those on low incomes. However, there is a danger that efforts at improving public transport services risk curbing their use by these groups. This is because enhancement of public transport services tends to be geared at enticing commuters to choose public transport over their private cars. This involves services which have to be of high quality, and promise maximum efficiency and reliability. This can prove costly and may involve increasing fares, or making routes more efficient by reducing the number of stops and diversions (Banister, 1993, in Lucas et al., 2001), both of which are measures which may stem their use by the less affluent non-commuting users.

In any case, despite greater attention being given to public transport, the primary emphasis within transport policy remains fixed on constructing and upgrading road networks. The key transport policy, *Transport 21*, is an investment programme for transport over 2006–15. As the National Development Plan describes it, *Transport 21*:

> ... will focus on the delivery of a modern state-of-the-art transport system that will, inter alia, promote sustainable transport solutions, including clean urban public transport, clean vehicle technologies and fuels, more fuel efficient driving techniques and zero emission transport modes such as walking and cycling. Crucially, investment in public transport will facilitate a modal shift from private to public transport and sustainable criteria will be mainstreamed into all transport investment policy development. (Government of Ireland, 2007c, p. 132)

On balance, however, the money committed to the programme still favours investment in road transport infrastructure, which facilitates private modes of transport. The investment strategy involves €34 billion overall, of which €18 billion is to be spent on roads and €16 billion between public transport and regional airports. However, these figures do represent something of a re-balancing of priorities; public transport received far less funding in comparison to investment in roads in the past. In the previous National Development Plan 2000–2006, for example, €4.7 billion was allocated to roads and €2.234 billion to public transport measures.

In addition to providing more public transport, other policy initiatives involve measures to reduce car use, by increasing the cost of ownership and use through ecological tax reform or green taxation. This option seems to be gaining attention, as evident in the *Sustainable Transport and Travel Consultation Document* (Department of Transport, 2008). The document acknowledges that measures in *Transport 21* will not by themselves achieve sustainable travel and that car use in particular will continue to rise. Greater emphasis is put on behavioural changes in this document, so that, where feasible, the car will be the mode of transport of last resort, and there will be a considerable shift to bus, rail, walking and cycling. To this end it gives consideration to the possibility of implementing more extensive ecological taxation measures, to incentivise the purchase of cars that emit less CO_2 and to reduce private car use in favour of public transport.

Tax reform measures to date have included the reform of vehicle registration tax and motor tax to calibrate charges according to levels of carbon emissions, as implemented for new cars in 2008. Other measures, which are frequently implemented at Budget time, involve higher levies on fuel, but primarily in the context of raising general tax revenue rather than as a green tax. A newer measure is the introduction of limited car parking charges in the 2009 Budget; again, however, this measure is primarily one of raising general tax revenue. The introduction of congestion charges is also being considered. In the absence of fully acknowledging the social dimension of sustainable transport, ecological tax reform is likely to be quite regressive and have a particularly negative effect on those on low incomes who are structurally dependent on cars. As Tindale and Hewett, (1999, p. 248) remark, 'unless environmental taxes are specifically designed to be progressive, they probably won't be.' Therefore, unless explicit efforts are made either to simultaneously provide public transport alternatives or to mitigate the regressive effects of ecological taxes, low-income families are further impoverished by green transport taxes. As Lucas et al. (2001, p. vii) point out, ecological tax measures which:

> ... make car ownership and use unaffordable for low-income groups without *first* significantly improving their local service provision are, by their very nature, inequitable and unjust. Such an approach not only represents a policy conflict with the social inclusion agenda but is also the least effective method for reducing environmentally damaging travel behaviour.

To date in Ireland, any attempts at curbing car use through fiscal measures have largely failed to reduce car use and to mitigate its environmental impact, as discussed earlier. Their primary impact has been to increase the cost of car travel for low-income families.

Lack of a social focus and lack of consideration of transport inequalities and travel poverty are evident across the range of policy documents, programmes and statements. Scant consideration is given to accessibility and social exclusion issues, and when these are raised, they are linked primarily to physical access to public transport facilities for people with disabilities. The one programme which does recognise issues of exclusion and the principle of equality of access is the Rural Transport Programme. Known as the Rural Transport Initiative until 2007, it was instigated under the National Development Plan (2000–2006) and began as a pilot programme, making €6 million available to communities proposing rural transport services, focusing in particular on older people and people with disabilities; 34 programmes were funded. In its new guise, the objective is to transform the pilot programme into a permanent national programme on a phased basis but to still rely on community initiatives to propose and deliver the services. In McDonagh's (2006) assessment the initial pilot programme was very successful in meeting the travel needs of older people, the unemployed and young people. Demand-responsive services were very positively received; they improved individuals' quality of life enormously, giving them new social outlets and independence. However, it seems that social policy-related principles such as equality of access and social inclusion, which ideally should inform all aspects of sustainable transport policy, are cordoned off and only applied to a very small element of transport policy.

To sum up, the focus on travel and transport policy here is but one example of how social and environmental issues are related. Other environmental policy areas such as waste, energy, water, and issues related to climate change, can and need to be analysed and assessed from the perspective of principles such as equity in terms of how reforms are being implemented and their impact on different social groups. In addition, the core areas of social policy, including health, housing and education, can also be examined in terms of how policies in these areas contribute to, or detract from, sustainable development and quality of life in various ways, and how environment-related issues and reforms in these areas impact on various social groups.

CHAPTER SUMMARY

▸ This chapter has considered the issue of the environment and sustainable development and their implications for the discipline of social policy. As environmental concerns and the concept of sustainable development have entered mainstream policy discourse, and have increasingly centred on issues of social relevance, such as quality of life and social sustainability, the connections between social policy and sustainable development have become stronger. However, sustainable development has come to mean many different things, which has perhaps weakened its impact, and it continues to be an aspiration rather than a practical reality.

▸ The evolution of environmental issues and sustainable development policy in the Irish context was examined in section two. While connections are made between social inclusion, quality of life and sustainable development, the dominant rhetoric has focused on the complementarity between economic growth and the environment. As a result, socio-economic trends related to economic growth which pose problems for the environment have mounted, and sustainable development has become more of a challenge and more difficult to realise.

▸ The third section examined the relationship between social policy, transport and the environment as one particular area in which sustainable development remains a serious challenge. As a result of the rhetoric regarding the complementarity between economic growth and the environment, transport and travel patterns which are ultimately unsustainable have grown in a largely unregulated manner which detracts from quality of life and is environmentally damaging. In addition, the economic lens through which transport policy is formulated has meant that little consideration is given to issues such as equity, access and inclusion in the way transport policy has evolved and how it has impacted on particular groups in society. The growing concern with sustainable transport policy, therefore, needs to give greater attention to the economic, the environmental and the social pillars of sustainable development.

Discussion points

▸ Explore the reasons why social policy has traditionally been sceptical about environmentalism.

▸ Explain the differences between weak and strong models of sustainable development.

▸ Think about the area in which you live and how public transport serves that area. Consider its adequacy, who uses it and whether it contributes to sustainable travel patterns.

Further reading

Baker, S. (2006) *Sustainable Development*, London: Routledge.

Jacobs, M. (1997) 'The Quality of Life: Social Goods and the Politics of Consumption' in Jacobs, M. (ed.) *Greening the Millennium? The New Politics of the Environment*, Oxford: Blackwell, pp. 47–61.

Lucas, K. (ed.) (2004) *Running on Empty – Transport, Social Exclusion and Environmental Justice*, Bristol: Policy Press.

Useful websites

Department of the Environment, Heritage and Local Government: www.environ.ie/en

Notes

1   The need for a new sustainable development strategy as an update to the 1997 strategy was agreed in *Towards 2016* and due in 2007; however, as of late 2008 it is yet to be published.

BIBLIOGRAPHY

Aalen, F.H.A. (1985) 'The Working-Class Housing Movement in Dublin, 1850–1920' in M.J. Bannon, ed. *The Emergence of Irish Planning, 1880–1920*, Dublin: Turoe Press, 131–88.

Abel-Smith, B. and Townsend, P. (1965) *The Poor and the Poorest: a new analysis of the Ministry of Labour's Family Expenditure Surveys of 1953–1954 and 1960*, London: Bell.

Acheson, N., Harvey, B., Kearney, J. and Williamson, A.P. (2004) *Two Paths, One Purpose: Voluntary Action in Ireland, North and South: A Report to the Royal Irish Academy's Third Sector Research Programme*, Dublin: IPA.

Adebowale, M. (2008) 'Understanding Environmental Justice: making the connection between sustainable development and social justice' in G. Craig, T. Burchardt and D. Gordon, eds., *Social Justice and Public Policy*, Bristol: The Policy Press, 251–75.

Adelantado, J. and Caderón, E. (2006) 'Globalisation and the welfare state: the same strategies for similar problems?', *Journal of European Social Policy* Vol.16 No.4 November, 374–86.

Age Action Ireland (2008) 'Elder abuse figures indicate widespread scale of problem in Ireland', Latest News 13/06/08. Accessed at: *http://www.ageaction.ie/news/article-13–06–08.asp* on 6 December 2008.

Ahern, B. (2006) 'Speech by An Taoiseach, Bertie Ahern, T.D., At the Annual Liam Mellows Commemoration, Castletown, Co. Wexford, Sunday, 10 December, 2006.' Accessed at: *http://www.taoiseach.gov.ie/index.asp?locID=200&docID=3087* on 6 October 2008.

Aiken, W. (1992) 'Human Rights in an Ecological Era', *Environmental Values* Vol.1 No.3 Autumn, 191–203.

Akenson, D. (1970) *The Irish Education Experiment, The National System of Education in the Nineteenth Century*, London: Routledge Kegan Paul.

Alber, J. (1988) 'Is There a Crisis of the Welfare State? Cross-National Evidence from Europe, North America and Japan', *European Sociological Review* Vol.4 No.3, December, 181–207.

Alexiadou, N. (2005) 'Social Exclusion and Educational Opportunity: the case of British education policies within a European Union context', *Globalisation, Societies and Education* Vol.3 No.1 March, 103–27.

Alford, R. (1975) *Health Care Politics: Ideological and Interest Group Barriers to Reform*, Chicago: The University of Chicago Press.

All-Party Oireachtas Committee on the Constitution (2006) *Tenth Progress Report: the family*, Dublin: Stationery Office.

Allen, K. (1997) *Fianna Fáil and Irish Labour: 1926 to the Present*, London: Pluto Press.

Allen, K. (2000) *The Celtic Tiger: the Myth of Social Partnership in Ireland*, Manchester: Manchester University Press.

Allen, K. (2007) 'Neo-liberalism and Immigration' in B. Fanning, ed., *Immigration and Social Change in the Republic of Ireland*, Manchester: Manchester University Press, 84–98.

Allen, M. (1998) *The Bitter Word: Ireland's Job Famine and Its Aftermath*, Dublin: Poolbeg.

Allen, R. and Jones, T. (1990) *Guests of the Nation: People of Ireland versus the Multinationals*, London: Earthscan.

Amerini, G. (1999) 'Social Protection in the European Union, Iceland and Norway', Eurostat, *Statistics in Focus*, 5/1999, Brussels: European Commission.

Archer, P. and Weir, S. (2005) *Addressing Disadvantage, A Review of International Literature and of Strategy in Ireland, Report to the Educational Disadvantage Committee*, Dublin: Educational Disadvantage Committee.

Arneson, R. (2008) 'Equality of Opportunity', in E.N. Zalta, ed., *Stanford Encyclopaedia of Philosophy*, Winter. Accessed at: *http://plato.stanford.edu/archives/fall2008/entries/equal-opportunity/* on 17 September 2008.

Arts, W.A. and Gelissen, J. (2002) 'Three worlds of welfare capitalism or more? A state-of-the-art report', *Journal of European Social Policy* Vol.12 No.2 May, 137–58.

Atkinson, T., Cantillon, B., Marlier, E. and Nolan, B. (2002) *Social Indicators: The EU and Social Inclusion*, Oxford: Oxford University Press.

Bacik, I. (2004) *Kicking and Screaming: Dragging Ireland into the 21st Century*, Dublin: The O'Brien Press.

Bacon, P. (1997) 'Economic Opportunities for the Twenty-First Century' in F. O'Muircheartaigh, ed., *Ireland in the Coming Times: Essays to Celebrate T.K. Whitaker's 80 Years*, Dublin: IPA, 231–52.

Baeten, G. (2000) 'The tragedy of the highway: empowerment, disempowerment and the politics of sustainable discourses and practices', *European Planning Studies* Vol.8 No.1 February, 69–86.

Baker, J., Lynch, K., Cantillon, S. and Walsh, J. (2004) *Equality: from theory to action*, Basingstoke: Palgrave Macmillan.

Baker, S. (1987) 'Dependent Industrialisation and Public Protest: Raybestos Manhattan in Ireland', *Government and Opposition* Vol.22 No.4 October, 353–58.

Baker, S. (1990) 'The Evolution of the Irish Ecology Movement' in W. Rudig, ed., *Green Politics One*, Edinburgh: Edinburgh University Press, 47–81.

Baker, S. (2006) *Sustainable Development*, London: Routledge.

Balanda, K. and Wilde, J. (2001) *Inequalities in Mortality 1989–1998: A Report on All-Ireland Mortality Data*, Dublin: IPH.

Balanda, K. and Wilde, J. (2003) *Inequalities in Perceived Health – A Report on the All-Ireland Social Capital and Health Survey*, Dublin: IPH.

Baradat, L.P. (2000) *Political Ideologies: Their Origins and Impact* (seventh edition), New Jersey: Prentice Hall.

Barnardos (2008) 'Children Placed at Serious Risk Due to Lack of Out of Hours Social Care Services', Press Release Friday, 8 August 2008. Accessed at: *http://www.barnardos.ie/media_centre/our-latest-news/Children-Placed-at-Serious-Risk-Due-to-Lack-of-Out-of-Hours-Social-Care-Services.html* on 6 December 2008.

Barot, R. and Bird, J. (2001) 'Racialization: the genealogy and critique of the concept', *Ethnic and Racial Studies* Vol.24 No.4 July, 601–18.

Barr, N. (2004) *The Economics of the Welfare State* (fourth edition), Oxford: Oxford University Press.

Barrientos, A. and Powell, M. (2004) 'The route map of the Third Way' in S. Hale, W. Leggett and L. Martell, eds., *The Third Way and beyond: Criticisms, futures, alternatives*, Manchester: Manchester University Press, 9–26.

Barrington, R. (1987) *The Politics of Health and Medicine, 1900–1970*, Dublin: IPA.

Barrington, R. (2004) *Poverty is Bad for your Health*, Discussion Paper, Dublin: CPA.

Barron, P. (1995) 'The Child Care Act 1991: An Overview' in H. Ferguson and P. Kenny, eds., *On Behalf of the Child: Child Welfare, Child Protection and the Child Care Act 1991*, Dublin: A. & A. Farmar, 9–16.

Barry, F. (1999) 'Introduction' in F. Barry, ed., *Understanding Ireland's Economic Growth*, Basingstoke: Macmillan, 1–11.

Barry, J. (1998) 'Social Policy and Social Movements, Ecology and Social Policy' in N. Ellison and C. Pierson, eds., *Developments in British Social Policy*, Basingstoke: Palgrave Macmillan, 218–32.

Barry, J. and Daly, L. (1988) *Travellers' Health Status Study Census of Travelling People 1986*, Dublin: Health Research Board.

Barry, J., Herity, B. and Solan, J. (1989) *The Travellers Health Status Study – Vital Statistics of the Travelling People, 1987*, Dublin: Health Research Board.

Bartley, B. (1998) 'Exclusion, Invisibility and the Neighbourhood in West Dublin' in A. Madanipour, G. Cars, and J. Allen, eds., *Social Exclusion in European Cities, processes, experiences and responses*, London: Jessica Kingsley, 131–56.

Bartley, B. (2007) 'Planning in Ireland' in B. Bartley and R. Kitchin, eds., *Understanding Contemporary Ireland*, London: Pluto Press, 31–43.

Beaumont, C. (1997) 'Women and the Politics of Equality: The Irish Women's Movement, 1930–1943' in M. Valiulis and M. O'Dowd, eds. *Women and Irish History*, Dublin: Wolfhound Press, 173–88.

Becker, S. (1997) *Responding to Poverty: the Politics of Cash and Care*, London: Addison Wesley Longman.

Beech, M. (2006) *The Political Philosophy of New Labour*, London: Tauris Academic Studies.

Begg, D. (2004) 'People, Work and Social Change' in J. Hourihane, ed., *Ireland and the European Union: The First Thirty Years, 1973–2002*, Dublin: The Lilliput Press, 40–53.

Begg, I. (2004) 'Policy Responses to Marginalization: The Changing Role of the EU' in D. Gallie, ed., *Resisting Marginalization: Unemployment Experience and Social Policy in the European Union*, Oxford: Oxford University Press, 243–63.

Bennett, J. (2007) 'ECEC Financing in Ireland' in N. Hayes and S. Bradley, eds., *A Decade of Reflection, Early Childhood Care and Education in Ireland 1996–2006*, Dublin: Centre for Social and Educational Research, 10–43.

Berend, I.T. (2005) 'Foucault and the Welfare State', *European Review* Vol.13 No.4 October, 551–556.

Berger, S. (2002) 'Democracy and Social Democracy', *European History Quarterly* Vol.32 No.1 January, 13–37.

Bertaux, D., Boje, F. and McIntosh, S., eds. (2002) *Between Integration and Exclusion: A comparative study of local dynamics in precarity and resistance to exclusion in urban contexts, Final Report of an EU-TSER Project.* Accessed at: *http://ec.europa.eu/research/social-sciences/pdf/finalreport/soe2ct983070-final-report.pdf* on 27 March 2008.

Bertens, H. (1995) *The Idea of the Postmodern: a history*, London: Routledge.

Beveridge, W. (1942) *Social Insurance and Allied Services: Report by Sir William Beveridge*, London: HMSO.

Bew, P., Hazelkorn, E. and Patterson, H. (1989) *The Dynamics of Irish Politics*, London: Lawrence and Wishart.

Billy Elliot (2000) Film, Directed by Stephen Daldry. UK, Arts Council of England.

Blackwell, J. (1982) 'Government, Economy and Society' in F. Litton, ed., *Unequal Achievement: The Irish Experience 1957–1982*, Dublin: IPA, 43–60.

Blackwell, J. (1990) 'Housing Finance and Subsidies in Ireland' in P. McLennan, and R. Williams, eds., *Affordable Housing in Europe*, York: Joseph Rowntree Foundation, 101–27.

Blair, T. (1998) *The Third Way: New Politics for the New Century*, Fabian Pamphlet No.588, London: Fabian Society.

Blair, T. and Schröder, G. (1999) *Europe: The Third Way/Die Neue Mitte*, London: Labour Party.

Boldt, S., Devine, B., MacDevitt, D. and Morgan, M. (1998) *Educational Disadvantage and early school-leaving: discussion papers*, Dublin: CPA.

Bonoli, G. (2007) 'Time Matters: Postindustrialization, New Social Risks, and Welfare State Adaptation in Advanced Industrial Democracies', *Comparative Political Studies* Vol.40 No.5 May, 495–520.

Bonoli, G. and Powell, M., eds. (2004) *Social Democratic Party Policies in Contemporary Europe*, London: Routledge.

Bonoli, G. and Sarfarti, H. (2002) 'Conclusions: the policy implications of a changing labour market-social protection relationship' in H. Sarfarti and G. Bonoli, eds., *Labour Market and Social Protection Reforms in International Perspective*, Aldershot: Ashgate, 453–86.

Boucher, G. (2008) 'Ireland's Lack of a Coherent Integration Policy', *Translocations* Vol.3 No.1 Spring, 5–28.

Boucher, G. and Collins, G. (2003) 'Having One's Cake and Being Eaten too: Irish Neo-liberal Corporatism', *Review of Social Economy* Vol.LXI No.3 September 2003, 295–316.

Bourdieu, P. (1986) 'The Forms of Capital' in J.G. Richardson, ed., *Handbook of Theory and Research for the Sociology of Education*, Westport CT: Greenwood Press, 241–58.

Bourdieu, P. and Passeron, J.-C. (1977) *Reproduction in Education, Society and Culture*, Sheffield: Sheffield Region Centre for Science and Technology.

Brandi, S. (2007) 'Unveiling the Ideological Construction of the 2004 Irish Citizenship Referendum: a critical discourse analysis approach', *Translocations* Vol.2 No.1 Summer, 26–47.

Brassed Off (1996) Film, Directed by Mark Herman. UK, Channel Four Films.

Braveman, P. (2006) 'Health Disparities and Health Equity: concepts and measurement', *Annual Review of Public Health* Vol.27, 167–94.

Braveman, P. and Gruskin, S. (2003) 'Defining Equity in Health', *Journal of Epidemiology and Community Health* Vol.57 No.4 April, 254–58.

Breathnach, A. (2006) *Becoming Conspicuous: Irish Travellers, Society and State, 1922–70*, Dublin: UCD Press.

Breen, R. (1987) 'The Costs of Unemployment', *Administration* Vol.35 No.3 Autumn, 225–49.

Breen, R., Hannon, D., Rottman, D. B. and Whelan, C.T. (1990) *Understanding Contemporary Ireland: State, Class and Development in the Republic of Ireland*, Dublin: Gill & Macmillan.

Brennan, P. (1982) 'Backlash and Blackmail: How a tiny Catholic pressure group privately won a commitment to a constitutional amendment on abortion', *Magill* July 1982, 14–24.

Brooke, S. and Clayton, V. (2005) 'The Changing Nature of the Housing Association Sector' in M. Norris, and D. Redmond, eds., *Housing Contemporary Ireland, Policy,*

Society and Shelter, Dublin: IPA, 205–23.

Brown, P. and Lauder, H. (2006) 'Globalisation, knowledge and the myth of the magnet economy', *Globalisation, Societies and Education* Vol.4 No.1 March, 25–57.

Brown, T. (1981) 'Poverty, Politics and Policies' in S. Kennedy, ed., *One Million Poor? The Challenge of Irish Inequality*, Dublin: Turoe Press, 145–63.

Brown, T. (2004) *Ireland: A Social and Cultural History 1922–2002*, London: Harper Perennial.

Browne, N. (1986) *Against the Tide*, Dublin: Gill & Macmillan.

Browne, V. (1981) 'If I were Taoiseach: Garrett FitzGerald interviewed by Vincent Browne', *Magill* April 1981, 26–34.

Browne, V., ed. (1982) 'Will the last TD to leave the Dáil please switch off the light at the end of the tunnel', *Magill* January 1982, 21.

Brownlee, A. (2008) 'Paradise Lost or Found? The changing homeless policy landscape in Ireland' in D. Downey, ed., *Perspectives on Irish Homelessness: past, present and future*, Dublin: Homeless Agency, 34–42.

Bryson, V. (1992) *Feminist Political Theory: An Introduction*, Basingstoke: Macmillan.

Buchanan, J.M. (2003) 'Public Choice: Politics Without Romance', *Policy* Vol.19 No.3 Spring, 13–18.

Buckley, H. (2002) *Child Protection and Welfare: Innovations and Interventions*, Dublin: IPA.

Buckley, H. (2005) 'Reviewing Children First: Some Issues for Consideration', *Irish Journal of Family Law* Vol.3, 2–8.

Burau, V. and Blank, R. (2006) 'Comparing Health Policy: an assessment of typologies of health systems', *Journal of Comparative Policy Analysis* Vol.8 No.1 March, 63–76.

Burke, H. (1987) *The People and the Poor Law in 19th Century Ireland*, Dublin: Women's Education Bureau.

Burke, S. (2007) *Addressing the Health Care Crisis*, ICTU/SIPTU Congress Briefing Paper, No.10.

Burke, S. (2008) 'Harney sets out to save the HSE – from itself' *The Irish Times*, 12 July 2008.

Burke, S., Keenaghan, C., O'Donovan, D. and Quirke, B. (2004) *Health in Ireland – an unequal state*, Dublin: Public Health Alliance Ireland.

Burningham, K. and Thrush, D. (2001) *Rainforests are a long way from here: the environmental concerns of disadvantaged groups*, York: Joseph Rowntree Foundation.

Burns, K., and Lynch, D., eds. (2008) *Child Protection and Welfare Social Work: Contemporary Themes and Practice Perspectives*, Dublin: A. & A. Farmar.

Burton-Jones, A. (1999) *Knowledge Capitalism: business, work and learning in the new economy*, Oxford: Oxford University Press.

Bytheway, B. (1995) *Ageism*, Buckingham: Open University Press.

Cabot, D., ed. (1985) *The State of the Environment*, Dublin: An Foras Forbatha.

Cahill, M. (1991) 'The Greening of Social Policy' in N. Manning, ed., *Social Policy Review, 1990–91*, Harlow: Longman, 9–23.

Cahill, M. (2002) *The Environment and Social Policy*, London: Routledge.

Cahill, M. (2003) 'The Environment and Green Social Policy' in J. Baldock, N. Manning and S. Vickerstaff, eds., *Social Policy*, (second edition) Oxford: Oxford University Press, 553–76.

Cahill, M. and Fitzpatrick, T., eds. (2002) *Environmental Issues and Social Welfare*, Oxford: Blackwell.

Callaghan, J. (2003) 'Social Democracy in Transition', *Parliamentary Affairs* Vol.56 No.1 January, 125–40.

Callan, T., Nolan, B., Whelan, B.J., Hannon, D. with Creighton, S. (1989) *Poverty, Income and Welfare in Ireland*, General Research Series, No.46 Dublin: ESRI.

Cantillon, S., Corrigan, C., Kirby, P. and O'Flynn, J., eds. (2001) *Rich and Poor: Perspectives on Tackling Inequality in Ireland*, Dublin: Oak Tree Press.

Carabine, J. (1998) 'New horizons? New insights? Postmodernism, social policy and the case of sexuality' in J. Carter, ed., *Postmodernity and the Fragmentation of Welfare*, London: Routledge, 121–35.

Carabine, J. (2004) 'Sexualities, Personal Lives and Social Policy' in J. Carabine, ed., *Sexualities, Personal Lives and Social Policy*, Bristol: Policy Press in association with the Open University, 1–48.

Carers Association in partnership with Caring for Carers Ireland and Care Alliance Ireland (2008) *Listen to Carers: Report on a Nation-wide Carer Consultation*. Accessed at: *http://www.carersireland.com/library_of_documents.htm#cc508* on 6 December 2008.

Carey, S. (2005) 'Land, Labour and Politics: Social Insurance in Post-War Ireland', *Social Policy and Society* Vol.4 No.3 July, 303–11.

Carter, J., ed. (1998) *Postmodernity and the Fragmentation of Welfare*, London: Routledge.

Carter, N. (2007) *The Politics of the Environment: ideas, activism, policy* (second edition), Cambridge: Cambridge University Press.

Cassell, R. (1997) *Medical Charities, Medical Politics, The Irish Dispensary System and the Poor Law, 1836–1872*, Suffolk: Boydell Press.

Castles, F.G., and Mitchell, D. (1993) 'Worlds of Welfare and Families of Nations' in F.G. Castles, ed., *Families of Nations: Patterns of Public Policy in Western Democracies*, Aldershot: Dartmouth, 93–128.

Cerny, P. (1997) 'Paradoxes of the Competition State: the dynamics of political globalisation', *Government and Opposition* Vol.32 No.2 April, 251–74.

Children's Rights Alliance (2008) 'Over One Million Reasons for Children's Rights Referendum' Press Release 8 October 2008. Accessed at: *http://www.childrensrights.ie/index.php?q=knowledgebase/irish-constitution/over-one-million-reasons-childrens-rights-referendum* on 6 December 2008.

Chitty, C. (1996) 'The Changing Role of the State in Education Provision' in J. Ahier, B. Cosin and M. Hales, eds., *Diversity and Change, Education, Policy and Selection*, London: Routledge, 249–64.

Christian Democratic Union of Germany (2008) Webpage 'The CDU of Germany: CDU – A Foundation of 50+ Years'. Accessed at: *http://www.cdu.de/en/3440_3455.htm* on 5 October 2008.

Christie, A. (2003) 'Unsettling the "social" in social work: responses to asylum seeking children in Ireland', *Child and Family Social Work* Vol.8 No.3 August, 223–31.

Christie, A. (2004) 'Difference' in B. Fanning, P. Kennedy, G. Kiely and S. Quin, eds., *Theorising Irish Social Policy*, Dublin: UCD Press, 147–64.

Churchill, W. (1911/2000) 'Speech on National Insurance Bill' in R. Goodin and D. Mitchell, eds., *The Foundations of the Welfare State*, Volume II, Cheltenham: Edward Elgar, 102–9.

Citizen Traveller (2000) *Attitudes to Travellers and Minority Groups*, Dublin: Citizen Traveller.

Citizens Information (2008) Webpage 'Upper age limits in Ireland' updated 22/07/2008. Accessed at: *http://www.citizensinformation.ie/categories/employment/equality-in-work/upper-age-limits-in-ireland* on 16 December 2008.

Clancy, M. (1999) 'Shaping the Nation: Women in the Free State Parliament, 1923–1937' in Y. Galligan, E. Ward and R. Wilford, eds., *Contesting Politics: Women in Ireland, North and South*, Boulder, Colorado: Westview Press, 201–18.

Clancy, P. (1982) *Participation in Higher Education: a national survey*, Dublin: HEA.

Clancy, P. (1988) *Who goes to College: a second national survey of participation in higher education*, Dublin: HEA.

Clancy, P. (1995) *Access to College, Patterns of Continuity and Change*, Dublin: HEA.

Clancy, P. (1996) 'Investment in Education, the equality perspective: progress and possibilities', *Administration* Vol.44 No.3 Autumn, 28–41.

Clancy, P. (2001) *College Entry in Focus: a fourth national survey of access to higher education*, Dublin: HEA.

Clancy, P. (2005) 'Education Policy' in S. Quin, P. Kennedy, A. Matthews and G. Kiely, eds., *Contemporary Irish Social Policy*, Dublin: UCD Press, 80–114.

Clancy, P. (2007) 'Education' in S. O'Sullivan, ed., *Contemporary Ireland: A Sociological Map*, Dublin: UCD Press, 101–119.

Clark, A. (2005) 'Wild Workhouse Girls and the Liberal Imperial State in Mid-Nineteenth Century Ireland', *Journal of Social History* Vol.39 No.2 Winter, 389–409.

Clarke, B. (1979) 'The Environment, 1945–70' in J.J. Lee, ed., *Ireland, 1945–70*, Dublin: Gill & Macmillan, 96–110.

Clarke, J. (2001) 'US Welfare: Variations on the Liberal Regime' in A. Cochrane, J. Clarke and S. Gewirtz, eds., *Comparing Welfare States: Family Life and Social Policy* (second edition), London: Sage in association with The Open University, 113–52.

Clarke, J. (2004) *Changing Welfare, Changing States*, London: Sage.

Clarke, J. and Piven, F.F. (2001) 'United States: An American Welfare State?' in P. Alcock and G. Craig, eds., *International Social Policy: Welfare Regimes in the Developed World*, Basingstoke: Palgrave, 26–44.

Clasen, J. (1994) 'Social security – the core of the German employment-centred social state' in J. Clasen and R. Freeman, eds., *Social Policy in Germany*, Herfordshire: Harvester Wheatsheaf, 61–82.

Clasen, J., Davidson, J., Ganßmann, H. and Mauer, A. (2006) 'Non-employment and the welfare state: the United Kingdom and Germany compared', *Journal of European Social Policy* Vol.16 No.2 May, 134–54.

Clear, C. (2004) "Too Fond of Going": Female Emigration and Change for Women in Ireland, 1946–1961' in D. Keogh, F. O'Shea and C. Quinlan, eds., *Ireland in the 1950s The Lost Decade*, Cork/Dublin: Mercier Press, 135–146.

Coakley, J. (1993) 'The foundations of statehood' in J. Coakley and M. Gallagher, eds., *Politics in the Republic of Ireland* (second edition), Dublin: Folens and PSAI Press, 1–24.

Coakley, J. and Gallagher, M., eds. (2005) *Politics in the Republic of Ireland* (fourth edition), London: Routledge in association with PSAI Press.

Cochrane, A. (1993) 'Comparative Approaches and Social Policy' in A. Cochrane and J. Clarke, eds., *Comparing Welfare States – Britain in an International Context* (first edition), London: Sage, 1–18.

Colantonio, A. (2007) 'Measuring social sustainability: best practice from urban renewal in the EU' 2007/1 EIBURS Working Paper Series. Accessed at: *http://*

www.brookes.ac.uk/schools/be/oisd/sustainable_communities/resources/SocialSustainability_Metrics_and_Tools.pdf on 12 October 2008.

Coleman, K. and Considine, J. (2006) 'The No Income Tax Campaign: Twenty-First-Century Tax Philosophy in 1920s', *Irish Economic and Social History* XXXIII, 1–17.

Colgan, A. (2006) 'People with physical disability: health policy and practice' in D. McCluskey, ed., *Health Policy and Practice in Ireland*, Dublin: UCD Press, 188–206.

Collins, N. (1999) 'Corruption in Ireland: a review of recent cases' in N. Collins, ed. *Political Issues in Ireland Today*, (second edition), Manchester: Manchester University Press, 64–88.

Collins, N. and Cradden, T. (1997) *Irish Politics Today* (third edition), Manchester: Manchester University Press.

Collins, N. and O'Shea, M. (2001) *Understanding Political Corruption in Irish Politics*, Cork: Cork University Press.

Collins, R. (2000) 'Comparative and Historical Patterns of Education' in M. Hallinan, ed., *Handbook of the Sociology of Education*, New York: Kluwer, 213–39.

Combat Poverty Agency (1987) *Poverty Today* Vol.1 No.1 December, 2–12.

Combat Poverty Agency (2003) *Educational Disadvantage in Ireland*, Poverty Briefing No.14, Dublin: CPA.

Combat Poverty Agency (2005) *Ending child poverty; policy statement*, Dublin: CPA.

Combat Poverty Agency (2007) *Health Policy Statement*, Dublin: CPA.

Combat Poverty Agency (2008) Combat Poverty Advice to Government Budget 2009, September 2008. Accessed at: *http://www.combatpoverty.ie/publications/submissions/2008_Sub_PBS2009.pdf* on 20 October 2008.

Commission on Assisted Human Reproduction (2005) *Report of the Commission on Assisted Human Reproduction*, Dublin: Stationery Office.

Commission on Health Funding (1989) *Report of the Commission on Health Funding*, Dublin: Stationery Office.

Commission on Itinerancy (1963) *Report of the Commission on Itinerancy*, Dublin: Stationery Office.

Commission on Social Justice (1994) *Social Justice: Strategies for National Renewal the Report of the Commission on Social Justice*, London: Vintage.

Commission on Social Welfare (1986) *Report of the Commission on Social Welfare*, Dublin: Stationery Office.

Commission on the Private Rented Residential Sector (2000) *Report of the Commission on the Private Rented Residential Sector*, Dublin: Stationery Office.

Commission on the Status of People with Disabilities (1996) *A Strategy for Equality*, Dublin: Stationery Office.

Commission on the Status of Women (1972) *Report of the Commission on the Status of Women*, Dublin: Stationery Office.

Committee to Monitor and Co-ordinate the Implementation of the Recommendations of the Task Force on the Traveller Community (2000) *First Progress Report of the Committee to Monitor and Co-ordinate the Implementation of the Recommendations of the Task Force on the Traveller Community*, Dublin: Stationery Office.

Committee to Monitor and Co-ordinate the Implementation of the Recommendations of the Task Force on the Traveller Community (2005) *Second Progress Report of the Committee to Monitor and Co-ordinate the Implementation of the Recommendations of the Task Force on the Traveller Community*, Dublin: Department of Justice, Equality and Law Reform.

Conference of Major Religious Superiors (1992) *Education and Poverty*, Dublin: Education Commission, Conference of Major Religious Superiors.

Connaughton, B., Quinn, B. and Rees, N. (2007) 'The Europeanization of Irish Environmental Policy: the EU as the Engine of Domestic Policy Change', *Administration* Vol.54 No.4 Winter, 77–93.

Connelly, A. (1999) 'Women and the Constitution of Ireland' in Y. Galligan, E. Ward and R. Wilford, eds., *Contesting Politics: women in Ireland, North and South*, Boulder, Colorado: Westview Press, 18–37.

Connolly, L. (1996) 'The Women's Movement in Ireland, 1970–1995', *Irish Journal of Feminist Studies* Vol.1 No.1 Spring, 43–77.

Connolly, L. and O'Toole, T. (2005) *Documenting Irish Feminisms – The Second Wave*, Dublin: Woodfield Press.

Connolly, T. (2004) 'The Commission on Emigration, 1948–1954' in D. Keogh, F. O'Shea and C. Quinlan, eds., *Ireland in the 1950s: The Lost Decade*, Cork/Dublin: Mercier Press, 87–104.

Conrad, K. (2001) 'Queer Treasons, Homosexuality and Irish National Identity', *Cultural Studies* Vol.15 No.1 January, 124–37.

Conroy, P. and Brennan, A. (2003) *Migrant Workers and Their Experiences*, Dublin: Equality Authority.

Conroy-Jackson, P. (1993) 'Managing Mothers: The Case of Ireland' in J. Lewis, ed., *Women and Social Policies in Europe, Work, Family and the State*, Aldershot: Edward Elgar, 72–91.

Conservative Party (2007) 'Raising the Bar, Closing the Gap: an action plan for schools to raise standards, create more good school places and make opportunity more equal', *Opportunity Agenda*, Green Paper No.1. Accessed at: *http://www.conservatives.com/pdf/New%20opportunity_proof.pdf* on 20 June 2008.

Constitution of Ireland (1937) *Bunreacht na hÉireann*, Dublin: Stationery Office.

Convery, F. (1982) 'The Physical Environment' in F. Litton, ed., *Unequal Achievement The Irish Experience, 1957–1982*, Dublin: IPA, 243–65.

Convery, F. (1992) 'Economy and the Environment – Towards Sustainability in Ireland' in J. Feehan, ed., *Environment and Development in Ireland*, Dublin: The Environmental Institute, UCD, 1–6.

Cook, G. (1986) 'Britain's legacy to the Irish social security system', in P.J. Drudy, ed., *Ireland and Britain since 1922*, Cambridge: Cambridge University Press, 65–85.

Cook, G. and McCashin, A. (1997) 'Male Breadwinner: A Case Study of Gender and Social Security in the Republic of Ireland' in A. Byrne and M. Leonard, eds., *Women in Irish Society: a sociological reader*, Belfast: Beyond the Pale, 167–80.

Coolahan, J. (1981) *Irish Education: History and Structure*, Dublin: IPA.

Corbett, M. (2008) 'Hidden Children: the Story of State Care for Separated Children' *Working Notes* No.59 November, 18–24.

Corcoran, M. (2000) 'Local Authority Residents: An Invisible Minority' in M. MacLachlan, and M. O'Connell, eds., *Cultivating Pluralism, Psychological, Social and Cultural Perspectives on a Changing Ireland*, Dublin: Oak Tree Press, 75–91.

Cornell, S. and Hartmann, D. (1998) *Ethnicity and Race: making identities in a changing world*, Thousand Oaks, California: Pine Forge Press.

Coughlan, A. (1987) 'The Constitution and Social Policy' *Administration* Vol.35 No.4 Winter, 143–161.

Coughlan, D. (2005) 'Postmodernism', *The Literary Encyclopedia*, December. Accessed at: *http://www.litencyc.com/php/stopics.php?rec=true&UID=889* on 20 September 2008.

Council of the European Union (2002) 'Fight against poverty and social exclusion: common objectives for the second round of National Action Plans – Endorsement, SOC 508' Brussels, 25 November 2002. Accessed at: *http://ec.europa.eu/ employment_social/spsi/docs/social_inclusion/counciltext_en.pdf* 13 September 2008.

Cousins, M. (1994) 'Social Security and Informal Caring – An Irish Perspective', *Administration* Vol.42 No.1 Spring, 25–46.

Cousins, M. (1995) *The Irish Social Welfare System: Law and Social Policy*, Dublin: Round Hall Press.

Cousins, M. (1997) 'Ireland's Place in the Worlds of Welfare Capitalism', *Journal of European Social Policy* Vol.7 No.3 August, 223–35.

Cousins, M. (1999) 'The Introduction of Children's Allowances in Ireland, 1939–1944', *Irish Economic and Social History* XXVI, 35–53.

Cousins, M. (2000) 'From the White Paper to the Commission on Social Welfare, 1949–1986', in A. Lavan, ed., *50 Years of Social Welfare Policy* (seminar proceedings), Dublin: Department of Social, Community and Family Affairs, 31–7.

Cousins, M. (2003) *The Birth of Social Welfare in Ireland, 1922–52*, Dublin: Four Courts Press.

Cousins, M. (2005a) *Explaining the Irish Welfare State. An Historical, Comparative and Political Analysis*, New York: Edwin Mellen Press.

Cousins, M. (2005b) *European Welfare States: Comparative Perspectives*, London: Sage.

Cousins, M., ed. (2007) *Welfare Policy and Poverty*, Dublin: IPA and CPA.

Cowen B. (2008) 'Taoiseach Addresses First Business Roundtable with Government of Ireland' Press Release 30 October 2008. Accessed at: *http://www.taoiseach.gov.ie/ index.asp?locID=584&docID=4070* on 16 December 2008.

Coyle, C. (1994) 'Administrative Capacity and the implementation of EU environmental policy in Ireland' in S. Baker, ed., *Protecting the Periphery – environmental policy in peripheral regions of the European Union*, London: Frank Cass, 62–79.

Coyne, E.J. (1951) 'Mother and Child Service', *Studies* Vol.XL No.158 June, 129–49.

Cromien, S. (2000) 'Serving in New Spheres' in R. O'Donnell, ed., *Europe: The Irish Experience*, Dublin: IEA, 148–58.

Crone, J. (1995) 'Lesbians: the Lavender women of Ireland' in I. O'Caroll and E. Collins, eds., *Lesbian and Gay Visions of Ireland, Towards the Twenty-first Century*, London: Cassell, 60–70.

Cronin, M. (2006) 'Place, Class and Politics' in J. Crowley, R. Devoy, D. Linehan, P. O'Flanagan, and M. Murphy, eds., *Atlas of Cork City*, Cork: Cork University Press, 202–08.

Crosland, A. (1956) *The Future of Socialism*, London: J. Cape.

Crowley, F. (2003) *Mental Illness: the Neglected Quarter, Summary Report Amnesty International (Irish Section)*, Dublin: Amnesty International (Irish Section).

Crowley, N. (1999) 'Travellers and Social Policy' in S. Quin, P. Kennedy, A. O'Donnell and G. Kiely, eds., *Contemporary Irish Social Policy*, Dublin: UCD Press, 243–265.

Crowley, N. (2005) 'Travellers and Social Policy' in S. Quin, P. Kennedy, A. Matthews and G. Kiely, eds., *Contemporary Irish Social Policy* (second edition), Dublin: UCD Press, 231–255.

Crowley, N. (2008) 'Age Discrimination Dominates Equality Authority Workplace Casefiles', Equality Authority Press Release, 23 July 2008. Accessed at: *http:// www.equality.ie/index.asp?locID=135&docID=733* on 6 December 2008.

CSO (2006) *Women and Men in Ireland 2006*, Cork: CSO.

CSO (2007a) *2006 Census of Population, Volume 11, Disability, Carers and Voluntary Activities*, Cork: CSO.

CSO (2007b) *EU Survey on Income and Living Conditions (EU-SILC) 2006*, Dublin: Stationery Office.

CSO (2007c) *2006 Census of Population, Volume 12, Travel to Work, School and College*, Cork: CSO.

CSO (2007d) *2006 Census of Population, Principal Socio-economic Results*, Cork: CSO.

CSO (various years) *Census of Population*, Dublin: Stationery Office.

CSO (various years) *EU Survey on Income and Living Conditions (EU-SILC)*, Dublin: Stationery Office.

Cullen Owens, R. (1984) *Smashing Times: A History of the Irish Women's Suffrage Movement 1889–1922*, Dublin: Attic Press.

Cullen, F. (2001) *Cleansing Rural Dublin, Public health and housing initiatives in the South Dublin Poor Law Union, 1880–1920*, Dublin: Irish Academic Press.

Cullen, P. (2006) 'One-half of Dublin drivers would never use bus – survey', *The Irish Times* 27 November 2006.

Culyer, A.J. and Wagstaff, A. (1993) 'Equity and Equality in Health and Health Care', *Journal of Health Economics* Vol.12 No.4 December, 431–57.

Currie, G. and Stanley, J. (2008) 'Investigating the Links between Social Capital and Public Transport', *Transport Reviews* Vol.28 No.4 July, 529–47.

Curry, J. (1986) 'Symposium on the Report of the Commission on Social Welfare', *Journal of the Statistical and Social Inquiry Society of Ireland* Vol.XXV Part IV, 1–7.

Curry, J. (1998) *Irish Social Services* (third edition), Dublin: IPA.

Curry, J. (2003) *Irish Social Services* (fourth edition), Dublin: IPA.

Curtin, C. and Varley, T. (1995) 'Community Action and the State' in P. Clancy, S. Drudy, K. Lynch and L.O'Dowd, eds., *Irish Society: Sociological Perspectives*, Dublin: SAI and IPA, 379–409.

Dahrendorf, R. (1999) 'The Newstatesman Essay – Whatever Happened to Liberty?' *New Statesman*, 6 September 1999. Accessed at: *http://www.newstatesman.com/199909060018* on 21 June 2008.

Dáil Éireann (1919) Volume 1 – 21 January, 1919 Democratic Programme. Accessed at: *http://historical-debates.oireachtas.ie/D/DT/D.F.O.191901210015.html* on 19 December 2006.

Dáil Éireann (1988) Volume 377 – 09 February 1988 Written Answers – Hospital Closures. Accessed at: *http://historical-debates.oireachtas.ie/D/0377/D.0377.198802090138.html* on 19 December 2006.

Dale, A. (1997) 'Women in the Labour Market: Policy in Perspective' in C. Ungerson and M. Kember, eds., *Women and Social Policy: A Reader* (second edition), Basingstoke: Macmillan, 57–71.

Daly, H. (1995) 'The Steady State Economy: Alternatives to Growthomania' in J. Kirby, P. O'Keefe and L. Timberlake, eds., *The Earthscan Reader in Sustainable Development*, London: Earthscan, 331–42.

Daly, M. (1989) *Women and Poverty*, Dublin: Attic Press (in conjunction with the CPA).

Daly, M. (2006) 'EU Social Policy after Lisbon', *Journal of Common Market Studies* Vol.44 No.3 September, 461–81.

Daly, M. (2008) 'Whither EU Social Policy? An Account and Assessment of Developments in the Lisbon Social Inclusion Process', *Journal of Social Policy* Vol.37 No.1 January, 1–19.

Daly, M. and Lewis, J. (2000) 'The concept of social care and the analysis of contemporary welfare states', *British Journal of Sociology* Vol.51, No.2 June, 281–98.

Daly, M. and Yeates, N. (2003) 'Common origins, different paths: adaptation and change in social security in Britain and Ireland', *Policy and Politics* Vol.31 No.1 January, 85–97.

Daly, M.E. (1981) *Social and Economic History of Ireland Since 1800*, Dublin: The Educational Company.

Daly, M.E. (1985) 'Housing Conditions and the Genesis of Housing Reform in Dublin, 1880–1920' in M.J. Bannon, ed., *The Emergence of Irish Planning, 1880–1920*, Dublin: Turoe Press, 77–129.

Daly, M.E. (1997) '"Turn on the Tap": the State, Irish Women and Running Water' in M. Valiulis and M. O'Dowd, eds., *Women and Irish History*, Dublin: Wolfhound Press, 206–219.

Daly, M.E. (1999a) 'The Irish Family Since the Famine: Continuity and Change', in *Irish Journal of Feminist Studies* Vol.3 No.2 Autumn, 1–21.

Daly, M.E. (1999b) '"An atmosphere of sturdy independence": the state and the Dublin hospitals in the 1930s' in E. Malcolm and G. Jones, eds., *Medicine, Disease and the State in Ireland, 1650–1940*, Cork: Cork University Press, 234–52.

Daniel, P. and Ivatts, J. (1998) *Children and Social Policy*, Basingstoke: Macmillan.

Dawson, C. (1910) 'The Children Act and the Oldham League', *Journal of the Statistical and Social Inquiry Society of Ireland* Vol.XII December, 388–395.

De Wispelaere, J. and Walsh, J. (2007) 'Disability Rights in Ireland: Chronicle of a Missed Opportunity', *Irish Political Studies* Vol.22 No.4 December, 517–43.

Deacon, A. (2002) *Perspectives on welfare: Ideas, ideologies and policy debates*, Buckingham: Open University Press.

Deacon, B. (2002a) 'Globalisation and the Challenge for Social Security' in R. Sigg and C. Behrendt, eds., *Social Security in the Global Village*, New Brunswick: Transaction Publishers, 17–29.

Deacon, B. (2007) *Global Social Policy and Governance*, London: Sage.

Deacon, B. (2008) 'Global and regional social governance' in N. Yeates, ed., *Understanding Global Social Policy*, Bristol: The Policy Press, 25–48.

Deacon, B., with Hulse, M. and Stubbs, P. (1997) *Global Social Policy: International Organisations and the Future of Welfare*, London: Sage.

Deakin, N. and Wright, A. (1995) 'Tawney' in V. George and R. Page, eds., *Modern Thinkers on Welfare*, Hertfordshire: Prentice Hall/Harvester Wheatsheaf, 133–148.

Dean, H. (2002) 'Green Citizenship' in M. Cahill and T. Fitzpatrick, eds., *Environmental Issues and Social Welfare*, Oxford: Blackwell, 22–37.

Dean, H. (2008) 'The Socialist Perspective' in P. Alcock, M. May and K. Rowlingson, eds., *The Student's Companion to Social Policy* (third edition), Oxford: Blackwell, 84–90.

Dean, H. and Taylor-Gooby, P. (1992) *Dependency Culture: the explosion of a myth*, Hertfordshire: Harvester Wheatsheaf.

Delaney, E. (2000) *Demography, State and Society, Irish Migration to Britain, 1921–1971*, Liverpool: Liverpool University Press.

Dench, G., ed. (2006) *The Rise and Rise of Meritocracy*, Oxford: Blackwell.

Department of Education and Science (2005) *Delivering Equality of Opportunity in Schools, An Action Plan for Educational Inclusion*, Dublin: Department of Education and Science.

Department of Education and Science (2006a) *Report and Recommendations for a Traveller Education Strategy*, Dublin: Department of Education and Science.

Department of Education and Science (2006b) *Survey of Traveller Education Provision*, Dublin: Department of Education and Science.

Department of Education and Science (2007) *Audit of School Enrolment Policies by Regional Offices Service*, Dublin: Department of Education and Science.

Department of Education and Science (2008) *Retention Rates of Pupils in Second Level Schools, 1999 Cohort*, Dublin: Department of Education and Science.

Department of Enterprise Trade and Employment (2003) *Strategy Statement, 2003–2005*, Dublin: Department of Enterprise Trade and Employment.

Department of Enterprise, Trade and Employment (2006) *Ireland, Implementation of National Reform Programme Progress Report, October, 2006*, Dublin: Department of Enterprise, Trade and Employment.

Department of Environment, Heritage and Local Government (2005) *Strategy Statement*, Dublin: Stationery Office.

Department of Environment, Heritage and Local Government (2007a) *Annual Housing Statistics Bulletin*, Dublin: Stationery Office.

Department of Environment, Heritage and Local Government (2007b) *Delivering Homes Sustaining Communities*, Dublin: Stationery Office.

Department of Environment, Heritage and Local Government (2007c) *Ireland's Progress Towards Environmental Sustainability*, Dublin: Stationery Office.

Department of Environment, Heritage and Local Government (2008a) *The Way Home: a strategy to address adult homelessness in Ireland 2008–2013*, Dublin: Stationery Office.

Department of Environment, Heritage and Local Government (2008b) Housing Statistics Excel Workbook. Accessed at: *http://www.environ.ie/en/Publications/Statisticsand RegularPublications/HousingStatistics/* on 18 October 2008.

Department of Environment, Heritage and Local Government (various years) *Annual Housing Statistics Bulletin*, Dublin: Stationery Office.

Department of Health (1994) *Shaping a Healthier Future*, Dublin: Stationery Office.

Department of Health and Children (1999) *Children – FirstNational Guidelines for the Protection and Welfare of Children*, Dublin: Department of Health and Children.

Department of Health and Children (2001a) *Quality and Fairness: A Health System for You – Health Strategy*, Dublin: Department of Health and Children.

Department of Health and Children (2001b) *Primary Health Care – A new direction*, Dublin: Department of Health and Children.

Department of Health and Children (2003) *Health Service Reform Programme*, Dublin: Department of Health and Children.

Department of Health and Children (2007) *Quality and Fairness Report. A Health System for You – Action Plan Progress Report 2006*, Dublin: Department of Health and Children.

Department of Health and Children (2008a) Webpage, Home Care Support Scheme for Carers. Accessed at: *http://www.dohc.ie/public/information/* health_services _for_ older_people/home_care_support_scheme_for_carers.html on 15 December 2008.

Department of Health and Children (2008b) The Nursing Homes Support Scheme "A Fair Deal" Information Leaflet. Accessed at: *http://www.dohc.ie/press/releases/pdfs/ fair_deal_info.pdf* on 15 December 2008.

Department of Justice, Equality and Law Reform (1999) *Integration: a two way process*, Dublin: Department of Justice, Equality and Law Reform.

Department of Justice, Equality and Law Reform (2004) National Disability Strategy 2004. Accessed at: *http://www.justice.ie/en/JELR/NDS.pdf/files/NDS.pdf* on 15 December 2008.

Department of Justice, Equality and Law Reform (2005a) Guide to the Disability Act. Accessed at: *http://www.justice.ie/en/JELR/DisabilityAct05Guide.pdf/ Files/DisabilityAct05Guide.pdf* on 16 December 2008.

Department of Justice, Equality and Law Reform (2005b) *Planning for Diversity, The National Action Plan Against Racism 2005–2008*, Dublin: Department of Justice, Equality and Law Reform.

Department of Local Government (1969) *Housing in the '70s*, Dublin: Stationery Office.

Department of Social and Family Affairs (2004) 'Mary Coughlan Minister for Social and Family Affairs to Announce new Social Welfare code restrictions', Press Release, 24 February 2004. Accessed at: *http://welfare.ie/EN/Press/Releases/2004/ Pages/pr240204.aspx* on 22 November 2008.

Department of Social and Family Affairs (2006a) *Government Discussion Paper: Proposal for Supporting Lone Parents*, Dublin: Department of Social and Family Affairs.

Department of Social and Family Affairs (2006b) 'Minister says further reforms and initiatives are needed if Ireland is to meet future jobs demand', Press Release, 22 May 2006. Accessed at: *http://www.welfare.ie/press/pr06/pr220506.pdf* on 5 October 2008.

Department of Social and Family Affairs (2006c) 'Minister announces he plans proposals for reform legislation that will deliver new opportunities for lone parents', Press Release, 27 April 2006. Accessed at: *http://www.welfare.ie/press/pr06/pr270406.pdf* on 5 October 2008.

Department of Social and Family Affairs (2007) *Statistical Information on Social Welfare Services 2006*, Dublin: Department of Social and Family Affairs.

Department of Social and Family Affairs (2008a) *Statement of Strategy 2008–2010*, Dublin: Department of Social and Family Affairs.

Department of Social and Family Affairs (2008b) *Statistical Information on Social Welfare Services 2007*, Dublin: Department of Social and Family Affairs.

Department of the Environment (1990) *An Environmental Action Programme*, Dublin: Stationery Office.

Department of the Environment (1995) *Social Housing – the Way Ahead*, Dublin: Stationery Office.

Department of the Environment (1997) *Sustainable Development: A Strategy for Ireland*, Dublin: Stationery Office.

Department of Transport (2008) *Sustainable Transport and Travel Consultation Document*, Dublin: Department of Transport.

Dieckhoff, M. and Gallie, D. (2007) 'The renewed Lisbon Strategy and social exclusion policy', *Industrial Relations Journal* Vol.38 No.6 November, 480–502.

Dixon, J. (1999) *Social Security in Global Perspective*, London: Praeger.

Donoghue, F. (1998a) 'The Politicisation of Disadvantage in the Republic of Ireland: the role played by the third sector', Paper presented at the International Society for Third Sector Research Conference, Geneva, Switzerland, 10 July 1998.

Donoghue, F. (1998b) 'Defining the nonprofit sector: Ireland', in L.M. Salamon and H.K. Anheier, eds., *Working Papers of the Johns Hopkins Comparative Nonprofit Sector Project*, No.28, Baltimore: The Johns Hopkins Institute for Policy Studies.

Donoghue, F. (1999) *Uncovering the Non-profit Sector in Ireland: Its Economic Value and Significance*, Dublin: The Johns Hopkins Institute for Policy Studies and National

College of Ireland.

Dowling, B. (1986) 'Symposium on the Report of the Commission on Social Welfare', *Journal of the Statistical and Social Inquiry Society of Ireland* Vol.XXV Part IV, 8–20.

Doyle, A. (1999) 'Employment Equality since Accession to the European Union' in G. Kiely, A. O'Donnell, P. Kennedy and S. Quin, eds., *Irish Social Policy in Context*, Dublin: UCD Press, 114–38.

Doyle, A. (2003) 'Disability policy in Ireland' in S. Quin and B. Redmond, eds., *Disability and Social Policy in Ireland*, Dublin: UCD Press, 10–27.

Doyle, N., Hughes, G. and Wadensjö, E. (2006) *Freedom of Movement for Workers from Central and Eastern Europe, Experiences in Ireland and Sweden*, Stockholm: Swedish Institute for European Policy Studies.

Drake, R. (2001) *The Principles of Social Policy*, Basingstoke: Palgrave.

Drennan, J., Treacy, M., Butler, M., Byrne, A., Fealy, G., Frazer, K. and Irving, K. (2008) 'The experience of social and emotional loneliness of older people in Ireland', *Ageing and Society* Vol.28 No.8 July, 1113–32.

Driver, S. and Martell, L. (1998) *New Labour: Politics after Thatcherism*, Cambridge: Polity Press.

Dross, F. (2002) 'Health Care Provision and Poor Relief in Enlightenment and 19th Century Prussia' in O.P. Grell, A. Cunningham and R. Jütte, eds., *Health Care and Poor Relief in 18th and 19th Century Northern Europe*, Aldershot: Ashgate, 69–111.

Drudy, P.J. (2006) 'Housing in Ireland: Philosophy, Problems and Policies' in S. Healy, B. Reynolds and M. Collins, eds., *Social Policy in Ireland, Principles, Practice and Problems* (second edition), Dublin: The Liffey Press, 241–69.

Drudy, P.J. and Punch, M. (2005) *Out of Reach – Inequalities in the Irish Housing System*, Dublin: Tasc at New Island.

Dryzek, J. (2005) *The Politics of the Earth: environmental discourses* (second edition), Oxford: Oxford University Press.

Dryzek, J. and Schlosberg, J.S., eds. (2005) *Debating the Earth: the environmental politics reader*, Oxford: Oxford University Press.

Duff, L. (1997) *The Economics of Governments and Markets, new directions in European Public Policy*, London: Longman.

Duffy, P. (2004) '"Disencumbering our crowded places": theory and practice of estate migration schemes mid-nineteenth century Ireland' in P. Duffy, ed., *To and From Ireland: Planned Migration Schemes c. 1600–2000*, Dublin: Geography Publications, 79–104.

Duignan, M. and Walsh, T. (2004) *Insights on Quality: A National Review of Policy, Practice and Research Relating to Quality in Early Childhood Care and Education in Ireland 1990–2004*, Dublin: The Centre for Early Childhood Development and Education.

Dukelow, F. (2005) 'The path towards a more "employment friendly" liberal regime? globalisation and the Irish social security system' in B. Cantillon, and I. Marx, eds., *International co-operation in social security – how to cope with globalisation?*, Antwerp: Intersentia, 125–54.

Dupriez, V. and Dumay, X. (2006) 'Inequalities in school systems: effect of school structure or of society structure?', *Comparative Education* Vol.42 No.2 May, 243–60.

Dwyer, P. (2004a) 'Creeping Conditionality in the UK: From Welfare Rights to Conditional Entitlements?', *Canadian Journal of Sociology* Special Issue on Social Policy: Canadian and International Perspectives, Vol.29 No.2 Spring, 265–287.

Dwyer, P. (2004b) *Understanding Social Citizenship: Themes and Perspectives for Policy and Practice*, Bristol: Policy Press.

Eames, M. (2006) *Reconciling Environmental and Social Concerns. Findings from the JRF research programme*, York: Joseph Rowntree Foundation.

Earner-Byrne, L. (2007) *Mother and Child: Maternity and Child Welfare in Ireland, 1920s-1960s*, Manchester: Manchester University Press.

Edgar, B., Doherty, J. and Meert, H. (2002) *Access to Housing, Homelessness and Vulnerability in Europe*, Bristol: Policy Press.

Educational Disadvantage Committee (2003) *A More Integrated and Effective Delivery of School-Based Educational Inclusion Measures, Submission to the Minister for Education and Science*, Dublin: Educational Disadvantage Committee.

Edwards, E. (2004) 'Get diagnosis right to cure blockages' *The Irish Times* Health Supplement, 3 February 2004, 4.

Elliot, J.A. (2005) *An Introduction to Sustainable Development* (third edition), London: Routledge.

Englander, D. (1998) *Poverty and Poor Law Reform in Britain: from Chadwick to Booth*, London: Addison Wesley Longman.

Environment Council (1979) *Towards an Environment Policy*, Dublin: Stationery Office.

Environment Council (1980) *A Policy for the Environment*, Dublin: Stationery Office.

Environmental Protection Agency (2008a) *Ireland's National Greenhouse Gas emissions inventory for 2007*, Wexford: EPA.

Environmental Protection Agency (2008b) *Ireland's Environment 2008*, Wexford: EPA.

Equality Authority (2002) *Implementing Equality for Lesbians, Gays and Bisexuals*, Dublin: Equality Authority.

Equality Authority (2005) *Implementing Equality for Carers*, Dublin: Equality Authority.

Equality Authority (2006) *Traveller Ethnicity*, Dublin: Equality Authority.

Equality Authority (2008) *The Equality Authority Annual Report 2007*, Dublin: Equality Authority.

Esping Andersen, G. (1990) *The Three Worlds of Welfare Capitalism*, Cambridge: Polity Press.

Esping Andersen, G., ed. (1996) *Welfare States in Transition: National Adaptations in Global Economies*, London: Sage.

European Commission (1997) Employment Summit 1997–Background-What to do? A European employment strategy based on four pillars. Accessed at: *http://ec.europa.eu/employment_social/elm/summit/en/backgr/pilars.htm* on 13 November 2008.

European Commission (2001a) *Making a European Area of Lifelong Learning a Reality*, Brussels: Commission of the European Communities.

European Commission (2001b) Communication from the Commission to the Council, the European Parliament, the Economic and Social Committee and the Committee of the Regions On the Sixth Environment Action Programme of the European Community 'Environment 2010: Our future, Our choice'-The Sixth Environment Action Programme /* COM/2001/0031 final */2001. Accessed at: *http://eur-lex.europa.eu/LexUriServ/LexUriServ.do?uri=CELEX:52001DC0031:EN:HTML* on 9 December 2008.

European Commission (2007a) EC Employment and Social Affairs-European Employment Strategy, Last updated 20/11/2007. Accessed at: *http://ec.europa.eu/employment_social/employment_strategy/develop_en.htm* on 13 September 2008.

European Commission (2007b) *Towards Common Principles of Flexicurity: More and better jobs through flexibility and security*, Luxembourg: Office for Official Publications of the European Communities.

European Commission (2008a) EC Employment and Social Affairs-Social Protection Social Inclusion, process, Last updated 13/11/2008. Accessed at: *http://ec.europa.eu/employment_social/spsi/the_process_en.htm* on 13 December 2008.

European Commission (2008b) EC Employment and Social Affairs-Social Protection Social Inclusion Common Objectives, New Common Objectives from 2006, Last updated 28/01/2008. Accessed at: *http://ec.europa.eu/employment_social/spsi/common_objectives_en.htm* on 13 September 2008.

European Environment Agency (2006) *Urban Sprawl in Europe The Ignored Challenge*, Copenhagen: European Environment Agency.

European Parliament (2000) 'European Parliament Fact Sheets: 4.8.1 Social and employment policy-General principles'. Accessed at: *http://www.europarl.europa.eu/factsheets/4_8_1_en.htm* on 13 September 2008.

Eurostat (2008) 'Causes of Death-standardised death rate per 100,000 inhabitants' Population and Social Conditions Dataset. Accessed at: *http://epp.eurostat.ec.europa.eu/portal/page?_pageid=1073,46870091&_dad=portal&_schema=PORTAL&p_product_code=HLTH_CD_ASDR* on 14 November 2008.

Eurostat (n.d.) 'At risk of poverty rate across EU'. Accessed at: *http://epp.eurostat.ec.europa.eu/tgm/table.do?tab=table&init=1&plugin=1&language=en&pcode=tsisc030* on 15 December 2008.

Eurydice (2000) *Two Decades of Reform in Higher Education in Europe: 1980s onwards*, Brussels: Eurydice.

Euzéby, A. (2002) 'The Financing of Social Protection in the Context of Economic Globalisation' in R. Sigg and C. Behrendt, eds., *Social Security in the Global Village*, New Brunswick: Transaction Publishers, 31–46.

Evason, E., Darby, J. and Person, M. (1976) *Social Need and Social Provision in Northern Ireland*, Coleraine: New University of Ulster.

Evetts, J. (1970) 'Equality of Educational Opportunity: the recent history of a concept', *British Journal of Sociology* Vol.21 No.4 December, 425–30.

Expert Working Group on the Integration of Tax and Social Welfare Systems (1996) *Integrating Tax and Social Welfare*, Dublin: Stationery Office.

Expert Group on Mental Health Policy (2006) *A Vision for Change: Report of the Expert Group on Mental Health Policy*, Dublin: Stationery Office.

Fahey, T. (1998) 'The Catholic Church and Social Policy' in S. Healy and B. Reynolds, eds., *Social Policy in Ireland: Principles, Practice and Problems* Dublin: Oak Tree Press, 411–29.

Fahey, T. (2001) 'Housing and Local Government' in M. E. Daly, ed., *County and Town, One Hundred Years of Local Government in Ireland*, Dublin: IPA, 120–29.

Fahey, T. (2002) 'The Family Economy in the Development of Welfare Regimes: A Case Study', *European Sociological Review* Vol.18 No.1 March, 51–64.

Fahey, T. (2007) 'The Case for an EU-wide Measure of Poverty', *European Sociological Review* Vol.23 No.1 February, 35–47.

Fahey, T. and Duffy, D. (2007) 'The Housing Boom' in T. Fahey, H. Russell and C. Whelan, eds. *Best of Times? The Social Impact of the Celtic Tiger*, Dublin: IPA, 123–138.

Fahey, T. and Fitz Gerald, J. (1997) *Welfare Implications of Demographic Trends*, Dublin: Oak Tree Press in association with CPA.

Fahey, T. and McLaughlin, E. (1999) 'Family and State' in A. Heath, R. Breen and C. Whelan, eds., *Ireland, North and South, Perspectives from Social Science*, Oxford: Oxford University Press, 117–40.

Fahey, T. and Russell, H. (2001) *Older People's Preferences for Employment and Retirement in Ireland*, National Council on Ageing and Older People Report No.67, Dublin: NCAOP.

Fahey, T. and Watson, D. (1995) *An Analysis of Social Housing Need*, General Research Series, No.168, Dublin: Economic and Social Research Institute.

Fahey, T., ed. (1999) *Social Housing in Ireland, A Study of Success, Failure and Lessons Learned*, Dublin: Oak Tree Press.

Fahey, T., Nolan, B. and Maître, B. (2004) *Housing, Poverty and Wealth in Ireland*, Dublin: IPA.

Fallon, J. (2005) 'Targeting disadvantage among young children in the Republic of Ireland', *Child Care in Practice* Vol.11 No.3 July, 289–311.

Fanning, B. (2002) *Racism and Social Change in the Republic of Ireland*, Manchester: Manchester University Press.

Fanning, B. (2003) 'The construction of Irish social policy 1953–2003' in B. Fanning and T. McNamara, eds., *Ireland Develops: Administration and Social Policy 1953–2003*, Dublin: IPA, 3–18.

Fanning, B. (2004) 'Locating Irish social policy' in B. Fanning, P. Kennedy, G. Kiely and S. Quin, eds., *Theorising Irish Social Policy*, Dublin: UCD Press, 6–22.

Fanning, B. (2006) 'The new welfare economy' in B. Fanning and M. Rush, eds., *Care and Social Change in the Irish Welfare Economy*, Dublin: UCD Press, 9–25.

Fanning, B. (2007a) 'Racism, Rules and Rights' in B. Fanning, ed., *Immigration and Social Change in the Republic of Ireland*, Manchester: Manchester University Press, 6–26.

Fanning, B. (2007b) 'Integration and Social Policy' in B. Fanning, ed., *Immigration and Social Change in the Republic of Ireland*, Manchester: Manchester University Press, 237–58.

Fanning, B. (2008) *The Quest for Modern Ireland: The Battle of Ideas 1912–1986*, Dublin: Irish Academic Press.

Fanning, B. and Rush, M., eds. (2006), *Care and Social Change in the Irish Welfare Economy*, Dublin: UCD Press.

Fanning, B. and Rush, M. (2006a) 'Introduction: Context, change, challenges and care' in B. Fanning and M. Rush, eds., *Care and Social Change in the Irish Welfare Economy*, Dublin: UCD Press, 1–8.

Fanning, B. and Veale, A. (2004) 'Child Poverty as Public Policy: Direct Provision and Asylum Seeker Children', *Child Care in Practice* Vol.10, No.3 April, 241–51.

Fanning, B., Veale, A. and O'Connor, D. (2001) *Beyond the Pale: Asylum Seeking Children and Social Exclusion in Ireland*, Dublin: Irish Refugee Council.

Farell, C., McAvoy, H., Wilde, J. and the CPA (2008) *Tackling Health Inequalities: an all-Ireland approach to social determinants*, Dublin: CPA with the IPH.

Farley, D. (1964) *Social Insurance and Social Assistance in Ireland*, Dublin: IPA.

Farnsworth, K. (2004) 'Welfare through Work: An Audit of Occupational Social Provision at the Turn of the New Century', *Social Policy and Administration* Vol.38 No.5 October, 437–455.

Farren, S. (1995) *The Politics of Irish Education, 1920–65*, Belfast: Institute of Irish Studies, Queens University Belfast.

Faughnan, P. and Woods, M. (2000) *Lives on Hold: seeking asylum in Ireland*, Dublin: University College, Social Science Research Centre.

Fawcett, B., Featherstone, B. and Goddard, J. (2004) *Contemporary Child Care Policy and Practice*, Basingstoke: Palgrave.

Fay, R. (2001) 'Health and Racism: a Traveller perspective' in F. Farrell and P. Watt, eds., *Responding to Racism in Ireland*, Dublin: Veritas, 99–114.

Feldman, A. (2008) 'Integration – mapping the terrain', *Translocations* Vol.3 No.1 Spring, 133–41.

Ferguson, H. (1995) 'Child Welfare, Child Protection and the Child Care Act 1991: Key Issues for Policy and Practice' in H. Ferguson and P. Kenny, eds., *On Behalf of the Child: Child Welfare, Child Protection and the Child Care Act 1991*, Dublin: A. & A. Farmar, 17–41.

Ferguson, H. and Kenny, P., eds. (1995) *On Behalf of the Child: Child Welfare, Child Protection and the Child Care Act 1991*, Dublin: A. & A. Farmar.

Ferguson, H. and O'Reilly, M. (2001) *Keeping Children Safe: Child Abuse, Child Protection and the Promotion of Welfare*, Dublin: A. & A. Farmar.

Fernandez, J. (1996) 'Homelessness: an Irish perspective' in D. Bhugra, ed., *Homelessness and Mental Health*, Cambridge: Cambridge University Press, 209–29.

Ferrera, M. (1996) 'The 'Southern Model' of Welfare in Social Europe', *Journal of European Social Policy* Vol.6 No.1 February, 17–37.

Ferris, J. (1991) 'Green Politics and the Future of Welfare' in N. Manning, ed., *Social Policy Review, 1990–91*, Harlow: Longman, 24–41.

Ferriter, D. (2004) *The Transformation of Ireland 1900–2000*, London: Profile Books.

Fine-Davis, M. (2004) 'The Childcare Policy Debate in Ireland' *Administration* Vol.52 No.2 Summer, 36–56.

Fine Gael (2008) Webpage 'Policy – Our Values' Accessed at: *http://www.finegael.ie// page.cfm/area/information/page/OurValues/pkey/1084* on September 3rd 2008.

Finnane, M. (1981) *Insanity and the Insane in post-famine Ireland*, London: Croom Helm.

Finnegan, F. (2001) *Do Penance or Perish, a study of Magdalen Asylums in Ireland*, Kilkenny: Congrave Press.

Fitz Gerald, J. (2000) 'The story of Ireland's failure – and belated success' in B. Nolan, P.J. O'Connell and C.T. Whelan, eds., *Bust to Boom? The Irish Experience of Growth and Inequality*, Dublin: IPA, 27–57.

Fitzgerald, E. (1981) 'The Extent of Poverty in Ireland' in S. Kennedy, ed., *One Million Poor? The Challenge of Irish Inequality*, Dublin: Turoe Press, 13–34.

Fitzgerald, E. (2007) 'Disability and poverty' in M. Cousins, ed., *Welfare Policy and Poverty*, Dublin: IPA and CPA, 229–58.

Fitzgerald, E. and Winston, N. (2005) 'Housing Equality and Inequality' in M. Norris and D. Redmond, eds., *Housing Contemporary Ireland, Policy, Society and Shelter*, Dublin: IPA, 224–44.

FitzGerald, G. (1998) 'Suits EU, Sir', *Magill* January 1998, 28–33.

FitzGerald, G. (2000) 'Diluting Lobbies and Unleashing Growth' in R. O'Donnell, ed., *Europe: The Irish Experience*, Dublin: IEA, 111–22.

FitzGerald, G. (2004) 'The Economics of EU Membership' in J. Hourihane, ed., *Ireland and the European Union: The First Thirty Years, 1973–2002*, Dublin: The Lilliput Press, 67–80.

Fitzpatrick Associates and O'Connell, P. (2005) *A review of higher education participation in 2003*, Dublin: HEA 2005.

Fitzpatrick, T. (1998) 'The Implications of Ecological Thought for Social Welfare', *Critical Social Policy* Vol.18 No.1 February, 6–26.

Fitzpatrick, T. (2001) *Welfare Theory: an introduction*, Basingstoke: Palgrave.

Fitzpatrick, T. (2002) 'Making Welfare for Future Generations' in M. Cahill and T. Fitzpatrick, eds., *Environmental Issues and Social Welfare*, Oxford: Blackwell, 38–52.

Fitzpatrick, T. (2003) 'Environmentalism and Social Policy' in N. Ellison and C. Pierson, eds., *Developments in British Social Policy*, Basingstoke: Palgrave Macmillan, 317–32.

Flora, P. (1981) 'Solution or Source of Crises? The Welfare State in Historical Perspective' in W.J. Mommsen, ed., *The Emergence of the Welfare State in Britain and Germany: 1850–1950*, London: Croom Helm on behalf of the German Historical Institute, 343–389.

Flynn, L. (1997) '"Cherishing all her children equally": the law and politics of Irish lesbian and gay citizenship', *Social and Legal Studies* Vol.6 No.2 December, 493–512.

Focus Ireland (2008) 'Football legend Paul McGrath teams up with Focus Ireland to launch campaign calling for a statutory right to aftercare for young people leaving state care', Press Release, 18 November 2008. Accessed at: *http://www.focusireland.ie/htm/press/2008/Nov08–Aftercare%20Magazine%20Launch.pdf* on 6 December 2008.

Foley, J., ed. (2004) *Sustainability and Social Justice*, London: Institute for Public Policy Research.

Fraser, D. (1984) *The Evolution of the British Welfare State: A History of Social Policy since the Industrial Revolution* (second edition), London: Macmillan Press.

Frazer, H. (2007) 'Promoting Social Inclusion: the EU Dimension', *Administration* Vol.55 No.2 Summer, 27–60.

Freeman, R. (2000) *The Politics of Health in Europe*, Manchester: Manchester University Press.

Fukuyama, F. (1992) *The End of History and the Last Man*, Harmondsworth: Penguin.

Gageby, D. (1979) 'The Media' in J.J. Lee, ed., *Ireland 1945–70*, Dublin: Gill & Macmillan, 124–35.

Galligan, Y. (1999) 'Women's issues in Irish politics' in N. Collins, ed., *Political Issues in Ireland Today* (second edition), Manchester: Manchester University Press, 177–89.

Galligan, Y. (2005) 'The Private Rented Sector' in M. Norris and D. Redmond, eds., *Housing Contemporary Ireland, Policy, Society and Shelter*, Dublin: IPA, 100–18.

Garavan, R., Winder, R. and McGee, H. (2001) *Health and Social Services for Older People (HeSSOP). Consulting Older People on Health and Social Services: A Survey of Service Use, Experiences and Needs*, Dublin: NCAOP.

Garner, R. (1996) *Environmental Politics*, London: Prentice Hall, Harvester Wheatsheaf.

Garner, S. (2004) *Racism in the Irish experience*, London: Pluto Press.

Garner, S. (2005) 'Guests of the Nation' *The Irish Review* No.33 Spring, 78–84.

Garner, S. (2007) 'Babies, Bodies and Entitlement: gendered aspects of access to citizenship in the Republic of Ireland', *Parliamentary Affairs* Vol.60 No.3 July, 137–51.

Garvin, J. (1944) 'Public Assistance' in F.C. King, ed., *Public Administration in Ireland*, Dublin: Parkside Press, 161–72.

Garvin, T. (2005) *Preventing the Future – Why was Ireland so poor for so long?*, Dublin: Gill & Macmillan.

Geary, L. (2004) *Medicine and Charity in Ireland 1718–1851*, Dublin: UCD Press.

General Medical Services (Payments) Board (various years) *General Medical Services (Payments) Board Annual Report*, Dublin: General Medical Services (Payments) Board.

George, V. and Page, R. (2004) 'Introduction' in V. George and R. Page, eds, *Global Social Problems*, Cambridge: Polity Press, 1–8.

George, V. and Wilding, P. (1985) *Ideology and Social Welfare*, London: Routledge and Kegan Paul.

George, V. and Wilding, P. (1994) *Welfare and Ideology*, Hemel Hempstead: Harvester Wheatsheaf.

George, V. and Wilding, P. (2002) *Globalization and Human Welfare*, Basingstoke: Palgrave.

Gibb, K. (2002) 'Trends and Change in Social Housing Finance and Provision within the European Union', *Housing Studies* Vol.17 No.2 March, 325–36.

Giddens, A. (1994) *Beyond Left and Right: the Future of Radical Politics*, Cambridge: Polity Press.

Giddens, A. (1998) *The Third Way: The Renewal of Social Democracy*, Cambridge: Polity Press.

Giddens, A. (2000) *The Third Way and Its Critics*, Cambridge: Polity Press.

Giddens, A. (2007) 'It's time to give the Third Way a second chance: Securing greater social justice depends on a strong economy, not the other way round', *The Independent* 28 June 2007. Accessed at: *www.independent.co.uk/opinion/ commentators/anthony-giddens-its-time-to-give-the-third-way-a-second-chance-454966.html* on 21 May 2008.

Gilbert, N. and Van Voorhis, R., eds. (2003) *Changing Patterns of Social Protection*, New Brunswick: Transaction Publishers.

Ginsburg, N. (1979) *Class, Capital and Social Policy*, London: Macmillan.

Ginsburg, N. (2001) 'Globalization and the Liberal Welfare States' in R. Sykes, B. Palier and P.M. Prior, eds., *Globalization and European Welfare States: Challenges and Change*, Basingstoke: Palgrave, 173–91.

Ginsburg, N. (2003) 'The Socialist Perspective' in P. Alcock, A. Erskine and M. May, eds., *The Student's Companion to Social Policy* (second edition), Oxford: Blackwell, 92–99.

GLEN/NEXUS (1995) *Poverty: Lesbians and Gay men: the economic and social effects of discrimination*, Dublin: CPA.

Glennerster, H. (1995) *British Social Policy since 1945*, Oxford: Blackwell.

Glyn, A. (2006) *Capitalism Unleashed, Finance, Globalisation and Welfare*, Oxford: Oxford University Press.

Goldsmith, E. and Allen, R. (1972) *A Blueprint for Survival*, London: Penguin.

Gough, I. (1979) *The Political Economy of the Welfare State*, London: Macmillan.

Government of Ireland (1958) *Programme for Economic Expansion*, Dublin: Stationery Office.

Government of Ireland (1987) *Programme for National Recovery*, Dublin: Stationery Office.

Government of Ireland (1990) *Programme for Economic and Social Progress*, Dublin: Stationery Office.

Government of Ireland (2006) *Towards 2016 – Ten Year Framework Social Partnership Agreement 2006–2015*, Dublin: Stationery Office.

Government of Ireland (2007a) *An Agreed Programme for Government 2007–2012*. Accessed at: *http://www.taoiseach.gov.ie/index.asp?locID=512&docID=-1* on 19 December 2008.

Government of Ireland (2007b) *National Action Plan for Social Inclusion 2007–2016*, Dublin: Stationery Office.

Government of Ireland (2007c) *National Development Plan 2007–2013, Transforming Ireland-A Better Quality of Life for All*, Dublin: Stationery Office.

Graham, H. (2007) *Unequal Lives, Health and Socio-economic inequalities*, Maidenhead, Berkshire: Open University Press.

Gray, A.W. (1997) 'Challenges for Ireland in the Integrated European Union' in F. O'Muircheartaigh, ed., *Ireland in the Coming Times: Essays to Celebrate T.K. Whitaker's 80 Years*, Dublin: IPA, 36–54.

Green, D.G. (1999) 'The Friendly Societies and Adam-Smith Liberalism' in D. Gladstone, ed., *Before Beveridge: Welfare Before the Welfare State*, Civitas, Choice in Welfare No.47 London: Civitas, 18–25.

Green Party (2007) 'Fairness and Prosperity: A Green approach to the economy' Green Party 2007. Accessed at: *http://www.greenparty.ie/en/policies/taxation* on 3 September 2008.

Green Party (2008a) Webpage 'A brief history of the party'. Accessed at: *http://www.greenparty.ie/en/about/history* on 3 September 2008.

Green Party (2008b) Webpage 'Party principles'. Accessed at: *http://www.greenparty.ie/en/about/party_principles* on 3 September 2008.

Griffin, S. and Shevlin, M. (2007) *Responding to Special Educational Needs: An Irish Perspective*, Dublin: Gill & Macmillan.

Guha, R. and Martinez-Alier, J. (1997) *Varieties of Environmentalism: essays North and South*, London: Earthscan.

Guinnane, T. (1993) 'The Poor Law and Pensions in Ireland', *Journal of Interdisciplinary History* Vol.24 No.2 Autumn, 271–91.

Guri-Rosenblit, S., Šebková, H. and Teichler, U. (2007) 'Massification and Diversity of Higher Education Systems: Interplay of Complex Dimensions', *Higher Education Policy* Vol.20 No.4 December, 373–89.

Hajer, M. (1995) *The Politics of Environmental Discourse Ecological Modernisation and the Policy Process*, Oxford: Oxford University Press.

Hale, S., Leggett, W. and Martell, L., eds. (2004) *The Third Way and beyond: Criticisms, futures, alternatives*, Manchester: Manchester University Press.

Ham, C. (2005) 'Lost in Translation? Health Systems in the US and the UK', *Social Policy and Administration* Vol.39 No.2 April, 192–209.

Hantrais, L. (2000) *Social Policy in the European Union* (second edition), Basingstoke: Macmillan.

Hantrais, L. (2007) *Social Policy in the European Union* (third edition), Basingstoke: Palgrave Macmillan.

Hantrais, L. (2008) 'Social Policy and the European Union' in P. Alcock, M. May and K. Rowlingson, eds., *The Student's Companion to Social Policy* (third edition), Oxford: Blackwell, 284–91.

Hardiman, N. (2005) *Partnership and Politics: How Embedded in Social Partnership?* Geary Discussion Paper Series, Geary WP 2005/8.

Hardiman, N. (2006) 'Politics and Social Partnership: Flexible Network Governance', *The Economic and Social Review* Vol.37 No.3 Winter, 343–74.

Harford, J. (2005) 'The Movement for the Higher Education of Women in Ireland: Gender Equality or Denominational Rivalry?', *History of Education* Vol.34 No.5 April, 473–92.

Harford, J. (2008) *The Opening of University Education to Women in Ireland*, Dublin: Irish Academic Press.

Harney, M. (1992) 'The Irish Environmental Protection Agency' in J. Feehan, ed., *Environment and Development in Ireland*, Dublin: The Environmental Institute, UCD, 28–32.

Harney, M. (2000) 'Remarks by Tánaiste, Mary Harney at a Meeting of the American Bar Association in the Law Society of Ireland, Blackhall Place, Dublin on Friday 21 July 2000' Department of Enterprise, Trade and Employment, Dublin. Accessed at: *http://www.entemp.ie/press/2000/210700.htm* on 3 September 2008.

Harney, M. (2006) 'A Fair Deal on Long-Term Nursing Home Care' Speech by Mary Harney, T.D., Minister for Health, 12 December 2006. Accessed at: *http://www.dohc.ie/press/speeches/2006/20061211.html* on 6 December 2008.

Harney, M. (2008) 'Minister Harney publishes Fair Deal Bill – "clear, coherent and totally fair support for the cost of long term care"', Department of Health and Children, 9 October 2008. Accessed at: *http://www.dohc.ie/press/releases/2008/20081009.html* on 6 December 2008.

Harvey, B. (1995) 'The Use of Legislation to Address a Social Problem: The Example of the Housing Act, 1988', *Administration* Vol.43 No.1 Spring, 76–85.

Harvey, B. (2003) *Guide to Equality and the Policies, Institutions and Programmes of the European Union*, Dublin: Equality Authority.

Harvey, B. (2008) 'Homelessness and the 1988 Housing Act, State Policy and Civil Society' in D. Downey, ed., *Perspectives on Irish Homelessness: past, present and future*, Dublin: Homeless Agency, 10–14.

Hayek, F. A. (1960/2006) *The Constitution of Liberty*, London: Routledge.

Hayes, M. (2006) 'Indigenous Otherness: Some Aspects of Traveller Social History', *Éire-Ireland* Vol.41 Nos.3/4 Fall/Winter, 133–61.

Hayes, N. (2007) 'Early Childhood Education and Care: A Decade of Reflection, 1996–2006' in N. Hayes and S. Bradley, eds., *A Decade of Reflection, Early Childhood Care and Education in Ireland 1996–2006*, Dublin: Centre for Social and Educational Research, 3–9.

Hayes, N. (2008) *The Role of Early Childhood Care and Education – an anti-poverty perspective*, Dublin: CPA.

Hayes, N. and Bradley, S. (2006) 'The childcare question' in B. Fanning and M. Rush, eds., *Care and Social Change in the Irish Welfare Economy*, Dublin: UCD Press, 163–78.

Hayward, K. and Howard, K. (2007) 'Cherry-picking the diaspora in B. Fanning, ed., *Immigration and Social Change in the Republic of Ireland*, Manchester: Manchester University Press, 47–62.

Hayward, T. (2005) *Constitutional Environmental Rights*, Oxford: Oxford University Press.

Health Insurance Authority (2008) *Annual Report and Accounts, 2007*, Dublin: The Health Insurance Authority.

Health Service Executive (2007a) *Finance Shared Services, Primary Care Reimbursement Service, Statistical analysis of claims and payments in 2006*, Kildare: HSE.

Health Service Executive (2007b) *Mental Health in Ireland: Awareness and Attitudes*, Kildare: HSE.

Health Service Executive (2007c) *National Intercultural Health Strategy 2007–2012*, Kildare: HSE.

Health Service Executive (2008) *Annual Report and Financial Statements 2007*, Kildare: HSE.

Healy, J. (2003) *Fuel Poverty and Policy in Ireland and the European Union*, Dublin: The Policy Institute, Trinity College Dublin in association with the CPA.

Hegedüs, J. and Tosics, I. (1996) 'The disintegration of the East European Housing Model', in D. Clapham, J. Hegedüs, K. Kintrea, and I. Tosics, eds., *Housing Privatisation in Eastern Europe*, London: Greenwood, 15–40.

Helleiner, J. (2000) *Irish Travellers and the politics of culture*, Buffalo: University of Toronto Press.

Hemerijck, A. (2003) 'The Reform Potential of the Welfare State in the Twenty First Century – an Essay in Social Pragmatism', paper presented to conference on 'Deliberation and Public Policy', Conference to Mark 30 years of the NESC, Dublin, 21 November 2003.

Hensey, B. (1988) *The Health Services of Ireland* (fourth edition), Dublin: IPA.

Hewitt, M. (2000) *Welfare and Human Nature – The Human Subject in Twentieth Century Social Politics*, London: Macmillan.

Heywood, A. (2002) *Politics* (second edition), Basingstoke: Palgrave Macmillan.

Heywood, A. (2003) *Political Ideologies: an introduction* (third edition), Basingstoke: Palgrave Macmillan.

Hill, M. (2003) *Understanding Social Policy* (seventh edition), Oxford: Blackwell.

Hockerts, H.G. (1981) 'German Post-war Social Policies against the Background of the Beveridge Plan. Some Observations Preparatory to a Comparative Analysis' in M.J. Mommsen, ed., *The Emergence of the Welfare State in Britain and Germany: 1850–1950*, London: Croom Helm on behalf of the German Historical Institute, 315–339.

Hodgins, M., Millar, M. and Barry, M. (2006) '"…it's all the same no matter how much fruit or vegetables or fresh air we get": Traveller women's perceptions of illness causation and health inequalities', *Social Science and Medicine* Vol.62, No.8 April, 1978–90.

Hoff, M.D. and McNutt, J.G. (2000) 'Social Policy and the Physical Environment' in J. Midgely, M. Tracy and M. Livermore, eds., *The Handbook of Social Policy*, Beverly Hills: Sage, 461–75.

Honohan, P. (1999) 'Fiscal Adjustment and Disinflation in Ireland: Setting the Macro Basis of Economic Recovery and Expansion' in F. Barry, ed., *Understanding Ireland's Economic Growth*, Basingstoke: Macmillan, 75–98.

hooks, b. (2000) *Feminism is for EVERYBODY: Passionate Politics*, Cambridge MA: South End Press.

Hoop, R. (2004) 'Social policy in Belgium and the Netherlands: Third Way or not?' in G. Bonoli and M. Powell, eds., *Social Democratic Party Policies in Contemporary Europe*, London: Routledge, 66–82.

Horgan, J. (2000) *Noël Browne: Passionate Outsider*, Dublin: Gill & Macmillan.

Horner, A. (1985) 'The Dublin Region, 1880–1982: An Overview on its Development and Planning' in M.J. Bannon, ed., *The Emergence of Irish Planning, 1880–1920*, Dublin: Turoe Press, 21–75.

Hourihan, K. (2006) 'The Suburbs' in J. Crowley, R. Devoy, D. Linehan, P. O'Flanagan, and M. Murphy, eds., *Atlas of Cork City*, Cork: Cork University Press, 278–89.

Huby, M. (1998) *Social Policy and the Environment*, Buckingham: Open University Press.

Huby, M. (2001) 'The Sustainable Use of Resources on a Global Scale', *Social Policy and Administration* Vol.35 No.5 October, 521–37.

Hughes, G. and Watson, D. (2005) *Pensioners' Incomes and Replacement Rates in 2000*,

Policy Research Series No.54, Dublin: ESRI.

Hutton, D. (1991) 'Labour in the post-independence Irish state' in S. Hutton and P. Stewart, eds., *Ireland's Histories, Aspects of state, society and ideology*, London: Routledge, 52–79.

Hutton, S. and Stewart, P., eds. (1991) *Ireland's Histories, Aspects of state, society and ideology*, London: Routledge.

Hyland, A. (1996) 'Multi-Denominational Schools in the Republic of Ireland 1975–1995' paper delivered at a conference Education and Religion organised by C.R.E.L.A. at the University of Nice, 21–22 June 1996. Accessed at: *http://www.educatetogether.ie/reference_articles_/Ref_Art_003.html* on 18 September 2008.

Inclusion Ireland (2008) 'Loss of Advocacy Service a massive Blow – Inclusion Ireland', Press Statement, July 2008. Accessed at: *http://www.inclusionireland.ie/Lossof AdvocacyServiceaMassiveBlow.htm* on 14 December 2008.

Inglis, T. (1998) *Moral Monopoly: The Rise and Fall of the Catholic Church in Modern Ireland*, Dublin: UCD Press.

Inglis, T. (2002) 'Sexual Transgression and Scapegoats: A Case Study from Modern Ireland', *Sexualities* Vol.5 No.1 February, 5–24.

Inglis, T. (2005) 'Origins and Legacies of Irish Prudery: Sexuality and Social Control in Modern Ireland', *Éire-Ireland* Vol.40 Nos.3/4 Fall/Winter, 9–37.

IOM (2005) *World Migration 2005: costs and benefits of international migration*, Geneva: IOM.

Irish Family Planning Association (n.d.) Irish Abortion Statistics. Accessed at: *www.ifpa.ie/abortion/iabst.html* on 2 April 2007.

Irish Human Rights Commission (2006) *The Rights of De-Facto Couples*, Dublin: Irish Human Rights Commission.

Isin, E.F. and Wood, P. (1999) *Citizenship and Identity*, London: Sage.

Jacobs, M. (1997) 'The Quality of Life: Social Goods and the Politics of Consumption' in M. Jacobs, ed., *Greening the Millennium? The New Politics of the Environment*, Oxford: Blackwell, 47–61.

Jacobs, M. (1999) 'Sustainable Development: a contested concept' in A. Dobson, ed., *Fairness and Futurity – Essays on Environmental Sustainability and Social Justice*, Oxford: Oxford University Press, 21–46.

Jacobsen, J.K. (1994) *Chasing Progress in the Irish Republic*, Cambridge: Cambridge University Press.

Jacobsson, K. (2004) 'Soft regulation and the subtle transformation of states: the case of EU employment policy', *Journal of European Social Policy* Vol.14 No.4 November, 355–70.

Jaeger, M. and Kvist, J. (2003) 'Pressures on State Welfare in Post-industrial Societies: Is More or Less Better?', *Social Policy and Administration* Vol.37 No.6 December, 555–72.

Jenkinson, H. (1996) 'History of Youth Work' in P. Burgess, ed., *Youth and Community Work: A Course Reader*, Centre for Adult and Continuing Education, Cork: Cork University Press, 35–43.

Jensen, C. (2008) 'Worlds of welfare services and transfers', *Journal of European Social Policy* Vol.18 No.2 May 2008, 151–62.

Jones, K. (2000) *The Making of Social Policy in Britain: From the Poor Law to New Labour* (third edition), London: The Athlone Press.

Jones, T. (1910) 'Pauperism and Poverty', *Journal of the Statistical and Social Inquiry*

Society of Ireland Vol.XII December, 358–70.

Joppke, C. (1999) 'How immigration is changing citizenship: a comparative view', *Ethnic and Racial Studies* Vol.22 No.4 July, 629–52.

Joppke, C. (2008) 'Comparative Citizenship: a restrictive turn in Europe?', *Law and Ethics of Human Rights* Vol.2 No.1 January, 1–41.

Kaim-Caudle, P. R. (1967) *Social Security in Ireland and Western Europe*, Dublin: ESRI.

Kartalova-O'Doherty, Y., Tedstone Doherty, D. and Walsh, D. (2006) *Family Support Study: A study of experiences, needs, and support requirements of families with enduring mental illness in Ireland*, Dublin: Health Research Board.

Katwala, S. (2004) 'In an Ideal World: As the Fabian Society marks its birthday, Sunder Katwala celebrates 120 years of practical utopianism' in *The Guardian* Tuesday, 6 January 2004. Accessed at: *http://politics.guardian.co.uk/comment/story/0,,1117051,00.html* on 11 April 2007.

Katz, M. (1986) *In the Shadow of the Poorhouse: A Social History of Welfare in America*, New York: Basic Books.

Kautto, M. and Kvist, J. (2002) 'Parallel Trends, Persistent Diversity: Nordic Welfare States in the European and Global Context', *Global Social Policy* Vol.2 No.2 August, 189–208.

Kellaghan, T. (2001) 'Towards a Definition of Educational Disadvantage', *The Irish Journal of Education* Vol.XXXII, 3–22.

Kellaghan, T., Weir, S., Ó hUallacháin, S. and Morgan, M. (1995) *Educational Disadvantage in Ireland*, Dublin: Department of Education.

Kelleher, C. (2007) 'Health and Modern Irish Society: the mother and father of a dilemma' in M. Cousins, ed., *Welfare Policy and Poverty*, Dublin: IPA and CPA, 201–28.

Kelly, J. (1999) 'The Emergence of Scientific and Institutional Medical Practice in Ireland, 1650–1800' in C. Malcolm and G. Jones, eds., *Medicine, Disease and the State in Ireland, 1650–1940*, Cork: Cork University Press, 21–39.

Kemeny, J. (1995) *From Public Housing to the Social Market*, London: Routledge.

Kemeny, J. (2006) 'Corporatism and Housing Regimes', *Housing, Theory and Society* Vol.23 No.1 March, 1–18.

Kennedy, F. (1997) 'The Course of the Irish Welfare State' in F. O'Muircheartaigh, ed., *Ireland in the Coming Times: Essays to Celebrate T.K. Whitaker's 80 Years*, Dublin: IPA, 129–55.

Kennedy, F. (2001) *Cottage to Crèche: Family Change in Ireland*, Dublin: IPA.

Kennedy, F. (2002) 'Abortion Referendum 2002', *Irish Political Studies* Vol.17 No.1, 114–28.

Kennedy, K. (1993) *Facing the Unemployment Crisis in Ireland*, Cork: Cork University Press.

Kennedy, K. A., Giblin, T. and McHugh, D. (1988) *The Economic Development of Ireland in the Twentieth Century*, Routledge: London.

Kennedy, S., ed. (1981) *One Million Poor? The Challenge of Irish Inequality*, Dublin: Turoe Press.

Kenny, C. (2005) *Moments That Changed Us*, Dublin: Gill & Macmillan.

Keogh, D. (1987) 'The Irish Constitutional Revolution: An Analysis of the Making of the Constitution', *Administration* Vol.35 No.4 Winter, 4–84.

Keogh, D. (2005) *Twentieth Century Ireland: Revolution and State Building* (second edition), Dublin: Gill & Macmillan.

Keohane, K. (1989) 'Toxic Trade-off: the price Ireland pays for industrial development',

The Ecologist Vol.19 No.4 July/August, 144–46.

Keohane, K. (2002) 'Model Homes for Model(led) Citizens: Domestic Economies of Desire in Prosperity Square', *Space and Culture* Vol.5 No.4 November, 387–404.

Kerrigan, G. (1983) 'The Moral Civil War', *Magill* September 1983, 6–15.

Kersbergen, van K. (2000) 'The declining resistance of welfare states to change?' in S. Kuhnle and M. Alestalo, eds., *Survival of the European Welfare State*, London: Routledge, 19–36.

Kilkelly, U. (2007) *Barriers to the Realisation of Children's Rights in Ireland*, commissioned by the Ombudsman for Children. Accessed at: *www.oco.ie/ policyResearch/research.aspx* on 17 October 2008.

Kilkey, M. and Bradshaw, J. (1999) 'Lone Mothers, Economic Well-Being and Policies' in D. Sainsbury, ed., *Gender and Welfare Regimes*, Oxford: Oxford University Press, 147–84.

Kilmurray, E. (1988) *Fight, Starve or Emigrate, A History of the Irish Unemployed Movements in the 1950s*, Dublin: Larkin Unemployed Centre.

Kirby, P. (2001) 'Inequality and Poverty in Ireland: clarifying social objectives' in S. Cantillon, C. Corrigan, P. Kirby and J. O'Flynn, eds., *Rich and Poor Perspectives on Tackling Inequality in Ireland*, Dublin: Oak Tree Press in association with CPA, 1–35.

Kirby, P. (2002) *The Celtic Tiger in Distress: Growth with Inequality in Ireland*, Basingstoke: Palgrave.

Kirby, P. (2006) 'The Changing Role of the Irish State: From Welfare to Competition State' in T. O'Connor and M. Murphy, eds., *Social Care in Ireland: Theory, Policy and Practice*, Cork: CIT Press, 112–25.

Kirby, P. (2008) *UNRISD Project on Poverty Reduction and Policy Regimes: Country paper on Ireland*, Geneva: UNRISD.

Kissane, B. (2003) 'The Illusion of State Neutrality in a secularising Ireland', *West European Politics* Vol.26 No.1 January, 73–94.

Klein, N. (2000) *No Logo*, London: Flamingo.

Kleinman, M. (1996) *Housing, Welfare and the State in Europe: a comparative analysis of Britain, France, and Germany*, Elgar: Aldershot 1996.

Kleinman, M. (2002) *A European Welfare State?: European Union Social Policy in Context*, Basingstoke: Palgrave.

Korpi, W. (1983) *The Democratic Class Struggle*, London: Routledge and Kegan Paul.

Korpi, W. (1992) *Welfare state development in Europe since 1930: Ireland in a comparative perspective*, Dublin: ESRI.

Kwon, H.J. (1997) 'Beyond European Welfare Regimes: Comparative Perspectives on East Asian Welfare Systems', *Journal of Social Policy* Vol.26 No.4 October, 467–84.

Labour Party (2008) Webpage 'What Labour stands for'. Accessed at: *http://www.labour.ie/party* on September 3rd 2008.

Lacey, B. (2008) *'Terrible Queer Creatures' Homosexuality in Irish History*, Dublin: Wordwell Books.

Laffan, B. (2000) 'Rapid Adaptation and Light Co-ordination' in R. O'Donnell, ed., *Europe: The Irish Experience*, Dublin: IEA, 125–147.

Laffan, B. (2004) 'Irish Politics and European Politics' in J. Hourihane, ed., *Ireland and the European Union: The First Thirty Years, 1973–2002*, Dublin: The Lilliput Press, 54–66.

Lane, F. and Ó Drisceoil, D., eds. (2005) *Politics and the Irish Working Class, 1830–1945*, Basingstoke: Palgrave Macmillan.

Langford, S. (1999) 'The Impact of the European Union on Irish Social Policy Development in Relation to Social Exclusion' in G. Kiely, A. O'Donnell, P.

Kennedy and S. Quin, eds., *Irish Social Policy in Context*, Dublin: UCD Press, 90–113.

Langford, S. (2007) 'Delivering Integrated Policy and Services for Children', *Journal of the Statistical and Social Inquiry Society of Ireland* Vol.XXXVI Annual Symposium, read before the Society 21 June 2007, 250–60.

Langhelle, O. (1999) 'Sustainable Development: Exploring the Ethics of Our Common Future', *International Political Science Review* Vol.20 No.2 April, 129–49.

Larragy, J. (2006) 'Origins and Significance of the Community and Voluntary Pillar in Irish Social Partnership', *The Economic and Social Review* Vol.37 No.3 Winter, 375–98.

Larsen, T.P. and Taylor-Gooby, P. (2004) 'New Risks at the EU Level; A Spillover from Open Market Policies?' in P. Taylor-Gooby, ed., *New Risks, New Welfare: The Transformation of the European Welfare State*, Oxford: Oxford University Press, 181–208.

Lavalette, M. (2006a) 'Marxism and Welfarism' in M. Lavalette and A. Pratt, eds., *Social Policy: Theories, Concepts and Issues* (third edition), London: Sage, 46–65.

Lavalette, M. (2006b) 'Globalisation and Social Policy' in M. Lavalette and A. Pratt, eds., *Social Policy: Theories, Concepts and Issues* (third edition), London: Sage, 274–89.

Lavalette, M. and Pratt, A. (2006) eds., *Social Policy: Theories, Concepts and Issues* (third edition), London: Sage.

Lavalette, M. and Pratt, A. (2006a) 'Introduction' in Lavalette, M. and Pratt, A., eds., *Social Policy: Theories, Concepts and Issues* (third edition), London: Sage, 1–5.

Law Reform Commission (2006) *Rights and Duties of Co-habitants*, Dublin: Law Reform Commission.

Layte, R., Fahey, T. and Whelan, C. (1999) *Income, Deprivation and Well-Being Among Older Irish People*, National Council on Ageing and Older People, Report No.55, Dublin: NCAOP.

Layte, R., Nolan, A. and Nolan, B. (2007) *Poor Prescriptions, Poverty and Access to Community Health Services* Dublin: CPA.

Ledden, P. (1999) 'Education and Social Class in Joyce's Dublin', *Journal of Modern Literature* Vol.22 No.2 Winter, 329–36.

Lee, J.J. (1979) 'Continuity and Change in Ireland, 1945–70' in J.J. Lee, ed., *Ireland 1945–70*, Dublin: Gill & Macmillan, 166–77.

Lee, J.J. (1989) *Ireland 1912–1985 Politics and Society*, Cambridge: Cambridge University Press.

Lee, P. and Raban, C. (1988) *Welfare Theory and Social Policy: reform or revolution?*, London: Sage.

LeGrand, J. (1982) *The Strategy of Equality*, London: George, Allen & Unwin.

LeGrand, J., Propper, C. and Robinson, R. (1992) *The Economics of Social Problems* (third edition), London: Macmillan.

Leibfried, S. (1992) 'Towards a European Welfare State? On Integrating Poverty Regimes into the European Community' in Z. Ferge and J.E. Kohlberg, eds., *Social Policy in a Changing Europe*, Frankfurt am Main: Campus Verlag, 245–80.

Lenaghan, J. (1997a) 'Introduction' in J. Lenaghan, ed., *Hard Choices in Health Care*, London: BMJ Publishing Group, 1–6.

Lenaghan, J. (1997b) 'Health Care Rights in Europe: a comparative discussion' in J. Lenaghan, ed., *Hard Choices in Health Care*, London: BMJ Publishing Group, 177–200.

Lenihan, B. (2005) Address by Mr Brian Lenihan T.D., Minister for Children Launch of the Office of the Minister for Children and Announcement of Youth Justice Reforms

Agreed by Government, Tuesday, 13 December 2005. Accessed at: *http://www.omc.gov.ie/viewdoc.asp?Docid=242&CatID=11&mn=&StartDate=01+January+2005* on 30 October 2008.

Lenihan, C. (2008) 'Governance Challenge for Future Primary School Needs' Address by Conor Lenihan TD, Minster for State for Integration at the opening of the open forum discussion, Conference on the Governance Challenges for Future Primary School Needs, 27 June 2008, Royal Hospital Kilmainham, Dublin. Accessed at *http://www.education.ie/servlet/blobservlet/*Conor_Lenihan_Speech.pdf on 30 August 2008.

Lentin, R. (2005) 'Black Bodies and "Headless Hookers": Alternative Global Narratives for 21st Century Ireland', *The Irish Review* No.33 Spring, 1–12.

Lentin, R. and McVeigh, R. (2006) *After optimism?: Ireland, racism and globalisation*, Dublin: Metro Éireann Publications.

Levitas, R. (2001) 'Against Work: A Utopian Incursion into Social Policy', *Critical Social Policy* Vol.21 No.4 November, 449–65.

Levitas, R. (2005) *The Inclusive Society? Social Exclusion and New Labour* (second edition), Basingstoke: Palgrave Macmillan.

Lewis, J. (1992) 'Gender and the Development of Welfare Regimes', *Journal of European Social Policy* Vol.2 No.3 August, 159–73.

Lewis, J. (1997) 'Gender and Welfare Regimes: Further Thoughts', *Social Politics* Vol.4 No.2 Summer, 160–77.

Lewis, J. (1999) 'The Voluntary Sector in the Mixed Economy of Welfare' in D. Gladstone, ed., *Before Beveridge: Welfare Before the Welfare State*, Civitas, Choice in Welfare No.47, London: Civitas, 10–17.

Lewis, J. and Åström, G. (1997) 'Equality, Difference and State Welfare: Labour Market and Family Policies in Sweden' in C. Ungerson and M. Kember, eds., *Women and Social Policy: A Reader* (second edition), London: Macmillan, 25–40.

Liberatore, A. (1991) 'Problems of transnational policymaking: environmental policy in the European Community', *European Journal of Political Research* Vol.19 Nos.1/2 January, 281–305.

Lightman, E.S. and Riches, G. (2001) 'Canada: One Step Forward, Two Steps Back?' in P. Alcock and G. Craig, eds., *International Social Policy: Welfare Regimes in the Developed World*, Basingstoke: Palgrave, 45–63.

Lister, R. (2002) 'Sexual Citizenship' in E. Isin and B. Turner, eds., *Handbook of Citizenship Studies*, London: Sage, 191–207.

Lister, R. (2003) *Citizenship: Feminist Perspectives* (second edition), Basingstoke: Palgrave Macmillan.

Lister, R. (2006) 'Ladder of Opportunity or Engine of Inequality?' in G. Dench, ed., *The Rise and Rise of Meritocracy*, Oxford: Blackwell, 232–36.

Lister, R., ed. (1996) *Charles Murray and the Underclass: The Developing Debate*, The IEA Health and Welfare Unit Choice in Welfare No.33, London: Civitas.

Littig, B. and Grießler, E. (2005) 'Social Sustainability: a catchword between political pragmatism and social theory', *International Journal of Sustainable Development* Vol.8 Nos.1/2 July, 65–79.

Litton, F., ed. (1982) *Unequal Achievement: The Irish Experience 1957–1982*, Dublin: IPA.

Lloyd George, D. (1908/2000) 'Old Age Pensions Bill. Order for Second Reading read', in R. Goodin and D. Mitchell, eds., *The Foundations of the Welfare State*, Volume II, Cheltenham: Edward Elgar, 91–101.

Lodge, A. and Lynch, K., eds. (2004) *Diversity at School*, Dublin: IPA for The Equality

Authority.

Loyal, S. (2003) 'Welcome to the Celtic Tiger: racism, immigration and the state' in C. Coulter and S. Coleman, eds., *The End of Irish History*, Manchester: Manchester University Press, 74–94.

Lucas, K. (2004a) 'Locating transport as a social policy problem' in K. Lucas, ed., *Running on Empty, Transport, Social Exclusion and Environmental Justice*, Bristol: Policy Press, 7–13.

Lucas, K., ed. (2004) *Running on Empty, Transport, Social Exclusion and Environmental Justice*, Bristol: Policy Press.

Lucas, K., Grosvenor, T. and Simpson, R. (2001) *Transport, the Environment and Social Exclusion*, York: Joseph Rowntree Trust.

Luddy, M. (1995) *Women in Ireland 1800–1918: A documentary history*, Cork: Cork University Press.

Luddy, M. (1999) '"Angels of Mercy": Nuns as Workhouse Nurses, 1861–1898, in C. Malcolm and G. Jones, eds., *Medicine, Disease and the State in Ireland, 1650–1940*, Cork: Cork University Press, 102–17.

Luddy, M. (2001) 'Moral Rescue and Unmarried Mothers in Ireland in the 1920s', *Women's Studies* Vol.30 No.6 December, 797–817.

Luddy, M. (2002) 'Women and Politics in Ireland, 1860–1918' in A. Bourke, S. Kilfeather, M. Luddy, M. Mac Curtain, G. Meaney, M. Ní Dhonnchadha, M. O'Dowd and C. Wills, eds., *The Field Day Anthology of Irish Writing, Volume V Irish Women's Writings and Traditions*, Cork: Cork University Press, 69–74.

Lund, B. (2002) *Understanding State Welfare: Social Justice or Social Exclusion?*, London: Sage.

Lund, B. (2006) 'Distributive Justice and Social Policy' in M. Lavalette and A. Pratt, eds., *Social Policy: Theories, Concepts and Issues* (third edition), London: Sage, 107–123.

Lynch, K. (1999) *Equality in Education*, Dublin: Gill & Macmillan.

Lynch, K. (2000) 'Research and Theory on Equality and Education' in M.T. Hallinan, ed., *Handbook of the Sociology of Education*, New York: Kluwer, 85–105.

Lynch, K. (2001) 'Equality in Education', *Studies* Vol.90 No.360 December, 395–411.

Lynch, K. (2007) 'Love labour as a distinct and non-commodifiable form of care labour', *The Sociological Review* Vol.55 No.3, 550–70.

Lynch, K. and Baker, J. (2005) 'Equality in Education An Equality of Condition Perspective', *Theory and Research in Education* Vol.3 No.2 July, 131–64.

Lynch, K. and Lyons, M. (2008) 'The Gendered Order of Caring' in U. Barry, ed., *Where are we now? New feminist perspectives on women in contemporary Ireland*, Dublin: Tasc at New Island, 163–83.

Lynch, K. and Moran, M. (2006) 'Markets, schools and the convertibility of economic capital: the complex dynamics of class choice', *British Journal of Sociology of Education* Vol.27 No.2 April, 221–35.

Lyons, M. (2003) 'Spatial Segregation in Seven Cities: A Longitudinal Study of Home Ownership, 1971–91', *Housing Studies* Vol.18 No.3 May, 305–26.

Mac Cormaic, R. (2007) 'Inside Story is Missing From Survey of Centres', *The Irish Times* 31 October 2007.

Mac Cormaic, R. (2008) 'Looking Beyond the Headscarf', *The Irish Times* June 14th 2008.

Mac Éinrí, P. (2001) 'Immigration Policy in Ireland' in F. Farrell and P. Watt, eds.,

Responding to Racism in Ireland, Dublin: Veritas, 46–87.

Mac Éinrí, P. (2006) 'Migration in Ireland: a changing reality' in S. Healy, B. Reynolds and M. Collins, eds., *Social Policy in Ireland, Principles, Practice and Problems*, Dublin: Liffey Press, 357–83.

Mac Éinrí, P. (2007) 'Integration Models and Choices' in B. Fanning, ed., *Immigration and Social Change in the Republic of Ireland*, Manchester: Manchester University Press, 214–36.

Mac Gréil, M. (1977) *Prejudice and Tolerance in Ireland*, Dublin: Research Section, College of Industrial Relations.

MacLaughlin, J. (1999) 'Nation Building, Social Closure and anti-Traveller racism in Ireland', *Sociology* Vol.33 No.1 February, 129–51.

Macnaghten, P. and Urry, J. (1996) *Contested Natures*, London: Sage.

Mac Sharry, R. (2000a) 'The Challenge of 1987' in R. Mac Sharry and P. White (in association with J. O'Malley), *The Making of the Celtic Tiger: the inside story of Ireland's boom economy*, Cork/Dublin: Mercier Press, 42–74.

Mac Sharry, R. (2000b) 'The Tallaght Strategy: Aid to Recovery' in R. Mac Sharry and P. White (in association with J. O'Malley), *The Making of the Celtic Tiger: the inside story of Ireland's boom economy*, Cork/Dublin: Mercier Press, 75–100.

Mac Sharry, R. and White, P. (2000) 'From Celtic Pauper to Celtic Tiger' in R. Mac Sharry and P. White (in association with J. O'Malley), *The Making of the Celtic Tiger: the inside story of Ireland's boom economy*, Cork/Dublin: Mercier Press, 356–78.

MacSweeney, A.M. (1915) 'A Study of Poverty in Cork City', *Studies* March 1915, 93–104.

Magill (1977) 'Two-thirds now favour divorce', *Magill* December 1977, 27.

Maguire, M. (1998) *Servants to the Public: A History of the Local Government and Public Services Union 1901–1990*, Dublin: IPA.

Maguire, M. and Ó Cinnéide, S. (2005) '"A Good Beating Never Hurt Anyone": the punishment and abuse of children in twentieth century Ireland', *Journal of Social History* Vol.38 No.3 Spring, 635–52.

Mair, P. and Weeks, L. (2005) 'The party system' in J. Coakley and M. Gallagher, eds., *Politics in the Republic of Ireland* (fourth edition), London: Routledge in association with PSAI Press, 135–159.

Maître, B., Nolan, B. and Whelan, C.T. (2006) *Reconfiguring the Measurement of Deprivation and Consistent Poverty in Ireland*, Dublin: ESRI.

Malcolm, E. (1999) '"The House of the Strident Shadows": the Asylum, the Family and Emigration in Post-Famine Rural Ireland' in E. Malcolm and G. Jones, eds., *Medicine, Disease and the State in Ireland, 1650–1940*, Cork: Cork University Press, 177–91.

Malcolm, E. (2003) '"Ireland's crowded madhouses": the institutional confinement of the insane in nineteenth-and twentieth-century Ireland' in R. Porter and D. Wright, eds., *The Confinement of the Insane: International Perspectives, 1800–1965*, Cambridge: Cambridge University Press, 315–33.

Manandhar, M., Share, M., Friel, S., Walsh, O. and Hardy, F. (2006) *Food, nutrition and poverty among asylum-seekers in North West Ireland*, Combat Poverty Agency Working Paper 06/01, Dublin: CPA.

Mangan, I. (1993) 'The Influence of EC Membership on Irish Social Policy and Social Services' in S. Ó Cinnéide, ed., *Social Europe: EC Social Policy and Ireland*, Dublin: IEA, 60–81.

Mangan, I. (2002) *Older People in Long Stay Care, report for the Irish Human Rights Commission*. Accessed at: *http://www.ihrc.ie/documents/article.asp?NID=45&NCID*

=5&T=N&Print on 30 October 2008.

Mann, K. (1998) '"One step beyond" critical social policy in a "postmodern" Britain?' in J. Carter, ed., *Postmodernity and the Fragmentation of Welfare*, London: Routledge, 85–102.

Mansergh, M. (1986) '119. The Spirit of the Nation: Presidential Address, 50th Fianna Fáil Ard-Fheis, 11 April 1981' in M. Mansergh, ed., *The Spirit of the Nation: The Speeches and Statements of Charles J. Haughey (1957–1986)*, Cork/Dublin: Mercier Press, 462–81.

Marshall, T. H. (1949/1964) 'Citizenship and Social Class' in T.H. Marshall, *Class, Citizenship and Social Development: Essays by T.H. Marshall*, New York: Double Day, 65–122.

Martin, D. Most Rev. (2008) 'Governance Challenge for Future Primary School needs' Speaking notes for Conference on the Governance Challenges for Future Primary School Needs, 27 June 2008, Royal Hospital Kilmainham, Dublin. Accessed at: *http://www.education.ie/servlet/blobservlet/Archbishop_Martin_Speech.pdf* on 30 August 2008.

Martin, J.P. (2008a) 'Opening Remarks' at Press Conference in Dublin for the release of *Sickness, Disability and Work: Breaking the Barriers*, Vol.3: Denmark, Finland, Ireland and the Netherlands, 20 November 2008. Accessed at: *http://www.oecd.org/dataoecd/51/44/41705015.pdf* on 15 December 2008.

Mayock, P. and O'Sullivan, E. (2007) *Lives in Crisis: Homeless Young People in Dublin*, Dublin: The Liffey Press.

McAleese, D. (2000) 'Twenty-five Years a Growing' in R. O'Donnell, ed., *Europe: The Irish Experience*, Dublin: IEA, 79–110.

McAvoy, S. (1999) 'The Regulation of Sexuality in the Irish Free State, 1929–1935' in E. Malcolm and G. Jones, eds., *Medicine, Disease and the State in Ireland, 1650–1940*, Cork: Cork University Press, 253–66.

McCann, M., Ó Siocháin, S. and Ruane, J., eds. (1994) *Irish Travellers: Culture and Ethnicity*, Belfast: Institute of Irish Studies, Queens University Belfast.

McCarthy, A. (2004) 'Aspects of Local Health in Ireland in the 1950s' in D. Keogh, F. O'Shea and C. Quinlan, eds., *Ireland in the 1950s, the lost decade*, Cork/Dublin: Mercier Press, 118–34.

McCarthy, J.P. (2006) *Kevin Higgins: Builder of the Irish State*, Dublin: Irish Academic Press.

McCashin, A. (1986) 'Discussion, Symposium on the Report of the Commission on Social Welfare', *Journal of the Statistical and Social Inquiry Society of Ireland* Vol.XXV Part IV, 29–37.

McCashin, A. (2004) *Social Security in Ireland*, Dublin: Gill & Macmillan.

McCashin, A. (2007) 'Income Support for Older People' in M. Cousins, ed., *Welfare Policy and Poverty*, Dublin: IPA and the CPA, 139–68.

McDonagh, J. (2006) 'Transport Policy Instruments and Transport-related social exclusion in rural Republic of Ireland', *Journal of Transport Geography* Vol.14 No.5 September, 355–66.

McDonagh, M. (2000) 'Ethnicity and Culture' in E. Sheehan, ed., *Travellers, Citizens of Ireland: Our Challenge to an Intercultural Irish Society in the 21st Century*, Dublin: The Parish of the Travelling People, 26–31.

McDonnell, P. (2003) 'Developments in special education in Ireland: deep structures and policy making', *International Journal of Inclusive Education* Vol.7 No.3 July –

September, 259–69.

McGarry, P. (2008) 'No Directive for Schools on Use of Islamic Headscarf', *The Irish Times* 15 August 2008.

McGinnity, F., O'Connell, P.J., Quinn, E. and Williams, J. (2006) *Migrants' experience of racism and discrimination in Ireland: survey report*, Dublin: ESRI.

McGrath, B. (1999) 'The sustainability of a car dependent settlement pattern: an evaluation of new rural settlement in Ireland', *The Environmentalist* Vol.19 No.2 June, 99–107.

McKee, E. (1986) 'Church-state relations and the development of Irish health policy: the mother-and-child scheme, 1944–53', *Irish Historical Studies* Vol.XXV No.98 November, 159–94.

McLaughlin, D. (2008) 'The Irish Christian Brothers and the National Board of Education: challenging the myths', *History of Education* Vol.37 No.1 January, 43–70.

McLaughlin, E. (2001) 'Ireland: From Catholic Corporatism to Social Partnership', in A. Cochrane, J. Clarke and S. Gewirtz, eds., *Comparing Welfare States: Family Life and Social Policy* (second edition), London: Sage in association with The Open University, 223–260.

McLaughlin, J. (2003) *Feminist Social and Political Theory: Contemporary Debates and Dialogues*, Basingstoke: Palgrave Macmillan.

McLoughlin, D. (1990) 'Workhouses and Irish Female Paupers, 1840–70' in M. Luddy and C. Murphy, eds., *Women Surviving*, Dublin: Poolbeg Press, 117–47.

McVeigh, R. (2007) '"Ethnicity in Denial" and racism: the case of the government against Irish Travellers', *Translocations* Vol.2 No.1 Summer, 90–133.

McVeigh, R. (2008) 'The "Final Solution": Reformism, Ethnicity Denial and the Politics of Anti-Travellerism in Ireland', *Social Policy and Society* Vol.7 No.1 January, 91–102.

Mead, L. (1992) *The New Politics of Poverty: the nonworking poor in America*, New York: Basic Books.

Meade, R. (2005) 'We hate it here, please let us stay! Irish social partnership and the community/voluntary sector's conflicted experiences of recognition', *Critical Social Policy* Vol.25 No.3 August, 349–73.

Meadowcroft, J. (2005) 'From Welfare State to Ecostate' in J. Barry and R. Eckersley, eds., *The State and the Global Ecological Crisis*, Cambridge MA: MIT Press, 3–23.

Meadows, D., Meadows, D., Randers, J. and Behrens III, W. (1972) *The Limits to Growth*, New York: Universe Books.

Medical Manpower Forum (2001) *Report of the Medical Manpower Forum*, Dublin: Department of Health and Children.

Memery, C. (2001) 'The Housing System and the Celtic Tiger: the state response to a housing crisis of affordability and access', *European Journal of Housing Policy* Vol.1 No.1 April, 79–104.

Mental Health Commission (2008) *Annual Report 2007 Mental Health Commission including the Report of the Inspector of Mental Health Services 2007 Book 1*, Dublin: MHC.

Migrant Rights Centre Ireland (2006a) *Realising Integration, Creating Conditions for Economic, Social, Political and Cultural Inclusion of Migrant Workers and their Families in Ireland*, Dublin: Migrant Rights Centre Ireland.

Migrant Rights Centre Ireland (2006b) *Social Protection Denied: the impact of the habitual residence condition on migrant workers*, Dublin: Migrant Rights

Centre Ireland.

Migrant Rights Centre Ireland (2007) *Realising Integration, Migrant Workers Undertaking Essential Low-Paid Work in Dublin City*, Dublin: Migrant Rights Centre Ireland.

Millar, J. (2003) 'Social Security: means and ends' in J. Millar, ed., *Understanding Social Security Issues for Policy and Practice*, Bristol: Policy Press, 1–8.

Miller, D. (1999) 'Social Justice and Environmental Goods' in A. Dobson, ed., *Fairness and Futurity: Essays on Environmental Sustainability and Social Justice*, Oxford: Oxford University Press, 151–72.

Millet, K. (1970) *Sexual Politics*, London: Virago.

Minton, S.J., Dahl, T., O'Moore, A.M. and Tuck, D. (2008) 'An Exploratory Survey of the experiences of homophobic bullying among lesbian, gay, bisexual and transgendered young people in Ireland', *Irish Educational Studies* Vol.27 No.2, 177–191.

Mishra, R. (1990) *The Welfare State in Capitalist Society: Policies of Retrenchment and Maintenance in Europe, North America and Australia*, New York: Harvester Wheatsheaf.

Mokyr, J. and Ó Gráda, C. (1988) 'Poor and getting poorer? Living standards in Ireland before the Famine', *Economic History Review* Vol.41 No.2 May, 209–35.

Mooney, G. (1983) 'Equity in Health Care: confronting the confusion', *Effective Health Care* Vol.1 No.4 December, 179–85.

Mooney, G. (1998) 'Remoralizing the Poor?: Gender, Class and Philanthropy in Victorian Britain' in G. Lewis, ed., *Forming nation, framing welfare*, London: Routledge in association with OUP, 49–91.

Mooten, N. (2006) *Making Separated Children Visible: The Need for a Child-Centred Approach*, Dublin: Irish Refugee Council.

Moran, G. (2004a) *Sending out Ireland's Poor Assisted emigration to North America in the Nineteenth Century*, Dublin: Four Courts Press.

Moran, G. (2004b) '"Shovelling out the poor": assisted emigration from Ireland from the great famine to the fall of Parnell' in P. Duffy, ed., *To and From Ireland: Planned Migration Schemes c. 1600–2000*, Dublin: Geography Publications, 137–54.

Moran, M. (1992) 'The health-care state in Europe: convergence or divergence?', *Environment and Planning C* Vol.10 No.1, 72–90.

Moran, M. (1999) *Governing the health care state: A comparative study of the United Kingdom, the United States and Germany*, Manchester: Manchester University Press.

Moran, M. (2000) 'Understanding the welfare state: the case of health care', *British Journal of Politics and International Relations* Vol.2 No.2 June, 135–160.

Moynihan, M., ed. (1980) *Speeches and Statements by Eamon de Valera, 1917–73*, Dublin: Gill & Macmillan.

Mullard, M. and Spicker, P. (1998) *Social Policy in a Changing Society*, London: Routledge.

Murie, A. (1997) 'The Social Rented Sector, Housing and the Welfare State in the UK', *Housing Studies* Vol.12 No.4 October, 437–61.

Murphy, J. A. (1979) '"Put them out!" Parties and Elections, 1948–69' in J.J. Lee, ed., *Ireland 1945–70*, Dublin: Gill & Macmillan, 1–15.

Murphy, M. (2006) 'The Emerging Irish Workfare State and its Implications for Local Development' in D. Jacobson, P. Kirby and D. Ó Broin, eds., *Taming the Tiger, Social Exclusion in a Globalised Ireland*, Dublin: Tasc at New Island, 85–111.

Murphy, M. (2007) 'Working-aged People and Welfare Policy' in M. Cousins, ed.,

Welfare Policy and Poverty, Dublin: IPA and CPA, 101–37.

Murphy, M. and Millar, M. (2007) 'The NESC developmental welfare state: a glass half empty or a glass half full approach to active social policy reform', *Administration* Vol.55 No.3 Autumn, 75–100.

Murray, C. (1984) *Losing Ground: American Social Policy, 1950–1980*, New York: Basic Books.

Murray, P. (2006) 'The Evolution of Irish Health Policy: a sociological analysis' in D. McCluskey, ed., *Health Policy and Practice in Ireland*, Dublin: UCD Press, 44–60.

NASC (2008) *Hidden Cork, the perspectives of asylum seekers on direct provision and the asylum legal system*, Cork: NASC.

National Childcare Strategy (1999) *The Report of the Partnership 2000 Expert Working Group on Childcare*, Dublin: Partnership 2000 Expert Working Group on Childcare.

National Children's Strategy (2000) *The National Children's Strategy, Our Children – Their Lives*, Dublin: Stationery Office.

National Consultative Committee on Racism and Interculturalism (2008) *Building Integrated Neighbourhoods – Towards an Intercultural approach to housing policy and practice in Ireland*, Dublin: NCCRI.

National Council for Curriculum and Assessment (2005) *Intercultural Education in the Primary School: Guidelines for Schools*, Dublin: National Council for Curriculum and Assessment.

National Council for Curriculum and Assessment (2006) *Intercultural Education in the Post-Primary School: Guidelines for Schools*, Dublin: National Council for Curriculum and Assessment.

National Council on Ageing and Older People (2005) *An Age Friendly Society: A Position Statement*, Report No.88, Dublin: NCAOP.

National Disability Authority (2005) *How Far Towards Equality? Measuring how equally people with disabilities are included in Irish society*, Dublin: NDA.

National Economic and Social Council (1975) *An Approach to Social Policy*, Dublin: Stationery Office.

National Economic and Social Council (1991) *The Economic and Social Implications of Emigration*, Dublin: NESC.

National Economic and Social Council (1999) *Opportunities, Challenges and Capacities for Choice*, Dublin: NESC.

National Economic and Social Council (2004) *Housing in Ireland: Performance and Policy*, Dublin: NESC.

National Economic and Social Council (2005) *The Developmental Welfare State*, Dublin: NESC.

National Economic and Social Council (2006) *Managing Migration in Ireland, A Social and Economic Analysis*, Dublin: NESC.

National Economic and Social Forum (2002a) *Equity of Access to Hospital Care*, Forum Report No.25, Dublin: NESF.

National Economic and Social Forum (2002b) *Early School Leavers*, Forum Report No.24, Dublin: NESF.

National Economic and Social Forum (2003) *Equality Policies for Lesbian, Gay and Bisexual People: implementation issues*, Forum Report No.27, Dublin: NESF.

National Economic and Social Forum (2005a) *Early Childhood Education and Care*, Forum Report No.31, Dublin: NESF.

National Economic and Social Forum (2005b) *Care For Older People*, Form Report

No.32, Dublin: NESF.

National Economic and Social Forum (2008) *Fifth Periodic Report of the Work of the NESF*, Forum Report No.37, Dublin: NESF.

National Office for Equity of Access to Higher Education (2008) *National Plan for Equity of Access to Higher Education 2008–2013*, Dublin: National Office for Equity of Access to Higher Education.

National Traveller Women's Forum and Pavee Point (2002) *A Submission to the National Plan for Women*, Dublin: National Traveller Women Forum.

National Treatment Purchase Fund (2008b) *Annual Report 2007*, Dublin: National Treatment Purchase Fund.

National Treatment Purchase Fund (2008a) *Report on the Patient Treatment Register May 2008*, Dublin: National Treatment Purchase Fund.

Navarro, V. (1989) 'Why some countries have national health insurance, others have national health services and the United States has neither', *International Journal of Health Services* Vol.19 No.3, 383–404.

Ní Shuinéar, S. (1998) '"Solving Itinerancy" – Thirty-five Years of Irish Government Commissions'. Accessed at: *http://www.history.ul.ie/heatravinit/documents/pdf/solving-itinerancy-final.pdf* on 4 November 2008.

Nicholls, G. (1856) *A History of the Irish Poor Law*, London: John Murray.

Nolan, B. (2003) 'Social Indicators in the European Union', Paper for the Statistics Users' Conference, "Measuring Government Performance", London 13 November 2003. Accessed at: *http://www.statistics.gov.uk/events/suc/downloads/Nolan_paper.doc* on 19 December 2008.

Nolan, B. (2006a) 'The EU's Social Inclusion Indicators and Their Implications for Ireland' in S. Healy, B. Reynolds and M. Collins, eds., *Social Policy in Ireland: Principles, Practice and Problems* (second edition), Dublin: The Liffey Press, 171–90.

Nolan, B. (2006b) 'The Interaction of Public and Private Health Insurance: Ireland as a case study', *Geneva Papers on Risk and Insurance* Vol.31 No.4 October, 633–49.

Nolan, B. and Maître, B. (2007) 'Economic Growth and Income Inequality: setting the context' in T. Fahey, H. Russell and C.T. Whelan, eds., *Best of Times? The Social Impact of the Celtic Tiger*, Dublin: IPA, 27–41.

Nolan, B. and Whelan, C. (1999) *Loading the Dice? A Study of Cumulative Disadvantage*, Dublin: Oak Tree Press.

Nolan, B. and Wiley, M. (2001) *Private Practice in Irish Public Hospitals*, Dublin: Oak Tree Press.

Nolan, B., O'Connell, J. and Whelan, C.T., eds. (2000) *Bust to Boom? The Irish Experience of Growth and Inequality*, Dublin: IPA.

Nolan, B., Whelan, C. and Williams, J. (1998) *Where are the poor households? The spatial distribution of poverty and deprivation in Ireland*, Dublin: Oak Tree Press.

Norris, M. (2005) 'Social Housing' in M. Norris and D. Redmond, eds., *Housing Contemporary Ireland, Policy, Society and Shelter*, Dublin: IPA, 160–82.

Norris, M., Coates, D. and Kane, F. (2007) 'Breaching the Limits of Owner Occupation? Supporting low-income buyers in the inflated Irish housing market', *European Journal of Housing Policy* Vol.7 No.3 September, 337–55.

Norris, M. and Redmond, D., eds. (2005) *Housing Contemporary Ireland, Policy, Society and Shelter*, Dublin: IPA.

Norris, M. and Winston, N. (2005) 'Housing and the Accommodation of Irish Travellers: From Assimilationism to Multiculturalism and Back Again', *Social Policy and*

Administration Vol.39 No.7 December, 802–21.

Nozick, R. (1974) *Anarchy, State and Utopia*, Oxford: Basil Blackwell.

NSPCC (n.d.) *A pocket history of the NSPCC*, Accessed at: *http://www.nspcc.org.uk/ whatwedo/aboutthenspcc/historyofnspcc/historyofnspcc_booklet_wdf33717.pdf* on 17 December 2008.

Nutley, S. (2000) 'Rural Transport: Time for Action?', *Geography* Vol.5 No.1 January, 85–87.

Oakley, A. (1994) 'Introduction' in A. Oakley and A.S. Williams, eds., *The Politics of the Welfare State*, London: UCL Press, 1–17.

O'Brien, C. (2008) 'Figures show 3,600 children awaiting psychiatric assessment', *The Irish Times* 24 July 2008.

O'Brien, G. (1999) 'State Intervention and Medical Relief of the Irish Poor, 1787–1850' in C. Malcolm and G. Jones, eds., *Medicine, Disease and the State in Ireland, 1650– 1940*, Cork: Cork University Press, 195–207.

O'Brien, L. and Dillon, B. (1982) *Private Rented: the forgotten sector*, Dublin: Mount Salus Press.

O'Brien, M. and Penna, S. (1998) *Theorising Welfare: Enlightenment and Modern Society*, London: Sage.

O'Callaghan, M. (2002) 'Women and Politics in Independent Ireland, 1921–68' in A. Bourke, S. Kilfeather, M. Luddy, M. Mac Curtain, G. Meaney, M. Ní Dhonnchadha, M. O'Dowd and C. Wills, eds., *The Field Day Anthology of Irish Writing, Volume V Irish Women's Writings and Traditions*, Cork: Cork University Press, 120–35.

O'Carroll, A. and O'Reilly, F. (2008) 'There's a hole in the bucket: the analysis of the impact of the medical card review process on patient entitlement to free health care', *Irish Medical Journal* Vol.101 No.1 January, IMJ Online 2008. Accessed at: *http:// www.imj.ie//Issue_detail.aspx?issueid=+&pid=2732&type=Papers* on December 16 2008.

O'Caroll, I. and Collins, E. eds. (1995) *Lesbian and Gay Visions of Ireland, Towards the Twenty-first Century*, London: Cassell.

Ó Cinnéide, S. (1969) 'The Development of the Home Assistance Service', *Administration* Vol.17 No.3 Autumn, 284–308.

Ó Cinnéide, S. (1970) *A Law for the Poor: A Study of Home Assistance in Ireland*, Dublin: IPA.

Ó Cinnéide, S. (1992) 'Social Policy' in P. Keatinge, ed., *Maastricht and Ireland: What the Treaty means*, Dublin: IEA, 56–61.

Ó Cinnéide, S. (1993) 'Ireland in a European Welfare State?' in S. Ó Cinnéide, ed., *Social Europe: EC Social Policy and Ireland*, Dublin: IEA, 117–46.

Ó Cinnéide, S. (1998/1999) 'Democracy and the Constitution', *Administration* Vol.46 No.4 Winter, 41–58.

Ó Cinnéide, S. (2000) 'The 1949 White Paper and the foundations of social welfare' in A. Lavan, ed., *50 Years of Social Welfare Policy* (Seminar Proceedings), Dublin: Department of Social, Community and Family Affairs, 18–30.

O'Connell, A. (2008) 'Very Ordinary People – Lesbian Mothers Talking' in U. Barry, ed., *Where are we now? New feminist perspectives on women in contemporary Ireland*, Dublin: Tasc at New Island, 96–129.

O'Connell, C. (2005a) 'The Collective Home? Recent experiences of social housing in Europe' in P.Herrmann, ed., *Utopia between corrupted public responsibility and contested modernisation: globalisation and social responsibility*, New York: Nova Science, 77–90.

O'Connell, C. (2005b) 'The Housing Market and Owner Occupation in Ireland' in M. Norris and D. Redmond, eds., *Housing Contemporary Ireland, Policy, Society and*

Shelter, Dublin: IPA, 19–43.

O' Connell, C. (2007) *The State and Housing in Ireland: ideology, policy and practice*, New York: Nova Science.

O'Connell, J. (2002) 'Travellers in Ireland: an examination of discrimination and racism' in R. Lentin and R. McVeigh eds., *Racism and Anti-Racism in Ireland*, Belfast: Beyond the Pale, 49–62.

O'Connell, M.J. (1880) 'Poor Law Administration as it affects Women and Children in Workhouses', *Journal of the Statistical and Social Society of Ireland* Vol.VII April, 20–31.

O'Connell, P.J. (1999) *Astonishing Success; Economic Growth and the Labour Market in Ireland*, ILO Employment and Training Papers No.44, Geneva: ILO.

O'Connell, P.J. (2000) 'The dynamics of the Irish labour market in comparative perspective' in B. Nolan, J. O'Connell and C.T. Whelan, eds., *Bust to Boom? The Irish Experience of Growth and Inequality*, Dublin: IPA, 58–89.

O'Connell, P.J. and McGinnity, F. (2008) *Immigrants at Work: ethnicity and nationality in the Irish labour market*, Dublin: ESRI/Equality Authority.

O'Connell, P., Clancy, D. and McCoy, S. (2006) *Who went to college in 2004? A national survey of new entrants to higher education*, Dublin: HEA.

O'Connor, C. (2003a), *Direct Discrimination? An analysis of the scheme of direct provision in Ireland*, Dublin: Free Legal Advice Centres.

O'Connor, J. (1973) *The Fiscal Crisis of the State*, New York: St. Martin's Press.

O'Connor, J. (1995) *The Workhouses of Ireland: The Fate of Ireland's Poor*, Dublin: Anvil Books.

O'Connor, J.S. (2003) 'Welfare state development in the context of European integration and economic convergence: situating Ireland within the European Union context', *Policy and Politics* Vol.31 No.3 July 2003, 387–404.

O'Connor, J.S. (2005) 'Policy coordination, social indicators and the social-policy agenda in the European Union', *Journal of European Social Policy* Vol.15 No.4 November, 345–61.

O'Connor Lysaght, D. (1991) 'A Saorstát is born: How the Irish Free State came into being' in S.Hutton and P. Stewart, eds., *Ireland's Histories Aspects of State, Society and Ideology*, London: Routledge, 36–51.

O'Dea, W. (2000) 'FF's social democracy is part of its heritage', *The Irish Times* 19 October 2000.

O'Donnell, A. (1999) 'Comparing Welfare States: Considering the Case of Ireland' in G. Kiely, A. O'Donnell, P. Kennedy and S. Quin, eds., *Irish Social Policy in Context*, Dublin: UCD Press, 70–89.

O'Donnell, R. (1992) 'Economic and Monetary Union' in P. Keatinge, ed., *Maastricht and Ireland: What the Treaty Means*, Dublin: IEA, 41–9.

O'Donnell, R. (2000a) 'The New Ireland in the New Europe' in R. O'Donnell, ed., *Europe: The Irish Experience*, Dublin: IEA, 161–214.

O'Donnell, R., ed. (2000) *Europe: The Irish Experience*, Dublin: IEA.

OECD (1965) *Investment in Education*, Dublin: Stationery Office.

OECD (1987) *Financing and Delivering Health Care: a comparative analysis of OECD countries*, Paris: OECD.

OECD (1992) *Economic Outlook: Historical Statistics 1960–1990*, Paris: OECD.

OECD (2000) *Education at a glance, 2000*, Paris: OECD.

OECD (2002) *OECD Historical Statistics 1970/2000*, 2001 Edition, Paris: OECD.

OECD (2004a) *Proposal for a taxonomy of health insurance*, Paris: OECD.

OECD (2004b) *Early Childhood Education and Care Policy: country note for Ireland*, Paris: OECD.

OECD (2004c) *Review of National Policies for Education: Review of Higher Education in Ireland*, Paris: OECD.

OECD (2006a) *Early Childhood Education and Care Policy: country note for Ireland*, Paris: OECD.

OECD (2006b) *Review of National Policies for Education: Review of Higher Education in Ireland*, Paris: OECD.

OECD (2007) *Health at a glance 2007–OECD Indicators*, Paris: OECD.

OECD (2008a) *OECD Factbook 2008 Economic, Environmental and Social Statistics*, Paris: OECD.

OECD (2008b) *OECD Health Data 2008*, Online Version, OECD, Accessed from: *www.sourceoecd.org* on 14 November 2008.

OECD (2008c) *Education at a glance, 2008*, Paris: OECD.

OECD (2008d) *Sickness, Disability and Work: Breaking the Barriers (Vol.3): Denmark, Finland, Ireland and the Netherlands*, Paris: OECD.

Offe, C. (1982) 'Some contradictions of the modern welfare state', *Critical Social Policy* Vol.2 No.5 September, 7–16.

Offe, C. (1984) *Contradictions of the Welfare State*, London: Hutchinson.

Office of the Minister for Children (2007) *Office of the Minister for Children Annual Report 2006* Dublin: Stationery Office.

Office of the Minister for Children and Youth Affairs (2008) *National review of compliance with Children First: National Guidelines for the Protection and Welfare of Children*, Dublin: Stationery Office.

Office of the Minister for Integration (2008) *Migration Nation: Statement on Integration Strategy and Diversity Management*, Dublin: Office of the Minister for Integration.

O'Flynn, J. and Murphy, M. (2001) 'The Politics of Redistribution' in S. Cantillon, C. Corrigan, P. Kirby and J. O'Flynn, eds., *Rich and Poor: Perspectives on Tackling Inequality in Ireland*, Dublin: Oak Tree Press in association with CPA, 37–80.

O'Gorman, C. (2008) RTE Radio 1 Drivetime Podcast, 'Article 8: Everyone has the right to ask for legal help when their basic rights are not respected', Colm O'Gorman, Amnesty Ireland 31/10/2008. Accessed at: *http://www.amnesty.ie/amnesty/ live/irish/action/article.asp?id=23195&page=15310* on 2 January 2009.

Ó Gráda, C. (1997) *A Rocky Road: The Irish economy since the 1920s*, Manchester: Manchester University Press.

Ó Gráda, C. (2002) '"The Greatest Blessing of All": The Old Age Pension in Ireland', *Past and Present* No.175 May, 124–61.

O'Hagan, J. and McIndoe, T. (2005) 'Population, Employment and Unemployment' in J. O'Hagan and C. Newman eds., *The Economy of Ireland: National & Sectoral Policy Issues*, Dublin: Gill & Macmillan, 76–106.

O'Hagan, J. and Newman, C., eds. (2005) *The Economy of Ireland: National & Sectoral Policy Issues*, Dublin: Gill & Macmillan.

O'Halloran, A. (2005) 'Transformation in Contemporary Ireland's Society, Economy and Polity: An Era of Post-Parliamentary Governance?', *Administration* Vol.53 No.1 Spring, 54–79.

O'Hanlon, G. (2004) 'Population Change in the 1950s: A Statistical Review' in D. Keogh, P. O'Shea and C. Quinlan, eds., *Ireland in the 1950s, the lost decade*,

Cork/Dublin: Mercier Press, 72–79.

O'Hara, P. and Commins, P. (2003) 'Ireland and the future of Europe: A regional perspective' in B. Reynolds and S. Healy, eds., *Ireland and the Future of Europe: Leading the way towards inclusion?*, Dublin: CORI Justice Commission, 29–64.

O'Hearn, D. (1997) 'The Celtic Tiger: The Role of the Multi-Nationals' in E. Crowley and J. MacLaughlin, eds., *Under the Belly of the Tiger: Class, Race, Identity and Culture in the Global Ireland*, Dublin: Irish Reporter Publications, 21–34.

O'Hearn, D. (2001) *The Atlantic Economy: Britain, the US and Ireland*, Manchester: Manchester University Press.

O'Hearn, D. (2003) 'Macroeconomic policy in the Celtic Tiger: a critical reassessment' in S. Coulter and S. Coleman, eds., *The End of Irish History? Critical reflections on the Celtic Tiger*, Manchester: Manchester University Press, 34–55.

Ó hÓgartaigh, M. (1999) 'Dr Dorothy Price and the elimination of childhood tuberculosis' in J. Augusteijn, ed., *Ireland in the 1930s New Perspectives*, Dublin: Four Courts Press, 67–82.

Oliver, M. (1996) *Understanding Disability: from theory to practice*, Basingstoke: Macmillan.

O'Loughlin, A. (2005) 'Social policy and older people' in S. Quin, P. Kennedy, A. Matthews, and G. Kiely, eds., *Contemporary Irish Social Policy* (second edition), Dublin: UCD Press, 206–30.

O'Mahony, C. (2005) *Cork's Poor Law Palace, Workhouse Life 1838–1890*, Cork: Rosmathún Press.

O'Malley, E. (2006) 'Populist Nationalists: Sinn Féin and Redefining the "Radical Right"', Paper Presented at the Elections, Public Opinion and Parties Conference, University of Nottingham, 9–11 September 2006. Accessed at: *http://www.psai.ie/conferences/papers2006/malley.pdf* on 13 September 2008.

Ombudsman for Children (2006) *Advice of the Ombudsman for Children on the proposed referendum on children's rights, 22 December 2006*. Accessed at: *http://www.oco.ie/whatsNew/advice_to_government.aspx* on 15 December 2008.

O'Reilly, J. and Wiley, M. (2007) *The Public/Private Mix in Irish Acute Public Hospitals: Trends and Implications*, ESRI Working Paper No.218, Dublin: ESRI.

Ó Riain, S. and O'Connell, P.J. (2000) 'The role of the state in growth and welfare' in B. Nolan, P.J. O'Connell and C.T. Whelan, eds., *Bust to Boom? The Irish Experience of Growth and Inequality*, Dublin: IPA, 310–39.

O'Riordan, T. (1981) *Environmentalism* (second edition), London: Pion Books.

O'Shea, E. (with contributions from Convery, J. and Larragy, J.) (2002) *Review of the Nursing Home Subvention Scheme*, Dublin: Stationery Office.

O'Shea, E. (2006) *Towards a National Strategy for Older People in Ireland*, Older and Bolder Campaign. Accessed at: *http://www.olderandbolder.ie/documents/1_Older&Bolder.pdf* on 6 December 2008.

O'Sullivan, D. (1989) 'The Ideational Base of Irish Educational Policy' in D. Mulcahy and D. O'Sullivan, eds., *Irish Educational Policy Process and Substance*, Dublin: IPA, 219–69.

O'Sullivan, D. (2005) *Cultural Politics and Irish Education Since the 1950s*, Dublin: IPA.

O'Sullivan, E. (2004) 'Welfare Regimes, Housing and Homelessness in the Republic of Ireland', *European Journal of Housing Policy* Vol.4 No.3 December, 323–43.

O'Sullivan, E. (2005a) 'Homelessness' in M. Norris and D. Redmond, eds., *Housing Contemporary Ireland, Policy, Society and Shelter*, Dublin: IPA, 245–67.

O'Sullivan, E. (2008) 'Researching Homelessness in Ireland: explanations, themes and approaches' in D. Downey, ed., *Perspectives on Irish Homelessness: past, present and future*, Dublin: Homeless Agency, 16–23.

O'Sullivan, S. (2007) 'Gender and the workforce' in S. O'Sullivan, ed., *Contemporary Ireland: A Sociological Map*, Dublin: UCD Press, 265–82.

O'Toole, F. (1988) 'Highbrow Robbery' *Magill* April 1988, 22–26.

O'Toole, F. (2003) *After the Ball*, New Island: Dublin.

Özüekren, S. and van Kempen, R. (2003) 'Special Issue Editors' Introduction: Dynamics and Diversity: Housing Careers and Segregation of Minority Ethnic Groups', *Housing, Theory and Society* Vol.20 No.4 December, 162–71.

Page, R. (2005) 'From democratic socialism to New Labour' in H. Bochel, C. Bochel, R. Page and R. Sykes, eds, *Social Policy: Issues and Development*, Essex: Pearson Education, 268–91.

Paris, C. (2007) 'International Perspectives on Planning and Affordable Housing', *Housing Studies* Vol.22 No.1 January, 1–9.

Parry, J. and Parry, N. (2000) 'The Equality of Bodies: Animal Exploitation and Human Welfare' in K. Ellis and H. Dean, eds., *Social Policy and the Body*, London: Macmillan, 160–79.

Pavee Point (2006) *Assimilation Policies and Outcomes: Travellers Experiences*, Dublin: Pavee Point.

Peck, B. (1966) 'Irish Education and European Integration', *Comparative Education* Vol.2 No.3 June, 197–207.

Penna, D. and O'Brien, M. (1996) 'Postmodernism and Social Policy: a small step forwards?', *Journal of Social Policy* Vol.25 No.1 January, 39–61.

Pepper, D. (1993) *Eco-socialism: From Deep Ecology to Social Justice*, London: Routledge.

Pepper, D. (1996) *Modern Environmentalism*, London: Routledge.

Pepper, D. (1999) 'Ecological modernisation or the "ideal model" of sustainable development? Questions prompted at Europe's periphery', *Environmental Politics* Vol.8 No.4 Winter, 1–34.

Peters, M. (2003a) 'Education Policy in the Age of Knowledge Capitalism', *Futures in Education* Vol.1 No.2, 361–80.

Peters, M. (2003b) 'Classical Political Economy and the Role of Universities in the New Knowledge Economy', *Globalisation, Societies and Education* Vol.1 No.2 July, 153–68.

Petrášová, A. (2008) 'Social Protection in the European Union', Eurostat, *Statistics in Focus*, 46/2008, Brussels: European Commission.

Phelan, E. and Norris, M. (2008) 'Neo-corporatist Governance of Homeless Services in Dublin: Reconceptualization, incorporation and exclusion', *Critical Social Policy* Vol.28 No.1 February, 51–73.

Pierce, M. (2006) 'Older people and social care' in B. Fanning and M. Rush, eds., *Care and Social Change in the Irish Welfare Economy*, Dublin: UCD Press, 190–205.

Pierson, P. (2001) 'Post-industrial Pressures on the Mature Welfare States' in P. Pierson, ed., *The New Politics of the Welfare State*, Oxford: Oxford University Press, 80–104.

Pillinger, J. (2006) *An Introduction to the situation and experiences of women migrant workers in Ireland*, Dublin: Equality Authority.

Pillinger, J. (2008) 'The Changing Face of Ireland – Gender and the Feminisation of Migration' in U. Barry, ed., *Where are we now? new feminist perspectives on women in contemporary Ireland*, Dublin: Tasc at New Island, 184–215.

Pinker, R. (2008) 'The Conservative Tradition' in P. Alcock, M. May and K. Rowlingson, eds., *The Student's Companion to Social Policy* (third edition), Oxford: Blackwell, 69–76.

Piven, F. and Cloward, R. (1993) *Regulating the Poor: The Functions of Public Welfare* (second edition), New York: Vintage Books.

Platt, L. (2008) '"Race" and Social Welfare' in P. Alcock, M. May and K. Rowlingson, eds., *The Student's Companion to Social Policy* (third edition), Oxford: Blackwell, 369–77.

Ploug, N. and Kvist, J. (1996) *Social Security in Europe, Development or Dismantlement?*, The Hague: Kluwer Law International.

Powell, F. (1989) 'Vagrancy and Deterrence', *Social Policy and Administration* Vol.23 No.1 May, 72–83.

Powell, F. (1992) *The Politics of Irish Social Policy 1600–1990*, New York: Edwin Mellen Press.

Powell, M., ed. (2002) *Evaluating New Labour's Welfare Reforms*, Bristol: Policy Press.

Powell, M. (2008) 'Third Way Perspectives' in P. Alcock, M. May and K. Rowlingson, eds., *The Student's Companion to Social Policy* (third edition), Oxford: Blackwell, 91–98.

Power, A. (1993) *Hovels to High Rise State Housing in Europe since 1950*, London: Routledge.

Pratt, A. (2006a) 'Neo-liberalism and Social Policy' in M. Lavalette and A. Pratt, eds., *Social Policy: Theories, Concepts and Issues* (third edition), London: Sage, 9–25.

Pratt, A. (2006b) 'Towards a "New" Social Democracy' in M. Lavalette and A. Pratt, eds., *Social Policy: Theories, Concepts and Issues* (third edition), London: Sage, 26–45.

Pratt, J. (2006) 'Citizenship, Social Solidarity and Social Policy' in M. Lavalette and A. Pratt, eds., *Social Policy: Theories, Concepts and Issues* (third edition), London: Sage, 124–140.

Preston, M. (1998) 'Discourse and Hegemony: Race and Class in the Language of Charity in Nineteenth-Century Dublin' in T. Foley and S. Ryder, eds., *Ideology and Ireland in the Nineteenth Century*, Dublin: Four Courts Press, 100–112.

Priemus, H. and Dieleman, F. (1999) 'Social Housing Finance in the European Union, Developments and Prospects', *Urban Studies* Vol.36 No.4 April, 623–33.

Primary Care Reimbursement Service (various years) *Primary Care Reimbursement Service Annual Report*, Dublin: HSE, Primary Care Reimbursement Service.

Prunty, M. (2007) *Older People in Poverty in Ireland: An Analysis of EU-SILC 2004*, Poverty Research Initiative: Combat Poverty Agency, Research Working Paper 07/02, April 2007.

Puirséil, N. (2005) 'Political and party competition in post-war Ireland' in B. Girvin and G. Murphy, eds., *The Lemass Era*, Dublin: UCD Press, 12–27.

Punch, M. (2005) 'Uneven Development and the Private Rental Market: Problems and Prospects for Low-Income Households' in M. Norris and D. Redmond, eds., *Housing Contemporary Ireland, Policy, Society and Shelter*, Dublin: IPA, 119–43.

Quin, S. (2006) 'Disability, children and social care' in B. Fanning and M. Rush, eds., *Care and Social Change in the Irish Welfare Economy*, Dublin: UCD Press, 179–89.

Quin, S. and Redmond, B., eds. (2003) *Disability and Social Policy in Ireland*, Dublin: UCD Press.

Quin, S. and Redmond, B. (2005) 'Disability and social policy' in S. Quin, P. Kennedy, A. Matthews and G. Kiely, eds., *Contemporary Irish Social Policy* (second edition), Dublin: UCD Press, 138–56.

Radaelli, C.M. (2003) *The Open Method of Coordination: A new governance architecture for the European Union?: Preliminary report*, Stockholm: Swedish Institute for

European Policy Studies.

Rafter, K. (2002) *Martin Mansergh: A Biography*, Dublin: New Island.

Raftery, D. and Nowlan-Roebuck, C. (2007) 'Convent Schools and National Education in Nineteenth Century Ireland: negotiating a place within a non-denominational system', *History of Education* Vol.36 No.3 May, 353–65.

Raftery, M. and O'Sullivan, E. (1999) *Suffer the Little Children*, Dublin: New Island.

Raftery, M. (2006) 'In danger of a siege mentality', *The Irish Times* September 9 2006.

Ratcliffe, P. (2004) *Race, Ethnicity and Difference: imagining an inclusive society*, Maidenhead: Open University Press.

Reay, D. (2001) 'Finding or Losing Yourself? Working Class Relationships to Education', *Journal of Education Policy* Vol.16 No.4 July, 333–46.

Redmond, D. (2001) 'Policy Review Social Housing in Ireland: under new management?', *European Journal of Housing Policy* Vol.1 No.2 August, 291–306.

Redmond, D. (2003) 'Defeat for Tenure Mix', *Cornerstone* April 2003, 12–13.

Redmond, D. and Norris, M. (2005) 'Setting the Scene: Transformation in Irish Housing' in M. Norris, and D. Redmond, eds., *Housing Contemporary Ireland, Policy, Society and Shelter*, Dublin: IPA, 1–20.

Reid, B. and Taylor, J. (2007) 'A Feminist Exploration of Traveller Women's Experiences of Maternity Care in the Republic of Ireland', *Midwifery* Vol.23 No.3 September, 248–59.

Reid, D. (1995) *Sustainable Development: an introductory guide*, London: Earthscan.

Rein, M. (1982) 'The Social Policy of the Firm', *Policy Science* Vol.14 No.2 April, 117–35.

Report of the Ferns Inquiry (2005) *The Ferns Report*, Presented to the Minister for Health and Children October 2005, Dublin: Stationery Office.

Rich, A. (1980) 'Compulsory Heterosexuality and the Lesbian Existence', *Signs* Vol.5 No.4 Summer, 631–60.

Richardson, D. (2000a) 'Constructing sexual citizenship: theorising sexual rights', *Critical Social Policy* Vol.20 No.1 February, 105–35.

Richardson, D. (2000b) 'Claiming Citizenship? Sexuality, Citizenship and Lesbian/Feminist Theory', *Sexualities* Vol.3 No.2 May, 255–72.

Richardson, D. (2004) 'Locating Sexualities: From Here to Normality', *Sexualities* Vol.7 No.4 November, 391–411.

Richardson, V. (2005) 'Children and social policy' in S. Quin, P. Kennedy, A. Matthews and G. Kiely, eds., *Contemporary Irish Social Policy* (second edition), Dublin: UCD Press, 157–85.

Ridge, T. (2008) 'Children' in P. Alcock, M. May and K. Rowlingson, eds., *The Student's Companion to Social Policy* (third edition), Oxford: Blackwell, 378–85.

Rieger, E. and Leibfried, S. (2003) *Limits to Globalization: Welfare States and the World Economy*, Cambridge: Polity.

Ring, E. and Travers, J. (2005) 'Barriers to inclusion: a case study of a pupil with severe learning difficulties in Ireland', *European Journal of Special Needs Education* Vol.20 No.1 February, 41–56.

Ritschel, D. (1995) 'Macmillan' in V. George and R. Page, eds., *Modern Thinkers on Welfare*, Hertfordshire: Prentice Hall/Harvester Wheatsheaf, 51–68.

Robbins, G. and Lapsley, I. (2008) 'Irish voluntary hospitals: an examination of a theory of voluntary failure', *Accounting, Business and Financial History* Vol.18 No.1 March, 61–80.

Robins, J. (1986) *Fools and Mad: A History of the Insane in Ireland*, Dublin: IPA.

Robins, J.A. (1960) 'The Irish Hospital – An Outline of its Origins and Development',

Administration Vol.8 No.2 Summer, 145–65.

Ronayne, T. and Creedon, M. (1991) *Life on the Dole: A Study of the Experiences and Views of the Long Term Unemployed in Tallaght*, Dublin: Tallaght Centre for the Unemployed.

Rose, K. (1994) *Diverse Communities, the evolution of lesbian and gay politics in Ireland*, Cork: Cork University Press.

Rosenbaum, D.E. (2005) 'Bush to Return to "Ownership Society" Theme in Push for Social Security Changes', *The New York Times* January 16 2005.

Rosenhaft, E. (1994) 'The historical development of German social policy' in J. Clasen and R. Freeman, eds., *Social Policy in Germany*, Hertfordshire: Harvester Wheatsheaf, 21–41.

Rowbotham, S. (1994) 'Interpretations of welfare and approaches to the state, 1870–1920' in A. Oakley and A.S. Williams, eds., *The Politics of the Welfare State*, London: UCL Press, 18–36.

Rowlingson, K. and McKay, S. (2005) 'Income Maintenance and Taxation' in H. Bochel, C. Bochel, R. Page and R. Sykes, eds., *Social Policy: Issues and Developments*, Harlow, Essex: Pearson, 39–65.

Ruddle, H., Donoghue, F. and Mulvihill, R. (1997) *The Years Ahead Report: A Review of the Implementation of its Recommendations*, National Council on Ageing and Older People Report No.48, Dublin: NCAOP.

Ruhs, M. (2004) 'Ireland: a crash course in immigration policy' Country profile prepared for the Washington Institute. Accessed at: *http://www.migrationinformation.org/Profiles/display.cfm?ID=260* on 17 October 2008.

Rush, M. (2006) 'The politics of care' in B. Fanning and M. Rush, eds., *Care and Social Change in the Irish Welfare Economy*, Dublin: UCD Press, 46–64.

Rush, M., Richardson, V. and Kiely, G. (2006) 'Family policy and reproductive work' in B. Fanning and M. Rush, eds., *Care and Social Change in the Irish Welfare Economy*, Dublin: UCD Press, 143–62.

Russell, H., Quinn, E., King O'Riain, R. and McGinnity, F. (2008) *The Experience of Discrimination in Ireland: Analysis of the QNHS Equality Module*, Dublin: ESRI/Equality Authority.

Ryan, L. (2000) 'Strengthening Irish Identity through Openness' in R. O'Donnell, ed., *Europe: The Irish Experience*, Dublin: IEA, 55–68.

Sainsbury, D. (2006) 'Immigrants' social rights in comparative perspective: welfare regimes, forms of immigration and immigration policy regimes', *Journal of European Social Policy* Vol.16 No.3 August, 229–44.

Salonen, T. (2001) 'Sweden: Between Model and Reality' in P. Alcock and G. Craig, eds., *International Social Policy: Welfare Regimes in the Developed World*, Basingstoke: Palgrave, 143–160.

Sanderson, M. (1987) *Educational Opportunity and Social Change in England*, London: Faber and Faber.

Sapouna, L. (2006) 'Tracing Evidence of Institutionalisation in the Process of De-Institutionalisation – The Irish Case' in L. Sapouna and P. Herrmann, eds., *Knowledge in Mental Health: Reclaiming the Social*, New York: Nova Science, 85–99.

Sarfarti, H. and Bonoli, G. (2002) 'Introduction: Tight Constraints; New Demands and Enduring Needs: Addressing the Labour Market versus Social Protection Challenge', in H. Sarfarti and G. Bonoli, eds., *Labour Market and Social Protection Reforms in International Perspective*, Aldershot: Ashgate, 3–7.

Sarokin, D. and Schulkin, J. (1994) 'Environmental Justice: Co-evolution of Environmental Concerns and Social Justice', *The Environmentalist* Vol.14 No.2 July, 121–9.

Sarup, M. (1993) *An Introductory Guide to Post-Structuralism and Postmodernism* (second edition), New York: Harvester Wheatsheaf.

Saunders, P. (1990) *A Nation of Home Owners*, London: Unwin Hyman.

Schultz, T. W. (1961) 'Investment in Human Capital', *The American Economic Review* Vol.51 No.1 March, 1–17.

Sevenhuijsen, S. (2003) 'The place of care: The relevance of the feminist ethic of care for social policy', *Feminist Theory* Vol.4 No.2, 179–97.

Sexton, J.J. (1986) 'Employment, Unemployment and Emigration' in K. A. Kennedy, ed., *Ireland in Transition: Economic and Social Change Since 1960*, Cork/Dublin: Mercier Press, 31–39.

Shannon, G. (1955) 'Woman: Wife and Mother', *Christus Rex* April.

Shannon Millin, S. (1917) 'Child Life as a National Asset', *Journal of the Statistical and Social Inquiry Society of Ireland* Part XCVI, Vol.XIII September, 301–16.

Sheehan, J. (1979) 'Education and Society in Ireland, 1945–70' in J.J. Lee, ed., *Ireland 1945–70*, Dublin: Gill & Macmillan, 61–72.

Sheehan, P. (2007) 'Migration and Homelessness in Cork, Ireland: the impact of European Union labour Mobility', *Feantsa Magazine Homeless in Europe* Autumn 2007, 5–7.

Siim, B. (2000) *Gender and Citizenship: Politics and Agency in France, Britain and Denmark*, Cambridge: Cambridge University Press.

Silke, D. (1999) 'Housing Policy' in S. Quin, P. Kennedy, A. O'Donnell and G. Kiely, eds., *Contemporary Irish Social Policy*, Dublin: UCD Press, 49–71.

Sinn Féin (2007) Others promise we deliver: Sinn Féin General Election Manifesto 2007. Accessed at: *http://www.sinnfein.ie/policies/manifesto/49* on 3 September 2008.

Sjöberg, O. (1999) 'Paying for Social Rights', *Journal of Social Policy* Vol.28 No.2 April, 275–97.

Skilbeck, M. (2001) *The University Challenged: a review of international trends and issues with particular reference to Ireland*, Dublin: HEA.

Smith, M. (1998) *Social Science in Question*, London: Sage with the Open University.

Smyth, A. (1988) 'The Contemporary Women's Movement in the Republic of Ireland', *Women's Studies International Forum* Vol.11 No.4 July-August, 331–41.

Smyth, A. (1993) 'The Women's Movement in the Republic of Ireland 1970–1990' in A. Smyth, ed., *Irish Women's Studies Reader*, Dublin: Attic Press, 245–69.

Smyth, E. (2008) 'Buying your way into college? Private tuition and the transition to higher education in Ireland', *Oxford Review of Education*, Published online 10 March 2008, DOI: 10.1080/03054980801981426.

Smyth, E., McCoy, S., Darmody, M. and Dunne, A. (2007) 'Changing Times, Changing Schools? Quality of Life for Students' in T. Fahey, H. Russell and C.T. Whelan, eds., *Best of Times? The Social Impact of the Celtic Tiger*, Dublin: IPA, 139–154.

Social Welfare Benchmarking and Indexation Group (2001) *Report of the Social Welfare Benchmarking and Indexation Group*, Dublin: Department of Social and Family Affairs.

Socialist Party (2008) Webpage 'About the Socialist Party'. Accessed at: *http://www.socialistparty.net/* on 3 September 2008.

Spaargaren, G. and Mol, A.P. (1992) 'Sociology, Environment and Modernity: Ecological Modernisation as a Theory of Social Change', *Society and Natural Resources* Vol.5

No.4, 323–44.

Spicker, P. (1988) *Principles of Social Welfare: an introduction to thinking about the Welfare State*, London: Routledge.

Stanley, J. and Lucas, K. (2008) 'Social exclusion: what can public transport offer?', *Research in Transportation Economics* Vol.22 No.1 July, 36–40.

Steffen, M., Lamping, W. and Lehto, J. (2005) 'The Europeanization of health policies' in M. Steffen, ed., *Health Governance in Europe: issues, challenges and theories*, London: Routledge, 1–17.

Steg, L. and Gifford, R. (2005) 'Sustainable Transportation and Quality of Life', *Journal of Transport Geography* Vol.13 No.1 March, 59–69.

Stevenson, J. (1984) 'From Philanthropy to Fabianism' in B. Pimlott, ed., *Fabian Essays in Socialist Thought*, London: Heinemann, 15–26.

Sweeney, J. (2007) 'Child poverty and child income supports' in M. Cousins, ed., *Welfare Policy and Poverty*, Dublin, IPA and CPA, 59–99.

Sweeney, P. (1999) *The Celtic Tiger: Ireland's Continuing Economic Miracle* (second edition), Dublin: Oak Tree Press.

Sweeney, P. (2003) 'Globalisation: Ireland in a global context' in M. Adshead and M. Millar, eds., *Public Administration and Public Policy in Ireland: Theory and Methods*, London: Routledge, 201–18.

Swift, A. (2001) *Political Philosophy: A beginners guide for students and politicians*, Cambridge: Policy Press.

Sykes, R. (2008) 'Globalisation and Social Policy' in P. Alcock, M. May and K. Rowlingson, eds., *The Student's Companion to Social Policy* (third edition), Oxford: Blackwell, 430–37.

Tallaght Travellers Youth Service/NEXUS (2006) *Moving Beyond Coping: an insight into the experiences and needs of Travellers in Tallaght in coping with suicide*, Dublin: NEXUS.

Tampke, J. (1981) 'Bismarck's Social Legislation: a Genuine Breakthrough?' in W.J. Mommsen, ed., *The Emergence of the Welfare State in Britain and Germany: 1850–1950*, London: Croom Helm on behalf of the German Historical Institute, 71–83.

Tansey, P. (1989) 'Paul Tansey on population and emigration. Falling Numbers Rising Costs', *Magill* July 1989, 41–5.

Task Force on the Travelling Community (1995) *Report of the Task Force on the Travelling Community*, Dublin: Stationery Office.

Tawney, R.H. (1922) *Secondary Education for All: a policy for Labour*, London: Allen & Unwin.

Tawney, R.H. (1931) *Equality*, London: Allen & Unwin.

Taylor, G. (1998) 'Conserving the Emerald Tiger: the politics of environmental regulation in Ireland', *Environmental Politics* Vol.7 No.4 Winter, 53–74.

Taylor, G. (2001) *Conserving the Emerald Tiger, the politics of environmental regulation in Ireland*, Galway: Arlen House.

Taylor-Gooby, P. (1994) 'Postmodernism and Social Policy: a great leap backwards?', *Journal of Social Policy* Vol.23 No.3 July, 385–404.

Taylor-Gooby, P. (2001) 'Polity, Policy-Making and Welfare Futures' in P. Taylor-Gooby, ed., *Welfare States Under Pressure*, London: Sage, 171–88.

Taylor-Gooby, P. (2004a) 'New Social Risks and Welfare States: New Paradigm and New Politics?' in P. Taylor-Gooby, ed., *New Risks, New Welfare: The Transformation of the European Welfare State*, Oxford: Oxford University Press, 209–38.

Taylor-Gooby, P. (2004b) 'New Risks and Social Charge' in P. Taylor-Gooby, ed. *New Risks, New Welfare: The Transformation of the European Welfare State*, Oxford: Oxford University Press, 1–28.

Thane, P. (1996) *Foundations of the Welfare State* (second edition), Essex: Longman.

The Cork Examiner (1847) 'City Opposition to Out-Door Relief' May 14th 1847. Accessed at: *http://adminstaff.vassar.edu/sttaylor/FAMINE/Examiner/Archives/May1847.html* on 11 May 2007.

Threshold (1987) *Policy Consequences: a study of the £5,000 Surrender Grant in the Dublin area*, Dublin: Threshold.

Timonen, V. (2003) *Irish Social Expenditure in a Comparative International Context*, Dublin: IPA.

Timonen, V. (2005) *Irish Social Expenditure in a Comparative International Context: Epilogue*, Dublin: IPA and CPA.

Timonen, V., Convery, J. and Cahill, S. (2006) 'Care revolutions in the making? A comparison of cash-for-care programmes in four European countries', *Ageing and Society* Vol.26 No.3 May, 455–74.

Timonen, V. and Doyle, M. (2007) 'Worlds apart? Public, private and non-profit sector providers of domiciliary care for older persons in Ireland', *Journal of Aging Studies* Vol.21 No.3 August, 255–65.

Timonen, V. and Doyle, M. (2008) 'From the workhouse to the home: evolution of care policy for older people in Ireland', *International Journal of Sociology and Social Policy* Vol.28 Nos.3/4, 76–89.

Timonen, V. and McMenamin, I. (2002) 'Future of Care Services in Ireland: Old Answers to New Challenges?', *Social Policy and Administration* Vol.36 No.1 February, 20–35.

Tindale, S. and Hewett, C. (1999) 'Must the Poor Pay More? Sustainable Development, Social Justice and Environmental Taxation' in A. Dobson, ed., *Fairness and Futurity, Essays on Environmental Sustainability and Social Justice*, Oxford: Oxford University Press, 232–48.

Titmuss, R. (1956/1987) 'The Social Division of Welfare: Some Reflections on the Search for Equity' in B. Abel-Smith and K. Titmuss, eds., *The Philosophy of Welfare, Selected Writings of Richard M. Titmuss,* London: Allen & Unwin, 39–59.

Titmuss, R. (1965/1987) 'The Role of Redistribution in Social Policy' in B. Abel-Smith and K. Titmuss, eds., *The Philosophy of Welfare, Selected Writings of Richard M. Titmuss,* London: Allen & Unwin, 207–19.

Titmuss, R. (1974) *Social Policy: An Introduction*, London: George Allen & Unwin Ltd.

Toolan, D. (2003) 'An emerging rights perspective for disabled people in Ireland: An activist's view' in S. Quin and B. Redmond, eds., *Disability and Social Policy in Ireland*, Dublin: UCD Press, 171–81.

Torgersen, V. (1987) 'Housing: the wobbly pillar under the welfare state' in B. Turner, J. Kemeny and L. Lundqvist, eds., *Between State and Market: housing in the post-industrial era*, Stockholm: Alqvist, 116–26.

Tormey, R. (2007) 'Education and Poverty' in M. Cousins, ed., *Welfare Policy and Poverty*, Dublin: IPA and CPA, 169–99.

Tovey, H. and Share, P. (2000) *A Sociology of Ireland*, Dublin: Gill & Macmillan.

Trattner, W.I. (1999) *From Poor Law to Welfare State: A History of Social Welfare in America* (sixth edition), New York: The Free Press.

Travelling People Review Body (1983) *Report of the Travelling People Review Body*, Dublin: Stationery Office.

Trench, B. and Brennan, P. (1980) 'Poverty in Ireland', *Magill* April 1980, 10–31.

Trench, B. with additional reporting by Herbert, C. and Fitzgerald, W. (1987) 'Short Cuts to Misery', *Magill* September 1987, 4–6.

Tussing, A.D. and Wren, M.A. (2006) *How Ireland Cares: the case for health care reform*, Dublin: New Island.

Tweedy, H. (1992) *A Link in the Chain: the story of the Irish Housewives' Association 1942–1992*, Dublin: Attic Press.

Ungerson, C. (1987) *Policy is personal: sex, gender, and informal care*, London: Tavistock.

Veale, A., Palaudaries, L. and Gibbons, C. (2003) *Separated Children Seeking Asylum In Ireland*, Dublin: The Irish Refugee Council.

Vij, R., ed. (2007) *Globalization and Welfare: A Critical Reader*, Basingstoke: Palgrave.

Vis, B. (2007) 'States of welfare or states of workfare? Welfare state restructuring in 16 capitalist democracies, 1985–2002', *Policy and Politics* Vol.35 No.1 January, 105–122.

Visser, A. (2005) 'Habitual Residence Condition', *Spectrum, Journal of the National Consultative Committee on Racism and Interculturalism* Issue 9 July, 18–21.

Walsh, A.M. (1999) 'Root them in the land: cottage schemes for agricultural labourers' in J. Augusteijn, ed., *Ireland in the 1930s – New Perspectives*, Dublin: Four Courts Press, 47–66.

Walsh, J. (2005a) 'The Politics of Educational Expansion' in B. Girvin and G. Murphy, eds., *The Lemass Era*, Dublin: UCD Press, 146–65.

Walsh, J. (2007) 'Monitoring Poverty and Welfare Policy 1987–2007' in M. Cousins, ed., *Welfare Policy and Poverty*, Dublin: IPA and CPA, 13–58.

Walsh, J., Craig, S. and McCafferty, D. (1998) *Local Partnerships for Social Inclusion?*, Dublin: Oak Tree Press in association with CPA.

Walsh, T. (2005) 'Constructions of Childhood in Ireland in the Twentieth Century: A View from the Primary School Curriculum 1900–1999', *Child Care in Practice* Vol.11 No.2 April, 253–69.

Warner, M. (1991) 'Introduction: Fear of a Queer Planet', *Social Text* No.29, 3–17.

Watson, D. and Williams, J. (2001) *Perceptions of the Quality of Health Care in the Public and Private Sectors in Ireland*, Dublin: ESRI.

Watt, P. and McCaughey, F., eds. (2006) *Improving Government Service Delivery to Minority Ethnic Groups, Northern Ireland, Republic of Ireland*, Scotland, Dublin: NCCRI.

Weir, S. and Archer, P. (with Flanagan, R.) (2005) *A Review of School-Based measures aimed at addressing educational disadvantage in Ireland, Report to the Educational Disadvantage Committee*, Dublin: Educational Research Centre.

Whelan, C.T., Layte, R., Maître, B., Gannon, B., Nolan, B., Watson, D. and Williams, J. (2003) *Monitoring Poverty Trends in Ireland: results from the 2001 Living in Ireland Survey*, Dublin: ESRI.

Whelan, T. (1987) 'The New Emigrants', *Newsweek*, 10 October 1987.

Whitaker, T.K. (1986) 'Economic Development 1958–1985' in K.A. Kennedy, ed., *Ireland in Transition: Economic and Social Change Since 1960*, Cork/Dublin: Mercier Press, 10–18.

Whyte, J. (1971) *Church and State in Modern Ireland 1923–1970*, Dublin: Gill & Macmillan.

Whyte, J. (1979) 'Church, State and Society, 1950–1970', in J.J. Lee, ed. *Ireland, 1945–1970*, Dublin: Gill & Macmillan, 73–82.

Wickham, J. (2004) *Public Transport and Urban Citizenship*, Working Paper No.9,

Dublin: The Policy Institute, Trinity College Dublin.

Wilensky, H.L. (1975) *The Welfare State and Equality: Structural and Ideological Roots of Public Expenditures*, Berkeley: University of California Press.

Wiley, M. (2005) 'The Irish health system: developments in strategy, structure, funding and delivery since 1980', *Health Economics* Vol.14, No.S1 September, S169–S186.

Williams, F. (1989) *Social Policy: A Critical Introduction: issues of race, gender and class*, Cambridge: Polity Press.

Williams, F. (1992) 'Somewhere over the rainbow: universality and diversity in social policy' in N. Manning and R. Page, eds., *Social Policy Review 4*, Canterbury: Social Policy Association, 200–19.

Wiliams, F. (1994) 'Social relations, welfare and the post-Fordism debate' in R. Burrows and B. Loader, eds., *Towards a Post-Fordist Welfare State*, London: Routledge, 49–73.

Williams, F. (2001) 'In and beyond New Labour: towards a new political ethics of care', *Critical Social Policy* Vol.21 No.4, 467–93.

Williams, K. (1999) 'Faith and the Nation: education and religious identity in the Republic of Ireland', *British Journal of Educational Studies* Vol.47 No.4 December, 317–31.

Williams, R.H. and Bjarnadottir, H. (1998) 'Environmental Protection and Pollution Control in the EU: problems and progress in the 1990s' in D.A. Pinder, ed., *The New Europe: economy, society and the environment*, Chichester: Wiley, 401–413.

Williamson, A. (2000) 'Housing Associations in the Republic of Ireland: Can they respond to the Government's challenge for major expansion?', *Housing Studies* Vol.15 No.4 July, 639–50.

Wilson, A. (2001) 'Social Policy and Homosexuality' in M. Lavalette and A. Pratt, eds., *Social Policy – a conceptual and theoretical introduction*, London: Sage, 121–40.

Winston, N. (2007) 'From Boom to Bust? An Assessment of the Impact of Sustainable Development Policies on Housing in the Republic of Ireland', *Local Environment* Vol.12 No.1 February, 57–71.

Wolfe, A. and Klausen, J. (1997) 'Identity Politics and the Welfare State', *Social Philosophy and Policy* Vol.14 No.2 Summer, 231–55.

Woods, M. (2006) 'The contours of learning/intellectual disability' in D. McCluskey, ed., *Health Policy and Practice in Ireland*, Dublin: UCD Press, 171–87.

Working Group on Elder Abuse (2002) *Protecting Our Future, Report of the Working Group on Elder Abuse*, Dublin: Stationery Office.

World Commission on Environment and Development (1987) *Our Common Future*, Oxford: Oxford University Press.

World Conservation Union (1991) *Caring for the Earth: a strategy for sustainable living*, Gland, Switzerland: World Conservation Union.

World Health Organization (1998) *Monitoring Equity in Health: a policy-oriented approach in low-and-middle-income countries*, Geneva: WHO.

World Health Organization (2008) *Closing the Gap in a Generation: health equity through action on the social determinants of health, Final Report of the Commission on Social Determinants of Health*, Geneva: WHO.

Wren, M.A. (2003) *Unhealthy State: Anatomy of a Sick Society*, Dublin: New Island.

Wren, M.A. (2004) 'The Case for Health System Reform. Can the universal health insurance system deliver? Or the arguments for going there if you have to start from here', Paper presented to Tasc discussion forum, 22 January 2004. Accessed at: *http://www.tascnet.ie/showPage.php?ID=89* on 23 September 2008.

Yearley, S. (1991) *The Green Case: A Sociology of Environmental Arguments, Issues and Politics*, London: Harper Collins.

Yeates, N. (1997) 'Gender and the Development of the Irish Social Welfare System' in A. Byrne and M. Leonard, eds., *Women and Irish Society: a sociological reader*, Belfast: Beyond the Pale, 145–166.

Yeates, N. (2001) *Globalization and Social Policy*, London: Sage.

Yeates, N. (2004) 'A Dialogue with 'global care chain analysis': nurse migration in the Irish context', *Feminist Review* Issue 77 Summer, 79–95.

Yeates, N. (2008a) 'The idea of global social policy' in N. Yeates, ed., *Understanding Global Social Policy*, Bristol: The Policy Press, 1–24.

Yeates, N., ed. (2008) *Understanding Global Social Policy*, Bristol: The Policy Press.

Young, I.M. (1989) 'Polity and Group Difference: A Critique of the Ideal of Universal Citizenship', *Ethics* No.9, 250–74.

Young, M. (1958) *The Rise of Meritocracy, 1870–2003: An Essay on Education and Equality*, London: Thames and Hudson.

Young, S. (2000) 'The origins and evolving nature of ecological modernisation' in S. Young, ed., *The Emergence of Ecological Modernisation: integrating the environment and the economy*, London: Routledge, 1–39.

Ziliak, S.T. (2004) 'Self-Reliance before the Welfare State: Evidence from the Charity Organisation Movement in the United States', *The Journal of Economic History* Vol.64 No.2 June, 433–61.

Zimmerman, B. (2006) 'Changes in Work and Social Protection: France, Germany and Europe', *International Social Security Review* Vol.59 No.4 October-December, 29–45.

INDEX